fifth edition
Criminal Justice

fifth edition
Criminal Justice

Sue Titus Reid, J.D., Ph.D.
Florida State University

BluePrints

coursewise
publishing
inc.

St. Paul • Bellevue • Boulder • Dubuque • Madison

Our mission at **coursewise** is to help students make connections—linking theory to practice and the classroom to the outside world. Learners are motivated to synthesize ideas when course materials are placed in a context they recognize. By providing gateways to contemporary and enduring issues, **coursewise** publications will expand students' awareness of and context for the course subject.

For more information on **coursewise,** visit us at our web site: http://www.coursewise.com

To order an examination copy, contact Houghton Mifflin Sixth Floor Media: 800-565-6247 (voice); 800-565-6236 (fax).

BluePrints is a series of core texts that provide the basic framework for college courses in brief, inexpensive paperbacks. Each title offers concise, current coverage of material for a specific course. **courselinks**™ and Chapter Plug-Ins™ provide statistical updates, late-breaking news, and additional resources and content.

coursewise publishing editorial staff

Thomas Doran, ceo/publisher: Journalism/Marketing/Speech
Edgar Laube, publisher: Political Science/Psychology/Sociology
Linda Meehan Avenarius, publisher: **courselinks**™
Sue Pulvermacher-Alt, publisher: Education/Health/Gender Studies
Victoria Putman, publisher: Anthropology/Geography/Environmental Science
Tom Romaniak, publisher: Business/Criminal Justice/Economics

coursewise production staff

Lori A. Blosch, permissions coordinator
Mary Monner, production coordinator
Victoria Putman, production manager

Interior design and cover design by Elise Lansdon

Printed in the United States of America by **coursewise publishing**, Inc., 1559 Randolph Avenue, St. Paul, MN 55105

10 9 8 7 6 5 4 3 2 1

About the Author

Sue Titus Reid

Sue Titus Reid, professor of the Rubin O'Donovan Askew School of Public Administration and Policy at Florida State University, Tallahassee, has taught law students, graduate students, and undergraduate students in many states. She has served on the board of the Midwest Sociological Society and the executive staff of the American Sociological Association. She has served as chairperson, associate dean, and dean. In 1985 she held the prestigious George Beto Chair in criminal justice at the Criminal Justice Center, Sam Houston State University, Huntsville, Texas.

Dr. Reid was influenced in her choice of career by her family background and early experiences in a small East Texas community. She graduated with honors from Texas Woman's University in 1960 and received graduate degrees in sociology (M.A. in 1962 and Ph.D. in 1965) from the University of Missouri–Columbia. In 1972 she graduated with distinction from the University of Iowa College of Law. She was admitted to the Iowa Bar that year and later to the District of Columbia Court of Appeals. She has been admitted to practice before the U.S. Supreme Court as well.

Dr. Reid is unique among authors in the criminal justice field because of her distinguished qualifications in both law and the social sciences. Her first major publication, *Crime and Criminology,* 1976, now in its eighth edition with the ninth in progress, has been widely adopted throughout the United States and in foreign countries. Dr. Reid's other titles include *The Correctional System: An Introduction,* and *Criminal Law,* Third Edition. She has contributed a chapter to the *Encyclopedia of Crime and Justice,* as well as to other books, in addition to publishing scholarly articles in both law and sociology. Dr. Reid's contributions to her profession have been widely recognized nationally and abroad. In 1982 the American Society of Criminology elected her a fellow "for outstanding contributions to the field of Criminology." Other national honors include the following: Who's Who among Women, Who's Who in Criminal Law, 2,000 Notable Women (Hall of Fame for Outstanding Contributions to Criminal Law, 1990); Personalities of America; and Most Admired Woman of the Decade, 1992. Her international honors include International Woman of the Year, 1991–1992; International Who's Who of Intellectuals; and International Order of Merit, 1993.

Dr. Reid has traveled extensively to widen her knowledge of criminal justice systems in the United States and in other countries. In 1982 she was a member of the People-to-People Crime Prevention delegation to the People's Republic of China. Her several trips to Europe included a three-month study and lecture tour of ten countries in 1985.

Preface

Preface

For many countries one of the most serious domestic problems is crime; the United States is no exception. With one of the highest crime rates and rates of incarceration in the world, the United States faces immense problems associated with national and international criminal activity. The concern for crime extends beyond the nature and frequency of occurrence to include official and unofficial reactions to crimes. Criminal justice systems appear inadequate to prevent crime and are questionable systems for coping with crimes that do occur.

Some bitterly criticize the criminal justice systems but have no meaningful suggestions for improvement. Others take the law into their own hands—fighting back, wounding, and in some cases, killing those who attempt to victimize them. Still others take a close look at the criminal justice systems and hope to retain the best parts and change those that need improvement.

I take the latter view in this text, which focuses on U.S. criminal justice systems but looks at the problems in general and includes some examples from other countries. The text also examines the interrelationships of the various parts of the systems because a change in one area of a system may and usually does have a significant impact on other areas of that system.

In the fourth edition of this text, I reduced the number of chapters from eighteen to fourteen. In this edition I have reduced the number of chapters further—to twelve. Why these changes? While teaching a criminal justice course and using the third edition of this text, I became aware that this text and its competitors have grown too long. Most contain eighteen chapters—too many to cover in the usual fourteen-week semester.

Increases in length, along with rising production costs (resulting from more color and greater photography), cause the prices of texts to escalate. Secondhand copies are expensive, too, with students receiving only a small portion of the original price for resale. Students may also have the additional cost of a Study Guide, should they choose to utilize one.

coursewise publishing and I decided that it is possible to write and produce a book that contains sufficient and up-to-date coverage of criminal justice, along with tables, illustrations, graphs, and other study aids, while keeping the price within the range of the average student budget. This text is the result, and we believe it provides an excellent alternative to the more expensive, four-color texts.

This fifth edition includes the most recent information on topics discussed. All topics have been checked for the latest information available at the time of publication. All legal citations, including cases and statutes, have been checked to determine whether they have been altered or overruled by legislation or subsequent court decisions. Where possible, issues are illustrated with recent cases, although some older cases are used because they represent "classic" statements on the law and are still in effect or because they represent the latest Supreme Court decision on that issue.

The recentness of some cases presents problems in that appellate courts will hear some of these cases while this book is in production or after it is published. Further, the personnel composition of the U.S. Supreme Court has changed significantly in recent years, and these changes are likely to be reflected in forthcoming decisions by the Court.

Along with presenting recent scholarly research in the social sciences, this fifth edition retains the practice of using recent current events from popular sources to illustrate what is happening in criminal justice. These have been updated right up to the book's publication. Even after the trials (or plea bargains), important events continue in many cases.

Chapter Format

Each chapter begins with an outline of the chapter's content and a list of learning objectives, which suggest to students what they should be learning as they progress through the chapter. Key terms are also listed at the beginning of each chapter, are boldfaced within the chapter, and are defined in the Glossary at the end of the text. Tables, figures, maps, and "Spotlight" boxes further emphasize and illustrate the material within each chapter. New to this edition are "Professions" boxes, which feature extensive information on careers in criminal justice. Each chapter concludes with a detailed summary called the "WiseGuide Wrap-Up," followed by essay questions ("Apply It") that help students to analyze and apply chapter concepts.

Text Organization and Important Content Changes

The text is divided into five sections. Section 1, "Introduction to Criminal Justice Systems," contains two chapters (rather than the previous five chapters). The first chapter, "Criminal Justice: An Overview," combines the main features of the first two chapters of the previous edition and discusses punishment, criminal law, the concept of crime, and defenses to crime. The Oklahoma City bombing trial is introduced in this chapter, with subsequent chapters containing additional references. Chapter 1 concludes with a discussion of criminal law, noting the problems that may arise when the law extends to areas that some might consider the realm of private behavior only.

Chapter 2, "Crime, Offenders, and Victims," covers data on crime as well as victimization, with an emphasis on the interrelationships between offenders and victims. The chapter also discusses fear of crime. Information on victims, misdemeanors, and recent efforts to expand the rights of crime victims is more extensive than was provided in the previous edition.

Section 2, "Entry into Criminal Justice Systems: Policing," now features three rather than two chapters. Chapter 3, "The Emergence and Structure of Police Systems," covers the history of policing, noting some of the problems of policing at the local, state, and federal levels. The yet unsolved case of the murder of JonBenet Ramsey in Boulder, Colorado, illustrates the interactions among policing at these levels. Recent problems with the FBI crime labs are noted, and the latest data on the Clinton administration's Community-Oriented Policing Services (COPS) program are underscored.

Chapter 4, "Policing in a Modern Society," explores the structure and function of policing, featuring additional information on the recruitment, training, and education of police. The chapter analyzes new legal cases on search and seizure, and discusses DNA testing and its use in freeing innocent persons.

Chapter 5 takes a close look at problems and issues in policing, such as the 1997 Supreme Court decision concerning the Brady Bill and gun control, and recent information on police corruption. The extreme stress that police officers may encounter is exemplified in accounts of police rescue efforts after the Oklahoma City bombing.

Chapter 5 also features such recent events as the killing by police of an unarmed black suspect in New York City and the alleged brutality against Abner Louima, who claims that police tortured and sodomized him in Brooklyn in 1997. The chapter features more coverage of racial and gender issues (including affirmative action hiring, with the latest legal developments and data on this topic).

Section 3, "Processing a Criminal Case: Criminal Court Systems," explores the procedures and issues that arise from the time of an arrest through sentencing and appeals. This section contains three chapters, in comparison to the five chapters in the previous edition. Chapter 6 provides an overview of court systems. Recent cases are used to delineate the concepts, such as that of judicial power to overturn a jury verdict, as illustrated by the au pair case of Louise Woodward. The chapter also notes some of the uses of the computer, especially the World Wide Web, in courts and court procedures.

Chapter 7, "Prosecution, Defense, and Pretrial Procedures," combines two chapters from the previous edition and begins with an analysis of the role of lawyers in criminal court systems and proceeds through the pretrial procedures. It examines the historical and current roles of prosecutors and defense attorneys. The cases of Terry Nichols, Ted Kaczynski, and Marv Albert are used to illustrate some of the chapter topics.

Chapter 8 describes the basic procedures of the trial, sentencing, and appeal phases of criminal cases. Since this chapter combines most of two chapters from the previous edition, much of the material, especially the description of a trial, has been streamlined. The chapter does, however, feature new issues in sentencing, such as "three strikes and you're out," truth in sentencing, and the issues surrounding *habeas corpus* appeals by inmates. Additionally, it covers the allegations of racism with respect to differentials in sentencing offenders found guilty of violating crack cocaine as compared with power cocaine statutes.

Section 4, "Confinement and Corrections," consists of three chapters (rather than the four of the previous edition) that examine the methods of confining offenders in total institutions or of placing them in the community under supervision. The discussion begins in Chapter 9, "The History and Structure of Confinement," with an overview of the history of prisons and jails, and a discussion of the federal and state prison systems. Attention is given to the problems of local jails and the current focus on boot camps. The discussion of privatization of prisons and jails has been updated, including notation of pending lawsuits against private corporations.

Chapter 10, "Life in Prison," combines the chapter in the previous edition on this subject with the chapter on inmates' rights, although that discussion has been shortened significantly to reflect the reduced legalistic approach of this edition. The chapter discusses inmates and correctional officers and the interactions between these two groups, especially the methods of social control. How inmates cope with the pains of imprisonment, and the distinction between the adjustment of women and men, are discussed as well. Special attention is given to AIDS in prison, as well as to the growing problems of dealing with disabled and aging inmates. The chapter also notes the special problems of female inmates and also of female correctional officers.

Section 4 closes with Chapter 11, "Probation, Parole, and Community Corrections," which examines the preparation of inmates for release, the problems inmates face upon release, and the supervision of offenders in the community. Recent legal developments (known as Megan's Laws) in the area of sex offender registration requirements are noted and explained.

The final section of the text, Section 5, "Juvenile Justice: A Special Case," consists of Chapter 12 on juvenile justice systems. Juvenile justice systems were developed to process juveniles in trouble with the law or in need of supervision or care because of neglectful parents or other guardians. This chapter explains juvenile justice systems, contrasts those systems with adult criminal court systems, and considers the changes in juvenile justice systems that have resulted from decisions of the U.S. Supreme Court as well as lower courts. The chapter includes discussions of the legal implications of racial and gender issues, and of recent legislative attempts to alter the juvenile court. For example, attention is given to the Juvenile Crime Control Act of 1997, which has passed the House but not the Senate.

Two appendices assist the reader with legal issues. Appendix A reprints selected amendments to the U.S. Constitution. Those amendments are cited throughout the text. Appendix B explains the abbreviations and references used in legal case citations. Individual indexes assist readers who desire quick access to names, subjects, and legal cases cited in the text.

Acknowledgments

The writing of a text is a labor of love for me, but in recent years, it has become more difficult because of physical limitations. This book is dedicated to the doctors who have helped me adjust to those limitations; to them I am most grateful.

As always, my family has been an enormous support. To Jill Pickett, my sister, her husband, Roger, and their children, Clint and Rhonda, I give my love and appreciation. Colleagues who have supported me throughout this revision are indispensable to writing, and I cannot name all of them, but special thanks goes to the following: David Fabianic, University of Central Florida; John Smykla, University of Alabama, Tuscaloosa; Laura Myers, Sam Houston State University; Marlyn Mather, retired, University of Iowa; Carlene Thornton and William Doerner, Florida State University; and Tony Cooper, University of Texas–Dallas. Thanks to all of you for your support, some of you for more than thirty years!

The employees of publishing companies may be anonymous to authors. In the publication of this book, mine have become "real people." The publisher, Tom Romaniak, was my editor as well as my friend on previous books, and his assistance in the writing and production of this text was most helpful. Chris Chapin-Tilton was a delightful copy editor; we laughed a lot as we wrote and rewrote passages. Vickie Putman, production manager, along with Mary Monner, production coordinator, kept us on schedule while observing with sincere reactions my limitations in getting the material returned on occasion. Finally, Kevin Campbell took a significant workload off my schedule by compiling the indexes.

Although I take full responsibility for the final book, I want to thank the following colleagues for their reviews of the manuscript:

Mark Dantzker

Jack E. Enter

W. Richard Janikowski

Jerry Dowling

Finally, I would like to express my appreciation to the students in my American Legal Systems classes, who have made my teaching life so exciting during the past two years, and to Lance deHaven-Smith, Director, and Governor Rubin O'Donovan Askew, Professor, both of the Rubin O'Donovan Askew School of Public Administration and Policy, Florida State University, for their support.

Dedication

To

Charles N. Aprill, M.D.
Magnolia Diagnostic Imaging, New Orleans

Walter C. Hellinger, M.D.,
and Prince K. Zachariah, Ph.D., Ph.D., M.D.
Mayo Clinic Jacksonville

Charles H. Wingo, M.D.
Tallahassee Orthopedic Center

with my sincere appreciation and gratitude
for your excellent medical care, understanding, and support.

Brief Contents

Contents

Section 2

Entry into Criminal Justice Systems: Policing 53

Chapter 3

The Emergence and Structure of Police Systems 55

Chapter 4

Policing in a Modern Society 79

Chapter 5

Problems and Issues in Policing 109

Section 3

Processing a Criminal Case: Criminal Court Systems 139

Chapter 6

Criminal Court Systems 141

Chapter 7

Prosecution, Defense, and Pretrial Procedures 165

Chapter 8

Trial, Sentencing, and Appeal 203

Section 4

Confinement and Corrections 237

Section 5

Juvenile Justice: A Special Case   337

Chapter 12

Juvenile Justice Systems   339

Introduction to Criminal Justice Systems

INTRODUCTION

Criminal justice systems throughout the world vary considerably; even within the United States there are differences among the various state systems. The federal system has unique features, too. All criminal justice systems, however, face common problems: a punishment philosophy; definitions of the conduct to be included in the criminal law; definitions of the elements of crimes; and crime data collection. Criminal justice professionals must decide how to respond to crime victims and how to process the accused and sanction the convicted.

INTRODUCTION—Continued

Section 1 of this text features U.S. criminal justice systems, although some of their procedures and issues that are common to other systems are noted. The first chapter presents an overview of criminal justice systems in general and in the United States in particular. The punishment philosophies on which criminal justice systems are based are explained, and the reality of how systems work is explored. In addition, Chapter 1 contains an overview of criminal law, beginning with the nature and philosophical bases of punishment. The chapter features an overview of criminal justice system components and discussions of the meaning of criminal law as compared with civil law, the sources of criminal law within the context of the adversary system, and the constitutional limits of criminal law. The concept of crime is explored in greater detail, with consideration given to the elements of crimes as well as to selected defenses to criminal behavior. The final section analyzes the reach of criminal law, looking in particular at sexual behavior and substance abuse.

Chapter 2 discusses the methods for securing and analyzing data on crime and victimization. It deals with characteristics of offenders and of victims.

The chapters in Section I set the stage for the subsequent and more extensive analysis of the basic parts of the criminal justice systems—police, prosecution and defense, courts, and corrections—that constitute the remainder of the text.

Criminal Justice: An Overview

The peace and tranquility of Oklahoma City and the nation were shattered on 19 April 1995 when a bomb ripped through the federal building, resulting in the deaths of 168 innocent people, including children and infants. In June of 1997 Timothy McVeigh was found guilty of those crimes and sentenced to death. Later in the year a second defendant, Terry L. Nichols, was tried for crimes associated with the bombing. He was found guilty of conspiracy and of manslaughter but not of murder.

Key Terms

administrative law
adversary system
battered-person syndrome
case law
causation
civil law
common law
crime
criminal justice system
criminal law
defenses
deterrence
discretion
due process
entrapment
equal protection
felony
general deterrence
incapacitation
individual deterrence
inquisitory system
jurisdiction
just deserts
mala in se
mala prohibita
mens rea
misdemeanor
plea bargaining
posttraumatic stress syndrome
rehabilitation
retribution
sanction
statutory law
torts

The senseless violence in Oklahoma City focused international attention once again on the criminal justice systems of a country that to some symbolizes random terror. On the other hand, the processing of the alleged crimes may have restored some of the confidence that had been lost during the "trial of the century," which culminated in the acquittal of O.J. Simpson. Simpson, a football icon and hero to many Americans, was tried for the murders of his ex-wife, Nicole Brown Simpson, and one of her friends, Ronald Goldman. Although Simpson was acquitted by the jury in the criminal trial, many thought him guilty and criticized the system that freed him. Simpson was found liable in his civil trial and was ordered to pay over $30 million in damages to the victims' estates. His lengthy, televised trial raised many questions about U.S. criminal justice procedures and led to extensive criticism of those procedures and of lawyers.

The purpose of this chapter is to analyze some of the issues regarding the imposition of punishment in criminal courts before looking briefly at the systems that impose that punishment and the criminal law on which punishment is based. Although the primary focus of this and other chapters is on U.S. criminal justice systems, some examples of other systems are included. Emphasis on careers is included too, as noted in Professions 1.1.

A criminal justice system comprises the agencies and personnel who are charged with the responsibility of enforcing the criminal law. This includes police, prosecution and defense, courts, and corrections, all of which are discussed in more detail later in the text. This chapter begins with a look at the nature and meaning of punishment, along with the *recognized* historical and current philosophies underlying punishment. But in reality societies punish for other reasons, some of which are illegal. It is important to understand the reality of any criminal justice system, and attention is given in this chapter to the wide discretion of decision making in criminal justice systems.

The basic components of criminal justice systems—police, prosecution, courts, and corrections—are noted. An overview of criminal law follows, with an examination of the distinction between criminal and civil law, an exploration of the adversary system, and a brief explanation of the constitutional limitations on criminal law. The sources of criminal law are mentioned briefly. The concept of crime is analyzed in terms of the ways in which crimes are classified and the basic elements of a crime. Brief attention is given to defenses to criminal allegations, with a closer look at a few particular defenses. The chapter closes with a discussion of how far the criminal law should reach in its efforts to control behavior.

Learning Objectives

Learning Objectives

After reading this chapter, you should be able to do the following:

- List, define, and illustrate the major punishment philosophies.
- Discuss the importance and impact of discretion in criminal justice systems.
- List and describe briefly the major components of criminal justice systems.
- Explain the difference between *civil law* and *criminal law* and illustrate with a discussion of *torts.*
- Contrast the *inquisitory* and the *adversary* systems.

- Explain what is meant by constitutional limits on criminal law.
- List and analyze the sources of law.
- Define *crime*; explain how crimes are classified, and discuss the meaning of the general elements of a crime.
- Explain crime *defenses*, comparing traditional with emerging defenses.
- Explain the pros and cons for including sexual behavior and the use of alcohol and other drugs within the reach of criminal law.

The Nature and Philosophical Bases of Punishment

A criminal justice system is designed to prevent people from violating its rules and to **sanction,** or impose legal punishments, on those who do. The issues arise, however, regarding the behavior that should be covered by criminal punishments, who should be sanctioned, and which sanctions should be applied. These issues are discussed in various chapters throughout the text, but at this point we look at the philosophical basis for punishment.

Consider the two cases described in Spotlight 1.1. Most people have no difficulty contrasting the cases of Florian and Brisbon, in view of the number and nature of the killings Brisbon committed. But the legal elements of first-degree murder might have been present in both cases.

The grand jury refused to indict Hans Florian, but similar cases have resulted in indictments, trials, convictions, and incarcerations. For example, consider another case that received national media attention. In 1990 Florida officials approved the release from prison of Roswell Gilbert, aged eighty-one, who was incarcerated for murdering his ailing wife in what he called a mercy killing.

PROFESSIONS 1.1

Most of the chapters of this text include a focus on careers. Although it is not possible to cover even a small portion of the careers available in criminal justice or to prepare students for applying for specific jobs, it is thought that some exposure to job possibilities is beneficial. This career focus constitutes a brief overview.

Careers in criminal justice encompass a wide range of activities, from custodial services to high levels of administrative and professional positions, such as that of a United States Supreme Court justice. They include professions in law, psychology, sociology and other social sciences, architecture, accounting, physical sciences, and many other fields. Persons in criminal justice may be investigating criminal activities on the streets or in the lab, engaging in administrative activities in a wide variety of settings, counseling adult or juvenile offenders, designing prisons or jails, supervising persons on parole or probation, training correctional officers or other personnel, supervising shop or other job assignments or training in correctional facilities, teaching college students in criminal justice, and many more kinds of activities.

These and other positions require training and education ranging from a high school education and on-the-job training to a Ph.D. or a law degree, perhaps with experience. But one fact is obvious: criminal justice is a growth industry; jobs are available and will continue to be waiting for those who wish to enter the field. The Bureau of Labor Statistics has reported that the future is bright for criminal justice employees.[1] As prison populations continue to grow, it can be expected that the department's projections will remain in effect for years to come.

The purpose of this text is to introduce you to criminal justice systems and their functions. Not all of you will become employed in the field, but even for those who do not, the information should be of general usefulness in related professions.

Enjoy your excursion through one of the most important and challenging areas of employment.

1. Bureau of Labor Statistics, *Occupational Projections and Training Data.* (Washington, D.C.: U.S. Department of Labor, April 1990), pp. 9, 11.

Gilbert was convicted of first-degree murder and sentenced to from twenty-five years to life. He served several years in prison before his release. Should Gilbert have been convicted of first-degree murder on facts similar to those of Florian and others? All these persons claim they acted out of love when they killed their terminally ill spouses, who begged to be relieved of their sufferings. If Gilbert deserved to serve time in prison, why should he have been released for medical reasons?[1] Gilbert died in 1994.

These cases may be analyzed in terms of four objectives recognized historically as bases for punishment: **incapacitation, retribution, rehabilitation,** and **deterrence**. These objectives are defined and analyzed in historical perspective in Spotlight 1.2, which mentions other factors that might be considered in punishment. The debate over which of these objectives ought to be the basis for punishment continues. The main punishment philosophies in vogue in this century have been rehabilitation and deterrence, with the former dominating the scene until recently and the latter dominating today. Both continue to influence legislation and court decisions.

Rehabilitation has been described as the rehabilitative ideal, which is based on the premise that human behavior is the result of antecedent causes that may be known by objective analysis and permit scientific control. The assumption is that the offender should be treated, not punished. Social scientists endorsed the rehabilitative ideal and began developing treatment programs for institutionalized inmates. The ideal was incorporated into some statutes, proclaimed by courts, and supported by presidential crime commissions.

The demise of the rehabilitative ideal was headlined in *Time* in 1982: "What Are Prisons For? No Longer Rehabilitation, but to Punish and to Lock the

Spotlight 1.1

Mercy Killing or Murder? A Comparison of Two Cases

A young woman driving a Chevrolet Caprice along Interstate 57 in southern Cook County, Illinois, on the night of 3 June 1973 was forced off the highway by a car occupied by four men. With one of the men pointing a gun at her, she was ordered to remove her clothing and climb through a barbed wire fence at the side of the road. Henry Brisbon Jr. responded to her pleas for life by thrusting a shotgun into her vagina and firing. She was in agony for several minutes before her assailant fired the fatal shot at her throat.

In less than an hour, Brisbon had committed two more murders. Brisbon's next victims, also riding in their car along I-57, were planning to be married in six months. When they pleaded that their lives be spared, Brisbon told them to lie on the ground and "kiss your last kiss," after which he shot each in the back. Brisbon took $54 in cash, two watches, an engagement ring, and a wedding band from his victims. He was arrested and convicted of these crimes; but because the death penalty in Illinois had been invalidated, he was given a term of 1,000 to 3,000 years. While serving that term he killed an inmate and was sentenced to death under the state's new death penalty statute.

During an earlier incarceration, Brisbon was involved in fifteen attacks on guards and inmates and was responsible for beginning at least one prison riot. He hit a warden with a broom handle and crashed a courtroom during a trial. Despite these acts of violence, Brisbon said, "I'm no bad dude. . . Just an antisocial individual." He blames his problems on the strict upbringing by his Muslim father, who taught him to dislike white people. The result: "I didn't like nobody." How does he feel about his victims? "All this talk about victims' rights and restitution gets me. What about my family? I'm a victim of a crooked criminal system. Isn't my family entitled to something?"[1]

How should society react to the crime of Henry Brisbon? At his trial that resulted in the death sentence, the prosecutor described Brisbon as "a very, very terrible human being, a walking testimonial for the death penalty." The attorney who prosecuted him for the I-57 murders said, "On the day he dies in the chair at Statesville, I plan to be there to see that it's done. Nobody I've heard of deserves the death penalty more than Henry Brisbon."[2]

In contrast to the case of Brisbon is that of Hans Florian. In March 1983, Florian, aged seventy-nine, went to the hospital to visit his sixty-two-year-old wife, who was suffering from a disease that eventually would make her senile and helpless. Florian had placed his wife in a nursing home because he was unable to care for her; but when she became too ill to be cared for properly in that facility, she was hospitalized. Florian visited his ailing wife daily. On each visit he placed her in a wheelchair and pushed her around the floor of the hospital to give her a change of scenery. On the day in question, he wheeled her into a stairwell and shot her in the head, ending her life quickly. Friends claimed that Hans was not a murderer. He killed his wife because he loved her so much that he wanted her to be rid of her suffering.[3]

Florian was charged with first-degree murder. Should he be convicted of that charge? Apparently his act was premeditated and without legal justification. If convicted, should he be sentenced to death?

1. "An Eye for an Eye," *Time* (24 January 1983), p. 30.
2. Ibid.
3. "When Is Killing Not A Crime?" *Washington Post* (14 April 1983), p. 23.

Worst Away." The article referred briefly to the original purpose of U.S. prisons: not only to punish, but also to transform criminals "from idlers and hooligans into good, industrious citizens." It concluded, however, that

> no other country was so seduced for so long by that ambitious charter. The language, ever malleable, conformed to the ideal: when a monkish salvation was expected of inmates, prisons became penitentiaries, then reformatories, correctional centers and rehabilitation facilities.[2]

Spotlight 1.2

Punishment Philosophies

1. **Incapacitation of the Offender.** In the past corporal punishment involved incapacitating the offender by making it impossible for him or her to commit further offenses of a like nature. The hands of a thief were cut off; the eyes of a spy were gouged; rapists were castrated; prostitutes were disfigured to make them unattractive. Another form of incapacitation in earlier days was to brand the offender with a letter indicating the crime. An adultress was branded with the letter *A* to indicate to everyone the crime she had committed. The assumption was that if people knew of this person's criminal activity, they would avoid her, although that defies logic in some cases, such as prostitution. In modern times incapacitation has been accomplished through incarceration.

2. **Retribution.** Seneca said that "revenge is an inhuman word," but historically revenge has been one of the most important justifications for punishment. The philosophy of revenge, or retribution, is the eye-for-an-eye doctrine, which can be traced back to the Bible and even further than biblical times in Persia. Among other provisions, it included the death penalty for stealing dogs, receiving stolen goods from a temple or house, stealing a child, inducing a male or female slave to leave the city, committing highway robbery, and breaking into a house. The eye-for-an-eye provisions differed by social class distinctions.

Not only was revenge acceptable, it was expected. The victim (or the victim's family) was expected to avenge the offender. Private revenge was replaced by official government punishment, and today the philosophy of retribution is recognized widely as an appropriate reason for punishment. The earlier "eye-for-an-eye, tooth-for-a-tooth" approach is not recognized legally today, but the U.S. Supreme Court has approved retribution as a basis for punishment.[1]

3. **Rehabilitation.** For years the rehabilitation philosophy dominated U.S. criminal justice policies. It is based on the belief that offenders may be changed through proper treatment and care. Some may be rehabilitated outside institutions; others may require confinement for this goal to be accomplished.

4. **Protection of Society: Deterrence Theory.** Punishment is imposed to keep people from victimizing others and is based on the assumption that it serves this purpose. Embodied in this societal goal is the philosophy of deterrence, both individual and general. **Individual deterrence** refers to stopping the apprehended offender from committing criminal acts, whereas **general deterrence** assumes that punishing that offender will keep others from engaging in criminal acts. Potential offenders will refrain from criminal behavior after seeing the punishment imposed on actual offenders.

5. **Preservation of Social Solidarity.** Some have suggested that the only justification for punishment is that it upholds the mores of society and prevents private revenge. According to sociologist Émile Durkheim, the true function of punishment "is to maintain social cohesion intact."[2] This theory raises the question of what would happen to law-abiding citizens who may be repressing their desires if society did not punish. Must there be a certain degree of punishment to keep citizens law abiding?

Friedrich Nietzsche said, "Distrust all in whom the impulse to punish is strong," from which a scholar concluded that punishment is one of the weapons people use to subdue their own desires that they cannot permit to be expressed. They feel guilty about those desires, so they enjoy punishing others who have been caught expressing them. "It is never he who is without sin who casts the first stone." Punishing the offender "not only relieves us of sin, but makes us feel actually virtuous."[3] Thus, punishment may serve to reinforce the morals of society and bind its members closer together in their fight against the offender.

6. **Reparation or restitution.** The reparation or restitution approach to punishment assumes that the victim should be returned to his or her former position. This approach has been used mainly in civil cases but recently has become more acceptable in criminal cases. Although injured persons (or the family of a deceased individual) may not be restored to their former positions by money, a financial contribution from offenders (or from society) eases the burdens caused by the crime. This type of punishment is more workable when victims have suffered crimes against property.

---

1. See Gregg v. Georgia, 428 U.S. 153 (1976).
2. Émile Durkheim, *The Division of Labor in Society* (New York: Free Press, 1984), p. 108.
3. Henry Weihofen, *The Urge to Punish* (New York: Farrar, Straus & Giroux, 1956), quoted in *Perspectives on Corrections,* ed. Donald E. J. MacNamara and Edward Sagarin (New York: Crowell, 1971), p. 71.

Spotlight 1.3

Punishment and Deterrence: Views from Other Countries

In 1982, in announcing that corrupt government officials would be executed, the government of the People's Republic of China articulated its belief in deterrence. "It is necessary to kill one to warn a hundred . . . the seriousness of a few economic offenses has reached such an extent that the death penalty may have to be employed to beat down the offenders' arrogance and to educate and save others."[1]

The list of capital offenses in the People's Republic was expanded to include crimes such as leading gangs, embezzling, and prostitution. In 1989 the government "gunned down hundreds, perhaps thousands, of unarmed pro-democracy demonstrators . . . in Beijing's Tiananmen Square." Later that year three of the protestors were executed publicly by a firing squad despite pleas from around the world that their lives be spared.[2]

In 1994 the caning of Michael Fay, an American teenager accused of vandalism in Singapore, demonstrated that government's strong belief in corporal punishment. President Clinton and others appealed to the Singapore government on Fay's behalf, and subsequently his sentence was reduced, but the caning was carried out. Prosecutors dropped charges against another teenager accused along with Fay of vandalism.[3]

Singapore deals harshly with drug offenders, too, as illustrated by the 1994 hanging of a Dutch engineer. He was sentenced to die under a statute that provides capital punishment for those who possess one-half ounce or more of heroin.[4]

1. "Peking to Execute Corrupt Officials, Paper Indicates," *Los Angeles Times* (11 March 1982), p. 10.
2. "Chinese Execute 3: More Condemned," *Atlanta Constitution* (22 June 1989), p. 1.
3. "Singapore Drops Charges Against Fay's Henchman," *Miami Herald* (18 May 1994), p. 12.
4. "Singapore Executes a Dutch Engineer Arrested on Drug Charges," *New York Times* (24 September 1994), p. 5.

The simple fact is that prisons did not work as intended. The result has been a movement toward more severe and definite sentences. For example, California, a state that employed the rehabilitation philosophy, led the way in returning to a punitive philosophy by declaring in its statutory changes in 1976 (to become effective the following year) that "the purpose of imprisonment for crime is punishment."[3]

In enacting sentencing guidelines (discussed later in this text), the U.S. Congress eliminated rehabilitation as a goal in the federal system.[4]

The second and more recognized punishment philosophy in vogue today is *deterrence*. Deterrence is based on the assumption that if punishments are unpleasant or severe enough, people will not engage in criminal behavior. This philosophy is one of the main justifications for punishment in U.S. criminal justice systems.[5] There are two types of deterrence: individual (or specific) and general. **Individual deterrence** (also called specific deterrence) refers to the effect of punishment in preventing a particular individual from committing additional crimes.[6] In the past this form of deterrence often involved incapacitation, or taking actions to make it impossible for a particular offender to repeat the crime for which he or she had been convicted. Today incapacitation takes the form of incarceration (or milder forms of restraint, such as house arrest) or capital punishment.

The second type of deterrence, **general deterrence**, is based on the assumption that punishing individuals convicted of crimes will set an example for potential violators who, being rational people and wishing to avoid such pain, will not violate the law. Pro and con reactions as to whether this is the case may be based on conjecture, faith, or emotion, with little significant empirical data. This approach leads to dogmatic statements, which cloud the issues and should be examined carefully. Deterrence philosophy is recognized in many countries today. Spotlight 1.3 discusses its use in the People's Republic of China and in Singapore.

A third punishment philosophy in vogue today is the justice approach or the **just deserts** model. It is based on two philosophies, deterrence and retribution, and constitutes a reaction against the perceived ineffectiveness of rehabilitation.[7] The retribution basis assumes that offenders will be assessed the punishment they deserve in light of the crimes they have committed. It assumes that appropriate punishments will deter those criminals from engaging in further criminal acts and deter others from committing crimes.

Under the justice model an incarcerated person should be allowed to choose whether to participate in rehabilitation programs. The only purpose of incarceration is to confine for a specified period of time, not to rehabilitate the criminal. The offender receives only the sentence he or she deserves, and that sentence is implemented according to fair principles.

The justice model sounds good. People should be punished in accordance with what they deserve. But try applying it to the cases discussed in Spotlight 1.1 and the accompanying text. Which, if any, of the offenders *deserve* to be executed? If Brisbon is not executed, will more people commit atrocious murders such as he committed? If he is executed, will people who contemplate such murders refrain from the killing? How about mercy killing? Did incarcerating a Florida mercy killer deter others from such acts? Would incarceration have deterred Gilbert from committing that offense again, or was imprisonment unnecessary for specific deterrence in his case? Or is it possible that regardless of the stated underlying punishment philosophies accepted by a society, the reality is that particular decisions are sometimes made for other reasons? It is true, too, that reasons for reacting to crime may be made for a variety of reasons, including politics.

The Role of Discretion in Punishment

It is characteristic of criminal justice systems throughout the world that decisions may be made for political reasons that have little if anything to do with the issues. A large body of scholarship has developed in an attempt to explain criminal justice systems as an area where critical decisions are made by those in power for the purpose of maintaining control over those not in power. It is alleged, for example, that in the United States, women, minorities, and the poor may expect the blunt end of justice whereas white men make all the important decisions legislatively, administratively, and judicially.[8]

Others disagree with this position, and the conflict may be expected to continue. But as long as **discretion** is possible, political decisions may result. *Discretion* means that individuals may use their own judgment to make important decisions. The text discussion of Spotlight 1.1 contains examples of the exercise of discretion. Hans Florian was not tried for the murder of his wife, but Roswell Gilbert, who took his wife's life under similar circumstances, was convicted and served prison time. The jury could have chosen not to convict him, as has been the case in some so-called mercy killings. Thus, the jury had considerable discretion. In Gilbert's case, the governor exercised his discretion in releasing Gilbert before the completion of his sentence.

Discretion may be exercised by various persons within criminal justice systems, including police, prosecutors, judges or magistrates, correctional officials, and paroling authorities. In addition, defense attorneys exercise discretion in determining which defenses to advance at trial. Defense and prosecutors exercise discretion in **plea bargaining**. In high profile cases, especially those that are televised, the media's exercise of discretion may influence public perceptions of the trial.

Discretion is inevitable within criminal justice systems, although the degree to which it is permitted varies. Discretion may be abused, but it is not necessarily a

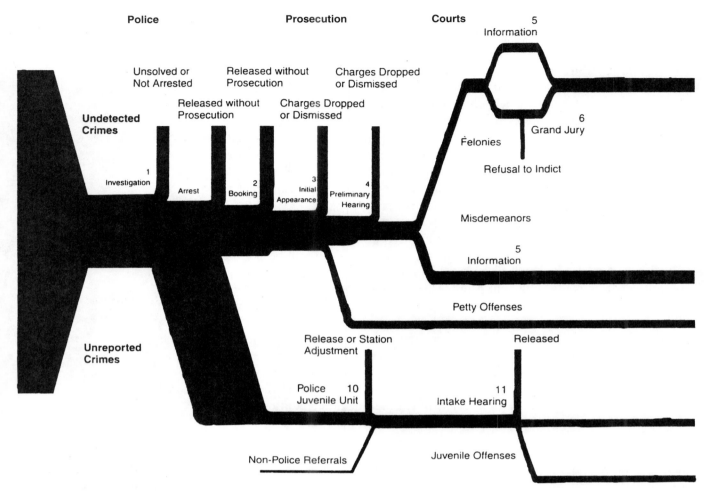

Figure 1.1
Institutions and Stages in American Criminal Justice Systems

Source: President's Commission on Law Enforcement and Administration of Justice, *The Challenge of Crime in a Free Society* (Washington, D.C.: U.S. Government Printing Office, 1967), pp. 8–9.

1. May continue until trial.
2. Administrative record of arrest. First step at which temporary release on bail may be available.
3. Before magistrate, commissioner, or justice of the peace. Formal notice of charge, advice of rights. Bail set. Summary trials for petty offenses usually conducted here without further processing.
4. Preliminary testing of evidence against defendant. Charge may be reduced. No separate preliminary hearing for misdemeanors in some systems.
5. Charge filed by prosecutor on basis of information submitted by police or citizens. Alternative to grand jury indictment; often used in felonies, almost always in misdemeanors.
6. Review whether government evidence sufficient to justify trial. Some states have no grand jury system; others seldom use it.

negative aspect of the system. It may be a positive factor. It is possible to establish guidelines for the exercise of discretion, but it is not possible to eliminate all need for discretion. In addition, attempts to abolish discretion in one area of the system may increase it in others. Thus, for example, if longer sentences are instituted to control crime but juries perceive these sentences as being too harsh, they might acquit rather than convict persons whom they believe are guilty. In such cases, the system would have no alternative but to free the accused. On the other hand, conviction of more offenders with longer sentences has clogged courts and prisons, creating serious problems of overcrowding in both areas.

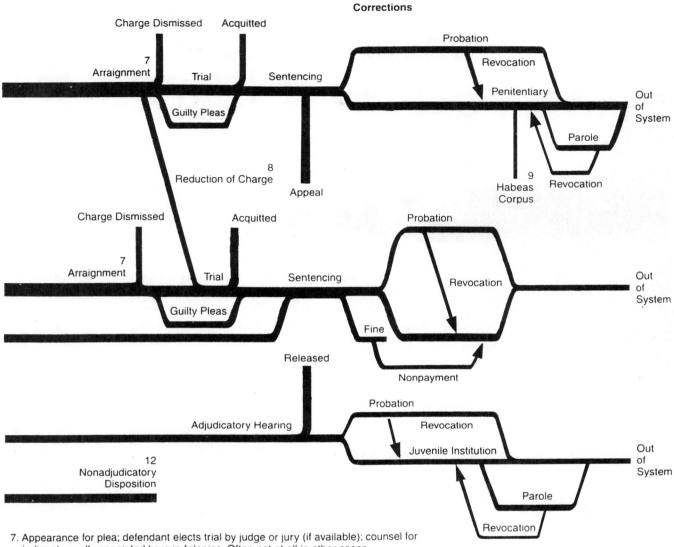

7. Appearance for plea; defendant elects trial by judge or jury (if available); counsel for indigent usually appointed here in felonies. Often not at all in other cases.
8. Charge may be reduced at any time prior to trial in return for plea of guilty or for other reasons.
9. Challenge on constitutional grounds to legality of detention. May be sought at any point in process.
10. Police often hold informal hearings, dismiss or adjust many cases without further processing.
11. Probation officer decides desirability of further court action.
12. Welfare agency, social services, counseling, medical care etc., for cases where adjudicatory handling not needed.

Components of Criminal Justice Systems

Criminal justice systems are composed of several components and processes, and they differ throughout the world. Figure 1.1 diagrams the most common model in the United States, although states organize and operate their systems in different ways. The federal system has some unique features as well. The various criminal justice systems have many common features, which are emphasized throughout this text.

In the United States, the most common organization of criminal justice systems is one consisting of four institutions: police, prosecution, courts, and corrections (noted at the top of Figure 1.1). The different stages are discussed in more detail where appropriate throughout the text.

A case may enter the system when a crime is reported to the police or when police observe behavior that appears to be criminal. After a crime has been reported, police may conduct a preliminary investigation to determine whether there is sufficient evidence that a crime was committed. If so and the suspect is a juvenile, he or she may be processed through the juvenile rather than the adult division of the system.

Not all arrested suspects proceed to the end of the criminal justice system. In fact, most cases do not go that far for a number of reasons. Police may decide that no crime has been committed or that a crime has been committed but there is not enough evidence on which to arrest a suspect. A suspect may be arrested but released quickly for lack of evidence. Persons who remain suspects through booking, the initial appearance, and the preliminary hearing, may be dismissed; or the charges may be dropped at any of those stages. These decisions may be made for lack of evidence or other reasons, some of them highly controversial, such as political pressures. Even after formal charges have been made against the accused, they may be dropped or reduced.

Suspects who proceed to trial may not be convicted. Despite strong evidence against them, they may be acquitted. They may be convicted but placed on probation, fined, or sentenced to work in the community in place of being sent to prison. Those sent to prison may not serve their full terms.

Criminal justice systems are a process as well as a set of stages, and many factors may affect how a suspect experiences the system. Throughout the text those factors are considered, but first, attention must be given to the basis of criminal justice systems, criminal law.

Criminal Law: An Overview

This section of the chapter contains an overview of criminal law, for that is the focus of the text. It begins with the differences between civil and criminal law.

Criminal and Civil Law Distinguished

Criminal law may be defined by contrasting it with **civil law**, which pertains to private rights. Criminal laws provide the basis for the actions that take place in criminal justice systems. They define acts that are so threatening to society (not just to the individual victim) that they require offenders be prosecuted by the government. They define punishments that may be imposed on offenders. Criminal and civil law, however, are not always distinguishable; in some instances they overlap.

Civil laws provide a vehicle for legal redress for those who are harmed by others. They are used to uphold certain institutions such as the family. Civil laws regulate marriage and divorce or dissolution, the handling of dependent and neglected children, and the inheritance of property. They protect legal and political systems, organize power relationships, and establish who is superordinate and who is subordinate in given situations.

Civil law governs many acts that are not discussed in this book, but one area of civil law that is related to criminal law is **torts**. The word *tort* comes from a Latin word that means twisted. In torts cases, the law permits the injured party to sue the person responsible for the death or injury (or damage to property) that results. If the suit is successful, the losing party may be ordered to pay for those damages.

Torts include varied actions such as injury and death caused by the negligence of others and damage to one's reputation caused when people make false comments that are slanderous, such as accusing a person of being a criminal or of having a sexually transmitted disease. Also included are unsafely designed or constructed products that result in injuries to persons or damage to property. An example from an area of tort law that has gained more recognition recently in the courts illustrates one type of tort, as well as the close relationship between torts and crimes. Some landlords have been required to pay damages to tenants who have been criminally attacked on rented premises. The legal theory is that the landlord was negligent in not providing adequate locks, lights, or security personnel.

When courts hold that landlords are liable in such cases, they are not saying that the individuals who committed the criminal acts are not responsible. The underlying assumption is that the criminal activities might have been prevented if the landlords had taken adequate precautions.

In cases constituting both a crime and a tort, how do the legal actions differ? In a torts case, the action is brought by the person who has been wronged. In a criminal case, the action is brought by the state or federal government because it is assumed that society's rights have been invaded, along with those of the victim. In a torts case, the losing party may be ordered to pay damages to the victim. In a criminal case, the defendant who is found guilty may be ordered to pay money to the victim as compensation for the crime; pay a fine to the state; engage in some type of community work service; or serve time in a correctional facility. Any combination of these activities may be ordered as well.

Civil and criminal cases are governed by different procedural rules; there are differences in the evidence that may be presented and in the extent of proof needed to win the case. Whether the action is civil or criminal may determine the type of court in which the trial occurs. In some cases, the action may not be considered a crime the first time it occurs. A first offense of driving while intoxicated is considered a traffic violation and not a crime in some jurisdictions, but a second or third offense may be a crime.

The distinction between a civil and a criminal violation is important. The repercussions of being accused of violating a criminal law are more serious than accusations of violating a civil law. In addition to the possibility of a prison sentence, persons accused of a crime may expect social repercussions even if they are acquitted. Some people lose their jobs as soon as they are charged with a crime, particularly when it involves sexual offenses. It is important that the criminal law not be taken lightly and that the term *criminal* be used only in referring to people who have been convicted of a *criminal* offense. Because of the serious impact of a criminal conviction, the law provides greater safeguards for those accused of crimes than for those facing civil suits. The most important safeguards are embodied in the concept of the adversary system.

The Adversary System

U.S. criminal justice systems are **adversary systems**, in contrast to the **inquisitory system** characteristic of some other countries. The two approaches may be distinguished in several ways. The adversary approach assumes that the accused are innocent. They do not have to prove their innocence; that burden lies with the state (or the federal government if it is a federal trial). In contrast, the inquisitory system assumes guilt, and the accused must prove that they are innocent. This difference between the two approaches is related to another basic contrast: the inquisitory approach places a greater emphasis on conviction than on the process by which that conviction is secured.[9]

The adversary approach requires following proper procedures designed to protect the rights of the accused. Those procedures are guided by two important principles: **due process** and **equal protection**, concepts considered necessary to create a system in which the accused has a fair chance against the tremendous powers of the prosecutor and the resources of the state. Theoretically, the protections prevent the prosecutor from obtaining a guilty verdict for an innocent defendant. In reality, justice does not always prevail.

The impossibility of explaining exactly what is meant by the concept of due process is illustrated by the comment of a former U.S. Supreme Court justice, who said that due process "cannot be imprisoned within the treacherous limits of any formula. 'Due process' is not a mechanical instrument. It is not a yardstick. It is a process."[10]

The basis for the right to due process and equal protection comes from the Fourteenth Amendment to the Constitution (see Appendix A), which guarantees that we shall not be deprived "of life, liberty, or property, without due process of law." Also, we may not be denied "the equal protection of the laws." The Supreme Court has decided numerous cases in which it has been argued that the due process or equal protection rights of individuals have been violated. It would take an extensive course in constitutional law to explore these concepts adequately, but we can look at them briefly. They are explained in more detail where relevant in subsequent chapters.

The concept of due process means that those who are accused of crimes and who are processed through a criminal justice system must be given the basic rights guaranteed by the Constitution. For example, defendants may not be subjected to unreasonable searches and seizures. When questioned by police about acts that, upon conviction, may involve a jail or prison term, they do not have to answer until they have an attorney. If they do not wish to talk then, they may remain silent. If they cannot afford an attorney, the state must provide one for them. They do not have to testify against themselves at trial. Certain rules of evidence must be followed during the trial.

Defendants may not be tried twice for the same offense; once a judge or jury has decided that the defendant is innocent, the state may not bring those same charges again in an effort to wear down the accused. In short, the state must conduct the criminal trial and the processes preceding and following that trial by the rules embodied in the Constitution, as interpreted by the Supreme Court of the United States and according to the established procedural statutes.

The equal protection clause of the Fourteenth Amendment is the focus of frequent lawsuits, too. That clause means that in general the government may not infringe on the rights of persons solely because of characteristics such as race, age, national origin, ethnicity, religion, or gender.

Constitutional Limitations on Criminal Law

The adversary model comes under attack frequently. Critics assert that it hinders law enforcement and, consequently, crime prevention and control. There is no question that observation of defendants' due process and equal protection rights creates obstacles for law enforcement. If authorities could accuse anyone of a crime regardless of available evidence, search and seize at will, interrogate suspects for unlimited periods of time when those suspects do not have an attorney, coerce confessions physically and psychologically, and so on, there might be more convictions, but the resulting loss of individual freedom and liberty is not tolerable in U.S. criminal justice systems.

In addition to the constitutional limits of due process and equal protection, state legislatures and Congress are limited by the federal Constitution (and interpretations of that document by lower federal courts and the Supreme Court) in how they may define criminal law. They are limited in criminal procedure as well. Throughout the text these limitations are discussed wherever relevant, but a few that are of importance to a general understanding of criminal law are noted here.

Criminal laws may not be vague or too broad. Laws may not specify everything that is prohibited; they must be flexible. However, to avoid being held unconstitutional due to vagueness, laws must meet three criteria: (1) give notice or warning to all who are subject to them; (2) protect against arbitrary and discriminatory enforcement; and (3) not unreasonably deny other rights, such as the First Amendment rights to free speech, religion, and so on (see Appendix A). With regard to breadth, a statute should not "sweep within its ambit other activities that constitute an exercise" of other constitutional rights.[11]

Another constitutional limitation of particular importance in the criminal justice field is that of the Eighth Amendment's prohibition against cruel and unusual punishment (see Appendix A). The issue arises frequently in capital punishment cases, and although the Court has ruled that capital punishment per se is not unconstitutional, it may be so if applied arbitrarily and capriciously.

The conflict between the legitimate concern of governments to maintain peace and control and the rights of citizens to be free of unreasonable governmental interference may be expected to continue. Throughout this text, examples of problems here and abroad are noted as illustrations of issues within criminal justice systems.

Sources of Criminal Law

Although many people think of law as those provisions written in the statute books after passage by legislatures, laws come from three sources: constitutions, statutes, and court decisions. State legislatures enact statutes that apply to actions in their respective states. Congress enacts statutes that apply to the federal government as well as to the District of Columbia. These statutes are called **statutory law**; they may apply to any type of activity, although they may not conflict with the constitutions of the respective **jurisdictions**. These statutes apply only to the jurisdiction in which they are passed, with the exception that no state may enforce statutes conflicting with the rights guaranteed by the U.S. Constitution. That document and state constitutions are sources of law, too.

Some statutes define the procedures that are appropriate for law enforcement. These are called *procedural laws*. Others define the elements that are necessary for an act to constitute a violation of the civil or criminal law. They are called *substantive laws*. For example, the crime of murder may be defined as the killing by one human being of another with malice aforethought. Convicting a person of murder under that statute requires proof of these elements: that a person has been killed, that the person was killed by the accused, and that the killing involved malice aforethought.

What does *malice aforethought* mean? It refers to the requirement of an intent to kill and the absence of any legal justification for that killing. But if the statute does not define that element, then court decisions, another source of law, may be used for a definition. Law that comes from court decisions is called **case law**. Much U.S. case law is derived from or influenced by English **common law**. *Common law* refers to those customs, traditions, judicial decisions, and other materials that guide courts in decision making but that have not been enacted by legislatures into statutes or embodied in the Constitution.

The common law developed in England after the Norman Conquest in 1066. Previously there was no distinction among law, custom, religion, and morality. Decisions might vary in different communities. The Normans wanted to establish some unity, so the king employed representatives to travel to the various jurisdictions. These representatives kept the king informed about the various decisions and carried news to each jurisdiction of what was happening in the others. "The result of all this was that the legal principles being applied began to be similar, or common, in all parts of England. Thus, the terms 'Common Law of England,' and 'Common Law.'"[12]

Another source that is important to an understanding of criminal law is **administrative law**. State legislatures and Congress delegate rule-making power to state and federal agencies. For example, prison officials are given authority to make rules that regulate the daily operations of their institutions; the Federal Bureau of Investigation is granted power to make rules governing the enforcement of laws under its jurisdiction. Such rules must be made according to specific procedures and guidelines. These rules are very important, but normally the violation of administrative rules is not viewed as criminal.

Violation of administrative rules may become criminal under some circumstances. Suppose that an administrative agency with the power to enforce rules concerning pure food discovers that a restaurant is serving spoiled food. Although this is not a criminal action, the agency may issue an order to the restaurant to stop the practice. If the practice is not stopped, the administrative agency may get a court order for enforcement; if that order is violated, the restaurant officials may be cited for a criminal offense. Even in those cases, however, violators are not viewed in the same way as those who violate the criminal law, and data on violations of administrative rules and regulations are not a part of official crime data.

The Concept of Crime

A **crime** may be defined as an "act or omission prohibited by law for the protection of the public, the violation of which is prosecuted by the state in its own name and punishable by incarceration."[13] Some jurisdictions define certain acts as violations or infractions. Those acts may be subject to fines or other minor penalties in the criminal law or to civil penalties, but the commission of those acts is not considered criminal. When an act is not defined or processed as a crime, it should not be labeled a crime.

Classification of Crimes

Crimes may be classified according to the seriousness of the offense; two main categories are used for this purpose. The term **misdemeanor** refers to the less serious offenses, while **felony** is used to classify the more serious ones. Generally misdemeanors are punishable by a short jail term, fine, probation, or some other penalty that does not involve incarceration in a prison. Felonies are punishable by more than a year in jail, incarceration in a prison, or capital punishment.

Crimes may be classified as *mala in se* and *mala prohibita*. *Mala in se* refers to acts that are considered criminal in nature, such as murder and rape. *Mala prohibita* refers to acts that are not regarded as criminal; they are criminal because the legislature has designated them as crimes. Examples of *mala prohibita* crimes are laws regulating the private, consensual sexual conduct of adults, the use of some drugs, and the use of alcohol by certain age groups.

Elements of Crimes

There are certain elements that must be proved before a person can be convicted of a crime. These vary from crime to crime and from jurisdiction to jurisdiction, but some common elements distinguish crime from noncrime.

An Act

In U.S. criminal justice systems, a person may not be punished for his or her thoughts; an act, or the omission of an act, must be committed, although some crimes do not require an act in the traditional definition of the term. For example, in the crime of conspiracy, which involves an agreement between two or more people to commit an illegal act, the agreement constitutes the act. Two parties may be convicted of conspiracy to commit a crime even though only one (or neither) was convicted of that crime. Thus, Timothy McVeigh was convicted of murder in the Oklahoma City bombings, while Terry Nichols was convicted of manslaughter, a lesser offense, although he was convicted of conspiracy to commit murder. In addition, a crime may be committed when a person is an accomplice to another who commits the criminal act.

In some cases, a crime may be committed when a person has made an attempt to commit an act defined as a crime but has not committed that act. The person must have made a substantial attempt to commit the crime. A very early English case established the crime of attempt. The defendant was accused of putting a lighted candle and some combustible materials in the house he was renting. The house was not burned, but the defendant was convicted. The court said, "The intent may make an act, innocent in itself, criminal; nor is the completion of an act, criminal in itself, necessary to constitute criminality."[14]

Failure to act may constitute a crime but only when a person has a legal duty to act. If a child is drowning and two people watch without making any effort to rescue the child, the lack of action of one may be a crime whereas that of the other might not meet the requirements of a criminal act of omission. In the first instance, the observer is a parent with a legal duty to aid the drowning child. Conversely, if the other person is not a close relative, has no contractual obligation to the child, and has not placed the child in that position of peril, he or she may not have a legal duty to come to the aid of the child. Failure to do so does not constitute a crime, no matter how reprehensible the lack of action may be from a moral point-of-view.

In order for an act to be criminal, it must be voluntary. A person who has a sudden epileptic seizure while driving a car, loses control, strikes another car and injures or kills another human being, would not necessarily have committed a crime. But the driver who has had prior attacks of a similar nature might be found guilty of a crime for recklessly creating a situation of danger to others by driving a car when he knows he may have such attacks and lose control of his car.

An Unlawful Act

A crime is an act prohibited by the criminal law. A person cannot be punished for acts that may be considered socially harmful but that are not prohibited by the criminal law. As noted earlier, the law must be reasonably clear about the conduct that is prohibited. A statute will be declared void when "men of common intelligence must necessarily guess at its meaning and differ as to its application."[15]

An Intent

For an act to be a crime, the law requires the element of intent or **mens rea**, a guilty mind. This is to distinguish those acts that may be harmful to others but for which the actor had no immoral or wrong purpose. Negligent actions may cause harm to others, who may recover damages in a civil tort suit, but the law requires a guilty or immoral mind for those acts to be considered criminal. Former Supreme Court Justice Oliver Wendell Holmes Jr. described the meaning of this distinction when he said, "Even a dog distinguishes between being stumbled over and being kicked."[16]

The intent requirement is complex. Neither court decisions nor scholarly legal writings provide an easily understood meaning. The intent requirement may

Spotlight 1.4

The Model Penal Code's Definition of Criminal Intent

Sec. 2.03. . . .
(2) Kinds of Culpability Defined:
  (a) Purposely.
  A person acts purposely with respect to a material element of an offense when:
  (i) if the element involves the nature of his conduct or a result therof, it is his conscious object to engage in conduct of that nature or to cause such a result; and
  (ii) if the element involves the attendant circumstances, he is aware of the existence of such circumstances or he believes or hopes that they exist.
  (b) Knowingly.
  A person acts knowingly with respect to a material element of an offense when:
  (i) if the element involves the nature of his conduct or the attendant circumstances, he is aware that his conduct is of that nature or that such circumstances exist; and
  (ii) if the element involves a result of his conduct, he is aware that it is practically certain that his conduct will cause such a result.

  (c) Recklessly.
  A person acts recklessly with respect to a material element of an offense when he consciously disregards a substantial and unjustifiable risk that the material element exists or will result from his conduct. The risk must be of such a nature and degree that, considering the nature and purpose of the actor's conduct and the circumstances known to him, its disregard involves a gross deviation from the standard of conduct that a law-abiding person would observe in the actor's situation.
  (d) Negligently.
  A person acts negligently with respect to a material element of an offense when he should be aware of a substantial and unjustifiable risk that the material element exists or will result from his conduct. The risk must be a of such a nature and degree that the actor's failure to perceive it, considering the nature and purpose of his conduct and the circumstances known to him, involves a gross deviation from the standard of care that a reasonable person would observe in the actor's situation.

Source: The American Law Institute, *Model Penal Code, Proposed Official Draft* (Philadelphia: The American Law Institute, May 4, 1962) Article 2, "General Principles of Liability." Copyright 1962 by The American Law Institute. Reprinted with the permission of The American Law Institute.

vary from crime to crime, but it is clear that some kind of intent must be present in order for an act to constitute a crime. In simple terms, an intent to do something means that the actor intends to bring about the consequences of his or her actions or engages in acts that are reasonably certain to bring about the negative effects. The actor does not have to intend the *specific* result that occurs. A person who fires a gun into a crowd intending to kill a specific person, misses that person, and kills another could be convicted of murder.

In this example, the intent comes from the evidence that the individual purposely and knowingly took the action that resulted in the death of another. Usually this is the easiest kind of case in which to prove intent, but the required intent need not be that obvious. Criminal intent may be found in cases in which the action is extremely reckless or negligent.

The definition of criminal intent in cases of reckless and negligent behavior is not easy. The Model Penal Code, reproduced in Spotlight 1.4, was drafted as a guide to use in defining those kinds of culpability as well as the two more common kinds of intent: purposely and knowingly.

Intent may not be required in some cases, such as those in which people are held responsible for the criminal acts of others. For example, the owner of a bar might be charged with a crime after one of his employees serves liquor to an underaged person who drives negligently and kills another. Nor is knowledge that a crime is being committed required in all circumstances. For example, sexual intercourse with a person under the legal age of consent may be defined as statutory rape even though the alleged victim consented to the act. Historically, the law has assumed that young women must be protected and thus cannot legally consent to sex. In recent years some of these laws have been revised or eliminated.

Attendant Circumstances

Acts may be criminal in some circumstances but not in others. As noted earlier, failure to act to save a drowning child constitutes a criminal omission only if the person has a legal duty to assist that child. It is true as well that some acts that normally are criminal, such as forcible rape, may not be criminal unless certain circumstances exist. Under the common law and under most criminal statutes in the United States, until very recently there was a marital exclusion for rape. That meant that a husband could not be convicted of raping his wife unless he forced her to have sexual intercourse with another man. Many states have changed their rape statutes to eliminate the marital exemption.

Concurrence of Act and Intent

For an act to be a crime, the act and the intent must occur together. It is not sufficient to have criminal intent today but not commit the act until later. *A* might intend to kill *B* today but not do so. One week later, after *A* and *B* have resolved their differences, they go hunting. *A* falls accidentally while preparing to shoot a deer, the gun fires, and *B* is killed. *A* should not be charged with murder because, at the time he fired, he did not have a criminal intent.

Causation

A final element of all crimes is that there must be proof that the result is caused by the act. If *A* shoots and hits *B*, wounding *B* slightly, *A* may be charged with attempted murder (if the elements of that crime can be proved). But *A* should not be charged with murder if *B* dies of causes unrelated to the act of shooting. **Causation** in criminal law is very intricate and complex. It is important to know, however, that legal cause is a crucial element that must be proved before a person is convicted of a crime.

Defenses to Crimes

The classical school of the 1800s believed that punishment should fit the crime and that there were no exceptions. All who committed a particular crime should have the same penalty. The positivists, who followed the classical school, advocated that some exceptions should be made. For example, because of their infancy, children should not have the same criminal liability as adults; indeed, children below a certain age should not be criminally liable at all. Those who have serious mental problems to the extent that either they do not know what they are doing, or cannot control their actions, should not be criminally liable. Exceptions or **defenses** thus crept into the law.[17]

Defenses to criminal liability have varied over the years, and like all areas of law, this one is in transition, with new attempts at criminal defenses occurring often, although some defenses have been traditional in many societies. Permitting sworn law enforcement officers to kill in self-defense or defense of others is an example.

Self-defense and defense of others may excuse persons outside the law enforcement field of criminal liability, too. Again, various laws specify the circumstances under which the defense is permitted, and many court decisions have interpreted these laws. Insanity is a defense that gained high visibility in the 1980s due to its successful use by John Hinckley, who attempted to assassinate then-President Ronald Reagan. This is a very controversial defense; a variety of tests are used to establish it, and there is much disagreement over the proper interpretation of those tests. Insanity is not used often, however, and generally it is not a successful defense. When it is successful, as in the case of Hinckley, generally the defendant is confined to a mental institution rather than released. Congress changed the insanity defense requirements in 1984 following the Hinckley case.[18] Other jurisdictions have abolished the insanity defense.[19]

Entrapment is another familiar defense. It is used by defendants who argue that they would not have engaged in the criminal conduct had a police officer (or other government agent) not induced them to commit the crime. The defense may be defeated by the government showing that the defendant was predisposed to commit the crime. The Supreme Court's general rule for determining whether government conduct constitutes entrapment was stated in 1958. In *Sherman* v. *United States*, the Court said, "To determine whether entrapment has been established, a line must be drawn between the trap for the unwary innocent and the trap for the unwary criminal."[20] Frequently that line is difficult to draw, and the entrapment defense raises many questions when the criminal law is used to control morality (discussed later in this chapter). It is difficult to get evidence of people committing sex crimes when consenting adults are involved and there is no complainant. Police may serve as decoys in an attempt to get evidence on prostitutes and others engaging in illegal sexual behavior. The involvement of police in such endeavors is controversial.

A defense that has been used previously but is gaining more attention today is one brought by Vietnam veterans and others who were subjected to great stress during combat. It is argued that these persons suffer from **posttraumatic stress syndrome** (PTSD). PTSD refers to stress that occurs after any traumatic event, such as war, rape, or other violent acts. Victims of these traumatic events continue to experience severe stress, manifested in nightmares and guilt; they lose their orientation and kill someone, thinking they are back in war (or some other traumatic event).

It is argued by some that PTSD victims should not be held accountable for their criminal acts. Where PTSD is permitted as a legal defense to criminal behavior, the defense may be used in various ways. The defendant may be found not guilty by reason of insanity caused by the PTSD syndrome. Testimony on PTSD may be used to mitigate a sentence or reduce a charge. It may be used also to exonerate a defendant.

A relatively new defense that is having some success in U.S. criminal justice systems is the **battered-person syndrome** defense. It has been used primarily by women who killed their husbands or other abusive men after an alleged long period of physical abuse. But the battered-person defense has been used in other contexts too, such as when a child kills an allegedly abusive parent. The defense recognizes that years of abuse may create in the victim a feeling of desperateness that she or he must act and act quickly. Some defendants who have been permitted to use the defense have been acquitted or convicted only of a lesser offense than the one charged. Some have been convicted but received lighter sentences. In addition, some governors have commuted the sentences of women who were convicted and served time for killing their spouses after years of alleged domestic abuse.[21]

The Reach of Criminal Law

An analysis of the legal definition of crime may answer the question of what kinds of acts are defined as criminal, but it does not answer the question of which acts *should* be included within the criminal law. Historically, the purpose of criminal law has been the subject of extensive debate. Some argue that only clearly criminal acts should be included and that criminal law should not be used to try to control behavior that many people do not consider wrong. Others take the position that the law is the most effective method of social control and therefore should embrace even those acts that some consider to be *mala prohibita* rather than *mala in se*. The issues arise most frequently when the criminal law embraces consensual adult sexual behavior and substance abuse.

Sexual Behavior

In a 1969 publication two scholars referred to U.S. criminal laws as the most moralistic in history—characterized by sex offense statutes designed "to provide an enormous legislative chastity belt encompassing the whole population and proscribing everything but solitary and joyless masturbation and 'normal coitus' inside wedlock."[22] In recent years many states have repealed criminal statutes that proscribe sexual behavior between consenting adults. They have limited criminal statutes to sexual behavior that is the result of force against any person, is committed consensually but with an underage person, or is committed in public. Many states retain the common law approach, however, and provide criminal penalties for adult consensual sexual behavior that is considered deviant by some members of the population. In a controversial decision in 1986 (*Bowers* v. *Hardwick*), the U.S. Supreme Court upheld the right of states to do so. This case involved consensual sexual behavior between two men in the privacy of their home where police had gone for legal reasons.[23]

Laws prohibiting oral and anal sex are enforced only occasionally against gay males or lesbians and rarely against heterosexuals. The historical argument for these laws was that such acts, along with sexual acts with animals, constituted "crimes against nature" and were forbidden by some religions. Occasionally such laws are enforced against aliens with the view of deporting them for immoral behavior.

Substance Abuse

Considerable debate is taking place throughout many countries in the world concerning the role of criminal law in attempting to regulate substance abuse. In recent years, many countries have increased penalties for the illegal sale and possession of alcohol and other drugs. Spotlight 1.3 gives a recent example of the harsh drug penalties in Singapore.

Restrictions on where people may smoke are becoming more widespread, especially in the United States, due to greater awareness of the health hazards of second-hand smoke. This movement toward controlling consensual behavior that may be a health hazard raises important questions regarding the purpose of the criminal law.

The critical question is not whether we should try to regulate some or all of these activities (although we do not even agree on that issue), but whether the criminal law is the best way to attempt control. For example, how does the offense of driving under the influence of alcohol or driving while intoxicated compare with another related act, public drunkenness, which is defined as criminal in some jurisdictions? Should the criminal law be used to regulate both offenses? Clearly, driving while intoxicated is a serious problem. Many fatal automobile accidents are caused by drunk drivers. But what about the public drunk who is wandering around but not harming anyone? Should that person be processed through the criminal justice system? If so, what do we do with the person after conviction? What is an appropriate penalty?

What has been the result of arresting people for public drunkenness? In most cases, the arrestees have overcrowded the jails and received no counseling or other services that would assist them in coping with the problem. Some jurisdictions have removed public drunkenness from the criminal law and provided alcohol treatment and other plans for handling the problem, while others have retained public drunkenness statutes.

Several reasons are given for including alcohol and other drug-related acts within the criminal law. First is the symbolic value of the legislation: by criminalizing the acts, society makes it clear that they are unacceptable. Second, it is assumed that criminalization has a deterrent effect; if the act is a crime, most people will decline to commit it. This reason requires more careful consideration. There is no significant evidence indicating that the threat of criminal punishment is a deterrent to public drunkenness. In fact, a California court concluded that jailing public drunks might even be counterproductive.[24]

Some researchers take the position that chronic alcoholism is a disease, not a condition over which the alcoholic has control. It is not clear which position the United States Supreme Court will take on the issue. In 1988 in *Traynor* v. *Turnage*, a case involving veterans' benefits, the Court classified alcoholism as "willful misconduct," but noted that it did not have to decide in that case whether alcoholism is a disease. "It is not our role to resolve this medical issue on which the authorities remain sharply divided."[25]

Since *Traynor* v. *Turnage*, some medical scientists have reported evidence of a hereditary basis for alcoholism. It has been suggested that an isolated gene may explain why many men can drink more than women without becoming intoxicated. If sufficient evidence suggests that the tendency toward substance abuse is inherited, we have to face the question of whether substance abuse should be decriminalized. And if so, in what way? Should the criminal law retain jurisdiction over the selling of alcohol and other drugs to minors? Should driving under the influence (DUI) of a controlled substance result in criminal liability if the driver cannot control his or her drinking? Given the high percentage of highway deaths that are caused by drunk drivers, one could argue that this criminalization should continue. But does it have a deterrent effect?

It is argued as well that because the use of alcohol (and other drugs) is related to criminal behavior, substance abuse should come under the jurisdiction of the criminal law. An earlier study of inmates revealed that many had been using alcohol or other drugs at the time of their criminal acts. Even if some of the inmates exaggerated their reports of alcohol use, the researchers concluded, "It is clear that alcohol has played a major role in the lives of many prison inmates." Furthermore, almost half the inmates said they had been drinking just before the commission of the criminal acts for which they were incarcerated at the time of the study. More than three-fifths reported that they had been drinking heavily.[26]

Later studies confirm that a large number of inmates as well as arrestees test positive for drugs. For example, a February 1997 publication from the White House, outlining the national strategy for drug control, refers to the latest National Institute of Justice Drug Use Forecasting data (1995), noting that from 51 percent to 83 percent of male arrestees tested positive for any drug. For female arrestees the range was from 41 percent to 84 percent.[27]

Substance-abuse violations account for a large percentage of the increase in crime and prison populations. According to the White House publication referred to previously, the "increase in drug offenders accounts for nearly three quarters of the total growth in federal prison inmates since 1980."[28] State prisons have also faced significant growth due to drug violations.

Studies of the effect of substance abuse on the crime rate must be analyzed carefully. Although it is unreasonable to ignore the possible effect of substance abuse present in so many instances when crimes are committed, the concurrence of alcohol or drug abuse and criminal activity does not necessarily mean that there is a direct cause-and-effect relationship. It is possible that the use of drugs and alcohol represents a lifestyle adopted by some offenders and has nothing to do with the commission of crimes. In those cases, attempts to enforce laws regulating the abuse of alcohol and drugs will not have a significant long-term effect on criminal activity.

Even if we decide that public drunkenness, driving while intoxicated, and substance abuse should be included within the criminal law, we should consider carefully what penalties to assess. What is accomplished by jailing a public drunk other than to get him or her off the streets? In most cases, there is no long-term positive result. For that matter, what is accomplished by jailing a person for DUI? Would it be more effective to impose a heavy fine and restrict or prohibit driving for a long period of time? Or is a jail term necessary to convince drivers that drunk driving will not be tolerated? If so, is that jail term worth the cost to society when new facilities must be constructed to handle the large populations of incarcerated people?

This discussion of criminalizing sexual behavior and substance abuse raises the issue of whether the criminal law is used too extensively, and therefore goes beyond the purpose of protecting the public's safety and welfare, and interferes with the behavior of private persons. Those who take this position argue that the criminal law is being used to encompass victimless crimes, or crimes without victims. They assert that the results are harmful in the long run: Police may invade personal rights of privacy in order to enforce the law; minorities and other unpopular groups may be harassed; courts, jails, and prisons may be overcrowded as a result of processing these people through criminal justice systems; black markets may develop to supply prohibited products such as drugs and alcohol; and attempts to enforce unpopular and unsupported criminal statutes may create disrespect for the law. Critical police resources may be diverted from more important functions.

Supporters argue that the criminal law is a necessary symbol of morality and that removal of *mala prohibita* acts from the criminal law would place society's stamp of approval on the behaviors in question. Resolution of these two positions regarding the use of the criminal law to control morality involves religious, moral, and ethical considerations as well as legal and empirical issues. In the final analysis, the answer may be a personal one. But it is clear that whatever position is taken, it will have important repercussions on criminal justice systems.

WiseGuide Wrap-Up This chapter begins the text with an overview of criminal justice systems and criminal law. Although the systems differ, all may be analyzed first in terms of punishment philosophies: retribution, incapacitation, social solidarity, revenge, rehabilitation, deterrence, and just deserts. In present-day United States the philosophies of deterrence and retribution, often combined in the just deserts approach, are dominant. Just a short time ago U.S. systems were dominated by the philosophy of rehabilitation, and today some efforts are being made to bring back that emphasis.

The role of discretion is discussed because it is crucial to criminal justice systems. It exists at all levels, and it cannot be eliminated. But it can be controlled by some measures, and if left unchecked, it can result in unfairness to defendants. After an overview of discretion the chapter turns to a brief look at the components of criminal justice systems, using a diagram of general U.S. approaches for illustrative purposes. All of the elements of the systems are discussed in more detail throughout the text.

Crucial to all criminal justice systems is the basis for those systems, criminal law. A criminal justice system is based on a society's willingness to grant legal authority to some individuals to impose punishment. Criminal law provides that basis in modern societies, and this chapter begins its overview of criminal law with a distinction between criminal and civil law.

Criminal law has existed for centuries, predating civil law and forming the basis for much of our civil law. In this country tort law is related closely to criminal law, and some acts constitute both crimes and torts. The distinctions are blurred, and they are changing.

Criminal justice systems may be based on the adversary or the inquisitory models. U.S. systems follow the adversary model, in which all accused are presumed innocent and the state must prove guilt. In contrast is the inquisitory system, in which the accused are presumed guilty and must prove their innocence. The adversary system is characterized by due process and equal protection. Other constitutional limitations include the requirements that statutes not be vague or too broad and that cruel and unusual punishment is prohibited.

Criminal law emerges from statutes enacted by the legislative branches of government, administrative rules and regulations, constitutions, and court decisions. All of these are important sources of law.

Criminal law is based on the concept of *crime*, which must be defined legally to fall within criminal justice systems. Crimes are classified as serious (felonies) or less serious (misdemeanors). Crimes may be classified as *mala prohibita*, criminal because they are so designated by society, or *mala in se*, criminal per se. Crimes have elements that must be proved before a person is convicted. Those include an illegal act that concurs with a guilty mind, attendant circumstances, and causation. Some acts that fit these elements may not be considered criminal because the accused has an acceptable defense. Attention is given to some traditional as well as some more recently recognized defenses to criminal acts.

Scholars, politicians, and the general public continue to debate what the reach of the criminal law should be. This chapter considers whether consensual sexual behavior between consenting adults in private and substance abuse should be included within the law's reach.

This overview chapter on criminal justice systems and criminal law sets the stage for more detailed analyses of the components of the systems. The next chapter focuses on another foundation important to the understanding of criminal justice systems—the collection and analysis of data on crime, offenders, and crime victims.

Apply It

1. Explain and distinguish deterrence, rehabilitation, incapacitation, and retribution. Explain how these punishment and sentencing philosophies relate to the justice model of punishment.

2. Discuss the punishment implications of the cases discussed in Spotlight 1.1.

3. How do you think discretion should be regulated in criminal justice systems? Be specific in discussing the process in terms of specific personnel, such as police, prosecutors, judges, juries, and so on. Consider your answer at the end of the course to determine whether your personal views have changed.

4. Contrast civil and criminal law and explain how the concept of tort law applies to both.

5. Discuss the similarities and differences between a crime and a tort.

6. Distinguish between the adversary and inquisitory systems.

7. Explain the meaning of due process and equal protection. What other constitutional limitations are placed on criminal law?

8. Do you think capital punishment is cruel and unusual punishment? A life sentence without parole for drug possession? For drug sales? Would your answer to the latter two questions depend on the volume of sales?

9. List and discuss the sources of criminal law.

10. How are crimes classified?

11. Discuss the basic elements of a crime.

12. What are criminal defenses? Illustrate.

13. Should the criminal law be used to control any or all of the following: premarital sex, extramarital sex, same-gender sex, driving while intoxicated, use of drugs, wearing seat belts?

Notes

1. See "Clemency Granted to a Mercy Killer," *New York Times* (2 August 1990), p. 9.
2. "What Are Prisons For? No Longer Rehabilitation, but to Punish—and to Lock the Worst Away," *Time* (13 September 1982), p. 38.
3. Cal. Penal Code, Article 1, Section 1170 (1997).
4. U.S. Code, Article 28, Section 994(k) (1997).
5. See, for example, United States v. Weaver, 920 F.2d 1570, 1576 (11th Cir. 1991).
6. See, for example, Douglas A. Smith and Patrick R. Gartin, "Specifying Specific Deterrence: The Influence of Arrest on Future Criminal Activity," *American Sociological Review* 54 (February 1989): 94–106.
7. See, for example, Ernest van den Haag, *Punishing Criminals: Concerning a Very Old and Painful Question* (New York: Basic Books, 1975); and David Fogel, *We Are the Living Proof: The Justice Model for Corrections* (Cincinnati, Ohio: Anderson, 1975).
8. For a brief overview of radical criminology, see Michael J. Lynch and W. Byron Groves, *A Primer in Radical Criminology*, 2d ed. (New York: Harrow & Heston, 1989).
9. For a discussion of the two systems in light of the English system, see Gregory W. O'Reilly, "England Limits the Right to Silence and Moves Towards an Inquisitorial System of Justice," *Journal of Criminal Law & Criminology* 85 (Fall 1994): 402–452.
10. Joint Anti-Fascist Refugee Committee v. McGrath, 341 U.S. 123, 162-163 (1951), Justice Frankfurter, concurring.
11. Thornhill v. Alabama, 310 U.S. 88, 97 (1940).
12. Hazel B. Kerper, *Introduction to the Criminal Justice System* (St. Paul, Minn.: West Publishing, 1972), p. 27.
13. Model Penal Code, Section 1.104(1).
14. Rex v. Scofield, Cald. 397, 400 (1784).
15. Connally v. General Construction Company, 269 U.S. 385, 391 (1926).
16. Oliver Wendell Holmes Jr., *The Common Law*, as cited in Morissette v. United States, 342 U.S. 246, 252 (1952).
17. For more details on defenses, see Sue Titus Reid, *Criminal Law*, 4th ed. (New York: McGraw-Hill, 1998), pp. 63–151.
18. The federal statute is the Insanity Defense Reform Act of 1984 (IDRA), U.S. Code, Title 18, Section 17, 4241–4247 (1997), which includes a new provision of "not guilty only by reason of insanity" and provides for a comprehensive civil commitment procedure. For a recent Supreme Court interpretation of this statute, see Shannon v. United States, 512 U.S. 573 (1994).
19. See Brian E. Elkins, "Idaho's Repeal of the Insanity Defense: What Are We Trying to Prove?" *Idaho Law Review* 31, no. 1 (1994): 151–171.
20. Sherman v. United States, 356 U.S. 369 (1958).
21. For a discussion of the application of the battered-person defense to clemency for children, see Jean Hellwege, "Battered Child Syndrome Is Basis for Successful Clemency Petitions," *Trial* 31 (April 1995): 19, 93. For a discussion of the use of the battered-person syndrome defense as applied to women, see Note, "The Battered Woman Syndrome and the Kentucky Criminal Justice System: Abuse Excuse or Legitimate Mitigation?" *Kentucky Law Journal* 85 (1996–97): 169–197. See also the symposium on Reconceptualizing Violence against Women by Intimate Partners: Critical Issues," in the *Albany Law Review* 58, no. 4 (1995): 959–1316.

22. Norval Morris and Gordon Hawkins, *The Honest Politician's Guide to Crime Control* (Chicago: University of Chicago Press, 1969), p. 15.

23. Bowers v. Hardwick, 478 U.S. 186 (1986). In 1996 the Georgia Supreme Court upheld a conviction for attempted sodomy, a misdemeanor. See Christensen v. State, 468 S.E.2d 188 (Ga. 1996). The statute is OCGA, Section 16-6-15(a) (1996).

24. Sundance v. Municipal Court, 729 P.2d 80 (Cal. 1986).

25. Traynor v. Turnage, 485 U.S. 535 (1988), *superseded by statute as stated in* Larrabee v. Derwinski, 968 F.2d 1497 (3d Cir. 1992).

26. Bureau of Justice Statistics, *Prisoners and Alcohol* (Washington, D.C.: U.S. Department of Justice, January 1983).

27. National Institute of Justice, *Drug Use Forecasting, Annual Report on Adult and Juvenile Arrestees 1995,* referred to in *The National Drug Control Strategy,* 1997 (Washington, D.C.: The White House, February 1997), p. 18.

28. *The National Drug Control Strategy,* 1997, ibid., pp. 19–20.

Crime, Offenders, and Victims

In early 1997 the Federal Bureau of Investigation (FBI) released preliminary crime data for the first six months of 1996, and for the fifth year, rates of serious crimes declined, led by a 7 percent decline in murder. Rates of robbery, aggravated assaults, and burglaries dropped by 5 percent. The only increase among serious crimes was a 2 percent increase in arson rates. Experts warned, however, that the declines may not be permanent. Some criminologists suggested that the declines represent only cyclical changes and may be expected to rise again in the near future.[1] Later in the year, when the final official data for 1996 were released, the FBI's report noted that the figures represented "the lowest annual serious crime count since 1986 and the fifth consecutive annual decline."[2]

These figures are encouraging, but crime data must be analyzed in light of changing demographics and other variables. Violent crime rates among young people have been rising in recent years, and by the year 2005, "the number of 14-to-17-year-old males will increase by 23 percent." Couple this with the fact that as a report compiled by a Princeton University professor notes, all major studies report that "after all is said and done the most serious criminals are males who begin committing crimes at a very early age," some even before they reach puberty.[3]

Violent crimes among young men are not confined to the United States. The beheading of an eleven-year-old Japanese boy in the port city of Kobe and the placing of his head in front of the gate to a junior high school shocked that nation in May 1997. Japan, a country with one-half the population of the United States, has only approximately 700 killings a year. That compares to over 20,000 in the United States.[4] Equally shocking was the June 1997 arrest of a fourteen-year-old male for the crime.[5]

Despite these recent statements concerning crime data, it must be understood that the collection of crime data is not as precise as some would have us believe. Not all crimes are reported to the

Key Terms

aggravated assault
arson
burglary
crime rate
crimes known to the police
domestic violence
forcible rape
hate crime
index offenses
larceny-theft
manslaughter
motor vehicle theft
murder
National Crime Victimization
   Survey (NCVS)
National Incident-Based
   Reporting System (NIBRS)
National Youth Survey (NYS)
property crimes
rape
robbery
self-report data (SRD)
statutory rape
Uniform Crime Reports (UCR)
victim compensation programs
victimology
victim precipitation
violent crimes
white-collar crime

police. Not all reported crimes are cleared by arrest; fewer still are cleared by conviction. This means that no data source is accurate in its measure of criminal activity. Additional problems exist when comparisons are made between local jurisdictions or between countries.

Despite the impossibility of detecting all criminal activity or prosecuting and convicting all guilty parties who are detected, crime data serve an important function. Crime data are needed by official agencies in determining policies and budgets. They are utilized by police officials who must decide the best use of their officers and their resources.

Crime data may be used by official agencies and by private citizens who are determined to make their communities safer for all who live there. Social scientists who study criminal behavior use crime data, both official and unofficial, in their analyses of why and under what circumstances people commit criminal acts. Crime data might be used also for political reasons in an effort to convince voters of the success or failure of crime prevention efforts.

The point is not to dismiss crime data because of problems of inaccuracy but rather to analyze carefully the various sources of data and determine which sources are best for a particular purpose. This chapter examines and analyzes the most common methods for collecting crime data: official reports of reported crimes; data secured from victims; and data from self-report studies. Following the description of data sources, the discussion compares those sources and analyzes the problems of collecting data by each method. The chapter contains an overview of the amount and types of crime and offenders as determined by official data as well as by data collected from victimization studies. Finally, the chapter looks at crime victims.

Learning Objectives

Learning Objectives

After reading this chapter, you should be able to do the following:

- List and evaluate the major sources of crime and victimization data.
- Recognize the importance of misdemeanors in criminal justice systems.
- List and explain four reasons why crime data may not be accurate.
- List and define the eight serious crimes as classified by the Federal Bureau of Investigation.
- Analyze and summarize recent crime data, noting changes in the rates of violent and of property crimes.
- Explain the meaning of *hate crime.*

- Discuss the demographic characteristics of offenders.
- Define *victimology* and describe and criticize the sources of victimization data.
- List the major variables used to analyze victimization data and explain the meaning of each.
- Explain the relationship between victims and offenders according to crime data, and predict your chances of becoming a crime victim given your current lifestyle.
- Discuss ways in which criminal justice systems have attempted to respond to the needs of victims; evaluate each.

Sources of Crime Data

There are two major sources of official crime data in the United States: the *Uniform Crime Reports (UCR)* and the National Crime Victimization Survey (NCVS). Table 2.1 explains the purposes of these two sources and their differences. The *UCR* reports crime data that come to the attention of police through their own observations or through reports from others. The *UCR*

T A B L E **2.1** Comparison of the *Uniform Crime Reports* and the National Crime Victimization Survey

	Uniform Crime Reports	National Crime Victimization Survey
Offenses measured	Homicide Rape Robbery (personal and commercial) Assault (aggravated) Burglary (commercial and household) Larceny (commercial and household) Motor vehicle theft Arson	Rape Robbery (personal) Assault (aggravated and simple) Household burglary Larceny (personal and household) Motor vehicle theft
Scope	Crimes reported to the police in most jurisdictions: considerable flexibility in developing small-area data	Crimes both reported and not reported to police: all data are available for a few large geographic areas
Collection method	Police department reports to FBI or to centralized state agencies that then report to FBI	Survery interviews: periodically measures the total number of crimes committed by asking a national sample of 49,000 households encompassing 101,000 persons age 12 and over about their experiences as victims of crime during a specified period
Kinds of information	In addition to offense counts, provides information on crime clearances, persons arrested, persons charged, law enforcement officers killed and assaulted, and characteristics of homicide victims	Provides details about victims (such as age, race, sex, education, income, and whether the victim and offender were related to each other) and about crimes (such as time and place of occurrence. whether or not reported to police, use of weapons, occurrence of injury, and economic consequences)
Sponsor	Department of Justice Federal Bureau of Investigation	Department of Justice Bureau of Justice Statistics

Source: Bureau of Justice Statistics, *Report to the Nation on Crime and Justice: The Data,* 2d ed. (Washington, D.C.: U.S. Government Printing Office, 1988), p. 1.

includes two crimes not included by the NCVS—murder and arson. Murder is not included in NCVS data because those data are based on interviews with crime victims. Arson is not included because it is too difficult to measure with the techniques used in the NCVS.

Of the two sources, the *UCR* is used more frequently. Despite their differences, the two sources may complement each other, but a comparison should be based on the realization of their differences. The *UCR* and the NCVS are based on different time periods, slightly different definitions of the included crimes, and different methods of counting crime.[6]

Each source has limitations, as noted in the respective discussions. But neither can estimate the extent to which a few offenders are responsible for large numbers of crimes. These reports disclose only how many crimes occurred, not how many of those crimes were traced to the same offenders; how many arrests were made, not how many times a particular person was arrested. More specialized studies disclose that a large percentage of those who enter prison to serve time have been convicted previously of other criminal offenses. Although these repeat offenders are relatively few in number, many authorities suspect that they account for an extremely large percentage of crime.[7]

Uniform Crime Reports (UCR)

The ***Uniform Crime Reports (UCR)*** includes crime data collected by the FBI. The FBI publishes the official report once a year. Originally seven crimes were selected, because of their seriousness and frequency, to constitute the *UCR* Crime Index. Known as Part I, or **index offenses,** they include murder and nonnegligent manslaughter, forcible rape, robbery, aggravated assault, burglary, larceny-theft, and motor vehicle theft. Congress added arson to the index in 1979.

Each month law enforcement agencies report the number of **crimes known to the police,** that is, the number of Part I offenses verified by police investigation of the complaint. A crime known to police is counted even if no suspect is arrested and no prosecution occurs. If a criminal activity involves several different crimes, only the most serious one is reported as an index offense. If a victim is raped, robbed, and murdered, only the murder is counted in the *UCR*. Offenses known to police do not show how many persons were involved in a particular reported crime. The data are used to calculate a **crime rate.** The national crime rate is calculated by dividing the number of Part I-reported crimes by the number of people in the country (data obtained from census reports). The result is expressed as a rate of crimes per 100,000 people.

In addition, the *UCR* reports the number of Part I offenses that are cleared. Offenses are cleared in two ways: (1) when a suspect is arrested, charged, and turned over to the judicial system for prosecution; and (2) by circumstances beyond the control of the police. For example, a suspect's death or a victim's refusal to press charges may signal the end of police involvement in a reported crime. Crimes are considered cleared whether or not the suspect is convicted.

Several persons may be arrested and one crime cleared, or one person may be arrested and many crimes cleared. The clearance rate is the number of crimes solved, expressed as a percentage of the total number of crimes reported to the police. The clearance rate is critical in policy decisions because it is one measure used to evaluate police departments. The higher the number of crimes solved by arrest, the better the police force looks in the eyes of the public.

Crimes of violence are more likely than property crimes to be cleared by arrest. This is because victims (or families in the case of murdered victims) are more likely to report violent crimes than to report property crimes and to report them more quickly. Victims of personal violence, as compared to victims of property crimes, are more likely to be able to give police pertinent information that might lead to an arrest. Murder is the crime most likely to be cleared by arrest; burglary is least likely, but motor vehicle theft and larceny-theft have low clearance rates, too.[8]

Arrest information in the *UCR* is presented in two forms: (1) the total estimated numbers of arrests by crime for each of the recorded offenses and (2) the number of arrests made during one year for each of the serious offenses per 100,000 population. The *UCR* does not report the number of persons arrested each year because some individuals are arrested more than once during the year. The actual number of arrested persons, therefore, is likely to be smaller than the total number of arrests.

In addition to data on crimes reported and arrest information for Part I offenses, the *UCR* publishes the number of arrests for less serious Part II offenses. Examples of these offenses are other assaults (simple), forgery and counterfeiting, fraud, embezzlement, stolen property, vandalism, prostitution and commercialized vice, other sex offenses, drug-abuse violations, driving under the influence (DUI), drunkenness, and disorderly conduct. Although some of the offenses included in Part II are felonies, others are misdemeanors; and they receive little attention in criminal justice texts, but they are important in criminal justice systems.

Recall that Chapter 1 noted that misdemeanors are the less serious criminal offenses, while felonies are more serious. Perhaps this is why so little attention is paid to misdemeanors in textbooks. But in terms of their impact on criminal justice systems and victims, misdemeanors can be extremely important. They occur more frequently than felonies, and attempts to apprehend offenders who commit misdemeanors often lead to a violation of constitutional rights. The importance of misdemeanors has been underscored by the Model Penal Code (MPC), which states that they "affect a large number of defendants, involve a great proportion of public activity, and powerfully influence the view of public justice held by millions of people."[9]

As noted in Chapter 1, some offenses may be misdemeanors the first time they are committed but classified as felonies for subsequent offenses. Chapter 1's discussion of whether the criminal law should be used to cover consenting sexual behavior between adults in private or minor drug offenses points to one of the reasons why misdemeanors are important. Attempts to enforce statutes covering the possession of small amounts of marijuana for one's own use or offenses, such as consensual and private instances of fornication, prostitution, or sodomy, may lead to invasions of privacy and the infringement of other constitutional rights. Attempts to enforce statutes regulating vagrancy and loitering may lead to violations of a person's right to be governed by statutes that are clear and concise and not too broad. Arrests in violation of constitutional rights offend our sense of fairness and justice and force our citizens to expend money and energy fighting criminal justice systems.

The lack of focus on misdemeanors is one problem with the *UCR*, but the FBI's reporting system has other limitations as well.

Limitations of the UCR

The most serious limitation of the *UCR* is that it does not include all crimes that are committed. Some have argued that *UCR* data are significantly lower than the actual incidence of crime. The UCR does not record all criminal activity for several reasons.

First, not all crimes are reported; in fact, most crimes are not reported to police. In 1992 victims reported only 39 percent of crimes to police. The following years the percentages fell, reaching 35.9 percent of all crimes reported to police in 1994. Four in ten violent and three in ten property crimes were reported in 1996, with reporting more likely among women and African Americans.[10] There are many reasons for not reporting a crime. Some victims think police will not do anything; others are embarrassed or believe they will be blamed for the crime. For example, **rape** victims may think that they will be suspected of encouraging the crime, particularly if the rape was committed by an acquaintance, as is often the case. Rape victims may not want to go through a trial in which they must face the alleged rapist and submit to intense cross-examination. They may be too embarrassed to relate the details of the crime to police or to their own families. In some cities there has been an increase in reported rapes after police have been given special training to deal with rape victims and counseling services have been made available. Some statutes have been enacted to protect the privacy of sexual assault victims and thus encourage them to report criminal activity. Some report the crime but refuse to testify against the alleged offender.

A second factor affecting crime data is the delay in reporting crimes. An earlier study in Kansas City disclosed that probabilities of arrest decline quickly as delays in reporting crimes increase.[11] Other studies have confirmed these findings and uncovered some of the reasons that citizens delay in reporting crimes.

Delay may be caused by an inability to decide whether to report the crime. There are three reasons for this indecisiveness. Some citizens want to verify that a crime has been committed. Others take some actions to cope with the crime before calling the police. Still others experience conflict about calling the police, so they try to avoid making a quick decision. Once the decision to call the police has been made, there may be further delays. A phone may not be available. The caller may not know the police number. The caller may have trouble communicating with the police complaint taker.[12]

Another factor affecting the *UCR* is police decisions. Crimes are included in the *UCR* only if the police decide there is sufficient evidence to believe that a crime has been committed. Police have wide discretion in making that decision, and factors such as the seriousness of the crime, the relationship between the complainant and the alleged offender, the desire for informal disposition of the case, deference showed the police, and so on may influence police decisions regarding arrest.[13]

Police individually, or as a department, may want to downplay the amount of crime in their areas; consequently, they do not record all reported crimes even when there is sufficient evidence that a crime was committed. In an earlier study of police reporting of thefts, investigators concluded that official crime data are misleading. Because they are used as official data by people who are under pressure to have those data show certain things, the data can be, and are, manipulated to show higher or lower crime rates.[14]

UCR crime data are affected by the fact that some crimes are not included within the list of crimes for which data are collected. As noted already, some misdemeanors are not included. Furthermore, some very serious crimes, such as those categorized as **white-collar crimes**, are handled informally, or they are handled by administrative agencies rather than by criminal courts and thus are not counted as crimes. Other kinds of crime are not recorded as either Part I or Part II offenses; for example computer crimes, organized crime, and corporate crimes. Yet the economic impact of these crimes is extensive, resulting in far greater total financial damage to the society than the theft crimes included in the *UCR*.

As already noted, arson was not included in the list of index crimes until 1979. Still other acts that are now defined as crimes, but previously were not, do not appear in any crime data.

NIBRS: The New Approach

The FBI recognizes that more data are needed. In 1988 the FBI published details of its new approach: **National Incident-Based Reporting System (NIBRS)**. NIBRS views crime, along with all its components, as an incident and recognizes that the data constituting those components should be collected and organized for purposes of analysis. The FBI refers to *elements* of crimes, among which are the following:

1. Alcohol and drug influence
2. Specified location of the crime
3. Type of criminal activity involved
4. Type of weapon used
5. Type of victim
6. Relationship of victim to offender

7. Residency of victim and arrestee
8. Description of property and their values.[15]

NIBRS collects data on twenty-two crime categories rather than limiting collection to the eight Part I offenses.[16] The new system is expected to improve the knowledge of crime, but it will take ten to fifteen years to implement the system completely. Data in this chapter are based on the traditional methods of collection because they are all that are available as of this publication.

The existence of unreported crime, often called the *dark figure of crime,* which never becomes part of official crime data, led to the establishment of another method of measuring crime. It was thought that if victims do not report crimes to the police, perhaps they will do so on questionnaires submitted to samples of the general population. Earlier victimization surveys revealed that many crimes were not reported to the police.[17]

Victimization surveys conducted by the Bureau of Justice Statistics (BJS) are called the **National Crime Victimization Survey (NCVS).** The NCVS is based on the results of interviews conducted each six months with persons in about 60,000 households. Household members are questioned about whether they have been the victims of rape, robbery, assault, household burglary, personal and household larceny, and motor vehicle theft. In addition, the NCVS conducts research on large samples in twenty of the largest cities in the country, along with eight impact cities. These surveys include questions on business as well as personal victimizations.

The NCVS is a valuable addition to the *UCR.* In addition to disclosing some crimes that are not reported to police, the surveys relate the reasons people give for not reporting crimes. However, the data are dependent on victim recall and perception, which may not be accurate. Despite this problem, victimization studies add to our knowledge of criminal activity. Following an evaluation by the National Academy of Sciences, efforts have been made to redesign the NCVS. This project began in 1979.[18]

In 1997 BJS reported that as a result of the changes in the design for collecting victimization data, the survey resulted in higher estimates of crime victimizations. Specifically, the rates for the following crimes were higher: "personal crimes (44% higher); crimes of violence (49%), rapes (157%), assaults (57%), property crimes (23%), burglaries (20%), and thefts (27%). A statistically significant difference could not be found for robbery, personal theft, and motor vehicle theft."[19]

National Crime Victimization Survey (NCVS)

In addition to the *UCR* data and surveys of the population that report how many people have been victimized, self-report studies are used to gather data on the extent and nature of criminal activity. **Self-report data (SRD)** are acquired by two methods: One is the interview, in which the person is asked questions about illegal activities. The other is the questionnaire, usually anonymous. Until recently, self-report studies were conducted mainly with juveniles, but increasingly the method is being used to study adult career criminals.[20]

SRD have been criticized on several grounds. The first problem is that of accuracy. Some respondents, especially juveniles, overreport their involvement in illegal activities, while others do not report some or all of their criminal activities. Other criticisms of SRD are that the surveys include too many nonserious, trivial offenses and sometimes omit serious crimes such as burglary, robbery, and sexual assault. Furthermore, self-report studies include too few minorities.

Self-Report Data

Taken together, these criticisms raise serious questions. White respondents tend to report greater involvement in less serious crimes that occur more frequently, and African Americans tend to report illegal acts that are less frequent but more serious. One study found that African American male offenders fail to report known offenses three times more often than white male offenders.[21]

Differences by gender have been reported, but such findings do not invalidate the use of self-reports. However, they do suggest that it may be necessary to compare these results with other measures and to develop more sophisticated methods for data analysis.[22]

Self-report studies may yield more useful data in the future. The **National Youth Survey (NYS)** is using interviews with adolescents over a five-year period to gather crime involvement data. The NYS has been structured to overcome many of the criticisms of other self-report studies.[23]

Crime and Offenders: An Overview

Before looking at crime data, it must be understood that all methods of counting and compiling crimes have problems. How crime is defined and how crimes are counted affect the results of all the methods. Crime is recorded and counted according to the policy used to determine whether one or more crimes occurred during the interaction between perpetrator and victim. Frequently, the issue arises in sex crimes. For example, in one rape case a defendant was convicted of three counts of forcible genital penetration (which includes rape by instrumentation). The defendant argued that he should have been convicted of only one count because each act lasted only a few seconds, and all three occurred during a brief period, seven to ten minutes. The court disagreed, stating that the statute's prohibition of "penetration, however slight, of the genital or anal openings of another person by any foreign object, substance, instrument, or device" against the victim's will means that *each penetration* is a separate act. A "violation is *complete* the moment such 'penetration' occurs." The court emphasized that the purpose of the statute is to punish those who commit the "outrage to the person and [violate] feelings of the victim" and that this outrage occurs "each time the victim endures a new, unconsented sexual insertion."[24] In some surveys measuring victimizations, however, these crimes might be recorded as three crimes but with only one victim. With these caveats, we will look at some crime data.

In the foreword to the 1982 *UCR*, the director of the FBI announced with cautious optimism that the rate of serious crime was down 3 percent from 1981. The cautiousness of his optimism stemmed from the fact that in the 1970s crime rates dropped twice, only to turn back upward shortly thereafter. In the 1984 *UCR,* the director announced that crime had declined for the third straight year with fewer index offenses reported to law enforcement that year than in any year since 1978. He cautioned that the unprecedented three-year period of decline might be coming to an end because there had been a slight increase in crime during the last quarter of 1984.[25]

According to the *UCR*, the number of crimes reported to the police and the crime rate began climbing in 1984, leading the director of the FBI to say, "There are few social statements more tragic than these."[26] The increase in the number of crime offenses continued through 1991 but began dropping between 1991 and 1992. The numbers continued to decline, and by 1996 had fallen to the lowest level since 1986, with a 10.3 percent decrease in the crime index total in 1996, the latest available official data, compared to 1992, as graphed in Figure 2.1. Experts do not agree on the reasons for these declines, now representing a five-year trend, but they warn that the rates can be expected to rise as more persons reach the ages between 13 and 21.[27]

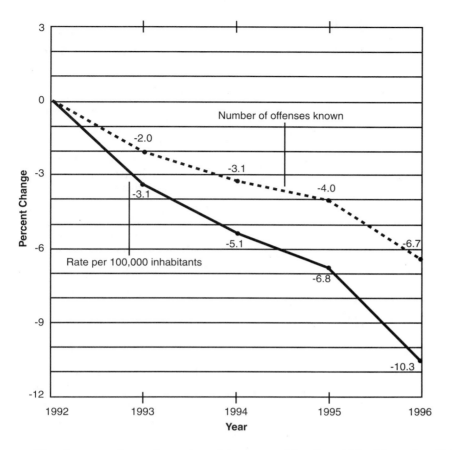

Figure 2.1
Crime Index Total: Percent Change, 1992–1996
Source: Federal Bureau of Investigation, *Crime in the United States: Uniform Crime Reports* 1996 (Washington, D.C.: U.S. Department of Justice, 1997), p. 7.

The downward trend continued in some cities for 1997, although official data were not available at the time this text went to press. In New York City, for example, the crime rate for violent felonies dropped 9.1 percent in 1997, continuing the decline that began in 1991. The highest drop was in murder, with a decrease of 22.1 percent. Officials attributed the continuing decrease to more successful efforts at drug control, but criminologists warned that the rates could be the result of decreasing numbers of young men and that they could change with population changes. Still, the decrease gives reason for optimism, especially since it was more significant in that large city than in many others.[28]

When measured by the NCVS, crime data also reveal a downward trend. According to the latest data, published in November 1997, victimizations for 1996 were the lowest since the NCVS was begun in 1973. Between 1995 and 1996 the violent crime rate declined by 10 percent, while the rate of property crime decreased by 8 percent. Spotlight 2.1 contains information on other changes in victimization data as reflected by the 1996 analysis.[29]

The FBI's division of index crimes into two categories—*violent crimes* (murder and nonnegligent manslaughter, robbery, aggravated assault, and forcible rape) and *property crimes* (burglary, larceny-theft, motor vehicle theft, and arson)—is used for further analysis of crime data.

Violent Crimes

Most of the reported serious crimes in the United States are property crimes, not violent crimes against the person. **Violent crimes** in the *UCR* include robbery, aggravated assault, murder and nonnegligent manslaughter, and forcible rape.

Frequently, the term **robbery** is used to refer to an act that constitutes theft rather than robbery. Since property is taken in both crimes, what is the difference? Robbery involves the same elements as larceny-theft but adds two elements that make it a violent crime: taking the property from the person or in the

Spotlight 2.1

Criminal Victimization 1996: Highlights of Changes between 1995 and 1996

- The 1994–95 general downward trend in criminal victimizations continued in 1996.

- The NCVS property and violent crime rates for 1996 are the lowest recorded since the survey's inception in 1973.*

- The murder rate dropped 10% between 1995 and 1996—the largest decrease in the past 4 years.

- Though overall violent crime rates decreased significantly from 1995 to 1996, the decline in the rates for robbery and aggravated assault were not statistically significant.

- In 1996 males experienced significantly higher victimization rates than females for all violent crimes except rape/sexual assault. Males were two times more likely than females to experience robbery and aggravated assault.

- In 48% of violent victimizations in 1996, the victim knew the offender.

- In 1996, 4 in 10 violent crimes and 3 in 10 property crimes were reported to the police. Females and blacks were more likely to report a crime to police than were males and whites.

- In 1996 violent crime rates were 16% lower and property crime rates 17% lower than they were in 1993.

- Between no two consecutive years from 1993 to 1996 did a violent, personal, or property crime rate increase a statistically significant amount.

- The decreasing victimization trends during 1993–96 were experienced about equally by both males and females and by the racial and income groups.

- Between 1993 and 1996 Hispanic households experienced a greater decrease than non-Hispanic households in the rate of property crime victimization.

Source: Bureau of Justice Statistics, National Crime Victimization Survey, *Criminal Victimization 1996* (Washington, D.C.: U.S. Department of Justice, November 1997), p. 1.

*After rates were adjusted following the 1992 NCVS redesign.

---

presence of the person and using force or threatening to use force. The FBI defines *robbery* as "the taking or attempting to take anything of value from the care, custody, or control of a person or persons by force or threat of force or violence and/or by putting the victim in fear."[30]

In some cases the line between larceny-theft and robbery is a very fine one, and not all scholars agree on how or where to draw that line. Thus, a crime such as purse snatching, which occurs so quickly that the victim does not have time to offer resistance or to be scared, may be classified as larceny-theft rather than robbery. But the fear that the victim suffers *after* the incident may be greater than the concern a victim has after a burglary or larceny-theft. It is this fear of violence, as well as the possibility of violence, that places robbery in the violent personal crime category.

Between 1995 and 1996, the number of robberies in the United States decreased by 7 percent. The average loss per robbery was $929. The total estimated loss was about $500 million.[31]

The second violent crime, **aggravated assault**, is a violent personal crime that involves an illegal attack on a person, which is committed for the purpose of causing death or serious bodily harm. Although some aggravated assaults are conducted without a weapon, many involve the use of a deadly weapon. Aggravated assaults are considered serious violent crimes because frequently they result in bodily harm or death. Between 1995 and 1996 the number of aggravated assaults decreased by 1.6 percent and accounted for 61 percent of all serious violent crimes. Twenty-two percent of the reported assaults were committed with firearms; 34 percent with blunt objects or other kinds of dangerous weapons other than knives; and 26 percent with hands, fists, and feet. Knives or other cutting instruments were used in the remainder.[32]

The third violent crime category is murder and nonnegligent manslaughter. The *UCR* defines **murder** and nonnegligent **manslaughter** as the "willful (nonnegligent) killing of one human being by another, but most jurisdictions separate the two crimes, which may be distinguished." In 1996 the volume of this crime decreased by 9 percent over 1995 and 17 percent over 1992. Most murder victims (77 percent) were men; 49 percent were African American, and 49 percent were white. Of the identified offenders whose race was known, 90 percent were men; 52 percent were African Americans, and 45 percent were white. Most of the white victims (85 percent) were killed by white offenders, while most of the African American victims (93 percent) were slain by members of their own race. Most men were killed by other men, but nine of every ten female victims were killed by men.[33]

The final violent crime is **forcible rape**, defined by the *UCR* as "the carnal knowledge of a female forcibly and against her will. Assaults or attempts to commit rape by force or threat of force are included; however, statutory rape (without force) and other sex offenses are not included in this category."[34] **Statutory rape** refers to consensual sexual intercourse that involves a female juvenile who is under the legal age of consent.

In 1996 reports of forcible rape were down 2 percent from those in 1995 according to the *UCR*. Over one-half of reported rapes were cleared by arrest in 1996.[35]

Property Crimes

Most of the serious crimes committed in the United States are not violent personal crimes; they are crimes against property. **Property crimes** declined 2 percent between 1995 and 1996 and represented the lowest total of property offenses for any year since 1986. Approximately $15 billion worth of property was stolen.[36] Four property crimes are included within the FBI's Index Offenses: larceny-theft, burglary, motor vehicle theft, and arson.

The most frequently committed property offense is larceny-theft, which accounted for 59 percent of serious crimes and 67 percent of all property crimes in 1996. **Larceny-theft**, which declined by 1.3 percent, is the "unlawful taking, carrying, leading, or riding away of property from the possession or constructive possession of another." It includes crimes such as shoplifting, pocket picking, purse snatching, thefts from motor vehicles, thefts of motor vehicle parts and accessories, and bicycle thefts in which no use of force, violence, or fraud occurs. In the *UCR*, this crime category does not include embezzlement, con games, forgery, and cashing worthless checks. Motor vehicle theft is excluded from this category, too, since it is a separate crime index offense.[37]

Burglary is defined by the FBI as "the unlawful entry of a structure to commit a felony or theft. The use of force to gain entry is not required to classify an offense as burglary." Burglary in the *UCR* is "categorized into three subclassifications: forcible entry, unlawful entry where no force is used, and attempted forcible entry." In 1996 two and one-half million burglaries were estimated to have occurred. These burglaries accounted for an estimated property loss of $3.3 billion, with an average loss of $1,332 per burglary. Most of the burglaries (66 percent) involved forcible entries.[38]

Motor vehicle theft, defined as "the theft or attempted theft of a motor vehicle," does not include thefts of items from within a motor vehicle; those are counted as larceny-theft. In 1996 an estimated 1,395,192 motor vehicle thefts occurred, representing a 5.2 percent decrease from 1995. The estimated annual loss was nearly $7.5 billion, with an average of $5,372 per stolen vehicle.[39]

The final serious property crime is **arson,** defined by the FBI as "any willful or malicious burning or attempt to burn, with or without intent to defraud, a dwelling, house, public building, motor vehicle or aircraft, personal property of another, etc." Arson did not become a Part I index offense until 1979; thus, trend data are not available for this crime as for other Part I offenses. Data are not available for all reporting agencies, and the FBI warns that as a result caution must be used in interpreting arson data. In 1996, 88,887 arson offenses were reported, but that represents only 68 percent of the U.S. population submitting reports for the entire year.[40]

This completes the overview of the four violent and four property crimes that constitute Part I offenses in the *UCR*. But beginning with the report on the 1996 data, the FBI included a section on **hate crime**.

Hate Crimes

In April 1990 the president signed the Hate Crime Statistics Act, which "mandates a five-year data collection of crimes motivated by religious, ethnic, racial, or sexual-orientation prejudice."[41] Subsequently, the statute was revised to include disability, although that addition is not reflected in the definition contained in the *UCR* because the collection of disability data did not begin until January 1997. Figure 2.2 graphs the distribution of hate crimes (also called bias motivation crimes) by the type of focus of the crime, noting that more were aimed at persons because of their race.

Hate crimes "are not separate, distinct crimes, but rather traditional offenses motivated by the offender's bias." Hate crimes may be aimed at property or at the person, but in 1996 the 10,702 reported hate crimes were aimed primarily against the person: 69 percent. Thirty-eight percent of the total hate crimes were crimes of intimidation; of the hate crimes committed primarily against the person, 56 percent were crimes of intimidation. Hate crimes against property more frequently involved destruction, damage, or vandalism, which accounted for 86 percent of the total.[42]

Characteristics of Offenders

A thorough study of crime includes not only an analysis of the number and type of crimes but also information on the characteristics of those who commit crimes. After a general overview of sources, data on offenders are discussed by the variables of age, race, and gender.

In the *UCR* arrest data, the variables of age, race, gender, and ethnic status are considered. Before the collection of self-report data, most studies of criminals were based on the *UCR* data, which revealed that a higher percentage of the arrestees were young African Americans from the lower socioeconomic class. Many people concluded that persons with these characteristics were more likely to commit crimes, while others argued that the data represented discrimination against these individuals.

When looking at the data here, we should understand that the differences between the crime rates of men and women and of African Americans and whites do not mean that gender or race *causes* the criminal activity or the reaction to that activity. There is some evidence that it is not race, age or gender that influences official reaction to the alleged offender but, rather, the seriousness of the offense committed and the degree of the offender's involvement in that offense.[43] There is evidence, too, that the differences in crime rates between the SRD and *UCR* data

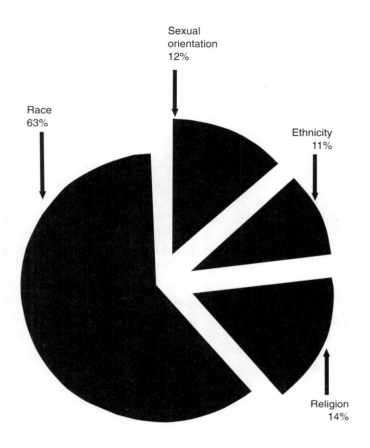

Sexual
orientation
12%

Race
63%

Ethnicity
11%

Religion
14%

Figure 2.2
Hate Crimes or Bias
Motivation Crimes, 1996,
Percent Distribution by
Category of Crime Target

Source: Federal Bureau of Investigation,
*Uniform Crime Reports: Crime in the
United States 1996* (Washington, D.C.:
U.S. Department of Justice, 1997),
p. 59.

may be explained by such factors as the fact that only a small number of African Americans were sampled in the self-report studies. Furthermore, some studies show that African Americans and whites differ in their tendencies to report certain crimes.[44] On the other hand, it is argued that the differences in crime rates by race are too great to be explained in any way other than discrimination.[45]

Age

Age is a variable most often associated with crimes, most of which are committed by young people. Of the 15.2 million arrests in 1996, 45 percent were of persons under the age of twenty-five; 32 percent were under twenty-one; 19 percent were under eighteen; and 6 percent were under fifteen.[46]

Various explanations have been given for the fact that crime decreases with age. Scholars who have studied career criminals have reported that the normal biological and sociopsychological maturation processes decrease criminal activity; that age enables people to calculate the probability of success in crime more accurately. Most criminals do not have great financial gains over a long period of years; nor do they avoid arrest, conviction, and incarceration with great success. Whatever the reasons, it appears that "the allure of crime diminishes substantially as offenders get older."[47]

There is more crime among the elderly, however. Although the figures are low when compared with the total number of arrests, crimes of the elderly could increase significantly in view of their increasing percentage in the population. Attention must be given to the processing and sentencing of the elderly offender as well as to custodial care for those who are incarcerated.[48]

Race

Another variable often associated with crime is race, although there is no general agreement on the impact of race on crime. Most arrestees are white (67 percent in 1996, compared with 31 percent for African Americans), but the percentages were much closer in the serious crimes. For serious violent crimes, 54.6 percent of all arrestees were white, compared with 43.7 percent African American. African Americans constituted 58.2 percent of the robbery arrests, but whites comprised 56.1 percent of arrests for forcible rape.[49]

For the less serious crimes, those designated as Part II offenses, 1996 arrestees showed wider differences by race. For example, the following data represent crimes of white offenders: 78.2 percent of arrests for runaways, 86.7 percent of arrests for driving under the influence, 80.9 percent of arrests for violating liquor laws, and 81.1 percent of arrests for drunkenness. Arrests for sex offenses (except forcible rape and prostitution) more often involved whites than African Americans, 73.9 percent compared with 23.7 percent.[50]

While analyzing these data, we must realize that even in cases in which the arrest rates are higher for whites than for African Americans, they may still be disproportionate, as African Americans constitute only approximately 11 percent of the total population. Second, we must consider not only arrest data but also the fact that official and unofficial crime data show differences between African Americans and whites at all levels of criminal justice systems.

Gender

A third demographic variable associated with crime is gender. Historically, crime rates for men have been significantly higher than those for women, with the exception of those crimes that by definition are predominantly female, such as prostitution. Men accounted for 79 percent of all arrests in 1996 and for 85 percent of all arrests for serious violent crimes. However, between 1987 and 1996 the percent change in total arrests of women increased by 35.9 percent compared to an increase of 12.1 percent for men. These overall arrests are even more interesting when broken down by crime. For example, between 1987 and 1996 the increase in arrests for aggravated assaults increased by 94.3 percent for women, compared to 35.4 percent for men. Arrests for robbery were up 31.6 percent for women but only 8.6 percent for men. Arrests for burglary increased 11.2 percent for women, while declining 20.8 percent for men.[51]

Among less serious crimes, the arrests for both men and women for offenses against family and children were up significantly in 1996 compared to 1987, but the increase for women was 196.7 percent compared to 104.1 percent for men. In the category of other assaults (excluding aggravated assaults), the change was a 117.7 percent increase for women, compared to an increase of 52.9 percent for men. On the other hand, the decrease in arrests for prostitution and commercialized vice of 18.1 percent for women compared to an increase of only 4.5 percent for men.[52]

Crime Victims

Until recently the study of victims was not an important focus among social scientists. This has changed in the past decade, with more attention being given to studying the characteristics and problems of victims as well as to improving the responses of criminal justice systems to victims' needs. Professional societies such as the National Organization for Victim Assistance (NOVA) have been instrumental in passing federal and state legislation concerning victims. NOVA has provided

PROFESSIONS 2.1

Careers in Victimology

The text notes that in recent years Congress has enacted legislation to provide assistance to crime victims. States have done so, too, creating numerous job opportunities in victimology. Provisions for financial assistance require persons to administer the programs. Counseling of crime victims requires specialized training in the treatment of victims of rape and other sexual crimes. Many jurisdictions have established rape crisis centers, while others have concentrated on training police and prosecutors to understand the trauma suffered by sex crime victims. School teachers must be informed regarding what to expect, especially from children who have become crime victims.

Background checks for employees in many jobs are important in order to avoid the negligent hiring of persons who might victimize those with whom they come into contact during work. All individuals who deal with victims must be sensitized to the privacy requirements regarding the records of crime victims. Preparing victim impact statements for court is a new area of crucial paper work required of probation officers and others. Requirements that victims be notified of pending court and other important hearings create jobs for persons charged with these reponsibilities.

Although we have a long way to go before victims receive sufficient assistance in our criminal justice systems, we have made progress at the national, state, and local levels, and interesting and challenging job opportunities exist for those who wish to work with crime victims.

assistance to thousands of victims and works directly with local organizations to improve services at that level. Workshops on **victimology** have increased knowledge and understanding of the problems.[53] Job opportunities have been developed in victimology, as illustrated by Professions 2.1

Concern with victims' needs has led to national legislation on their behalf. In response to the Victim and Witness Protection Act of 1982,[54] a federal statute, the U.S. Attorney General's office issued detailed guidelines concerning the treatment of crime victims and witnesses by prosecutors and investigators in the Department of Justice. These guidelines are designed to protect the privacy of victims and witnesses and provide medical and social services as well as counseling. Notification of court proceedings, restitution, and other programs available for the assistance of victims and witnesses are provided as well. Some states have gone beyond the federal provisions and enacted additional legislation to aid victims, and in the 1994 crime bill Congress included some provisions to enhance victims' rights, with a major focus on domestic violence victims.[55]

The NCVS data include information on characteristics such as the age, gender, and race of crime victims. For many years analyses of victimization data have revealed differences in the rates of victimization of specific groups within the population. Young people, men (except for rape and sexual assault), African Americans, Hispanics, divorced or separated people, the unemployed, the poor, and residents of central cities are the most frequent violent crime victims.[56]

Victimization data show that African Americans suffer higher rates of violent and household crimes than whites, and generally violent crimes against African Americans are more serious than those committed against whites. Offenders who victimize African Americans are more likely to use weapons; violent crimes against African Americans involved a gun in twice as many cases as compared to whites. African American victims are more likely than whites to be attacked physically during the crime's commission.[57]

Characteristics of Victims

African Americans are victimized by robberies three times as frequently as whites, and they are twice as likely as whites to be the victims of aggravated assaults. For overall assaults or simple assaults, the differences in victimization of African Americans as compared to whites is not significant.[58]

Victimization data distinguish Hispanic victims as well. Earlier analyses of data disclosed that Hispanics, whose growth is expanding more rapidly than any other racial or ethnic group in the United States, were more often victimized by violent crimes than were non-Hispanics. They endured a higher rate of household crimes as well. These differences may be explained in part by the higher rates of poverty, residence in cities, and youth among Hispanics.[59]

According to the most recent victimization data, Hispanics are more frequently the victims of completed violent crimes although the overall rates of violent crimes and of attempted violent crimes do not differ significantly when Hispanics are compared with non-Hispanics. The crimes of robbery and personal theft, however, are twice as likely to be committed against Hispanics as against non-Hispanics.[60]

Differences in property victimizations appear by race and ethnicity as well. In the most recent victimization data, "For overall property crime, household burglary, motor vehicle theft and theft, black and Hispanic households were more likely to experience property crimes than white or non-Hispanic households, respectively." Motor vehicle thefts victimized African Americans and Hispanics twice as frequently as whites and non-Hispanics.[61]

A final, significant variable in victimizations is that of age. Young adults and teenagers are more likely than senior citizens to become victims of serious violent crimes. A 1997 publication of the Bureau of Justice Statistics reports that persons in the age group eighteen to twenty-one were the most likely targets for violent crimes, with race and ethnicity apparently factors as well. BJS reported 72 victimizations per 1,000 African Americans; 50 per 1,000 Hispanics, and 46 victimizations per 1,000 whites in that age group. Women below the age of 25 were victims in over 52 percent of all rape/sexual assaults.[62]

The Relationship Between Victims and Offenders

According to the latest BJS victimization data, approximately one-half of the victims of nonfatal violent crimes knew their assailants, with 68 percent of rape victims knowing their offenders. Robberies, on the other hand, are usually committed by strangers, and only 23 percent of victims knew their assailants.[63]

Violent crimes committed by relatives are much more likely to be against women than against men, while violent crimes committed by strangers are more likely to have male than female victims. Crimes committed by strangers are more likely to involve more than one offender and to involve a weapon.[64]

Social interaction between offender and victim is an important variable in some crimes. Normally, violence in the form of assault or murder is preceded by social interaction, and physical violence is more likely if both the offender and the victim define the situation as one calling for violence. If only one is prone toward physical violence, generally the altercation will not become a physical one. In this sense, the victim may contribute to his or her own injury or death, but that does not mean the victim caused or is responsible for the crime.

In recent years considerable attention and focus have been placed on the type of relationships between victims and offenders, and the magnitude of the problems of **domestic violence** have been highlighted in widely publicized trials.

In 1994 Erik and Lyle Menendez, who admitted that they killed their parents, alleged that they were abused by their parents over a period of years and that they feared their parents would kill them. Their first trial ended in hung juries; their second trial ended with convictions for both; they were sentenced to life in prison.

The second crime was the double murder of Nicole Brown Simpson and her friend, Ronald Goldman. Nicole's ex-husband, O. J. Simpson, national hero and former football star, was charged with both murders. As early evidence in the prosecution's case revealed, the Simpsons had experienced domestic problems prior to the divorce, with Nicole calling the police to report that her husband was attacking her. After Simpson was acquitted of both murders, some jurors stated that the domestic violence evidence was not influential in their decision with regard to Simpson's guilt. Subsequently Simpson was found liable for the murders in a civil trial brought by the Brown and Goldman families.

It is difficult to estimate the extent of violence committed by those who know each other, especially within the domestic setting. Such crimes are not always reported by the victims or by other family members because of fear, embarrassment, or for other reasons, such as a hope that the situation will improve. With the hope of improving data collections, NCVS officials spent ten years redesigning their survey instruments. For example, the new techniques involve asking about a broader scope of sexual assaults, ranging from a completed rape to a threat of sexual violence by a domestic partner. The first results, based on 1992–1993 data, were reported in 1995. Highlights of that report are contained in Spotlight 2.2.

Another victimization focus is on the fear of random violence, resulting in crimes such as the one noted in Spotlight 2.3, which describes the random victimization of Americans visiting in another country but has numerous counterparts in the United States. The fear of violent crime by strangers, who often pick their victims randomly, led U.S. Supreme Court Chief Justice Warren E. Burger to refer in 1981 to the "reign of terror in American cities." One privately funded study of crime concluded that "the fear of crime is slowly paralyzing American society."[65]

In 1996, however, the National Association of Police Organizations (NAPO) released the results of its survey, which revealed that although Americans believe that crime is getting worse overall, they do not express that concern with their own communities. According to the NAPO, approximately three out of five Americans do not express a fear of becoming a crime victim.[66] On the other hand, a poll of 2,000 teenagers conducted by Louis Harris & Associates and released in 1996, reported that the fear of crime is high among teens. One out of nine said they stayed away from school at times because of this fear, while one in eight teens reported that at times they carry a weapon for protection. That figure rises to two in five in high-crime neighborhoods.[67]

The fear of crime may not always be realistic in terms of the probability that crimes will occur, but fear leads to lifestyle changes for many, especially the elderly. A purse snatching may have a far more serious effect on an elderly person than it would have on younger victims. The elderly are more likely to be injured seriously in any altercation between the assailant and the victim. Such direct contact may be much more frightening to an elderly person. The loss of money may be more serious to a person living on a fixed income. For many elderly, fear of crime leads to severe changes in lifestyle, to the point that they refuse to leave their dwellings.[68]

Women may adjust their lifestyles to decrease their chances of becoming crime victims. They may be advised by police and others to do so. In various cities police have reported that a high percentage of rapes are committed against victims

The Fear of Crime and Citizens' Reactions

Spotlight 2.2

Violence Against Women: Estimates from the Redesigned Survey

- Women age 12 or older annually sustained almost 5 million violent victimizations in 1992 and 1993. About 75% of all lone-offender violence against women and 45% of violence involving multiple-offenders was perpetrated by offenders whom the victim knew. In 29% of all violence against women by a lone offender, the perpetrator was an intimate (husband, ex-husband, boyfriend, or ex-boyfriend).

- Women were about 6 times more likely than men to experience violence committed by an intimate.

- Women annually reported about 500,000 rapes and sexual assaults to interviewers. Friends or acquaintances of the victims committed over half of these rapes or sexual assaults. Strangers were responsible for about 1 in 5.

- Women of all races and Hispanic and non-Hispanic women were about equally vulnerable to violence by an intimate.

- Women age 19 to 29 and women in families with incomes below $10,000 were more likely than other women to be victims of violence by an intimate.

- Among victims of violence committed by an intimate, the victimization rate of women separated from their husbands was about 3 times higher than that of divorced women and about 25 times higher than that of married women. Because the NCVS reflects a respondent's marital status at the time of the interview, which is up to 6 months after the incident, it is possible that separation or divorce followed the violence.

- Female victims of violence by an intimate were more often injured by the violence than females victimized by a stranger.

Source: Bureau of Justice Statistics, *Violence against Women: Estimates from the Redesigned Survey* (Washington, D.C.: U.S. Department of Justice, August 1995): 1.

Spotlight 2.3

Random Violence Claims Young American Victim

He was only seven years old when he was killed by gunfire while riding with his parents and sister on an Italian highway. Nicholas Green was a lively young brother and son full of life and vigor when he was killed while vacationing with his family. His distraught parents donated his organs to several children who were waiting for a chance at a longer life. They won the hearts of the Italian people who gave them a gold medal for their generosity in the face of tragedy. The family expressed its confidence in the Italian government's efforts to apprehend, try, and punish the offenders even after a trial of suspects resulted in acquittals.

Source: Summarized by the author from media sources.

who have been careless. They were walking alone at night, hitchhiking, sleeping in apartments with unlocked doors or windows, or going out with someone they met at a bar. Other women, because of their fear of crime, may avoid going places they would like to go and thereby reduce the probability that they will be victimized. But they deprive themselves of a lifestyle they prefer. For them, one cost of crime is diminished personal freedom.

Women and the elderly are not the only ones who make changes in lifestyle as a result of a concern with crime. Many people move or install expensive burglar alarms. Others refrain from going out at night or from traveling to certain areas. After terrorist incidents from 1985 to 1986 in several foreign countries where Americans were visiting, many Americans changed their plans to travel abroad. The fear of crime might not have been the only reason for such changes, but it certainly was one factor, along with the falling value of the American dollar. Although the dollar continued to fall in 1987, Americans in increasing numbers traveled abroad, and the figures rose again in 1988, only to fall during the 1990–91 Persian Gulf crisis. The apparent increase in fear of crime, with resulting changes in lifestyle, has led some scholars to conclude that fear of crime is a serious problem. "Left unchecked, it can destroy the fabric of civilized society, causing us to become suspicious of each other, locking ourselves in our homes and offices, and relinquishing our streets to predators."[69]

Research in the 1980s and 1990s provides information on how victims react to crime. Findings of this research have led to significant changes in criminal justice systems. It has not been an easy journey for crime victims; nor are all of their problems solved. Victim reaction, however, has been a key factor in these changes.

Criminal Justice Systems and Crime Victims

In 1982 President Ronald Reagan established the President's Task Force on Victims, which was followed in 1984 by the Attorney General's Task Force on Family Violence. Both commissions interviewed crime victims and others. Most of the victims spoke negatively about their treatment in criminal justice systems.

The criminal justice system's reaction to some crime victims means that they are victimized twice: once by the criminal and once by the system in a variety of ways. First, the victim may be blamed for the crime. Particularly in the case of sexual assault, the response of the system may be that the victim asked for it by being in a questionable place such as a bar, or by hitchhiking on the highway, or by having a questionable reputation. This is referred to as **victim precipitation**.

In addition to being blamed for the crime, victims may perceive that police and others will not be sympathetic to domestic violence or other crimes committed by known persons, that they view those actions as domestic problems, not violence. Some rape victims have complained about the reactions of police and prosecutors, alleging that they have not tried to understand the problems suffered by the victims.

Third, some victims (and others) complain that U.S. criminal justice systems favor defendants over victims.[70] This response should be analyzed in light of later discussions of defendants' rights, but basically the position is that criminal justice systems have gone too far in protecting defendants to the exclusion of victims. In an effort to combat this perception, some jurisdictions have enacted statutes (or constitutional amendments) designed to give more rights to victims. By 1997 twenty-nine states had victims' rights provisions in their constitutions, and the federal government was attempting to do likewise with the U.S. Constitution.[71]

There have been some legal challenges to victim involvement in criminal proceedings. In 1987 the U.S. Supreme Court ruled in *Booth* v. *Maryland* that at death sentence hearings the constitutional rights of defendants are not consistent with evidence of a Victim Impact Statement to the extent that that statement contains information on any of the following: the severe emotional impact of the crime on the family, the personal characteristics of the victim, and the family members' opinions and characterizations of the crime and of the offender.[72]

In 1991 the Supreme Court reversed itself in part. In *Payne* v. *Tennessee*, the Court held that a VIS may be used at capital sentencing hearings. Writing for the majority, Chief Justice Rehnquist said that the two previous cases were decided wrongly. Rehnquist noted that if the victim is a "faceless stranger at the penalty phase of a capital trial," the state may be deprived of "the full moral force of its evidence and may prevent the jury from having before it all the information necessary to determine the proper punishment for a first-degree murder."[73]

Other changes designed to benefit victims have been made within criminal justice systems. Many jurisdictions have started training police and prosecutors to be sensitive to the needs of particular types of victims, such as victims of rape and domestic violence, as well as very young victims. Some departments have special units of officers designated to handle allegations of rape, domestic violence, or child abuse.

Many jurisdictions have changed their arrest policies. Domestic violence victims have complained that police view their problems as domestic problems, not as violence, and that police do not arrest the offenders. If police do arrest, prosecutors will not file charges. Police response to that complaint has been that most victims will not cooperate and without their cooperation, most prosecutions of domestic violence cases will not be successful. Victims respond that they are afraid that if they cooperate the alleged offenders will retaliate.

In an attempt to remove the responsibility (and thus increased chances of retaliation by the accused) from the victim, some police departments have instituted a policy of mandatory arrests in domestic battery cases. Mandatory arrests remove from police the discretion to avoid the situation, mediate, or recommend civil action only. If called to the scene of a domestic battering, police must arrest if they have probable cause to believe that battering has occurred.[74]

Changes have been made in arrests of alleged offenders in domestic violence cases, and there is some evidence that the policies are effective.[75] Although many are still reluctant to do so, an increasing number of public welfare professionals, teachers, and doctors do report suspected child abuse, and all states now have legislation requiring them to do so. Despite this, underreporting remains a problem.

Legislative and administrative changes in the roles of prosecutors and judges have been made. Training programs for prosecutors have given them greater understanding of the unique problems suffered by domestic abuse victims. Provision of counseling services for victims, court-ordered counseling for those found guilty of child abuse or domestic violence, greater restrictions on pretrial release of suspects, and many other changes have occurred.[76]

Some changes have been made in court procedures to make it more comfortable and less embarrassing for victims to testify. Testifying in court is a difficult experience for most people, but that experience may be traumatic for a crime victim, particularly a victim of a sensitive personal crime such as rape. In the past, rape victims could be asked questions about their prior sexual experiences. Today, many jurisdictions prohibit such questions on the grounds that the information is not relevant to the case on trial, will prejudice the jury, and will discourage rape victims from agreeing to testify. Exceptions may be made, as in the case of the victim's prior sexual experience with the defendant.

Court rules have been relaxed in some cases in which children are sexual abuse victims. Many children do not understand the sexual experience and find it very difficult to explain what happened. Prosecutors may use anatomically correct dolls and ask the children to demonstrate what happened. Rules regarding direct testimony of complaining witnesses have been relaxed in some courts when the victims are children. Some courts permit the testimony of a child victim to be presented to the court by videotape. Others permit doctors or nurses to testify concerning what the child said to them and thus eliminate the child's direct testimony in court.

There are legal problems with some evidence changes. State and federal courts are not in agreement over whether the defendant's right to confront his or her witnesses and cross-examine them in court is violated when the state permits doctors, nurses, parents, or others to testify regarding what the child said, rather than having the child testify in court.[77]

Easing the fear and frustration of testifying for child witnesses has led some jurisdictions to make such arrangements as physical shields so that the child does not see the defendant, but the U.S. Supreme Court refused to uphold Iowa's procedure. In *Coy* v. *Iowa* the Court said that the defendant (father of the complaining witness) was denied his constitutional rights to confront his accuser. The Court did not hold that shields would never be permitted; rather, individualized facts must be considered in each case in which the issue is in question.[78]

A final area in which some criminal justice systems have responded to victims' needs is by the provision of **victim compensation programs.** Beginning in 1965 with California, the first state to adopt a victim compensation program, the trend toward adoption of these programs moved quickly. Unfortunately, many states have not provided adequate funding, leaving victims with an illusion that they will receive financial aid, medical care, and counseling assistance for the injuries and losses they have suffered as the result of crime. The provisions of state victim compensation programs vary considerably. The state plans differ also in methods of application, eligibility requirements, and minimum and maximum awards.

Despite their popularity, state victim compensation programs have been criticized severely. The passage of legislation in this area gives the impression that something is being done for the victim. But, for many reasons, many crime victims are not compensated adequately, if at all. Also, it is not clear that the programs meet other goals, such as increased crime reporting.

Some jurisdictions have enacted legislation to benefit witnesses as well as crime victims. Congress passed a victim compensation bill that applies to victims and witnesses involved in federal crimes, the Victim and Witness Protection Act of 1982 (VWPA), which has been amended subsequently. The act contains various provisions designed to prevent harassment of victims and witnesses. It establishes guidelines for fair treatment of crime victims and witnesses in criminal justice systems. It requires Victim Impact Statements at sentencing, contains more stringent bail requirements, and provides that the sentencing judge order defendants to pay to victims or state reasons for not so ordering.[79]

The restitution provisions of the VWPA have been challenged in the courts. Those decisions are discussed in more detail in a subsequent chapter. Here it is relevant to note that the basic problem is one of conflict between defendants' rights and victims' rights.

Congress also passed the Comprehensive Crime Control Act and the Victims of Crime Act of 1984, which authorizes that federal funds be distributed by the Office of Justice Programs through its Office for Victims of Crime and Bureau of Justice for state victim compensation and assistance programs. That law, which is often called VOCA, provided that federal funds stop after 30 September 1988, but Congress reauthorized the program to continue through amendments to the statute.[80]

In 1997 the federal victims' fund reached a record high of $528.9 million, and as a result the Office for Victims of Crime (OVC) awarded twice as many grants to state victim compensation and victim assistance programs as it had awarded the previous year. The funds are generated through fines paid by federal criminal offenders.[81]

One final act that may enhance the plight of crime victims is the action taken in 1997 by the American Bar Association (ABA). At its annual meeting in August, the ABA House of Delegates adopted a victims' rights resolution, which contains the following seven principles:

- Defendants' rights should not be diminished.
- Victims' rights should not diminish the ability of the trial court to 'efficiently and fairly' manage courtroom proceedings.
- Victims' rights should not diminish prosecutorial discretion in charging and plea negotiations.
- Violations of a victim's rights should not give rise to a new cause of action against any public official or public office.
- Government resources for implementing victims' rights should be fully funded.
- The term 'victim' should be defined.
- Each jurisdiction should be able to develop its own victims' rights procedures.[82]

WiseGuide Wrap-Up This chapter provides an overview of data on crime, offenders, and crime victims and discusses how those data are secured. The three basic methods for collecting crime data are described and analyzed. The official data of the *Uniform Crime Reports* (*UCR*) report the amount of crime as recorded by police departments and reported to the FBI.

In recent years, the FBI has recognized the limitations of its method of collecting and recording crime data. Its most significant change, the National Incident-Based Reporting System (NIBRS), is in operation in many states. NIBRS views crime as an incident that involves many elements, including alcohol and drug abuse; types of victims, weapons, and criminal activity; the victim's and arrestee's residency; the relationship between victim and offender; and a description of property and property values. Collection of these additional elements of criminal acts will enhance significantly our ability to analyze crime.

The second source of crime data, the National Crime Victimization Survey (NCVS), is an official source of crime data, too. It is valuable because it reveals that many victims do not report their victimizations to the police. The NCVS provides data on why people do not report victimizations. It does not give any information on arrests, and it is dependent on the accuracy of perception and reporting of crime victims.

The third major source of crime data—self-report data (SRD)—contains data that are not secured by either of the official methods. Through this method we get information on characteristics of people who say they have committed crimes. SRD provide valuable information for social scientists who study why crimes are committed, as well as for officials who must make decisions concerning the use of resources aimed at crime control and prevention. SRD allow us to study repeat offenders. The major problem with this approach is that respondents may underreport or overreport crimes.

All the data sources may be used to analyze the nature and extent of crime, but it is important to analyze carefully the time periods and the definitions of crimes being measured before comparing data from the various sources. Data in this chapter come primarily from the *UCR*, with victimization data coming from the NCVS. The data on criminal offenders are analyzed by three major variables: age, race, and gender.

Following the look at data, the chapter explores the recently developed and rapidly expanding study of victimology. It discusses the characteristics of crime victims, along with the problems those victims face in criminal justice systems. The chapter notes that although they are the most frequently studied, women, the elderly, and children are not the most frequent crime victims. Most violent crimes are committed against African American men, and in general men are more frequent crime victims than women.

The chapter notes some of the specific problems crime victims face within criminal justice systems. The chapter closes with a discussion of efforts to assist crime victims, mentioning such measures as victim compensation, revised court procedures, and victim participation in criminal justice processes.

Like most changes in the system, recognizing the rights of victims creates other needs, such as training programs for professionals within the system and financial backing for those programs as well as for victim compensation plans. Furthermore, victims' rights and defendants' rights may come into conflict. Nevertheless, changes made in the system to help victims may produce positive results such as increased crime reporting and more arrests and convictions. But what appear to be positive results could create problems for the system and society because of the increased need for jails and prisons. Thus, a study of crime victims provides another example of the need to assess the effect that changes in one aspect of the system will have on the rest of the system and on society.

This completes the introductory chapters. We turn now to a look at policing, the element through which many people enter criminal justice system processing.

Apply It

1. Describe and contrast the major sources of crime data.

2. Why should attention be paid to misdemeanors?

3. Explain and evaluate the FBI's new system of data reporting.

4. What are the advantages and disadvantages of self-report studies?

5. What have been the major changes in the amount of crime in the United States in the past decade?

6. What are the major differences between violent crimes and property crimes? List and define the four crimes in each of these categories.

7. What is *hate crime?* Discuss.

8. Discuss the relationship between crime and each of the following variables: age, race, and gender.

9. What progress has been made recently in the study of victims?

10. Discuss the characteristics of crime victims.

11. What lifestyle changes might you consider because of the risk of crime?

12. Is the fear of crime realistic?

13. What changes have been made in criminal justice systems to improve the plight of crime victims?

Notes

1. Geoffrey A. Campbell, "Putting a Crimp on Crime: Experts Differ over Reasons for Falling Rates of Serious Offenses," *American Bar Association Journal* 83 (May 1997): 24.

2. Federal Bureau of Investigation, *Crime in the United States: Uniform Crime Reports 1996* (Washington, D.C.: U.S. Department of Justice, 1997), p. 6.

3. "Experts on Crime Warn of a 'Ticking Time Bomb,'" *New York Times* (6 January 1996), p. 6.

4. "A Boy Is Killed, and All Japan Is Stunned," *New York Times* (31 May 1997), p. 3.

5. "Fourteen-Year-Old Held in Japan in Brutal Slaying of a Child," *New York Times* (29 June 1997), p. 6.

6. See David McDowall and Cohn Loftin, "Comparing the UCR and NCS Over Time," *Criminology* 30 (February 1992): 125–132. For additional information on the differences between the UCR and the NCS, see Albert D. Biderman and James P. Lynch, *Understanding Crime Incidence Statistics: Why the UCR Diverges from the NCS* (New York: Springer-Verlag, 1991).

7. Bureau of Justice Statistics, *Examining Recidivism* (Washington, D.C.: U.S. Department of Justice, 1985).

8. See Federal Bureau of Investigation, *Crime in the United States: Uniform Crime Reports 1995* (Washington, D.C.: U.S. Government Printing Office, 1996), p. 197.

9. American Law Institute, *Model Penal Code and Commentaries*, Part II, vol. 3 (Philadelphia: American Law Institute, 1980), Article 250, "Riot, Disorderly Conduct, and Related Offenses," p. 309.

10. Bureau of Justice Statistics, *Criminal Victimization 1992* (Washington, D.C.: U.S. Department of Justice, October 1993), p. 5; Bureau of Justice Statistics, *Criminal Victimization 1994* (Washington, D.C.: U.S. Department of Justice, April 1996), p. 6; Bureau of Justice Statistics, *Criminal Victimization 1996* (Washington, D.C.: U.S. Department of Justice, November 1997), p. 1.

11. Kansas City Police Department, *Response Time Analysis*, vol. 1, *Methodology*; vol. 2, *Crime Analysis* (Kansas City, Mo.: 1977).

12. William Spelman and Dale K. Brown, *Calling the Police: Citizen Reporting of Serious Crime* (Washington, D.C.: National Institute of Justice, October 1984), pp. xxiv–xxvii.

13. See, for example, Donald J. Black, "Production of Crime Rates," *American Sociological Review* 35 (August 1970): 733–748.

14. David Seidman and Michael Couzens, "Getting the Crime Rate Down: Political Pressure and Crime Reporting," *Law and Society Review* 8 (Spring 1974): 457–493.

15. See Federal Bureau of Investigation, *Uniform Crime Reporting: National Incident-Based Reporting System*, vol. 1, *Data Collection Guidelines* (Washington, D.C.: U.S. Department of Justice, 1 July 1988). See also Bureau of Justice Statistics, *Using NIBRS Data to Analyze Violent Crime* (Washington, D.C.: U.S. Department of Justice, October 1993).

16. Those categories are as follows: arson, assault, bribery, burglary, counterfeiting, destruction of property, drug offenses, embezzlement, extortion, fraud, gambling, homicide, kidnapping, larceny, motor vehicle theft, pornography, prostitution, robbery, sex offenses forcible, sex offenses nonforcible, stolen property, and weapons violation.

17. For a discussion of early victimization surveys, see Michael Hindelang, *Criminal Victimization in Eight American Cities: A Descriptive Analysis of Common Theft and Assault* (Cambridge, Mass.: Ballinger Publishing, 1976). See also R. M. O'Brien, *Crime and Victimization Data* (Beverly Hills, Calif.: Sage Publications, 1985); and W. G. Skogan, *Issues in the Measurement of Victimization* (Washington, D.C.: U.S. Government Printing Office, 1981).

18. For details of these changes, see Bureau of Justice Statistics, *New Directions for the National Crime Survey* (Washington, D.C.: U.S. Department of Justice, March 1989).

19. Bureau of Justice Statistics, National Crime Victimization Survey, *Effects of the Redesign on Victimization Estimates* (Washington, D.C.: U.S. Department of Justice, Office of Justice Programs, April 1997), p. 2.

20. See "Career Criminals and Criminal Careers," *Criminal Justice Research at Rand* (Santa Monica, Calif.: Rand, 1985), pp. 3–7. See also Minu Mathur et al., "Inmate Self-Report Data: A Study of Reliability," *Criminal Justice Review* 17 (Autumn 1992): 258–267; Michele S. Motiuk et al., "A Comparison Between Self-Report and Interview-Based Inventories in Offender Classification," *Criminal Justice and Behavior* 19 (June 1992): 143–159; and Julie Horney and Ineke Haen Marshall, "Measuring Lambda Through Self-Reports," *Criminology* 29 (August 1991): 471–496.

21. Michael J. Hindelang, Travis Hirschi, and Joseph G. Weis, "Correlates of Delinquency: The Illusion of Discrepancy Between Self-Report and Official Measures," *American Sociological Review* 44 (December 1979): 995–1014. See also a book by the same authors, *Measuring Delinquency* (Beverly Hills, Calif.: Sage publications, 1981). For a review of these and other criticisms of self-report studies, see Delbert S. Elliott and Suzanne S. Ageton, "Reconciling Race and Class Differences in Self-Reported and Official Estimates of Delinquency," *American Sociological Review* 45 (February 1980): 95–110.

22. See Douglas A. Smith and Laura A. Davidson, "Interfacing Indicators and Constructs in Criminological Research: A Note on the Comparability of Self-Report Violence Data for Race and Sex Groups," *Criminology* 24 (August 1986): 473–488.

23. For an extensive discussion of the new structure of the NYS, see Elliott and Ageton, "Reconciling Race," pp. 95–110.

24. People v. Harrison, 768 P.2d 1078, 1081, 1082 (Cal. 1989).

25. Federal Bureau of Investigation, *Crime in the United States: Uniform Crime Reports 1984* (Washington, D.C.: U.S. Government Printing Office, 1985), p. iii.

26. Federal Bureau of Investigation, *Crime in the United States: Uniform Crime Reports 1985* (Washington, D.C.: U.S. Government Printing Office, 1986), p. iii.

27. Geoffrey A. Campbell, "Putting a Crimp in Crime: Experts Differ over Reasons for Falling Rates of Serious Offenses," *American Bar Association Journal* 83 (May 1997): 24.

28. "Crime Continues to Decline in New York City, Statistics Show," *New York Times* (3 January 1998), p. 10.

29. Bureau of Justice Statistics, *Criminal Victimization 1996*, p. 1.

30. *Uniform Crime Reports 1996*, p. 26.

31. Ibid., p. 27.

32. Ibid., pp. 31, 32.

33. Ibid., p. 14.

34. Ibid., p. 23.

35. Ibid., p. 24. For an analysis of the legal issue of consent and rape, see the recent discussion of the Glen Ridge rape case involving a woman who is mentally disabled. Peter Laufer, *A Question of Consent: Innocence and Complicity in the Glen Ridge Rape Case* (San Francisco: Mercury House, 1994). For an analysis of victimization studies of rape, see Mary P. Ross, "The Measurement of Rape Victimization in Crime Surveys," *Criminal Justice and Behavior* 23 (March 1996): 55–69.

36. *Uniform Crime Reports 1996*, p. 36.

37. Ibid., pp. 43, 44.

38. Ibid., p. 39.

39. Ibid., pp. 49, 50.

40. *Uniform Crime Reports 1996*, pp. 53, 54.

41. Federal Bureau of Investigation, *Crime in the United States: Uniform Crime Reports 1990* (Washington, D.C.: U.S. Department of Justice, 1991), pp. 5–6. The statute is codified in U.S. Code, Chapter 28, Section 534 (1997).

42. *Uniform Crime Reports 1996*, p. 58.

43. See Charles R. Tittle, "Labelling and Crime: An Empirical Evaluation," in *The Labelling of Deviance: Evaluating a Perspective*, 2d ed., ed. Walter Gove (Beverly Hills, Calif.: Sage Publications, 1980), pp. 241–270.

44. Hindelang, "Variations in Sex-Race-Age-Specific Incidence Rates," p. 462. See also Hindelang, Hirschi, and Weis, "Correlates of Delinquency"; and Delbert S. Elliott and David Huizinga, "Social Class and Delinquent Behavior in a National Youth Panel: 1976–1980," *Criminology* 21 (May 1983): 149–177.

45. See William Wilbanks, *The Myth of a Racist Criminal Justice System* (Monterey, Calif.: Brooks/Cole, 1987), and Joan Petersilia et al., *Racial Equity in Sentencing* (Santa Monica, Calif.: Rand, February 1988).

46. *Uniform Crime Reports 1996*, pp. 213, 214.

47. Neal Shover and Carol Y. Thompson, "Age, Differential Expectations, and Crime Desistance," *Criminology* 30 (February 1992): 88. See this article for a review of the literature in this area, along with the results of the authors' own research. See also Shover, *Aging Criminals* (Beverly Hills, Calif.: Sage Publications, 1985). For an analysis of age and delinquency, see Scott Menard, "Demographic and Theoretical Variables in the Age-Period-Cohort Analysis of Illegal Behavior," *Journal of Research in Crime and Delinquency* 29 (May 1992): 178–199.

See also Darrell Steffensmeier and Miles D. Harer, "Did Crime Rise or Fall During the Reagan Presidency? The Effects of an 'Aging' U.S. Population on the Nation's Crime Rate," *Journal of Research in Crime and Delinquency* 28 (August 1991): 330–359.

48. See Sol Chaneles and Cathleen Burnett, eds., *Older Offenders: Current Trends* (New York: Haworth Press, 1989); Letitia T. Alson, *Crime and Older Americans* (Springfield, Ill.: Chas. C Thomas, 1986), pp. 123, 124; and William E. Adams Jr., "The Incarceration of Older Criminals: Balancing Safety, Cost, and Humanitarian Concerns," *Nova Law Review* 19 (1995): 465–486.

49. *Uniform Crime Reports 1996*, pp. 214, 232.

50. Ibid., pp. 214, 219.

51. Ibid., p. 219.

52. Ibid., p. 219.

53. For a recent account of the history of victimology, see William G. Doerner and Steven P. Lab, *Victimology,* 2d ed., (Cincinnati: Anderson, 1998), pp. 1–18.

54. U.S. Code, Title 18, Section 3663 (1997).

55. See, for example, Title IV, Violence Against Women, of the Violent Crime Control and Law Enforcement Act of 1994, Public Law 103-322 (13 September 1994). For an overview of domestic violence victims, see the following chapters in Doerner and Lab, *Victimology:* Chapter 5, "Sexual Assault," pp. 83–109; Chapter 6, "Spouse Abuse," pp 111–135; Chapter 7, "Child Maltreatment," pp. 137–159; and Chapter 8, "Elder Abuse," pp. 161–181.

56. Bureau of Justice Statistics, *Criminal Victimization 1996*, pp. 4–5.

57. Bureau of Justice Statistics, *Black Victims* (Washington, D.C.: U.S. Department of Justice, April 1990), p. 1.

58. Bureau of Justice Statistics, *Criminal Victimization 1996*, p. 4.

59. Bureau of Justice Statistics, *Hispanic Victims* (Washington, D.C.: U.S. Department of Justice, January 1990): 1; Bureau of Justice Statistics, *Criminal Victimization 1994*, p. 4.

60. Bureau of Justice Statistics, *Criminal Victimization 1996*, p. 4.

61. Ibid., p. 7.

62. Bureau of Justice Statistics, Special Report, *Age Patterns of Victims of Serious Violent Crime* (Washington, D.C.: U.S Department of Justice, September 1997), p. 1.

63. Bureau of Justice Statistics, *Criminal Victimization 1996*, p. 7.

64. Bureau of Justice Statistics, *Violent Crime by Strangers and Nonstrangers* (Washington, D.C.: U.S Department of Justice, January 1987), p. 1. See also Bureau of Justice Statistics, *Murder in Families* (July 1994).

65. "The Curse of Violent Crime: A Pervasive Fear of Robbery and Mayhem Threatens the Way America Lives," *Time* (23 March 1981), p. 16.

66. "Fear of Crime Is Generalized, not Local, NAPO Survey Finds," *Criminal Justice Newsletter* 17 (3 September 1996): 4.

67. "Crime Fear Is Seen Forcing Changes in Youth Behavior," *New York Times* (17 February 1996), p. 6.

68. For studies of the elderly as victims, see James Alan Fox and Jack Levin, "Homicide Against the Elderly: A Research Note," *Criminology* 29 (May 1991): 317–327; and Ezzat A. Fattah and Vincent F. Sacco, *Crime and Victimization of the Elderly* (Secaucus, N.J.: Springer-Verlag, 1989).

69. Hubert Williams and Antony M. Pate, "Returning to First Principles: Reducing the Fear of Crime in Newark," *Crime & Delinquency* 33 (January 1987): 53.

70. "Survey: Americans Think System Favors Defendants over Victims," *Criminal Justice Newsletter* 22 (1 May 1991): 5.

71. For a discussion see Peggy M. Tobolowsky, " 'Constitutionality' Crime Victim Rights," *Criminal Law Bulletin* 33 (September/October 1997): 395–423. The proposed federal constitutional amendment may be found at the following: Senate version: S.J.Res. 52, 104th Cong. (1996); House version, H.R.J. Res. 173, 174, 104th Cont. (1996).

72. Booth v. Maryland, 482 U.S. 496 (1987), *overruled in part*, Payne v. Tennessee, 501 U.S. 808 (1991).

73. Payne v. Tennessee, 501 U.S. 808 (1991). The other case that was overruled is South Carolina v. Gathers, 490 U.S. 805 (1989).

74. See, for example, "The Impact of Arrest on Domestic Assault," a special issue of *American Behavioral Scientist* 36 (May 1994); and J. David Hirschel et al., "Review Essay on the Law Enforcement Response to Spouse Abuse: Past, Present, and Future," *Justice Quarterly* 9 (June 1992): 247–283.

75. See, for example, Eve S. Buzawa and Carl G. Buzawa, eds., *Do Arrests and Restraining Orders Work?* (Thousand Oaks, CA: Sage Publications, 1996); David A. Klinger, "Policing Spousal Assault," *Journal of Research in Crime and Delinquency* 32 (August 1995): 308–324; and all articles in the special issue, "Responding to Violence against Women," in *Crime & Delinquency* 41 (October 1995).

76. For a discussion of these and other changes, see Gail A. Goolkasian, *Confronting Domestic Violence: The Role of Criminal Court Judges* (Washington, D.C.: U.S. Department of Justice, 1986).

77. See Cassidy v. State, 536 A.2d 666 (Ct.Spec.App.Md. 1988), *cert. denied*, 541 A.2d 965 (Md. 1988), holding inadmissible the testimony of a doctor who testified that the alleged victim said that her "Daddy" abused her.

78. Coy v. Iowa, 487 U.S. 1012 (1988), *on remand*, 433 N.W.2d 714 (1988).

79. U.S. Code, Title 18, Section 3663 (1997).

80. U.S. Code, Title 42, Section 10601 et seq. (1997). For an excellent discussion of changes in victim's rights, see James R. Acker, "Social Sciences and the Criminal Law: Victims of Crime—Plight vs. Rights," *Criminal Law Bulletin* 28 (January–February, 1992): 64–77.

81. "1997 Aid to Crime Victim Programs Is More than Double Last Year's," *Criminal Justice Newsletter* 28 (15 July 1997): 5.

82. Quoted in "ABA Takes Stand on Victims' Rights, Needle Exchange Programs," *Criminal Law Reporter* 61 (20 August 1997): 1457–1458.

Entry into Criminal Justice Systems: Policing

Chapter 3
The Emergence and
Structure of Police Systems

Chapter 4
Policing in a Modern Society

Chapter 5
Problems and Issues
in Policing

INTRODUCTION

The President's Commission on Law Enforcement and Administration of Justice emphasized in its 1967 report that police occupy the front line. In a real sense our ability to do what we want, free from the fear of crime, depends on the police. But despite the responsibilities and powers granted to the police, they cannot deal effectively with crime without the cooperation of victims and witnesses. We have noted that such cooperation is not always given. Yet, police are blamed if crime rates increase and if reported crimes are not solved.

INTRODUCTION—Continued

Section 2 explores the nature, organization, function, and problems of policing in an attempt to place this important aspect of criminal justice systems in proper perspective. Chapter 3 covers the history of policing and explains how formal police systems emerged. It differentiates the levels of public police systems in the United States, looks briefly at international policing, and reviews the nature and problems of private policing. The organization and administration of police systems are considered, with a focus on community-oriented policing.

Chapter 4 describes what police actually do, ranging from performing many services within the community to the dangerous job of apprehending criminals. Police functions are discussed in the context of legal requirements and empirical social science research. Section 2 closes with Chapter 5, which focuses on the major problems and issues in policing.

The Emergence and Structure of Police Systems

WiseGuide Intro

Policing is one of the most important functions in criminal justice systems. "The strength of a democracy and the quality of life enjoyed by its citizens are determined in large measure by the ability of the police to discharge their duties."[1] Yet, the ability of U.S. police to discharge their duties effectively and properly has come into serious question in recent years, as when television cameras around the world replayed the amateur photographer's recording of police officers beating an African American suspect, Rodney King. The acquittal of four white officers in their state trial was followed by massive rioting. Subsequently, two of the officers were convicted and two were acquitted in federal trials. Mr. King settled his suit with the Los Angeles Police Department (LAPD).

The tarnished image of the LAPD was not diminished by the allegations of sloppy and negligent work in collecting evidence in their investigations of O. J. Simpson, their sole suspect in the 1994 slayings of Simpson's ex-wife, Nicole Brown Simpson, and her friend, Ronald Goldman. Defense attorneys offered evidence of racist attitudes and behavior on the part of detective Mark Fuhrman and implied that he planted the bloody glove found at Simpson's estate. They accused the LAPD of leaking false evidence to the media and of mishandling evidence crucial to the investigation. Prosecutors denied these charges and made efforts to refute them, but after Simpson's acquittal several jurors noted that the mishandling of evidence was a factor in their decision.

The LAPD is not the only police department under fire, and most recently allegations of internal bickering and a lack of cooperation between the police and prosecution in Boulder, Colorado, have emerged as reasons for the failure to arrest anyone in the brutal slaying of JonBenet Ramsey. JonBenet, a six-year-old girl known for her success in beauty pagents, was found murdered in her own home on

Key Terms

Bow Street Runners
constable
frankpledge system
hundred
INTERPOL
Law Enforcement Assistance
    Administration (LEAA)
Law Enforcement Education
    Program (LEEP)
magistrate
marshal
Molly Maguires
police
posse
private security forces
sheriff
tithing
vigilantism
watch system

26 December 1996. No arrests have been made in the case, and JonBenet's parents, who have moved to Atlanta, Georgia, have not been excluded as suspects. Two detectives originally assigned to the case were on medical leaves because of stress. The lead detective, for whom this was his first homicide investigation, was openly looking for another job and was subsequently replaced as the head of the investigation. Furthermore, for six weeks the police department refused to share the results of DNA blood tests with the district attorney's office.[2] Some predict there will never be an arrest in this case.

This chapter and the following two chapters discuss policing: its past, present, and future. The discussion begins with a history of policing to explain the reason for the formal systems of present-day public policing. The history is traced from its informal beginnings in other countries to today's formal systems in the United States. The decentralized system of policing that exists in this country is examined by its major categories: local, state, and federal policing systems, along with a brief look at international policing. Private policing is also examined.

The chapter then focuses on the organization and administration of police departments and closes with a discussion and analysis of two policing models: the professional model and community-oriented policing.

Learning Objectives

Learning Objectives

After reading this chapter, you should be able to do the following:

- Discuss the history of U.S. policing, paying special attention to the contributions of the British police.
- Explain the meaning of decentralized policing.
- Distinguish local, state, and federal policing systems.
- State and evaluate the role and function of the FBI.

- Explain the difference between private and public policing, and discuss their comparative growth and importance.
- Note early reform efforts in the organization and administration of policing systems.
- Distinguish the professional model and the community-oriented policing models, and evaluate each.

History of Policing

Although formal policing is a relatively modern development, some form of policing has existed for centuries. When societies were small and cohesive, with most members sharing common goals and activities, usually it was possible to keep order without a formal police structure. The rules and regulations of the society were taught to new members as they were socialized, and most people observed the rules. Others could be coerced into observing those rules by informal techniques of social control. If that did not work and if rules were violated, crime victims might handle the situation informally. The victim might be permitted to take private revenge against the offender, too.

In some countries informal policing was organized beyond the immediate family or individual concerned. England had the **frankpledge system,** in which families were organized into a **tithing** (ten families) and a **hundred** (ten tithings) for purposes of protecting each other as well as for enforcing laws. The frankpledge was a system of mutual pledge or mutual help, with all adult members responsible for their own conduct and that of others in the system. If the group failed to apprehend a lawbreaker, the English Crown fined all members.

Individual private policing had its limits, however, and as societies grew in size and complexity, public policing was needed. The appointment of constables in England in the twelfth century signaled the beginning of public policing in that country. The **constable,** an unpaid adult male, was responsible for taking care of the weapons and the equipment of the hundred, as well as keeping the peace by enforcing laws.

A second kind of police officer emerged when hundreds were combined to form shires, which were analogous to counties. The king appointed a shire-reeve to supervise each shire. The shire-reeve was the forerunner of the **sheriff.** Originally, the shire-reeve was responsible only for ensuring that citizens performed their law enforcement functions adequately, but later the duties were expanded to include apprehending law violators. The shire-reeve was assisted in his duties by his constables, but he was the only paid official.

During the reign of Edward I (1272–1307), the **watch system,** the immediate forerunner to modern police systems, emerged in England. The watch system was developed as a means of protecting property against fire and for guarding the walls and gates of the cities. Watchmen were responsible for maintaining order and monitoring public behavior and manners. The London watchmen carried clubs and swords. They did not wear uniforms and could be distinguished from other citizens only by the lanterns and staffs they carried. Originally, they were to patrol the streets at specified intervals during the night, announcing that all was well. As the city grew, a day shift was added.

In 1326 Edward II supplemented the shire-reeve supervised mutual pledge system by creating an office of justice of the peace. The justices were appointed by the king, and their original function was to assist the shire-reeve with policing the counties. Later the justices assumed judicial functions. As the central government took on greater responsibility for law enforcement in England, the constables lost their independence as officials of the pledge system and were under the authority of the justices, who were assisted by volunteers.

Constables performed functions such as supervising night watchmen, taking charge of prisoners, serving summonses, and executing warrants. The justices performed judicial functions, thus beginning the separation of the functions of the police and the judiciary. This distinction between the police functions of the constable and the judicial functions of the justices, with the constables reporting to the justices, remained the pattern in England for the next 500 years.

The mutual pledge system began to decline, however, as many citizens failed to perform their law enforcement functions within the system. The early police officials were not popular with citizens; nor were they effective. Citizens were dissatisfied with the watch system and its inability to maintain order and prevent crime. English life was characterized by rising levels of crime, a perceived increase and greater severity of public riots, and an increase in public intoxication resulting from a rise in drinking among the lower classes.

Public drunkenness became a serious problem. Not used to drinking, people were unpredictable and often violent in their behavior on the streets. The result was a significant increase in violent crimes and theft. The government responded by improving city lighting, increasing the number of watchmen, and increasing the punishment for all crimes. But the watchmen were not able to control the frequent riots that occurred; neither could they protect citizens and their possessions. The public responded by refraining from entering the streets at night without a private guard and by arming themselves. The rich moved to safer areas, leaving behind them the residential segregation characteristic of contemporary society.[3]

The rise of industrialization in England contributed to the need for a formal police force. As more people moved to cities and life became more complex, maintaining law and order became more difficult, and the less formal system of policing was not sufficient.

Modern Policing: The London Beginning

Although scholars debate how and why formal police systems emerged, usually the beginning is traced to England, where Londoners protested the ineffectiveness of the watch system and agitated for a formal police force. Some believed that a police force constantly patrolling the town would reduce and eventually eliminate crime in the streets. Others feared that the concentration of power necessary for a formal police force would lead to abuses, especially if the force were a national one. Eventually, the tension between these two positions was resolved by the establishment of local police systems.[4]

Dissatisfaction with the constable system led the English to experiment with other systems. In the mid-eighteenth century John Fielding and Henry Fielding, London **magistrates,** instituted a system called the **Bow Street Runners.** The Fieldings selected constables with a year of experience and gave them police powers of investigation and arrest. The constables were given some training and were paid a portion of the fines in the cases they prosecuted successfully.

Increased concern about safety and security in London led to pressures from citizens to improve police protection. Between 1770 and 1828, a total of six commissions appointed by the English Parliament investigated policing and made suggestions, but an attempt in 1785 to establish a metropolitan police force was defeated by the opposition of powerful commercial interests. None of the English efforts were successful in establishing a satisfactory police force until 1829.[5]

That year the first modern police force, the Metropolitan Police of London, was founded in London by Sir Robert Peel. The men employed by the force were called Peelers or Bobbies after the founder. Working full-time and wearing special uniforms, the officers' primary function was to prevent crime. They were organized by territories, and they reported to a central government. Candidates had to meet high standards to qualify for a job as a police officer in London. The system has been described as follows:

> Peel divided London into divisions, then into "beats." The headquarters for the police commissioners looked out upon a courtyard that had been the site of a residence used by the Kings of Scotland and was, therefore, called "Scotland Yard." . . . [I]n 1856 Parliament required every borough and county to have a police force similar to London's.[6]

London set the example; the rest of England was slow to follow, but other countries began establishing modern, formal police systems. Some countries developed a centralized police system, but a decentralized system developed in the United States.[7] Most European countries followed the British practice of not arming the police, but the amount of violence led the British to change that tradition slightly by 1994. In May of that year, a few dozen specially trained Bobbies began carrying guns.[8]

People in the United States saw a variety of policing systems in the early days. English immigrants brought many aspects of their system to this country. The constable was in charge of towns, and the sheriff had jurisdiction over policing counties. Before the American Revolution, these positions were filled by governors appointed by the British Crown, but subsequently, most constables and sheriffs obtained their positions by popular elections.

The Emergence of Policing in the United States

The English watch system was adopted by many of the colonies. As early as 1631, Boston had a watch system; New Amsterdam (later New York) developed a watch system in 1643. The New York City system was said to be typical of that system of policing in this country. Bellmen walked throughout the city, ringing bells and providing police services. Later they were replaced by a permanent watch of citizens and still later by paid constables. Professional, full-time police were not appointed in New York City until 1845.

One of the most familiar kinds of policing, still in use in rural areas today, was the **posse.** Under the posse system, a sheriff could call into action any number of citizens over a certain age if they were needed to assist in law enforcement.

In some early systems in this country, law enforcement officials were paid by local government. Others were paid by private individuals. By the early nineteenth century, American law enforcement was a hodgepodge of small jurisdictions staffed by various officials with different powers, responsibilities, and legal standing. There was no system, although there were ample precedents for public policing.[9]

It did not take long, however, for Americans to realize that these methods of policing did not produce the efficiency and expertise necessary to control the urban riots and increasing rates of crime and violence that accompanied the industrialization, increased complexity, and growth of American cities. A professional police system was needed; the movement toward that goal began in Boston in 1837. By the late 1880s, most American cities had established municipal police forces, although the county sheriff system continued to provide policing services in rural areas. State police systems were added gradually, followed by the federal system. The state and federal systems, however, were not to supercede the local systems.[10]

One final type of policing that should be mentioned is **vigilantism,** which means *watchman,* a person who is alert and on guard, cautious, suspicious, ready to take action to maintain and preserve peace. The phrase *vigilantibus et non dormientibus jura subveniunt* expresses the reason for vigilantism. It means that laws aid persons who are vigilant and who do not sleep on their rights. In colonial days people (usually only men) formed vigilante committees to stop rebellions and other problems and to catch and punish criminals. These groups operated outside the law, but apparently they viewed themselves as preserving law.[11]

Vigilante committees and groups continue to operate within our society, and often they aim their efforts at suppression of racial and other minority groups, thus constituting a serious threat to the rights of these people. The issue of vigilantism arose in 1988 in Detroit after two neighbors, agitated by the drug activities taking place in two crack houses in their neighborhood, proudly admit-

Spotlight 3.1

Revenge or Justice: A Mother Takes Aim and Fires

She was distraught over the sexual abuse of her young son, allegedly by a man who had been convicted of sexual abuse previously but never served prison time. On 2 April 1993, Ellie Nesler took the law into her own hands when she entered the court room and fired five bullets into the back of the head of Daniel Driver, her son's alleged molester. Driver, who was handcuffed and awaiting that day's court session on his trial for sexually abusing four boys, including Nesler's only son, died instantly.

Nesler received sympathy from around the world, along with approximately $40,000 for her defense. The jury was not completely sympathetic, however, convicting Nesler of voluntary manslaughter (for which she received a six-year prison sentence) and using a gun to carry out the crime (for which she received a four-year sentence). Nesler said the sentences were fair, and after serving a few months in a California maximum-security prison, Nesler admitted that she should not have taken the law into her own hands. Declaring that she is not a hero, as some claimed, Nesler lamented that she had ruined her life and that of her family by her act.

Not everyone thought Nesler a hero. The judge said, "This crime was in fact an execution. . . . It was an intentional and intolerable assault on our system of justice. She's proud of what she's done, and if given the chance would do it again."[1]

There was evidence that Nesler's son was sodomized repeatedly by the defendant, who went to the Nesler home with his Bible, allegedly to teach Bible lessons to the child. Instead, he took the child to the back and abused him sexually. Nesler claimed that she was distraught and concerned that justice would not be served through the courts. Her insanity defense was rejected by the jury.

Before her sentencing, Nesler was diagnosed with breast cancer. Doctors said she had only a fifty-fifty chance of living five years, the period at which she would be eligible for parole. Her cancer was treated with chemotherapy while she was in prison, but she refused a recommended mastectomy, saying that she did not have confidence in prison medical personnel. After she began serving her term, she was granted a retrial because of juror misconduct. She was permitted to plead guilty to voluntary manslaughter rather than be retried, and in October of 1997 she was freed by a judge after having served four years, which was over one-half of the seven years to which she was sentenced after her plea agreement. Under California law, the judge was permitted to release her. Outside that courtroom, Nesler hugged her children and asked for forgiveness. She denied that she was a vigilante.[2]

Source: Summarized by the author from media sources.

1. "Mother in Courtroom Slaying Calls Jail Term Fair," *New York Times* (9 January 1994), p. 11.
2. "Mom Who Slew Son's Molester Freed from Jail," *Buffalo News* (2 October 1997), p. 4.

ted in court that they set those houses on fire. They were acquitted of arson, with one juror stating later that he would have burned the house, too, and suggesting that actually he would have been even more violent! Noted Harvard law professor and defense attorney Alan Dershowitz denounced the jury as a "vigilante jury," while other criminal justice professionals noted that sometimes juries dispense justice in terms of what they think is deserved. Residents argued that the police could not protect them; they had to take action. But one resident said, "I thought we had gotten away from lynchings. I thought we were more civilized than that."[12] Spotlight 3.1 relates the results of one woman's decision to take the law into her own hands.

Decentralized Policing: U.S. Systems

In the United States formal police systems are decentralized, operating at local, state, and federal levels.

Local policing includes police agencies at the rural, county, and municipal levels. Most studies of police focus on municipal policing. Few criminal justice texts discuss rural policing, and usually only slight attention is given to county police systems, leaving the impression that these levels of policing are not important. This conclusion is erroneous because local and county levels of policing cover significant geographical areas of the country. In fact, the majority of police agencies in the United States are located in small towns, villages, or boroughs.

Local Policing

Rural Policing

Throughout the United States, but particularly in southern and western regions, many towns and villages are too small to support a police department. Some of these areas depend on the county police system for protection. Others have their own systems, usually consisting of an elected official. This official may be called a *constable,* who has policing duties similar to those of the county sheriff. Constables may not be trained in law or policing. However, they have the power to enforce laws, to arrest, to maintain order, and to execute processes from the magistrate's courts, which are courts of limited jurisdiction, often called *justice of the peace courts.*

Rural policing is very important but often plagued with financial and personnel problems. One officer cannot police even a small area for twenty-four hours a day. Frequently, citizens are without police protection; local police officers are overworked; and in many jurisdictions funds are not available for the support services necessary for adequate policing.[13]

Many rural officers do not have sufficient resources for investigating criminal activity. They are more isolated from other officers. Quick backup services from other officers may be a scarce luxury rather than a daily reality. Working conditions of rural police may be less desirable than those of police officers at other levels. Most salaries are low and not necessarily compensated for by a lower cost of living. Initial training is more limited and may not be geared to the unique problems of rural policing. Most officers must train in urban settings because in many areas there are not enough rural police to justify separate training centers. As a result, those officers may have unrealistic expectations of rural policing. In addition, many rural officers do not have the opportunity for continued education and training.

Budget planning and other activities concerning policing in rural areas might be town projects, with police officers involved in heated discussions from which their urban counterpart might be shielded by police administrators. This high visibility and total immersion in local problems and politics might affect the social life of the officer, who finds it impossible to go anywhere in the area without being viewed as a police officer. For rural officers, long periods of inactivity may lead to boredom and lowered self-concept. In comparison to urban police, rural police may face even greater citizen expectations for a variety of services not connected with law enforcement.[14]

On the positive side, some rural officers enjoy the greater involvement in community activities with local citizens. The lower crime rates, particularly the lower rates of violence, may increase police security. The lack of complexity in the police system might be seen as a positive rather than a negative factor. Problems associated with a lack of security, when only one officer is assigned to an area, might be eliminated or greatly reduced by cooperation from the next level, county

PROFESSIONS 3.1

The County Sheriff

At the county level of government, the sheriff is the primary law enforcement officer. He is an elected official whose term usually spans from two to four years and whose jurisdictional responsibility primarily covers unincorporated portions of each county. His functions include keeping the peace, executing civil and criminal process, patrolling the area, maintaining the county jail, preserving order in county courts, and enforcing court orders. The sheriff as a rule performs only restricted law enforcement functions in incorporated areas within a county and then usually only when the city requests his participation in such activities as patrol or investigation.

Source: The President's Commission on Law Enforcement and Administration of Justice, *Task Force Report: The Police* (Washington, D.C.: U.S. Government Printing Office, 1967), p. 8.

policing. In many areas, rural police are limited to traffic functions and some ministerial duties, with the major law enforcement activities being handled by the county sheriff and county police officers. The county may contract with the rural community to provide these services.[15]

County Policing

Some county police agencies are rural, but the county system is larger and usually employs as the primary law enforcement officer a sheriff whose main law enforcement functions are described in Professions 3.1. The county sheriff may have numerous other functions unrelated to law enforcement, such as acting as the county coroner, collecting county taxes, or supervising any number of county government activities. If the department is large enough, the county police department might have a deputy sheriff and law enforcement officers assigned to patrol the county and enforce order.

The sheriff is considered the most important law enforcement officer in the county, but in practice, the functions of the sheriff's office usually are limited to the unincorporated areas of the county, with law enforcement in the incorporated areas handled by the municipal police in the larger cities. As Professions 3.1 notes, the sheriff is an elected official. Previously, most sheriffs served for very long periods. But one Texas study noted that with changing times, it is becoming difficult if not impossible for long sheriff tenures to continue. Political activists have been successful in unseating several sheriffs who have served for years, leading some authorities to refer to the office of incumbent sheriff as "an endangered species."[16]

Larger county police departments may contract their services to smaller county or rural departments. The county department may employ a county **marshal,** a sworn officer whose primary function is to perform civil duties for the courts, such as delivering papers to initiate civil proceedings or serving papers for the arrest of criminal suspects.

Larger county police departments have investigative units that service the district attorneys who bring the prosecutions in the county. These departments are staffed by sworn officers and support personnel. Departments too small for investigative units may contract for such services from the municipal or urban police departments in the area or from the Federal Bureau of Investigation (FBI).

Municipal Policing

Most studies of policing focus on municipal departments; consequently, the discussions in the following two chapters apply mainly to municipal policing. Here some comments are made about the differences between municipal, or urban, policing and the other local levels.

Municipal police departments differ from other local police agencies mainly in their size, organization, complexity, and services. Although they may service smaller geographic areas than rural or county systems, most municipal police systems have more employees and provide more extended services. The complexity of the departments leads to greater problems in staffing, organization, and meeting the public's needs. Usually, municipal departments have more resources within the department and from the community. In some cases, these resources are shared with rural and county systems on a contract basis. On the other hand, the expectations of citizens for services from municipal police departments may be greater than expectations at the rural or county levels, whereas the mandate of the department may be less defined and more openended.[17]

Municipal departments, in contrast to departments at other levels, may encounter more difficult political problems with their governing bodies. The police department competes with other agencies for funding. The costs of policing are highest in urban areas, where population changes may present more problems. Many large cities have experienced significant changes in the numbers of people who live in the city, compared to the number who come in daily to work. The residential tax base goes down as the need for services, order maintenance, and law enforcement increases.

Generally, crime rates are much higher in urban than rural or county areas. The composition of the urban population may present greater policing problems. Urban areas have a more heterogeneous population as well as a greater number of unemployed, transients, and those who have been in trouble with the law.[18]

State Policing

State police patrol highways and regulate traffic. They have the primary responsibility for enforcing some state laws and providing services such as a system of criminal identification, police training programs, or a communications system for local law officials. The organization and services provided by state police vary from state to state. No national or central control exists, except for some standards of the U.S. Department of Justice and the U.S. Department of Transportation.

This lack of centralization stems from the historic distrust of national police systems, as well as from the different law enforcement needs of the individual states. For example, in 1835 the Texas Rangers, a group of uneducated and untrained men, were recruited and given authority to protect the Texas border from the Mexicans. After Texas was admitted to the Union, the Rangers were retained, along with their primary duty of patrolling the southern border of Texas.

The Texas Rangers became the first state-supported organization of police in the United States. As police functions expanded, the role of the Texas Rangers was enlarged, as was their training. In 1988 the Texas Rangers appointed their first African American of this century. It is believed that African Americans served with the Texas Rangers in the 1800s, but in recent years the National Association for the Advancement of Colored People charged that in this century African Americans had been excluded systematically from serving in the Texas Rangers.[19]

The industrialization and expansion of the country led to many problems that could not be handled adequately at the local level, and although Texas had the first state police agency, Pennsylvania's system became the early model for state police in the United States. In the late 1870s, a powerful secret organization, the **Molly Maguires,** responded to anti-Irish riots in Pennsylvania by forming Irish labor unions that used violence to terrorize the state's coal-producing regions. The Molly Maguires controlled all hiring and firing. Some employers who ignored their mandates were killed. The terrorists threatened the growing Pennsylvania economy, which was heavily dependent on mineral wealth. The state was settled sparsely, and local police authorities could not control the Molly Maguires. "The Pinkerton Detective Agency, a private national organization, was eventually brought in to infiltrate the Molly Maguires, and twenty of its members were convicted of murder and other crimes."[20] The Pinkerton's Agency is discussed later in this chapter.

In 1905 the governor of Pennsylvania succeeded in convincing the state legislature to appropriate funds for a constabulary to help prevent future disasters such as those caused by the Molly Maguires. The movement toward state policing did not happen quickly, however, for many still feared that the next step would be national police and political repression. But the use of automobiles and increased problems with traffic on state roads and highways in the twentieth century created an obvious need for state police.

State police are similar to the state patrol. Both have uniformed, sworn officers who carry weapons, and "When the activities of the state patrol are added to the services provided by the county sheriffs and a state bureau of investigation, the services rendered are very close to those offered by a state police system."[21] The state patrol and the state police differ primarily in their law enforcement powers. Most state patrol officers engage in traffic control primarily. Although they may be empowered to enforce criminal laws violated in their presence, on the highway, or within sight of or adjacent to the highway, they do not have general powers of law enforcement for all state laws as state police have. State police, in contrast to state patrol, may have their own investigation units as well as a forensic science laboratory.

State police and state patrol differ also in that many state police systems include specialized forms of policing, such as control over fishing and gaming laws, regulation of gambling and horse racing, and regulation of alcohol sales. The Alcohol Board of Control is a state agency responsible for investigating requests for liquor licenses and may have the power to establish rules concerning the conditions under which liquor is sold. This same board may be in charge of enforcing state laws concerning the sale of dangerous drugs.

Federal Policing

Enforcement of criminal laws in the United States historically has been viewed as the function of states, although states may and do delegate some of their powers to local police agencies. The Constitution does not provide for a central police agency. It gave the federal government specific power to enforce only a limited number of crimes. The Constitution provides also that all powers not delegated to the federal government are reserved to the states.[22] The Constitution gives Congress the power to pass laws that are "necessary and proper" for the exercise of congressional powers. Over the years Congress has passed statutes on federal crimes. The U.S. Supreme Court has upheld the power of Congress to do so.

Federal law enforcement includes federal prosecutors and federal police agencies. The federal policing level is complex and encompasses more than fifty enforcement agencies, as enumerated in Professions 3.2. One agency is that of the U.S. Marshals Service, the oldest federal law enforcement agency. The U.S. president, with the advice and consent of the Senate, appoints one person to each federal judicial district. These marshals are assisted by deputy marshals.

The primary function of U.S. marshals is to transport federal inmates between prison and court and to escort them to homes or jobs when they have temporary leaves. Witnesses at federal trials who need protection receive that protection from federal marshals. The marshals are in charge of seizing and auctioning property that has been taken by officers under federal court orders. As sworn police officers, U.S. marshals make arrests for federal offenses and perform other police functions such as controlling riots.

In addition to the U.S. Marshals Service and other agencies, the Department of Justice encompasses other major investigative agencies (see Professions 3.2), the largest of which is the FBI.

The Federal Bureau of Investigation (FBI)

On 26 July 1908 President Theodore Roosevelt directed the attorney general to issue an order creating the agency now known as the Federal Bureau of Investigaton (FBI). In 1924 J. Edgar Hoover was appointed director of the organization and remained in that position until his death in May 1972. The FBI is the largest federal criminal law enforcement agency (with the exception of the military). The department is the primary agency charged with enforcing all federal laws not assigned to other special agencies. The FBI headquarters are located in Washington, D.C. Field officers are located in major cities throughout the United States and in San Juan, Puerto Rico. The director of the FBI is appointed by the President of the United States, by and with the consent of the Senate.

The investigative work of the FBI is performed by special agents, who are trained at the FBI Academy, located on the U.S. Marine Corps Base at Quantico, Virginia. In addition to special agents, the FBI employs individuals who perform such investigative functions as fingerprint examinations, clerical and receptionist duties, computer programming, and laboratory work. Attorneys, accountants, and other professionals are employed as well.

The FBI is not a national police force. Primarily, it is an investigative agency. FBI agents may investigate crimes over which the federal government has jurisdiction by statute; they may investigate state and local crimes when requested by those agencies. There is no charge for these services.

The training facilities of the FBI Academy are used by other agencies for training law enforcement officers; some foreign officers are accepted into the program. The academy provides continued education and training for officers. Another important function of the FBI is the collection of national data on crimes known to the police and on arrests.

Throughout its history, particularly during the long years it was headed by J. Edgar Hoover, the FBI has been criticized severely as well as praised highly. During most of its existence, the FBI has had only loose directives from Congress. A strong leader like Hoover was able to take advantage of that situation and build a powerful, extremely influential organization that allegedly held extensive control even over the presidents under whom Hoover served. A book focusing on the activities of the FBI describes the organization's status historically as follows:

Professions

PROFESSIONS 3.2

Federal Agencies with Authority to Carry Firearms and Make Arrests

Agency	Selected Key Responsibilities
Department of Agriculture	
U.S. Forest Service	Protect National Forest lands, animals, resources, and users
Office of Inspector General	Investigate fraud and other criminal acts related to USDA operations
Department of Commerce	
National Oceanic and Atmospheric Administration	Enforce Federal laws and international treaties on hunting and fishing
National Marine Fisheries Service	
Department of Defense	
Office of Inspector General	Investigate fraud and other criminal acts related to DOD operations
Department of the Interior	
Bureau of Indian Affairs - Law Enforcement	Enforce Federal and tribal laws on Indian reservations
Bureau of Land Management	Enforce Federal laws and regulations relating to public lands and resources
National Park Service - Ranger Activities Division	About a third of the 4,500 full-time rangers nationwide are commissioned to investigate crimes and make arrests in the National Park system, as are 800 seasonally employed rangers
National Park Service - U.S. Park Police	Provide police services for the National Park system
Department of Justice	
Drug Enforcement Administration	Investigate major narcotics violators at interstate and international level
Federal Bureau of Investigation	Investigate a broad range of Federal crimes
Federal Bureau of Prisons	Control and transport prisoners; arrest prisoners
Immigration and Naturalization Service	The Border Patrol interdicts aliens and narcotics or other contraband between ports of entry; other INS programs investigate crimes committed within INS jurisdiction, detain and deport illegal aliens, and perform intelligence functions related to INS responsibilities
U.S. Marshals Service	Provide security for Federal courts; protect Federal judges, prosecutors, and jurors; enforce Federal court orders; execute Federal fugitive warrants; transport Federal prisoners; provide custody for Federal pretrial detainees; arrest violators; manage Federal Witness Security Program; control riots on Federal lands, in prisons, or for court orders; administer DOJ programs for judicial forfeiture

At the time of his death in 1972, J. Edgar Hoover had spent a lifetime creating the most powerful law enforcement agency in the United States. The Federal Bureau of Investigation enjoyed one of the most favorable images of any federal agency. Not only had it been relatively immune from public criticism for nearly five decades, but it had also been insulated from any meaningful legislative oversight and had carved out a semiautonomous status within the U.S. Justice Department. The bureau's decade-old multimillion-dollar Washington headquarters, which overshadows the Department of Justice building, is symbolic of this Hoover legacy.[23]

The book goes on to analyze many of the problems, including corruption, other scandals, and lawlessness that have characterized the FBI. In recent years the FBI has experienced additional charges of scandals, corruption, favoritism, discrimination against minorities and women, sexual harassment, and other problems. In 1993 President Clinton appointed Judge Louis J. Freeh to head the FBI. Freeh's appointment followed the resignation under fire of the former director, William Sessions, who was plagued by allegations of ethics violations. Freeh has

PROFESSIONS 3.2 (Continued)

Agency	Selected Key Responsibilities
Department of Transportation	
Federal Air Marshals	Armed in-flight intervention
Department of the Treasury	
Bureau of Alcohol, Tobacco and Firearms	Investigate criminal use of firearms and explosives; enforce Federal alcohol and tobacco regulations
Bureau of Engraving and Printing Police	Enforce laws and regulations at Bureau facilities
U.S. Customs Service	Interdict and seize contraband entering the United States; process persons and property at ports of entry; investigate revenue fraud
Internal Revenue Service	Investigate tax fraud
U.S. Secret Service	Protect dignitaries and investigate threats against them; investigate counterfeiting and computer fraud; provide security for Treasury buildings in Washington, D.C.
Department of Veterans Affairs	Employed about 2,300 personnel with arrest authority who were providing security at VA facilities; however, only 11 met the firearms authorization criteria of this survey
Other	
Administrative Office of the U.S. Courts	Supervise Federal offenders on probation and parole; arrest violators
Amtrak Police	Provide police services for Amtrak facilities and equipment nationwide
U.S. Capitol Police	Provide police services for U.S. Capitol buildings and grounds
Environmental Protection Agency-Office of Criminal Enforcement	Enforce criminal environmental statutes
GSA Federal Protective Services	Provide security for Federal buildings and property nationwide
Government Printing Office Police	Provide security for GPO facilities
U.S. Postal Inspection Service	Enforce laws pertaining to the mails; provide security for postal facilities and employees
Smithsonian National Zoological Park Police	Provide police services at National Zoo and perimeter grounds
U.S. Supreme Court Police	Provide police services for Supreme Court buildings and grounds
Tennessee Valley Authority - Public Safety Service	Provide police and fire services for TVA facilities and lands

Source: William A. Geller and Norval Morris. "Relations between Federal and Local Police," in *Modern Policing*, vol. 15, eds. Michael Tonry and Norval Morris. Chicago: University of Chicago Press, 1992: 322–35, as reprinted in Bureau of Justice Statistics, *Federal Law Enforcement Officers 1993* (Washington, D.C.: U.S. Department of Justice, December 1994), p. 7. Reprinted with permission. © 1992 University of Chicago Press.

been criticized but thus far remains in office despite recent allegations of disagreements with the White House as well as reports that the FBI's world renowned crime lab has serious problems.

Complaints by Frederic Whitehurst, a chemist in the FBI's explosives unit, began in 1995, resulting in investigations of the lab. Attorneys for O. J. Simpson, Timothy McVeigh (convicted in the bombing of the federal building in Oklahoma City in 1995), and lesser known defendants have blasted the agency's analysis of crime data. Whitehurst was put on paid suspension after an investigation confirmed some of his allegations, but many questions about the accuracy of FBI lab reports remain unanswered.[24]

After a U.S. Department of Justice report criticized the FBI crime lab, in the fall of 1997 an outsider, nuclear-weapons physicist, Donald M. Kerr Jr., was appointed to head the lab. According to Director Freeh, Kerr will bring management experience as well as scientific experience to the FBI although he has no forensic experience. "His remarkable background will be invaluable as the F.B.I. carries out its priority efforts to prevent terrorists from using nuclear, biological or chemical weapons in the United States," said Freeh. Kerr formerly headed the Los Alamos National Laboratory, which is a nuclear weapons and research institute, and held high-level management positions at the U.S. Department of Energy.[25]

The FBI, like other federal law enforcement agencies, should be viewed as a supplement to, not a replacement of, state and local agencies. The agency provides outstanding career opportunities for young people who want to be involved in law enforcement, which is especially true now that many agents are facing retirement. The agency is experiencing a loss of large numbers of mid-career agents for the first time in its history as the FBI, like other law enforcement agencies, has failed to keep pace with the private sector in salary increases. For example, in December of 1997, New York FBI Chief James Kallstrom retired to take a position with a banking and credit card firm. Having served in the FBI since 1970, Kallstrom was well known for his role in the investigation of TWA Flight 800, which killed all passengers and crew when it crashed shortly after takeoff on 17 July 1996.[26]

Other Federal Law Enforcement Agencies

In addition to the FBI, the Department of Justice contains two other major law enforcement agencies: the Drug Enforcement Administration (DEA) and the Immigration and Naturalization Service (INS). The DEA previously was part of the Treasury Department and called the *Bureau of Narcotics*. It was shifted to the Justice Department in 1973. The FBI has some drug enforcement powers, too, and engages in some cooperative work with the DEA. The INS polices the borders of the United States, trying to prevent the entrance of illegal aliens. In addition, the INS is in charge of admitting foreigners who qualify for U.S. citizenship.

Some federal law enforcement agencies are part of the Treasury Department. The Customs Service handles inspections at points of entry into the United States. The Internal Revenue Service (IRS) is in charge of laws regulating federal income tax and its collection. The Secret Service is responsible for protecting the president, vice president, and other specific officials, as well as for investigating forged government checks, other securities, and counterfeiting activities.

The Bureau of Alcohol, Tobacco, and Firearms (ATF) has jurisdiction over laws and licensing requirements regarding the sale of alcohol and drugs, and over federal gun control laws and the collection of taxes connected with these areas. The ATF came under close scrutiny when federal agents assaulted the Branch Davidian compound near Waco, Texas in 1993, described as "one of the most disastrous law enforcement operations in the nation's history." Four agents were killed during the February siege, while many cult members and their children perished in a subsequent siege. In 1994 a jury acquitted eleven surviving Davidians of all charges of murder and conspiracy. Seven of the eleven were convicted of lesser charges, while four were acquitted of all charges.[27] After public hearings in 1995 and 1996, a subcommittee of the U.S. House of Representatives accepted a report stating among other findings that the actions of Attorney General Janet Reno were seriously negligent.

Other federal agencies are concerned with law enforcement, licensing, or both. The Food and Drug Administration (FDA) oversees the enforcement of the vast number of laws regulating the sale and distribution of pure food and drugs. The Department of Agriculture has an office that investigates fraud in the areas of food stamps, aid to disaster victims, subsidies to farmers and rural home buyers, and other activities of the department. Additional criminal law enforcement divisions are found in the Securities and Exchange Commission (SEC), the Department of Labor, the U.S. Postal Service, and other federal organizations as well.

The function that federal agencies may provide for local and state police is illustrated by the participation of the federal government in **INTERPOL,** a world police organization established for cooperation among nations involved in common police problems. INTERPOL was founded in 1923 but did not function actively until after its reorganization in 1946. The United States became a member in 1938. INTERPOL is to "track and apprehend criminal fugitives, thwart criminal schemes, exchange experience and technology, and analyze major trends of international criminal activity. Any police official of any member country may initiate a request for assistance on a case that extends beyond his country's territory."[28]

The International Level

In addition to public policing, an important development all over the world is the growth of private policing, which by the 1990s cost approximately twice as much as public policing.[29] Businesses employ security guards to protect their premises from shoplifting and to secure the personal safety of employees and shoppers. Security guards are employed to escort female employees from their places of work to their automobiles at night, particularly in high-crime areas. Apartment owners have increased their use of private security forces, as have neighborhood associations. Increasingly common are guard gates at which drivers entering the association's area are required to stop and present adequate identification before being granted permission to enter the premises.

Private Police and Security Forces

On many college campuses **private security forces** are hired for night work in addition to the regular security of the institution. Some serve as escorts for female students who attend night classes. In many large cities private security forces are hired to patrol housing and business areas. The demand for private security and private police has risen as citizens have felt a lack of sufficient security provided by public police.

Private security may be *proprietary* or *contractual.* In the case of proprietary, organizations or individuals have their own private investigators and security personnel. For those who cannot afford this approach or who choose not to do so, contracts may be made with professional agencies to provide private security. Regardless of the type of system, a variety of components exist, including security managers, uniformed officers, undercover agents, or electronic specialists or equipment.

Types of Systems

The oldest and largest of the firms providing investigative and security services is Pinkerton's, founded in 1850 by Allan Pinkerton. Pinkerton was the first detective of the Chicago Police Department. Local, state, and federal agencies, as well as private companies and individuals, employed the services of Pinkerton's. The term *private eye* had its source in the unblinking eye that was Pinkerton's trademark for many years. The primary business of Pinkerton's, headquartered in New York City, is to supply private security guards, but the firm also provides private consultants, electronic surveillance devices, and some investigation services.[30]

Private security is provided by alarm companies, too. The most frequently used security program is alarm systems; increasing numbers of systems are being installed in private residences and in businesses. Fire and burglar alarm systems are most common, but alarm companies install access control systems, fixed security equipment, and perimeter security systems as well. Most alarm systems are installed by relatively small companies, although some companies have services available nationally. The most sophisticated systems are monitored constantly for increased protection and may involve extensive, and very expensive, systems.

Private security is provided by armored vehicles with armed guards for transporting precious jewels, money, and other valuables. Courier services provide fast delivery of valuables and papers that must be transported quickly and safely. Private security services may be employed for emptying cash machines, delivering money from businesses to bank drops after hours, and many other activities in which business persons or private citizens feel a need for added security. Other services include security training courses, screening of personnel for businesses, technical countersurveillance to determine whether bugging devices have been installed, security consultation, and drug detection. Some people who want access to their valuables after regular banking hours use private security vaults.[31]

Private employment of public police for additional security is utilized as well. Noted expert on policing, sociologist Albert J. Reiss Jr., has emphasized the increased use of public police for private security. In fact, while on patrol with the police, Reiss remarked that it was impossible to tell which officers were performing as public employees and which off-duty public employees were working in a private capacity. Reiss researched the problems and issues of off-duty police employment with special emphasis on particular departments noted in Spotlight 3.2, which also enumerates the three models for off-duty police employment.

Some police departments place restrictions on off-duty employment. Reiss found that generally officers are forbidden to take any assignments that involve a "conflict of interest between duties as a police officer and duties for the outside employer" and those that constitute "threats to the status or dignity of the police" as well as those that pose an "unacceptable risk of injury that would disable an officer for regular duty." In addition, police departments may limit the jurisdiction in which officers work, the compensation received, and the number of hours worked.[32]

Public and Private Policing Compared

Some attempts have been made to study the relationships between public law enforcement and private security systems. An earlier national government study highlighted some of the problems between the two systems as well as some of the progress in solving those problems. It was found that the two systems share many common goals, such as recovering stolen property, protecting life and property, and deterring and discovering criminal activity. In addition, the study disclosed that public law enforcement officials rate private security personnel poorly in almost every area of their work and that they do not have a high regard for the ability of private security to prevent crime.

The study concluded that there is a "climate of suspicion and distrust between private security and law enforcement," although some progress toward cooperative efforts has been made. There was evidence of a willingness to cooperate and to transfer some responsibilities from public law enforcement to private security. Some efforts have been made to integrate the activities and increase the understanding between private security personnel and public law enforcement officers.[33]

Other issues have arisen concerning private police protection. Despite recent legislation in many states, some still do not have licensing requirements for private security. In those jurisdictions, there are few if any checks on the quality of security services or on the training of security personnel.

Spotlight 3.2

Models of Off-Duty Police Employment

Officer Contract Model

- Each officer finds own secondary employment

- Officer independently contracts conditions of work, hours, pay

- Officer then applies for permission to accept off duty job

- Department grants permission provided job meets minimum standards

- Employer pays officer in cash (work is "called cash detail")

Departments in Atlanta, Charlotte, Cincinnati, Minneapolis, and Omaha generally follow this mode differing on what work is permitted.

Arlington County permits uniformed employment only by permission of the police chief and only at activities funded or sponsored by the county, state, or U.S. government. Any other work must be nonpolice in nature.

In Peoria, most secondary employment is independently contracted, but the department itself contracts for civic center jobs, lets department heads broker other work, and permits officers to broker work for other officers.

In Cincinnati, work for private parties is independently contracted, but the department contracts work for city, county, or State agencies.

Union Brokerage Model

- Union, guild, or association finds paid details

- Union assigns officers who have volunteered

- Union sets assignment conditions for paid details

- Union bargains with the department over status, pay, and conditions of paid details

Most off-duty employment of Seattle police is coordinated by the Seattle Police Officers' Guild, although the officers act as independent contractors. For privately sponsored special events at the Seattle Center complex, off duty officers are employed by the center's security officer and paid through an outside accounting firm.

Department Contract Model

- Police agency contracts with employers

- Agency assigns officers and pays them from reimbursements by employers

- Agency assigns an Off-Duty Employment Coordinator to receive employer requests, issue off-duty work permits, and assign officers to paid details

- Agency negotiates with union or guild on pay, conditions, and regulations governing employment

Boston, Colorado Springs, New Haven, and St. Petersburg fit this model. Metro Dade contracts for police-related work (including, unlike most departments, work for private security firms), but lets officers contract for nonpolice jobs, each of which requires a permit.

Source: Albert J. Reiss Jr., *Private Employment of Public Police* (Washington, D.C.: U.S. Department of Justice, December 1988), p. 3.

Many states have enacted statutes providing for regulation of private security, but even in those cases, issues remain to which there has been opposition. Some question licensing fees, required psychological tests, and statutes that are not broad enough to include all types of private security. Increased reliance on private security forces raises the moral and ethical question of whether society can afford to have a system in which necessary police protection is available only to those who can pay for it.

On the other hand, there is evidence that in some jurisdictions the age, experience, and training of private security officers is approaching that of public officers, with private policing showing greater growth in diversity by hiring more minorities and women than public policing.[34]

The Organization and Administration of Police Systems

The organization, administration, and management of any large department presents numerous challenges and problems, but these may be particularly acute in publicly supported police departments. The police department is the largest and most complex department in many criminal justice systems, with officers at the lower levels exercising immense authority over citizens. The functions performed by these people are varied and complex, although the training for the job is focused primarily on only one of those functions—law enforcement.[35]

Despite the importance of police administration, until recently little attention was given to the issues and problems of organization or administration. Indeed, in contrast to the well-planned development of the English police system, the American police system's development was preceded by little planning because of a basic mistrust of a professional police force. Early systems were characterized by corruption and inefficiency. The result was that, at the turn of this century, police forces in our metropolitan areas "were caught in a vicious circle of political manipulation, low prestige, small public expectations, and neither the will nor the pressure to improve."[36]

Early Reform Efforts

Widespread corruption, inefficiency, and a realization of the often negative impact of partisan politics on police systems gave rise in the early 1900s to a study of the role of police organization and administration in improving the quality of policing and to the increased use of private security guards. These early efforts were assisted by the work of the major reformer August Vollmer, often referred to as the father of modern police management systems or the dean of American chiefs of police. As chief of the Berkeley, California, Police Department, Vollmer instituted a summer program in criminology at the University of California at Berkeley and began an emphasis on the importance of educating police formally.

In 1931 the School of Criminology was founded at Berkeley. In 1933 it granted the first police degree, an A.B. degree with a minor in criminology. In 1930 the first two-year college police program was begun at San Jose Junior College, but the first grants to such programs were not offered until 1966. These programs comprised courses in liberal arts, behavioral sciences, public administration, law, and government. Many changes have occurred in the past two decades in criminal justice education, with other programs developing and some, such as Berkeley's, being abolished.[37]

Others who were influential were Bruce Smith, who contributed to police professionalism through his writings and as a professional police consultant, and O. W. Wilson. Wilson was influential as a police chief who emphasized advanced training for officers in Wichita, Kansas, in the late 1920s. He was dean of the School of Criminology at Berkeley and authored a widely acclaimed text on police administration.[38] Perhaps he is best known for his contributions in the 1960s as superintendent of police in Chicago.

Vollmer, Smith, and Wilson influenced the emergence of a professional model for policing, including not only the use of management skills at the administrative levels of policing, but also the application of modern technology in improving police work. The result was a model characterized by "a tight quasi-military organization; rigorous discipline; a streamlined chain of command; higher recruitment standards; a lengthy period of preservice training; the allocation of available personnel according to demonstrated need; and extensive use of vehicles, communications, and computer technology."[39]

The organization and management of police departments received considerable attention from the President's Commission on Law Enforcement and Administration of Justice. Some of the commission's conclusions, stated in its 1967 report on police, were the lack of qualified leadership; resistance to change; lack of trained personnel in research and planning, law, business administration, and computer analysis; inefficient use of personnel; and departmental organization that does not incorporate "well-established principles of modern business management."[40]

Policing Models

A Professional Model of Policing

The commission graphed one model of departmental organization, the traditional or professional model, characterized by a hierarchical structure with the police chief as the central authority in the organization. Heads of departments such as internal investigation, community relations, administration bureau, operations bureau, and services bureau, report directly to the chief. Each of these heads has subordinate administrators reporting directly to him or her. Under this model, the police department is organized around specialized functions such as patrol, traffic, personnel and training, and data processing, all of which are subunits of the major divisions of administration, operations, and services. This particular model has major units concerned with internal investigations and community relations. Some departments have a unit specializing in crime prevention.

The chain of command in this traditional model is clear. Subordinates in each unit report directly to their division heads, who report to the chief. This authoritarian model involves many rules and regulations, with little input from subordinates in developing them. It may be a very efficient model for making some kinds of quick decisions, for prescribing safety measures, and for internal control of subordinates, and frequently it results in high production output.

The professional model of policing gained momentum with the reports of the President's Commission on Law Enforcement and Administration of Justice in 1967 and the National Advisory Commission on Criminal Justice Standards and Goals in 1973. According to the 1981 report of the U.S. Commission on Civil Rights, "These two commissions, in particular, gave added impetus to some specific suggestions, such as the more effective use of police personnel and, most emphatically, the requirement that police officers have some college education."[41]

The need for professional police systems became obvious in the 1960s when television brought into American homes the violent clashes between police and minorities, including the young as well as racial and ethnic groups. The urban riots of the 1960s demonstrated the need to train police in handling orderly protests as well as violence and law enforcement.

During the 1960s, police and other elements of criminal justice systems became the focus of the federal government. In 1965 President Lyndon Johnson appointed the President's Commission on Law Enforcement and Administration of Justice. This commission issued several reports in 1967. In 1965 Congress established the Office of Law Enforcement Assistance, and in 1968 the **Law Enforcement Assistance Administration (LEAA).** Until its demise in 1982, LEAA provided over $7 billion for research, development, and evaluation of various programs in criminal justice, some of which went for hardware in police departments (a source of criticism of the LEAA). Money was provided for police education through the **Law Enforcement Education Program (LEEP).** The result was the development of criminal justice departments throughout the country. Most of them focused on police education or training, discussed in Chapter 4.

The professional model is criticized for being too authoritarian and for establishing policing units that are too specialized. For example, if a police officer assigned to the patrol division encounters a problem with a juvenile, under the traditional model that person should be turned over to the juvenile division, even though the patrol officer in that district may have more knowledge of the individual juvenile and his or her background. Controlling traffic and issuing traffic citations is the specialty of the officers in the traffic division; they should be called for handling these problems in the patrol officer's district. The officer may arrest a suspect for violating a crime, but the investigation of that crime will be conducted by a detective in another division. There may be overlap in the record keeping of these various divisions, in addition to the obvious fragmentation of functions.

Criticism of the traditional method of organizing police departments has led to adoption of other organizational models.

Community-Oriented Policing

Dissatisfaction with the professional model has led to a recent emphasis on a problem-solving approach to policing, which may focus on the community. The popular term is *community-oriented policing*. The problem-solving nature of this approach focuses on a less extensive division of labor, fewer rules and regulations, and few levels of authority. The emphasis is on solving problems, and power comes from the ability of employees to succeed in that goal, not from the titles of their positions. Its emphasis is on gaining knowledge and using that knowledge to adapt to new situations. This model provides greater flexibility, which may be necessary for some decisions, while permitting greater involvement of subordinates in the police force. It is based on the belief that police effectiveness may be increased if the expertise and creativity of line officers are utilized to develop innovative methods for solving the underlying problems that cause or influence criminal behavior.

Since much of police work requires officers to make on-the-spot decisions, the problem-solving model may be more effective than the professional model in developing the ability to make decisions effectively. Problem-oriented policing may focus on underlying problems in any or all of the three traditional areas of policing: order maintenance, law enforcement, and community service (discussed in Chapter 4). It is not designed to eliminate police reaction to citizen calls but, rather, to enhance the effectiveness of policing by identifying underlying problems and attempting to solve those problems.

The problem-solving approach to policing has been emphasized in the writings of Herman Goldstein, who developed his earlier published ideas in a 1990 book. Among other examples, Goldstein discussed a Philadelphia case involving a police sergeant who noted that many noise complaints (505 separate calls in a six-month period) about the same bar had been made to police, who responded to all of these complaints. The officers who responded did not find the noise to be in violation of the city ordinance. After some time, however, officers discovered that the noise about which the neighbors complained was coming from the vibration of the jukebox located at the common wall. The jukebox was moved to another wall, and the noise complaints stopped.[42] In this case, police used their common sense to solve the problem, which resulted in the cessation of calls regarding that issue.

Focus on problem-solving policing does not mean that police will not respond to calls for service, but the demands created by these calls may lead administrators to rationalize that they do not have the personnel to engage in innovative policing, such as problem-solving approaches. It is necessary to integrate the traditional calls for service approach with problem-solving policing, and this cannot be done without better management of police time. As a retired chief noted, "The crisis in American policing is not a money or resource scarcity but a management problem, and one that has not been recognized, much less addressed."[43]

Goldstein responds to the time issue also:

> A common reaction to problem-oriented policing is that the agency has no time available for it. . . . This type of reaction assumes that problem-oriented policing is an add-on. It fails to recognize that the concept raises fundamental questions about how police currently spend their time, both in responding to calls for assistance and in the intervals between calls.[44]

It is argued that the time police may waste in patrol under the professional policing model can be utilized more effectively if they are involved in problem-solving approaches. For example, give police daily assessments of specific problems in their patrol areas, and let them work on those problems. "Many of the citywide crime problems would appear more manageable if officers could deal with them at the neighborhood level."[45]

Community-oriented policing is based on the concept that officers should become less anonymous and more integrated into the communities in which they patrol. Returning to foot patrol, as in earlier days, or using horses or bicycles assists officers in this effort. Police become more visible and more accountable to the public, and they are encouraged to view citizens as partners in crime prevention. Furthermore, more decision making at the patrol level means that those who are best informed of the problems in the community are the ones making important policing decisions.[46]

Assessment of Community-Oriented Policing   Criminologist Gary W. Cordner has evaluated community-oriented policing by stating that, "In less than two decades, community policing has evolved from a few small foot patrol studies to the preeminent reform agenda of modern policing. . . . [It has become] the dominant strategy of policing.[47]

The measure of Cordner's statement is underscored by the support given to community policing by President Bill Clinton and Attorney General Janet Reno. In early 1994 the administration announced the "down payment" on its campaign promise to put 100,000 more police on the street by offering federal grants for hiring police. Later that year Congress enacted a new crime bill that contains a provision for the 100,000 promised officers.[48] Community-oriented policing is in vogue, complete with funds for implementation. But will it work? Many say it will not make a significant improvement in crime.[49] Two programs are illustrative of the variance in assessment.

Community policing begun in one precinct of Seattle, Washington, was considered so successful in reducing crime that it spread to the city's other precincts. Evaluators claim that the emphasis on community policing provides benefits to police as well as to citizens, who have developed a real partnership in the battle against crime.[50] In Houston, Texas, investigators evaluating the community-oriented policing system put in place by Chief Lee P. Brown (who later began a similar program in New York City, and, after holding two other positions, has returned to Houston as mayor) were not so positive. They claimed the program was an "end in itself" rather than a "tool to reduce crime and improve service." The investigators endorsed the concept but found that community-oriented policing had not significantly changed citizens' feelings about security.[51]

In the summer of 1994 an entire issue of a major criminology journal was devoted to community policing. The lead article of that journal contains an evaluation and assessment of community policing, described by the authors as the "latest reform in law enforcement," a reform that is "quite popular among politicians, citizens, and police managers." The authors conclude that although some questions remain unanswered, evaluations of community policing suggest "that community policing-type programs can have some positive effects on the community's perceptions and feelings about crime, disorder, and the police."[52]

Despite opposition by Republicans to President Clinton's Community-Oriented Policing Services (COPS) program, in 1996 the president won budget approval of $1.4 billion to continue the program for hiring and training law enforcement officers. Other activities, such as operating drug courts, drug testing, and many other programs may be aided with the funds, too.[53] By early 1997 the Clinton Administration had passed the halfway mark of its goal to put 100,000 new state and local police in action. At that point $2.7 billion had been provided in COPS grants. This money will provide for the hiring of 52,000 officers, 22,000 of whom were already at work.[54] By the middle of 1997 the two-thirds mark had been reached, with more than 62,000 new community-oriented policing positions having been filled with federal grants.[55]

WiseGuide Wrap-Up Earlier chapters introduced the subject of social control and explored the differences between informal and formal methods of control. This chapter illustrates those differences, with reference to the need for a formal police system. The history of informal and formal policing methods in England and the United States is examined. Many factors contributed to the need for formal policing, but in both countries the increasing complexity that resulted when society became industrialized was a crucial factor. The rising levels of criminal activity, public unrest, and riots that accompanied industrialization demonstrated the inability of informal methods of policing to provide adequate protection.

The formal system of policing that evolved in the United States, a decentralized system having local, state, and federal levels, results in overlap and gaps between levels. It also permits states and localities to experiment with methods that might be effective in light of the problems that distinguish their policing needs from those of the federal government. The various levels of policing cooperate in some functions, such as investigation and training. Numerous law enforcement agencies exist at the federal level, and they are available to assist states and local agencies as well.

Formal, public policing systems have been the object of criticism for a long time; some citizens have reacted by employing private police or by having security devices installed in their homes or businesses. Conflict between public and private policing developed and continues, although there is some evidence of cooperation between the two. Some states have established minimum requirements for licensing private security firms.

The type of police organization and administration may have a significant effect on policing. The chapter discusses early reform efforts in police organization and administration and then focuses on differentiating the two major models of policing: the traditional or professional model and community policing. The choice of model will affect the way people perform their jobs; thus, this chapter provides a framework in which to examine the nature and functioning of policing, the focus of Chapter 4.

Apply It

1. Why do we have a formal system of policing?

2. Explain the meaning of the following to the development of modern policing: Bow Street Runners, Peelers or Bobbies, posse, and Molly Maguires.

3. Compare local, state, and federal police systems. What are the advantages and disadvantages of decentralized policing?

4. What are some of the unique problems of rural law enforcement?

5. What is the function of U.S. marshals?

6. Discuss the strengths and weaknesses of the FBI.

7. What is the role of private police agencies? Evaluate.

8. How would you describe the administration of early police systems in the United States?

9. Evaluate the traditional, authoritarian model of organizational structure of police departments.

10. Trace the development of the professional model of policing.

11. Describe and analyze the concept of community-oriented policing.

Notes

1. Herman Goldstein, *Policing in a Free Society* (Cambridge, Mass.: Ballinger Publishing, 1977), p. 1.
2. "Case of JonBenet Ramsey Stalls on Error and Rivalry," *New York Times* (2 July 1997), p. 10.
3. Jonathan Rubinstein, *City Police* (New York: Ballantine Books, 1973), p. 5. See also Phillip Smith, *Policing Victorian London* (London: Greenwood Press, 1985).
4. For a summary of the work in this area, see Alexander W. Pisciotta, "Police, Society, and Social Control in America: A Metahistorical Review of the Literature," *Criminal Justice Abstracts* 14 (December 1982): 514–39.
5. David H. Bayley, "Police: History," in *Encyclopedia of Crime and Justice*, vol. 3, ed. Sanford H. Kadish (New York: Free Press, 1983), pp. 1122–23.
6. Louis B. Schwartz and Stephen R. Goldstein, *Law Enforcement Handbook for Police* (St. Paul, Minn.: West Publishing, 1970), p. 34.
7. For more recent analyses of the British police system, see Avrom Sheer, *Public Order and the Law* (New York: Basil Blackwell, 1988), which explores the role of the police in British society; and Simon Holdaway, *Inside the British Police: A Force at Work* (New York: Basil Blackwell, 1983). Written by a sociologist who was previously employed as a police sergeant, this book examines the modern British police system on the basis of his observations of everyday policing in Great Britain.
8. "A First: Some Bobbies Will Wear Pistols," *Miami Herald* (17 May 1994), p. 7.
9. Bayley, "Police: History," p. 1124.
10. Ibid.
11. See, for example, Arnold Madison, *Vigilantism in America* (New York: Seabury Press, 1973); Richard M. Brown, *Strain of Violence: Historical Studies of American Violence and Vigilantism* (New York: Oxford University Press, 1975); and William C. Culberson, *Vigilantism: Political History of Private Power in America* (Westport, Ct.: Greenwood Press, 1990). For a recent study, see Francis Bailey, "Real Life Vigilantism and Vigilantism in Popular Films," *The Justice Professional* 8 (Summer 1993): 33–52.
12. " 'Crack House' Fire: Justice or Vigilantism?" *New York Times* (22 October 1988), p. 7.
13. For an overview of rural policing, see Ralph A. Weisheit et al., *Crime and Policing in Rural and Small-Town America* (Prospect Heights, IL: Waveland Press, 1996).
14. For a discussion of rural policing, see Bureau of Justice Assistance, *Neighborhood-Oriented Policing in Rural Communities: A Program Planning Guide* (Washington, D.C.: U.S. Department of Justice, 1994).
15. For a discussion and analysis of rural crime and rural policing, see Ralph A. Weisheit et al., *Rural Crime and Rural Policing,* National Institute of Justice Research in Action (Washington, D.C.: U.S. Department of Justice, October 1994).
16. "Sheriffs Losing Posts in Southeast Texas: Political Activist Cites Changing Times," *Dallas Morning News* (18 April 1988), p. 13.
17. Egon Bittner, "Police: Urban Police," *Encyclopedia of Crime and Justice*, vol. 3, ed. Kadish, p. 1133.
18. For a discussion of urban policing and crime, see Roger Lane, "Urban Police and Crime in Nineteenth-Century America," in *Modern Policing*, ed. Michael Tonry and Norval Morris (Chicago: University of Chicago Press, 1992), pp. 1–50. For a history of urban policing, see the same source, Eric H. Monkkonen, "History of Urban Police," pp. 547–580.
19. "Milestones," *Time* (19 September 1988), p. 97.
20. Robert Borkenstein, "Police: State Police," in *Encyclopedia of Crime and Justice*, vol. 3, ed. Kadish, p. 1133.
21. Ibid., p. 1134.
22. For a discussion of the relationship between federal and local policing, see William A. Geller and Norval Morris, "Relations between Federal and Local Police," in *Modern Policing*, ed. Tonry and Morris, pp. 231–348.
23. Tony Poveda, *Lawlessness and Reform: The FBI in Transition* (Pacific Grove, Calif.: Brooks-Cole Publishing Co., 1990), p. 1.
24. "Trouble in the F.B.I. Lab," *New York Times* editorial (2 January 1997), p. 6; "F.B.I. Suspends an Agent who Criticized Crime Lab," *New York Times* (28 January 1997), p. 8.
25. "F.B.I. Names an Outsider as New Head of Crime Lab," *New York Times* (22 October 1997), p. 15.
26. "Kallstrom Quits FBI; Led Probe of Jet Blast," *USA Today* (10 December 1997), p. 3.

27. "Eleven in Texas Sect Are Acquitted of Key Charges," *New York Times* (27 February 1994), p. 1.

28. Michael Fooner, "INTERPOL," in *Encyclopedia of Crime and Justice,* vol. 3, ed. Kadish, p. 912. See also Fooner, *Interpol: Issues in World Crime and International Criminal Justice* (New York: Plenum, 1989).

29. See William C. Cunningham et al., *Private Security: Patterns and Trends* (Washington, D.C.: National Institute of Justice, August 1991), p. 1. For an analysis of the emergence of private police, see Les Johnston, *The Rebirth of Private Policing* (New York: Routledge, 1992).

30. James S. Kakalik and Sorrel Wildhorn, *The Private Police: Security and Danger* (New York: Crane Russak and Co., 1977; copyright Rand Corp.), p. 68.

31. William C. Cunningham and Todd H. Taylor, *Crime and Protection in America: A Study of Private Security and Law Enforcement Resources and Relationships: Executive Summary* (Washington, D.C.: U.S. Government Printing Office, May 1985), pp. 19–22.

32. Albert J. Reiss Jr., *Private Employment of Public Police* (Washington, D.C.: U.S. Department of Justice, December 1988), pp. 2–3. For practical information on private policing, see John L. Coleman, *Practical Knowledge for a Private Security Officer,* 2d ed. (Springfield, Il.: Charles C Thomas, 1993). For an analysis of private policing, see Clifford D. Shearing, "The Relation between Public and Private Policing," in *Modern Policing,* ed. Tonry and Morris, pp. 399–434.

33. William C. Cunningham and Todd H. Taylor, "Ten Years of Growth in Law Enforcement," *Police Chief* 1 (June 1983): 32. For a more recent analysis of the rapid growth of private policing and the effect it has had on public policing, see Clifford D. Shearing and Philip C. Stenning, *Private Policing* (Beverly Hills, Calif.: Sage Publications, 1987). See also the study describing the efforts of the police department and private security companies in Oakland, California, to collaborate on crime prevention as well as the problem of residents' fear of crime. Albert J. Reiss Jr., *Policing a City's Central District—The Oakland Story,* National Institute of Justice (Washington, D.C.: U.S. Department of Justice, 1985).

34. Cunningham et al., *Private Security,* p. 4.

35. The basis for this discussion is the article by Herman Goldstein, "Police Administration," in *Encyclopedia of Crime and Justice,* vol. 3, ed. Kadish, pp. 1125–31.

36. Bruce Smith, *Police Systems in the United States* (New York: Harper Bros., 1960), pp. 104-5, quoted in George D. Eastman and James A. McCain, "Education, Professionalism, and Law Enforcement in Historical Perspective," *Journal of Police Science and Administration* 9 (June 1981): 122.

37. For an analysis of criminal justice doctoral programs in the early 1990s, see Timothy J. Flanagan, "Criminal Justice Doctoral Programs in the United States and Canada: Findings from a National Survey," *Journal of Criminal Justice Education* 1 (Fall 1990): 195–213. For other discussions of criminal justice education, see the following two articles in *Journal of Criminal Justice Education* 1 (Spring 1990): Frank J. Remington, "Development of Criminal Justice as an Academic Field," pp. 9–20; and Leslie T. Wilkins, "The Future of Graduate Education in Criminal Justice: Keeping Curriculum Fashionable? A Personal View," pp. 21–32. For an assessment on student learning in the field, see the recent article by Thomas Kelley and Steven Stack, "Achievement in Criminal Justice: An Analysis of Graduating Seniors," *Journal of Criminal Justice Education* 8 (Spring 1997): 37–50.

38. See O. W. Wilson and Roy Clinton McLaren, *Police Administration,* 4th ed. (New York: McGraw-Hill, 1977). McLaren took over the revisions after Wilson's death.

39. Goldstein, "Police Administration," p. 1126.

40. The President's Commission on Law Enforcement and Administration of Justice, Task Force on the Police, *Task Force Report: The Police* (Washington, D.C.: U.S. Government Printing Office, 1967), p. 44.

41. United States Commission on Civil Rights, *Who Is Guarding the Guardians? A Report on Police Practices,* (Washington, D.C.: U.S. Government Printing Office, 1981), p. 6.

42. Herman Goldstein, *Problem-Oriented Policing* (New York: McGraw-Hill, 1990), p. 81 (n. 6).

43. Anthony Bouza, *The Police Mystique: An Insider's Look at Cops, Crime, and the Criminal Justice System* (New York: Plenum, 1990), p. 138.

44. Goldstein, *Problem-Oriented Policing,* p. 151.

45. David A. Kessler, "Integrating Calls for Service With Community- and Problem-Oriented Policing: A Case Study," *Crime & Delinquency* 39 (October 1993): 506.

46. "Community Policing in the 1990s," *National Institute of Justice Journal* 225 (August 1992): 3. See also Robert Trojanowica and Bonnie Bucqueroux, *Community Policing: A Contemporary Perspective* (Cincinnati: Anderson, 1990). For a discussion of some of the problems of implementing community policing, see George L. Kelling and William J. Bratton, *Implementing Community Policing: The Administrative Problem* (Washington, D.C.: National Institute of Justice, July 1993). See also Mark Harrison Moore, "Problem-Solving and Community Policing," in *Modern Policing,* ed. Tonry and Morris, pp. 99–158.

47. Gary W. Cordner, "Community Policing: Elements and Effects," in *Critical Issue in Policing: Contemporary Readings,* 3d ed., ed. Roger G. Dunham and Geoffrey P. Alpert (Prospect Heights, Illinois: Waveland Press, 1997), pp. 451–468. Quotation is on p. 451. The chapter was originally published in *Police Forum* (1995).

48. Violent Crime Control and Law Enforcement Act of 1994, Public Law 103-322 (13 September 1994).

49. For a discussion of community policing, see *The Challenge of Community Policing: Testing the Promises,* ed. Dennis P. Rosenbaum (Thousand Oaks, Calif.: Sage Publications, 1994). For a discussion of the need for evaluation, see David M. Kennedy and Mark H. Moore, "Underwriting the Risky Investment in Community Policing: What Social Science Should be Doing to Evaluate Community Policing," in *Critical Issues in Policing,* 3d ed., ed. Dunham and Alpert, pp. 469–488.

50. *Community Policing in Seattle: A Model Partnership Between Citizens and Police* (Washington, D.C.: National Institute of Justice, August 1992).

51. "Houston Study Criticizes Community Policing," *New York Times* (8 August 1991), p. 11.

52. Dennis P. Rosenbaum and Arthur J. Lurigio, "An Inside Look at Community Policing Reform: Definitions, Organizational Changes, and Evaluation Findings," *Crime & Delinquency* 40 (July 1994): 299–314. Quotation is on p. 309. The reader is referred to this Special Issue on Community Policing. See also Ralph A. Weisheit et al., "Community Policing in Small Town and Rural America," *Crime & Delinquency* 40 (October 1994): 549–567.

53. "August 9 Deadline Set for Law Enforcement Block Grants," *Criminal Justice Newsletter* 27 (3 June 1996): 6.

54. "Justice Department Cites Progress in 'Cops' and Prison Grants," *Criminal Justice Newsletter* 28 (16 January 1997): 5.

55. "62,000 New Officers Funded with COPS Grants, Justice Department Says," *Criminal Justice Newsletter* 28 (15 July 1997): 6.

Policing in a Modern Society

Police in the United States are expected to prevent crime, apprehend and arrest criminals, enforce traffic ordinances and other laws, maintain order in domestic and other kinds of disputes, control riots and other disturbances, and perform numerous miscellaneous services. Police must perform these functions in the context of political, legal, and popular expectations that may be unrealistic and conflicting.

Some of the functions assigned to police are shared by other persons or agencies, which often results in conflict concerning police roles. But police are given greater discretion and power in performing their tasks than are other agencies. Why? The possibility that disorder, or even violence, may occur convinces us that the force of the police should handle the situation. Therefore, we are willing to grant police the power to intervene when such intervention is necessary. "This lends homogeneity to such diverse procedures as catching a criminal, driving the mayor to the airport, evicting a drunken person from a bar, directing traffic, crowd control, taking care of lost children, administering medical first aid, and separating fighting relatives."[1]

This chapter focuses on what police do in a modern society, but those functions should be examined in the context of the extensive discretion police have in performing their jobs. The importance of discretion and the possibility of its abuse require that high standards be maintained by those who occupy policing roles. The chapter's discussion of discretion is thus preceded by a look at preparing for policing.

Key Terms

arrest
contraband
curtilage
frisk
informant
Miranda warning
probable cause
search and seizure
search warrant
warrant

Learning Objectives

Learning Objectives

After reading this chapter, you should be able to do the following:

- Describe the importance of police recruitment and training.
- Discuss the role of higher education in policing.
- Explain the meaning of discretion in policing.
- List the three major areas of police functions and explain each.
- Present an overview of the U.S. constitutional provisions that govern policing.
- Discuss recent U.S. Supreme Court decisions regarding traffic stops and searches.

- Explain the difference between an investigatory stop and an arrest.
- Discuss the meaning of probable cause and explain the purpose of requiring a warrant for most searches.
- Explain what police can and cannot do in searching the home, the automobile, and the person.
- Compare the police role of interrogation with that of investigation.
- Explain and evaluate the *Miranda* rule and its exceptions.

Preparing for Policing

T he importance of policing demands that careful attention be given to the recruitment and training of persons in policing. Part of the preparation involves education. Attention is given here to these three areas.

Recruitment

Recruitment and training are critical processes in the establishment of an efficient and effective police force; yet the 1981 report of the U.S. Commission on Civil Rights noted that standards for selecting police recruits did not reflect and measure the qualities needed for adequate job performance. In addition, the standards contributed to discrimination against women and minorities. The commission recommended the review of selection standards "to ensure that they are job-related. Those standards that tend to disqualify minorities and women disproportionately should be subjected to a high degree of scrutiny." The commission emphasized the importance of psychological testing as well.[2]

The difficulty, however, is that desirable qualities and characteristics are never defined in acceptable and measurable terms. Perhaps the problem is that in the past the focus has been on the people and their qualities, the assumption being that if different types of people were attracted to policing, the profession would improve. Some have assumed that certain types of people, for example, authoritarian and cynical people, are attracted to policing. Others argue that policing creates these personalities.[3]

In an analysis of the literature on police personalities, two researchers concluded that it is not possible to draw conclusions about whether police possess a distinct personality, and if so, when and how it is acquired. Nor is it possible to eliminate all undesirable candidates by the use of psychological testing as part of the recruitment and selection process. However, psychological tests are useful in conjunction with other recruitment and selection methods, although at least one authority argues that, "Unfortunately, the psychological tests used to identify and select police officer candidates are neither effective nor efficient."[4]

Despite the lack of conclusive data on the predictability of psychological and other tests or job interviews, all should be used in recruiting and selecting police recruits. It is important as well to give the recruits an understanding of the context in which policing occurs as well as the nature of the job. This information might alleviate the stress caused by recruits' unrealistic expectations.

Successful recruitment of police officers requires more research into the characteristics most highly associated with effective policing. We do know that good policing requires many qualities, including intelligence and the abilities to think independently, to switch roles, to understand other cultures and subcultures, to switch functions, and to understand the importance of freedom and the dangers of abusing authority.

We also know that it is crucial to recruit into policing people who have high moral and ethical standards and who have not been engaged in previous infractions with the law. The next chapter discusses corruption in policing; avoiding that problem requires recruiting persons who will not succumb to the temptations facing law enforcement officers. This is difficult to do, however, as police departments throughout the country have discovered. Officers are recruited from a generation of young people who have grown up in a culture in which it may be considered appropriate to engage in some law violations, such as using illegal drugs. Trying to recruit persons who have never used drugs may be an impossible task, especially in some of the larger cities. Of course, recruiting ethical candidates for jobs is important in most jobs, but as one authority on police ethics notes, it is particularly crucial in policing. On the cover page of his text, John Kleinig states:

> Few occupations make as significant moral demands on their practitioners as policing. Yet no occupation has been as poorly prepared for the moral demands laid on it.[5]

The issue of police integrity was addressed by the National Institute of Justice (NIJ) and the COPS office (Community Oriented Policing Services), which together sponsored a symposium on police integrity in 1996. Among other issues, the more than 200 participants discussed ways to establish and maintain integrity in police departments and to "offer positive reinforcement to new recruits to help them retain the ideals they held on entering the force." The participants sought to direct future research into the area of police integrity.[6]

The success of efforts to recruit persons with high moral and ethical standards into policing and to encourage them to maintain those standards may be analyzed in terms of the subsequent behavior of recruits. In that respect, the New York City Police Department is often the focus of attention. For example, a major investigation into policing in that city occurred upon the arrest of four police after a brutal sexual attack on Abner Louima, a Haitian immigrant, outside a Brooklyn station house on 9 August 1997. In testimony before the New York City Council, Frank Serpico stated, "We must create an atmosphere where the crooked cop fears the honest cop, and not the other way around." Serpico, a former New York City police officer, testified against other officers in the early 1970s, turning in those who engaged in corrupt or other forms of illegal behavior. He almost lost his life in his fight against the problems of the department, and his story became a best-selling book and movie, *Serpico*.[7]

Training

In its 1967 report, the Task Force on Police of the President's Commission on Law Enforcement and Administration of Justice emphasized the importance of adequate police training, noting that the problem was particularly acute in small police departments. Many larger departments had expanded police training, but the task force concluded that "current training programs, for the most part, prepare an officer to perform police work mechanically but do not prepare him to understand his community, the police role, or the imperfections of the criminal justice system." Few of the programs reviewed by the commission provided training on the use of police discretion.[8]

The commission recommended that police training include instruction on "subjects that prepare recruits to exercise discretion properly and to understand the community, the role of the police, and what the criminal justice system can and cannot do." The commission recommended "an absolute minimum of 400 hours of classroom work spread over a four-to-six month period so that it can be combined with carefully selected and supervised field training." In-service training at least once a year, along with incentives for officers to continue their education, should be provided.[9] In 1973 the National Advisory Commission on Criminal Justice Standards and Goals put police training into perspective with some harsh comments: "Perhaps no other profession has such lax standards or is allowed to operate without firm controls and without licensing."[10]

In 1981 the Commission on Civil Rights emphasized the need for formal police training and concluded that most of the examined programs "do not give sufficient priority to on-the-job field training, programs in human relations, and preparation for the social service function of police officers, including intervening in family-related disturbances." The commission found that in many jurisdictions even firearms training was inadequate and, in addition, "subject to the ambiguities found in statutes and departmental policies." Because of this ambiguity, the commission concluded that it is imperative that police training expose recruits to situations in which the use of firearms might or might not be appropriate. Alternatives to deadly force should be demonstrated, too. Finally, the commission recommended that police receive training in the social services they are expected to perform.[11]

The importance of adequate police training was emphasized by a 1989 U.S. Supreme Court decision in which the Court held that inadequate police training may result in civil liability for the municipality under which the police department operates. The Court placed limitations on this liability, stating that liability may exist "only where the failure to train amounts to deliberate indifference to the rights of persons with whom the police come into contact."[12] The case is discussed in Chapter 5.

Other forms of negligence, in addition to negligence in training, may lead to police liability. These include negligence in hiring, assignment, supervision, direction, entrustment, and investigation or discipline.[13]

Higher Education

College education for police first received significant attention from August Vollmer in 1917, when he recruited part-time police officers from students at the University of California. Despite his emphasis on the importance of higher education and his reputation as an outstanding police administrator, Vollmer did not succeed in getting many police departments to follow his lead. During the Depression, when jobs were scarce, college-educated men were recruited by police departments, but that practice ceased with the end of the Depression. The employment of college-educated police officers has been questioned.

In 1967, when the average police officer had barely more than a high school diploma, the President's Commission on Law Enforcement and the Administration of Justice recommended that the "ultimate aim of all police departments should be that personnel with general enforcement powers have baccalaureate degrees."[14] The government provided financial incentives and support for the development of programs for higher education of police. In 1989 it was estimated that approximately 55 percent of police officers had received some college training, but the average police officer had completed only fourteen years of education.

Spotlight 4.1

Police Training and Education: The Baltimore Approach

As part of the 1994 crime bill, Congress provided for changes in policing. President Clinton supported putting more police on the streets, and community policing became the focus of changes in law enforcement. Congress began providing funds for support of improvements in policing. One of the programs is called the Police Corps and is modeled after the military's Reserve Officers Training Corps.

Funds are provided for jurisdictions that submit proposals for improving police education and training. One of the programs that received the largest funding is that of Baltimore, Maryland, whose police commissioner, Thomas C. Frazier, had conceived the idea of a police corps in the late 1960s while working as an aide to Robert F. Kennedy. Along with one of Kennedy's daughters, Kathleen Kennedy Townsend, Maryland's lieutenant governor, Frazier proposed the Maryland plan, which received $6.5 million in federal funds.

The Maryland program emphasizes sensitivity training, social skills, community understanding, the demographics of neighborhoods, and communication skills along with self-defense and other skills taught traditionally in police academies. Role playing is a central part of the training, giving an opportunity for recruits to simulate experiences of neighborhoods far different from the ones they have

Lieutenant Governor Kathleen Townsend of Maryland and Baltimore's Police Commissioner, Thomas C. Frazier, Support the Police Corps.

(Marty Katz/NYT Pictures, The New York Times Company, 229 West 43rd Street, 9th floor, NYC 10036)

experienced. In Maryland the new program will eventually replace the traditional police-academy approach. Other programs funded by the federal government are in South Carolina, Oregon, North Carolina, Arkansas, and Nevada. Other states have applied for funding in the 1997 budget year, and President Clinton has requested additional funding for 1998.

Source: Summarized from "Baltimore Tries Training Police in a New Way," *New York Times* (30 March 1997), p. 10.

In the early 1980s the federal funding was cut; many programs were reduced or abolished; local budgets were cut; and some departments that had established policies requiring police officers to have a college degree either were changing those requirements or extending the date for their enforcement requirements.

As noted in Chapter 3, one of the provisions of the 1994 crime control bill was to put more police on the streets. The money provided by Congress for community-oriented policing, the COPS program, has been used in some jurisdictions for enhanced training and education of police. The 1994 statute provided funds for the development in six states (Maryland, North Carolina, Oregon, Nevada, Arkansas, and South Carolina) of programs that are modeled after the military's Reserve Officers Training Corps. For college graduates who agree to serve four years in policing, the program will reimburse up to $30,000 in educational costs. One of the featured programs is that of Maryland, whose Lieutenant Governor, Kathleen Kennedy Townsend, daughter of the late Robert F. Kennedy (former U.S. attorney general and brother of President John F. Kennedy), strongly supported the program. The plan for a Police Corps was generated by Thomas C. Frazier, Baltimore's police commissioner, when he was an aide to Robert Kennedy in the 1960s. More details on the Police Corps are contained in Spotlight 4.1.

In 1996 the Bureau of Justice Statistics reported that many local police departments were increasing educational requirements for police officers as well as recruiting more Hispanics, women, and African Americans. Reporting on 1993 data, the BJS noted a doubling over the 1990 requirements for higher education, with 12 percent of local police departments requiring some college education, 8 percent requiring a degree of some type (which could be a two-year, associate of arts degree), and one in 100 requiring a four-year degree.[15]

Not all agree that higher education should be required for policing. First, there is concern that raising educational requirements might discriminate against minority applicants. Second, there is concern that the applicant pool may be too small. Third, there is concern that some police unions are opposed to higher educational requirements.[16] Finally, many of the criminal justice programs that provided police education have come under attack. Critics argue that there is too much emphasis on technical skills at the expense of a broad educational background. The purpose of current federal and some local efforts to expand the program of training and education, such as that characteristic of Baltimore's program discussed above, are attempts to remedy an excessive emphasis on technical skills.

In 1989 the Police Executive Research Forum released a study of police education in which it noted the perceived advantages and disadvantages of higher education of police. The authors concluded that overall, college-educated officers are more responsible and better decision makers than their less educated counterparts. As such, the former are not only more effective in performing their jobs but are more efficient in that costs associated with lost personnel time are lower.[17]

In a later study a criminologist/police officer found that today's officer is more educated although less dedicated to the job of policing. "What we are seeing is college kids getting their education and graduating and being hired by police agencies."[18] However, the controversy remains over the nature and quality of that education. In professions such as law, dentistry, and medicine, the profession has considerable control over the nature of education. This is not true in policing, in which "the implementation of a professional educational program for a professionalizing ideology is barely under way."[19]

Discretion in Policing

Chapter 1 includes a discussion of discretion and notes that wide discretion exists in criminal justice systems. Perhaps that discretion is greatest in policing. Police have wide discretion in determining whether to begin the formal processing of the criminal justice system. When they see a person who appears to be violating the law, police may refuse to acknowledge that action. Or they may investigate the situation and decide that they do not have sufficient reason to think a crime has been committed. They might decide that a crime has been committed but not by the suspect, or that the suspect may have committed the crime but for some reason should not be arrested.

How the officer exercises discretion may be determined by a number of factors. Consider the following hypothetical scenario: A police officer, while out on patrol at midnight on a Friday night, observed a car weaving down the highway, going five miles over the speed limit. The officer turned on his siren and lights and directed the driver to stop. After checking the operator's driver's license, the officer inquired where the person was going and why he was speeding. The driver replied that he did not realize he was speeding but that he was in a hurry to get home because his contact lens was causing pain. Something apparently flew into his eye and blurred his vision temporarily. He considered it unsafe to stop by the side of a busy highway. He was trying to get to his home only a mile away.

When asked where he had been, the driver replied that he was an A student in a criminal justice program and had been at a friend's house studying since the library closed at 11 P.M. When asked whether he had been drinking, the driver replied that he drank one beer. The driver answered all questions politely and nondefensively.

What would you do if you were the police officer? Would you ticket the driver for speeding? Would you believe his response about the contact lens? Would you believe what he told you about drinking only one beer? Would it make any difference in your decision if you had stopped him at 3 A.M. rather than at midnight? You could, of course, give the driver a verbal warning and let him go. You could give him a speeding ticket. If you had sufficient reason to think that he had been drinking to the point that he was legally drunk, you could ask him to get out of the car and perform some simple tests. Or you might arrest him and take him to the police station to begin the official processing in the criminal justice system.

Now, think about the results of your decision. If the driver is telling the truth and you decide to arrest him, what have you accomplished by your action? Is it not possible that the negative effect of the arrest and subsequent experiences he has in the criminal justice system will outweigh any benefit that society would get from this arrest? On the other hand, if he has been drinking too much, is it not possible that an arrest will cause him to think before he gets in a car again after drinking? Or will it not affect his behavior at all? What about the behavior of his friends, who will certainly hear about your actions?

Perhaps by now you have decided what action you would take. Let's add some factors to the scenario. Suppose that, when you begin to talk to the driver, he curses you and tells you to mind your own business. Would this affect your decision to write a speeding ticket or give him roadside tests for intoxication?

Police must make such decisions as these daily. Selective enforcement of laws is necessary because our system cannot process all cases of law violations even if we choose to do so. Police discretion is important because most often police are responsible for the initial entry of a person into the criminal justice system. The necessity to exercise discretion without adequate guidelines puts tremendous pressure on police.

> The police really suffer the worst of all worlds: they must exercise broad discretion behind a facade of performing in a ministerial fashion; and they are expected to realize a high level of equality and justice in their discretionary determinations though they have not been provided with the means most commonly relied upon in government to achieve these ends.[20]

In its 1967 report, the President's Commission on Law Enforcement and Administration of Justice emphasized the importance of police discretion and questioned why more articulate guidelines had not been developed for that discretion. Citing police manuals that detail many rules and regulations for police officers, the report noted that these manuals rarely discuss the difficult choices that police make numerous times a day. "Yet these decisions are the heart of police work. How they are made determines to a large degree the safety of the community, the attitude of the public toward the police and the substance of court rulings on police procedures."[21]

The commission report suggested reasons that police discretion is not given sufficient guidelines. First, it is very difficult to articulate how to make decisions in situations that differ. Second, the guidelines might be controversial. For example, if the police manual stated that under the circumstances of the speeding hypothetical no arrest should be made, there would be serious objections by some. To avoid the controversy, they avoid drafting guidelines! Finally, police may not realize that they are making informal policy during many of their daily decisions.[22]

In recent years attention has been given to the need to prepare police for the appropriate use of discretion. The need for guidelines is recognized, although there is no agreement on what those guidelines should be or which agency should formulate them. Legislatures enact statutes for general guidance and delegate to police departments, as administrative agencies, the power to develop more specific rules. Courts have the responsibility of interpreting the guidelines, statutes, and policies in terms of state and federal constitutions.

Numerous studies have been made of police discretion, with most of them emphasizing that in some circumstances that discretion is exercised on the basis of extralegal rather than legal factors.[23] For example, one study of the reasons police exercise their discretion to report rather than ignore alleged child abuse revealed that the most significant reason to report the behavior was the officer's definition of the behavior as serious, and the definition was "*not* out of line with societal standards and definitions concerning child abuse." The study also found that race was a factor in some cases, with white families more likely than African American families to be reported. These findings on race differ from some others that find police taking action more frequently against African Americans than whites. It is important to note that in this study the race of the victim and of the alleged suspect were the same. It is possible, noted the authors, that police are more willing to accept violence among African American families than among whites.[24]

The Role of the Police: An Overview

Although in the popular image police may spend most of their time apprehending and arresting criminals, these functions constitute a very small part of the daily life of a police officer. In reality, police perform a variety of functions not directly related to law enforcement. Police functions may differ also by the size of the department, as noted in Professions 4.1, which gives an overview of the duties of local police.

In addition to law enforcement, a major function of policing is order maintenance. Although some use order maintenance synonymously with the function of providing various services, the two are distinct. James Q. Wilson says the key to order maintenance is the management of conflict situations to bring about consensual resolution. Wilson believes that order maintenance is the main function of the police and that it is important because police encounter more problems in this area than in social service or law enforcement (with the exception of traffic violations). Police face danger in performing the order maintenance function, too.[25] A third function of policing is the provision of services, ranging from helping people with directions when they are lost to driving them to the service station for gas when they are stranded on the highway.

There appears to be agreement that law enforcement, order maintenance, and community services are the three basic areas of police functions; but there is no agreement over whether they should be the basic functions. Nor is there agreement on how police time and resources should be allocated among the three

PROFESSIONS 4.1

Duties of Sworn Personnel in Local Police Departments

Departments with 100 or More Officers

About 10% of the officers in departments with 100 or more sworn personnel primarily performed duties outside the area of field operations. About half of these officers worked in administrative areas (5%), including finance, personnel, and internal affairs.

Another 4% of the officers in these larger departments provided technical support services. These sworn personnel primarily performed duties related to dispatch, recordkeeping, data processing, communications, fleet management, and training.

Depending on a particular department's responsibilities, some local police officers may have been assigned to jail or court operations. Departments with 100 or more officers reported about 1% of their officers worked primarily in these areas.

Departments with 100 or more officers

Primary area of responsibility	Percent of full-time officers
Field operations	90%
Administration	5%
Technical support	4%
Other*	1%

*Includes jail and court operations

Among the 90% of officers classified as working in field operations, an estimated 3 in 4 were uniformed officers whose regularly assigned duties included responding to calls for service. The other fourth included supervisors and those whose primary duties were investigative in nature, such as detectives. Other examples of field operation officers whose primary duties did not include responding to calls for service included those assigned to special operations or traffic-related duties.

All Departments

Overall, an estimated 252,000 local police officers, 67% of all such officers nationwide, were uniformed personnel whose regularly assigned duties included responding to calls for service.

The percentage of full-time sworn personnel in local police departments who were uniformed officers assigned to respond to calls for service was highest in jurisdictions with fewer than 25,000 residents. For example, an estimated 75% of sworn personnel in departments serving a population of 10,000 to 24,999 were assigned to respond to calls for service. The percentage was even higher in departments serving a population of 2,500 to 9,999 (85%) or under 2,500 (95%).

Possible explanations for this pattern include the fact that smaller departments have less need for administrative personnel such as those handling budgetary and personnel matters. Smaller departments also tend to be less technologically advanced and may need fewer employees for technical support duties related to computerized functions. Smaller departments also often rely on larger departments for their training needs rather than employ personnel to handle such duties.

In some small departments it may also be more common for sworn personnel to handle multiple areas of responsibility, including but not limited to responding to calls for service.

Source: Bureau of Justice Statistics, *Local Police Departments*, 1993 (Washington, D.C.: U.S. Department of Justice, April 1996), p.3.

areas. It is clear, however, that the areas are not discrete; there is considerable overlap. Attention to an order maintenance problem or provision of a particular service may prevent the situation from escalating into criminal behavior. Engaging in order maintenance functions and services may alert the police to criminal law violations as well. Police are also expected to prevent crime, and that function may occur within any of the three main functions.

Before these three main functions of policing are discussed in more detail, it is important to emphasize that all functions involve an enormous amount of paper work that consumes considerable police time, a fact that is mentioned rarely in discussions on policing. Perhaps this oversight is typical of other professions, and those who enter have no prior concept of the incredible detail expected of them in filing reports. With police, however, expectations are particularly important because if the paper work is not done properly, cases may be dropped or evidence may be excluded. The defendant may be acquitted or civil action may be brought against the police. Reports must be filed immediately to preserve accuracy, and police rarely have access to sufficient staff assistance in writing and filing their reports. Thus, paper work is a tedious and time-consuming function of policing.

Order Maintenance

Police are charged with maintaining order, particularly in areas in which crime might erupt. James Q. Wilson defined *order* as the absence of disorder, by which he means behavior that tends to disrupt the peace and tranquility of the public or that involves serious face-to-face conflict between two or more persons. According to Wilson, the maintenance of order, "more than the problem of law enforcement, is central to the patrolman's role for several reasons."[26]

First, many police departments receive more calls for help in order maintenance than in enforcing the law. Some of these complaints may result in arrests, but most do not. Police may be called to quiet down noisy neighbors; they may be asked to intervene in disputes between friends and associates who cannot solve their differences and who appear to be on the brink of fighting. Public drunks wandering around the city alarm some people, who call the police to handle the situation. Some of these activities may violate local ordinances, but many of the situations involve activities that are not criminal, although they may be obnoxious to those who call the police.

Order maintenance is an important function of policing for a second reason. Maintaining order may subject the police and others to physical danger. A large protest group may turn into a riot. Some domestic disputes lead to violence between the participants or against the police, although there is some evidence that the danger has been overstated.[27] Many domestic problems occur late at night when other resources are not available to the complainant.

A third reason listed by Wilson as underscoring the importance of order maintenance is that in this area police exercise

> substantial discretion over matters of the greatest importance (public and private morality, honor and dishonor, life and death) in a situation that is, by definition, one of conflict and in an environment that is apprehensive and perhaps hostile.[28]

Emphasis on Order Maintenance: The Controversy

Not all scholars and practitioners agree on the emphasis that should be placed on order maintenance. George L. Kelling analyzes order maintenance in the context of the reforms of policing popular in this century. As professionalism in policing was emphasized, evaluation of individual police and of police departments focused on tangibles such as arrests and quick response time of police to citizen calls.

> Police behavior that did not lead to arrests . . . was neither organizationally recognized nor rewarded. Police actions were rarely seen as ends in themselves but instead were viewed as means to 'process persons' into the justice system.

Police concentrated on crime prevention, arrests, and apprehension of criminals, thus emphasizing law enforcement over order maintenance or provision of services. This approach, says Kelling, decreased police corruption and improved the internal management of policing, but it resulted in less emphasis on order maintenance.[29]

Kelling argues that the focus on law enforcement has not lowered crime rates significantly but that a decreased involvement of police in order maintenance has had negative effects. His position is that increased police attention to order maintenance improves relationships between the police and the community, which results in greater cooperation of citizens with the police. Citizen fear of crime is reduced, community support of the police is improved, police feel less isolated from the community, and crime detection and prevention increase.[30] Kelling, along with James Q. Wilson, advocates a significant enlargement of order maintenance in policing. Neither believes this approach would endanger law enforcement.[31]

The Kelling and Wilson position has been challenged by Carl B. Klockars, who argues that American police, historically and today, maintain "an extraordinarily strong crime-fighting mandate," seen by them and others as the primary mission of policing. To reduce that emphasis by increasing resources for order maintenance is undesirable. It would not reduce crime significantly because the police do not have control over many of the factors that produce crime. The financial cost would be much greater and would be at the sacrifice of a reduction in the number of calls for service to which police could respond quickly.

Klockars suggests one solution might be to use foot patrols in high-density areas, particularly business areas. The increased costs might be financed partially by voluntary, tax-deductible contributions by business people, who stand to gain the most from the increased presence of police in the area. The problem with that suggestion, warns Klockars, is that a study of a foot patrol experiment in Newark disclosed that commercial residents perceived "a deterioration in their neighborhoods: more activity on the street, more crime-related problems, reduced safety, more victimization, poorer police service, and greater use of protective devices." Klockars is not arguing against order maintenance, but only against an extended and more systematic and costly approach that would require significant changes in the administrative structure of police departments.[32]

In his support of order maintenance, which he calls *street justice,* one scholar emphasizes that at the local level order maintenance is the main police function. It can be justified "on moral grounds as part of the community building and maintaining functions." Further, "to deny to citizens this police role has profound moral consequences and abandons those less capable of protecting themselves to the unchecked forces of private power."[33]

Community Service

Police perform a variety of services unrelated to law enforcement. James Q. Wilson maintains that such services are performed by police as a result of historical accident and community convenience, that there is no good reason for police to perform such services, and that the services should "be priced and sold on the market."[34]

The President's Crime Commission was concerned about the amount of time police spend in community services. The commission looked at the pros and cons. Performing community services takes away police time that otherwise might be spent in law enforcement. Conversely, the performance of certain community services by police might deter criminal activity as well as improve the public's image of police. The commission concluded that a careful analysis should be made of these service functions with the aim of deleting those that have little or no relationship to law enforcement or order maintenance.[35]

Removal of unnecessary community services does not mean that the police should not continue to be involved in community services either directly or indirectly related to crime prevention or order maintenance. For example, Operation Identification is a service that relates directly to crime prevention. Police departments provide the equipment and officers to visit community groups and individual homes to assist residents in marking their possessions so that stolen items may be identified more quickly and easily. Officers give talks on crime prevention, emphasizing to residents what they can do to diminish the possibility that they will become crime victims. Educating women on rape prevention is a frequent topic of these sessions. Visiting with school children to educate them in crime prevention is another type of police community service.

One way to solve the time commitment problem of police is to train and assign special officers for community services, one of the suggestions made by the President's Crime Commission. Community service officers complete less training than other officers. Usually less education is required, and the salary is lower. The community service program, however, provides career opportunities for qualified young people who cannot or do not wish to fulfill all of the requirements for regular police officers. Most community service officers are certified law enforcement officers who carry guns and may have the authority to arrest law violators. They have provided excellent services in many communities.

Law Enforcement

The third major area of police functions is law enforcement. Police are empowered to detect and prevent crime even if to do so means using force, although there are limitations to the force that may be used. However, the ability of police to handle crime is limited, and they are dependent on citizens for assistance, although they do not always get that assistance.

The law enforcement function of policing cannot be understood adequately except in the context of the legal requirements that must be observed by police officers performing this function. Thus, before discussing particular law enforcement activities, it is necessary to look at the legal context of law enforcement.

Constitutional Provisions

The power to use coercive force to intervene in the daily lives of people is a tremendous power. It is a power necessary for police to perform their functions properly and efficiently. If police were empowered to engage in crime control without the limitations imposed by our earlier discussions of due process, their jobs could be performed more efficiently and more quickly. But the adversary system recognizes basic fundamental rights of due process. Observation of those rights is viewed by some as creating unreasonable obstacles for police; by others it is seen as important to the philosophy on which the U.S. Constitution is based.

The Constitution's Bill of Rights contains many provisions critical to an understanding of U.S. criminal justice systems. The first eight amendments to the Constitution specify twenty-three separate rights, twelve of which concern criminal procedures. These provisions of the Bill of Rights of the Constitution require interpretation. Over the years the Supreme Court has heard and decided many cases involving these basic rights (which govern the federal system) and their application to states through the Fourteenth Amendment (see Appendix A). Legislative branches of government have passed numerous statutes for enforcing these rights. It is not possible to consider all of those statutes or decisions, for criminal procedure is a complex area of law. But it is possible to consider the overall picture of due process rights as they relate to policing.

Subsequent chapters discuss other amendments to the Constitution. This discussion is concerned primarily with the Fourth Amendment and a portion of the Fifth Amendment (see Appendix A). These amendments apply also to certain pretrial procedures that involve police, issues that are discussed in a subsequent chapter. This chapter considers the application of constitutional rights to the police functions of stopping and questioning suspects; arresting and conducting searches of the person, home, or automobile of a suspect; and the practices of custodial interrogation and initial investigation. The discussion begins with a brief look at traffic control, an area of law enforcement in which many police officers engage and one that may lead to the detection of serious crimes.

Traffic control is an important aspect of law enforcement. The flow of traffic is controlled primarily by stop signs and lights, but during high peak times police may direct traffic. Police enforce state and local ordinances governing the operation of motor vehicles. This function includes enforcing requirements that vehicles be licensed and inspected, as well as ticketing motorists who commit moving violations. Normally, violations of this type involve a simple procedure in which the police officer signs a statement noting the violation and gives a copy to the driver, explaining that the ticket, if unchallenged, may be handled by mail or in person at the police station. Court appearances are not required unless the motorist decides to challenge the ticket. Most people do not challenge these tickets. The officer may decide not to issue a ticket; a verbal or written warning may be given instead.

Enforcement of statutes and ordinances designed to regulate the flow of traffic and to create safe conditions for drivers and pedestrians is an important police function, too. Excessive speed on any street or highway, speeding in school zones or failing to stop for school buses, and driving under the influence of alcohol or other drugs are dangerous. Apprehension of people who violate traffic ordinances may lead to disorder and violence. Thus, it is important that trained police officers be in charge of such apprehensions, which may lead police to evidence of criminal activity such as stolen automobiles, violations of substance abuse laws, escaped felons, wanted persons, burglaries, and other crimes.

The problem arises when police go too far in making the pretextual traffic stop. During its last two terms, the U.S. Supreme Court has decided three important cases involving traffic stops, each one undercutting the protections of the Fourth Amendment (see Appendix A). In the first, the U.S. Supreme Court decided *Whren* v. *United States*, an automobile search case based on the so-called "pretextual traffic stop." In this case, decided in 1996, the initial stop was made by plainclothes vice officers in unmarked cars in an area known for illegal trafficking in drugs. The officers observed two young African American males in a Nissan Pathfinder waiting for an unusually long time at a stop sign, with the driver looking into the lap of his passenger. When officers made a U-turn to follow the vehicle, the driver turned without signaling and took off at what the officers considered an unreasonable speed. The officers signaled the driver to stop; and as the officers approached the car, they observed through the driver's window two large plastic bags of what appeared to be crack cocaine. The defense argued that if such searches are permitted the police might use them to harass persons for whom they otherwise could not make a stop for lack of reasonable suspicion that a violation had occurred. The Court held, however, that an officer who is suspicious of the behavior of occupants of a motor vehicle but does not have grounds for stopping them may do so when a traffic violation occurs. The stop may then be used to pursue the other suspicions of illegal acts.[36]

In the second case, also decided in 1996, the Court examined the issue of whether police must tell drivers detained for alleged traffic violations that they are free to leave before they ask them for permission to search their vehicles. In *Ohio* v. *Robinette*, decided by a vote of eight-to-one, the justices held that "sweet-talking" a driver into consenting to a vehicle search is permitted and that police are not required to tell the drivers that they are free to leave and thus do not have

Traffic Control and
Enforcement of
Traffic Laws

to consent to the search. After all, drivers should know enough to resist pressure from police. This might be questioned when it is understood that the officer does have the power to write a ticket for the alleged traffic violation.[37]

In the third and most recent case, *Maryland* v. *Wilson,* decided in 1997, the Court held that during a routine traffic stop, police may order occupants of the car (as well as the driver) out of the car without any reason to suspect them of wrong-doing. In this case the officer pulled over a car going 64 in a 55 mile-per-hour area. During the one and one-half mile pursuit before the car stopped, the officer noticed three passengers in the car, each turning from time to time to look at the officer and then retreating. After the car stopped, the driver exited and walked back to the officer's car. The driver was trembling and appeared very nervous, but he did produce a valid state driver's license. The officer instructed the driver to return to the car and retrieve the rental papers. When the driver complied, followed by the officer, the officer noted that one of the passengers was sweating and acting nervous. He asked that passenger to exit the vehicle, and when he did, a quantity of crack cocaine fell to the ground. The passenger was arrested and charged with possession of cocaine with intent to distribute. His motion to suppress the evidence was granted by the county circuit court. The decision was upheld by the court of special appeals. The Supreme Court reversed. As part of its reasoning that the evidence should have been admitted, the Court stated:

> [D]anger to an officer from a traffic stop is likely to be greater when there are passengers in addition to the driver in the stopped car. While there is not the same basis for ordering the passengers out of the car as there is for ordering the driver out, the additional intrusion on the passenger is minimal. We therefore hold that an officer making a traffic stop may order passengers to get out of the car pending completion of the stop.[38]

A law professor has stated that as a result of these three cases, motorists are left "to fend for themselves when confronted with the authority and power of the police."[39] Others would argue that in all cases the officer in question observed facts that could constitute a reason for believing that additional law infractions were being committed.

Whatever the case, the apprehension of traffic violators and their passengers, as well as of persons suspected of having committed crimes in other environments, begins with the investigatory stop, which may or may not lead to an arrest.

The Investigatory Stop

The police may be notified or they may observe a situation that gives them a reasonable basis for stopping and questioning a person. At this initial stop, police have wide discretion. They can decide not to make the stop. They can stop but not arrest the suspect. They can release the suspect with a verbal or a written warning. The police must make important judgment calls at the stage of stopping and questioning suspects, for it would be an inefficient use of police time and a violation of a suspect's constitutional right to arrest suspects when there is not probable cause to believe they are violating the law. Spotlight 4.2 discusses the *Lawson* case, which illustrates police abuse of the discretion to stop and question a suspect. For several reasons this case is very important despite the fact that it was decided in 1983. First, it is still good law. Second, it was decided by the U.S. Supreme Court. Third, it stands against the recent decisions, discussed earlier, in which the Court has refused to restrict police in stopping and searching, especially in the area of traffic control. Finally, it is argued by some that the stop in *Lawson* represented a case of racial bias, which is not permitted.

Spotlight 4.2

The *Lawson* Case and the Abuse of Police Discretion to Stop and Question

Thirty-six-year-old Edward Lawson—tall, black, muscular, and longhaired—walked almost everywhere he went. Lawson was stopped by police approximately fifteen times between March 1975 and January 1977. Police in California were relying on a California statute that prohibited a person from loitering or wandering

> Upon the streets or from place to place without apparent reason or business and who refuses to identify himself and to account for his presence when requested by any peace officer to do so, if the surrounding circumstances are such as to indicate to a reasonable man that the public safety demands such identification.[1]

Each time he was stopped, Lawson refused to identify himself. He was arrested five of the times he was stopped, convicted once, and spent several weeks in jail. The *Lawson* case illustrates the tension between the police who claim that in order to combat crime they must be able to stop and question people who look suspicious, and the right of citizens to be free of intrusions into their privacy.

Lawson appealed his convictions to the U.S. Supreme Court, which reversed them on the grounds that the statute under which Lawson was convicted was vague. The problem with the California statute was not the initial police stop. According to the Court, "Although the initial detention is justified, the State fails to establish standards by which the officers may determine whether the suspect has complied with the subsequent identification requirement." The Court indicated that giving a police officer such discretion "confers on police a virtually unrestrained power to arrest and charge persons with a violation," and therefore "furnishes a convenient tool for 'harsh and discriminatory enforcement by local prosecuting officials against particular groups deemed to merit their displeasure.' "[2]

1. Cal. Penal Code, Section 647(e) (1977).
2. Kolender et al. v. Lawson, 461 U.S. 352, 360, 361 (1983).

The *Lawson* case makes it clear that police may not use a vague statute for purposes of stopping, questioning, and otherwise harassing individuals. But the case makes it clear, too, that police may stop and question individuals. How can the police tell when they can go beyond initial questioning and make an arrest? Some basic legal principles must be explained.

Stop and Frisk

Some discretion must be allowed the police officer who, based on experience, perceives that a crime might have been committed and that the suspect may be armed, thus constituting a threat to the life or health of the officer and others who are present. It is permissible for the police to conduct pat-down searches, or **frisk** the suspect in some cases, as illustrated by the following example.

In *Terry* v. *Ohio* Detective Martin McFadden of the Cleveland Police Department noticed two men standing on a street corner in front of several stores. The men made many trips up and down the street, peering into store windows. They talked to a third man, whom they followed up the street after his departure. McFadden, who had thirty-nine years of experience as a police officer, suspected that the men were casing the stores for a robbery. He approached the men, identified himself as a police officer, and asked their names. The men mumbled responses, at which point the detective spun Terry around and patted his breast pocket. Officer McFadden removed the pistol that he felt and then frisked the second man, on whom he also found a pistol. The third man was frisked but did not have a weapon.[40]

In *Terry* the Supreme Court emphasized that even brief detention of a person without probable cause for an arrest is a seizure of that person. These stops constitute a serious intrusion that can lead to strong resentment. On the other hand, the Supreme Court recognized that police officers are injured and killed in the line of duty. They cannot be expected to take unreasonable risks; thus, they may conduct a search that is limited in time and scope.

In *Terry* the Court held that if during the pat-down search the police feel an object that might be a weapon, they may continue the search until they are satisfied that it is not a weapon. The Court, however, did not answer the question of whether they could seize a **contraband** item that is not a weapon. In 1993 the Court decided that issue. In *Minnesota* v. *Dickerson* the Court held that if during a *Terry* search and before an officer has concluded that the suspect is not armed the officer feels an item "whose contour or mass makes its identity immediately apparent," that item may be seized without a warrant. The discovery of the contraband would not constitute any greater invasion of privacy than had occurred during the permissible weapons search and thus is acceptable. The Court referred to this as the *plain feel* doctrine, analogous to the *plain view* doctrine discussed on page 98. But officers may not go beyond the permissible scope of the weapons search to examine the item suspected of being contraband but not a weapon.[41]

In a subsequent case a federal court upheld a search and seizure involving a frisk in which an officer used his fingertips to press and probe a defendant's crotch. When the officer felt a hard object that felt to him like crack cocaine, he asked the suspect to drop his pants. During this process the officer used his own body to shield the suspect from the view of others, thus preserving his privacy to a reasonable extent according to the court.[42]

Arrest, Search, and Seizure

The process of stopping and questioning suspects may lead to an **arrest,** which is a crucial step in criminal justice proceedings because most cases are initiated by arrest. **Search and seizure** may accompany arrest, but a clear understanding of these processes is impossible without a brief introduction to the Fourth Amendment of the Constitution. That amendment prohibits *unreasonable* searches and seizures (see Appendix A). This provision of the Constitution is pertinent to the discussion here because under some circumstances stopping and arresting a person may constitute a seizure of the person and therefore must follow proper procedures or be ruled unreasonable by the courts.

Warrants and Probable Cause

With some exceptions, arrests and searches may not be made until the police secure a **warrant.** A 1948 decision emphasized the purpose of the **search warrant,** but the principle applies also to arrests. According to the Court,

> The point of the Fourth Amendment, which often is not grasped by zealous officers, is not that it denies law enforcement the support of the usual inferences which reasonable men draw from evidence. Its protection consists in requiring that those inferences be drawn by a neutral and detached magistrate instead of being judged by the officer engaged in the often competitive enterprise of ferreting out crime . . . . When the right of privacy must reasonably yield to the right of search is, as a rule, to be decided by a judicial officer, not by a policeman or government enforcement agent.[43]

The Fourth Amendment requires that a warrant shall not be issued except upon a finding of **probable cause.** Probable cause is required as well in those exceptions, to be discussed, in which arrest, search, and seizure are permitted without a warrant. To constitute probable cause, the facts of the situation must be such that upon hearing those facts, a reasonable person would conclude that in all probability a crime had been committed.[44]

How is probable cause established? Facts sufficient to lead a reasonable person to conclude that a crime has been committed by a particular person or that a particular kind of contraband may be found at a specified location may be secured in various ways. One of the most controversial ways occurs when the facts come from an **informant,** who may have a history of criminal activity, or from an anonymous source. The Supreme Court considered the latter in *Illinois* v. *Gates.* In *Gates* the police received an anonymous letter alleging that two specified people, a husband and wife, were engaging in illegal drug sales and that on May 3 the wife would drive their car, loaded with drugs, to Florida. The letter stated that the husband would fly to Florida to drive the car back to Illinois with the trunk loaded with drugs and that the couple had about $100,000 worth of drugs in their Illinois basement.

After receiving this information, a police detective secured the address of the couple. He found that the husband had a May 5 reservation to fly to Florida. The flight was put under surveillance, which disclosed that the suspect took the flight. It was confirmed that he spent the night in a motel room registered to his wife and that the next morning, he left the motel in a car with a woman. The license plate of the car was registered to the husband suspect. The couple were driving north on an interstate highway used frequently for traffic to Illinois.

The police detective in possession of these facts signed a statement under oath concerning the facts and submitted that statement to a judge, who issued a search warrant for the couple's house and automobile. The police were waiting for the couple when they returned to their Illinois home. Upon searching the house and car, the police found drugs that the state attempted to use against the couple at trial. The Gates's motion to have the evidence suppressed at trial was successful, and the Illinois Supreme Court upheld the lower court on this issue.

The U.S. Supreme Court disagreed, established a new test, the "totality of circumstances," and held that in this case, independent police verification of the allegations from the anonymous source provided sufficient information on which a magistrate could have probable cause to issue the warrants. The Court emphasized that probable cause is a fluid concept based on probabilities, not hard certainties. All of the circumstances under which information is secured must be considered and weighed in determining whether probable cause exists for issuing a warrant.[45]

The Supreme Court has established rules that must be followed when police secure information from known informants. There must be underlying circumstances that would lead a reasonable person to conclude that the informant is reliable and credible in what he or she is saying, and there must be underlying circumstances that provide a basis for the conclusions drawn by the informant[46]. If the informant is a police officer, credibility might not be questioned, although it is necessary to show why that person has reason to have such information. When the informant is a known or suspected criminal, as is frequently the case, establishing credibility is more difficult.[47]

Some searches and seizures are permissable without a warrant and without probable cause.[48] One exception to the warrant requirement is a search that occurs when an officer makes a lawful arrest.[49] This type was considered by the Supreme Court in 1914; but in a 1948 decision, the Court emphasized that the right to search the person, even when the arrest is proper, is a limited privilege.[50] After arrest, some warrantless searches, such as searches of possessions or of the

Spotlight 4.3

Exigent Circumstances and Warrantless Searches

Police are permitted to conduct warrantless searches in limited cases, including those with exigent circumstances. The issue arose in the initial search of O. J. Simpson's yard and home shortly after police were notified of the deaths of Simpson's ex-wife, Nicole, and her friend, Ronald Goldman. Police claimed there were exigent circumstances for entering the estate without a warrant; defense attorneys questioned that position. Judge Lance Ito rebuked police for their efforts but denied the defense motion to suppress evidence obtained from a warrantless search of Mr. Simpson's home. Legal experts had predicted that Judge Ito would not suppress the evidence. According to one defense lawyer, "The state of the law is now such that it is difficult for the defense to win search-and-seizure motions."[1]

In another recent California case the court refused to suppress evidence seized in a warrantless search of a home by police who were responding to an anonymous call concerning domestic violence. Police were greeted at the door by a woman who said she was alone and safe. But police saw a man in the house, and the woman appeared to have been hit recently. The woman told police she had just fallen down the stairs.

Police entered the home and seized the illegal drugs that were in plain view. The court held that the officers entered the home under exigent circumstances. They knew that the woman was lying about being alone, and they had reason to suspect she had been hit recently, perhaps by the man they saw in the home. For her protection, they had a right to enter. While they were in the home legally, police were justified in seizing illegal drugs that were in plain view.[2]

---

1. "Once Again, Simpson's Lawyers Will Try to Throw Out Evidence," *New York Times* (19 September 1994), p. 1.
2. People (California) v. Higgins, 26 Cal. App. 4th 247 (4th Dist. 1994), *review denied*, 1994 Cal. LEXIS 5620 (Cal. 13 October 1994).

---

person when the suspect is booked into jail (inventory searches), may be proper.[51] Routine searches at the border may be permitted as well.[52] Inspections and searches of regulated industries are permitted, too,[53] as are searches at certain fixed checkpoints, such as checks for drivers under the influence of controlled substances.[54] As Spotlight 4.3 notes, warrantless searches may be permissable under exigent circumstances.[55]

Warrantless searches may be conducted legally when a person consents to the search.[56] This consent may be given prior to arrest, at the time of arrest, or later at the police station. It may involve searching possessions, automobiles, homes, or persons. The critical factor is whether the consent was made knowingly and voluntarily. In some circumstances, consent to a search may be given by a third party, but these circumstances are limited.[57]

In 1996 in *Ornelas* v. *United States,* the Supreme Court held that when judges are confronted with a warrantless search they are to consider the facts that led to the stop or search and then determine whether those facts "viewed from the standpoint of a reasonable police officer," constitute probable cause. The decisions of trial judges on this matter are to be reviewed by appellate judges only for clear error, and during that review due weight must be given to the consideration of the facts by local law enforcement officers and trial judges. Appellate review of such cases should be undertaken *de novo* (from the beginning). Again, the Court emphasized its "strong preferences for searches conducted pursuant to a warrant."[58]

Arrests may be made without an arrest warrant under some circumstances.[59] Historically, under English common law, police were permitted to make lawful arrests without an arrest warrant if they had probable cause to believe that a felony had been committed and that it was committed by the person to be arrested. Today, either by court decisions or by statutes, this rule exists in most jurisdictions.

On the other hand, under common law, in cases of a less serious offense, a misdemeanor, police were permitted to arrest without a warrant only if the act constituted a breach of peace that occurred within the presence of the officer.

Today most jurisdictions permit police to make a warrantless arrest for any misdemeanor committed in their presence. If the offense is not committed in the officer's presence, however, most jurisdictions require a warrant for an arrest of a suspected misdemeanant, even if the officer has overwhelming evidence that the suspect committed the offense. "Committed in the presence of the officer" does not mean that the officer must have seen the crime committed; usually it is interpreted to mean that the officer has probable cause to believe that the misdemeanor was committed in his or her presence.

An arrest without a warrant is a serious matter, however, and the Court has placed restrictions on this procedure. Persons arrested without a warrant are entitled to a prompt judicial determination of whether probable cause exists.[60] The Court has interpreted *prompt* to be forty-eight hours under most circumstances. If a weekend is involved and the judicial determination of probable cause will not be held within forty-eight hours, the state has the burden of showing that the delay beyond that period is reasonable.[61]

Home Searches

The U.S. Supreme Court has said that the "physical entry of the home is the chief evil against which the wording of the Fourth Amendment is directed."[62] The Court recognizes a difference between searches and seizures within a home or office and the search of a person's property in other places.[63]

An example of an unreasonable entry into and search inside of a home occurred in *Mapp* v. *Ohio*. When police arrived at the home of Mapp without a search warrant, she called her attorney and denied entrance to the officers. The police advised their headquarters of that response and put the house under surveillance. About three hours later, with more officers on the scene, police attempted entry again. When Mapp did not come to the door quickly, the officers forced their way into the house. Mapp's attorney arrived, but the police would not let him enter the house or see Mapp.[64]

Mapp demanded to see a search warrant. The officers produced a paper they claimed to be a search warrant. Mapp grabbed that paper (which was not a warrant) and tucked it into her bosom. The officers retrieved the paper and handcuffed Mapp for being belligerent. Mapp complained that the officers were hurting her. The officers took the complaining and handcuffed suspect to her bedroom where they conducted a search. They searched other rooms as well and found obscene materials in a basement trunk.

The seized evidence was used against Mapp at trial, and she was convicted of "knowingly having had in her possession and under her control certain lewd and lascivious books, pictures, and photographs." The U.S. Supreme Court reversed the conviction.

Scope of the Search   Even if police have a right to search a home, there is an issue of the permissible scope of that search. Several factors must be considered. In *Chimel* v. *California* police officers searched a house thoroughly after they entered with an arrest warrant but without a search warrant. The U.S. Supreme Court reversed the defendant's conviction and limited the areas that may be searched for weapons, if necessary, to protect the life of the officer and others. The suspect may be searched to the extent necessary to prevent destruction of evidence. The officer may search the area "within the immediate control" of the arrestee, such as a gun lying on a table near the suspect.[65]

In 1971 the Court held that police may seize evidence without a warrant while they are within the home to execute a lawful arrest, provided that evidence is in plain view.[66] The *plain view doctrine* is illustrated by the cases discussed earlier in Spotlight 4.3. In 1987 the Court held that probable cause is required to invoke the plain view doctrine.[67]

In 1990 the Court held that an officer who is executing an arrest warrant within a private dwelling may search rooms other than the one in which the arrest is made. The Court called this a *protective sweep* search, but there are limitations. Although the search does not require probable cause or even reasonable suspicion, it is permitted only for the purpose of locating another person who might pose danger. Thus, the officers may "look in closets and other spaces immediately adjoining the place of arrest from which an attack could be immediately launched." To go further, the officers must have "articulable facts which, taken together with the rational inferences from those facts, would warrant a reasonably prudent officer in believing that the area to be swept harbors an individual posing a danger to those on the arrest scene." The Court emphasized that this warrantless search is permissible only for the protection of those present and cannot extend to a full search of the premises, "but may extend only to a cursory inspection of those spaces where a person may be found." The protective sweep must be brief; it may last "no longer than is necessary to dispel the reasonable suspicion of danger and in any event no longer than it takes to complete the arrest and depart the premises."[68]

The Supreme Court has elaborated on the scope of the lawful search of a home's **curtilage.** The Court has held that a barn sixty yards from the house and outside the area surrounding the house enclosed by a fence was not part of the curtilage. The Court stated that

> curtilage questions should be resolved with particular reference to four factors: the proximity of the area claimed to be curtilage to the home, whether the area is included within an enclosure surrounding the home, the nature of the uses to which the area is put, and the steps taken by the resident to protect the area from observation by people passing by.[69]

The Supreme Court has ruled that the Fourth Amendment does not prohibit warrantless searches and seizures of garbage that is left outside a home's curtilage. The Court reasoned that since the garbage is readily accessible to the public, its owner has no reasonable expectation of privacy.[70] The Court left unanswered the issue of whether the Fourth Amendment prohibits warrantless searches of garbage left within the curtilage. In January 1991 a federal court of appeals ruled that the search would not be unlawful, provided the garbage was left under circumstances in which it was readily accessible to the public. That test was interpreted to include garbage left on a driveway fifty feet south of the house and twenty feet from the unattached garage, twenty-five to thirty feet west of the street, and eighteen feet west of the public sidewalk. The garbage in question was halfway up the driveway, a bit closer to the sidewalk than to the garage and technically within the curtilage. The court ruled that despite that location the garbage was abandoned and exposed to the public; consequently, its owner had no reasonable expectation of privacy. The U.S. Supreme Court refused to review the case.[71]

State constitutions and statutes may provide greater protection than the federal Constitution. For example, the New Jersey Supreme Court has held that police need a search warrant to open and examine garbage bags left at curbside for collection.[72]

Another type of search regarding the home and its curtilage is the aerial search. The Supreme Court has held that aerial searches may be conducted without a warrant.[73]

One final but very important issue concerning searches of the home is a long-standing principle of "knock and announce," meaning that police who arrive at a dwelling to search with or without a warrant must knock and announce their presence prior to entering. In 1995 the Court elevated that principle to a constitutional dimension.[74] The rule may be relaxed under exigent circumstances, such as if there is reason to believe the evidence sought will be destroyed or the suspects are armed and dangerous,[75] and the Court left it to lower courts to devise rules under which the principle could be waived. However, in 1997 in *Richards* v. *Wisconsin,* the Court struck down a blanket exception to the knock-and-announce rule. In this case the rule applied to felony drug investigations. The Court held that a case-by-case analysis was required but that in *Richards* the defendant's Fourth Amendment rights were not violated.[76]

Automobile Searches

Some of the rules concerning warrantless automobile searches were discussed earlier in connection with traffic violation stops, but the Supreme Court has decided a number of cases that go beyond that scenario.

In *Carroll* v. *United States,* the Court held that when police stop an automobile and have probable cause to believe it contains contraband, it is not unreasonable to search that vehicle. However, the Court did not deal with the scope of that permissible search. In *Chambers* v. *Maroney,* the Court held that a search warrant is not necessary "where there is probable cause to search an automobile stopped on the highway; the car is moveable; the occupants are alerted; and the car's contents may never be found again if a warrant must be obtained." Each case must be judged on its facts, for the Court has made it clear that not all warrantless car searches are lawful.[77]

In 1991 the Court clarified some of the procedural problems in *Carroll* and *Maroney* and other cases, holding that "the police may search an automobile and the containers within it where they have probable cause to believe contraband or evidence is contained."[78]

In 1981 in *Robbins* v. *California,* the Court held that when police stopped a car for proceeding erratically, smelled marijuana smoke as the door was opened, searched the car, and found two packages wrapped in opaque plastic, they went beyond the scope of a legitimate search without a warrant when they opened the packages.[79] One year later in *United States* v. *Ross,* the Court reconsidered its position by examining the extent to which police officers, who have stopped an automobile legitimately and who have probable cause to believe that contraband is concealed somewhere within it, may conduct a probing search of compartments and containers within the vehicle whose contents are not in plain view. "We hold that they may conduct a search of the vehicle that is as thorough as a magistrate could authorize in a warrant 'particularly describing the place to be searched.'" The Court emphasized that such searches must be based on probable cause.[80]

In 1985 the Court held that a warrantless search of packages held for three days after seizure by customs officials was not unreasonable. Customs officials had been observing what appeared to be a drug-smuggling operation. They saw several packages removed from two small airplanes that had landed in a remote section of the airport. The packages were loaded onto two pickup trucks. The customs officers approached the trucks, smelled marijuana, and saw packages that were wrapped in plastic bags and sealed with tape. Some of the individuals were arrested, and the packages were seized and placed in a Drug Enforcement Agency (DEA) warehouse. Three days later, without a search warrant, officers opened the packages and found marijuana. In ruling that the search was proper even without a warrant, the Supreme Court held that the warrantless search of a vehicle need not occur contemporaneously with the lawful seizure of the items. The Court emphasized, however, that officers may not hold vehicles and their contents indefinitely before they complete a search.[81]

As noted earlier, police may conduct warrantless searches of vehicles in some cases. This may be done to protect the police from danger; to protect the owner's property while the police have custody of the vehicle; and to protect police against claims that items were stolen from the vehicle while it was in police custody.[82] Furthermore, the Court has held that when a driver who was stopped for an illegal turn consents to a search of his car, police may search the contents of a closed container within that car.[83]

The search of vehicles may include buses, too. The Court has held that when police board long-distance buses and ask passengers for permission to search their luggage for narcotics without any reasonable suspicion that anyone on those buses is smuggling drugs, they are not violating those passengers' constitutional rights per se.[84]

Body Searches

The search of body cavities is the most controversial search and seizure issue. Some searches are permitted, but there are limitations on the type, time, place, and method of search. The classic case involving body searches was decided in 1949 when three deputy sheriffs of Los Angeles County, relying on some information that a man named Rochin was selling narcotics, went to Rochin's home and entered the home through an open door. They forced open the door of the second-floor bedroom, where they found Rochin, partially clothed, sitting on the bed where his wife was lying. The officers saw two capsules beside the bed and asked, "Whose stuff is this?" Rochin grabbed the capsules and swallowed them. The officers, applying force, tried to remove the capsules, and when they were unsuccessful, handcuffed Rochin and took him to the hospital. They ordered his stomach pumped, and the drugs were used as evidence in the subsequent trial, at which Rochin was convicted. The U.S. Supreme Court stated why this search and seizure were illegal:

> [T]he proceedings by which this conviction was obtained do more than offend some fastidious squeamishness or private sentimentalism about combating crime too energetically. This is conduct that shocks the conscience, illegally breaking into the privacy of the petitioner, the struggle to open his mouth and remove what was there, the forcible extraction of his stomach's contents—this course of proceeding by agents of government to obtain evidence is bound to offend even hardened sensibilities. They are methods too close to the rack and the screw to permit of constitutional differentiation.[85]

Body cavity searches are permitted under some circumstances. Safety and security within jails and prisons are sufficient reasons for strip searching prison inmates, but a distinction may be made between prison inmates and detained suspects. Thus, the Ninth Circuit has invalidated a blanket policy of strip searching all felony arrestees.[86]

Likewise, the same court held that it was illegal to conduct a strip and visual search of the vagina and anus of each of three women who were arrested for shoplifting rings. No rings were found, and no charges were filed. The court noted that even if the women had secreted rings in their body cavities, they were in no danger to themselves. Furthermore, officials could have monitored their behavior until a search warrant was secured. Thus, no exigent circumstances existed for conducting a warrantless body cavity search.[87]

Earlier we noted that border searches are permissible. Body cavity searches may be conducted at the borders into the country whenever customs officials have reason to believe a person is smuggling contraband by carrying the contraband, usually illegal drugs, therein. This crime is referred to as *alimentary canal smuggling*. Probable cause is not required for the search of body cavities in these cases; customs officials need only have a reasonable suspicion that a traveler is committing the crime of alimentary canal smuggling to conduct the search.

The Supreme Court has decided a case on this issue. *United States v. Montoya de Hernandez*[88] involved a woman who arrived in Los Angeles from Bogota, Colombia. Customs officials became suspicious when, while examining her passport, they noted that she had made numerous recent trips to Miami and Los Angeles. She was carrying $5,000 in cash and told officers that she planned to purchase goods for her husband's store, but she had made no hotel reservations nor any appointments with merchandise vendors. Customs officials suspected that she was smuggling drugs within her body. A patdown search by a female officer disclosed that the suspect's abdomen was firm and that she was wearing plastic underpants lined with a paper towel.

Officials asked the suspect to consent to an X-ray, which at first she agreed to do, but she withdrew her consent subsequently. At that point she was given three choices. She could return to Colombia on the next available flight, submit to an X-ray, or remain in detention until she produced a bowel movement that would be monitored. She chose to return to Colombia, but no flight was available, so she was detained for sixteen hours. During that time she refused to use the toilet facilities provided for her (a wastebasket placed in a restroom). She refused to eat or drink. Officials obtained a court order for an X-ray and body search of her rectum. They found a cocaine-filled balloon. During the next four days of detention, the suspect excreted numerous balloons filled with cocaine, totaling more than half a kilogram of the drug.

In upholding the body search as legal, the Supreme Court stated that the right to privacy is diminished at the border. The rights of suspects are important, but the government has an interest in preventing drug smuggling. The test used by the Court for border searches is whether, after considering all of the facts involved, customs officials reasonably suspect that the traveler is smuggling contraband in her alimentary canal.

In contrast is a case involving proposed surgery to remove a bullet from a suspect who refused to consent to the surgery. The Court held that this search and seizure would be unreasonable. The prosecution claimed that the bullet would link the suspect to the crime. Initial investigation had shown that the surgery would involve only a minor incision that could be conducted with a local anesthetic; on the basis of that evidence, the lower court granted the request to conduct the surgery. Further evidence indicated that the bullet was imbedded deeply and that removal would require a general anesthetic.

The Court noted that the interest of individuals in their right to privacy as well as health and life must be considered against the government's interest in combating crime. A surgical procedure to remove evidence may be unreasonable and therefore illegal if it "endangers the life or health of the suspect . . . and [intrudes] upon the individual's dignitary interest in personal privacy and bodily integrity." In this case the Court said there was considerable medical uncertainty regarding the safety of the procedure.[89]

Interrogation

Another important law enforcement function of policing is interrogation. Police must be able to question suspects, but that need to question must be balanced with the Fifth Amendment provision that no person "shall be compelled in any criminal case to be a witness against himself" (see Appendix A). For most of our history, it was assumed that most decisions regarding police interrogation and the admission of evidence in court obtained by those interrogations were governed by state, not federal, law. Jurisdictions recognized various police practices, and coercion of confessions was not uncommon. In 1964 the Supreme Court declared that "today the admissibility of a confession in a state criminal prosecution is tested by the same standard applied in federal prosecutions since 1897," which meant that the Fifth Amendment's prohibition against self-incrimination was applicable to the states.[90]

In 1964 in *Escobedo* v. *Illinois*, the Court spoke of "the right of the accused to be advised by his lawyer of his privilege against self-incrimination." Although Escobedo concerned the Sixth Amendment right to counsel (see Appendix A), it was considered important in the movement toward interpreting the Fifth Amendment as constituting a right not to testify against oneself.[91]

In 1966 the Court decided *Miranda* v. *Arizona* by a five-to-four decision, which set off a flurry of reaction from liberals and conservatives but established the constitutional rights of the accused concerning interrogation. The Court engaged in a lengthy examination of police manuals, which stated, among other things, how to use psychological coercion to elicit the suspect's confession. The Court examined the facts of the *Miranda* case. Briefly stated, Miranda was arrested, taken into custody, and identified by a complaining witness. He was held and interrogated for two hours by police who admitted that they did not tell him he had a right to have an attorney present. The police obtained from Miranda a written confession that said his confession was voluntary, made with full knowledge that it could be used against him, and that he understood fully his legal rights. That confession was admitted into evidence at the trial, and Miranda was convicted.

The Arizona Supreme Court upheld the conviction, emphasizing that Miranda did not ask for an attorney. The U.S. Supreme Court reversed the conviction in a lengthy decision discussing the dangers of establishing psychological environments in which the accused, even if innocent, would confess. To protect suspects from impermissible psychological interrogation, the Court handed down the ***Miranda* warning,** which consists of the following:

1. the right to remain silent

2. the right to notice that anything said by the suspect may and will be used against him or her at trial

3. the right to the presence of an attorney who will be

4. appointed (that is, paid for by the government) if the suspect is indigent[92]

The suspect may waive the right to an attorney, but that waiver must be made voluntarily, knowingly, and intelligently. If the suspect indicates a willingness to talk but subsequently wishes to remain silent, police should not continue their interrogation.

Numerous articles in scholarly journals and popular news sources have been written since the Court decided *Miranda,* including many in 1991, the twenty-fifth anniversary of the decision. The Court has decided numerous cases interpreting *Miranda.*[93] One recent case is *Davis* v. *United States,* in which the Court voted five-to-four to uphold the conviction of a defendant who was convicted of murdering a fellow serviceman on naval grounds. After he received the *Miranda* warnings, the suspect signed a waiver of his right to counsel and began talking. Later he stated, "Maybe I should see a lawyer." At that point officers stopped questioning him about the crime and began inquiring whether he wanted counsel. The suspect said he did not wish to speak with an attorney, and interrogation was resumed. The suspect's statements were used against him, and he was convicted. On appeal, the Court upheld the admission of this evidence. In the opinion written for the Court, Justice Sandra Day O'Connor stated that the Court was not willing to go beyond previous cases and hold that police may not question a suspect who *might* want an attorney. The suspect must request an attorney.[94] This case is not to be confused with the Court's previous holdings that once a suspect has invoked the right to counsel police must cease interrogation.[95]

The Supreme Court continues to answer questions on the issues surrounding police interrogation and suspect confessions, with the justices disagreeing among themselves on the resolution of the issues. In this area of criminal procedure, we must analyze carefully the facts of each case and how the Court applied its decision to those facts.

In analyzing the *Miranda* rule and the subsequent interpretations of that rule, we should recall the purpose of the adversary system: the search for truth, coupled with the belief that truth is not to be obtained by unreliable confessions from bewildered, beaten, or terrified suspects. The purpose of the *Miranda* requirement is not to suppress the truth but, rather, to avoid violating suspects' rights during police interrogations. Those rights may differ according to the facts in a particular situation.[96]

Despite immense criticism, the *Miranda* rule remains, with noted law professor Yale Kamisar stating that "overturning *Miranda* seems to be an idea whose time has come and gone."[97]

Investigation

Searching and seizing, along with interrogation, illustrate the investigative function of policing. The success or failure of the prosecution of a suspect for a particular crime may—and often does—depend on the investigative abilities of the police before, during, or after the suspect's arrest. Evidence may be destroyed quickly or never found. Without physical evidence, it may be impossible to link the alleged criminal activity with the suspect. The investigation of the JonBenet Ramsey case, for example, is cited often as a case in which authorities are apparently unable to link physical evidence to the extent that an arrest or arrests may be made.

In larger departments criminal investigation may be the responsibility of specialists, and police officers may not be involved closely in the process. In many cases, however, the police officer who makes the arrest is a critical element in the investigative process. In large police departments the investigative function of the patrol officer is limited. Most of the investigation, at least in serious cases, is conducted by specialized officers in the criminal investigation unit of the department. These investigators conduct various kinds of activities, ranging from maintaining field activity records to total crime scene management, including such other activities as collecting body fluid, photographing crime scenes, following up on investigations, sketching crime scenes, obtaining search/arrest warrants, conducting interviews/interrogations, attending autopsies, and others.

Police use many investigative techniques. Fingerprinting is one of the most effective methods. This technique has been available in the United States since it was first used around 1900 by London's Scotland Yard. The use of computers to assist with fingerprint identification has increased investigative techniques in this area.

Another new technique is the use of DNA, or deoxyribonucleic acid, "which carries the genetic information that determines individual characteristics such as eye color and body size." Some argue that DNA is close to 100 percent accurate, compared to traditional blood and semen tests, which are only 90 to 95 percent accurate. Advocates call this process *DNA genetic fingerprinting.*[98]

DNA results have been used to free some inmates who were convicted and have served years in prison.[99] The results have been used to win acquittals for defendants as well as to convict others. But DNA remains controversial; and courts do not agree on whether testimony regarding DNA should be admitted, although the trend is toward admitting the evidence.[100] Still, some courts have concluded that DNA results are not sufficiently accepted for admissability in criminal cases. Some courts, however, have admitted certain methods of DNA testing while excluding others or have instructed trial courts to examine the testing methods more carefully.[101]

WiseGuide Wrap-Up

This chapter is the second of two on policing, and it begins with a discussion of preparing for policing, which looks at the issues surrounding the recruitment, training, and higher education of police. At a time when police departments face the need to recruit more officers, it is becoming increasingly difficult to find candidates who have no background of law violations and whose records for morality and integrity are beyond question.

Police exercise wide discretion in criminal justice systems, and the chapter devotes a section to the explanation and analysis of why discretion is necessary and how it might be abused. Discretion cannot be abolished; controlling it is thus a necessity. The primary focus of the chapter, however, is on the functions that police must perform in an increasingly complex society. Those functions are numerous, but they are categorized as law enforcement, order maintenance, and community service. The latter two are discussed briefly before greater attention is given to law enforcement.

The controversy over the importance of order maintenance is noted within the context of the contributions of several experts on policing. Order maintenance may be a crucial function of policing, as the absence of order may lead to law violations, even serious criminal acts such as the violent crimes of aggravated assault and murder. Likewise, the community-service function of policing may prevent or reduce actions that might lead to law violations. Furthermore, many of the activities police are called upon to perform occur after hours, when other organizations have closed for the day.

The discussion of law enforcement begins with a brief overview of the constitutional limitations on policing, for it is clear that police could make more arrests and conduct more thorough investigations if they did not have to observe the due process rights of defendants. U.S. criminal justice systems place great emphasis on the right of individuals to be free from unreasonable governmental intrusion. This does not mean that police cannot arrest, search and seize, interrogate, and investigate, but only that these functions must be performed within the limits of state and federal statutes, constitutions, and court decisions.

The Fourth Amendment's prohibition against unreasonable search and seizure and the Fifth Amendment's provision that a person may not be forced to incriminate him- or herself are the key constitutional bases of what police may and may not do in law enforcement. The investigatory stop, brief detention, arrest, and searching and seizing are important police activities regulated by constitutional requirements, court interpretations of those requirements, and departmental policies.

A look at a few key cases on the law of stop, arrest, search, and seizure should make it obvious that it is impossible to state what *the law* is in these areas. The facts of a particular case must be analyzed carefully in light of previous court decisions, statutes, and constitutional provisions. Reasonable minds may differ as to the conclusion in any given case. It is important to analyze case law carefully, looking at the rule of a case as well as the reasons for that rule.

In some situations police are permitted to stop, arrest, search, and seize without a warrant, although the Supreme Court prefers warrants. Again, it is impossible for police to know in every case whether they face exceptions to the warrant requirement. Frequently, law enforcement is ambiguous, leaving considerable discretion to the individual officer, who may be second-guessed by the courts. Despite the need to analyze individual cases in terms of their unique facts, there are some general principles of constitutional law governing the law enforcement function of policing. Those are discussed, with attention paid to some of the major U.S. Supreme Court cases governing each aspect of law enforcement, from the initial stop to the searching and seizing of homes, automobiles, and persons.

Interrogation is another important law enforcement function of policing. The Supreme Court has decided many cases in this area. The *Miranda* warning must be given in cases in which a person might be deprived of his or her liberty, but it is not always clear when interrogation has begun and the warning must be given. Failure to comply with *Miranda* requirements may result in the exclusion of evidence from the trial, an issue discussed in the next chapter.

Investigation is the final police function discussed in this chapter. Traditionally, police have spent considerable time investigating crimes at the scene of their occurrence without significant effectiveness. Recently, investigative techniques have been improved by the use of forensic science, especially DNA. Some continue to question its reliability or challenge the scientist's work on DNA.

Policing has changed in many ways in recent years. This chapter touches on only a few areas in which changes have been attempted. Chapter 5 focuses on the primary problems and issues of policing.

Apply It

1. If you were in charge of recruiting persons into policing, what characteristics would you emphasize? What emphasis would you place on higher education, and why? What type of training would you require, and why? How would you assess the ethics and moral standards of recruits? What standards would you require for policing, and what efforts would you suggest for maintaining those standards within police forces?

2. Discuss the importance of discretion in policing.

3. What is meant by *order maintenance* in policing?

4. What should be the role of police with regard to service functions within the communities they serve?

5. Explain briefly the constitutional provisions that govern policing.

6. What functions do police have in traffic control and enforcing traffic laws and ordinances? Discuss the recent U.S. Supreme Court cases in this area.

7. Under what circumstances may police stop, question, and arrest a suspect? When may police frisk?

8. Why are warrants usually required for arrest and search?

9. Under what circumstances may police search without a warrant? Arrest without a warrant?

10. What is the meaning of *probable cause* and how may it be established?

11. When may police search a home? How much of the home may be searched? Explain the *plain view* doctrine and define curtilage.

12. Explain the *plain touch* doctrine.

13. Under what circumstances may an automobile be searched?

14. Under what circumstances may bodily searches be conducted?

15. What is the *Miranda* warning? Why is it important?

16. What exceptions has the Court made to the *Miranda* warning?

17. What is DNA testing, and why is it controversial?

Notes

1. Egon Bittner, "The Police Charge," *The Functions of the Police in Modern Society* (Bethesda, Md.: National Institute of Mental Health, 1970); quoted in *Police Behavior: A Sociological Perspective,* ed. Richard J. Lundman (New York: Oxford University Press, 1980), p. 38.

2. United States Commission on Civil Rights, *Who Is Guarding The Guardians? A report on Police Practices* (Washington, D.C.: U.S. Government Printing Office, 1981), pp. 154–155. See also Note, "Psychological Health Tests for Violence-Prone Police Officers: Objectives, Shortcomings, and Alternatives," *Stanford Law Review* 46 (July 1994): 1717–1770.

3. See Arthur Niederhoffer, *Behind the Shield: The Police in Urban Society* (Garden City, N.Y.: Anchor Books, 1969), pp. 109–160.

4. Geoffrey P. Alpert, "Hiring and Promoting Police Officers in Small Departments—The Role of Psychological Testing," *Criminal Law Bulletin* 27 (May/June 1991): 261.

5. John Kleinig, *The Ethics of Policing* (New York: University of Cambridge, 1996), front cover, as cited in a review of the text by Richard N. Holden, *Criminal Justice Review* 22 (September 1997): 113. See also Tom Barker, *Police Ethics: Crisis in Law Enforcement* (Springfield, Ill.: Charles C Thomas, 1996); and Joycelyn M. Pollock, "Ethics and Law Enforcement," in *Critical Issues in Policing,* 3d ed.

(Prospect Heights, Ill.: Waveland Press, 1997), ed. by Roger G. Dunham and Geoffrey P. Alpert, pp. 336–354.

6. National Institute of Justice Research Report, *Criminal Justice Research Under the Crime Act—1995 to 1996* (Washington, D.C.: U.S. Department of Justice, 13 September 1997), p. 12.

7. "Ex-Cop Serpico Testifies on NYPD," *Miami Herald* (24 September 1997), p. 8.

8. The President's Commission on Law Enforcement and Administration of Justice, *Task Force Report: The Police* (Washington, D.C.: U.S. Government Printing Office, 1967), p. 138.

9. The President's Commission on Law Enforcement and Administration of Justice, *The Challenge of Crime in a Free Society* (Washington, D. C.: U.S. Government Printing Office, 1967), pp. 112–113.

10. National Advisory Commission on Criminal Justice Standards and Goals, *A National Strategy to Reduce Crime* (Washington, D.C.: U.S. Government Printing Office, 1973), p. 83.

11. *Who is Guarding the Guardians?*, p. 155.

12. City of Canton, Ohio v. Harris, 489 U.S. 378 (1989). For a discussion, see Geoffrey P. Alpert and William C. Smith, "Defensibility of Law Enforcement Training," *Criminal Law Bulletin* 26 (September/October 1990): 452–458.

13. For a discussion, see Rolando V. del Carmen and Michael R. Smith, "Police, Civil Liability, and the Law," in *Critical Issues in Policing: Contemporary Readings,* 3d ed., ed. by Roger G. Dunham and Geoffrey P. Alpert (Prospect Heights, Ill.: Waveland Press, 1997), pp. 225–242.

14. President's Commission on Law Enforcement, *The Challenge of Crime in a Free Society,* p. 109.

15. Bureau of Justice Statistics, *Local Police Departments, 1993* (Washington, D.C.: U.S. Department of Justice, April 1996), p. 1.

16. See Patrick Murphy, foreword to *The State of Police Education: Policy Direction for the 21st Century* by David L. Carter et al. (Washington, D.C.: Police Executive Research Forum, 1989), pp. iii–iv.

17. David L. Carter et al., *The State of Police Education: Policy Direction for the 21st Century* (Washington, D.C.: Police Executive Research Forum (PERF), 1989), p. 15.

18. "Today's Cops Are a New Breed," *Tampa Tribune* (11 July 1993), p. 1 Florida/Metro.

19. Albert J. Reiss Jr., "Police Organization in the Twentieth Century," in *Modern Policing,* ed. Michael Tonry and Norval Morris (Chicago: University of Chicago Press, 1992), p. 90. For more recent articles on the nature of police education, see Marilyn B. Peterson, "Practical Analytical Techniques: A Necessary Addition to Police Education," *Journal of Criminal Justice Education* 8 (Spring 1997): 19–36, and Michael G. Breci, "What Motivates Officers to Continue their College Educations?" in the same journal, pp. 51–60.

20. Michael R. Gottfredson and Don M. Gottfredson, "The Decision to Arrest," in *Decision Making in Criminal Justice: Toward the Rational Exercise of Discretion* (Cambridge, Mass.: Ballinger Publishing Co., 1980), p. 87.

21. President's Commission on Law Enforcement and Administration of Justice, *The Challenge of Crime in a Free Society,* p. 103.

22. Ibid., pp. 103–4. For an often cited discussion of police discretion in general, see Kenneth Culp Davis, *Police Discretion* (St. Paul, Minn.: West Publishing Co., 1975).

23. See, for example, the following research: domestic disputes, Michael G. Breci and Ronald L. Simons, "An Examination of Organizational and Individual Factors That Influence Police Response to Domestic Disturbances," *Journal of Police Science and Administration* 15 (June 1987): 93–104; traffic offenses, John A. Gardiner, *Traffic and the Police: Variations in Law Enforcement Policy* (Cambridge, Mass.: Harvard University Press, 1969); public disorder, Egon Bittner, "The Police on Skid Row: A Study of Peace Keeping," *American Sociological Review* 32 (1967): 699–715; and juvenile offenses, Irving M. Piliavin and Scott Briar, "Police Encounters with Juveniles," *American Journal of Sociology* 70 (1964): 106–214.

24. Cecil L. Willis and Richard H. Wells, "The Police and Child Abuse: An Analysis of Police Decisions to Report Illegal Behavior," *Criminology* 26 (November 1988): 695–715. For research showing that police and others are more likely to consider a criminal act serious if the victim is white, see Donald Black, *The Manners and Customs of the Police* (New York: Academic Press, 1980); and Douglas A. Smith, "Police and Violent Disputes: Defining the Parameters of Legal Control," *Social Forces* 65 (1987): 767–82. For information concerning a perception that violence is more "normal" among African Americans than whites, see Darrel F. Hawkins, "Beyond Anomalies: Rethinking the Conflict Perspective on Race and Punishment," *Social Forces* 65 (1987): 719–45.

25. James Q. Wilson, *Varieties of Police Behavior: The Management of Law and Order in Eight Communities* (Cambridge, Mass.: Harvard University Press, 1968), p. 21.

26. Ibid., pp. 16, 17.

27. See, for example, Joel Garner and Elizabeth Clemmer, *Danger to Police in Domestic Disturbances—A New Look* (Washington, D.C.: U.S. Department of Justice, November 1986).

28. Wilson, *Varieties of Police Behavior,* p. 21.

29. George L. Kelling, "Order Maintenance, the Quality of Urban Life, and Police: A Line of Argument," in *Police Leadership in America: Crisis and Opportunity,* ed. William A. Geller (Chicago: American Bar Foundation, 1985), p. 297.

30. Ibid., p. 308.

31. See James Q. Wilson and George L. Kelling, "Police and Neighborhood Safety: Broken Windows," *Atlantic Monthly* 249 (March 1982): 29–38.

32. Carl B. Klockars, "Order Maintenance, the Quality of Urban Life, and Police: A Different Line of Argument," *Police Leadership,* ed. Geller, p. 316, quoting *The Newark Foot Patrol Experiment* (Washington, D.C.: Police Foundation, 1981), p. 88.

33. Gary W. Sykes, "Street Justice: A Moral Defense of Order Maintenance Policing," *Justice Quarterly* 3 (December 1986): 510.

34. Wilson, *Varieties of Police Behavior,* p. 5.

35. President's Commission, *The Challenge of Crime,* pp. 97-98.

36. Whren v. United States, 517 U.S. 806 (1996).

37. Ohio v. Robinette, 519 U.S. 33 (1996).

38. Maryland v. Wilson, 519 U.S. 408 (1997).

39. Tracey Maclin, "Open Door Policy: Court Rulings on Traffic Stops Undercut Fourth Amendment Protections," *American Bar Association Journal* 83 (July 1997): 46.

40. Terry v. Ohio, 392 U.S. 1 (1968).

41. Minnesota v. Dickerson, 508 U.S. 366 (1993). For a discussion see "Fourth Amendment—The Plain Touch Exception to the Warrant Requirement," *Journal of Criminal Law & Criminology* 84 (Winter–Spring 1994): 743–768.

42. United States v. Ashley, 37 F.3d 678 (D.C.Cir. 1994).

43. John v. United States, 333 U.S. 10, 13–14 (1948).

44. For a discussion, see Peter J. Kocoras, "The Proper Appellate Standard of Review for Probable Cause to Issue a Search Warrant," *DePaul Law Review* 42 (1993): 1413–1459.

45. Illinois v. Gates, 462 U.S. 213 (1983); and United States v. Miller, 925 F.2d 695 (4th Cir. 1991), *cert denied,* 502 U.S. 833 (1991).

46. Aguilar v. Texas, 378 U.S. 108 (1964), *overruled in part by* Illinois v. Gates, 472 U.S. 213 (1983).

47. See United States v. Simpson, 813 F.2d 1462 (9th Cir. 1987), *cert. denied,* 484 U.S. 898 (1987) (upholding the use of a prostitute to obtain information on a drug dealer).

48. See, for example, Katz v. United States, 389 U.S. 347, 357 (1967).

49. See Chimel v. California, 395 U.S. 752 (1969); and United States v. Rodriguez, 995 F.2d 776 (7th Cir. 1993), *cert. denied,* 510 U.S. 1029 (1993).

50. Weeks v. United States, 232 U.S. 383 (1914); *overruled in part by* Elkins v. United States, 364 U.S. 206 (1960); Trupiano v. United States, 334 U.S. 699 (1948), *overruled in part by* United States v. Robinowitz, 339 U.S. 56 (1950).

51. See Colorado v. Bertine, 479 U.S. 367, 371 (1987).

52. See United States v. Ludlow, 992 F.2d 260 (10th Cir. 1993), stating, "Border patrol agents have virtually unlimited discretion to selectively refer cars to the secondary inspection area."

53. See New York v. Burger, 482 U.S. 691 (1987).

54. See Michigan Department of State Police v. Sitz, 496 U.S. 444 (1990), upholding brief stop of motorists at sobriety checkpoints. For a discussion see Thomas J. Hickey and Michael Axline, "Drunk-Driving Roadblocks Under State Constitutions: A Reasonable Alternative to Michigan v. Sitz," *Criminal Law Bulletin* 28 (May–June 1992): 195–217.

55. See, for example, Schmerber v. California, 384 U.S. 757 (1966) (permitting warrantless seizure of blood from person suspected of driving under the influence; reduction of alcohol in the blood over time constituted exigent circumstances).

56. Schneckloth v. Bustamonte, 412 U.S. 218 (1973).

57. See United States v. Varona-Algos, 819 F.2d 81, 83 (5th Cir. 1987), *cert. denied,* 484 U.S. 929 (1987). The U.S. Supreme Court has upheld the *apparent authority doctrine* under which police enter private premises without a warrant if they are acting with the reasonable but incorrect belief that a third party who gives consent

had some common authority over those premises. See Illinois v. Rodriguez, 497 U.S. 177 (1990).

58. Ornelas v. United States, 517 U.S. 690 (1996).

59. See Gerstein v. Pugh, 420 U.S. 103 (1975).

60. Gerstein v. Pugh, 420 U.S. 103 (1975).

61. County of Riverside v. McLaughlin, 500 U.S. 44 (1991).

62. United States v. U.S. District Court, 407 U.S. 297 (1972).

63. See Coolidge v. New Hampshire, 403 U.S. 443 (1971).

64. Mapp v. Ohio, 367 U.S. 643 (1961).

65. Chimel v. California, 395 U.S. 752 (1969).

66. Coolidge v. New Hampshire, 403 U.S. 443 (1971).

67. Arizona v. Hicks, 480 U.S. 321 (1987). For a discussion see "Fourth Amendment-Requiring Probable Cause for Searches and Seizures Under the Plain View Doctrine," *Journal of Criminal Law and Criminology* 78 (Winter 1988): 763–791.

68. Maryland v. Buie, 494 U.S. 325 (1990), *cert. denied,* 498 U.S. 1106 (1991). For a discussion see "Fourth Amendment—Protective Sweep Doctrine: When Does the Fourth Amendment Allow Police Officers to Search the Home Incident to a Lawful Arrest?" *Journal of Criminal Law and Criminology* 81 (Winter 1991): 862–882. In United States v. Akrawi, 920 F.2d 418 (6th Cir. 1990) the court held that the protective sweep was not valid when police spent forty-five minutes on the premises and could not show that this amount of time was necessary.

69. United States v. Dunn, 480 U.S. 294 (1987).

70. California v. Greenwood, 486 U.S. 35 (1988).

71. United States v. Hedrick, 922 F.2d 396 (7th Cir. 1991), *cert. denied,* 502 U.S. 847 (1991).

72. State v. Hempele, 576 A.2d 793 (N.J. 1990).

73. See California v. Ciraolo, 476 U.S. 207 (1986); and Florida v. Riley, 488 U.S. 445 (1989).

74. Wilson v. Arkansas, 514 U.S. 927 (1995).

75. See, for example, United States v. One Parcel of Real Property, 873 F.2d 7, 9 (1st Cir. 1989), *cert. denied,* 493 U.S. 891 (1989).

76. Richards v. Wisconsin, 117 S.Ct. 1416 (1997).

77. Carroll v. United States, 267 U.S. 132 (1925); Chambers v. Maroney, 399 U.S. 42 (1970). See also Florida v. Myers, 466 U.S. 380 (1984) (*per curiam*), upholding the warrantless search by police of a car that was impounded and had been subjected to a previous legitimate inventory search.

78. California v. Acevedo, 500 U.S. 565 (1991).

79. Robbins v. California, 453 U.S. 420 (1981).

80. United States v. Ross, 456 U.S. 798 (1982).

81. United States v. Johns, 469 U.S. 478 (1985).

82. See Colorado v. Bertine, 479 U.S. 367 (1987); and Florida v. Wells, 495 U.S. 1 (1990)

83. Florida v. Jimeno, 500 U.S. 248 (1991). For a discussion of automobile consent searches, see "Fourth Amendment—Expanding the Scope of Automobile Consent Searches," *Journal of Criminal Law & Criminology* 82 (Winter 1992): 773–796.

84. Florida v. Bostick, 501 U.S. 421 (1991), *on remand,* 593 So.2d 494 (Fla. 1992). For a discussion see "Fourth Amendment—Protection Against Unreasonable Seizures of the Person: The Intrusiveness of Dragnet Styled Drug Sweeps," *Journal of Criminal Law & Criminology* 82 (Winter 1992): 797–828;

85. Rochin v. California, 342 U.S. 165 (1952), *overruled as stated in* Lester v. Chicago, 830 F.2d 706 (7th Cir. 1987).

86. Fuller v. M.G. Jewelry, 950 F.2d 1437 (9th Cir. 1991).

87. Fuller v. M.G. Jewelry, 950 F.2d 1437 (9th Cir. 1991).

88. United States v. Montoya de Hernandez, 473 U.S. 531 (1985).

89. Winston v. Lee, 470 U.S. 753 (1985).

90. Malloy v. Hogan, 378 U.S. 1 (1964).

91. Escobedo v. Illinois, 378 U.S. 478 (1964).

92. Miranda v. Arizona, 384 U.S. 436, 478–479 (1966).

93. See, for example, Oregon v. Mathiason, 429 U.S. 492 (1977) (*Miranda* warnings not required when a person goes to the police station and confesses after an investigator has left a card at his home); Minnesota v. Murphy, 465 U.S. 420 (1984) (*Miranda* warnings not required when a probation officer speaks to his client about another crime that client may have committed); Edwards v. Arizona, 451 U.S. 477 (1981) (although the police may not interrogate a suspect who invokes the right to remain silent, they may do so if the suspect *initiates* the discussion about the crime for which the suspect is being held); Arizona v. Roberson, 486 U.S. 675 (1988) (Edwards bars police-initiated interrogation following the suspect's request for counsel in the context of a *separate* investigation); and Duckworth v. Eagan, 492 U.S. 195 (1989) (*Miranda* warning does not have to be given in the exact form described in the decision). See also the discussion of the exclusionary rule in Chapter 5 of this text.

94. Davis v. United States, 512 U.S. 452 (1994).

95. See Edwards v. Arizona, 451 U.S. 477 (1981); and Minnick v. Arizona, 498 U.S. 146 (1990).

96. See, for example, Pennsylvania v. Muniz, 496 U.S. 582 (1990), holding that police are not required to give the *Miranda* warnings before they videotape the behavior of alleged drunk drivers. The Court held that this evidence is physical, not testimonial, and therefore does not fall within the *Miranda* rule concerning the right of suspects not to testify against themselves. For a discussion of this case, see "Fifth Amendment—Videotaping Drunk Drivers: Limitations on *Miranda's* Protections," *Journal of Criminal Law and Criminology* 81 (Winter 1991): 883–925.

97. Yale Kamisar, Remarks at Constitutional Law Conference, sponsored by *United States Law Week* (12 September 1987), Washington, D.C. For further discussion concerning interpretations of *Miranda,* see Fred Cohen, "*Miranda* and Police Deception in Interrogation: A Comment on *Illinois v. Perkins*," *Criminal Law Bulletin* 26 (November–December 1990): 534–46. Illinois v. Perkins, 496 U.S. 292 (1990) held that *Miranda* warnings were not required when an undercover officer posed as an inmate and engaged Perkins in a conversation about a crime that allegedly he had committed.

98. Debra Cassens Moss, "DNA—The New Fingerprints," *American Bar Association Journal* 74 (1 May 1988): 66.

99. "DNA Tests Are Unlocking Prison Cell Doors," *New York Times* (5 August 1994), p. 1.

100. See, for example, Commonwealth v. Lanigan, 641 N.E.2d 1342 (Mass. 1994); and People v. Wesley, 633 N.E.2d 451 (N.Y.Ct.App. 1994).

101. See, for example, State v. Bloom, 516 N.W.2d 159 (Minn. 1994), *review denied,* 1996 Minn. LEXIS 237 (Minn. 1996). For analyses of the use of DNA evidence in criminal cases, see the following articles, both from *Journal of Criminal Law & Criminology* 84 (Spring 1993): William C. Thompson, "Evaluating the Admissibility of New Genetic Identification Tests: Lessons from the 'DNA War,'" pp. 22–104; and Rockne P. Harmon, "Legal Criticisms of DNA Typing: Where's the Beef?" pp. 174–188.

Problems and Issues in Policing

Policing is a job that arouses great controversy. Police may use deadly force and, in some circumstances, they would be negligent if they did not use force. Police are expected to stop and question persons who appear to have violated laws, but they may be criticized for doing so. Police are expected to obey all laws, but not all of them meet that expectation. Police are expected to be well trained and have enough education to use reasonable judgment and discretion, but they may be stressed and bored if they are too highly educated or trained. They are expected to be alert on the job, but the dull aspects of many patrol assignments may make it difficult to remain alert at all times. In short, policing is stressful and raises many issues and problems.

Police officers may or may not experience more stress than persons in other jobs or professions,[1] but stress is a part of policing. Some officers handle that stress successfully with the aid and support of other officers and their families; however, some become involved in the police subculture to the exclusion of other social contacts. This may lead to negative rather than positive reinforcement.

In considering the problems and issues in policing, we must realize that no problem is pervasive. Our purpose is to discuss problems and issues that arise in policing, not to suggest that all police, or even most police, encounter the problems and do not resolve them successfully. Policing, like all jobs, has some persons who are corrupt, incompetent, or in some other way unprofessional; but many police officers work very hard to serve the public, and they do an excellent job. And many police officers find their work to be challenging and rewarding.

Policing presents officers and administrators with some serious dilemmas. Conflicts arise over allocation of the officer's time; investigations may compromise the officer's integrity or lead the public to question the officer's investigative techniques. Processing domestic violence calls, confronting the drug scene, and dealing with the reality that some

Key Terms

acquired immune deficiency
   syndrome (AIDS)
deadly force
exclusionary rule
fleeing felon rule
good faith exception
inevitable discovery rule
proactive
reactive
subculture
torts

suspects or victims may have **acquired immune deficiency syndrome (AIDS)**, are situations that, among others, may create serious problems for police.

Role conflicts, the threat of danger, methods of evaluating job performance and the degree of job satisfaction, and other problems may create stressful situations that lead to professional and personal problems. Some police react in the same way many people react to stress: they confront the issues and deal with them successfully. Some police become involved in a police subculture, in which they feel comfortable and accepted while off duty. Others may become involved in corruption or in overzealous law enforcement. A few turn to brutality against crime suspects. The line between appropriate use of deadly force and brutality is not easy to draw, but court decisions give some guidelines. When the line is crossed, civil liability attaches, and civil lawsuits against police are increasing.

The final section of the chapter focuses on affirmative action policies. The efforts of police departments to recruit minority and female applicants have increased the representation of these groups, but it is not clear whether these policies will continue. Court cases are chipping away at affirmative action policies, and many organizations are abandoning their efforts. Thus far policing has not succumbed significantly to what may be a trend; the future is unclear.

Learning Objectives

Learning Objectives

After reading this chapter, you should be able to do the following:

- Explain the meaning of dilemmas in policing.
- Summarize the external political pressures of policing.
- Explain time allocation pressures in policing.
- Define *proactive* and *reactive* policing and discuss each in the context of domestic violence.
- Discuss the impact of AIDS and other conditions or situations that create stress in policing.
- Explain and analyze the impact of police subcultures.
- Discuss the nature and extent of police misconduct.
- Explain the proper use of deadly force in the context of fleeing felons and vehicle pursuits.

- Discuss the nature and implications of police brutality.
- Discuss violence against police.
- Explain how police activities may be controlled by police departments.
- Explain and evaluate the exclusionary rule.
- Discuss the control of policing by community relations and through tort actions.
- Explain the legal actions that citizens may take if they are mistreated by negligently trained police officers.
- Discuss the impact that affirmative action programs have had on policing and what might be expected in the future.

Dilemmas in Policing

In any work environment it is necessary to make adjustments to conflicting demands and pressures, but conflicts may be greater in policing than in most jobs or professions. We expect the police to solve and prevent crimes. We expect them to respond cheerfully, quickly, and efficiently to a host of public services. At the same time, police are expected to be polite, even when being attacked verbally, and to be effective in securing evidence of crimes without violating suspects' constitutional rights. They are expected to use violence when necessary, not when unnecessary, and the line between those two is not articulated clearly. They are expected to report ethical and legal violations of their colleagues, but frequently internal pressures are against such actions. All of the dilemmas police face are enhanced by external political pressures.

Although external political pressures impact many if not all work environments, policing may involve greater pressures than most. Many of these pressures are legal, but they create serious problems for police administrators and line officers, who are more visible than workers in most other jobs and professions. In addition, police often experience greater and more varied demands for their services than is required of most other people. Failure in policing is highly visible, and the consequences may be far more severe to police and to the public than failure in other work environments. Accountability is difficult, and temptations are great for those who wield so much power over our daily lives.

External Political Pressures

Police are accountable to local, state, and federal agencies. Legal restrictions may be placed on police by any of these levels. This chapter's discussion of U.S. Supreme Court decisions demonstrates the increasing role that federal courts are playing in policing at all levels. Furthermore, police departments must compete with other public agencies for funding, and, to be competitive, they must show that although they are using their existing resources efficiently and prudently, local, state, or federal problems have grown beyond their ability to cope without additional resources.

The wide discretion police have in law enforcement may create political problems. Police are supposed to enforce laws that are violated, but if they arrest a prominent, influential citizen, they may find that strict enforcement is not expected. Failure to enforce laws whenever prominent, influential citizens are involved creates political pressures from those against whom those laws are enforced. Political pressure from those in power for the police to control the poor and minorities leads to allegations by the latter that policing is for the purpose of protecting the majority's status quo, with little regard for the rights of all people. A police administrator might find it impossible to be responsive to the needs of all of his or her constituents because of political influences that could cause the administrator to lose a job. Political pressures from local, state, and federal levels permeate policing and cannot be ignored. The fact that these external pressures may conflict with internal pressures makes the situation even more difficult and stressful for police.

The internal values of a police department may be and often are at odds with those of the external constituency. "This breeds confusion, distrust, and cynicism rather than clarity, commitment, and high morale."[2] To make the situation even more complicated, both the external and the internal values and pressures may not be suitable for the current challenges of policing. One issue that creates conflict within and outside of the police department is how police time should be allocated.

There is little agreement on how police should allocate their time among law enforcement, order maintenance, and social services. Part of this conflict might be solved if recruits were informed about the time pressures of policing. Studies of why people call police departments illustrate this time pressure. Earlier studies of police time allocation gained considerable attention. James Q. Wilson sampled calls to the Syracuse New York Police Department in 1966 and found that only 10.3 percent of those calls related to law enforcement, compared to 30.1 percent for order maintenance. Requests for services dealing with accidents, illnesses, and lost or found persons or property constituted 37.5 percent (the largest category of calls), whereas 22.1 percent called for information.[3]

Allocation of Police Time

In another study Albert J. Reiss Jr. analyzed calls to the Chicago Police Department. His findings were similar to those of Wilson in one respect: 30 percent of the calls were for noncriminal matters. But Reiss found that 58 percent of the calls were related to law enforcement matters.[4] Richard J. Lundman, in studying police activities in five jurisdictions, found law enforcement to be the most frequent category of functions in which police engaged, consuming slightly less than one-third of all police time.[5]

The inconsistent findings of these studies may be attributed to the different methodology used for assessing police time allocation. Wilson and Reiss analyzed calls made to police departments; Lundman observed officers on patrol. Perhaps a more important variable in explaining the difference lies in the failure to specify carefully which activities would be included in each category.

Carefully defined, narrow categories may produce a more accurate picture of police time allocation. Eric J. Scott categorized over 26,000 calls to police departments. According to Scott, 21 percent of the calls were for information; 17 percent concerned nonviolent crimes; 12 percent were for assistance; 22 percent for public nuisances; 9 percent for traffic problems; 8 percent were citizens offering information; and 7 percent were concerned with interpersonal conflict. Other categories were violent crimes (representing only 2 percent of the calls), medical assistance, dependent persons, and calls regarding internal operations. Each of the categories was subdivided into more specific categories. For example, the category *assistance* included animal problems, property checks, escorts and transports, utility problems, property discoveries, assistance to motorists, fires, alarms, crank calls, unspecified requests, and other.[6]

According to Scott, the failure of other investigators to define each category carefully is a serious problem because "the addition or subtraction of a particular call from some categories can cause a large change in the percentage of calls attributable to that category."[7] Scott was concerned with the problem of coding calls as crime or noncrime. Many police activities involve a little of each and cannot be coded accurately into two discrete categories. As a result, the various studies are not comparable as it is not possible to determine how specific types of calls in the various studies were coded.

These studies of the allocation of police time have important implications for police recruitment, as well as for understanding the role conflicts of those already in policing. If people are attracted to policing because they think most of the officer's time will be spent in exciting chases of dangerous criminals and have no concept of the often dull periods of waiting for action, they might be quite unhappy as police officers. If they have no concept of the service functions of policing and are not trained to perform those functions, life on the beat might come as an unpleasant surprise.

An additional problem is that police officers may encounter supervisors who do not give equal credit to successful performance of the three police functions. Catching dangerous criminals might result in a faster promotion than performing order maintenance or social service functions successfully. Police officers may experience a similar response from their colleagues and from the community.

Proactive Versus Reactive Policing

Regardless of how police activities are categorized, it is clear that police do not spend most of their time engaging in the stereotype held by many: catching dangerous criminals. In fact, many police officers spend very little time in actual crime detection. Most police work is **reactive,** not **proactive;** that is, police are dependent on the assistance of victims, witnesses, and other citizens to report crimes.

There have been some changes in recent years. In the previous chapter we examined problem-oriented policing, whereby police identify problems that may be creating the criminal situation and try to eliminate those problems. Police have become proactive in other areas, too, such as identifying and arresting domestic violence offenders.

Police and Domestic Violence

In recent years more attention has been paid to domestic violence, which involves spouses abusing each other, parents abusing children, and children abusing each other or their parents. Some studies include courtship violence. Although data are questionable, all of these types of violence are thought to be on the increase.[8] Data show that domestic violence is rising in the military[9] and among police.[10]

In earlier times, violence within the family was considered a domestic problem, not a crime, and if police intervened at all they did so mainly as mediators, not as law enforcement officers. Rarely were arrests made. In recent years, with emphases on victimization and women's rights, more attention has been given to domestic violence. Many police officers receive training in how to handle domestic violence, and some jurisdictions have instituted a policy of mandatory arrests in domestic violence cases.[11] But the evidence on the results of police arrests in domestic violence cases is contradictory.

Under a mandatory arrest policy, the police officer must arrest the alleged perpetrator of domestic violence if there is sufficient evidence that violence has occurred. This approach has resulted in more arrests in domestic violence cases in which police act on their own without waiting for victims to insist on pressing charges.

Some of the earlier evaluations of higher arrest rates in domestic violence cases show that this approach is more successful in preventing further domestic violence than a nonarrest policy. In assessing the results of the Minneapolis Domestic Violence Experiment, Lawrence W. Sherman and Richard A. Berk concluded that

> arrest was the most effective of three standard methods police use to reduce domestic violence. The other police methods—attempting to counsel both parties or sending assailants away—were found to be considerably less effective in deterring future violence in the cases examined.[12]

Such findings led the Attorney General's Task Force on Family Violence (appointed in 1984) to recommend that "to provide the most effective response, operational procedures should require the officer to presume that arrest, consistent with state law, is the appropriate response in cases of family violence."[13]

The Minneapolis findings were not replicated in a similar study in Omaha, Nebraska, leading its authors to suggest that their findings

> will undoubtedly cast some doubt on the deterrent power of a mandatory or even a presumptory arrest policy for cases of misdemeanor domestic assault. At this point, researchers and policymakers are in the awkward position of having conflicting results from two experiments and no clear, unambiguous direction from the research on this issue.[14]

Other studies report that the first time an offender is apprehended by police after a domestic violence call is the most potent one and that arrest is most effective at that time. Arrest is more effective if followed by court-mandated treatment.

Subsequent monitorings of these offenders reveal that the more educated an offender, the more likely it is that he will not repeat domestic violence offenses.[15]

In a recent journal that featured a symposium on domestic violence Lawrence W. Sherman examined what we know and do not know about domestic violence and particularly the effect of arrest. Sherman concluded that,

> after more than a decade of evaluating arrest for midemeanor domestic violence, we still have much to learn. The jigsaw puzzle of diverse results in different cities has not been put together, and too many pieces are still missing.[16]

Another recently published study regarding policing spousal violence reports that although police are not likely to arrest in such cases (arrests were not made in 76 percent of the cases), arrests are no more likely in other types of violence cases.[17] And a recent analysis of police responses to domestic violence in the past few decades concludes that we have yet to develop a set of tools or responses that "work well across a variety of situations in reducing the likelihood of future violence" with domestic environments.[18]

These and other studies suggest that we need to continue evaluating the best ways to handle domestic violence, a situation that remains one of conflict for police. Even where mandatory arrest policies are in effect, police encounter alleged victims who refuse to cooperate. Many spouses do not want their partners arrested; if police insist and make the arrest, the complaining partner may become hostile, belligerent, even violent. Thus, what appears to be a positive change in policing may result in greater role conflict for police officers, including violence against them.[19]

One final problem created by domestic disturbance situations is that police (and their employers) may face civil liability suits if they do not provide adequate protection for women who report that they have been beaten or threatened with violence by their partners. Providing protection in all cases is costly, however, and in many instances, it is unnecessary. Deciding when to provide protection is a critical decision that some police officers and administrators are not trained to make.[20]

Concern with domestic violence and the need to prevent it as well as provide legal recourse for victims led Congress to include within the 1994 crime control legislation a provision known as the Violence Against Women Act.[21] In 1996 the Department of Justice published its final rules covering federal grants authorized by this legislation. Included are provisions for programs that provide training police for handling domestic violence cases; developing policies providing sanctions for officer who refuse to arrest in such cases; developing guidelines for when to arrest in domestic violence cases; and so on.[22]

Stress

In recent years increasing attention has been given to stress and the effects it has on people in various occupations and professions. A variety of harmful physical results may occur when individuals do not handle stress successfully. Whereas all people may be affected in some way by on-the-job stress, studies have found evidence of particularly high stress rates in some jobs; policing has been called the most stressful. The effect goes beyond the individual officer. "Police work affects, shapes, and at times, scars the individuals and families involved."[23] Several cases illustrating police stress are discussed in Spotlight 5.1.

Spotlight 5.1

Police Reaction to Stress

The bombing of the federal building in Oklahoma City in 1995, resulting in the deaths of 168 persons at that time, has claimed at least one police officer who was on duty during the tragedy. In 1996 Sgt. Terrance Yeakey, aged thirty, took his own life. He left no note, but friends suggested that although he saved four people in that disaster he may have felt guilty about not saving more. Sgt. Yeakey was one of the first officers to arrive on the scene, but after he rescued the four persons he fell two stories in the building, injuring his back.[1]

Like all other professionals, police react to stress in a variety of ways. One reaction to stress is violence against others or against oneself. In September 1994, *Time* featured a story on police suicides as one reaction to stress. The article reported that ten New York City police had committed suicide to date in 1994, the record for one entire year (1987) in that department. Authorities continued to analyze explanations, but some facts were evident. Female officers were far less likely than male officers to commit suicide. Alcohol was involved in most cases, and suicides could be expected to occur after exposure of corruption within the police department.[2]

In February 1994 a St. Petersburg, Florida, police officer who had been praised for preventing a suicide took his own life with his gun.[3] In 1993 suicides among police in Jacksonville, Florida, were higher than the combined suicides during the same period for the police departments in New York, Atlanta, Miami, Charlotte, N.C., and two Florida cities, Tampa and St. Petersburg. Struggling to understand the causes, one young officer blamed accumulated stress. He cited the difficulties of leaving the stress at the office or on patrol. "We become very cynical and suspicious . . . For example,

instead of having a normal father-to-son or husband-to-wife relationship, you come home and you interrogate everyone in your house."[4] His analysis was echoed by the ex-husband of an officer who stated that his wife had gotten into the police role so much "that she regarded any challenge to her authority as an attack."[5]

One source of stress for officers is the necessity of using deadly force. One police sergeant said that after ten years he still had flashbacks of the scene in which he killed a suspect after the man had shot another officer. According to the International Association of Chiefs of Police, 70 percent of police who are involved in a shooting leave policing within ten years after the event.[6]

Officers who fire their weapons and injure and kill suspects may be disciplined or charged with criminal behavior by those in a position to consider the behavior more analytically at a later time. Criminal charges may result even when the officer believes he or she is firing to protect others or in self-defense. Miami police officer William Lozano, who shot a motorcyclist in self-defense, resulting in the deaths of the cyclist and his passenger, was charged with manslaughter. At his first trial, Lozano was convicted of two counts and sentenced to prison. Those convictions were reversed on appeal. Lozano was acquitted at his second trial, but the proceedings took almost five years.[7]

Increased recognition of the importance of identifying stress early has led some police administrators to initiate special programs or hire psychologists. Some have been successful, but officers may reject the services of psychologists. "Police officers have far more cause to succumb to stress than most people, and, sadly, far more reason to fear stigma if they ask for help."[8]

1. "Policeman in Bombing Rescue in Oklahoma City Is a Suicide," *New York Times* (11 May 1996), p. 9.
2. "Officers on the Edge," *Time* (26 September 1994), p. 62.
3. "Officer Kills Himself with Roommate's Gun," *St. Petersburg Times* (8 February 1994), p. 7.
4. "Jacksonville Police Suicides Alarming," *St. Petersburg Times* (19 July 1993), p. 5B.
5. "Officers on the Edge," p. 63.
6. "Police Who Shoot Suspects Face Flashbacks, Guilt, Anger," *Miami Herald* (19 July 1992), p. 6.
7. Lozano v. State, 584 So.2d 19 (Fla.Dist.Ct.App.3d Dist. 1991), *review denied,* 595 So.2d 558 (Fla. 1992).
8. "Stress, Cops and Suicide," *New York Times* (1 December 1993), p. 16. See also the symposium on police psychology in *Criminal Justice and Behavior* 19 (September 1992).

Some studies suggest that police have higher rates of divorce, suicide, and other manifestations of stress than those found among people in other occupations and professions;[24] but most of the research contains serious methodological problems, and we should be cautious about accepting the conclusions.

Stress in policing is not confined to patrol officers. Undercover officers may experience the same stresses as patrol officers, along with some stressors, such as the need for secrecy, unique to undercover work.[25] Police administrators may experience stress for the following reasons: dependence on others such as staff to get the work done (after being trained to be relatively independent as line officers); concerns for personnel and their needs (in contrast to the line officer, whose daily concerns are mainly with "equipment, supplies, and support which directly and individually pertains to them"); lack of resources; increased community demands and pressures; impact of the external bureaucracy; political nature of the job; sedentary nature of the job; lack of preparation for the job (special programs for police chiefs and other administrators are relatively recent developments and still not sufficiently available); conflict with employee organizations; difficulty of effecting lasting change; and separation from the police subculture.[26]

This discussion suggests that stress in policing may be no different from stress in other occupations and professions. But there is one major difference; police are trained to injure or kill, and if the situation requires, they are expected to use that ability. Indeed, they may be sanctioned for not using their weapons. It is this requirement, say some officers, that is unique in creating stress in policing.

A psychologist notes that in war, military officers may cope by defining the opposition as bad. "The role is so well accepted and shared." But that is not true of police officers, who may be highly criticized, even sanctioned, for a killing. Officers who kill may be isolated socially from their colleagues. Routine procedure is to suspend officers pending investigation of a shooting. Said one officer, "I felt as alone as I ever had in my whole life. They take you out of a group and make you stand alone." Another officer spoke of the nightmares, the flashbacks, and the social isolation that he felt after he had killed a person while on patrol. "I consider myself part of a class of people other people don't understand."[27]

Professors at Michigan State University have found that officers who kill in the line of duty suffer postshooting trauma that may lead to severe problems, perhaps even ruining their careers. Some research reports that 70 percent of these officers leave the police force within seven to ten years after the shooting.[28] As Spotlight 5.1 relates, some police departments have recognized the need for psychological counseling as part of the professional assistance provided for police.[29] In one Florida county, for example, police and firefighters who are involved in "crisis calls" are required to undergo debriefings after those calls. These sessions do not focus on what went wrong and what went right but, rather, on how the professionals felt about seeing human pain and death.[30]

The Commission on Civil Rights emphasized the need to provide stress management programs and services for police. Citing Los Angeles as a city having this type of comprehensive program, the commission noted that unfortunately, most police departments lack such programs, despite the recent emphasis on stress as "an important underlying factor in police misconduct incidents."[31]

The Impact of AIDS

One source of stress for police is the fear of contracting the human immunodeficiency virus (HIV) that causes *acquired immune deficiency syndrome* (AIDS). AIDS is a deadly disease that affects the immune system, leaving the body unable to fight infections. It may be acquired through exchanges of bodily fluids with an infected person, through use of an unsterile needle, or by means of a transfusion of tainted blood. The virus may also be transmitted by a pregnant woman to her fetus.

One other issue of concern is police officers who have AIDS. Although there is no evidence that AIDS is transmitted by casual contact, many people are concerned about contacts with persons infected with AIDS. Colleagues may react negatively to an officer who has AIDS.[32]

The Police Subculture

One way of handling dilemmas, role conflicts, and stress is to withdraw into a more comfortable situation. If sufficient numbers of a group do so, a subgroup or **subculture** is formed. The subculture has values and expectations that distinguish it from the dominant culture but that solidify its members.[33]

Police can become isolated from people who might be their friends if it were not for the police officer's authority and responsibility to regulate the daily lives of citizens. Traffic violations and laws regulating the use of alcohol and other drugs are examples. "The nature of the policeman's role tends to overflow the norms of friendship and to violate the integrity of trust on which friendships must rest." It would be difficult to form an intimate relationship with someone who is expected "to arrest you for common and petty violations which intimates would ordinarily know about."[34]

Earlier studies suggested that police were a homogeneous group who formed subcultures and manifested a distinct personality type. They were said to be authoritarian, cynical, punitive, rigid, physically aggressive, assertive, and impulsive risk takers.[35] Police were viewed as people who looked for negatives and who stereotyped situations, making quick judgments whenever they thought crime was involved. Such attitudes may lead to violence.

It was assumed that the best way to alleviate police cynicism was to increase professionalism, but some studies reported that although "commitment to a professional ideology reduces cynicism among police," the relationship between these two variables was more complex than earlier researchers thought.[36] Thus, it is necessary to look more carefully at the dimensions of each of the variables: cynicism and professionalism.[37]

There is some evidence of a relationship between professionalism and cynicism among police chiefs, although there are some differences when comparing chiefs to other police officers. Also there are differences based on duration of service. For example, cynicism "is highest for police chiefs during their early years and gradually declines with experience." Cynicism varies according to the size of the chief's police agency, with those in larger agencies showing lower cynicism.[38]

There is some evidence that police officers, like police chiefs, become less cynical as their length of service increases.[39] Taken as a whole, research on police cynicism underscores the importance of looking carefully at all variables that might account for cynicism and analyzing those variables in their full complexity. It is not sufficient to find cynicism and professionalism (or any other trait) among police officers or chiefs and draw the conclusion that the relationship is a simple one. On the other hand, professionalism is important in policing as in other occupations and professions.

Police Misconduct

Police officers have many opportunities for engaging in improper behavior, and they have the power to coerce or force individuals to comply. One area of misconduct that has received some attention lately is sexual misconduct. In recent years

Florida papers have carried reports of allegations that a police officer was apprehended for running naked through apartment complexes; another pleaded no contest to a misdemeanor battery charge after he was accused of fondling a woman's breast when she was stopped for a traffic violation; another was arrested and charged with sexual misconduct with four women. Experts say it is particularly difficult for individuals to cope with such victimizations by police, whom they have been taught to trust.[40] In March 1997 one Florida newspaper reported that evidence of serious misconduct among police in the state was on the rise but that punishments were less severe.[41]

Although most reports of sexual abuse by officers are allegations against male officers, one Florida female officer was accused of providing underage boys with alcohol and drugs and engaging in sexual relations with one of them. After pleading guilty to some of the charges, the officer was sentenced to weekends in jail, probation, and house arrest. She must perform 200 hours of community service and attend psychotherapy, drug, and alcohol treatment and support groups. In sentencing her, the judge said, "You're a police officer. . . . People expect more. Quite frankly, I think they're entitled to expect more."[42]

Most reported police misconduct involves corruption, defined as follows:

> A public official is corrupt if he accepts money or money's worth for doing something that he is under a duty to do anyway, that he is under a duty not to do, or to exercise a legitimate discretion for improper reasons.[43]

The possibility for corruption varies with greater opportunities available in larger cities, but corruption may be found in all types of police departments. Corruption occurs in police departments of other countries, too.[44]

James Q. Wilson analyzed police corruption according to the type of organization in the police department. He defined three types of law enforcement styles and found those styles to be related to the degree of police corruption.[45] According to Wilson, the greatest degree of police corruption is found in departments characterized by the *watchman style,* in which police are expected to maintain order, not regulate conduct. Low salaries and the expectation that police will have other jobs increase the probabilities that police will be involved in corruption.

Corruption is found to a lesser degree in departments characterized by the *legalistic style,* with its emphasis on formal police training, recruiting from the middle class, offering greater promotional opportunities, and viewing law as a means to an end rather than an end in itself. Formal sanctions are used more frequently than informal ones, with police giving less attention to community service and order maintenance than to law enforcement.

Corruption is not a serious problem in the third type of style, the *service style.* In this management style, law enforcement and order maintenance are combined, with an emphasis on good relationships between the police and the community. Police command is decentralized, with police on patrol working out of specialized units. Higher education and promotional opportunities are emphasized, and police are expected to lead exemplary private lives.

Police corruption has been analyzed according to types, too. The first, the *rotten apples,* refers to a department characterized by a few police officers who accept bribes and engage in other forms of corruption. Generally, those people are uniformed patrol officers, but they are loners who will accept bribes for overlooking traffic violations, licensing ordinances, or crimes. Some work in groups, termed *rotten pockets,* accepting bribes for nonenforcement of the law. Many members of the vice squad are found in this type.[46]

A second type of corruption is *pervasive organized corruption,* describing the highly organized hierarchical organization of the political processes of the community, which goes beyond the police force. Some police departments are characterized by widespread but unorganized corruption, labeled as *pervasive unorganized corruption.* In addition to identifying these types, the external opportunities that might be conducive to police corruption have been analyzed. [47]

In 1970 in response to allegations of corruption in New York City, Mayor John V. Lindsay issued an executive order establishing the Knapp Commission. The 1972 commission's report disclosed widespread police corruption. Rookies were initiated into the system quickly; many became corrupt; some grew cynical. The commission found that police were involved with organized crime (the most lucrative form of corruption); payoffs from citizens, especially for traffic citations; and accepting money for overlooking violations of licensing ordinances. [48]

New York Police Department officials contend that only a very small percentage of city officers are involved in corruption. They say that undercover tests of integrity, whereby some officers are assigned to make secret reports on the behavior of other officers, have eliminated most corruption. Others contend that corruption has not been eliminated in the New York City Police Department or any other; they hold that it is inevitable.

> Corruption is endemic to policing. The very nature of the police function is bound to subject officers to tempting offers . . . . Solutions, so far, seem inadequate and certainly are not likely to produce permanent results. [49]

Recent reports from New York City confirm that corruption remains in the police department. In the fall of 1993 the Mollen Commission began another study of police corruption in New York City. In referring to the commission's interim report, published in December of that year, a *New York Times* editorial stated these findings:

> [P]ockets of police corruption and brutality exist because the ingrained culture of the Police Department tolerates wrongdoing, even protects the wrongdoer. The panel recommends shaking up the department's anti-corruption bureaucracy, and appointing an outside panel to conduct investigations. [50]

The final report of the commission was issued in July 1994. This report concluded that corruption was less common in New York City than it was during the Knapp Commission report but that its nature had changed. In 1994 more officers sought opportunities to move beyond bribery to violating other laws. Some officers stole routinely from drug dealers after stopping them for traffic violations, and some used violence to carry out their thefts. The commission found that corruption flourished in some parts of New York City because of opportunities but also because the police culture placed a greater emphasis on loyalty than on integrity. The majority of New York City's officers were not involved in corruption, but they feared reporting those who were. [51]

The nation's declared war on drugs presents criminal justice systems and police with one of their most frustrating problems. The escalation of drug trafficking is resulting in violence, distorted and ruined lives, enormous expense, and a crushing blow to all elements of criminal justice systems. As subsequent chapters disclose, jails and prisons are overcrowded, due in large part to drug offenders, many of whom are creating "a new underworld" within prisons; the result is that some prison correctional officers have been corrupted. [52] Civil cases are backed up for years to enable courts to process the drug cases.

The Knapp Commission and Its Aftermath

Police face the difficulty of confronting the massive drug problem without sufficient resources, while drug offenders have resources to tempt officers who earn relatively low salaries in highly stressful jobs. In 1997 in Chicago 124 narcotics cases were dismissed because the primary witness for the prosecution in each case was one of the police officers apprehended the previous year for extorting and robbing undercover officers who were posing as drug dealers. Furthermore, the police department's superintendent, Matt Rodriguez, resigned in November after the disclosure that he violated department policy by maintaining a close friendship with a convicted felon.[53] The problem of police corruption by drugs and drug offenders is sufficient to lead some to propose random drug testing of police.[54]

Finally, in 1996 the city of Philadelphia took action to counteract police corruption by establishing an Office of Integrity and Accountability within the police department. James B. Jordan, who was in charge of the city solicitor department's litigation group, was named head of the new office. The creation of the office was part of a settlement agreement approved by a federal judge after the American Civil Liberties Union and the National Association for the Advancement of Colored People threatened the city with a lawsuit. Jordan will have broad powers to combat corruption with Philadelphia's police department.[55]

Violence and the Police

Historically, police have been viewed as agents who are necessary for establishing law and order, often by applying justice on the spot. Although violence between police and citizens was reported earlier, the violence and unrest that occurred in the 1960s led to demands for larger and better-trained police forces. During that decade predominantly white police and minority citizens clashed in hot, crowded cities. Many student protesters found themselves in conflict with the police, and the police experienced disillusionment with a system that they did not believe protected their interests. They, too, became more active. Police unions were established; these were viewed by many as a representation of hostility by the police.

In short, the decade of the 1960s brought open violence between police and citizens, and the 1970s brought more cases of police violence and corruption. Meanwhile, crime rates began to rise and citizens demanded greater police protection. Demands for a more professionalized police force were heard, along with allegations of police misconduct.

Police are, however, entitled to use force, even deadly force. The issue is under what circumstances.

Police Use of Deadly Force

The use of **deadly force** by police has been defined as "such force as under normal circumstances poses a high risk of death or serious injury to its human target, regardless of whether or not death, serious injury or any harm actually result."[56] Police officers may use deadly force under some circumstances. If they use deadly force improperly, the officers (and the police department) may be liable to the injured person (or, in the event of death, to the family of the deceased) in a civil suit. Most rules for the use of deadly force come from federal statutes or administrative decisions. In 1995 the Department of Justice (DOJ) issued a uniform policy on the use of deadly force. The policy applies to all law enforcement and corrections officers who are employed by the DOJ.[57]

Excessive use of force may occur while police are chasing suspects either on foot or in vehicles; or it may occur when suspects are already apprehended. We will consider first the use of force in attempts to apprehend suspects.

Fleeing Felon Rule

Shooting any fleeing felon was permitted historically. Because all felonies were punishable by death, it was assumed that any felon would resist arrest by all possible means. The **fleeing felon rule** developed during a time when apprehending criminals was more difficult. Police did not have weapons that could be used for shooting at a long distance; nor did they have communication techniques that would enable them to notify other jurisdictions quickly that a suspect had escaped arrest. Therefore, it was possible for fleeing felons to escape if not immediately apprehended and begin a new life in another community without fear of detection by the local police.[58]

As more efficient weapons were developed, it became easier for police to apprehend felons, and many did so by use of deadly force, even though the fleeing felons were not dangerous. Such actions were not necessary to protect the officer and others, nor were they necessary to apprehend felons. Despite these developments, however, many states codified the common law rule that permitted police officers to use deadly force in apprehending fleeing felons. This practice was condemned by many commentators and scholars, but the practice was not prohibited by most courts before 1985.

On 27 March 1985, the U.S. Supreme Court ruled that Tennessee's fleeing felon statute was unconstitutional under the facts of the case. *Tennessee* v. *Garner* involved an unarmed boy who was killed by a police officer as the youth fled from an unoccupied house. The officer could see that the fleeing felon was a youth and apparently unarmed. But the officer argued that he knew that if the youth got over the fence, he could escape; so he fired at him. The Tennessee statute allowed an officer to shoot a suspect if it appeared to be necessary to prevent the escape of a felon.[59]

In *Garner* the Court emphasized that the use of deadly force by police officers must be reasonable to be lawful. It is reasonable in the following circumstances:

1. To prevent an escape when the suspect has threatened the officer with a weapon
2. When there is a threat of death or serious physical injury to the officer or others
3. If there is probable cause to believe that the person has committed a crime involving the infliction or threatened infliction of serious physical harm and, where practical, some warning has been given by the officer.

The Tennessee statute that permitted an officer to shoot a fleeing felon may be constitutional in some instances. But used against a young, slight, and unarmed youth who was suspected of burglary, deadly force was unreasonable and therefore unlawful.[60]

Vehicle Pursuits

A second area in which police may be involved in violence is in vehicle pursuits. High-speed chases may end in injury or death to the suspect, the police pursuer, or innocent bystanders. Earlier studies report some data indicating that these pursuits are not worth the results in property damage, human injury, and death. Likewise, some courts have held police departments liable for the consequences of such pursuits. Consequently, some police departments have restricted the types of cases in which vehicle pursuits are permitted or have eliminated hot pursuits entirely.

In a recent national study of 1,200 police departments, Geoffrey P. Alpert found that 90 percent have written policies governing police vehicle pursuits. Although some of those policies are old, dating back to the 1970s, one-half had been revised or drafted within the last two years. Most of the changes involved making the policies more restrictive. Alpert reported "strikingly effective" results after changes were made in policies. For example, in Miami, Florida, a change in policy in 1992, stating that only violent felonies warrant pursuits, was followed by an 82 percent drop in pursuits. On the other hand, Omaha, Nebraska's policy was changed to a more permissive one in 1993 and was followed by an increase in pursuits of over 600 percent the following year.[61]

Police use of deadly force is necessary, but when used improperly, it violates suspects' rights and may lead to serious injuries or death as well as a loss of confidence in the police. How much abuse occurs is unknown, although some researchers report that abuse is relatively rare.[62] Even if that is true, and many question the conclusion, the *perception* citizens have about police brutality is crucial. For example, presidential commissions studying urban riots have noted the effect of police brutality on such incidents. When the public perceives an act by a police officer to be unfair, unreasonable, unnecessary, or harassing, especially when minorities are the victims, that perception may provide the impetus for urban riots.[63] This is not to suggest that police actions *cause* the riots. Police have no control over the root causes of civil disturbances, such as unemployment, lack of educational opportunities, poor housing, and inadequate health care facilities; but police may escalate or reduce violent confrontations by the policies they adopt. And they must confront the allegations that they use excessive violence, especially against minorities, as the following discussion of police brutality suggests.

Police Brutality

In a classic and frequently cited article on police brutality published in 1968, Albert J. Reiss Jr. began his discussion with a 1903 quotation by a former New York City police commissioner:

> For three years, there has been through the courts and the streets a dreary procession of citizens with broken heads and bruised bodies against few of whom was violence needed to affect an arrest. Many of them had done nothing to deserve an arrest. In a majority of such cases, no complaint was made. If the victim complains, his charge is generally dismissed. The police are practically above the law.[64]

During the summer of 1966, Reiss conducted a study of police-citizen interactions in Boston, Chicago, and Washington, D.C. In discussing the results of that study, Reiss pointed out the difficulty of defining police brutality, but he emphasized the importance to the citizen of the status degradation aspect of police behavior, "the judgment that they have not been treated with the full rights and dignity among citizens in a democratic society."[65] Police brutality may cause serious injury or even death, and the use of deadly force by the police is the root of most controversy surrounding police behavior. Some of the most publicized allegations of police brutality of the 1990s are discussed in Spotlight 5.2.

Allegations of police brutality such as those discussed in Spotlight 5.2 draw widespread media attention. Some of the attention is justified, and in some cases, as illustrated by that spotlight, police are found guilty of crimes for their use of force toward citizens. But it is important to put these incidents in perspective and note that most people who have encounters with police report that those interactions do not include violence. A recent publication of the Bureau of Justice Statistics (BJS) reports that less than 1 percent of persons who come into contact with police report that officers threatened to use or did use force against them. During the years studied by the BJS, one in five respondents had some contact with police. Of those, one-third were seeking help or offering assistance; another one-third were reporting that they were victims of or witnesses to crimes, while less than one-third reported that the police initiated the contact. But as one authority pointed out, the report "probably doesn't really speak to the strained relations between the police and minority communities in America."[66]

A second type of violence involving police occurs when citizens engage in violence *against* the police.

Violence Against the Police

In 1995 the number of felonious killings of law enforcement officers reached a six-year high, but in 1996 the number of officers killed in the line of duty was the lowest it had been since 1960. The 117 federal, state, and local officers killed feloniously in 1996 represented a 30 percent decrease over the number killed in 1995. Criminologist Alfred Blumstein cites several possible reasons for the decline in officer deaths: the waiting period imposed by the Brady gun control law; more carefully designed and aggressive efforts to remove handguns from the streets, especially in large cities such as New York City; efforts to reduce the number of licensed firearms dealers; and increased efforts to reduce the number of young people involved in gangs and violence.[67]

Blumstein's analysis may or may not be correct, but in 1997 the U.S. Supreme Court ruled unconstitutional the portion of the Brady Handgun Violence Prevention Act that requires local law enforcement officers to conduct background checks on persons who attempt to purchase handguns. A significant drop in these background checks might affect violence rates, and if so, killings of police might increase.[68]

It is important to understand that not all police deaths in the line of duty are felonious deaths—that is, caused by the criminal acts of others. Approximately 40 percent of police deaths are the results of accidents.[69] Furthermore, not all police who are confronted with violence by others are killed. Some are, however, injured seriously. In addition, police encounter growing hostility that may result in verbal abuse and physical attacks short of murder. Although it is debatable which comes first and which causes which, there are indications that violence against police officers is accompanied by violence by police officers. In their report of a Police Foundation study focusing on police use of deadly force, the authors stated that they were "acutely aware of the interrelationship between acts committed *by* the police and acts committed *against* them."[70]

Violence against police has serious repercussions. Officers who survive may have physical injuries or psychological problems that preclude further work as police officers. Families and friends of those who are killed are victims of such violence as well. There is evidence that these family members develop feelings of hostility and fear; they have difficulty making decisions; they feel alone in social situations; they have emotional problems; they develop sleep disorders; and they may have guilt feelings about their interactions with the deceased prior to his or her death.[71]

The Control of Policing

Although only a minority of police officers may be guilty of misconduct, any misconduct should be subject to discipline. Policies and programs should be developed to avoid as much misconduct as possible. Police misconduct may be controlled from within the department or by outside agencies.[72]

Spotlight 5.2

Alleged Police Brutality in the 1990s

Allegations of police brutality in the 1990s focused on several highly publicized cases in New York City, Detroit, and Los Angeles.

New York City, 1997

On 25 December 1997 police officer Michael Davitt shot and killed twenty-two-year-old William J. Whitfield, unarmed, as he ran into a grocery store. The officer and his partner were in the area looking for a gunman. The officer who shot Whitfield said he thought the victim had a gun; he was carrying only a set of keys on a long leather strap. It was alleged that Davitt may have thought the strap was a gun. Officer Davitt's firing was his ninth in fourteen years as a police officer, which was more shootings than any other officer in the 38,000-person force.

The funeral of Mr. Whitfield was attended by over 500 people, many of whom did not know him but came to express their concern for the family and their outrage at what they perceived as unreasonable force used by police against African Americans. One of the mourners was a Haitian immigrant, Abner Louima, who, flanked by his attorneys, came to "show our support for the family. Because in our time of sorrow, everyone supported us." A family friend who spoke at the funeral, closed with an address to the officer. "So now you know, Officer Davitt: We are devastated, devastated. And our lives, and your life, won't ever be the same."[1]

Mr. Louima has alleged that in August 1997 he was beaten and sodomized by police with a broom in the bathroom of the Brooklyn stationhouse. As an investigation into that allegation began, Police Commissioner Howard Safir reassigned the two top supervisors, suspended a desk sergeant, and placed nine other officers on desk duty. That investigation continues, but the intense publicity it has already engendered has tarnished the image of New York City police significantly.[2]

Detroit, 1992

After a controversial trial, two white police officers, Walter Budzyn and Larry Nevers, were convicted of second-degree murder in the death of an African American suspect, Malice Wayne Green. In July 1997 the Michigan Supreme Court ordered a new trial for Budzyn, based on improper procedures during the trial. Subsequently, Budzyn was released from prison. The state court refused to order a new trial for Nevers, but he was released on 31 December 1997, after serving four years in prison. A federal judge ordered his release and a new trial based on prejudicial pretrial publicity as well as improper procedures at trial. One such procedure included the showing of the movie, "Malcolm X," which begins with footage from the police beating of Rodney King, discussed next.[3]

In April 1998 Budzyn was sentenced to four to fifteen years for involuntary manslaughter and remained free while the judge decided how much more time, if any, he would have to serve. Budzyn had spent four and one-half years in prison after his first conviction.

Los Angeles, 1991

The brutality of white police officers against an African American suspect might have gone unnoticed, but an eyewitness taped the actions of 3 March 1991. National television brought the details of a police beating into

Regulation by Police Departments

The efficient operation of any department requires internal discipline of employees; in the case of police departments, it is important that the public's image of internal operations be positive. The Commission on Civil Rights emphasized that it is essential that police departments have an effective system of internal discipline that will "include clear definition of proper conduct, a reliable mechanism for detecting misconduct, and appropriate sanctions, consistently imposed, when misconduct has been proven." Policies must be articulated clearly.[73]

Police departments should enforce their written policies actively and fairly. If officers believe that they will not be reprimanded for violating departmental policies, those policies may be ineffective in curbing abuse of discretion. The Commission on Civil Rights recommended that "every police department should have a clearly defined system for the receipt, processing, and investigation of civil-

Spotlight 5.2 *continued*

our homes as we saw Rodney King, a twenty-five-year-old African American suspect, fired on by a white police officer carrying a 50,000-volt Taser stun gun. Three other officers kicked and beat the suspect on his head with their nightsticks, causing injuries to his neck, legs, and kidneys. King suffered multiple skull fractures, a broken ankle, crushed cheekbone, internal injuries, severe bruises, and some brain damage.

All four officers in the King incident were charged with assault with a deadly weapon and excessive force by an officer under color of authority: Two were charged with filing a false police report, and one was charged with being an accessory after the fact. In the spring of 1992, the officers were tried by a jury in Simi Valley, California, a predominantly all-white community to which the trial had been moved when defense attorneys argued successfully that their clients could not get a fair trial in Los Angeles. All of the officers were acquitted of the assault and secondary charges, but the jury could not reach a verdict on the excessive force charge against one officer. The judge declared a mistrial on that charge. The prosecutor announced plans to retry the officer, and the judge ruled that the trial would be held in Los Angeles.

The reaction in Los Angeles was violent. The resulting rioting and looting led to the deaths of sixty persons, although later reports indicated that approximately fifteen of those deaths were not related to the rioting. Still, it was the "most deadly U.S. disturbance in the twentieth century." In the weeks following the rioting, authorities reduced their estimates of fires from more than 5,000 to 623 and their estimates of arrests from over 19,000 to about one-half of that number.[4] Approximately one billion dollars in property damage occurred in the Los Angeles area, while lesser riots causing property damage occurred in other cities, too.

All four police officers were tried on federal charges of violating Mr. King's civil rights. Two officers, Timothy Wind and Ted Briseno, were acquitted. Officer Laurence Powell and Sgt. Stacey Koon were found guilty and sentenced to prison for two-and-one-half years. A federal appeals court upheld the convictions but ordered the trial court to reconsider the sentences, ruling that they were too short. The case was appealed to the U.S. Supreme Court, which upheld some but not all of the reasons for the trial court judge's sentence. The case was sent back for reconsideration by the trial judge in light of the Supreme Court's analysis of federal sentencing guidelines. On reconsideration, the original sentence was not changed.[5]

Source: Summarized by the author from media sources.

1. "500 Attend Funeral of Man Killed by Police Officer," *New York Times* (1 January 1998), p. 4; "Panel Defies Rudy, Listens to Gripes about B'klyn Cops," *Newsday* (3 January 1998), p. 3.
2. "A Clean Sweep for a Stained Station House," *New York Times* (15 August 1997), p. 1.
3. "Detroit Braces for the Rerun of a Divisive Murder Trial," *New York Times* (2 January 1998), p. 10. The state case is People v. Budzyn, 566 N.W.2d 229 (MI. 1997).
4. "One-Fourth of L.A. Riot Deaths Found Unrelated to Violence," *St. Petersburg Times* (2 June 1992), p. 4.
5. "Court Recommends Longer Sentences in Beating of King," *New York Times* (20 September 1994), p. 1. The case is United States v. Koon, 34 F.3d 1416 (9th Cir. 1994), *aff'd. in part, rev'd. in part, remanded,* 518 U.S. 81 (1996).

ian complaints." Once a violation of policy is found, "discipline imposed should be fair, swift, and consistent with departmental practices and procedures."[74] Police departments should take measures to identify violence-prone officers in an attempt to avert problems.

Regulation by Courts

Police departments do not control themselves sufficiently, and the courts must be utilized for some types of control. Courts have two major ways of controlling policing: excluding evidence and providing a forum for civil lawsuits against police officers and their departments.

The Exclusionary Rule and Its Exceptions

If police seize evidence illegally or secure confessions improperly, the evidence may be excluded from trial. This procedure is the result of the U.S. Supreme Court's **exclusionary rule.** In 1914 the Supreme Court held that the Fourth Amendment (which prohibits unreasonable searches and seizures; see Appendix A) would have no meaning unless courts prohibited the use of illegally seized evidence. Consequently, when the police violate that provision, the evidence they seize may not be used in *federal* cases. In 1961 the Court held that the exclusionary rule applies to the states.[75]

The exclusionary rule is controversial, mainly because it applies after the fact. When the illegally seized evidence is excluded from the trial, we know who the suspect is and, in many cases, believe that guilt is obvious. Thus, when the judge rules that the gun allegedly used in a murder cannot be used against a suspect because the evidence was obtained illegally by the police, and the suspect goes free because we do not have enough legal evidence for a conviction, there is strong public reaction of disbelief and outrage.

The exclusionary rule serves a symbolic purpose. It is "a symbol of our system of criminal procedure. It is lauded as a crowning achievement of a free society."[76] If police violate individual rights to obtain evidence to convict alleged criminals, the government, in a sense, is supporting crime. When this occurs, the government becomes a lawbreaker, and "it breeds contempt for law; it invites . . . anarchy."[77]

The symbolic purpose is important, but the second reason for the exclusionary rule is a practical one: it is assumed that the rule prevents police from engaging in illegal searches and seizures. According to the Supreme Court, the exclusionary rule "compels respect for the constitutional guarantee in the only effectively available way—by removing the incentive to disregard it."[78]

It is difficult to know whether that statement is true because most illegal searches that may be conducted to harass or punish take place in secret and may not be reported. Research on the issue reports inconclusive evidence. There is evidence, however, that the rule has led some police departments to increase the quantity and quality of police training, thus educating officers in what they may and may not do regarding search and seizure.[79]

In recent years the exclusionary rule has come under severe attack, with many people calling for its abolition or modification. Most of their arguments are the reverse of the arguments in favor. First is the argument of the symbolism of abolition, based on the view that, when people see guilty persons going free as a result of a technicality, they lose respect for law and order, and the entire criminal justice system is weakened. The public's perception of letting guilty people go free is crucial.

Second, the abolitionists contend that the exclusionary rule should be eliminated because it results in the release of guilty people. The rule "is attacked as one of the chief technical loopholes through which walk the guilty on their way out of the courthouse to continue their depredations."[80] It makes no difference how many: one is too many, argue the abolitionists. Third, the possibility of having evidence excluded from trial because it was not seized properly leads defendants to file numerous motions to suppress evidence, which consumes a lot of court time and contributes to their congestion. In criminal cases, objections to search and seizure are the issues raised most frequently.[81]

Criticism of the exclusionary rule has not led to its abolition, but some exceptions to the rule have been recognized by the U.S. Supreme Court. Under the

good faith exception, illegally obtained evidence is not excluded from trial if it can be shown that police secured the evidence in good faith; that is, they had a reasonable belief that they were acting in accordance with the law. The good faith exception has been adopted by some state legislatures. For example, the Colorado statute provides that "evidence which is otherwise admissible in a criminal proceeding shall not be suppressed by the trial court if the court determines that the evidence was seized . . . as a result of a good faith mistake."[82]

In *Massachusetts* v. *Sheppard,* the Supreme Court adopted the good faith exception, holding that when police conduct a search in good faith, even though the technical search warrant is defective, the seized evidence should not be excluded from the trial.[83] In 1995 the Court ruled that an unconstitutional arrest resulting from errors made by a court's clerical employee may be admitted against the accused at trial.[84]

The Court has interpreted the Constitution to permit the use of evidence seized by officers who had a warrant to search one apartment but searched the wrong apartment and found illegal drugs. In *Maryland* v. *Garrison,* the Court reasoned that because the search was in good faith and excluding its use in such cases would not deter police, who thought they were searching an apartment included in the warrant, nothing positive would be gained by applying the exclusionary rule.[85]

The Court has held that a defendant's constitutional rights are not violated when police officers lose or destroy evidence that might have been used to establish the defendant's innocence, provided the officers' actions were made in good faith. The case, *Arizona* v. *Youngblood,* involved an Arizona case in which Larry Youngblood was convicted of the kidnapping, molestation, and sexual assault of a ten-year-old boy.

The police in *Youngblood* had failed to refrigerate the victim's semen-stained clothing or to make tests capable of showing whether the semen came from Youngblood. Results of such tests might have shown that Youngblood was not the offender. Justice Rehnquist, writing for the majority, argued that omission can "at worst be described as negligent."[86]

Since the Supreme Court adopted the good faith exception to the exclusionary rule, some state courts have held that it does not apply under their state constitutions and thus all illegally seized evidence must be excluded at trial, regardless of the motivation of the officer who seized the evidence. Because this involves enlarging, not reducing, a Supreme Court interpretation of the federal Constitution, as it decreases the amount of evidence that can be used against a defendant, such interpretations are permissible.[87]

Numerous efforts have been made recently to enact legislation to abolish or alter the exclusionary rule. The most recent is referred to as the Exclusionary Rule Reform Act of 1997 and is part of the 1997 Omnibus Crime Control Act, which was introduced in January 1997. The last action on this bill was in June 1997, when it was referred to committee.[88]

The Supreme Court has approved a second major exception to the exclusionary rule: the **inevitable discovery rule.** According to this rule, evidence that police seize illegally will be admitted at trial if it can be shown that eventually the evidence would have been discovered by legal methods. Writing for the Court in *Nix* v. *Williams,* Chief Justice Warren E. Burger said, "Exclusion of physical evidence that would inevitably have been discovered adds nothing to either the integrity or fairness of a criminal trial."[89]

In a 1990 case the Court demonstrated its relaxing of the exclusionary rule. In 1980 the Court had held that the Fourth Amendment prohibits police from entering a suspect's home without a warrant and without the suspect's consent to effect a felony arrest. The Court stated that its reason for this rule was to protect the physical integrity of the home. In 1990 the Court ruled that even a violation of this earlier case would not invalidate a statement made by the accused *after* the warrantless entry of the home if the accused makes a statement to police *outside* the home. It is not necessary to exclude the statement despite the illegal entry into the home. The prohibition against the warrantless entry of the home is to protect the home's physical integrity, "not to grant criminal suspects protection for statements made outside their premises where the police have probable cause to make an arrest."[90]

In March 1991 a sharply divided Supreme Court demonstrated the impact of its recently appointed associate justice, David Souter, who joined the majority in a five-to-four decision that permits the use of coerced confessions in some circumstances. In 1967 the Court had articulated the *harmless error rule,* which holds that if a confession is coerced, it must be excluded at trial. In *Arizona* v. *Fulminante* the Court held that the Constitution does not require the automatic exclusion of the coerced confession. Rather, it is to be considered like any other trial error; it is to be analyzed under the circumstances and the trial court is to make a decision regarding whether it was a harmless error beyond a reasonable doubt. If so, it must be excluded; if not, it may be used against the suspect.[91]

In addition to the exclusionary rule, courts assist in the regulation of police actions through civil cases, as noted in the following discussion.

Tort Actions

Earlier the text discussed the meaning of *torts,* noting that civil suits may be brought in some cases that involve crimes as well as torts. The use of civil suits to bring actions against police (or other authorities) who violate civil rights of citizens is thought to be an effective deterrent for such illegal actions. Even if they do not deter other violations, tort actions permit abuse victims (or their survivors) to recover monetary damages for their physical injuries (or death) and also for emotional and psychological as well as economic damages.

Tort actions are brought under the Civil Rights Act and commonly called *1983 actions,* after the section of the U.S. Code in which the provision for such action is codified.[92] Section 1983 actions may be brought by persons injured as a result of police negligence, as, for example, in high-speed chases that result in injuries (or death) to bystanders. Suits may be brought for police mistreatment as well. Civil actions against police represent a growing body of tort law and increasing expenses for the municipalities that are responsible for those actions. In New York City, for example, payouts to settle claims against the police were $27.3 million in 1996. That represents an increase of $19.5 million over 1995. The number of brutality claims against police in that city tripled during the decade ending in 1996, but not all of those claims are substantiated. Still, the increase in payouts the city is willing to spend to settle cases is significant.[93]

Civil suits against police may be brought not only for intentional or malicious conduct. Negligence is also a basis for liability, especially negligence in hiring and training. In 1989, for example, the U.S. Supreme Court held that inadequate police training may result in civil liability for the municipality under which the police department operates. The following excerpt from *City of Canton, Ohio* v. *Harris* gives the facts and a portion of the Court's view:[94]

In this case, we are asked to determine if a municipality can ever be liable . . . for constitutional violations resulting from its failure to train municipal employees. We hold that, under certain circumstances, such liability is permitted . . .

In April 1978, respondent Geraldine Harris was arrested by officers of the Canton Police Department. Harris was brought to the police station in a patrol wagon.

When she arrived at the station, Harris was found sitting on the floor of the wagon. She was asked if she needed medical attention, and responded with an incoherent remark. After she was brought inside the station for processing, Mrs. Harris slumped to the floor on two occasions. Eventually, the police officers left Mrs. Harris lying on the floor to prevent her from falling again. No medical attention was ever summoned for Mrs. Harris. After about an hour, Mrs. Harris was released from custody, and taken by an ambulance (provided by her family) to a nearby hospital. There, Mrs. Harris was diagnosed as suffering from several emotional ailments; she was hospitalized for one week, and received subsequent outpatient treatment for an additional year.

Some time later, Mrs. Harris commenced this action alleging many state laws and constitutional claims against the city of Canton and its officials. Among these claims was one seeking to hold the city liable . . . for its violation of Mrs. Harris' right, under the Due Process Clause of the Fourteenth Amendment, to receive necessary medical attention while in police custody. . . .

We hold today that the inadequacy of police training may serve as the basis for liability only where the failure to train amounts to deliberate indifference to the rights of persons with whom the police come into contact. . . . Only where a municipality's failure to train its employees in a relevant respect evidences a "deliberate indifference" to the rights of its inhabitants can such a shortcoming be properly thought of as a city "policy or custom" that is actionable. . . .

Moreover, for liability to attach in this circumstance the identified deficiency in a city's training program must be closely related to the ultimate injury. Thus in the case at hand, respondent must still prove that the deficiency in training actually caused the police officers' indifference to her medical needs. Would the injury have been avoided had the employee been trained under a program that was not deficient in the identified respect? Predicting how a hypothetically well-trained officer would have acted under the circumstances may not be an easy task for the factfinder, particularly since matters of judgment may be involved, and since officers who are well-trained are not free from error and perhaps might react very much like the untrained officer in similar circumstances. But judge and jury, doing their respective jobs, will be adequate to the task.

Community Relations

Another method of controlling police activities is through community involvement and improved police-community relationships. It is vital that relationships between police and the community be improved. Police are not able to apprehend most criminals without the support of citizens. The U.S. Commission on Civil Rights emphasized that the men and women who are authorized to make arrests depend to a great extent on the cooperation of the public. "Perhaps the most valuable asset these officers can possess is credibility with the communities they serve."[95]

The importance of these contacts is emphasized by studies showing that citizens who have positive images of the police are more likely to report crimes than those who have negative images. Those most likely to have negative images of the police are members of the lower class, African Americans, and other nonwhites—persons who feel a general alienation from the political process and those who perceive an increase in crime in their neighborhoods.[96]

Previously, we discussed community-oriented policing (COP) as being in vogue today. Earlier studies disclosed that some positive results, such as crime reduction, follow COP.[97] Crime prevention programs are important, too. Police educate the community about various approaches to crime prevention. Community organization activities in which police and the community work together to identify community problems are helpful.[98] Herman Goldstein, who has written extensively on numerous criminal justice issues, concludes that full development of the overall concept of community policing, including a "concern with the substance of policing as well as its form," could "provide the integrated strategy for improving the quality of policing."[99]

We have noted already that violence by the police may evoke violence against the police. Earlier commissions underscored police violence as a catalyst in urban rioting in the 1960s.[100] But earlier commissions also noted the impact of race in explaining violence by and against the police. For example, the U.S. Commission on Civil Rights emphasized the importance of hiring more racial minorities and upgrading their positions on police forces when it cited the study of the National Minority Advisory Council on Criminal Justice, which stressed the far-reaching effects of police brutality.[101] Efforts to increase diversity in policing deserve analysis.

Affirmative Action Recruitment and Hiring

Diversity in police departments is recognized increasingly as one way to improve the services police offer to the community as well as the community's perception of police.

The need to recruit women and racial minorities was emphasized by the Commission on Civil Rights, which concluded:

> Serious underutilization of minorities and women in local law enforcement agencies continues to hamper the ability of police departments to function effectively in and earn the respect of predominantly minority neighborhoods, thereby increasing the probability of tension and violence.

> While there has been some entry of minorities and women into police service in recent years, police departments remain largely white and male, particularly in the upper-level command positions. Utilization figures for women hardly approach tokenism, although studies have indicated that as a rule women perform at least as well as men on the force.

In light of that finding, the commission recommended that "[p]olice department officials should develop and implement affirmative action plans so that ultimately the force reflects the composition of the community it serves."[102]

The Commission on Civil Rights found that efforts by police departments to recruit women and racial minorities may be hindered by the community's perceptions that the department is not committed to such recruitment. Such perceptions are created in different ways. For example, newspaper reports of the way police handle cases involving women and racial minorities, complaints of former members of the police force, and the treatment received by women and minorities who applied but were turned down as recruits by the police department may affect perceptions. Perceptions of race and gender discrimination are created by the lack of advancement opportunities for women and racial minorities within police departments, as well as by the high rates of attrition during training. The commission concluded that in addition to an emphasis on recruitment, "Minorities and women, through the implementation of equal opportunity programs, should hold positions that lead to upward mobility in the ranks, allowing them to compete for command positions."[103]

Recruitment of women and minority officers has had some help from the courts, with both groups having filed successful affirmative action cases under federal statutes. Women have argued successfully that they were discriminated against in hiring, on-the-job assignments, and promotions. After a decade of decisions on affirmative action policies concerning minorities and women, in 1987 the Supreme Court held that it is permissible for employers to give preferential treatment in jobs on the basis of gender and race. *Johnson* v. *Transportation Agency* involved a white man who argued that he was discriminated against when his employer promoted a white woman to a position for which he, too, was qualified.[104]

In *Johnson,* the Court upheld the voluntary affirmative action plan of the transportation agency. Under this plan, in making promotions to positions in which women and minorities traditionally have been excluded or underrepresented, the agency was authorized to consider gender or race as a reason for a promotion. No quota was mentioned, but the policy did call for short-range goals of actively promoting women and minorities.

In 1987 in *United States* v. *Paradise,* the Court upheld an Alabama affirmative action plan that established a one-for-one racial quota for promotions. The Court said this action is permissible because of the long history of excluding African Americans from employment as state troopers.[105]

Some have argued, however, that affirmative action discriminates against whites, and in recent years the programs designed to increase diversity have come under fire. The cases are complicated, and they involve settings other than policing, but several are significant.

In June of 1995 the U.S. Supreme Cout decided *Adarand Constructors, Inc.* v. *Pena,* a decision that may be the legal death blow to affirmative action programs. Although the Court did not use the words *affirmative action,* by a five-to-four decision the Court held that *federal government* programs that classify persons by race are presumably unconstitutional. To survive, such programs must pass a test of "strict scrutiny" and be "narrowly tailored" to meet a purpose in which the government has a "compelling state interest." The case involved federal government contracts, but it has implications for affirmative action hiring by federal agencies as it restricts severely the leeway the government has in minority (and by analogy gender) hiring. The case created considerable controversy, and within two weeks after its announcement, a spokesperson stated that the Federal Communications Commission was making plans to scale back a program that gave preferences to women and minorities in the awarding of wireless communication licenses.[106]

In 1995 the California Board of Regents ended affirmative action in that state's colleges and universities, and in 1996 a federal court in Texas refused to uphold the affirmative action policies of the University of Texas Law School. The U.S. Supreme Court refused to review the case, thus letting the decision stand.[107] The Court did agree, however, to hear a New Jersey case during its 1997–98 term.

The New Jersey case, *Piscataway Board of Education* v. *Taxman,* involved the dismissal of a white teacher rather than a similarly situated black teacher when the school district thought it necessary to cut back its payroll. The case was settled out of court prior to a decision by the U.S. Supreme Court, and in December of 1997 the Court dismissed the case. Thus, the issue remains unresolved by the highest Court.[108]

The legal and administrative changes regarding minority admission are resulting in smaller admissions to African American students by some colleges and universities. For example, California's most renowned university, Berkeley,

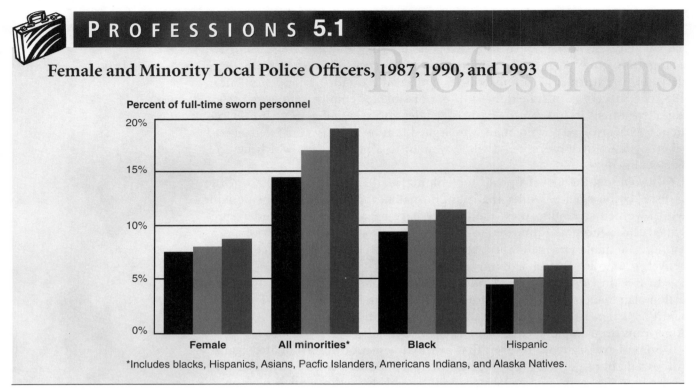

PROFESSIONS 5.1

Female and Minority Local Police Officers, 1987, 1990, and 1993

Percent of full-time sworn personnel

Female   All minorities*   Black   Hispanic

*Includes blacks, Hispanics, Pacfic Islanders, Americans Indians, and Alaska Natives.

Source: Bureau of Justice Statistics, *Local Police Departments, 1993* (Washington, D.C.: U.S. Department of Justice, April 1996), p. 1.

issued admission invitations to only 191 African American students for the fall class of 1998. A total of 8,034 students were offered admission. It was feared that the incoming freshman class would be comprised of only 2 percent African American, compared to 7.3 percent of the class that entered a year earlier. Some students who were offered admission said they would not enroll because of their concern that they will not be welcomed by other students. Others are angry that their friends have not been admitted.[109]

These changes in school enrollments may be a forecast with regard to what might happen in other settings, including police hiring. If minorities believe that their representation in a given police force will be too small, they may not apply. On the other hand, both women and minorities have been involved in policing for a long time although they represent a small percentage of law enforcement officers, and most hold subordinate roles. Still, their numbers have been increasing, and it may be hoped that the recent court decisions on affirmative action programs will not be followed by a reduction in efforts to recruit women and minorities in policing.

A 1996 publication by the Bureau of Justice Statistics reported that the percentage of women in local police departments rose from 7.6 percent in 1987 to 8.8 percent in 1993. During the same period the percentage of African American officers rose from 9.3 percent to 11.3 percent, while the percentage of Hispanics increased from 4.5 percent in 1987 to 6.2 percent in 1993. These data are graphed in Professions 5.1.

WiseGuide Wrap-Up This chapter focuses on some problems and issues connected with policing in a complex society. Political pressures from within the department, along with pressures from the community and other outside forces create problems. Problems may be related to role conflicts of policing. Most officers receive more training in law enforcement than in order maintenance and performance of services. Many of them view policing primarily as law enforcement; superiors may evaluate them by their work in that area. Yet studies reveal that officers spend less time in law enforcement than in other police functions. Nor are the lines always clear regarding law enforcement. For example, today most departments view domestic violence as a law enforcement issue, not a social problem, but not all police administrators, officers, or the public agree. The spread of AIDS has created further problems for police.

Police encounter stress due to the nature of the job and varying citizen expectations, and many citizens have no hesitation in complaining if all police functions are not performed quickly, efficiently, and adequately. The real problem may lie in our unrealistic expectations of police. In theory, we expect them to enforce all laws; but in reality, we will not tolerate full enforcement—police will not and cannot do that, anyway. We expect the police to prevent crime. They have the same expectation, but that is not always possible either. We expect them to be authoritarian in enforcement situations, yet maintain a supportive and friendly approach in others. We expect them to handle all kinds of emergencies, yet we do not provide them the resources or authority for these functions. No matter what police do, they encounter conflicts.

Most important, we cannot separate policing and its context from the rest of our society. The actions of the police "mirror the social relations of American society. Until those relations change we will continue to have a police problem."[110]

Police misconduct is another problem and has been studied widely. Reports vary as to the pervasiveness and nature of misconduct, but it is clear that at least some police are involved in drug transactions and other illegal acts such as sexual harassment and sexual battery. Departmental efforts to eradicate this illegal behavior are not always successful.

Police use of deadly force has become a critical issue in some departments. Police are permitted to use some force, but the *abuse* of that responsibility is the focus of concern. Court decisions have required changes in the use of deadly force, for example, and some police departments have responded with a greater emphasis on proper training in the use of deadly force. In addition, some have established more detailed departmental policies on the use of vehicular pursuits. Despite these changes, some police use excessive force, leading to allegations of police brutality.

Police violence and brutality came into national focus in the widely publicized beating of Rodney King, an African American, by white police officers. Violence against police and police violence against citizens lead to serious repercussions, as illustrated by the deadly and destructive Los Angeles riots after the state acquittals of the officers tried in the Rodney King case. Recent allegations of police violence in New York City have refocused attention on this serious problem of policing.

Efforts to control improper policing have come from department regulations, court decisions, tort actions against police, and improvement of community-police relations. The most controversial of these efforts has been the Supreme Court's exclusionary rule, whereby evidence obtained by police in violation of a suspect's constitutional rights may be excluded from use in that individual's subsequent trial. Recently, the Court has created some exceptions to the exclusionary rule, such as good faith and inevitable discovery. Civil actions against police may serve as a deterrent to improper police behavior, and an increasing number of these suits are being filed under the federal code.

Further problems and issues in policing surround affirmative action programs aimed at employing more women and racial minorities in policing. These groups argue that police cannot understand their problems and gain the support of their members unless they (the group) are represented adequately among police officers and administrators. Others argue that recruitment efforts have lowered standards or that court decisions upholding affirmative action programs for increasing the number of women and racial minorities on a police force are unfair and create internal problems for police. Changes in affirmative action policies in Texas and California are already showing significant decreases in the enrollment of African American applicants; this may be expected in other areas, such as policing, if affirmative action is abolished.

Despite problems in policing, many officers are satisfied with their profession. Problems exist in any profession; and, perhaps, it is good that we are never free of the opportunities for improvement that problems present. Policing is not for everyone; but for those who enjoy a challenging, exciting job in which there is opportunity for service as well as hard work, policing is a viable choice.

Joseph Wambaugh, a former police officer and currently an author of best-selling novels, has assessed his life in both professions. He does not miss the tedium and the bureaucracy of policing, but he does miss the loyalty and camaraderie of his police colleagues. "I find a lot of disloyalty in show business. In police work, it's totally different . . . for the period of time that you're working together [in policing] you are absolutely loyal to each other." In the final analysis, Wambaugh emphasizes that driving a Mercedes rather than a VW is nice, but that he does not consider himself a success now and a failure when he was a police officer. "Being a cop was a good life."[111]

Apply It

1. What external political situations might affect policing?

2. How should police spend most of their time? Why?

3. What is meant by *proactive* and *reactive* policing, and what changes are being made in the former?

4. Describe the problems AIDS creates for police.

5. What is meant by *subculture*? How does that concept apply to policing?

6. Discuss the extent and result of police corruption, with particular reference to the influence of drugs.

7. What is meant by the *fleeing felon rule*? Contrast its historical meaning with the Supreme Court's ruling currently in effect.

8. Discuss police brutality in the context of a recent example.

9. What is the relationship between violence against the police and violence of the police?

10. Distinguish police department regulations and tort actions as methods of controlling policing.

11. State the purpose of the *exclusionary rule* and analyze whether that purpose is being met. What exceptions has the Supreme Court permitted?

12. Explain what is meant by Section 1983 actions.

13. Discuss civil liability that may result from inadequate training of police.

14. What has been the result of efforts to recruit women and racial minorities into policing? What would you recommend for the future?

Notes

1. It is argued that policing does not meet all of the criteria of a profession. See, for example, M. L. Dantzker, "Being a Police Officer: Part of a Profession?" in *Contemporary Policing: Personnel, Issues, and Trends* (Butterworth-Heinemann, 1997).

2. Robert Wasserman and Mark H. Moore, *Values in Policing* (Washington, D.C.: U.S. Department of Justice, November 1988), p. 1.

3. James Q. Wilson, *Varieties of Police Behavior: The Management of Law and Order in Eight Communities* (Cambridge, Mass.: Harvard University Press, 1968), p. 19.

4. Albert J. Reiss Jr., *The Police and the Public* (New Haven, Conn.: Yale University Press, 1971), pp. 63, 64, 71.

5. Richard J. Lundman, "Police Patrol Work: A Comparative Perspective," in *Police Behavior: A Sociological Perspective*, ed. Richard J. Lundman (New York: Oxford University Press, 1980), p. 55.

6. Eric J. Scott, *Calls for Service: Citizen Demand and Initial Police Performance,* National Institute of Justice (Washington, D.C.: U.S. Department of Justice, July 1981), pp. 24–30.

7. Ibid., p. 27.

8. For example, see Bureau of Justice Statistics, *Violence against Women: A National Crime Victimization Survey Report* (Washington, D.C.: U.S. Department of Justice, January 1994); Margo I. Wilson and Martin Daly, "Who Kills Whom in Spouse Killings? On the Exceptional Sex Ratio of Spousal Homicides in the United States," *Criminology* 30 (May 1992): 189–216.

9. "Military Struggling to Stem an Increase in Domestic Violence," *New York Times* (23 May 1994), p. 1.

10. "Domestic Violence Involving Police Growing," *Miami Herald* (18 October 1994), p. 5B.

11. For a brief review of the literature on police training, see Joanne Belknap, "Police Training in Domestic Violence: Perceptions of Training and Knowledge of the Law," *American Journal of Criminal Justice* 14 (Spring 1990): 248–267.

12. Lawrence W. Sherman and Richard A. Berk, *The Minneapolis Domestic Violence Experiment* (Washington, D.C.: Police Foundation, 1984), p. 1.

13. *Attorney General's Task Force on Family Violence,* Final Report (Washington, D.C.: U.S. Department of Justice, 1984), p. 20. For analyses of the research in this area, see Lawrence Sherman, *Police Change Policy on Domestic Violence* (Washington, D.C.: Crime Control Institute, 1986).

14. Franklyn W. Dunford et al., "The Role of Arrest in Domestic Assault: The Omaha Police Experiment," *Criminology* 28 (May 1990): 204.

15. Maryann Syers and Jeffrey L. Edleson, "The Combined Effects of Coordinated Criminal Justice Intervention in Woman Abuse," *Journal of Interpersonal Violence* 7 (December 1992): 490–502.

16. Lawrence W. Sherman, "The Influence of Criminology on Criminal Law: Evaluating Arrests for Misdemeanor Domestic Violence," *Journal of Criminal Law and Criminology* 83 (Spring 1992): 1–45, quotation is on pp. 44–45. See the entire journal for additional information on domestic violence and police intervention. See also *American Sociological Review* 57 (October 1992), which contains four articles on domestic violence, including the relationship between arrest and deterrence; and Jeffrey Fagan, "The Social Control of Spouse Assault," in *New Directions in Criminological Theory*, vol. 4, *Advances in Criminological Theory*, ed. Freda Adler and William S. Laufer (New Brunswick, N.J.: Transaction Publishers, 1993), pp. 187–237. For an overall legal discussion, see "Developments in the Law—Legal Responses to Domestic Violence," *Harvard Law Review* 106 (May 1993): 1501–1507.

17. David A. Klinger, "Policing Spousal Assault," *Journal of Research in Crime and Delinquency* 32 (August 1995): 308–324.

18. Robert C. Davis and Barbara Smith, "Domestic Violence Reforms: Empty Promises or Fulfilled Expectations?" *Crime & Delinquency* 41 (October 1995): 541–552; quotation is on p. 541.

19. For a recent analysis see Eve S. Buzawa and Carl G. Buzawa, "Traditional and Innovative Police Responses to Domestic Violence," in *Critical Issues in Policing: Contemporary Readings* (Prospect Heights, Ill.: Waveland Press, 1997), ed. by Roger G. Dunham and Geoffrey P. Alpert, pp. 243–264.

20. See Watson v. City of Kansas City, Kan., 857 F.2d 690 (10th Cir. 1988). See also Note, "Due Process and Equal Protection Challenges to the Inadequate Reponse of the Police in Domestic Violence Situations," *Southern California Law Review* 68 (July 1995): 1295–1334.

21. Violence against Women Act of 1994, U.S. Code, Title 42, Chapter 136, Section 1381 (1997).

22. The final rule is published in the *Federal Register,* Volume 61, Section 40727-34 (6 August 1996), and is discussed in "DOJ Finalizes Rule Covering Grant Program on Arrest Policies in Domestic Violence Cases," *Criminal Law Reporter* 59 (28 August 1996): 1491–1492.

23. Jerry Dash and Martin Reiser, "Suicide Among Police in Urban Law Enforcement Agencies," *Journal of Police Science and Administration* 6 (March 1978): 18. For an analysis of some of the coping techniques police officers use to adjust to stress, see M. T. Charles, *Policing the Streets* (Springfield, Ill.: Charles C. Thomas, 1986). For a recent analysis of the relationship between stress and suicide among police, see Bruce A. Arrigo and Karyn Garsky, "Police Suicide: A Glimpse Behind the Badge," in *Critical Issues in Policing,* 3d ed., ed. by Dunham and Alpert, pp. 609–628.

24. For a bibliography and discussion of earlier studies, see W. Clinton Terry III, "Police Stress: The Empirical Evidence," *Journal of Police Science and Administration* 9 (March 1981): 67–68, 70. For a more recent overview of police stress, see Larry Miller and Michael Braswell, *Human Relations & Police Work,* 3d ed. (Prospect Heights, Ill.: Waveland Press, 1993).

25. See, for example, the study of Charles E. Faupel and Charles A. Watson, "Undercover Law Enforcement Stress: Some Lessons from the Analogy of Academic Field Research," *Justice Professional* 3 (Fall 1988): 235–254. See also John P. Crank, Robert Regoli, John D. Hewitt, and Robert G. Culbertson, "Institutional and Organizational Antecedents of Role Stress, Work Alienation, and Anomie among Police Executives," *Criminal Justice and Behavior* 22 (June 1995): 152–171.

26. James D. Sewell, "The Boss as Victim: Stress and the Police Manager," *FBI Law Enforcement Bulletin* 57 (February 1988): 15–19.

27. Quoted in Anne Choen, "I've Killed That Man Ten Thousand Times," *Police Magazine* (July 1980), pp. 17–23.

28. *Justice Assistance News* 4 (April 1983): 5.

29. In general see William H. Kroes, *Broken Cops: The Other Side of Policing* (Springfield, Ill.: Charles C. Thomas, 1988). See also Theodore H. Blau, *Psychological Services for Law Enforcement* (New York: Wiley, 1994), reviewed by George T. Bergen in *Criminal Justice and Behavior* 23 (September 1996): 508–515; and Curt R. Bartol, "Police Psychology: Then, Now, and Beyond," *Criminal Justice and Behavior* 23 (March 1996): 70–89.

30. "Stress Therapy Ordered for Cops on Crisis Calls," *Miami Herald* (2 May 1989), p. 2.

31. The U.S. Commission on Civil Rights, *Who Is Guarding the Guardians? A Report on Police Practices* (Washington, D.C.: U.S. Government Printing Office, October 1981), p. 156. The Los Angeles police psychology program, designed to provide therapy for police officers and their families, was begun in 1968 when a pioneer in police psychology, Martin Reiser (sometimes called the father of police

psychology), was employed by the department and given the title of department psychologist.

32. For a discussion of the various problems with AIDS and officers encountered by police departments, see Mark Blumberg, "The AIDS Epidemic and the Police," in *Critical Issues in Policing*, 3d ed., ed. Dunham and Alpert, pp. 214–224. See also Blumberg, ed., *AIDS: The Impact on the Criminal Justice System* (Columbus, Ohio: Merrill Publishing, 1990). For an overview of AIDS, see Clyde B. McCoy and James A. Inciardi, *Sex, Drugs, and the Continuing Spread of AIDS* (Los Angeles: Roxbury Publishing, 1995).

33. See William A. Westley, *Violence and the Police: A Sociological Study of Law, Custom, and Morality* (Cambridge, Mass.: MIT Press, 1970).

34. Rodney Stark, *Police Riots: Collective Violence and Law Enforcement* (Belmont, Calif.: Focus Books, 1972), p. 93.

35. See Arthur Niederhoffer, *Behind the Shield: The Police in Urban Society* (Garden City, N.Y.: Doubleday Publishing Co., 1969).

36. Eric D. Poole and Robert M. Regoli, "An Examination of the Effects of Professionalism on Cynicism among Police," *Social Science Journal* 16 (October 1979): 64.

37. Robert M. Regoli et al., "Police Professionalism and Cynicism Reconsidered: An Assessment of Measurement Issues," *Justice Quarterly* 4 (June 1987): 269. See also the following articles in that journal: Robert H. Langworthy, "Comment—Have We Measured the Concept(s) of Police Cynicism Using Niederhoffer's Cynicism Index?" pp. 278–280; and Regoli et al., "Rejoinder—Police Cynicism: Theory Development and Reconstruction," pp. 281–286.

38. John P. Crank et al., "Cynicism among Police Chiefs," *Justice Quarterly* 3 (September 1986): 343–352. See also Crank et al., "The Measurement of Cynicism Among Police Chiefs," *Journal of Criminal Justice* 15 (1987): 37–48.

39. Dennis Jay Wiechman, "Police Cynicism Toward the Judicial Process," *Journal of Police Science and Administration* 7 (September 1979): 340–345.

40. "Officers' Sexual Attacks Traumatic, Hard to Punish," *Tallahassee Democrat* (30 March 1994), p. 6B.

41. "Reports of Police Misconduct on the Rise," *Tampa Tribune* (16 March 1996), Florida/Metro, p. 4.

42. "Teens Tell of Sex and Drugs with Officer," *St. Petersburg Times* (17 June 1993), p. 3B; *St. Petersburg Times* (15 April 1994), p. 3B.

43. Lawrence W. Sherman, ed., *Police Corruption: A Sociological Perspective* (Garden City, N.Y.: Doubleday, 1974), p. 6.

44. For example, see "Mexico to Combat Police Corruption," *New York Times* (5 June 1991), p. 6.

45. Wilson, *Varieties of Police Behavior*, Ch. 5–7, pp. 140–226.

46. Sherman, ed., *Police Corruption*, pp. 7–8. For a discussion of corruption in four police departments, see Sherman, *Controlling Police Corruption: The Effects of Reform Policies: Summary Report* (Washington, D.C.: U.S. Government Printing Office, 1978). See also Sue Titus Reid, "The Police," in *Current Perspectives on Criminal Behavior*, 2d ed., ed. Abraham S. Blumberg (New York: Alfred A. Knopf, 1981), pp. 124–129.

47. See Sherman, ed., *Police Corruption*, pp. 1–39.

48. *The Knapp Commission Report on Police Corruption* (New York: Braziller, 1972).

49. Herman Goldstein, *Policing a Free Society* (Cambridge, Mass.: Ballinger Publishing, 1977), p. 218.

50. "Pursuing Corrupt Cops," *New York Times* (30 December 1993), p. 12.

51. "Police Corruption in New York Found Rarer but More Virulent," *Criminal Justice Newsletter* 25 (15 July 1994): 1–2.

52. "Explosive Drug Use in Prisons Is Creating a New Underworld," *New York Times* (30 December 1989), p. 1.

53. "Drug Cases Are Upended by the Police in Chicago," *New York Times* (27 December 1997), p. 6.

54. See Thomas J. Hickey and Sue Titus Reid, "Testing Police and Correctional Officers for Drug Use after *Skinner* and *Von Raab*,"

Public Administration Quarterly 19 (Spring 1995): 26–41. The cases are *Skinner* v. *Railway Labor Executives' Association*, 489 U.S. 602 (1989), upholding drug testing among railway workers; and *National Treasure Employees Union* v. *Von Raab*, 489 U.S. 656 (1989), upholding a drug testing program in the U.S. Customs Service for employees who sought promotions to positions involving such activities as carrying firearms or interdiction of illegal drugs.

55. "Anti-Corruption Officer Named to Monitor Philadelphia Police," *Criminal Justice Newsletter* 21 (1 November 1996): 5.

56. Catherine H. Milton et al., *Police Use of Deadly Force*, (Washington, D.C.: Police Foundation, 1977), p. 41. For a recent discussion of police use of excessive force, see Geoffrey P. Alpert and William C. Smith, "How Reasonable Is the Reasonable Man?: Police and Excessive Force," *Journal of Criminal Law and Criminology* 85 (Fall 1994): 481–501.

57. These rules are reprinted in the *Criminal Law Reporter* 58 (25 October 1995): 2001–2006. See also Jeffery T. Walker, "Police and Correctional Use of Force: Legal and Policy Standards and Implications," *Crime & Delinquency* 42 (January 1996): 144–156.

58. Lawrence W. Sherman, "Execution without Trial: Police Homicide and the Constitution," *Vanderbilt Law Review* 33 (January 1980): 74–75.

59. Tennessee v. Garner, 471 U.S. 1 (1985).

60. For a review of changes in the use of deadly force, see Mark Blumberg, "Controlling Police Use of Deadly Force: Assessing Two Decades of Progress," in *Critical Issues in Policing*, 3d ed., ed. Dunham and Alpert, pp. 507–530; and James J. Fyfe, "The Split-Second Syndrome and Other Determinants of Police Violence," in *Critical Issues in Policing*, pp. 531–546. See also Geoffrey P. Alpert, "The Management of Police Driving: Assessing the Risks," in Ibid., pp. 547–565.

61. Geoffrey P. Alpert, National Criminal Justice Reference Service, *Police Pursuit: Policies and Training* (Washington, D.C.: U.S. Department of Justice, 1997), as cited in "Police Tightening Policies on High-Speed Chases, Study Finds," *Criminal Justice Newsletter* 28 (1 July 1997), p. 6.

62. See, for example, David H. Bayley and James Garofalo, "The Management of Violence by Police Patrol Officers," *Criminology* 27 (February 1989): 1–25.

63. See Milton et al., *Police Use of Deadly Force*, pp. 3–4, for a discussion of such findings.

64. Albert J. Reiss Jr., "Police Brutality," *Transaction Magazine* 5 (1968), reprinted in *Police Behavior: A Sociological Perspective*, ed. Richard J. Lundman (New York: Oxford University Press, 1980), pp. 274–275.

65. Ibid., p. 276. See also Albert J. Reiss Jr., *The Police and the Public* (New York: Ballantine Books, 1973).

66. "In Study of Contact with Police, Less than 1% Cite Use of Force," *New York Times* (23 November 1997), p. 14.

67. "Number of Slain Police Officers Is Lowest Since 1960," *New York Times* (1 January 1997), p. 7.

68. Printz v. United States, 117 S. Ct. 2365 (1997).

69. For a discussion of the official FBI data on this topic, see the recently published chapter by Lorie A. Fridell and Antony M. Pate, "Death on Patrol: Killings of American Law Enforcement Officers," in *Critical Issues in Policing*, 3d ed., ed. by Dunham and Alpert, pp. 580–608.

70. Milton et al., *Police Use of Deadly Force*, p. 3.

71. Frances A. Stillman, *Line-of-Duty Deaths: Survivor and Departmental Responses*, National Institute of Justice (Washington, D.C.: U.S. Department of Justice, January 1987), pp. 2, 3.

72. For a history and analysis of controlling policing, see Samuel Walker, "Controlling the Cops: A Legislative Approach to Police Rulemaking," *University of Detroit Law Review* 63 (Spring 1986): 361–391.

73. *Who Is Guarding the Guardians?* p. 35.

74. Ibid., pp. 157, 159. See also pp. 58–79.

75. Weeks v. United States, 232 U.S. 383 (1914); Mapp v. Ohio, 367 U.S. 643 (1961). For a discussion of the implications of Mapp and subsequent cases, see Lawrence Crocker, "Can the Exclusionary Rule be Saved?" *Journal of Criminal Law & Criminology* 84 (Summer 1993): 310–351.

76. Crocker, "Can The Exclusionary Rule Be Saved?," pp. 310–311.

77. Olmstead v. United States, 277 U.S. 438, 485 (1928), Justice Brandeis, dissenting.

78. Elkins v. United States, 364 U.S. 206, 217 (1960).

79. See Stephen H. Sachs, "The Exclusionary Rule: A Prosecutor's Defense," *Criminal Justice Ethics* 1 (Summer/Fall 1982). This journal contains a symposium on the pros and cons of the exclusionary rule and is an excellent source on the topic.

80. Crocker, "Can The Exclusionary Rule Be Saved?" p. 311.

81. See Comptroller General of the United States, *Impact of the Exclusionary Rule on Federal Criminal Prosecutions* (Washington, D.C.: U.S. Government Printing Office, 19 April 1979), p. 1.

82. Colo. Rev. Stat. 8A, Section 16-3-308 (1994).

83. Massachusetts v. Sheppard, 468 U.S. 981 (1984). See also United States v. Leon, decided the same day, 468 U.S. 897 (1984).

84. Arizona v. Evans, 514 U.S. 1 (1995).

85. Maryland v. Garrison, 480 U.S. 79 (1987).

86. Arizona v. Youngblood, 488 U.S. 51 (1988).

87. See People v. Sundling, 395 N.W.2d 308 (Mich.App. 1986).

88. Exclusionary Rule Reform Act of 1997, Omnibus Crime Control Act of 1997, 105th Congress, 1st Session, U.S. senate, U.C. 3 (introduced 21 January 1997).

89. Nix v. Williams, 467 U.S. 431 (1984).

90. New York v. Harris, 495 U.S. 14 (1990), referring to the previous case, Payton v. New York, 445 U.S. 573 (1980).

91. Arizona v. Fulminante, 499 U.S. 279 (1991).

92. U.S. Code, Chapter 42, Section 1983 (1997).

93. "Using Settlements to Gauge Police Abuse," *New York Times* (17 September 1997), p. 1. For an overview of police liability, see Rolando V. del Carmen and Michael R. Smith, "Police, Civil Liability, and the Law," in *Critical Issues in Policing*, 3d ed., ed. Dunham and Alpert, pp. 225–242. See also Victor E. Kappeler and Michael Kaune, "Legal Standards and Civil Liability of Excessive Force," in the same source, pp. 565–578.

94. City of Canton, Ohio v. Harris, 489 U.S. 378 (1989), citations and footnotes omitted. For a discussion, see Geoffrey P. Alpert and William C. Smith, "Defensibility of Law Enforcement Training," *Criminal Law Bulletin* 26 (September/October 1990): 452–58; and Alpert, "*City of Canton, Ohio* v. *Harris* and the Deliberate Indifference Standard," *Criminal Law Bulletin* 25 (September/October 1989): 466–72.

95. *Who Is Guarding the Guardians?* p. 2.

96. For a discussion of these findings, see Paul S. Benson, "Political Alienation and Public Satisfaction with Police Services," *Pacific Sociological Review* 24 (January 1981): 45–64.

97. See Jerome H. Skolnick and David H. Bayley, *The New Blue Line: Police Innovation in Six American Cities* (New York: Free Press, 1986); Albert J. Reiss Jr., *Policing in a City's Central District: The Oakland Story* (Washington, D.C.: National Institute of Justice, 1985).

98. See S. W. Greenberg et al., *Informal Citizen Action and Crime Prevention at the Neighborhood Level: Executive Summary* (Washington, D.C.: National Institute of Justice, 1985).

99. Herman Goldstein, "Toward Community-Oriented Policing: Potential, Basic Requirements, and Threshold Questions," *Crime & Delinquency* 33 (January 1987): 28. See also Peter K. Manning, "Community-Based Policing," pp. 421–432 and Geoffrey P. Alpert and Rogert G. Dunham, "Community Policing," pp. 432–450 in *Critical Issues in Policing*, 2d ed., ed. Dunham and Alpert.

100. *Who Is Guarding the Guardians?* p. vi.

101. National Minority Advisory Council on Criminal Justice, *The Inequality of Justice: A Report on Crime and the Administration of Justice in the Minority Community* (October 1980), pp. 15–16, as quoted in *Who Is Guarding the Guardians?* p. 2.

102. *Who Is Guarding the Guardians?* p. 2.

103. Ibid., p. 154. For a discussion of women in policing see Dorothy Moses Schulz, *From Social Worker to Crime Fighter: Women in United States Municipal Policing* (Westport, CT: Praeger, 1995).

104. Johnson v. Transportation Agency, 480 U.S. 616 (1987).

105. United States v. Paradise, 480 U.S. 149 (1987). For a discussion of the legal issues in affirmative action, see Thomas J. Hickey, Sue Titus Reid, and K. Lee Derr, "Legal Issues in Affirmative Action Policy Development," forthcoming, *International Journal of Public Administration* 19, no. 1 (January 1996): 123–149.

106. See Adarand Constructors, Inc., v. Pena, 515 U.S. 200 (1995), sending a Colorado case back to the lower federal court for retrial under the test articulated by the Court. The case applies only to federal contracts, for the facts involved a federal agency. The Court had held previously that state and local agency policies involving racial classifications should be analyzed under strict scrutiny. See Richmond v. J. A. Croson Co., 488 U.S. 469 (1989).

107. Hopwood et al. v. Texas, 78 F.3d 932 (5th Cir. 1996), *cert. denied,* 116 S.Ct. 2580 (1996).

108. Taxman v. Board of Education, 91 F.3d 1547 (3d Cir. 1996), *cert. granted,* Piscataway Township Board of Education v. Taxman, 117 S.Ct. 2506 (1997), *and cert. dismissed,* 118 S. Ct. 595 (1997).

109. "Black Students May Prefer to Say No to Berkeley," *New York Times* (2 April 1998), p. 1.

110. Michael K. Brown, *Working the Street: Police Discretion and the Dilemmas of Reform* (New York: Russell Sage, 1981).

111. Quoted in Claudia Dreifus, "A Conversation with Joseph Wambaugh," *Police Magazine* (May 1980), pp. 37–38.

Processing a Criminal Case: Criminal Court Systems

INTRODUCTION

The processing of a criminal case involves a complex series of stages that center on the criminal courts. The chapters in Section 3 examine the pretrial, trial, and appellate procedures of criminal court systems. Chapter 6 explores the structure of courts, how they are administered, what role judges play in the court system, and what might be done about the current crisis in courts created by the increase in cases at the trial and the appellate levels.

Attorneys play important roles in the trial of criminal cases. Prosecutors and defense attorneys are seen popularly as fighting their battles in the drama of criminal courtrooms. Their roles are far more complex, however, than the media portrays. Chapter 7 looks at the differences between the prosecution and the defense and analyzes their roles in

INTRODUCTION—Continued

criminal justice systems. Particular attention is given to prosecutorial discretion. The prosecution and defense of a criminal case begin long before the actual trial; in fact, most cases do not go to trial. Chapter 7 also covers pretrial procedures, including the frequently used and highly controversial process of plea bargaining.

Chapter 8 focuses on the trial of a criminal case, examining each step of the trial and explaining the roles of defense, prosecution, and judge in the criminal trial. But perhaps the most controversial process in criminal justice systems is the sentencing of persons who are found guilty. Chapter 8 examines recent trends in sentencing, along with the sentencing process and an analysis of issues raised by sentencing. The chapter closes with a discussion of appeals.

6

Criminal Court Systems

WiseGuide Intro

In recent years, increasing attention has been focused on the role of courts in American criminal justice systems. The importance of courts cannot be overemphasized. Courts supervise most aspects of criminal justice systems. Judges determine whether there is sufficient reason to hold a suspect brought in by the police and whether to grant bail for those who are not dismissed. Judges supervise the actions of the prosecution and defense in pretrial procedures. They decide whether to accept or deny a guilty plea. Judges preside over pretrial hearings and determine crucial issues such as whether evidence may be admitted at trial. They grant or deny motions on other issues, such as motions to dismiss, and they decide whether juries should be sequestered in high profile cases where media exposure may taint jury decision making.

Trials are supervised by courts. The process of sentencing occurs within courts. All motions after conviction, such as motions for a new trial, and all appeals take place within courts. Thus, courts are critical, and the actions that occur within them affect all other aspects of criminal justice systems.

This chapter begins with an introduction to some legal concepts that must be understood for an adequate examination of courts. It examines court structures, pointing out the distinctions between federal and state court systems. Both systems have trial and appellate courts, and those types are discussed and distinguished. The highest court in the United States, the Supreme Court, is examined in more detail.

The second major section of the chapter examines the judge's role. The final section focuses on court congestion and discusses solutions to this major problem.

Key Terms

acquittal
appeal
appellant
appellee
concurring opinion
continuance
dicta
judge
judicial review
magistrate
moot
recusal
sentence disparity
standing
stare decisis
writ of *certiorari*

Learning Objectives

After reading this chapter, you should be able to do the following:

- Discuss the judicial branch of government; define basic legal terminology regarding courts; and distinguish trial and appellate courts.
- Diagram the levels of state and federal court systems and explain what happens at each level.
- Discuss the history and purpose of the U.S. Supreme Court and explain and evaluate its functions and operations.
- Describe the role of judges in criminal trials.

- Explain and evaluate the sentencing role of trial judges.
- Contrast the role of the appellate judge with that of the trial judge.
- List and explain two methods for selecting judges.
- Explain briefly the training, retention, and control of judges.
- Describe court congestion and suggest remedies.

The Judicial Branch of Government

The framers of the U.S. Constitution established three branches of government at the national level—legislative, executive, and judicial—and provided for the establishment of one supreme court. They envisioned a separation of the powers of these three branches, although there is some overlap. Federal judges and justices of the U.S. Supreme Court are appointed by the president, representing the executive branch, and confirmed by the Senate, representing the legislative branch. Because courts have limited enforcement powers, they rely on the executive branch for enforcement of their decisions. The court system must depend on the legislative branch of government for financial appropriations.

In U.S. criminal justice systems a separate judicial branch is viewed as necessary for assuring that the constitutional and statutory rights of citizens are not controlled by political pressures. In practice, however, political pressures may enter into the selection of judges as well as into the organization and administration of courts and the judicial decision making process.

Definitions of Legal Terms

At the outset it is necessary to understand some legal terms and concepts. *Jurisdiction* refers to a court's power to hear and decide a case. This power is given by the constitution or statute that created that court. A court's jurisdiction may be limited to a certain age group (e.g., juvenile courts, with jurisdiction over juvenile delinquency, child custody, and adoption proceedings) or to a particular type of law (e.g., bankruptcy). Some courts have jurisdiction only over minor offenses or *misdemeanors*. Others may hear only the more serious kinds of offenses, called *felonies*. Some courts may hear only civil cases, others only criminal cases. This chapter is concerned primarily with courts that have jurisdiction over criminal cases, although at appellate levels, most courts hear both criminal and civil cases. Thus, civil cases become important to an understanding of court congestion.

It is important to distinguish original and appellate jurisdiction. *Original jurisdiction* refers to the jurisdiction of the court that may hear a case first; that is, the court that may try the facts. *Appellate jurisdiction* refers to the jurisdiction of the court that may hear the case on appeal. When more than one court may hear a case, the courts have *concurrent jurisdiction*. When only one may hear a case, that court has *exclusive jurisdiction*.

Another limitation on courts is that they hear only cases and controversies. Courts do not decide hypothetical issues, and normally they do not give advisory opinions. Only when a dispute involves a legal right between two or more parties will a court hear the case. If the controversy ends before the completion of the trial or the appeal, usually the court will not decide the case because the issue is **moot,** meaning that it is no longer a real case because no legal issue between the parties remains to be resolved. Thus, if a defendant has appealed the exclusion of evidence at trial but the case is decided on a plea bargain, there is no reason for the appellate court to hear the appeal on the evidence issue: that issue is moot once the defendant and the prosecution have agreed to a plea, which has been accepted by the trial court judge.

Because law needs stability, courts follow the rule of *stare decisis* ("to abide by, or adhere to, decided cases"), whereby previous decisions become precedents for current and future decisions. But law is flexible, and courts may overrule (specifically or by implication) their previous decisions, although this is not done often.

It is important to distinguish between the rule of the court and the **dicta** of the judges or justices. *Dicta* refers to judicial comments on issues that are not part of the court's ruling. These comments, even if they represent the opinion of a majority of the court, must be recognized as dicta and not confused with the holding or rule of law of the court. It is not uncommon, for example, for lower court judges or justices or even U.S. Supreme Court justices to state their opinions on capital punishment. In most cases, however, those opinions are just that and are not part of the court's ruling on the facts. For this reason it is necessary to read cases carefully.

Most appellate court judges and justices issue written opinions that are recorded in official reports. Decisions of the Supreme Court are recorded officially in the *United States Reports,* but this official printing takes a couple of years after a case has been decided. Thus, when recent U.S. Supreme Court cases are cited in this text, endnotes reference those cases as printed in the *Supreme Court Reporter* (S.Ct.); the *U.S. Law Week* (USLW); or a legal computer service, such as Lexis or Westlaw, which also provide access to important information, such as the prior decisions in those cases as well as any subsequent court action. Today U.S. Supreme Court cases are available on the World Wide Web shortly after announcement, thus making them available almost immediately to anyone with access to a computer.

Decisions of the Supreme Court are binding on all federal courts and on state courts where applicable; that is, where federal statutory or constitutional rights are involved.

Trial and Appellate Courts

It is important to distinguish trial and appellate courts. Both exist at the state and federal levels. Both are involved in making and interpreting laws, but generally it is said that trial courts try the facts of the case and appellate courts are concerned only with law. There are exceptions.

Trial courts are the major fact finders in a case. The trial jury (or judge if the case is not tried by a jury) answers the basic questions of fact. In a criminal trial, for example, the trial jury decides whether the accused committed the crime for which he or she is being tried; whether a defense (such as insanity) was proved; and so on. In making these findings, the jury considers evidence presented by both the defense and the prosecution. Because the trial judge and jury hear and see the witnesses, it is assumed that they are in a better position than the appellate court to decide whether those witnesses are credible. Thus, it is argued, the appellate court should be confined to issues of law and not be permitted to reverse a trial court's decision regarding ultimate fact issues, such as guilt or innocence.

After the judge or jury has made a decision at the trial level, the defendant, if found guilty, may **appeal** that decision. In a criminal case, the defendant has a right of appeal in state and federal court systems, although he or she does not (except in a few specific cases) have the right to appeal to the highest court.

At the appellate level, the **appellant,** the defendant at trial, alleges errors in the trial court proceeding (for example, admission of an illegal confession or exclusion of minority groups from the jury) and asks for a new trial. The **appellee,** the prosecution at trial, argues that either errors did not exist, or if they did, they did not prejudice the appellant, and therefore a new trial should not be granted.

Appeal cases are heard by judges or justices rather than by juries. The appellate court looks at the trial court record, considers written briefs submitted by attorneys who use these briefs to establish and support their legal arguments, and may hear oral arguments from counsel for the defense and the prosecution regarding alleged errors of law during the trial. The appellate court makes a ruling on those issues. The court may hold that no errors were committed during the trial, in which case the appellate court *affirms* the lower court's decision. It may hold that there were errors but that they did not prejudice the defendant, and thus the conviction stands. The court may hold that there were errors and that one or more of those errors prejudiced the defendant, which means that the defendant could not have received a fair trial. In that case, the appellate court may reverse the case and send it back for another trial with instructions concerning the errors. This process is referred to as *reversed and remanded.* The court may reverse the case *with prejudice,* meaning that no further trials are permitted.

In essence, appellate courts are trying trial courts. This system allows appellate courts to exercise some administrative control over trial courts, thus achieving more uniformity among courts than would exist otherwise. Trial court judges and juries exercise considerable power in criminal justice systems, however, as many cases are not appealed. In cases that are appealed and retried, frequently the lower court reaches the same decision on retrial.

In addition to the power to hear and decide cases on appeal on facts of law in criminal trials, appellate courts have the power of **judicial review** over acts of the legislative and executive branches of government if those acts infringe on freedoms and liberties guaranteed by the state constitutions and the U.S. Constitution. This power of judicial review represents the great authority of courts. The Supreme Court has the power to declare acts of the president or of Congress unconstitutional.

The highest court of each state determines the constitutionality of that state's statutes in relation to its constitution. The Supreme Court is the final decision maker in the process of judicial review of the U.S. Constitution.

The Dual Court System

The United States has a dual court system consisting of state and federal courts, as diagrammed in Figure 6.1. State crimes are prosecuted in state courts and federal crimes are tried in federal courts. State crimes are defined by state statutes. Federal crimes are defined by Congress.

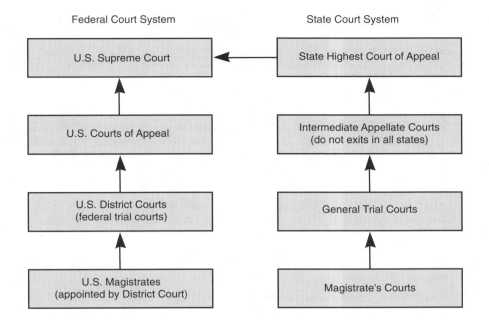

Federal Court System

State Court System

Figure 6.1
The U.S. Dual Court System.
Note: Arrows indicate avenues of appeal generally; there may be some exceptions. State court systems are explained in more detail in Spotlight 6.1.

Some acts violate both federal and state statutes, in which case the defendant may be tried in a state or a federal court or both. For example, the four Los Angeles police officers who were acquitted of charges in a California state court were tried in a federal court for violation of Rodney King's *federal* civil rights; two were convicted.

Lower federal courts and state courts constitute separate systems. Cases may not be appealed from a state court to a federal court except to the U.S. Supreme Court and then only when a federal statutory or constitutional right is involved. Federal and state courts may hear only cases over which they have jurisdiction. Many of the cases brought in federal courts by state inmates are appropriate to those courts because the inmates are alleging that federal rights have been violated.

A close look at the structure and organization of state and federal court systems facilitates understanding of the subsequent material in this chapter, as well as the analyses of pretrial and trial processes in subsequent chapters. This discussion begins with the state court systems since most criminal cases are tried in state and local courts.

State Courts

Considerable variation exists in the organization of state court systems. Diversity exists within states, too, leading to problems that have prompted some states to move toward a unified court system. Despite the variety in systems, it is possible to make some general observations that provide an overview of state court systems. This discussion focuses on courts that process criminal cases (although they may process civil cases, too). The main aspects of the structure, function, and jurisdiction of state courts are summarized in Spotlight 6.1.

Spotlight 6.1

Structure and Jurisdiction of State Court Systems

Court	Structure	Jurisdiction
Highest State Appellate Court (usually called the Supreme Court)	Consists of five, seven, or nine justices who may be appointed or elected; cases decided by this court may not be appealed to the U.S. Supreme Court unless they involve a federal question, and then there is no right of appeal except in limited cases.	If there is no intermediate appellate court, defendants convicted in a general trial court will have a right of appeal to this court, if there is an intermediate appellate court, this court will have discretion to limit appeals with few exceptions such as in capital cases.
Intermediate Appellate Court (also called court of appeals; exists in approximately half of the states)	May have one court that hears appeals from all general trial courts; or may have more than one court, each with appellate jurisdiction over a particular area of the state. Usually has a panel of three judges.	Defendants convicted in general trial court have right of appeal to this level.
General Trial Courts (also called superior courts, circuit courts, district courts, court of common pleas)	Usually state is divided into judicial districts with one general trial court in each district, often one per county. Courts may be divided by function, such as civil, criminal, probate, domestic.	Jurisdiction to try cases usually begins where jurisdiction of lower court ends, so this court tries more serious cases. May have appellate jurisdiction over cases decided in lower courts.
Courts of Limited Jurisdiction (also called magistrate's courts, police courts, justice of peace courts, municipal courts)	Differs from state to state, some states divide state into districts, with each having the same type of lower court. In other states, courts may be located in political subdivisions such as cities or townships, in which case the structure may differ from court to court. May not be a court of record, in which case the system will permit trial *de novo* in general trial court. Particularly in rural areas, magistrates may not be lawyers and may work only part-time.	May be limited to specific proceedings such as initial appearance, preliminary hearing, issuing search and arrest warrants, setting bail, appointing counsel for indigent defendants. Jurisdiction of cases is limited to certain types, usually the lesser criminal and civil cases. Some jurisdictions may hear all misdemeanors; others are limited to misdemeanors with minor penalties.

Courts of Limited Jurisdiction

In discussions about courts, frequent references are made to lower courts. These are the courts of limited jurisdiction, so called because legally they are entitled to hear (that is, have jurisdiction over) only specific types of cases. Usually jurisdiction is limited to minor civil cases and criminal misdemeanors. Jurisdiction over criminal cases may be limited to certain kinds of misdemeanors such as those that carry a jail or short prison term or some other less serious sanction.

Jurisdiction may be limited to certain activities of the courts. The judge or **magistrate** who presides over courts of limited jurisdiction may conduct some pretrial procedures such as issuing warrants for searches or arrests, deciding bail, appointing counsel for indigent defendants, or presiding over the initial appearance or preliminary hearing.

Lower courts, which are called by various names, as noted in Spotlight 6.1, should not be considered unimportant due to their limited jurisdiction. Subsequent chapters illustrate the importance of the pretrial procedures occurring in these lower courts. Certainly the power to grant or deny bail or some other method of pretrial release is a tremendous power. Despite the importance of lower courts, many are underfinanced and staffed by part-time judges who may be political appointees or elected officials in small towns where politics and courts are interrelated.

General Trial Courts

General trial courts are called by various names, too, as noted in Spotlight 6.1. Usually these courts have a wider geographic base than lower courts. In large areas, the general trial court may be divided by functions: traffic cases; domestic cases; civil cases (excluding domestic and traffic cases); probate; estates and wills; and criminal cases. Smaller jurisdictions may have fewer divisions. A civil and a criminal division is one model used frequently.

In most systems the jurisdiction of general trial courts begins where the jurisdiction of the lower courts ends and includes the more serious cases. If the lower court is not a court of record, meaning that the court does not make provision for a transcript of the proceedings, a case appealed from the lower court to the general trial court may be tried *de novo,* which means that the case will be tried again. In that instance, the evidence will be presented again. Over time, however, evidence may be destroyed, and witnesses may die or forget. So the probability of being convicted when a case is tried *de novo* at this level may be lower than the probability of conviction in the lower court.

Administrative Personnel in Trial Courts Both of the court levels discussed thus far are at the trial level. Before considering state appellate courts, we must look briefly at the day-to-day operations of these trial courts. These procedures and their personnel vary among jurisdictions. Some positions and procedures are fairly common.

The *court clerk* is the court officer charged by statute or court rules with the responsibility of maintaining all court records. The court clerk files the pleadings and motions and records any decisions made by the court. These are very important functions because judgments are not enforceable if they have not been filed properly. The court clerk is assisted by a staff, which in large jurisdictions may include a deputy for each of the court's divisions (such as traffic, probate, civil, and criminal). Various personnel may be employed to handle the paperwork of the court.

The *bailiff,* perhaps best known for pronouncing "Hear ye, hear ye, this court of the Honorable Judge Smith is in session, all rise" before the judge's entry into the courtroom, has a variety of functions associated with keeping order. The bailiff may eject or otherwise discipline people who do not observe proper courtroom decorum. The bailiff may transport defendants to and from the court, pass papers and exhibits to and from attorneys and the judge, run errands for the judge, and guard the jury during its deliberations. In some courts a deputy sheriff performs the functions of the bailiff. In federal courts a deputy marshal may serve as bailiff. And in state courts the bailiff's position may carry a different title, such as *court service officer,* or a similar title.

In courts of record, a verbatim account of all proceedings is kept by a *court reporter.* The proceedings are not transcribed unless the parties request it, in which case there is a fee. If a criminal defendant is indigent, the state pays for the transcript when it is required for an appeal. Court reporters may transcribe proceedings outside of court when attorneys are securing evidence for trial by questioning witnesses.

The *minute clerk* is an employee of the court who records an outline of what happens during the proceedings but does not maintain a verbatim account. The minute clerk might record the charges against the defendant, summarize the process of selecting the jury, perhaps note the time spent in that process, list the names of the jurors and alternates, summarize the presented evidence, and record the court's decision.

Intermediate Appellate Courts

All states provide for at least one appeal from an adverse decision in a criminal trial, but only about half of the states have an intermediate appellate court, sometimes called a *court of appeals*. In states that have an intermediate appellate court, only one court may hear all appeals, or courts in various districts may hear appeals from their respective geographical areas. Defendants who have been convicted in general trial courts have a right to appeal to this court where it exists. If it does not exist, they have a right of appeal to the highest court; but if the state has an intermediate appellate court, the defendant may not have a right to appeal to more than one appellate court, except in capital (death penalty) cases. Thus, the defendant who loses an appeal at the intermedial appellate level may have no other appeal unless he or she has other legal issues that might be raised, for example, in a federal court.

Highest State Appellate Courts

If the state does not have an intermediate appellate court, cases may be appealed from the general trial courts to the highest court, which in most states is called the *state supreme court*. Justices of this court may be elected or appointed, and the court may have five, seven, or nine justices. In states having intermediate appellate courts, except in a few types of cases, the highest appellate court has the power to limit the cases it hears and decides. This court has the final decision on cases that involve legal issues pertaining to the constitution or statutes of the state in which the case is brought. If the case involves any federal issues, the defendant may appeal to the U.S. Supreme Court, although that Court hears only a limited number of the cases for which review is requested.

Other states have two final appellate courts. For example, both Texas and Oklahoma have a final court of appeals for criminal cases and a second one for civil cases. Cases may not be appealed from one of these courts to the other.

Federal Courts

In the federal court system, U.S. magistrates, judicial officers appointed by the district court (as noted in Figure 6.1), may have full jurisdiction over minor offenses along with jurisdiction over some of the pretrial steps of more serious offenses. The basic trial courts in the federal system are the U.S. district courts. These courts hear cases in which individuals have been accused of violating federal criminal laws. They try civil cases that meet specified criteria. Each state has at least one federal district court, and some states have several. In the federal district courts, cases are prosecuted by U.S. attorneys and presided over by federal trial judges. These are appointed positions.

Cases appealed from federal district courts go to the appropriate intermediate federal appellate courts. These courts, referred to as *circuit courts*, are called the United States Court of Appeals for the First (Second, and so on) Judicial District. Decisions of the federal courts of appeals are not binding on state courts unless they involve federally created procedural rights that have been held to apply to the states or federally protected constitutional rights such as the right to counsel. The

Careers in Criminal Court Systems

A wide variety of positions exist in criminal court systems. Not all require a law degree, but those of lawyers and judges generally do.

Lawyers perform various functions in court systems. Prosecutors represent the government and prosecute cases, but lawyers also serve as attorneys for those who are accused of violating the criminal law. Lawyers must receive a law degree (usually a three-year program) and pass the bar. Although some states are reciprocal and permit attorneys from other states to practice, many require that the state bar be taken in that state. Some permit attorneys from other states to become members of the bar by taking only part of the exam provided they have passed the bar of another state and engaged in some years of practice.

Most *judges* are lawyers. Some of them have practiced; others have not. Judges may or may not have received special training for their new roles, although it is becoming more common to provide judicial training.

Paralegals may perform some legal functions in criminal court systems, but they are not recognized as lawyers and generally must be supervised by attorneys. They have some legal training, but it is not as extensive as that required for a law degree. *Legal assistants* and *law clerks* may assist attorneys, but they, too, must be supervised. Although the position of law clerk (generally held by law students) usually does not pay well, that is not the case with legal assistant and paralegal positions, which, in some jurisdictions, are relatively high-paying.

Court clerks are in charge of much of the paper work of the court, including scheduling. They are not required to have legal training. *Bailiffs* are court officers who are in charge of keeping order and otherwise facilitating court functions. Often they are sworn deputies and are in charge of security in the courtroom; transporting the accused; escorting the jury to and from the courtroom and ensuring that no one approaches jurors.

Court reporters, who may be contracted by the court, are responsible for taking down verbatim everything that is said "on the record" during the court proceedings, including depositions as well as in-court testimony. Most use a tape recorder in addition to typing by code the exact statements as they are made. Court reporters will provide a transcript of the proceedings should that be needed by the attorneys or the judge. The training for these positions is extensive, and generally the pay is very good. Many court reporters have their own businesses; others are employed by the court.

In larger court systems other professionals might be employed. *Counselors* or *social workers* may be available, along with *psychologists*, *statisticians*, *probation officers*, and clerical personnel.

decision of one federal court of appeals is not binding on another federal court of appeals. If circuit courts decide similar cases differently, the resulting conflict may be resolved only by the U.S. Supreme Court, the final court of appeals in the federal system. The importance of that Court warrants a closer look.

The U.S. Supreme Court, traditionally held in high esteem, has been subjected to criticism since 1982 when some of its own members criticized the Court. In that year a *New York Times* editorial criticized the "diminishing quality of the Court's final product," referring to "wordy opinions ghost-written by law clerks" with little input from justices. But despite the criticisms, the *Times* concluded that the U.S. Supreme Court "remains one of the world's most trusted institutions."[1]

The United States Supreme Court

The Supreme Court is the only specific court established by the Constitution, which designates a few cases in which the Supreme Court has original jurisdiction. The Court has appellate jurisdiction under such exceptions and regulations as determined by Congress. During the debates of the Constitutional Convention, it was recognized that the Supreme Court would have the power to review state court decisions whenever such decisions affected federal rights.

History and Purpose of the Court

The basic function of the Supreme Court is to interpret federal laws and the U.S. Constitution. In fulfilling this function of judicial review, often the Court is accused of making law or of reshaping or changing the Constitution. In response to this allegation, constitutional law expert Paul A. Freund said, "Like a work of artistic creation, the Constitution endures because it is capable of responding to the concerns, the needs, the aspirations of successive generations."[2]

If the Court is to interpret the Constitution according to the concerns, needs, and aspirations of the day, it will be subjected to criticism because these are issues on which reasonable minds differ. Technically, then, the Court does not make, but rather interprets, law. A former member of the Court said that the justices "breathe life, feeble or strong, into the inert pages of the Constitution and of statute books." One constitutional lawyer pointed out that "it matters who does the breathing."[3]

Composition of the Court

Nine justices sit on the Supreme Court. The Court began its 1998–99 term with seven men, one of whom is African American, and two women. William H. Rehnquist is the chief justice and presides over the Court. After controversial confirmation hearings in 1986, Rehnquist was elevated to the position of chief justice, replacing Warren E. Burger, who retired. The vacancy was filled by Anthony Scalia, who was confirmed by a unanimous Senate vote, but subsequent appointments have not been so easy, and most demonstrate the political nature of elevation to the U.S. Supreme Court.

In the summer of 1987, associate Justice William A. Powell, who was frequently the swing vote in the Court's five-to-four decisions, announced his retirement. President Reagan's first nominee was Judge Robert H. Bork, a strong conservative who was on the U.S. Court of Appeals for the District of Columbia. After a bitterly fought (and expensive) confirmation battle, the Senate refused to confirm Bork's nomination. The second nominee, Douglas H. Ginsburg, another conservative, withdrew after admitting that on a few occasions in the 1960s (while he was a college student) and 1970s (while he was a Harvard law professor), he had smoked marijuana.

President Reagan's third appointment was Anthony McLeod Kennedy, a federal appellate judge from California. Judge Kennedy's appointment was confirmed by a Senate vote of ninety-seven to zero. In July 1990 Justice William Brennan announced his retirement. President Bush nominated a relatively unknown judge, David Hackett Souter, a fifty-one-year-old jurist from a small New Hampshire town. Judge Souter was confirmed by the Senate by a ninety-to-nine vote and sworn in as the 105th justice of the Court.

At the end of the Court's 1990–1991 term, Justice Thurgood Marshall, the only African American to sit on the Court, announced his retirement. Justice Marshall was a controversial figure on the Court, highly praised by his supporters and criticized severely by others. Following Marshall's resignation, President Bush nominated another African American, Clarence Thomas, a conservative whose nomination generated considerable debate. Thomas was confirmed, but he received only fifty-two senate votes after lengthy and bitter nationally televised hearings into allegations of sexual harassment. Thomas described the hearings as a "high-tech lynching for uppity blacks," while his accuser, University of Oklahoma (OU) law professor Anita Hill, testified in graphic words of the alleged improprieties. Hill, whose actions provoked debate internationally but especially in Oklahoma, subsequently resigned her position at OU.

In 1993 associate Justice Byron White retired and was replaced by Judge Ruth Bader Ginsburg, a former Columbia University law professor. In 1994 associate Justice Harry Blackmun retired and was replaced by Judge Stephen G. Breyer.[4]

The term of the Court that ended in July 1997 was one of its most notable. Among other issues, the Court upheld the right of states to prohibit physician-assisted suicide; struck down Congress's efforts to regulate indecency on the Internet; held that states may confine some sexual offenders in mental hospitals even after they have served their prison terms; and ruled that Congress does not have the power to force local law enforcement officers to perform background checks on those who wish to purchase handguns. The Court handed down eighty opinions, almost one-half of which were decided by a unanimous vote.[5]

A case gets before the U.S. Supreme Court if the Court grants a **writ of *certiorari*** on an appealed case. A *writ* is an order from a court authorizing or ordering that an action be done. *Certiorari* literally means "to be informed of." When the Supreme Court grants a writ of *certiorari*, in effect, it is agreeing to hear the case appealed from a lower court and ordering that court to produce the necessary documents for that appeal. If the Court denies *certiorari*, it is refusing to review the case. In those instances, the decision of the lower court stands. Four of the justices must vote in favor of a writ in order for it to be granted. If an even number of justices is sitting and there is a tie vote, the decision being appealed is affirmed. In an average term, the Court hears only about 3 percent of the cases filed.[6]

One of the obvious reasons for limiting the number of cases is the time required for oral arguments as well as for the deliberations and opinion writing of the justices. The second reason the Court hears only a percentage of the cases filed was emphasized by a former chief justice of the Court:

> To remain effective, the Supreme Court must continue to decide only those cases which present questions whose resolution will have immediate importance far beyond the particular facts and parties involved.[7]

The Supreme Court may hear cases when lower court decisions on the issues in question have differed. The Court's decision becomes the final resolution of the issue, unless or until it is overruled by a subsequent U.S. Supreme Court decision; by a constitutional amendment; or, in some cases, by congressional legislation.

Cases that are accepted for review by the Supreme Court must be filed within a specified time before oral argument. The attorneys who argue before the Court are under considerable pressure. They may be interrupted at any time by a justice's question. Attorneys are expected to argue their cases without reading from the prepared briefs. Each is limited to thirty minutes (sometimes an hour) for oral arguments. When the Court is in session, Fridays are reserved for conferences during which the justices discuss cases argued before them and decide which additional cases they will hear.

Most Supreme Court decisions are announced in written opinions, which represent majority opinions in most cases. **Concurring opinions** may be written by justices who vote with the Court but disagree with one or more of its reasons; agree with the decisions but for reasons other than those in the Court's opinion; or agree with the Court's reasons but wish to emphasize or clarify one or more points. Thus, in some cases, the opinion of the Court may represent the views of a plurality of the justices. Opinions concurring in part, dissenting in part, and dissenting entirely may be written as well.

Operation
of the Court

Judicial opinions are a very important part of U.S. legal systems. They are read carefully by lawyers, who use the arguments in future cases. The justices circulate among themselves drafts of their opinions, which are printed in secret and remain secret until the Court announces its decision in the case. In this way the entire Court participates in formulating an opinion; rarely is a written opinion the sole product of the justice whose name appears as writer.

Decisions of the Court are handed down on opinion days, usually three Mondays of each month of the term. The announced decisions are public, and the media pick up portions of the decisions thought to be of greatest interest.[8] As noted earlier, decisions of the Court are available on the World Wide Web.

Judges in Criminal Court Systems

Historically, **judges** have been held in high esteem by the U.S. public. In recent years, however, judges have come under severe criticism. In their decisions on pretrial releases, they have been accused of releasing dangerous persons who prey on the public, commit more crimes, and terrorize citizens. In their sentencing decisions, they have been accused of coddling criminals. Judges are easy scapegoats, and some critics are taking the opportunity to accuse judges of causing most of the critical problems in the handling of criminals. Although some of the criticism is justified, much of it is not.

The Role of Judges in Criminal Cases

Judges begin their participation in criminal justice systems long before the trial occurs. Judges determine when there is probable cause to issue a search warrant or an arrest warrant. After arrest, a suspect must be taken before a neutral magistrate, who will determine whether there is probable cause to hold the alleged offender. Judges determine whether the accused is released on bail or some other pretrial procedure or detained in jail awaiting trial.

Judges hear and rule on motions made by the defense and the prosecution before trial. They approve plea bargains made between the prosecution and the defense. Judges play a critical role in the criminal trial. They hear and rule on motions made before, during, and after the trial; and, in most cases they determine the sentences of convicted offenders. Judges at the appellate level determine whether cases should be reversed or affirmed.

The Judge at Trial

At the trial, judges are referees. Theoretically they are neither for nor against a particular position or issue, but rather are committed to the fair implementation of the rules of evidence and law. They are charged with the responsibility of ensuring that attorneys follow the rules.

In the role of referee, the judge has immense power. If the defense makes a motion to have some important evidence suppressed on the grounds that it was obtained illegally, the judge's decision whether or not to grant that motion might be the deciding factor in the case. Without the evidence, the prosecution might not be able to prove its case. Likewise, the judge's decision to admit evidence offered by the defendant, such as the testimony of a psychiatrist regarding the defendant's mental state, may be the deciding factor in the ability of the defense to convince the jury of its position.

Although trial judges' decisions may be appealed, most are not. Many decisions that are appealed are not reversed, and even if the defense wins on appeal, considerable time has been lost—time that might have been spent by the accused in jail. Furthermore, the U.S. Supreme Court has emphasized that it is important to *prevent* problems at trial whenever possible, and that responsibility of prevention lies with the trial judge.[9]

An important responsibility of the trial judge is to rule on whether expert testimony may be admitted. Many issues in criminal cases are beyond the common knowledge of jurors; so it is necessary to submit expert testimony. In addition to deciding whether the area of expertise is acceptable, the judge must determine whether the offered expert is qualified to testify about that evidence. Generally judges make these decisions after hearing oral argument from the defense and the prosecution, and some judges require written motions by attorneys prior to those arguments.[10]

Another responsibility of the trial judge is to decide whether there is sufficient evidence to send the case to the jury for a decision on the facts being argued or whether the case should be dismissed for lack of evidence. Even if the judge sends the case to the jury and the jury finds the defendant guilty, the trial judge may reverse that decision if he or she believes the evidence is not sufficient to determine guilt beyond a reasonable doubt. This power is given to judges so they may serve as a check on jurors who might be influenced by passion or prejudice despite the evidence in the case.

The role of the trial judge in deciding whether to accept a jury verdict is illustrated by the recent case of the trial and conviction of Louise Woodward. This case, called the au pair case, is discussed in Spotlight 6.2.

After hearing the evidence in a case, a judge may direct the jury to return a verdict of **acquittal**. This may be done even before the judge hears all the evidence, or it may be done even after a jury verdict of guilty. Once the verdict of acquittal has been entered, however, the defendant may not be retried on the same issue; to do so would violate the defendant's constitutional right not to be tried twice for the same offense.

Another role of the judge is to instruct the jury regarding the law in the case it must decide. In addition, the judge must monitor all activities of the trial, making certain that the defendant's constitutional and statutory rights are protected, that all rules and regulations are followed, and that all participants and spectators (including the media) behave appropriately. This is a difficult task in some cases, as illustrated by the Unabomber trial, which began in January 1998. The defendant, Theodore J. Kaczynski, accused of mailing bombs that injured and killed some of the recipients, led police and the FBI on the longest manhunt in history. Kaczynski, a former math professor, had disagreed with his court-appointed defense attorneys over the use of an insanity defense, which he opposed. On the first day of the scheduled trial, Mr. Kaczynski said he had important matters to discuss with the judge, and that led to a delay in the trial.[11] Before the rescheduled trial began, a plea bargain was reached. Kaczynski's guilty plea spared him the death penalty.

In all of these and other activities at trial, not only the decision but also the demeanor and the attitude of the judge are important. The judge's behavior may influence the attitudes and decisions of jurors, witnesses, and victims at trial as well as the general public's image of criminal justice systems. In addition, the judge influences the flow of cases through the criminal courts. Poor management of the caseload contributes to court congestion and risks impairing the rights of defendants to a fair and speedy trial.

Spotlight 6.2

Judicial Power in Question: The Au Pair Case

In a case that gained international media attention in 1997, Louise Woodward, aged nineteen, was convicted of second-degree murder in the death of Matthew Eappen, eight months old. Woodward is the British au pair whom Matthew's parents hired to take care of the baby and his older brother. Woodward was charged with murder after she called 911 on February 4 to report that Matthew was not responsive. The prosecution argued that Woodward shook the baby and knocked his head against a wall or the tub. The defense claimed that Matthew died of a skull injury that he had incurred several weeks prior to his death.

The defense asked the judge to instruct the jury on murder charges only, taking the gamble that if the jury had to choose between murder and acquittal for Woodward, they would choose acquittal. They were wrong. After deliberating for twenty-seven hours, the jury found Woodward guilty of second-degree murder.

Trial judge Hiller B. Zobel listened to arguments from both the defense and the prosecution; took a few days to contemplate; then announced his decision: Louise Woodward's conviction of second-degree murder was not supported by the evidence. "Having considered the matter carefully, I am firmly convicted that the interests of justice . . . mandate my reducing the verdict to manslaughter. I do this in accordance with my discretion and my duty."[1]

The judge ruled that had the jury been instructed on manslaughter, it might have chosen that option, which he believed was one rational conclusion based on the evidence. He did not believe the evidence supported a murder conviction. At a subsequent hearing the judge sentenced Woodward to the time she had already served and set her free. Woodward has returned to England. Her appeal seeking a declaration of her innocence in Matthew's death was unsuccessful.

The Woodward case illustrates the power of the judge to change a jury's decision if he or she believes such is required in light of the evidence. Some argue that is a plus in the system; others argue that it is unreasonable and unfair. The Massachusetts Society for the Prevention of Cruelty to Children published a letter signed by forty-nine child abuse specialists, stating that the prosecution's expert evidence at trial was overwhelmingly supportive of the theory that Woodward shook the baby and thus caused his death. The defense argued that the blood clots that caused Matthew's death were several weeks ago. The case appeared to turn on the controversial scientific evidence, and perhaps one result of the case will be a closer look at the presentation of such evidence in criminal trials.[2]

Judge Zobel has been the subject of high praise for his courage and the object of criticism, with one columnist referring to him as the "second coming of Lance Ito," the controversial judge in the O.J. Simpson case. The judge has vowed not to talk about the Woodward case.[3]

1. "Excerpts from the Judge's Decision Reducing Conviction of Au Pair," *New York Times* (11 November 1997), p. 16.
2. "Pediatric Experts Express Doubt on Au Pair's Defense," *New York Times* (12 November 1997), p. 14.
3. "Judge in Au Pair Case now Is Being Judged," *St. Petersburg Times* (21 November 1997), p. 4.

The Judge at Sentencing

The role of the judge at sentencing is one of the most important of all judicial functions. Despite the tremendous importance of sentencing, until recently little attention was paid to preparing judges for this decision. Nor was there any emphasis on the importance of thorough presentence reports by probation or other officers of the court, to assist judges in making the decision. Likewise, little attention was given to appellate review of judicial sentencing.

Concern with the extensive power judges had over sentencing, along with other sentencing issues, have led to sentence reform, which is discussed in Chapter 8. Clearly the purpose of most of the reform efforts has been to reduce judicial sentencing power. Some of the alleged disparity results from a consideration of legally acceptable factors, such as prior record and nature of the current offense.

Spotlight 6.3

Controversial Judicial Sentences

A Florida judge angered citizens when he overrode a jury's recommendation for the death sentence for Lavarity Robertson, who had shot and killed two teenage sweethearts six years previously. When the judge announced his decision, the mother of one of the victims "threw herself on the floor outside the courtroom and howled in protest, . . . My daughter begged for her life and he shot her nine times. . . . Now her killer asks for mercy and they give it to him."[1]

Like all judicial decisions this one should be analyzed more carefully. The jury sentence had been appealed, with the state supreme court sending the case back for resentencing, ruling that the state had not proven the elements of a death penalty case. A second jury recommended the death penalty, but the judge ruled that there were more mitigating and aggravating factors in the case and sentenced the defendant to life.

National public reaction and outrage followed another judicial sentencing in 1994. A defendant found guilty of murdering his wife after he found her in bed with another man was sentenced to eighteen months in prison and fifty hours of community service in a domestic violence program. The defendant shot his wife in the head shortly after he had found her, consumed wine and beer, and argued with her, with a time lapse between when he caught her with her lover and when he fired the first shot. This lapse of time might lead one to conclude that a "heat of passion" defense was not applicable and thus should not have been considered in sentencing.

The judge compounded the issue by stating, "I seriously wonder. . . . how many men married five, four years would have the strength to walk away without inflicting some corporal punishment," adding that he imposed a prison term because he felt obligated to "make the system honest." A *New York Times* editorial on the case was headlined, "She Strays, He Shoots, Judge Winks."[2] A subsequent investigation concluded that the judge had not abused his discretion in this case.

The other side of the controversy over judicial sentencing is that judges complain that mandatory minimum sentences are too strict in many cases and that they are powerless to impose what they consider to be reasonable sentences.[3]

1. "Life Sentence Outrages Victims' Kin," *Miami Herald* (29 July 1994), p. 1B. The case is Robertson v. State, 611 So.2d 1228 (Fla. 1993).
2. *New York Times* (22 October 1994), p. 14.
3. "Judges Irked by Tough-on-Crime Laws," *American Bar Association Journal* 80 (October 1994): 18.

However, some of the differences may be the result of unacceptable factors such as gender, age, and race of defendants, as well as of the personalities, backgrounds, and prejudices of the sentencing judges. Therefore, before concluding that judicial sentencing differences are unfair, unreasonable, or unconstitutional, it is important to consider all the variables involved in the decision-making process.

The sentencing decision is a difficult one; it may be impossible to achieve justice at this stage. As one judge concluded, "I am sure that I speak for my many colleagues when I state that the imposition of a criminal sentence is the most delicate, difficult, distasteful task for the trial judge."[12] This may be the case, but citizens will continue to express anger at judicial sentences such as those noted in Spotlight 6.3.

The Appellate Judge

Appellate court judges have a tremendous responsibility. In those courts having the power to decide which cases they will hear, judges or justices must decide whether to hear a case.

We have noted that the decisions of trial judges may be reversed on appeal. In most cases, however, appellate courts defer to trial courts on issues in which the trial judge has an advantage because of his or her direct observation of the events that occurred at trial. Only a fraction of cases are reversed on appeal, but those cases are important not only to the individual defendants but to the justice system as well.

Frequently, appellate judges and justices are faced with interpreting the laws and constitutions of their jurisdictions in ways that will have an effect on more than the parties before the court. In that respect, their decisions have a much broader impact than the decisions of trial courts. Usually their decisions, in contrast to those of trial courts, are accompanied by written opinions, thus placing an even greater responsibility on judges to articulate why they decided a specific issue in a particular way.

Judicial Selection, Training, and Retention

The first issue in deciding how to select, train, and retain judges is to decide which qualities are desired. Historically, judges have been white, male, and Protestant, with conservative backgrounds. Only recently have more women and minorities joined the judiciary, and scholars continue to debate whether race and gender impact judicial decision making. Most recently, for example, two scholars studied judicial decision making of female as compared to male judges and found women to be "somewhat harsher (i.e., more likely to incarcerate and impose longer sentences)," especially "toward repeat black offenders."[13]

Although President Clinton promised that the judges he appointed to the federal bench would look more like the average American, a 1997 report emphasized that the average net worth of Clinton's 1996 appointees was $1,024,188, a record at that time. His appointees in 1997, however, had (with their spouses) an average net worth of $1,798,670. Fifteen of those nominees, including seven women, are millionaires.[14]

Although minority judges remain in short supply, the number of women has increased in recent years. In 1997 nine women served as chief justice of state supreme courts and seventy women had been appointed to state supreme courts; the total serving was 357. The 1997 figures, compared to those of 1995, represent a tripling of women serving on the highest state courts.[15]

Judges should be impartial and fair. They should be able to approach a case with an objective and open mind concerning the facts. If for any reason a judge cannot be objective in a case, he or she should withdraw from that case, a process known as **recusal**. Objectivity enables the judge to be fair, to insist that attorneys play by the rules of the game, and to see that due process is not violated. Judges should be well educated in substantive law, procedural rules, and evidence. Judges should be able to think and write clearly. Their opinions are of great importance to attorneys and other judges who use them to analyze how future cases might be argued and decided. Judges should have high moral and ethical standards, enabling them to withstand political and economic pressures that might influence decisions. They should be in good physical, mental, and emotional health. They should be good managers, because judges have considerable power over the management of the court system. They should be able to assume power sensibly, without abuse, and to exercise leadership in social reform where necessary and desirable.

The late Irving R. Kaufman, a federal judge on the Second Circuit, addressed the issue of the qualities and characteristics that should be considered in the selection of federal judges, but his suggestions are applicable to state and local judges. According to Kaufman,

> a judge's comportment must at all times square with the ideals of justice and impartiality that the public projects on us in our symbolic role. A judge must be reflective, perhaps even a bit grave, but must always demonstrate an openness consistent with our tradition of giving each side its say before a decision is rendered. [A judge should be able to] separate the dignity of the office from a sense of self-importance.[16]

Finding persons with the desired judicial qualifications is not always easy. Several methods have been used for selecting judges in the United States. During the colonial period, judges were appointed by the king, but after the Revolution, this practice ceased. In a majority of the colonies, judges were appointed by the legislators. In some the appointment was made by the governor, with or without the required approval of his council, depending on the colony.

As the colonies became states, gradually they began to select judges by popular election, but that method came under criticism, with frequent allegations that undue political influence led to the selection of incompetent and corrupt judges. In 1991 forty-one states used the election process for some of their judges. In that year the U.S. Supreme Court held that the Federal Voting Rights Act, which provides that it is illegal to maintain voting practices that have the effect of discriminating on the basis of race, covers judicial elections.[17]

Another method of selecting judges, the merit plan, is traced to Albert M. Kales, one of the founders of the American Judicature Society. The first state to adopt the merit plan was Missouri in 1940. This method is referred to as the *Missouri plan* or, less commonly, the *Kales plan* or the *commission plan.*

Merit selection plans vary extensively from state to state, but most plans include a nonpartisan commission that solicits, investigates, and screens candidates when judicial openings occur. The commission sends a select number of names (usually three to five) to the executive branch, where an appointment is made. The new judge may serve a probationary period (usually a year) and may be required to run unopposed on a general election retention ballot. Voters are polled with a yes or no vote to decide whether this judge should be retained in office. A judge who receives a majority of votes (which is usually the case) will be retained. A merit selection plan does not assure that politics will not enter into the selection process, but arguably the prescreening by a nonpartisan commission places only qualified candidates in a position for election. Criticisms remain, however, and politics plays an important role.[18]

In an effort to avoid public pressures on judicial decision making, federal judges are appointed and hold their jobs for life. Technically, they are appointed by the president of the United States and confirmed by the Senate, but usually the recommendations to the president are made by the attorney general or the deputy attorney general, and the president accepts those recommendations. Members of the House and Senate are influential in nominating these judges, although the Justice Department consults bar associations such as the American Bar Association. The constitutional provision for the appointment of federal judges and justices has been interpreted to mean that they hold their appointments for life. They may be removed only for bad behavior, but this seldom occurs.

Most U.S. jurisdictions do not have required formal training for judges, although training is required in many other countries. Despite the lack of a requirement for judicial training in order to be eligible to become a judge, we are making progress in providing training programs for newly appointed or elected judges. Most states provide some training, and many are offering continuing education courses for judges already on the bench.

Recruiting the right kind of attorneys and giving them proper training in the judiciary is important, but retention of our best judges is becoming a serious problem. In the past a judicial appointment, especially to the federal bench, was the ultimate aim of many lawyers. But the increasing number of resignations of federal judges has led some to refer to the "revolving door" of the federal judiciary, with some of the best candidates refusing nominations or accepting them, staying a few years, and then leaving. For those who do stay, morale may be affected as they realize the substantial pay cut they take by leaving private practice to accept an appointment to the bench.

Judicial salaries vary significantly from state to state. Although generally salaries are higher at the federal level, the level of compensation of federal judges was described by the late Judge Irving R. Kaufman, in an open letter to President Reagan: "And as you know, we receive for our services little more than those fresh-faced lads a few years out of Harvard at the larger New York firms."[19] Salaries of federal judges have been increased since Judge Kaufman made that statement, but they remain too low to attract many qualified attorneys.

Added to the problems of low pay (compared to attorneys of their experience in private practice) and heavy workloads is the stress that judges experience. Judges handle issues that are very important and highly controversial but must be decided. As Judge Kaufman said, "Much tension accompanies the job of deciding the questions that all the rest of the social matrix has found too hard to answer."[20]

In addition to stresses that may be faced by any professional person, judges face several stressors not common to other professions. There is a lonely transition from the practice of law to a profession about which they may know very little except as outside observers. Usually at the peak of their legal careers when they become judges, they must give up many of their positions and even their friendships. Additional stresses on judges come from the judicial code of conduct that places limitations on a judge's financial and social life. For example, contacts that might compromise a judge's decisions must be avoided; close associations with attorneys who might appear before them must be restricted; and they are restricted in terms of when and with whom they may discuss cases.

One final area of stress is the increased violence encountered by judges, as courtrooms in some parts of the country have been invaded by the violence that threatens peace and safety in the rest of American society. In high profile cases it is customary now to have extra courthouse security, such as metal detectors and additional security personnel.

Judicial Control

At the opposite extreme of the problem of how to retain good judges is the delicate issue of how to get rid of bad ones. Like all other professions, the judiciary is characterized by some who fall below the line in their professional and personal lives. Their shortcomings may affect their abilities to function effectively as judges. Although the sexual behavior of most adults may be considered their private business as long as it is consensual and does not involve minors, the public considers it their business when judges engage in questionable sexual behavior. Sexual harassment by anyone is unacceptable, but sexual harassment by a judge is even more shocking. Excessive drinking may be tolerated in some circles, but excessive drinking by a judge, particularly one charged with driving while intoxicated, is another matter.

How do we control such judicial activities? It is not easy to unseat judges even after they have been convicted of a crime. Usually they are asked to resign, but if they do not do so, it may take a lot of time to go through disciplinary channels to unseat them. Elected judges may be unseated by a recall vote. When judges are appointed, however, the process is more difficult. At the federal level, where judges serve for life and may be removed only by impeachment, legislation provides some avenues for disciplining judges. The Judicial Councils and the Judicial Conduct and Disability Act of 1980 provide for several sanctions: certify disability, request the judge to retire, strip the judge of his or her caseload "on a temporary basis," and censure or reprimand privately or publicly.[21]

Another method for controlling judicial misconduct and compensating those who are victimized by judges is to permit federal civil rights charges to be brought against the judges. In 1997 the U.S. Supreme Court considered a case appealed from a lower federal court, which had held that the federal civil rights statute involved in a Tennessee case does not provide notice that it covers simple or sexual assault crimes. The Court held that the statute need not specify the *specific* conduct covered and sent the case back for the lower court to reconsider the issue in light of the Court's holding that the rule is "whether the statute, either standing alone or as construed [by other federal courts or the U.S. Supreme Court], made it reasonably clear at the relevant time that the defendant's conduct was criminal."[22]

The case of *United States* v. *Lanier* involves allegations that Judge David Lanier sexually assaulted five women in his judicial chambers. Judge Lanier had presided over the divorce and custody hearings of one of the complainants. It was alleged that when the woman interviewed for a secretarial position at the courthouse in which he worked, Judge Lanier suggested to her that he might have to reexamine her daughter's custody case. The woman charged that as she left the interview the judge "grabbed her, sexually assaulted her, and finally committed oral rape."

Judge Lanier was convicted in 1992 and served two years of his twenty-two year sentence before a federal appeals court released him on his own recognizance after its decision that the statute did not apply to the facts of his case. After the U.S. Supreme Court heard the case, ruled that the statute in question does apply, and sent the case back to the lower court, that court ordered Judge Lanier to appear on 22 August 1997 for a hearing. He did not appear; the court issued a warrant for his arrest and subsequently dismissed his appeal. The judge was located and arrested two months later in Mississippi, where he was living under an assumed name. In December 1997 he entered a plea of guilty to eluding arrest to avoid prison.[23] The judge is back in prison, now serving a twenty-five-year sentence.

Crisis in the Courts

Numerous problems exist in our criminal courts, some of which are mentioned in the discussions in this chapter. But by far the most serious problem is the pressure placed on courts, on defendants, and on society by the increased numbers of cases tried and appealed. This increase has led to a crisis in our courts, and the crisis continues despite the addition of more judges in state and federal courts. For example, at the end of fiscal year 1996, the backlog of criminal cases in federal district courts was 41,731 cases involving 68,867 defendants. Of those, 67 percent had been pending for thirty-six months or less; 58 percent had been pending for 24 months or less. In federal civil courts 101,209 cases were pending.[24] Spotlight 6.4 contains additional information about the increases in federal civil and criminal caseloads.

The greatest number of criminal offenses in federal criminal courts fall into the categories concerned with drugs, leading the Federal Courts Study Committee to recommend in a 1990 report that most drug cases be tried in state courts.[25] In addition to drug cases, federal court cases have increased because of the increased number of offenses that have been made *federal* offenses by statute. Chief Justice Rehnquist has warned against this trend of "one new federal statute after another," but his warnings have not been heeded.[26]

Shifting federal cases to state courts might ease the problem in federal courts, but state courts face case backlogs, too. Chief Justice Rehnquist has emphasized that the crises in state courts are greater than those in federal courts, with many

Spotlight 6.4

Fiscal Year 1998 Statistical Highlights: U.S. Federal Courts

Criminal Prosecutions

Criminal case filings increased by four percent

- Immigration filings up by 42 percent
- Environmental offense filings up by 38 percent
- Government regulatory offense filings up by 13 percent
- Health care fraud filings up by seven percent

Civil Litigation

Civil cases increased by six percent

- Affirmative civil litigation up by three percent
- Defensive civil litigation up by eight percent

Settlements increased by nine percent

- Thirty percent of all civil cases settled

Eighty-four percent of judgments rendered in favor of the United States

- Ninety-six percent of judgments in affirmative cases in favor of the United States

Criminal and Civil Appeals

Total number of appeals increased by four percent

- Criminal appeals up by one percent
- Post-sentence motions filed by incarcerated defendants up by 59 percent
- Civil appeals up by nine percent
- Eighty-three percent of criminal appeals terminated in favor of the United States
- Eighty-two percent of civil appeals terminated in favor of the United States

Source: *United States Attorneys Annual Statistical Report, Fiscal Year 1996* (Washington, D.C.: U.S. Department of Justice, March 1997), front matter, no page numbers.

systems facing serious funding cuts. Rehnquist concluded, "It seems likely for the foreseeable future that a regime of fiscal austerity will predominate at the national and state levels."[27]

The Chief Justice continued his fight for decreasing the caseload in federal courts by alleging in early 1998 that part of the problem of backlog is the result of the failure of the Senate to confirm President Clinton's recent appointments to the federal judiciary. In addition, Rehnquist argued that overcrowding in federal courts has resulted from the failure of Congress to provide more positions for federal judges while increasing the jurisdiction of federal courts. The Senate's chair of the Judiciary Committee, Senator Orrin G. Hatch, dismissed that allegation, noting that we have more federal judges now than ever before, and shifted the blame to the White House and President Clinton for slowness in making nominations.[28]

The rapid increase in court caseloads has raised serious questions: is public safety jeopardized when the outcome of criminal cases can be delayed for many months or even longer, and when, in order to accommodate criminal cases, courts delay civil cases for years?

Court congestion results in delayed trials. It is argued that justice delayed is justice denied. That concept is based on the belief that when a trial is delayed, there is a greater chance for error. Witnesses may die or forget. Crowded court dockets have created pressures that encourage plea bargaining and mass handling of some cases. Delayed trials may deny defendants their constitutional right to a speedy trial.

For the accused who are not released before trial, court congestion may mean a long jail term in already overcrowded facilities. Because their court-appointed attorneys are so busy with other cases, defendants may not see them during that period. The accused are left with many questions, no answers, and a long wait, often under inhumane conditions in local jails. Those who are incarcerated before trial face more obstacles in preparation for trial.

Obvious injustices are created by overcrowded courts that must decide cases presented by overworked prosecutors and defense attorneys. The image of inefficiency and injustice that the crowded court dockets and delayed trials project colors public perceptions of the legal system.

In addition to the overcrowded court dockets, there are other reasons for court delays. One is the use of **continuances,** or postponements. The purpose of granting continuances is to guarantee a fair hearing. The defense or the prosecution may need more time to prepare; additional evidence might have come to light and need evaluating; additional witnesses may need to be located. Too often, however, continuances are used by defense attorneys to collect their fees.

A second reason for congestion in criminal courts is that courts must handle some cases that perhaps should be processed in some other way. The criminal law is used in an effort to control behaviors such as some types of alcohol and drug abuse, consenting sexual behavior between adults in private, prostitution, and gambling. This is not to suggest that we should be unconcerned with these activities but only to question the reasonableness of using the criminal law for their regulation. Removal of some or all of these actions from the criminal court system would reduce the number of cases in those courts.

A third reason for court congestion may be the filing of frivolous lawsuits. This occurs in civil cases, but some inmates have filed numerous and frivolous lawsuits as well. These lawsuits may involve allegations of violations of federal constitutional rights in prison, but some of them are civil cases. For example, one plaintiff filed five products liability lawsuits in one year in New York. He alleged that a scoop of yogurt contained glass that cut his mouth and paralyzed his lip; his head was burned by Revlon's Flex protein conditioner; a can of shaving cream exploded in his face; a television set caught fire and burned his clothes; and a Nuprin tablet caused severe kidney damage and left him comatose. The judge dismissed the cases, stating that the court "cannot tolerate this type of cynical abuse of the judicial process." The normal punishment is to fine the abuser, but in this case the plaintiff is serving time in prison; so the judge removed his word processor, computer, printer, and any other instruments used in filing the frivolous claims. The plaintiff-inmate was barred from filing any new products liability cases with the court without the judge's permission, and he was ordered to pay a $5,000 fine to the court clerk.[29]

Many suggestions have been made for solving court congestion. The first is to reduce the number of offenses covered by criminal law. Building new court facilities and expanding the number of judges, prosecutors, defense attorneys, and support staff is another possible solution. Better management of court proceedings and court dockets is another. Court personnel need to update their equipment and make use of improved technology. Some courts are using computers to speed up the paperwork. Other courts have been reorganized for greater efficiency.

Other suggestions are to utilize lay judges, volunteers who would handle misdemeanor cases such as disorderly conduct, petit larceny, prostitution, and criminal mischief, as a method of relieving pressures in the regular court system. Volunteers may be used as prosecutors in some cases, while special courts, such as drug courts, are "better than standard courts at keeping addicts from repeating their crimes."[30]

Another suggestion is the use of alternatives to courts, based on the assumption that in many cases courts could be avoided. Although most of the alternatives, such as arbitration and mediation, apply primarily to civil cases, some are used in criminal cases. The expanded use of plea bargaining, whereby defense and prosecution reach an agreement out of court, is an example. This practice is used frequently and is discussed in a subsequent chapter, along with the controversy that surrounds its use.

The costs of these proposals must be evaluated. We are not talking only about the cost of increasing the judiciary. Expanding courts and increasing the number of judges involve the direct cost of the expansions along with support staff and an increase in the number of prosecutors, defense attorneys, courtrooms, other facilities, and police and correctional personnel and facilities.

WiseGuide Wrap-Up   An understanding of the nature and structure of criminal court systems is necessary for a study of the activities taking place within those systems. Terminology is important, too. If a court does not have jurisdiction, it cannot hear and decide a case. Cases must be brought before the proper court, and this may be determined by the seriousness of the offense, the type of offense, or both. Some courts may hear criminal cases; others may hear civil; some may hear both. Some may hear petty offenses or misdemeanors, whereas others may hear felony cases.

Trial courts must base their decisions on facts that will or will not establish whether the defendant committed the alleged criminal act or acts. Usually appellate courts are concerned only with questions of law. They ask, "During the trial, did the trial court commit any serious errors in law, such as the admission of evidence that should have been excluded, and if so, was that error prejudicial to the defendant's right to a fair trial?" If so, the case is reversed and sent back for retrial. The appellate court might find less serious errors in law and not reverse the case.

Criminal cases may be appealed but not necessarily to the highest court. Cases in the state system may not be appealed to the lower federal appellate courts. If a federal constitutional right is involved in a state case, the Supreme Court of the United States may hear that case. Cases decided in state courts must be followed in the states in which they are decided but are not binding on other states' courts.

Decisions on one level or jurisdiction may be used by other courts as reasons for their decisions if the judges choose to do so. Decisions of the U.S. Supreme Court are binding on state and lower federal courts. But, because the Supreme Court hears only a few of the cases it is asked to hear, many issues remain unsettled, for courts in different jurisdictions decide similar cases differently.

The primary figure in court efficiency and administration is the judge. Despite the importance of judges in U.S. court systems, many who become judges are not trained in judicial decision making or trial and appellate procedures. Some have had limited experience as trial lawyers. Yet they are given vast powers in criminal justice systems. Most perform admirably; some need to be disciplined or removed, but the system is not very well equipped for those processes.

Today courts are criticized for being in a state of crisis as a result of the large backlog of cases, criminal and civil, at both the trial and the appellate levels. Some steps must be taken to reduce this backlog; lawyers and judges have a great responsibility to solve this problem. But the role of the public is important, too.

Significant changes cannot be made in court systems without public support, especially financial. It is imperative to realize that changes must be made in all areas of criminal justice systems. Significant changes in the courts have an effect on the other elements of criminal justice systems. If we create more courts so we can try, convict, and sentence more people to prison and do not build sufficient and adequate facilities to accommodate that increase, we push the problems from one area of the systems to another. Courts must be analyzed and altered in the total social context in which they operate.

Apply It

1. Distinguish the judicial from other branches of government.

2. What is meant by *jurisdiction*? How does it apply to the dual court system?

3. What is the difference between trial and appellate courts?

4. What is the relationship between state and federal courts?

5. What are the levels of courts in each of the two main court systems, state and federal?

6. What is the purpose of the U.S. Supreme Court, and how does a case get before that Court? What happens to a case that is appealed to but not accepted by that Court? What changes would you suggest in the operation of the Supreme Court in order to handle the increasing workload it faces?

7. What are the main roles of judges in trial courts? In appellate courts?

8. How are judges and justices selected? What are the advantages and disadvantages of each method?

9. Should an effort be made to recruit more female and minority judges? Why or why not? What methods would you suggest if you think more should be recruited?

10. What actions do you think should be sufficient to disqualify a person for a state judgeship? A federal judgeship? Appointment to the U.S. Supreme Court?

11. To what extent, if any, should public opinion be permitted to influence judicial appointments? Judicial retention?

12. How would you suggest that the current caseload crisis in trial and appellate courts be resolved?

Notes

1. "Supreme Court Blues," *New York Times* (4 October 1982), p. 18.
2. Paul A. Freund, *On Law and Justice* (Cambridge, Mass.: Harvard University Press, 1986), p. 54.
3. "Court at the Crossroads," *Time* (8 October 1984), p. 28, referring to a remark by Floyd Abrams in response to the earlier remark by former U.S. Supreme Court Justice Felix Frankfurter.
4. For a concise, overall view of those who have served on the U.S. Supreme Court, see the article by Alexander B. Smith and Harriet Pollack, "Quality Control and the Supreme Court," *Criminal Law Bulletin* 29 (January/February 1993): 3–18.
5. "Benchmarks of Justice," *New York Times* (1 July 1997), p. 1.
6. "Quiet Times: The Supreme Court Is Reducing Its Workload—But Why?" *American Bar Association Journal* 80 (October 1994), p. 40. For a concise but comprehensive guide to the operation of the Supreme Court, as well as a discussion of the political influences on the Court, see Lawrence Baum, *The Supreme Court*, 3d ed. (Ridgely, Md.:

Congressional Quarterly Books, 1989). For an analysis of the first one hundred years of the Court, see William H. Rehnquist, "The Supreme Court: 'The First Hundred Years Were the Hardest,'" *University of Miami Law Review* 42 (January 1988): 475–490.
7. Chief Justice Fred M. Vinson, quoted in *Criminal Justice Procedure*, 2d ed., Ronald L. Carlson (Cincinnati, Oh.: Anderson, 1978), p. 243.
8. For more information on how the Supreme Court operates, see the account by Chief Justice William Rehnquist, *The Supreme Court: How It Is. How It Was* (New York: Morrow, 1987).
9. See, for example, Sheppard v. Maxwell, 384 U.S. 333 (1966).
10. For a case illustrating the power of the trial judge regarding the admission of expert testimony, see State v. Hansen, 751 P.2d 951 (Ariz. 1988).
11. "Unabomber Trial Halted Abruptly as Suspect Battles his Defense," *New York Times* (6 January 1998), p. 1.
12. United States v. Wiley, 184 F.Supp. 679 (D.Ill. 1960).

13. Darrell Steffensmeier and Chris Hebert, "Women and Men Policymakers: Does the Judge's Gender Affect the Sentencing of Criminal Defendants?" submitted for publication.

14. "Courting the Young and the Rich," *USA Today* (17 March 1997), p. 3.

15. "Idaho's New Chief Justice Helps Break Glass Ceiling," *New York Times* (23 February 1997), p. 20.

16. Irving R. Kaufman, "An Open Letter to President Reagan on Judge Picking," *American Bar Association Journal* 67 (April 1981): 443.

17. "High Court Considers Election of Judges," *New York Times* (23 April 1991), p. 11. The case is Houston Lawyer's Association v. Attorney General of Texas, 501 U.S. 380 (1991).

18. See, for example, "ABA Judicial Ratings Draw Fire," *American Bar Association Journal* 80 (November 1994): 38.

19. Kaufman, "An Open Letter," p. 444.

20. Quoted in "By and Large We Succeed," *Time* (5 May 1980), p. 70.

21. Judicial Councils Reform and Judicial Conduct and Disability Act of 1980, Pub. L. No. 96-458, incorporated into Complaints of Judicial Misconduct or Disability, USCS Ct. App. Fed. Cir. R 51 (1994). See also Michael J. Broyde, "Expediting Impeachment: Removing Article III Federal Judges after Criminal Conviction," *Harvard Law Journal & Public Policy* 17 (1994): 157–222.

22. United States v. Lanier, 117 S.Ct. 1219 (1997), *and vacated,* 114 F.3d 84 (6th cir. 1997), *subsequent appeal,* 120 F.3d 640 (6th Cir.), *appeal dismissed,* 123 F.3d 945 (6th Cir. 1997).

23. "Former Judge, a Sex Offender, Pleads Guilty to Fleeing," *Buffalo News* (31 December 1997), p. 5.

24. *United States Attorneys Annual Statistical Report, Fiscal Year 1996* (Washington, D.C.: U.S. Department of Justice, March 1997, front matter), no page numbers.

25. "Panel Recommends Shifting Drug Cases to State Courts," *Criminal Justice Newsletter* 21 (16 April 1990): 1.

26. "Troubling Review: Rehnquist Sees Rough Times Ahead of Federal and State Courts," *American Bar Association Journal* 80 (January 1994): 94.

27. Ibid.

28. "Senator Blames White House for Concerns in Rehnquist Report," *USA Today* (2 January 1998), p. 9.

29. "Judge Ensures Frivolous Suits Will Stop," *St. Petersburg Times* (30 March 1994), p. 9.

30. Michael Higgins, "Drug War on the Cheap," *American Bar Association* 83 (August 1997): 24.

Prosecution, Defense, and Pretrial Procedures

WiseGuide Intro

The adversary philosophy that characterizes U.S. criminal justice systems applies not only to the trial and appeal of a criminal case but to many activities that occur prior to trial. The purpose of this chapter is to discuss those critical pretrial procedures, but first, it is necessary to examine the role that lawyers play. Underlying the adversary philosophy is the belief that the best way to obtain the facts of a criminal case is to have an advocate for each side, presenting witnesses who are subjected to examination by the opposing side. The advocates are the attorneys: the prosecutor or **prosecuting attorney** (also referred to as the district attorney, the state's attorney, the attorney general, deputy attorney general, assistant attorney general, and so on) representing the state (or federal government in a federal case) and the **defense attorney** representing the accused. Each side may have more than one attorney assisting in the case.

The prosecutor and the defense attorney are important figures at various stages in criminal justice systems. This chapter examines the important functions of each side and then focuses on the pretrial procedures in which they engage, along with the judge and other participants in criminal cases. The chapter begins with a general overview of lawyers and the legal profession.

Key Terms

arraignment
assigned counsel
bail
bond
booking
defense
defendant
defense attorney
depositions
discovery
expert witness
grand jury
indictment
information
initial appearance
interrogatories
lineup
motion
nolo contendere
plea bargaining
preliminary hearing
presentment
preventive detention
pro se
prosecuting attorney
prosecution
public defender
right to counsel
showup
subpoena
true bill
venue
waiver

Learning Objectives

Learning Objectives

After reading this chapter, you should be able to do the following:

- Discuss briefly the historical background of the legal profession.
- Explain the organization and structure of prosecution systems.
- Recognize the importance and problems of prosecutorial discretion regarding whether to prosecute.
- Explain the role of the defense attorney.
- Explain and analyze the right to be represented by defense counsel.
- Discuss the reasons for private defense counsel in contrast to public defense counsel.
- Distinguish public defender systems, assigned counsel, and contract systems for defense counsel.

- Explain the meaning of effective assistance of counsel and the right to refuse counsel.
- List and explain the major steps in the criminal justice process before trial.
- Explain the importance of bail to defendants.
- List and explain the ways in which a defendant may be released pending trial.
- Explain the process of entering a plea in a criminal case.
- Discuss the arguments for and against plea bargaining.

Lawyers and the Legal Profession

Lawyers have created controversy historically throughout the world. One of Shakespeare's characters in *Henry VI* exclaims, "The first thing we do, let's kill all the lawyers." The English poet John Keats said, "I think we may class the lawyer in the natural history of monsters." Lawyers have been "charged with the practice of witchcraft, demagoguery, corrupting justice, hypocrisy, charging outrageous fees, pleading unjust causes, and misusing language."[1]

During the seventeenth century, the American colonies operated under a legal system without lawyers. Lawyers were so distrusted and scorned that most people handled their own cases. The Puritans preferred to keep law and religion as one. Their "law" was the Bible, and many of their criminal laws were taken verbatim from the Bible. In Massachusetts it was illegal for a lawyer to take a fee for his work. For seventy years after Pennsylvania was settled, the colony had no lawyers.[2]

As legal matters became more complicated, people began to recognize the need for experts trained in law, and the legal profession developed into one of power and wealth. In the fifty years before the American Revolution, the profession flourished. Of the fifty-five men who served in the Continental Congress, thirty-one were lawyers; twenty-five of the original signers of the Declaration of Independence were lawyers.

Between 1830 and 1870, as a result of the rejection of anything English and out of fear of a legal aristocracy, the American bar fell into disfavor again. During this frontier era, with its dislike for specialists, practicing law was considered a natural right. Michigan and Indiana permitted any person of good moral character to practice law if he were a voter. After 1870 there was a move toward professionalism, which resulted in the improvement of legal education, licensing of lawyers, higher admission standards, and the beginning of a strong bar association.[3]

The image of lawyers improved in the United States, and in the 1900s public opinion polls revealed that generally lawyers were accorded high prestige.[4] In 1975, however, a Louis Harris public opinion poll found that "the public had more confidence in garbage collectors than in lawyers, or doctors or teachers."[5]

The image of the legal profession in the United States was tarnished by the criminal activities of high-level politicians during the administration of President Richard M. Nixon. Prosecution of some of those politicians in the Watergate scandal (so-called because of the illegal entrance into offices in Washington, D.C.'s Watergate, a building containing condominiums as well as offices and businesses) led to prison terms. Many of the people involved in Watergate were attorneys. In addition to violating the law and the ethics of the legal profession, they violated the ethical principles of many Americans. According to one writer, the result was that "the pedestal on which lawyers traditionally have been placed is crumbling faster than at any other time in history."[6]

During the years since the Watergate scandal, the image of the legal profession has remained tarnished. The highly publicized and internationally televised trial of O. J. Simpson, acquitted of murder in the deaths of his ex-wife and her friend, also exacerbated that tarnished image.

Attacks on lawyers have come from within the legal profession, too. The 1977 criticisms by Chief Justice Warren Burger of the U.S. Supreme Court were publicized widely. Burger warned that society was moving toward excessive litigation, and he predicted that if we did not stop that trend and devise "substitutes for the courtroom process . . . we may well be on our way to a society overrun by hordes of lawyers hungry as locusts competing with each other, and brigades of judges in numbers never before contemplated." Justice Burger recognized the great contribution lawyers have made in the United States but warned that "unrestrained, they can aggravate the problem."[7]

A lack of understanding of the adversary system may influence the public's image of lawyers, especially of those who practice in criminal justice. The public's image of justice may be confused with the attorney's obligation to protect the adversary system. It is said that on one occasion a federal judge drove Supreme Court Justice Oliver Wendell Holmes in a horse-drawn carriage to a session of the U.S. Supreme Court. The judge said, "Well, sir, good-bye. Do justice." Justice Holmes turned and scowled. "That is not my job. My job is to play the game according to the rules."[8]

The discussion looks first at the prosecution—then at the defense.

Prosecution

The **prosecution** of a criminal case refers to the process by which formal charges are brought against a person accused of committing a crime. Formal prosecutions are a modern phenomenon. In the American colonies, although an attorney general or prosecutor had the authority to initiate prosecutions, many criminal prosecutions were left to the alleged victims. There was considerable abuse of the system, with some victims initiating criminal prosecutions in order to pressure a **defendant** to make financial settlements with them. Because the penalties for many criminal offenses were severe, it was not uncommon for the accused to settle financially, thus, in effect, buying freedom from criminal prosecution.

Such abuses led to the exercise of the power of public prosecution by the colonial attorney general. Soon it became evident that one attorney general and one colonial court could not handle all the prosecutions in a colony. Gradually, a system developed by which prosecutors in each county would bring local prosecutions in the emerging county courts. These county prosecutors were viewed as local and autonomous, not as arms of the colonial government.[9]

The system of public prosecution differed from colony to colony. Some counties distinguished between violations of state statutes and of local ordinances and had a separate prosecution system for each. Today all states have local and state prosecution systems. Local jurisdictions may have local ordinances applicable only to those jurisdictions, and local prosecutors are responsible for prosecuting violations of those ordinances. Serious offenses are designated by state statutes, although generally they are prosecuted in local courts by local prosecutors. A federal system of prosecution exists as well.

The Organization and Structure of Prosecution Systems

Most local and state prosecutors are elected officials, although the elected prosecutor may appoint other attorneys to serve as deputy (or assistant) prosecutors within the office. Election means that prosecutors may be subject to the pressures of local and state politics, but it is argued that the election of this important official makes the person more accountable to the people. Prosecution systems may be categorized as local, state, or federal.

Local prosecution systems exist at the rural, suburban, and urban levels. The advantages of rural prosecution are numerous. Generally, small towns and rural areas have lower crime rates, and case processing may be more informal. Caseloads are lighter, so rural district attorneys may have more time to prepare cases. Most prosecutors are acquainted with the other lawyers, judges, and court personnel on a professional as well as a social level. Most cases are handled individually; and most personnel, from the judge to the probation officer, may give each case considerable attention.

In rural areas most cases are settled by guilty pleas. Since rural judges and juries tend to give harsher sentences, defense attorneys are less likely to advise taking cases to trial, and more defendants are willing to plead guilty without a trial. Rural prosecutors handle a different type of population and different types of cases than urban prosecutors. Violent crimes such as armed robbery or murder are rare.[10]

One disadvantage of *rural prosecution* is that salaries are low; many prosecutors maintain a private law practice in order to survive financially. Another disadvantage is that many rural prosecutors must function without a full-time staff, adequate office equipment, or resources to investigate crimes. Criminal justice systems may be affected, too: when the sole prosecutor has an unexpected illness or emergency, the court cannot process cases. The *suburban prosecutor* has more funds and resources than the rural office. The land development, population increases, and growth in the tax base in suburban areas provide greater resources for their criminal justice systems.[11]

The third type of local prosecution system is that of *urban prosecution*, which is more complex than rural and suburban prosecution because the volume of crime is higher in most large urban areas and includes the more serious personal crimes of violence, such as armed robbery and murder. Caseloads are higher, too. Some urban prosecutors are so busy that they may not see the files of cases involving less serious offenses until a few minutes before they arrive in court to prosecute the cases.

Generally, the salaries of urban prosecutors are not competitive with those of attorneys in private practice, and for that reason it is difficult to attract the most qualified attorneys. Many who do become prosecutors may not stay long because of low salaries or job burnout, or because they view the job as only a training ground. On the positive side, most salaries for urban prosecutors are higher than those in suburban and rural areas. Offices are also better equipped and better staffed, and some attorneys find the variety in the types of crime prosecuted in large cities to be a challenge not found in other areas of legal work.

Urban prosecution offices may include programs not available in smaller offices. In recent years, many urban prosecution offices have added programs for crime victims and witnesses. Special prosecutors may be trained to work with rape victims and children who are victims of sexual and other forms of abuse.

A second major type of prosecution occurs at the state level. These systems differ from state to state, but most are headed by a state attorney general, usually an elected official, who is the chief prosecutor for the state. The attorney general has jurisdiction throughout the state for prosecuting violations of state statutes, although some of that responsibility may be delegated to local levels. The attorney general may issue opinions on the constitutionality of state statutes. He or she may appoint assistant attorney generals.

Many young attorneys view the office of the state attorney general as an excellent place to begin a legal career. The legal experience to be gained at this level of prosecution is excellent preparation for other kinds of law practice. It provides young lawyers with valuable contacts in the legal profession.[12]

The final type of prosecution system occurs at the federal level and was provided for by the Judiciary Act of 1789. Federal prosecutors are called *U.S. attorneys.* They are appointed by the president (who often accepts the recommendations of the members of the Senate and House of Representatives from the area in which the U.S. attorney will work) and approved by the Senate. These officials and their assistant U.S. attorneys, along with other lawyers in the U.S. Department of Justice, have jurisdiction for prosecuting alleged violations of federal statutes. Additional information on federal prosecutors is featured in Professions 7.1

The U.S. Department of Justice (DOJ) is headed by the attorney general, an attorney who is appointed by the president and confirmed by the Senate. After President Bill Clinton made two unsuccessful nominations, his third appointee, Janet Reno, was confirmed. She is the first female U.S. attorney general.[13]

U.S. attorneys are responsible to the attorney general, to whom they report through the deputy attorney general, but generally they are free to develop their own priorities within the guidelines provided by the DOJ. This freedom may result in greater job satisfaction for the attorneys who occupy these positions and provide the needed flexibility for federal prosecutions to be concentrated on the types of crime characteristic of specific areas. But it may also result in different types of law enforcement throughout the federal system, which in turn may lead to charges of unjust practices.

The Prosecutor's Role

According to the American Bar Association, the "duty of the prosecutor is to seek justice, not merely to convict."[14] In a criminal case the prosecutor is responsible for bringing charges against persons accused of committing crimes, assessing the evidence and deciding whether to plea bargain a case, recommending to the judge that the charges be dropped, or, if the case goes to trial, developing and presenting the evidence against the accused. Prosecutors also participate in the sentencing phase of a trial. Most of these functions are discussed later; the importance of this section is to assess the role of discretion in prosecutorial decisions whether to charge or proceed with a case.

The prosecutor in most jurisdictions has virtually unlimited discretion in deciding whether to bring formal charges against the accused. Statutes vary among the states, but generally they provide that the prosecutor or assistant prosecutors of a particular jurisdiction shall appear at all trials and shall prosecute all actions for crimes committed in their jurisdictions. These statutes have been

PROFESSIONS 7.1

Federal Prosecutors

At the federal level cases are prosecuted by attorneys who are called *United States Attorneys* or U.S. Attorneys. The chief prosecutor is the Attorney General, currently Janet Reno. The positions are political appointments and require a law degree. Special prosecutors may be appointed by the attorney general. An example is the appointment of Kenneth Starr to head the investigation of allegations of impropriety by President Bill Clinton, his wife, and their associates in the failed Whitewater venture. Although he was criticized for taking his investigations further and delving in allegations of sexual improprieties by the president, Mr. Starr was authorized by attorney general Janet Reno to extend his investigation into those allegations.

Some of the functions of U.S. attorneys, along with their method of appointment, are described in this excerpt:[1]

> The United States Attorneys serve as the chief Federal law enforcement officers within their respective districts. They are appointed by the President, confirmed by the Senate, and report to the Attorney General through the Deputy Attorney General. Each United States Attorney is responsible for establishing law enforcement priorities within his or her district. Each United States Attorney is also the chief litigator representing the United States in civil judicial proceedings in the district. The United States Attorneys, too, carry out the important role of liaison with Federal, state and local law enforcement officers and members of the community on programs such as the Attorney General's Anti-Violent Crime Initiative, juvenile violent crime and drug demand reduction, and the Weed and Seed Program. . . .
>
> Assistant United States Attorneys constituted 54 percent of all Department of Justice attorneys and about 60 percent of those Department attorneys with prosecution or litigation responsibilities. Most new Assistant United States Attorneys have prior litigation experience with a prosecuting attorney's office, a law firm, or another government agency. In addition to their prior legal experience, Assistant United States Attorneys nationwide have an average of eight years' experience in United States Attorneys' offices.
>
> While the civil caseload is larger numerically, about 75 percent of the United States Attorneys' personnel were devoted to criminal prosecutions and 25 percent to civil litigation. Ninety percent of all attorney work hours spent in United States District Court were devoted to criminal prosecutions and ten percent to civil litigation. . . .
>
> The United States Attorneys continued to make the best use of resources during Fiscal Year 1996 by promoting coordination and cooperation among Federal, state and local law enforcement through continued use of their Law Enforcement Coordinating Committees (LECC). The LECCs bring together Federal agencies such as the Federal Bureau of Investigation, Drug Enforcement Administration and Bureau of Alcohol, Tobacco and Firearms, along with state and local prosecutors' offices, state police agencies, and local sheriffs' and police departments, thereby enhancing the effectiveness of the criminal justice system. . . .
>
> The United States Attorneys, their Assistants, Victim-Witness Coordinators and other members of their staffs worked with community, business, and social service representatives to provide assistance to the victims and witnesses of crime, to identify and address the particular violent crime problems within their local communities, to develop and implement prosecution and redevelopment strategies for selected neighborhood sites under the Weed and Seed program, and to encourage and initiate local activities to deter both drug use and violent crime among America's children.

1. *United States Attorneys Annual Statistical Report* (Washington, D.C.: U.S. Department of Justice, 1997), pp. 1–3.

interpreted to mean that prosecutions must be brought by prosecutors or their assistants and not that *all* crimes brought to the attention of the prosecutor must be prosecuted. Consequently, prosecutors have the discretion to refuse to prosecute; this discretion is virtually unchecked.

> A decision to prosecute or not to prosecute is to be accorded judicial deference in the absence of a showing of arbitrariness, gross abuse of discretion or bad faith. . . . It is fundamental that the mental processes of public officials by means of which governmental action is determined are generally beyond the scope of judicial review.[15]

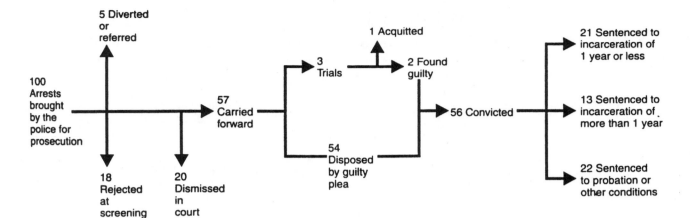

Figure 7.1

Typical Outcome of One Hundred Felony Arrests Brought by the Police for Prosecution.

Source: Barbara Boland et al., *The Prosecution of Felony Arrests, 1987* (Washington, D.C.: U.S. Department of Justice, August 1990), front cover.

Potential abuse of prosecutorial discretion has led to suggestions that limits be placed on that power.[16] It is clear that most people accused of crime are not prosecuted, and there may be rational reasons for this practice, one of which is the limitation of time and resources. Of those who are prosecuted, most do not proceed through all stages of the criminal justice system. Figure 7.1 graphs what happens to one hundred typical arrestees. Note that five are diverted or referred, which means the prosecutor refers them to another agency, such as a drug treatment facility. Of each one hundred cases, eighteen are rejected at screening, meaning that the prosecutor refuses to prosecute those cases. Over one-half, fifty-seven, are carried forward; fifty-four of those are disposed of by a guilty plea, while three are tried, resulting in one acquittal and two guilty verdicts. Of the fifty-six convicted by either a plea before trial or a trial verdict, only thirteen are incarcerated for more than one year.

What influences decisions whether or not to prosecute? It is, of course, possible that extra-legal factors such as race, ethnicity, or gender may influence a prosecutorial decision. If so, the accused may have legal recourse, but it is difficult to win these cases. In 1996 the U.S. Supreme Court decided an important case on prosecutorial discretion. In *United States* v. *Armstrong* the Court held that a defendant who alleges racial bias regarding a prosecutorial decision must show that similarly situated persons of other races were not prosecuted. In *Armstrong* African American defendants argued that because of their race they were selected for prosecution for alleged crack cocaine violations. The Court held that they had not met the requirements for proving race discrimination.[17] In an earlier case involving alleged prosecutorial discrimination, the Supreme Court said, "The conscious exercise of some selectivity in enforcement is not in itself a federal constitutional violation."[18]

It is important to understand that practical reasons such as lack of resources may lead to a refusal to prosecute, especially cases that involve a lot of time, resources, and expense. Other reasons are summarized in Spotlight 7.1. These reasons may apply also to a prosecutor's decision to request a dismissal after a case has been filed.

Once the prosecutor decides to prosecute, he or she must decide the appropriate charge(s) to bring. Many criminal statutes overlap. Some offenses are defined by degrees of seriousness, such as first- or second-degree murder. There may be sufficient evidence that the suspect has committed a number of crimes. The prosecutor must decide which charges to make in each case, and there is no

Spotlight 7.1

Reasons for Prosecutorial Rejection or Dismissal of Some Criminal Cases

Many criminal cases are rejected or dismissed because of

- *Insufficient evidence* that results from a failure to find sufficient physical evidence that links the defendant to the offense

- *Witness problems* that arise, for example, when a witness fails to appear, gives unclear or inconsistent statements, is reluctant to testify, is unsure of the identity of the offender or where a prior relationship may exist between the victim/witness and offender

- *The interests of justice,* wherein the prosecutor decides not to prosecute certain types of offenses, particularly those that violate the letter but not the spirit of the law (for example, offenses involving insignificant amounts of property damage)

- *Due process problems* that involve violations of the Constitutional requirements for seizing evidence and for questioning the accused

- *A plea on another case,* for example, when the accused is charged in several cases and the prosecutor agrees to drop one or more of the cases in exchange for a plea of guilty on another case

- *Pretrial diversion* that occurs when the prosecutor and the court agree to drop charges when the accused successfully meets the conditions for diversion, such as completion of a treatment program

- *Referral for other prosecution,* such as when there are other offenses, perhaps of a more serious nature in a different jurisdiction, or deferral to Federal prosecution.

Source: *Report to the Nation on Crime and Justice,* 2d ed. Washington, D.C.: U.S. Department of Justice, 1988), p. 73.

requirement that the suspect be charged with all possible crimes. In jurisdictions in which separate charges may not be prosecuted in the same trial, or for other reasons, prosecutors may bring charges only in the more serious charges.

Once the prosecutor has decided on specific charges, formal charges must be made. The law specifies where and how those charges are to be filed with the court. The prosecutor prepares an **information,** a document that names a specific person and the specific charge(s) against that person. The information is only one method by which formal charges are made. The second method is an **indictment** by a **grand jury,** which is discussed on p. 187. There are cases in which the law requires a formal grand jury indictment, but even then, the prosecutor may have considerable influence over the grand jury's decision. Although the grand jury is viewed as a safeguard against unfounded criminal charges, and thus serves as a check on the prosecutor, most grand juries follow prosecutors' recommendations,[19] especially in urban jurisdictions faced with a large number of alleged criminal violations, many of which may be serious crimes. In smaller jurisdictions, especially in rural areas, grand juries may have more time to consider cases and thus be less influenced by prosecutors.

When charging decisions are made, most prosecutors have scant evidence about the defendant or the alleged crime. Charging decisions may be based on intuition, personal beliefs about the usefulness of punishment, the relation of the crime to the possible penalty, or even personal bias or prejudice. Most prosecutors must make charging decisions without adequate guidelines or established goals. Where goals and guidelines exist, they differ from one jurisdiction to another. However, some general goals of prosecution are commonly accepted.

One goal for charging decisions is crime reduction. Prosecutors attempt to control crime by prosecuting and, therefore, incapacitating offenders and presumably deterring potential criminals. Charging practices may be affected by decisions to concentrate on cases involving repeat offenders and the use of habitual criminal statutes with enhanced penalties. In other words, persons convicted of multiple specified crimes may be given larger prison terms than they could receive for each crime cumulatively.[20] In addition, crime control efforts may focus on high-rate, dangerous offenders, as mentioned earlier.

Another goal of charging decisions is the efficient use of resources in the prosecutor's office. Funds and staff limit the number of cases that can be processed. The cost of prosecuting some cases may be too great, and charging decisions must emphasize early case disposition in offices that cannot afford many full trials. Still another goal may be the rehabilitation of the defendant. The prosecutor may set the level of charge for a defendant with the goal of moving that person into an alternative treatment program such as job training or alcohol or drug rehabilitation rather than incarceration in prison.

Prosecutors have even more discretion than police. The arrest power of the police may be minimized by prosecutors who refuse to file formal charges against arrestees. Although the prosecutor has no direct control over the police, this power to decline prosecution may affect the way police operate. If the prosecutor refuses to prosecute certain types of cases, the police may stop making arrests when suspects appear to have violated those offenses. On the other hand, vigorous prosecution of some kinds of offenses might encourage police to be more diligent in arresting for those offenses. In some cases, prosecutors and police cooperate in their efforts to reduce crime.[21]

Prosecutorial discretion cannot be eliminated, but it can be subjected to some controls. One method is for the prosecutor's office to establish guidelines and policies. This has been done in some offices as prosecutors realize the need for innovative practices. Another method is the establishing of statutory guidelines. For some years, the U.S. Department of Justice has had the *United States Attorney Manual*, which contains some guidance for prosecutorial decision making. However, not until a 1980 directive from the attorney general of the United States did we see "the first public pronouncement of prosecutorial policies ever issued by the Department of Justice."[22] Some states have established prosecutorial guidelines.[23]

A third way to control prosecutorial discretion is by the exercise of judicial review. Defendants who think they have been treated unfairly might appeal their convictions on the basis of prosecutorial misconduct. This is possible but difficult, as noted in the discussion above concerning the *Armstrong* case. The landmark case using the equality principle to overturn a prosecutor's decision is a century old. In 1886 the U.S. Supreme Court held that if the prosecutor uses a law that is fair and impartial as written and applies it with "an evil eye and an unequal hand" so that the prosecutor creates discrimination, the defendant has been denied equal protection of the laws, and the decision may be overturned.[24]

Overcharging is another type of prosecutorial abuse for which judicial review may be a remedy. Prosecutors abuse their discretion when they file charges that are not reasonable in light of the evidence available at the time the charges are filed. Overcharging may be done on purpose to coerce the defendant to plead guilty to a lesser charge.

Allegations of overcharging are difficult to prove. Prosecutors may charge a suspect with any crime for which there is sufficient evidence to connect that person. If the prosecutor decides not to file the most serious charges that could be filed, and if the defendant refuses to plead guilty to the lesser charges, the prosecutor may file the more serious charges. This is not an abuse of discretion.

Prosecutorial misconduct may involve withholding evidence that would be favorable to the defense. A landmark 1963 Supreme Court case held that prosecutors who suppress evidence favorable to defendants are violating the due process rights of those defendants.[25] A more recent example of alleged prosecutorial misconduct involves the production of a training film that teaches prosecutors "how to lie to judges and exclude young blacks from juries." Among other comments, Jack McMahon, candidate for the position of district attorney in Philadelphia, states on the tape that low-income blacks are less likely to convict; thus, efforts should be made to exclude them from juries. It has been alleged that the tape tainted some cases, with the possibility that they would need to be retried.[26] McMahon lost the election to the incumbent district attorney by a large margin.

Finally, prosecutorial misconduct may occur in or out of court in the manner in which the prosecutor talks or acts. Spotlight 7.2 elaborates on the point.

Defense

One of the most effective ways to control prosecutorial misconduct is to provide adequate defense counsel for those accused of crimes. This section focuses on the role of the attorney as defense counsel in U.S. criminal justice systems, giving particular attention to the right to counsel.

The Defense Attorney's Role

Defense attorneys are charged with the responsibility of protecting defendants' constitutional rights at all stages of the legal proceedings, which begin long before trial. The first encounter that a defense attorney usually has with a client is at the jail. Normally, after arrest and booking a suspect is permitted one phone call. That call is frequently to a lawyer or friend, requesting that the friend find a lawyer. If the suspect cannot afford an attorney, counsel is appointed by the judge at the first court appearance. Usually, defendants who can afford to retain attorneys are visited by their attorneys before that court appearance.

The first responsibility of the defense attorney is to interview the client and obtain as many facts as possible. The attorney must gain the confidence of the client to the extent that the defendant is willing to disclose the important facts. The attorney should explain that this information is confidential between the attorney and the defendant. The defense attorney may begin an investigation by interviewing witnesses or friends, going to the scene of the alleged crime, and securing physical evidence. The attorney will talk to the prosecutor to see what information the police and prosecution have secured against the defendant.

The initial interview with the defendant is a very important one. Defendants may be confused about the law. They may have little or no recognition of their constitutional rights. They may not understand the importance of certain facts to the defense. The attorney must be able to elicit the needed information while maintaining a sense of perspective and understanding.

As soon as the defense attorney has enough information, he or she should advise the defendant concerning the strategy that might be used in the case. It might be reasonable for the defendant to plead guilty rather than go to trial. Negotiating pleas before trial—a frequent and very important procedure—is discussed

Spotlight 7.2

Prosecutorial Misconduct In and Out of Court

All attorneys who serve the courts should be held to a high standard of conduct. This includes how they act and what they say both in and out of court. Defense and prosecution attorneys may be placed under a complete or restricted gag order by the judge. If they violate the order and discuss the case with anyone other than those working on the case, including the press, they may be sanctioned. Attorneys may be sanctioned also for what they say during court proceedings. When their statements or actions are questioned, courts analyze them in light of the Supreme Court's decisions requiring that the words be read in context and that the effect of the words is to deny the defendant a fair trial.[1]

Consider the case of *Darden v. Wainwright*. Among other questionable comments, the prosecutor stated that the defendant "shouldn't be out of his cell unless he has a leash on him and a prison guard at the other end of that leash. I wish [Mr. Turman] had had a shotgun in his hand when he walked in the back door and blown [sic] his [Darden's] face off. I wish I could see him sitting here with no face, blown away by a shotgun."[2]

The crime involved in *Darden* was a particularly heinous one. Darden was attempting the armed robbery of Mrs. Turman in a furniture store in 1973. When Mrs. Turman's husband unexpectedly came in the back door, Darden shot him. As Mr. Turman was dying, Darden attempted to force Mrs. Turman into a sexual act. A young neighbor entered the store and tried to help Mr. Turman but was shot three times by Darden, who fled after the assault. In his rush to escape, Darden had an automobile accident. A witness to that accident testified that Darden was zipping his pants and buckling his belt. Officers traced the car, and with this evidence, charged Darden with the crimes against the Turmans.

During the trial, in addition to the comment quoted above, the prosecutor said repeatedly that he wished Darden had used the gun to kill himself. The Supreme Court held that although the prosecutor's comments were improper, they were not sufficient to deny Darden a fair trial. Four justices dissented. In 1988 Darden was executed in Florida's electric chair.

In a recent Florida case, a highly regarded prosecutor misbehaved in public after a trial and found it necessary to resign his position as a U.S. attorney. Kendall B. Coffey, who was in charge of one of the largest federal prosecution offices in the country, resigned after allegedly engaging in "boisterous behavior" in a nightclub. It was alleged that Mr. Coffey bit a dancer on the arm in a bar a few days after his office lost a major drug case. Because he believed he would win the case, Coffey had refused the defense's offer to forfeit $20 million to the government. Noted defense attorney Roy Black, who represented one of the defendants in the case, expressed his concern that Coffey was forced out because of these allegations. "If he had done things professionally, that's one thing, but not this," said Black, who continued, "I didn't always agree with him but he served the U.S. as well as anyone."[3] Coffey entered the private practice of law.

1. See Greer v. Miller, 483 U.S. 756 (1987).
2. Darden v. Wainwright, 477 U.S. 168 (1986).
3. "U.S. Attorney in South Florida Resigns after Inquiry into His Bar Altercation," *New York Times* (18 May 1996), p. 7.1.

on p. 194. The defense attorney should explain to the defendant the pros and cons of pleading guilty, but the attorney must be careful about encouraging a guilty plea when the evidence is strong that the defendant is not guilty. Even in those cases, a particular defendant, because of his or her prior record or the nature of the alleged offense, might be well advised to plead guilty to a lesser offense rather than risk conviction on the more serious charge. All of these issues involve trial strategy, which includes knowing what to expect from the prosecutor as well as trying to predict what the judge and jury will do should the case go to trial.

In some cases defense attorneys talk to the families of their clients and inform them of what to expect during the initial stages of the criminal justice process. Families and friends might be valuable sources of information useful to the attorney in preparing a defense and in preparing sentencing recommendations if the defendant is found guilty. Getting the facts from defendants and their families and friends is a difficult task in many cases. It is emotionally draining as well, and it is a process for which many defense attorneys are not trained. Defense attorneys devise many strategies to elicit information from clients. Some use sworn police statements to shock the defendant into being honest. Others appear nonjudgmental and use hypothetical questions to allow clients to save face. Some attorneys admit that they browbeat their clients by being tyrannical. Others try to be friendly, but they may resent the time required to discover the facts.

The defense attorney must keep track of the scheduled procedures for the remainder of the time the case is in the criminal justice system. Defense attorneys are criticized for missing deadlines, being unprepared for hearings, or attempting to delay the proceedings by asking for a continuance. Sometimes continuances are justified because there has not been sufficient time to prepare for the hearing. At other times the delays are unreasonable.

Private defense attorneys have been known to attempt to delay proceedings because they have not been paid by their clients. It is difficult to collect fees after a case has ended, particularly when the defendant is not pleased with the result. Some attorneys handle this problem by requiring that defendants pay in advance. They require a retainer fee, and when that amount of money has been exhausted by the time and expenses of the attorney, another fee is required before the attorney continues with the case.

It is important for the defense attorney to keep the defendant informed of what is happening in the case. Some defendants complain that they have not been told what is happening in their cases; some do not know when they will go to court for the pretrial hearing or for the trial until shortly before time for their appearances.

Even while obtaining facts and other forms of evidence from defendants and others, most defense attorneys will begin preparing the case for trial, should that occur. Trial strategy is important, and an unprepared attorney will do a great disservice to the defendant. If the case results in a trial and the defendant is convicted, the defense attorney must be prepared to file an appeal if the case warrants one.

Defense and the Right to Counsel

The **defense** of a criminal case is extremely important in an adversary system. If the prosecutor tries to prove the case against the defendant by introducing evidence that has been seized or a confession that has been elicited in violation of the defendant's rights, the defense attorney may ask the court to exclude that evidence. If the prosecutor files charges for which there is insubstantial evidence, the defense attorney may ask the court to dismiss those charges.

The primary job of a defense attorney is to protect the legal rights of the defendant and thereby preserve the adversary system. It is not the function of the defense attorney to judge the guilt or innocence of the defendant; that is an issue to be decided by the judge or jury. The defense attorney gathers and presents evidence and witnesses that support the defense and examines the evidence and witnesses produced by the prosecutor.

It is important to understand this basic defense function. The adversary system requires that for a person to be convicted of a criminal offense all of the elements of that offense must be proved by the prosecutor and the question of guilt decided by a jury or judge. The evidence must be strong enough to determine the defendant's guilt beyond a reasonable doubt, a much tougher burden than that required in a civil case. The prosecution may fail in this burden, as illustrated by the recent high-profile case of Terry Nichols. He, along with Timothy McVeigh, was accused of the crimes associated with the bombing of the federal building in Oklahoma City in April 1995. After the verdicts some jurors said they based their decisions on the prosecutor's failure to prove guilt beyond a reasonable doubt. Nichols was found guilty not of murder but of the lesser charges of manslaughter, along with the conspiracy charges. Some of the jurors, who spoke after the jurors deadlocked on the penalty issue, said the government did not prove beyond a reasonable doubt that Nichols was guilty of murder or that he should be given the death penalty.

The drafters of the U.S. Constitution recognized that in a criminal trial the state's powers are immense compared to those of the defendant. The Sixth Amendment to the U.S. Constitution provides that "in all criminal prosecutions, the accused shall enjoy the right . . . to have the Assistance of Counsel for his defense" (see Appendix A). Many scholars consider the **right to counsel** the most important of all the defendant's constitutional rights. The use of counsel by those who can hire attorneys has been accepted, but the right to have counsel appointed at the expense of the state (or federal government in a federal trial) has been the subject of considerable litigation.

It is important to an understanding of this emerging right to counsel to note that the Bill of Rights, the first ten amendments of the U.S. Constitution, was included to restrain the federal government's power. Today most of those rights have been applied to the states through the Due Process Clause of the Fourteenth Amendment, which specifies that states may not deny "life, liberty, or property" without "due process of law" (see Appendix A). It took the Court over a century, however, to apply most of the rights contained in the Bill of Rights to the states. The evolution of the right to appointed counsel is an example.

Appointed Counsel

The right to appointed counsel, which means counsel provided at government expense, has not always been recognized in the United States. In 1932 in *Powell v. Alabama*, the Supreme Court gave limited recognition to the right.[27] In *Powell* a state case, nine African American youths were charged with the rape of two white Alabama women. Eight of the defendants were convicted and sentenced to death. Several issues were raised on appeal; two of them pertained to the lack of counsel.

In *Powell* the Court focused on the issue of whether appointed counsel should have been provided for defendants because they could not have afforded to retain counsel even if they had been given the opportunity to do so. In discussing the right to counsel, the Court emphasized that the right to be heard would have little meaning unless accompanied by a right to counsel. The Court held that there was a right to appointed counsel but limited that right to the facts of *Powell*, in which the crime committed carried the death penalty. At the time *Powell* was decided, almost half the states provided a right to appointed counsel in capital cases. In federal trials that right was provided by a congressional statute.

In a 1938 *federal* case the Supreme Court held that there is a right to appointed as well as to retained counsel and that this right is not limited to capital cases.[28] In 1942 the Supreme Court refused to apply the right to appointed counsel to state cases. In *Betts* v. *Brady* the Court established a fundamental fairness test, holding that an indigent defendant in a state trial would be entitled to appointed counsel in a noncapital case only where it could be shown that circumstances necessitated appointed counsel for the defendant to receive a fair trial.[29] *Betts* v. *Brady* was a controversial case, but it remained the law until 1963, when it was overruled.

On 8 January 1962, the Supreme Court received a large envelope from Florida inmate number 003826. Clarence Earl Gideon, a pauper who had been in and out of prison most of his life, had printed his request in pencil. He was not a violent man, but he had committed several nonviolent crimes. In this case, he was charged with breaking and entering a poolroom with the intent to commit a misdemeanor, which was a felony under Florida law. Gideon requested that the state appoint an attorney for him. The judge responded that he was sorry but that the laws of Florida did not provide for appointed counsel except in capital cases. Gideon responded, "The United States Supreme Court says I am entitled to be represented by Counsel." Gideon conducted his own defense. He was convicted and sentenced to five years in the state prison.

Gideon appealed to the U.S. Supreme Court, which agreed to hear the case and appointed a prestigious law firm in Washington, D.C., to defend him. The result was one of the few occasions in which the Court has overruled an earlier decision by name. In *Gideon* v. *Wainwright* the Court reversed its ruling in *Betts* v. *Brady* and applied the right to appointed counsel to state cases. According to the Court,

> In our adversary system of criminal justice, any person haled into court, who is too poor to hire a lawyer, cannot be assured a fair trial unless counsel is provided for him. This seems to us to be an obvious truth. . . . [The Court quotes *Powell*] "He lacks both the skill and knowledge adequately to prepare his defense, even though he may have a perfect one. He requires the guiding hand of counsel at every step in the proceedings against him. Without it, though he be not guilty, he faces the danger of conviction because he does not know how to establish his innocence."[30]

Gideon was convicted of a felony; consequently, his case extended the right to appointed counsel in felony cases only. In 1972 the Supreme Court extended the right to misdemeanors when the conviction of a particular misdemeanor might result in the "actual deprivation of a person's liberty." In *Argersinger* v. *Hamlin* the Court held "that absent a knowing and intelligent waiver, no person may be imprisoned for any offense, whether classified as petty, misdemeanor, or felony unless he was represented by counsel at his trial."[31]

The Court clarified *Argersinger* in *Scott* v. *Illinois*, decided in 1979. Scott was fined but not given a prison sentence although the statute under which he was convicted for shoplifting provided for either punishment. In ruling that Scott was not entitled to appointed counsel, the Court emphasized the difference between actual imprisonment and any other form of punishment.[32]

Gideon, *Argersinger*, and *Scott* concern the right to appointed counsel at trial. In 1967 the Court held that the Sixth Amendment right to counsel applies during "critical stages" in criminal proceedings.[33] The right applies when the court begins adversarial judicial proceedings, which may be a preliminary hearing, an indictment, a formal charge, or an arraignment.[34] It is not necessary for the defendant to ask for an attorney. At the stage when the right to counsel begins, if an attorney is not provided, any further judicial proceedings are improper and will result in a reversal of a conviction.[35]

The right to counsel does not apply to all pretrial stages, although it has been applied to most. The right to appointed counsel applies to some but not all appeals.[36] States may extend constitutional rights beyond those mandated by Supreme Court interpretations of the federal Constitution, and some have done so;[37] but, if they do not do so in appeals that the Court considers discretionary rather than mandatory, the fact that one person may retain private counsel does not mean the state must provide appointed counsel for indigents.[38]

The right to counsel involves a right to refuse counsel. Defendants may choose to give up their right to counsel and represent themselves.[39] The **waiver** of the right to counsel must be made voluntarily and knowingly. Judges know that the trial process is complicated, and they guard against the possibility that defendants will create an unfair disadvantage by appearing *pro se* (representing themselves). Judges question defendants carefully about their knowledge of criminal law and procedure and their understanding of the advantages of having counsel present. Some judges require standby counsel to be present with the defendant to explain the basic rules, formalities, and etiquette in the courtroom.[40]

A recent widely publicized case in which a defendant sought to represent himself was the Unabomber trial of Theodore J. Kaczynski. Kaczynski lost in his attempts to have the judge order new attorneys, a request made at the beginning of the trial and thus not a timely one. The defendant reportedly disagreed with his court-appointed attorneys over the use of a defense of mentally ill, with Kaczynski insisting that he was not mentally ill. He had refused to be examined by psychiatrists, but two days after Kaczynski's initial disruption on the first scheduled day of the trial in January 1998, the judge ruled that the defendant would be examined by a psychiatrist to determine whether he was competent to stand trial. Kaczynski had refused to be examined by a government psychiatrist, but during the first week of the scheduled trial, Judge Garland E. Burrell Jr. warned defense counsel that if their client continued to refuse, "[H]e will be on a plane and I will fly him to a psychiatric institution immediately."[41]

Private Defense Counsel

Many defendants prefer to retain their own defense counsel, and they must do so if they are not eligible for an attorney provided at public expense. It is a common belief that the defense attorney with the best reputation for winning cases is one who works privately and charges very high fees. The belief that private attorneys are more likely to win acquittals (or lesser sentences) for their clients receives support from articles noting that the wealthy do not live on death row.[42]

A few high-profile defense attorneys are easily recognizable; some of them have been on television as attorneys in well publicized cases or as commentators in other cases, but their fees preclude many defendants from retaining them. Nor are they always the best attorneys. The high-profile image may backfire with some jurors, especially if the attorney is from out of town or has been involved in a questionable case in which he or she was viewed as unprofessional or just arrogant. In many jurisdictions the attorneys who try cases regularly and are familiar with the local prosecutors and judges, may have a better chance of gaining an acquittal in a difficult case.

Finding a good defense attorney one can afford may be quite difficult. Few standards exist for measuring the competency of attorneys in criminal defense work. Some are selected by references from former clients. Others may be selected from advertising on radio or television. In some cities, the local bar association makes referrals on request. Defendants should choose an attorney who is a competent trial lawyer and negotiator, but the personality and style of the attorney might be important as well. It is wise to avoid attorneys who guarantee results or who have a reputation of plea bargaining all or most cases rather than going to trial. On the other hand, an attorney who insists on a trial might not provide the best representation for some clients.

Whether defendants have private or appointed counsel, they are entitled to effective counsel, although the nature and meaning of that right is not clear.

The Right to Effective Assistance of Counsel

The right to effective assistance of counsel is not mandated by the Constitution, but it has been held to be implied by that document. After all, the right to counsel would have little or no meaning without effective counsel. The Court used the concept of "effective and substantial aid" in *Powell* v. *Alabama* and in several subsequent cases referred to the effective assistance of counsel.[43]

The definition and application of the terms *effective assistance of counsel* were left to the lower courts. In 1945 the District of Columbia Circuit Court articulated the standard that representation would not be considered ineffective unless counsel's actions reduced the trial to a "farce or mockery of justice." Other lower courts adopted this standard; some courts developed higher standards, such as "reasonably effective assistance."[44] In 1984 the Supreme Court adopted the "reasonably effective assistance" standard then used by all the lower federal courts and stated that no further definition was needed than the establishing of a two-prong test, explained in *Strickland* v. *Washington* and defined as follows:

> First, the defendant must show that counsel's performance was deficient. This requires showing that counsel made errors so serious that counsel was not functioning as the 'counsel' guaranteed the defendant by the Sixth Amendment. Second, the defendant must show that the deficient performance prejudiced the defense. This requires showing that counsel's errors were so serious as to deprive the defendant of a fair trial, a trial whose result is reliable.[45]

Although a court may conclude that counsel was ineffective based on a single error,[46] *Strickland* requires the court to consider the *totality of circumstances* of the case, and there is a strong presumption that counsel provided effective assistance.[47] Spotlight 7.3 contains more information about ineffective assistance of counsel.

The Organization and Structure of Defense Systems for Indigents

Court appointed counsel for indigent defendants represents a critical part of U.S. criminal justice systems. Approximately 80 percent of jail inmates and 75 percent of prison inmates were represented by appointed rather than retained counsel. In recent years funding of indigent defense programs has been threatened as demand has increased. Underfunding of public defender systems at all levels may have a greater impact on minorities than on white defendants, leading to accusations of racism.[48]

Defense counselors' caseloads are too high; salaries are too low to attract many of the brightest law graduates; capital cases are growing at an alarming rate and consume far more time than other criminal cases; other serious felony cases are expanding, too. Funding and availability of attorneys are not keeping up with this growth. These and other problems led one expert on criminal defense systems to conclude in 1989 that "the indigent defense delivery system is in a state of crisis throughout the country."[49]

Spotlight 7.3

When Is a Defense Attorney Ineffective?

Although numerous defendants have argued that their attorneys were ineffective in representing them, few have won on this issue. For example, a lower federal court held that a defendant was not denied effective assistance of counsel when his attorney fell asleep during the trial. The trial judge did not awaken the attorney because he did not think he was missing anything important. The appellate court held that counsel's action did not make a "farce or mockery of justice" out of the trial![1]

This case illustrates the need to look more carefully at all the facts before drawing a conclusion. It is possible to conclude that when an attorney falls asleep during trial, the trial becomes a "farce or mockery," or under the *Strickland* guidelines discussed in the text on p. 180, the defendant was denied "reasonably effective assistance of counsel," and the two-prong test was met. It is possible, however, that nothing important happened during that brief period of sleep. Perhaps this issue could be analyzed in light of your experiences with class lectures or reading a text.

A state court has held that a defense attorney's efforts to further his own career rather than pursue the best interests of his client constituted ineffective assistance of counsel. The defendant was charged with first-degree murder for killing her sleeping husband, who had abused her previously. Counsel advised her to plead not guilty on the grounds of self-defense, apparently believing that an acquittal on that basis would enhance his career. Technically, self-defense does not apply in such cases; however, the defense has been permitted in some battered-person syndrome cases, in which the defendant (usually a woman) had been abused previously (and frequently) by her partner but was not threatened at the time she committed the otherwise criminal act. Considerable publicity is given to cases in which the defense is used successfully. Counsel's advice to his client concerning the case implied his motives, leading the appellate court to reverse the defendant's conviction for first-degree murder.[2]

1. United States v. Katz, 425 F.2d 928 (2d Cir. 1970).
2. Lawson v. State, 766 P.2d 261 (Nev. 1988). For a Supreme Court case finding ineffective assistance of counsel, see Penson v. Ohio, 488 U.S. 75 (1988). For a case in which the Court found that counsel was not ineffective, see Lockhart v. Fretwell, 506 U.S. 364 (1993), in which the Court held that a defendant did not prove ineffective assistance of counsel by showing that the defense attorney failed to object to a decision that was overruled subsequently.

The magnitude of the problem was illustrated by the 1994 strike of public defenders in New York City. After the mayor threatened to fire the city's public defenders, who were striking for higher pay, most returned to work. At the time of the strike, the average salary of a Legal Aid lawyer in New York City was $45,000.[50] Highlights of a recent study of indigent defense are contained in the second portion of Spotlight 7.4.

Legal aid services at the federal level have struggled in recent years. Legal Services Corporation, which provides legal aid services, had a $415 million budget in 1995. The following year Congress cut that to $278 million. In 1996 the Senate voted to appropriate $300 million for the 1997 budget, the House $250. The compromise appropriation was $283 million. The budget remained the same for 1998.[51]

Three models have been used for organizing the provision of defense counsel for indigent defendants: the public defender, assigned counsel, and the contract models. Each is defined briefly in Spotlight 7.4. The public defender system is a public law firm whose mission is to provide counsel in criminal cases for defendants who cannot afford to retain private counsel. Most public defender systems are located in metropolitan areas. They are supported publicly and administered by an attorney, usually called the **public defender.**

Spotlight 7.4

Indigent Defense

Types of Delivery Systems

Although the U.S. Supreme Court has mandated that the States must provide counsel for indigents accused of crime, the implementation of how such services are to be provided has not been specified. The States have devised various systems, rules for organizing, and funding mechanisms for indigent defense programs. As a consequence, each State has adopted its own approach for providing counsel for poor defendants.

Three systems have emerged throughout the country as the primary means to provide defense services for indigent defendants.

Public defender programs are public or private nonprofit organizations with full- or part-time salaried staff. Local public defenders operate autonomously and do not have a central administrator.

By contrast, under a statewide system, an individual appointed by the governor, a commission, council, or board is charged with developing and maintaining a system of representation for each county of the State. In 30 States a public defender system is the primary method used to provide indigent counsel for criminal defendants. (For a more detailed description see *State-wide Defender Programs: The Lay of the Land,* National Legal Aid and Defender Association, 1992.)

Assigned counsel systems involve the appointment by the courts of private attorneys as needed from a list of available attorneys. Assigned counsel systems consist of two types. Ad hoc assigned counsel systems are those in which individual private attorneys are appointed by an individual judge to provide representation on a case-by-case basis. Coordinated assigned counsel systems employ an administrator to oversee

the appointment of counsel and to develop a set of standards and guidelines for program administration.

Contract attorney systems involve governmental units that reach agreements with private attorneys, bar associations, or private law firms to provide indigent services for a specified dollar amount and for a specified time period.

Highlights of Indigent Defense

- States and localities use several methods for delivering indigent defense services: public defender programs, assigned counsel, and contract attorney systems.

- Twenty-eight percent of State court prosecutors reported that their jurisdictions used public defender programs exclusively to provide indigent counsel.

- In 1990 State and local governments spent approximately $1.3 billion on public defenders services. In 1979 this figure was about $300 million.

- About three-fourths of the inmates in State prisons and about half of those in Federal prisons received publicly-provided legal counsel for the offense for which they were serving time.

- In 1992 about 80% of defendants charged with felonies in the Nation's 75 largest counties relied on a public defender or on assigned counsel for legal representation.

- Little current information is available regarding the workload, staffing, procedures, or policies for indigent defense services across the Nation.

Source: Steven K. Smith and Carol J. DeFrances, Bureau of Justice Statistics Selected Findings, *Indigent Defense* (Washington, D.C.: U.S. Department of Justice, February 1996), pp. 1–2.

Like prosecutors, public defenders have the advantage of specializing in criminal cases. This increases their expertise and efficiency, but it may contribute to professional burnout. Like prosecutors, many public defenders work with tremendous caseloads, leaving them insufficient time to devote to any particular case. In addition, inadequate budgets result in a lack of support staff and equipment.[52]

Better recruitment and more adequate training of attorneys would improve public defender programs. Training programs should include an emphasis on efficiency and ethical standards as well as negotiating and trial skills. If the office does not have a formal training program, efforts might be made to assign new personnel to a more experienced attorney for a period of observation or to contract with private agencies or other public defender offices for training programs.

The burden of improving public defender services rests in two places. Both the legal profession and society must assume the responsibility for protecting constitutional guarantees. Criminal defendants will never be popular, but the public must provide the money and resources necessary to make the system work as a protective device to ensure that no one is denied the constitutional right to be defended by counsel.

The second method of providing counsel for indigents is the **assigned counsel** system. Under this model, attorneys are assigned to defend particular indigent defendants. Normally, assignments are made by the judge scheduled to preside over that trial, but some jurisdictions have moved to a more formal and organized system in an attempt to coordinate assignments throughout a jurisdiction. Most assignments are made from lists of attorneys who have volunteered to participate in the program, although in some jurisdictions all attorneys are expected to participate in the assigned counsel program. A minority of jurisdictions have some procedures for assessing qualifications of attorneys who participate in assigned counsel cases, but the majority have no qualifications beyond a license to practice law. Most areas that have assigned counsel systems do not have formal provisions for removing names from the list of participating attorneys.

Assigned counsel are paid on a fee schedule that may be determined by state statute or by local bar regulations. In some jurisdictions, however, the requirement is that attorneys assigned to represent indigent defendants must receive "reasonable compensation" for their work. This gives judges wide discretion in determining fees for assigned counsel. Attorneys have complained about different fees for the same types of cases. In general, the money received by assigned counsel is less than the average fees paid to private attorneys, and in most jurisdictions, considerably less. In some jurisdictions maximum fees are established, making it impossible for assigned counsel to be paid an adequate fee for all hours worked in a complicated case.

The final method is that of the *contract system*, which is not used widely. Most of the counties that utilize this method are small (fewer than 50,000 people). In the contract system, a bar association, private law firm, or individual attorney contracts with a jurisdiction to provide legal assistance for indigent defendants.

The prosecution and the defense begin playing their respective roles and interacting with each other during a series of important pretrial procedures, the focus of the second half of this chapter.

Pretrial Procedures

This section explores the important processes and procedures that occur prior to the trial of a criminal case. It is important to understand, however, that the stages in the criminal justice process of any trial are not discrete. They do not always happen one after the other; some stages overlap. Nor are the functions of the police, prosecutors, defense attorneys, and judges limited to particular stages. Citizens—as victims, witnesses, or members of a jury—function at different levels as well.

Spotlight 7.5

Steps in the Criminal Justice Process before Trial

1. Report of a crime
2. Investigation prior to arrest
3. Arrest
4. Booking
5. Postarrest investigation
6. Prosecutor's decision to charge suspect with a crime
7. Initial appearance
8. Preliminary hearing
9. Grand jury review
10. Arraignment
11. Pretrial motions
12. Pretrial conferences

Steps in the Criminal Justice Process

Figure 1.1 in Chapter 1 diagrams the steps in the criminal justice process. References to that figure are made in this chapter to help you to visualize the processes discussed here. The specific stages occurring before trial are enumerated in Spotlight 7.5 for easy reference in this chapter.

The stages in the criminal justice process are very important for two reasons: First, most people who are arrested are not tried in a criminal court. Figure 7.1 on p. 171 points out how the system loses cases before trial. After the initial investigation, there may not be sufficient evidence for an arrest. There may be sufficient evidence, but the police may not be able to locate the suspect, or for some other reason the police may not arrest. Those who are arrested may not be prosecuted for any number of reasons discussed previously. Second, after the prosecutor files charges, those charges may be dismissed by the judge or they may be dropped by the prosecutor. This action may occur during any of the court sessions before trial. The charge may be dropped or the case dismissed after the trial begins.

The procedures listed in Spotlight 7.5 begin with the report of an alleged crime, which may be followed by a formal arrest and **booking.** The second step is that the alleged crime must be investigated. Early investigation of a reported crime is very important. Evidence may be lost or destroyed. Witnesses may disappear. Thus, police prefer to question potential witnesses at or near the scene of a crime as soon as they can do so. Various methods are used by police in investigating an alleged crime. Defense attorneys may use the same methods or even retain private investigators to search for evidence that would assist in the defense of the case. They check for physical evidence by analyzing the clothing of the victims and looking for hair, blood, or other evidence that might associate the accused with the reported crime. They look for a weapon or weapons that might have been used in the crime. They question all parties who might know something about the crime or the alleged offender, looking for information such as motive as well as any evidence linking a specific individual with the crime.

Securing physical evidence that a crime has occurred may involve searching the automobile, home, or office of the suspect. It may involve securing physical evidence from the accused as well. For example, police may obtain body fluid or hair samples from the suspect. Police cannot compel suspects to testify against themselves. That would be a violation of the Fifth Amendment (see Appendix A), discussed on p. 102 in connection with police interrogation, but the Supreme Court has held that some forms of evidence may be secured from suspects without violating their due process rights.[53] Samples of hair, fiber, blood, and saliva are tested for deoxyribonucleic acid, or DNA, a genetic code by which individuals may be identified. Although some courts initially rejected the use of DNA evidence, its usage is rather common today.[54]

The results of tests on evidence may lead the prosecution to decide not to file charges or to drop charges already filed. In earlier stages, the police may decide not to arrest after a preliminary investigation. For example, a driver suspected of driving under the influence may be given a field test for alcohol and perform so well that the officer decides not to pursue the matter.

Police may be required to file detailed reports even if they decide not to pursue the investigation, and this is true especially if the reported crime is a felony. Usually, the reports are filed on a printed form that contains questions about the offense, location, description of vehicle, weapons, injuries, and location of the injured parties.

These initial investigations at the time of a crime or shortly after a crime has been reported may be followed by more intensive investigations by the police or prosecution. Investigations may continue throughout the case and for a very long time before a case is settled—even before arrest. In the case of the Unabomber, the investigation went on for seventeen years before Theodore "Ted" Kaczynski was arrested. Kaczynski, aged fifty-three at the time of his arrest in 1996, was suspected of carrying out sixteen mail bombings, which killed three people and wounded twenty-three others over a seventeen-year period. Kaczynski is a former math professor who received his Ph.D. from the University of Michigan at Ann Arbor and taught at the University of California at Berkeley.

Examinations may be required of violent crime victims to secure physical evidence of the alleged crime. Psychological examinations of victims may be given to obtain evidence that might be useful to the prosecution. Psychological or psychiatric examinations of defendants may be ordered at some point before trial in order to determine whether the defendant is mentally competent to stand trial. In the case of Kaczynski, the trial was postponed after the judge ordered the suspect be examined to determine whether he was competent to stand trial. Kaczynski had been judged competent previously, but his actions shortly before and during the week the trial was to begin led the judge to order the competency examinations. In addition to the suspect's behavior in attempting to fire his attorneys and represent himself, it was believed that he attempted to commit suicide by hanging himself with his underwear in his jail cell during the week the trial was scheduled to begin.

During investigations, both sides look for testimonial as well as for physical evidence. Both sides may employ the services of an **expert witness** to testify regarding a crucial element of the case. An expert witness is an individual who has specialized knowledge in a recognized area such as medicine. Both the prosecution and the defense look for eye witnesses to the crime. One frequently used method of obtaining eye-witness identification of a suspect is to conduct lineups or showups. A *lineup* involves several people. The witness (who may be the victim as well) is asked to look at all of the people in the lineup and decide whether he or she can identify the person(s) who allegedly committed the crime. Lineups are permissible provided they are conducted properly.[55]

It is improper in most instances to ask a witness to identify the suspect in a **showup** that involves only that suspect. This kind of identification procedure has been condemned by courts but allowed under limited circumstances. Pictures may be shown to witnesses for identification of suspects, although restrictions are placed on this procedure. It must be shown that the witnesses had a good opportunity to see the suspect. The pictures must be viewed soon after the alleged crime while the memory of the witnesses is clear. Multiple witnesses may not view the pictures in the company of each other. The police may not make suggestive comments regarding the pictures and the suspect.[56] Usually, it is not permissible to offer the witness only one photograph, that of the accused.[57]

If the investigation convinces the prosecutor that sufficient evidence is available to lead a reasonable person to think that a particular suspect committed the crime, and if the prosecutor decides to file formal charges against the suspect, in most cases that suspect must be taken before a magistrate for an **initial appearance.** The initial appearance is for the purpose of having the court determine whether there is probable cause to charge the suspect with this crime.

A suspect who has been retained in custody must be taken before the magistrate without unreasonable delay. The time involved in processing the suspect at the police station usually means that the initial appearance cannot take place until the following day. If the suspect is booked on a weekend, the initial appearance cannot take place until the following Monday unless special provisions have been made. In some metropolitan areas, because of the high volume of weekend arrests, magistrate's courts hold special sessions on weekends to permit initial appearances earlier than usual and thus decrease the amount of time suspects must spend in jail before their initial appearances.

Usually, the initial appearance is brief. Magistrates verify the names and addresses of the defendants and inform them of the formal charges and of their constitutional rights. Although the procedures differ among jurisdictions, at this stage in many areas the process of appointing counsel is started. Most defendants who have retained counsel have their attorneys with them at their initial appearances.

If the defendant is charged with a minor offense, such as a misdemeanor, he or she may enter a plea at the initial appearance. Many defendants enter guilty pleas at this stage. If that is not the case, the defendant is informed of the next stage in the proceeding. Defendants charged with felonies may not enter a plea at the initial appearance. In some felony cases the defendant does not have to appear at this stage, although defense counsel will do so. For defendants who have been retained in custody to this point, magistrates make determinations whether to release or retain them pending trial. If defendants have been released by the police after booking, at the initial appearance magistrates review the terms of those releases and decide whether they were made properly under the circumstances.

In some jurisdictions, the initial appearance is followed by a **preliminary hearing,** at least in cases involving felonies. Normally, the preliminary hearing occurs between one and two weeks after the initial appearance. During the interval between these two stages, some or all charges may be dropped as prosecutors discover that there is insufficient evidence to proceed with all charges or even with some cases. If charges are not dropped, the preliminary hearing is held to determine whether there is probable cause to continue with those charges. A preliminary hearing is not required in all jurisdictions. If it is not required, prosecutors may take the case directly to a grand jury (see p. 187) where that is required. If a grand jury is not required, prosecutors may proceed on their own.

At the preliminary hearing, the prosecution and the defense present sufficient evidence to enable the magistrate to decide the issue of probable cause. Normally, the preliminary hearing is open because of the First Amendment right (see Appendix A) of the press to cover and of the public to know about such hearings. The hearing may be closed if a defendant shows that he or she can not get a fair hearing without closure.[58] Defendants may waive the preliminary hearing and many choose to do so, but that waiver must be a knowing and intelligent one.

In the United States, the official accusation of a felony begins in one of two ways. First, the prosecutor may initiate the proceedings by returning an information. That may be done in cases not requiring action by the grand jury or when the grand jury review is waived. Second, the case may begin with a grand jury indictment, required in felony cases in some states although they differ in the crimes for which an indictment is required. Some states limit the requirement to serious felonies. In federal courts, grand jury indictments are required for prosecution of capital or otherwise infamous crimes, with the exceptions noted in the Fifth Amendment (see Appendix A).

The grand jury is composed of private citizens, usually twenty-three persons, although some states have reduced the number. Originally, a majority vote was required for a decision, but today some states, particularly those with grand juries smaller than twenty-three, require more than a majority vote. The grand jury review differs from the initial appearance and the preliminary hearing in that evidence in this review is presented only by the prosecutor. The defendant does not have a right to present evidence or to be present. The grand jury is not bound by all the rules of evidence that are required at trial. The deliberations are secret.

The basic function of the grand jury is to hear the evidence presented by the prosecutor and to decide whether there is probable cause to return the indictment presented by the prosecutor. If they return the indictment, that is called a **true bill.** The *indictment* is the official document stating the name of the accused, the charge, and the essential facts supporting that charge. In returning that indictment, the grand jury is not bound by the decision of the magistrate at the preliminary hearing. Generally, a grand jury indictment is not required in misdemeanor or petty offense cases. Those are begun officially when the prosecutor returns an *information.*

Once it is in session, the grand jury may initiate investigations. This may be done when there are allegations of widespread corruption in public agencies. The grand jury may be used to investigate organized crime, too. When the grand jury begins an official prosecution in this manner, that is, by action on its own knowledge without the indictment presented by the prosecutor, it returns a **presentment.** A *presentment* is an official document that is an accusation asking for the prosecutor to prepare an indictment.

In theory, the grand jury serves as a check on prosecutorial discretion. The Supreme Court recognized this important function when it said that the grand jury serves the invaluable function in our society of standing between the accuser and the accused, whether the latter be an individual, minority group, or other, to determine whether a charge is founded on reason, or was dictated by an intimidating power, or by malice and personal ill will.[59]

In many cases, however, the grand jury is an arm of the prosecution. In fact, in most cases presented by prosecutors to grand juries, the indictment is returned as a true bill. Of course, some procedures must be observed by the grand jury, and the body of case law is extensive and at times conflicting. Like that of trial juries (discussed in the next chapter), the selection of the grand jury may not involve systematic exclusion because of race[60] or other suspect categories, such as gender.

After the indictment or information is filed officially with the court, the **arraignment** is scheduled. At that hearing, judges or magistrates read the indictments or informations to defendants, inform them of their constitutional rights, and ask for a plea to the charges. If the defendant pleads not guilty, a date is set for trial. If the defendant pleads guilty, a date is set for formal sentencing, unless that takes place at the arraignment, as is often the case with less serious offenses.

In some jurisdictions a defendant is permitted to plead ***nolo contendere,*** which literally means, "I do not contest it." That plea in a criminal case has the legal effect of a guilty plea. The difference is that the plea may not be used against that defendant in a civil case. Thus, if the defendant pleads *nolo contendere* to felony charges of driving while intoxicated and leaving the scene of an accident, that plea may not be used in a civil case by a victim who suffered injuries and property damage in the accident.

In 1991 the Supreme Court considered the issue of how quickly a jurisdiction must hold an arraignment for the purpose of determining probable cause to detain a suspect arrested without a warrant (in such a case, no probable cause determination would have been made earlier for purposes of issuing an arrest warrant). Although probable cause may be determined prior to the arraignment, it was the policy to combine that determination with arraignment procedures in the county of Riverside, California. This prompted the case of *County of Riverside* v. *McLaughlin.* Procedures in that jurisdiction required that the arraignment be held within two days of arrest, not counting holidays. For example, a suspect arrested without a warrant could wait seven days for an arraignment, and thus a probable cause hearing, if arrested just before the Thanksgiving holiday.

In an earlier case, the Supreme Court had held that in cases of a warrantless arrest, a probable cause hearing must be held "promptly," but the Court did not define that word.[61] In *McLaughlin* the Court held that a forty-eight-hour period was presumptively reasonable but emphasized that under some circumstances, it might not be. The Court said that in order to satisfy the promptness requirement, "A jurisdiction that chooses to combine probable cause determinations with other pretrial proceedings must do so as soon as is reasonably feasible, but in no event later than 48 hours after arrest."[62]

Throughout the pretrial proceedings both sides may file motions. A **motion** is a document submitted to the court asking for a rule or an order. Some motions are inappropriate before trial; a motion for a new trial is an example. Other motions may be made before the trial begins. The defense may make a motion to suppress evidence on the allegation that the evidence was secured in violation of the defendant's rights. Defendants may make motions to dismiss the case because of insufficient evidence. There could be other reasons: the defense might attack the technical sufficiency of the charging document, question the composition of the grand jury, or claim prosecutorial misconduct.

It is common for the defense to file a motion requiring the prosecutor to produce evidence, a process called **discovery.** Discovery procedures are defined by court rules and procedural statutes, but the nature of discovery rules varies from permitting extensive discovery to rather limited discovery. Discovery is a two-way street. The prosecution and the defense are entitled to certain information that the other side plans to use at trial. Lists of witnesses, prior statements obtained from those witnesses, and the nature of physical evidence are the kinds of information that the prosecution and defense might obtain. Both prosecutors and defense attorneys may be sanctioned for violating discovery rules.

Under some circumstances, both the prosecution and the defense may obtain oral statements from witnesses outside of court and before trial. These statements are called **depositions.** They are taken under oath, recorded verbatim (usually by a court reporter), and may be used in court. They are permitted when there is a court order or rules of procedure that allow depositions. Attorneys for both sides are present. Witnesses or other parties may be given **interrogatories,** a series of questions that are to be answered truthfully, with the respondent signing a notarized statement of oath that the answers are correct.

Discovery is very important in criminal as well as in civil cases. The deposition is one of the best tools for gathering information (although it is not permitted in criminal cases in all jurisdictions). Although we are accustomed to movies and television in which surprise witnesses appear unexpectedly in court and change the nature of the case, or known witnesses blurt out an incriminating fact to the surprise of everyone, normally this is not the case in real practice.

An exception to the "lack of surprises rule" came to light in the fall of 1997, when sports newscaster Marv Albert was on trial for charges of forcing a woman to perform a sexual act on him and for biting that alleged victim. Another complaining witness was called to testify, and when her testimony of allegations of Albert's behavior corroborated the same pattern as those allegations of the victim at trial, Albert entered into a plea agreement in the case. Defense attorney Roy Black complained that the defense was not given time to secure evidence concerning the surprise witness and thus could not cross-examine her effectively. Apparently, Albert thought the testimony damaging enough that it was reasonable to plea bargain the case. He entered a plea of guilty to a misdemeanor account of assault and battery. Albert is on probation and engaging in therapy, but if he does not violate the terms of his probation within a year, his criminal record will be expunged.

Another motion the defense might file is for a change of **venue,** which refers to the place of trial. If the case has received considerable media attention, the defense may succeed with the argument that the defendant could not get a fair trial in that jurisdiction, and therefore a change of venue should be granted.

Although many defense motions might be filed before trial, these motions do not result in dismissals very often. The prosecutor might file motions, too, including a motion to drop the case or change the charges. In some jurisdictions, however, once formal charges have been filed, prosecutors may not drop or change those charges without the permission of the court. Frequently, the prosecutor files a motion to drop or lower charges as the result of plea bargaining, discussed on p. 194.

In addition to motions that the prosecution and defense might wish to make individually or other issues they want to discuss with the judge, there are times when both sides want to meet with the judge to ask for more time to secure evidence, to prepare pretrial motions, to negotiate a plea, or to handle any other pretrial matters. In some instances these arrangements may be made between the attorneys and not require the presence or approval of the judge. In other cases, the judge might keep a tight hold on the management of the case and not permit any changes (such as an extension of the discovery period) without judicial approval.

Pretrial conferences may be referred to as *status conferences.* They may be informal, with the prosecution and the defense discussing the status of the case, enumerating the issues on which they agree so that no time is wasted in court arguing issues that are not in dispute. The judge may ask each attorney to give an estimate of the time he or she expects to take to present the case. The answer is important for time management in courts, and the defense and prosecution might be limited by their predictions during these conferences; so the estimates should be made only after a close scrutiny of the evidence the attorney thinks should be presented.

Both the prosecution and the defense use the pretrial period to prepare for trial. Preparation may include further investigations and tests of physical evidence, repeated attempts to locate witnesses who have not yet been found, interviews with witnesses, obtaining depositions of expert and other witnesses, and reviewing those depositions, along with all other information pertinent to the trial. Attorneys spend time with their own witnesses, making sure they know what information each will give at trial and preparing them for the questions that might be asked by opposing counsel.

Attorneys are involved in keeping records of the expenses of trial preparation, which include costs of their own time (even if they are public defenders paid by the case and not by the hour, or prosecutors on salary, they probably keep an hourly record of their activities) as well as out-of-pocket costs for investigations, depositions, interrogatories, expenses for expert witnesses, and other expenses. Most attorneys who require retainers in advance for criminal cases will, in all probability, still keep an annotated record of the time they spend on the case.

Lists of witnesses who will be called for trial must be prepared, and the proper papers for notifying those witnesses must be filed. If the witnesses do not want to appear, the attorney may request a court order to **subpoena** them. A *subpoena* is an order to appear in court at a particular time and place and to give testimony on a specified subject or issue. As a precautionary measure, subpoenas might be issued to all potential witnesses to make it more difficult for them to change their minds and refuse to appear in court or at a deposition to testify. Witnesses may be ordered to produce documents or papers that are important to the trial.

Pretrial conferences are very important to attorneys as they assess and prepare their cases. For example, the prosecutor may decide that the defense position is strong enough to weaken the case sufficiently that a guilty verdict is unlikely. The attorneys may offer and accept (or reject) plea bargains for a plea to the charge(s) or to lesser charges. Many issues may be discussed during these pretrial conferences.

Release or Detention: Bail or Jail?

Once a person has been charged with a crime and arrested, the decision whether to release or detain that individual pending trial is an important one. According to the Supreme Court, for the defendant it is a time "when consultation, thorough going investigation and preparation . . . [are] vitally important."[63] During this period, the defendant retains an attorney or is assigned counsel. The defense counsel and the prosecutor negotiate and consider plea bargaining. Witnesses are interviewed and other attempts are made by both sides to secure evidence for the trial. Uncovering additional evidence may change the nature of the case and may even result in dropping or reducing charges before trial.

The Bail Decision

For society, the issue of whether the defendant is released or detained before trial is critical. Public outcries, accusing courts of coddling criminals, are common when persons charged with serious crimes are released. When they commit crimes during their release, the response is even more critical.

The procedures by which the **bail** decision is made vary among jurisdictions, but a hearing is required and the defendant is entitled to the benefit of counsel at that hearing. In the federal system, the hearing must take place within twenty-four hours of arrest. In some jurisdictions there are statutes specifying what types of offenses are bailable. In others there are specifications concerning what the magistrate may consider in making the decision. In many cases, however, the magistrate has wide discretion in the bail decision, and there is virtually no check on this decision.

The magistrate has wide latitude in setting the amount of bail. In the federal system, the factors most closely related to the level of bail, in order of importance, are: the seriousness of the current charge, the district in which the bail hearing occurs, and the criminal record of the offender.[64]

A defendant who is detained may petition the court to reduce the amount of bail or to grant bail if it were denied previously. Some judges grant these motions, particularly when the defense has had more time to gather evidence that favors pretrial release of the defendant.

The Eighth Amendment to the U.S. Constitution prohibits requiring excessive bail (see Appendix A). This provision has been interpreted to mean that when bail is used, its amount may not be excessive, but there has been no clear definition of what that means. In 1951 in *Stack* v. *Boyle,* the Court considered this issue and stated that bail set at a "figure higher than an amount reasonably calculated to fulfill this purpose [assuring the presence of the defendant at trial] is 'excessive' under the Eighth Amendment."[65]

Until recently the only legitimate purpose of bail was to secure the presence of the accused at trial. In 1970, with the passage of the District of Columbia Court Reform and Criminal Procedure Act, **preventive detention** was recognized as a legitimate purpose of bail. The statute was upheld in 1981.[66] It permits judges to deny bail to defendants charged with dangerous crimes if the government has clear evidence that the safety of others would be endangered if the accused were released. In addition, bail could be denied in cases involving persons who had been convicted of violent crimes while on probation or parole. Other jurisdictions followed the District of Columbia in passing statutes or changing their constitutions to permit the denial of bail for preventive detention. And in 1984 in *Schall* v. *Martin* the Supreme Court upheld preventive detention of juveniles.[67]

The most controversial change in bail, however, occurred in the Bail Reform Act of 1984, a federal statute that permits judges to deny bail if they have sufficient reason to think a defendant poses a dangerous threat to the community. The defendant is entitled to a prompt hearing on that issue, but if the hearing is not prompt, the government is not required to release a defendant who otherwise meets the criteria for detention.[68] If there is sufficient evidence to charge the defendant with a serious drug offense or certain other serious offenses, there is a presumption of dangerousness. This means that bail may be denied unless the defendant can prove to the court that he or she is not dangerous. This burden is a difficult one to sustain.

In 1987 the Supreme Court decided a case challenging the Bail Reform Act's provision for the preventive detention of dangerous persons. *United States* v. *Salerno* involved the detention of defendants charged with numerous acts associated with organized crime. At the pretrial detention hearing, the government presented evidence that both defendants were in high positions of power in organized crime families. The government contended that the only way to protect the community was to detain these persons pending trial.[69]

In *Salerno* the Court upheld pretrial detention but did not answer all questions about its constitutionality. Lower federal courts continue to disagree on its constitutionality regarding other issues. Extensive litigation may be expected to continue on the constitutionality of the Bail Reform Act of 1984, but it seems clear that at least some forms of preventive detention are recognized, and state legislatures will continue to pass statutes or amend their constitutions to provide for preventive detention.

Spotlight 7.6

Methods of Pretrial Release

Both financial bonds and alternative release options are used today.

Financial Bond

Fully secured bail The defendant posts the full amount of bail with the court.

Privately secured bail A bondsman signs a promissory note to the court for the bail amount and charges the defendant a fee for the service (usually 10 percent of the bail amount). If the defendant fails to appear, the bondsman must pay the court the full amount. Frequently, the bondsman requires the defendant to post collateral in addition to the fee.

Deposit bail The courts allow the defendant to deposit a percentage (usually 10 percent) of the full bail with the court. The full amount of the bail is required if the defendant fails to appear. The percentage bail is returned after disposition of the case, but the court often retains 1 percent for administrative costs.

Unsecured bail The defendant pays no money to the court but is liable for the full amount of bail should he or she fail to appear.

Alternative Release Options

Release on recognizance (ROR) The court releases the defendant on the promise that he or she will appear in court as required.

Conditional release The court releases the defendant subject to his or her following specific conditions set by the court, such as attendance at drug treatment therapy or staying away from the complaining witness.

Third party custody The defendant is released into the custody of an individual or agency that promises to assure his or her appearance in court. No monetary transactions are involved in this type of release.

Citation release Arrestees are released pending their first court appearance on a written order issued by law enforcement personnel.

Source: Bureau of Justice Statistics, *Report to the Nation on Crime and Justice: The Data*, 2d ed. (Washington, D.C.: U.S. Department of Justice, 1988), p. 76.

The Bail System

The bail system developed for practical reasons. It began in England, probably before 1000 A.D. Before urbanization and the development of modern courts, judges traveled from jurisdiction to jurisdiction to hold court sessions. They could not get to any one place often; consequently, it was necessary to devise a way of detaining the accused before the judges arrived. The bail system developed because the detention facilities were recognized as horrible places of confinement and were expensive.

An opportunity to make money in the bail system resulted in the development of the bail **bond** system. In return for a fee, the bail bondsman/woman posts bond for the defendant. If the defendant does not appear at trial, theoretically the bond money must be forfeited to the court. In reality the forfeiture provision is rarely enforced, but since some bondsmen/women post bond without having the money available, some jurisdictions require bondsmen/women to prove that they can pay the forfeiture should that be necessary. Abuses of the bond system led to alternative methods for pretrial release. They are defined in Spotlight 7.6.

The Guilty Plea

The guilty plea is very important in U.S. criminal justice systems because approximately 90 percent of defendants plead guilty.[70] Although many guilty pleas are entered after plea bargaining begins, defendants may choose to plead guilty without any negotiation between the prosecution and the defense. Various reasons may account for this decision. Many defendants are guilty and may see no reason to go to trial, thinking that they have no chance of an acquittal or even a conviction of a lesser offense. They may not want to engage in any kind of plea bargaining because that, like a trial, might take more time than they are willing to devote to the process. Some defendants want a quick decision. This may be true particularly if they have been denied bail and must wait in jail until a plea bargain is reached or the trial occurs. Still other defendants may not want to experience the public exposure of the evidence the prosecution will present at trial. Again, in the Marv Albert case, the defendant wanted to avoid the embarrassment to himself and to his family that would have resulted from further testimony regarding his alleged bizarre sexual behavior. In addition, had he been convicted of the felony charges, he could have been sentenced to a long prison term; but if he pleaded guilty to the misdemeanor charge, he could expect to be placed on probation and not serve any jail or prison time unless he violated probation.

In cases involving minor offenses, most defendants are placed on probation. That means they do not have to serve time in jail or prison. They might prefer to plead guilty and get on with their lives. Pleading guilty may save the family money in the case of defendants who do not qualify for publicly supported counsel. Getting back to work enables defendants to continue supporting their families and to reduce the stress placed on everyone by an indecisive situation.

Defendants who plead guilty may be familiar with the court process and the reputation of the prosecutor in that jurisdiction. If the prosecutor has a reputation for recommending stricter sentences for defendants who insist on trials, compared to those who plead guilty, the defendant may be willing to enter a guilty plea. If juries in that jurisdiction have a reputation for being tough on defendants, that reputation might lead the defendant to plead guilty.

The defense attorney may encourage the defendant to plead guilty. In many cases, this is the best advice that the attorney can give the defendant and should not be viewed as a dereliction of the defense attorney's duty to the client. It may be bad advice in some cases; but if the defendant has little chance of acquittal at trial, the defendant is entitled to know that. In addition, most attorneys will explain what may be expected financially and otherwise if the case goes to trial. In all cases, however, the final decision whether to plead guilty should be made by the defendant.

In deciding whether to plead guilty, the defendant may consider carefully the implications of studies showing that defendants who plead guilty are less likely to be sentenced to prison than defendants who go to trial and are convicted. Many who plead guilty receive shorter sentences than those who go to trial. The difference may be related to the nature of the offense or to other factors that are not in themselves related to whether guilt is determined by a guilty plea or by a trial.

Jurisdictions vary in the processes by which defendants plead guilty, but generally the plea is entered in open court and recorded on a form signed by the defendant and defense counsel. By signing this form, defendants swear that they are of sound mind, that they are not under the influence of alcohol or other drugs, that they understand fully that they are waiving the rights associated with a trial, and that nothing has been promised in return for their signatures on this form. The form contains the sentence recommended by the prosecutor. The judge does not have to abide by that recommendation but usually does.

After the form is completed, the defendant, the defense attorney, and the prosecutor appear before the magistrate or judge for formal entering of the plea. At that time the judge questions the defendant. Before the plea is accepted, the judge must be convinced that the plea is a knowing and intelligent one and made voluntarily. The Supreme Court has made it clear that, because a defendant who pleads guilty gives up several constitutional rights, including the right to a trial by an impartial jury, that guilty plea requires "an intentional relinquishment or abandonment of a known right or privilege" and must be declared void if it is not a knowing and intelligent plea.[71]

If the judge decides that the plea is a knowing and intelligent one, he or she may accept that plea, in which case a formal record will be made with the court. Generally, the form specifies how long the defendant has for an appeal on a sentence imposed by the court. Defendants who change their minds and wish to withdraw their guilty pleas may petition the court to do so. If that request is made prior to sentencing, the judge may grant it; usually motions to withdraw a guilty plea after sentencing are not granted. There is no absolute right to withdraw a guilty plea at any time.[72]

Plea Bargaining

One of the most controversial practices in U.S. criminal justice systems is **plea bargaining,** a process in which the prosecution and the defense attempt to negotiate a plea. The negotiation may involve reducing charges, dropping charges, or recommending a sentence. Plea bargaining became a part of U.S. criminal justice systems after the Civil War but was not practiced widely until this century. Little attention was paid to the process until crime commissions began their studies in the 1920s.[73]

It was not until the 1970s that the Supreme Court recognized plea bargaining as appropriate and even essential to criminal justice systems. In 1971 the Court approved plea bargaining as a means of managing overloaded criminal dockets, referring to the process as "an essential component" of the criminal process, which "properly administered . . . is to be encouraged."[74] The plea bargaining process may not involve threatened physical harm or mental coercion that might result in an involuntary plea by the defendant.[75]

There is no right to plea bargaining. According to the Supreme Court, states and Congress may abolish plea bargaining, but where it does exist, it is not improper to offer leniency "and other substantial benefits" to defendants in exchange for a guilty plea.[76] In 1984 the Court upheld a prosecutor's withdrawal of an offer that had been accepted by the defendant. After he accepted the prosecutor's offer, the defendant was told that the offer was a mistake and was being withdrawn. He appealed; the federal appellate court agreed with the defendant that the withdrawal was not permissible. The Supreme Court disagreed, reversed the lower federal court, and stated that an agreement to a plea bargain is an "executory agreement that does not involve the constitutional rights of the accused until it is embodied in the formal pleas." In upholding the prosecutor's withdrawal of the plea, the Court said, "The Due Process Clause is not a code of ethics for prosecutors" but rather is concerned "with the manner in which persons are deprived of their liberty."[77]

The reasons for allowing plea bargaining, as well as some of the prosecutorial activities permissible in the process, were articulated by the Supreme Court in *Bordenkircher* v. *Hayes*, decided in 1978. This case involved a defendant who was indicted by a grand jury on the charge of uttering a forged instrument (passing a hot check), an offense carrying a prison term of two to ten years. After the arraignment on the charge, the prosecutor offered to recommend a five-year sentence if the defendant would plead guilty to the indictment. If he did not do so, the prosecutor said that he would return to the grand jury and ask for an indictment under the Kentucky Habitual Criminal Act (since repealed). Conviction under that act would have resulted in a life term in prison because the defendant had two prior felony convictions.

Defendant Hayes did not plead guilty. The prosecutor secured the indictment under the Habitual Criminal Act. The jury found Hayes guilty of uttering a forged instrument and in a separate proceeding found that he had two prior felony convictions. As required by statute, upon conviction under that act, he was sentenced to life in prison. The Supreme Court noted the need for plea bargaining; acknowledged that it is not a right; and held that although one may not be punished for exercising constitutional rights, the "give-and-take" of plea bargaining leaves the defendant free to accept or reject an offer. "To hold that the prosecutor's desire to induce a guilty plea is an 'unjustifiable standard,' which, like race or religion, may play no part in his charging decision, would contradict the very premises that underlie the concept of plea bargaining itself."[78] Four justices dissented in *Bordenkircher,* arguing that the facts of the case constituted prosecutorial vindictiveness, which the Court had held was impermissible.

In 1995 the Court decided a plea bargaining case that might reduce the use of this practice. Although the Court was interpreting a federal statute, the principle of the case may be used in other situations. *United States* v. *Mezzanatto* involved a statute specifying that incriminating statements made by a defendant in the course of a plea bargain may not be used against him or her at trial. The defendant agreed to the prosecutor's demand during plea bargaining that if the informal process were not effective and the case went to trial, he would not invoke that provision. Thus, the issue was whether the defendant should be permitted to waive the statutory provision. The Court held that the exclusionary provision of the federal rule could be and was waived by the defendant. Lower federal courts had split in their decisions on the issue.[79] It is possible that some defendants will be less candid in plea bargaining sessions as a result of this decision.

Plea bargaining may occur during any stage of the criminal process, but most defense attorneys begin negotiations as soon as possible. The longer a defendant has been in the system, the less likely prosecutors are to plea bargain because of the time and effort already spent on the case. The prosecutor may want to initiate plea bargaining early to dispose of a heavy caseload. On the other hand, he or she might stall on the process, thinking that defendants will be more cooperative the longer they have to wait, especially if they are being detained in jail.

Plea bargaining may be initiated by the prosecution or the defense, but the defendant has no right to a plea bargain. The prosecutor may refuse to discuss any kind of bargain and insist on a trial. Likewise, the defendant may refuse to bargain and insist on a trial, but a defendant who enters a guilty plea cannot withdraw it merely because he or she chose the wrong strategy.[80]

Normally, plea bargaining begins early in the pretrial procedures and is completed before the date set for trial. It is possible for the parties to negotiate a final plea after the trial has begun (as in the case of Marv Albert). In the case of Ted Kaczynski, a few weeks before the scheduled date of the trial the defense offered to plead guilty in exchange for a sentence of life without parole. The U.S. Department of Justice, however, recommended that the plea be rejected, and it was. This decision was questioned by some who pointed out the irony that after the defendant's alleged attempt at suicide, "having insisted on the death penalty, the Government is now engaged in the bizarre exercise of trying to prevent Mr. Kaczynski from killing himself so that it can continue to spend enormous amounts of money and court time trying to execute him." The *New York Times* editorialist concluded that pressing a capital trial in this case "will only prolong this costly legal farce." The amount of evidence suggesting that the defendant is mentally ill probably would have been sufficient to trigger a successful appeal if he were convicted.[81] A plea was accepted in this case, and the defendant was sentenced to life without parole.

Once the plea bargain is reached, the defense and prosecution submit formal papers to the judge, who must accept or reject the agreement. The judge is not required to abide by any promise made by the prosecution. Thus, after plea negotiations, it is possible for the defendant to enter a guilty plea with the understanding that a particular sentence will be imposed and subsequently be faced with a different, even harsher sentence.[82]

Generally, judges may not participate in plea negotiations in federal cases, although some state and local jurisdictions permit this practice. When judges participate in plea bargaining, they may suggest directly or indirectly the sentence that might be imposed in the case, encourage defense attorneys and prosecutors to reach a settlement, nudge defendants to accept the plea negotiation decision, or intervene actively in the negotiations.

One final participant in plea bargaining should be mentioned. Some jurisdictions permit victims to be a part of the negotiations if they choose to do so. Some victims do not want to participate; others may be too vindictive or too lenient, but at a minimum victims should be kept informed of the proceedings at all stages in the pretrial procedures. Whether they should participate actively in plea negotiations is controversial. Some argue that it would give defendants a chance to begin the rehabilitation process by being confronted with the victim. It would give victims an opportunity to see the defendant as a whole person. Others take the position that the participation of victims would be disruptive to the system and have a negative impact on victims.

WiseGuide Wrap-Up This chapter discusses the attorneys who prosecute and defend in criminal cases and continues through an overview of the pretrial procedures in which they engage. It begins with an historical overview of the legal profession before turning to the prosecution of a criminal case. In its analysis of prosecution, the chapter looks briefly at the historical emergence of public prosecution, contrasting that approach with the method of private prosecution that was its predecessor in the United States and that still exists in some other countries.

U.S. public prosecution systems are varied. Although most prosecutors are elected officials, their functions and the structures of their offices differ, depending on the size of the jurisdiction and the complexities of local needs. State systems of prosecution, like those at the federal level, may be quite large. They differ from local systems in some respects. State and federal prosecutors may issue opinions on the constitutionality of their respective state and federal statutes. In addition, they are charged with the prosecution of state and federal crimes, and like local prosecutors, they must make important decisions on which cases to prosecute and which charges to bring in each case.

This authority to determine whom to prosecute and which charges to bring when there are several options gives prosecutors tremendous power. Generally, a decision not to prosecute ends the case. Once the initial decision to prosecute has been made, prosecutors may drop charges. Charges may be dropped for a lack of evidence or for political or personal reasons. This power is virtually unchecked. Even when the prosecutorial decision to drop charges occurs after the defendant has made a court appearance and the judge must approve the prosecutor's decision, the prosecutor has immense power in the final determination. Frequently, judges defer to prosecutors who may insist that they are overworked, that their resources are limited, and that there is not enough evidence to continue this prosecution.

Such extensive power may lead to abuse. Prosecutors may abuse their discretion in many ways. They may charge defendants with crimes for which they have little or no evidence in order to coerce the defendants to plead guilty to crimes for which they have sufficient evidence. This avoids trials and reduces the prosecutors' caseloads while providing them with "victories."

The second focus of the chapter is on the defense of a criminal case. It begins with an overview of the defense attorney's role, followed by a discussion of the right to counsel. The evolution and current status of the right to appointed counsel for indigent defendants is explored, culminating with the critical *Gideon* decision in 1963, in which the Court held that the right to appointed counsel for indigents was not limited to capital cases but applies to other felonies as well. In 1972 the right to appointed counsel for indigents was extended. In *Argersinger* v. *Hamlin* the Court held that no one may be sentenced to incarceration, even for a short time or for a petty offense, without having had benefit of counsel at trial.

The right to appointed counsel does not exist at all pretrial and posttrial stages, although it does exist at critical stages. *Actual imprisonment,* not the mere threat of imprisonment, appears to trigger the right to appointed counsel in criminal cases.

The right to counsel involves a right to refuse counsel as well. Defendants may serve as their own attorneys, provided their waivers of counsel have been made knowingly and intelligently. They may retain private counsel if they prefer and can afford to do so.

The right to counsel implies a right to effective counsel, which has been defined by the Supreme Court in *Strickland* v. *Washington* as involving a two-prong test. The defendant must show that counsel was deficient and that deficiency resulted in prejudice to the defendant who, as a result, did not get a fair trial. This standard is very difficult to prove, but the courts must consider the totality of the circumstances in making their decisions concerning whether a defendant had effective assistance of counsel.

The discussion of defense closes with an explanation of the three major systems by which appointed counsel are provided: the public defender system, the assigned counsel system, and the contract system, noting how they differ from each other and from the use of privately retained defense counsel.

The interaction of the defense attorney and the prosecutor is important during the criminal proceedings. The pretrial procedures that are the focus of their interaction are the subject of the final section of the chapter. These procedures include some of the most critical issues and most difficult procedures in criminal justice systems. All of the pretrial court hearings are crucial, for at any stage failure to find probable cause must result in the release of the defendant. If any rights of the accused are violated during arrest, interrogation, investigation, or search and seizure, the evidence secured as a result of those violations may be excluded from the trial. Without the illegally seized evidence, many cases must be dismissed for lack of probable cause. The initial appearance, the preliminary hearing, the grand jury review, and the arraignment are concerned with the issue of determining whether there is sufficient evidence to continue the case.

The critical roles of the prosecution and the defense in these stages cannot be overemphasized. Prosecutorial discretion to drop the charges after the police have arrested a suspect may negate police crime control efforts. However, that discretionary power may serve as a check on overzealous police officers. Even after the formal charges are filed with the court, either through a prosecutorial information or a grand jury indictment, the prosecutor has considerable influence in getting those charges dismissed. This dismissal may be done for good reasons, such as lack of evidence, or for bad reasons, such as discrimination or political pressure. Prosecutors have great power at the stage of grand jury review, because grand juries usually return a true bill on indictments submitted by the prosecution.

The role of the defense attorney is to protect defendants' rights at all pretrial stages and to plan the defense strategy should the case go to trial. The role of the judge is important as well. He or she presides over all formal court hearings and has the power to grant or deny motions, to grant or deny bail in most cases, and to accept or reject guilty pleas. To a great extent, the judge controls the timing of all the stages, as he or she sets dates for the court hearings and for the trial. If a guilty plea has been accepted, usually the judge has the power to impose sentencing at that time.

Two critical procedures discussed in this chapter raise controversial issues in our criminal justice systems: the decision whether to release or detain defendants pending trial and the practice of plea bargaining. The decision whether to release a defendant on bail or to allow some other alternative requires the judge to predict whether that person would appear for trial if released prior to trial. With recent legislation in some jurisdictions permitting pretrial detention for preventive purposes, some judges have the power to detain if they think the defendant is a danger to society. These are not easy decisions in a world in which predicting human behavior is inaccurate. Yet, the decision to detain imposes great burdens on defendants, who are inconvenienced and may lose their jobs, suffer the indignities and embarrassments of a jail term, and in some cases suffer physical attacks by other inmates. For those who are acquitted of the crimes for which they are charged, pretrial detention is an incredible injustice. For society, pretrial release may mean more crime; but pretrial detention creates the need for more facilities, thus increasing the cost of criminal justice systems.

Plea bargaining is another procedure that raises many issues. The practice is necessary as long as we have high crime rates and insufficient facilities and personnel to try all cases. The practice allows the flexibility necessary if the system is to respond with any degree of concern for circumstances of individual cases. But that flexibility may lead to abuse of discretion, resulting in bitter defendants, some of whom have reasonable justification for believing that they have been treated unfairly by the system. Plea bargaining may entice defendants to plead guilty to crimes they did not commit rather than risk their constitutional right to trial. Such a choice might, and usually does, result in conviction.

Many of the subjects discussed in this chapter are important to the next as well. Attorneys and judges are the major professionals in the trial as well as during pretrial procedures. Plea bargaining may continue. Many of the motions made at pretrial may be made during the trial. The issue of whether a detained defendant should be released from jail may be reconsidered; likewise, the decision to release a defendant pending trial may be revoked when changes in the circumstances warrant that decision. Both prosecution and defense may continue investigation to secure more evidence to present at trial, particularly during a long trial. The stages in criminal justice systems are not separable. Some procedures and issues, however, are peculiar to the criminal trial, the focus of Chapter 8, which also discusses the stages of sentence and appeal.

Apply It

1. Contrast the current versus historical views of U.S. lawyers.

2. Why did a system of public prosecution develop, and what is the difference between public and private prosecution? Which system do you think is better?

3. Compare local, state, and federal prosecution systems.

4. What is the main function of the prosecutor? Why is the prosecutor allowed so much discretion in fulfilling that role? What are the problems with allowing such discretion?

5. How can prosecutorial discretion be kept within reasonable limits?

6. What is meant by the *right to counsel*? Describe briefly what that right means today compared to its historical meaning in the United States.

7. What is the importance of the *Gideon* case?

8. What is the scope of the right to appointed counsel? Should it be expanded?

9. Do you think a defendant should have the right to refuse counsel? Explain your answer.

10. What does the Supreme Court mean by *effective assistance of counsel*? If you had the opportunity to define that term for the Court, what would you include?

11. Enumerate and explain the three major systems by which appointed counsel is provided.

12. How would you suggest improving the availability and quality of legal defense counsel?

13. Would you prefer to be a defense attorney or a prosecuting attorney? Why would you choose one over the other?

14. Define each of the major steps in the criminal justice process before trial.

15. What restrictions are placed on the securing of physical evidence from a suspect?

16. Describe the main purposes of the *initial appearance, preliminary hearing*, and *arraignment*.

17. What is a *grand jury indictment*? How does that process differ from a prosecutor's *information*?

18. Distinguish between *depositions* and *interrogatories*.

19. What should be considered in deciding whether to release a defendant prior to trial?

20. What is the *bail bond system*, and why is it controversial today?

21. Which of the alternatives to a bail bond system do you think is most feasible? Why?

22. Describe the process of pleading guilty before trial. Does it make any difference whether the plea is a negotiated one?

23. Do you think plea bargaining should be abolished? Why? If it is, what might result?

Notes

1. "Those #*X!!! Lawyers," *Time* (10 April 1978), p. 66.
2. Alexis de Tocqueville, "The Temper of the Legal Profession in the United States," in *Before the Law: An Introduction to the Legal Process*, ed. John J. Bonsignore et al. (Boston: Houghton Mifflin, 1974), p. 151.
3. James Willard Hurst, *Growth of American Law* (Boston: Little, Brown, 1950), p. 6.
4. See Peter H. Rossi, "Occupational Prestige in the United States, 1925–1963," *American Journal of Sociology* 70 (November 1964): 286–302. See also Quintin Johnstone and Don Hopson Jr., *Lawyers and Their Work: An Analysis of the Legal Profession in the United States and England* (Indianapolis: Bobbs-Merrill, 1967).
5. Bailey Morris, "Lawyers' Images of Yesteryear Are Crumbling Fast," *Washington Star* (13 September 1976), p. 1A.
6. Ibid.
7. Quoted in "Burger Warns About a Society Overrun by Lawyers," *New York Times* (28 May 1977), p. 1.
8. Whitney North Seymour Jr., *Why Justice Fails* (New York: Morrow, 1973), p. 7.
9. See Abraham S. Goldstein, "Prosecution: History of the Public Prosecutor," in *Encyclopedia of Crime and Justice*, vol. 3, ed. Sanford H. Kadish (New York: Macmillan, 1983), pp. 1286–1289.
10. "For the People: Richard McQuate Has Prestige, Little Crime as a Rural Prosecutor," *Wall Street Journal* (6 May 1976), p. 1.
11. Joan E. Jacoby, *The American Prosecutor: A Search for Identity* (Lexington, Mass.: D. C. Heath, 1980), pp. 55–61, 64–65, 71–74, 275, 277, 278.
12. For an overview of state prosecution system, see Bureau of Justice Statistics, *Prosecutors in State Courts, 1992* (Washington, D.C.: U.S. Department of Justice, December 1993).
13. For a summary of the criminal and civil prosecutions made by U.S. attorneys, along with a description of the systems, see the most recent annual report, *United States Attorneys Annual Statistical Report Fiscal Year 1996* (Washington, D.C.: U.S. Department of Justice, March 1997).

14. *ABA Standards for Criminal Justice: The Prosecution Function*, Standard 3-1.2, approved by the ABA House of Delegates February 1992. For a journalistic account of prosecutors and their work, based on interviews with famous prosecutors, see James Stewart, *The Prosecutors* (New York: Simon & Schuster, 1987).

15. State v. Mitchell, 395 A.2d 1257 (Sup.Ct.App.Div. N.J. 1978).

16. See, for example, Bruce Fein, "Time to Rein in the Prosecution: New Rules Are Necessary to Limit Potential Abuse of Power," *American Bar Association Journal* 80 (July 1994): 96.

17. United States v. Armstrong, 517 U.S. 456 (1996).

18. Oyler v. Boles, 368 U.S. 448, 456 (1962).

19. See Abraham S. Goldstein, *The Passive Judiciary: Prosecutorial Discretion and the Guilty Plea* (Baton Rouge: Louisiana State University Press, 1981), p. 9.

20. See Peter W. Greenwood, "The Violent Offender in the Criminal Justice System," in *Criminal Violence*, ed. Marvin E. Wolfgang and Neil Alan Weiner (Beverly Hills, Calif.: Sage Publications, 1982), p. 334.

21. See John Buchanan, "Police-Prosecutor Teams: Innovations in Several Jurisdictions," *National Institute of Justice Reports* (May–June 1989): pp. 2–8.

22. *Principles of Federal Prosecution* (Washington, D.C.: U.S. Department of Justice, 1980).

23. See, for example, Rev. Code Wash., Section 9.94A.440(1) (1997).

24. Yick Wo v. Hopkins, 118 U.S. 356 (1886). In the *Yick Wo* case, a public board that was authorized to issue laundry licenses denied licenses to Chinese applicants and granted licenses to nearly all white applicants.

25. Brady v. Maryland, 373 U.S. 83 (1963).

26. "Former Prosecutor Accused of Bias in Election Year," *New York Times* (3 April 1997), p. 10.

27. Powell v. Alabama, 287 U.S. 45 (1932). See also Wayne R. LaFave and Jerold H. Israel, *Criminal Procedure* (St. Paul, Minn.: West Publishing, 1985), pp. 473–475. This source was used for this historical background of the right to counsel.

28. Johnson v. Zerbst, 304 U.S. 458 (1938).

29. Betts v. Brady, 316 U.S. 455 (1942), *overruled,* Gideon v. Wainwright, 372 U.S. 335 (1963).

30. Gideon v. Wainwright, 372 U.S. 335 (1963). For a detailed account of this case, see Anthony Lewis, *Gideon's Trumpet* (New York: Random House, 1964).

31. Argersinger v. Hamlin, 407 U.S. 25, 37 (1972).

32. Scott v. Illinois, 440 U.S. 367 (1979).

33. United States v. Wade, 388 U.S. 218 (1967).

34. Kirby v. Illinois, 406 U.S. 682, 689 (1972) (plurality opinion).

35. Gideon v. Wainwright, 372 U.S. 335 (1963).

36. See Douglas v. California, 372 U.S. 353 (1963), holding that an indigent defendant must be appointed counsel for the initial appeal that he or she is granted as a matter of right; that is, the appeal is mandatory, not discretionary.

37. See Walker v. McLain, 768 F.2d 1181 (10th Cir. 1985), *cert. denied,* 474 U.S. 1061 (1986), extending the right to appointed counsel to *civil* cases that might result in a jail term.

38. See Commonwealth v. Finley, 481 U.S 551 (1987).

39. See Faretta v. California, 422 U.S. 806, 807 (1975).

40. See McKaskle v. Wiggins, 465 U.S. 168 (1984).

41. "Judge Requires Mental Testing for Kaczynski," *New York Times* (9 January 1998), p. 1; "Judge Orders Unabom Suspect to Cooperate in Psychiatric Tests," *New York Times* (10 January 1998), p. 1.

42. See "Thanks to Good Lawyers, the Wealthy Don't Live on Death Row," *Miami Herald* (11 September 1994), p. 6.

43. Powell v. Alabama, 287 U.S. 45 (1932); Avery v. Alabama, 308 U.S. 444 (1940); Glasser v. United States, 315 U.S. 60 (1942); Michel v. Louisiana, 350 U.S. 91 (1955); McMann v. Richardson, 397 U.S. 759 (1970).

44. Diggs v. Welch, 148 F.2d 667 (D.C.Cir. 1945); *cert denied,* 325 U.S. 889 (1945); Rummel v. Estelle, 590 F.2d 103 (5th Cir. 1979), *remanded,* 498 F.Supp. 793 (W.D.Tex. 1980), *aff'd.,* 445 U.S. 263 (1980).

45. Strickland v. Washington, 466 U.S. 668 (1984). See also United States v. Cronic, 466 U.S. 648 (1984); and Burger v. Kemp, 483 U.S. 776 (1987).

46. See Murray v. Carrier, 477 U.S. 478 (1986).

47. Strickland v. Washington, 466 U.S. 668, 689 (1984).

48. Note: "Racism in Our Courts: The Underfunding of Public Defenders and Its Disproportionate Impact upon Racial Minorities," *Hastings Constitutional Law Quarterly* 22 (Fall 1994): 219–267.

49. Robert L. Spangenberg, "We Are Still Not Defending the Poor Properly," *Criminal Justice* 3 (Fall 1989): 11–13, 44–45.

50. "New York Plans to Replace Striking Legal Aid Lawyers," *New York Times* (14 October 1994), p. 16.

51. "LSC Funds Stable," *Chicago Daily Law Review* (14 November 1997), p. 1.

52. For an account of the job of public defender, based on a study of Cook County, Illinois, see Lisa J. McIntyre, *The Public Defender: The Practice of Law in the Shadows of Repute* (Chicago: University of Chicago Press, 1987). For a more recent analysis of burnout and other problems of public defenders, see Charles J. Ogletree Jr., "Beyond Justifications: Seeking Motivations to Sustain Public Defenders," *Harvard Law Review* 106 (April 1993): 1239–1292.

53. See, for example, Holt v. United States, 218 U.S. 245 (1910), upholding the requirement that the defendant model a blouse. Holt was referred to in 1966 as the "landmark case." In Schmerber v. California, 384 U.S. 757 (1966), the Court permitted securing blood samples from the defendant.

54. See, for example, State v. Bible, 858 P.2d 1152 (Ariz. 1993), *cert. denied,* 511 U.S. 1046 (1994), holding that probability calculations used by Cellmark labs were not admissible because the techniques used were not generally accepted in the scientific community. To the contrary, see United States v. Jakobetz, 955 F.2d 786 (2d Cir. 1992), *cert. denied,* 506 U.S. 834 (1992), a federal case upholding the admission of DNA evidence. The two important cases on the issue of expert witnesses that affect the DNA issues are Frye v. United States, 293 F. 1013 (1923), effectively replaced by Daubert v. Merrell Dow Pharmaceuticals, 509 U.S. 579 (1993). Daubert relaxes the rules concerning expert testimony on scientific evidence.

55. See, for example, United States v. Wade, 388 U.S. 218 (1967).

56. See Simmons v. United States, 390 U.S. 377 (1968).

57. See Commander v. State, 734 P.2d 313 (Okla.Crim.App. 1987).

58. Press-Enterprise Co. v. Superior Court of California, 478 U.S. 1 (1986).

59. Wood v. Georgia, 370 U.S. 375, 390 (1962).

60. See, for example, Vasquez v. Hillery, 474 U.S. 254 (1986); and United States v. Mechanik, 475 U.S. 66 (1986).

61. See Gerstein v. Pugh, 420 U.S. 103 (1975).

62. County of Riverside [California] v. McLaughlin, 500 U.S. 42 (1991).

63. Powell v. Alabama, 287 U.S. 45, 57 (1932).

64. See U.S. Code, Title 18, Section 3142(c)(1) (1997).

65. Stack v. Boyle, 342 U.S. 1 (1951).

66. United States v. Edwards, 430 A.2d 1321 (D.C.Ct.App. 1981), *cert. denied,* 455 U.S. 1022 (1982).

67. Schall v. Martin, 467 U.S. 253 (1984).

68. United States v. Montalvo-Murillo, 495 U.S. 711 (1990). The Bail Reform Act may be found in U.S. Code, Chapter 18, Sections 3141 et.seq. (1997).

69. United States v. Salerno, 481 U.S. 739 (1987).

70. Bureau of Justice Statistics, *Felony Sentences in State Courts 1988* (Washington, D.C.: U.S. Department of Justice, December 1990), p. 1.

For a detailed study of the guilty plea, see Peter F. Nardulli et al., *The Tenor of Justice: Criminal Courts and the Guilty Plea Process* (Chicago: University of Illinois Press, 1988).

71. Johnson v. Zerbst, 304 U.S. 458 (1938).
72. See United States v. Buckles, 843 F.2d 469 (11th Cir. 1988), c*ert. denied*, 490 U.S. 1099 (1989).
73. For a brief history, see Joseph B. Sanborn Jr., "A Historical Sketch of Plea Bargaining," *Justice Quarterly* 3 (June 1986): 111–138.
74. Santobello v. New York, 404 U.S. 257, 260–61 (1971).
75. Brady v. United States, 397 U.S. 742 (1970).
76. Corbitt v. New Jersey, 439 U.S. 212 (1978).
77. Mabry v. Johnson, 467 U.S. 504 (1984).
78. Bordenkircher v. Hayes, 434 U.S. 357, 360–365 (1978).

79. United States v. Mezzanatto, 513 U.S. 196 (1995).
80. Brady v. United States, 397 U.S. 742, 757 (1970).
81. "The Unabomber Travesty," *New York Times* (10 January 1998), p. 24.
82. Although the case involves complications not discussed here, in Rickets v. Adamson, 483 U.S. 1 (1987), the Supreme Court held that defendant's right not to be tried twice for the same offense was not violated under these facts. Defendant, one of three charged with first-degree murder, entered a guilty plea in return for a specific prison term and his testimony against codefendants. He complied with that agreement and received a prison term. But he refused to testify when the codefendants were retried after their first convictions were overturned on appeal. Defendant was tried for first-degree murder, convicted, and sentenced to death.

8

Trial, Sentencing, and Appeal

WiseGuide Intro

Chapter 7 notes that most cases are not tried, but for those that are tried it is important to know the rules and constitutional principles that govern the processes involved in a criminal trial. This chapter begins with a discussion of defendants' constitutional rights at trial and explains the major processes that occur during the trial and sentencing. The decisions made during those stages may be appealed; thus, appeals and writs are explained as well.

Key Terms

beyond a reasonable doubt
capital punishment
circumstantial evidence
community work service
concurrent sentence
consecutive sentence
contempt of court
corporal punishment
cross examination
demonstrative evidence
determinate sentence
direct examination
direct evidence
directed verdict
fine
good time credits
habeas corpus
harmless errors
hearsay evidence
incarceration
indeterminate sentence
jury
mandatory sentence
mistrial
pardon
peremptory challenge
petit jury
prejudicial errors
presentence investigation (PSI)
presumption of innocence
presumptive sentence

probation
recidivist
restitution
sentence
sentence disparity
summons
three strikes and you're out
trial
truth in sentencing
voir dire
writ

Learning Objectives

Learning Objectives

After reading this chapter, you should be able to do the following:

- State an overview of defendants' constitutional rights.
- Explain the defendant's right to a speedy, public trial by an impartial jury.
- Discuss the variables of gender, race, age, and disability in jury selection.
- List and explain the stages in the trial and appeal of a criminal case in the United States.
- Explain how evidence is presented in a criminal trial, and discuss the various types of evidence and objections to evidence.
- Distinguish the prosecution's case from the case of the defense.
- Discuss the role of the jury in deciding a criminal case.

- Explain and analyze the concept and process of sentencing and sentencing strategies.
- Discuss the sentencing hearing and decision.
- List and define the major types of sentences.
- Define *sentence disparity,* and analyze the impact of race and gender on sentencing.
- Describe the use of sentencing guidelines by states and the federal government.
- Explain the difference between indeterminate and determinate sentencing and evaluate each.
- Describe *appeals* and *writs*.

Constitutional Issues at Trial

Earlier chapters contain general discussions of the adversary system and the concepts of due process and equal protection, as well as defendants' specific constitutional rights. The legitimate police practices of reasonable searches and seizures, as well as interrogation of suspects, are examined in light of the constitutional prohibition against unreasonable searches and seizures and the right of defendants not to be compelled to testify against themselves. The right to counsel at all critical stages in the criminal justice process is discussed, along with the right to effective assistance of counsel and the right to refuse counsel. All these rights are important at trial; they were discussed earlier because they are important during pretrial procedures as well. This analysis of constitutional issues at trial is not meant to be exclusive. It must be understood in the context of the earlier discussions, but it focuses on the constitutional issues and rights that have not been presented earlier or that pertain primarily to a criminal trial.

Speedy Trial

The right to a speedy **trial** is embodied in the Sixth Amendment (see Appendix A). The Supreme Court has held that this right "is as fundamental as any of the rights secured by the Sixth Amendment."[1]

In 1974 Congress passed the Speedy Trial Act, which, with its subsequent amendments, provides that, for suspects in federal cases, an indictment or an information must be filed within thirty days of the arrest or of the time when the defendant is served with a summons on the charge. That period may be extended for thirty days in a felony charge if the grand jury was not in session during that time. It is possible that the defendant could be tried so quickly that there would not be adequate time for preparing a defense. The Speedy Trial Act provides that, without the consent of the defendant, "the trial shall not commence less than thirty days from the date on which the defendant first appears through counsel or expressly waives counsel and elects to proceed pro se."[2]

Some delays are permissible under the Speedy Trial Act. Several are listed in the act, including the obvious ones, such as those delays caused by examinations to determine whether the defendant is competent to stand trial; delays caused by the defendant's mental incompetence to stand trial; and delays caused by deferred prosecution when that is agreed on by the prosecutor, the defendant, and the court. The act permits delays caused by continuances granted to the defense or to the prosecution when they are granted to serve the ends of justice.

The Speedy Trial Act applies only to prosecutions in federal courts, but most states have constitutional provisions for the right to a speedy trial. Those provisions are similar to the Sixth Amendment. In addition, most states have procedural or statutory rules denoting how many days may elapse between arrest and trial. Texas, for example, provides as follows:

> Insofar as is practicable, the trial of a criminal action shall be given preference over trials of civil cases, and the trial of a criminal action against a defendant who is detained in jail pending trial of the action shall be given preference over trials of other criminal actions.[3]

The Texas rules of criminal procedure provide specifically that the court shall entertain a motion to set aside an indictment, information, or complaint if the state is not prepared to go to trial within a specified time after these methods of beginning criminal cases have begun. The time permitted is 180 days for a felony case; 90 days for a misdemeanor punishable by more than 180 days in prison; and 60 days for a misdemeanor punishable by less than 180 days in prison or by a fine only.[4]

Public Trial

The Sixth Amendment guarantees the right to a public trial. This right does not mean that the defendant may be tried by the media. If it can be shown that the defendant cannot get a fair trial because of publicity in the jurisdiction where the case is to be tried, the trial should be moved to another jurisdiction.

Media publicity in criminal cases raises a delicate problem: the conflict between the First Amendment (see Appendix A) free speech right of the press and the public's right to know and the defendant's right to a trial by an impartial jury not biased by media information.

The Supreme Court has had several occasions to consider the conflict between the defendant's right to a fair trial and the First Amendment rights of the press. In a 1966 case, the Court overturned the conviction of Dr. Sam Sheppard, who had served ten years in prison after his conviction for murdering his wife. On retrial Sheppard received an **acquittal**, but he was not allowed to return to the practice of medicine. He tried to begin a new life in France after suffering intense rejection in the United States, but subsequently committed suicide. In overturning Sheppard's conviction, the Court said:

> Murder and mystery, society, sex and suspense were combined in this case in such a manner as to intrigue and captivate the public fancy to a degree perhaps unparalleled in recent annals. Throughout the preindictment investigation, the subsequent legal skirmishes and the nine-week trial, circulation-conscious editors catered to the insatiable interest of the American public in the bizarre. . . . In this atmosphere of a "Roman holiday" for the news media, Sam Sheppard stood trial for his life.[5]

Sheppard's case became the subject of a 1960s TV series and a 1994 movie, "The Fugitive." In late 1997 Dr. Sheppard's son, Sam Reece Sheppard, and his attorneys for his father's estate won permission to present their arguments on

13 January 1998 to the Ohio Supreme Court. The Court is considering whether the estate should be entitled to damages for wrongful imprisonment for the ten years Dr. Sheppard spent in prison.[6]

In subsequent cases the Court has continued to wrestle with the rights of defendants versus the First Amendment free speech right of the press and of the public. The Court has held that under some circumstances the former must give way to the latter.[7] Later cases have examined what some of those circumstances might be. For example, in *Globe Newspaper Co.* v. *Superior Court*, the Court invalidated a Massachusetts statute that had been interpreted to mean exclusion of the press from *all* trials when sexual offense victims under the age of eighteen were testifying. The Court ruled that each case must be examined in terms of its own facts, such as "the minor victim's age, psychological maturity and understanding, the nature of the crime, the desires of the victim, and the interests of parents and relatives."[8]

Trial by Jury

The Sixth Amendment (see Appendix A) guarantees the defendant in a criminal case the right to trial by **jury**. In 1968 in *Duncan* v. *Louisiana* the Court held that this right applies to the states through the Fourteenth Amendment.[9] Technically, the jury that sits in a trial is called the **petit jury**. The word *petit* means minor, small, or inconsequential, but in this context it is used to distinguish the trial jury from the larger grand jury, not to carry the connotation of inconsequential.

The importance of the right to a jury trial, along with a brief history of its evolution, was emphasized by the Supreme Court in *Duncan* v. *Louisiana*. This case involved a defendant who was charged with simple battery, a misdemeanor punishable by a maximum of two years' imprisonment, and a $300 fine. Duncan's request for a trial by jury was denied by a Louisiana trial court. At that time, the Louisiana Constitution granted jury trials only in cases in which convicted defendants could be sentenced to imprisonment at hard labor or to capital punishment. Duncan was convicted of the crime charged, sentenced to sixty days in the parish prison, and fined $150. The Louisiana Supreme Court denied his request for appeal. Duncan appealed to the U.S. Supreme Court, alleging that he had been denied his constitutional right to a jury trial. The Court agreed, as illustrated by the following brief excerpt from the case:[10]

> A right to jury trial is granted to criminal defendants in order to prevent oppression by the Government. . . . Providing an accused with the right to be tried by a jury of his peers gave him an inestimable safeguard against the corrupt or overzealous prosecutor and against the compliant, biased, or eccentric judge. . . . [T]he jury trial provisions in the Federal and State Constitutions reflect a fundamental decision about the exercise of official power—a reluctance to entrust plenary powers over the life and liberty of the citizen to one judge or to a group of judges. . . . The deep commitment of the Nation to the right of jury trial in serious criminal cases as a defense against arbitrary law enforcement qualifies for protection under the Due Process Clause of the Fourteenth Amendment, and must therefore be respected by the States.

Although it held that Duncan was entitled to a trial by jury, the Court did say in passing "that there is a category of petty crimes or offenses which is not subject to the Sixth Amendment jury trial provision."[11] The right may be waived provided the waiver is made knowingly, intelligently, voluntarily, and in writing and is accepted by the court.

The Constitution does not specify how many jurors must be present in order for the defendant's right to a jury trial to be legal. Although twelve is the usual number of petit jurors, the U.S. Supreme Court has upheld the use of smaller juries in some cases. There must be at least six jurors,[12] and a jury that small must be unanimous.[13] The Court had held previously that a unanimous vote is not required in a twelve-person state jury trial,[14] although the Court has recognized the right to unanimity in federal jury trials.[15]

The Sixth Amendment provides for the right to trial by an *impartial* jury, which means a number of things, including the right to a jury not prejudiced unduly by media publicity. We have noted that in some cases it is necessary to move the location of the trial to eliminate the impact of extensive publicity in the area in which the crime occurred. In some cases that might not be possible because of extensive national publicity. In those instances the trial judge may order the jury sequestered for the trial, but a very long sequestration might work against the defense (or the prosecution if it is perceived as prolonging the trial unnecessarily) and certainly is disruptive to the lives of jurors, their families, and employers.

The Sixth Amendment provides for a trial by a jury of the defendant's peers, which has been interpreted by the Court to involve implications for the exclusion of people from the jury on the basis of specific characteristics, such as gender, race, religion, and so on. Despite the acceptance of the process of excusing some potential jurors, our statutes and court decisions establish guidelines on exclusions that may be made in the composition of juries.[16]

Juries must be representative of the community, but that does not mean that

> juries must mirror the community and reflect the various distinctive groups in the population. Defendants are not entitled to a jury of any particular composition, but the jury wheels, pools of names, panels, or venires [list of persons summoned to serve in the jury pool for a particular case] from which juries are drawn must not systematically exclude distinctive groups in the community and thereby fail to be reasonably representative thereof.[17]

It is not clear what is meant by *the community*, but it is clear that exclusions based on race and gender are impermissible. It is the *systematic exclusion* of particular groups of persons from the jury pool or jury selection that constitutes the problem, illustrated primarily by the Court's rulings regarding the exclusion of African Americans from juries. In 1880 the Supreme Court held that a statute permitting only white men to serve on juries was unconstitutional. In 1965 the Court held that it was permissible to exclude individual African Americans through *peremptory challenges* (discussed on p. 211), but the Court left open the possibility that systematic exclusion of African Americans would not be acceptable.[18]

Other decisions were made in the intervening years, but the key decision did not come until 1986 in *Batson* v. *Kentucky*, in which the defendant proved that he was a member of a cognizable racial group whose members were excluded from the jury under circumstances that raise an inference that they were excluded because of race.[19] Portions of *Batson* are included in Spotlight 8.1.

Since *Batson*, lower courts and the Supreme Court have dealt with variations in fact patterns in which the case might apply,[20] including holding that a criminal defendant does not have to be of the same race as the excluded juror to object to race-based exclusions because excluded jurors have a constitutional right not to be excluded from juries based on their race;[21] that *Batson* applies equally to the removal of white as well as African American potential jurors and to defense as well as prosecution;[22] that a defendant may challenge a prosecutor's race-based exclusion of a potential juror regardless of whether the defendant and the

Spotlight 8.1

Race and Jury Selection: The *Batson* Rule

In *Batson* v. *Kentucky*, the U.S. Supreme Court held that it is unconstitutional to exclude African Americans from juries when there is evidence that the exclusion is based on race. The Court stated:

Petitioner, a black man, was indicted in Kentucky on charges of second-degree burglary and receipt of stolen goods. The prosecutor used his peremptory challenges to strike all four black persons on the venire, and a jury composed only of white persons was selected. . . .

Exclusion of black citizens from service as jurors constitutes a primary example of the evil the Fourteenth Amendment was designed to cure. . . .

The Equal Protection Clause guarantees the defendant that the State will not exclude members of his race from the jury venire on account of race, or on the false assumption that members of his race as a group are not qualified to serve as jurors. . . .

Racial discrimination in selection of jurors harms not only the accused whose life or liberty they are summoned to try. Competence to serve as a juror ultimately depends on an assessment of individual qualifications and ability impartially to consider evidence presented at a trial. A person's race simply "is unrelated to his fitness as a juror.". . .

The harm from discriminatory jury selection extends beyond that inflicted on the defendant and the excluded juror to touch the entire community. Selection procedures that purposefully exclude black persons from juries undermine public confidence in the fairness of our system of justice. . . .

Although a prosecutor ordinarily is entitled to exercise permitted peremptory challenges "for any reason at all, as long as that reason is related to his view concerning the outcome" of the case to be tried, the Equal Protection clause forbids the prosecutor to challenge potential jurors solely on account of their race or on the assumption that black jurors as a group will be unable impartially to consider the State's case against a black defendant.

[The Court discussed procedures for contesting the peremptory challenges and concluded that the conviction in this case should be reversed.]

Source: Batson v. Kentucky, 476 U.S. 79 (1986), citations and footnotes omitted.

excluded juror are of the same race;[23] and that *Batson* applies to civil as well as to criminal cases.[24]

Gender is another important category in jury selection. Women have a right to serve on juries; defendants have a right to have women serve on juries. Lower court decisions varied on the issues, but in 1994 the U.S. Supreme Court settled the controversy. The Court's decision in *Batson* was extended to include gender. *J.E.B.* v. *Alabama ex. rel. T.B* is a civil rather than a criminal case, but it is likely that the holding will apply to criminal cases as well. Justice Harry Blackmun (who has since retired from the Court) delivered the Court's opinion, stating, "We hold that gender, like race, is an unconstitutional proxy for juror competence and impartiality."[25]

Two other categories that might be the basis for exclusion or failure to include are age and disability. The Court has not held that defendants have a right to a jury of peers of their own ages. In 1985 a federal court reversed one of its earlier decisions and held that a young defendant did not have a right to a new trial because young adults from ages eighteen to thirty-four were underrepresented on the jury. The court held that a "mere statistical disparity in the chosen age group" is not sufficient to establish a violation of the Sixth Amendment right to a jury of peers. The defendant must show that the underrepresented group is defined and limited by a factor or characteristics that can be defined easily, that the group may be characterized by a common thread of similarity in attitude, ideas, or experience, and that the group has a community of interest. The U.S. Supreme Court refused to hear the case, thus permitting the lower court's decision to stand.[26]

Finally, with the current emphasis on the rights of disabled persons, exemplified by the passage of and the numerous cases being brought under the Americans with Disabilities Act (ADA), consideration must be given to extending the right to serve on juries to those whose physical or mental disabilities might have precluded such service in the past.[27]

Some constitutional rights of defendants discussed earlier in connection with the police or with pretrial procedures may be applicable during the trial of a criminal case as well. Some of those rights take on their fullest meaning during the trial. For example, defendants must be notified of the charges against them. That notice must occur during the early pretrial stages, but formal charges must be read to the defendant at the trial. A confession obtained or evidence secured in violation of a defendant's rights should be excluded from the trial under the exclusionary rule.

Other Constitutional Issues at Trial

Defendants have the right to compel witnesses to testify on their behalf and the right to confront and to cross examine witnesses who testify against them. These rights and others have been interpreted to mean that defendants have a right to be present at the trial. The right to be present at the trial, however, is subject to the defendant's good behavior, as illustrated by the classic case of *Illinois* v. *Allen.*[28]

Illinois v. *Allen* involved a defendant, Allen, who appealed his conviction for armed robbery on the grounds that he was excluded improperly from his own trial. At the beginning of the trial, Allen insisted on being his own lawyer, rejecting the services of his court-appointed counsel. When Allen began questioning prospective jurors, the judge interrupted him and asked him to confine his questions to the matters relating to their qualifications. Allen responded in an abusive and disrespectful manner. The judge asked appointed counsel to proceed with the examination of prospective jurors. Allen continued to talk, "proclaiming that the appointed attorney was not going to act as his lawyer. He terminated his remarks by saying, 'When I go out for lunchtime, you're [the judge] going to be a corpse here.'"

Allen took a file from his attorney, tore it, and threw it on the floor. The judge warned Allen that he would remove him from the trial if he continued in this manner, but the warning had no effect on Allen's conduct. Allen was removed from the courtroom, and the examination of the jury continued in his absence. Later he was returned to the court but was removed again after another outburst. During the presentation of the state's case, occasionally Allen was brought to the courtroom for identification, but during one of those visits he used vile and abusive language in responding to a question from the judge. After assuring the court he would behave, Allen was permitted to be in the courtroom while his attorney presented the case for the defense.

Justice Hugo Black delivered the opinion for the Court, which upheld the right of the trial judge to exclude Allen from his own trial. Black pointed out that the trial judge had three constitutionally permissible options in this case. He could cite Allen for **contempt of court**, exclude him from the trial, or bind and gag him and leave him in the trial. Each option was discussed, with the Court noting the possible prejudicial effect binding and gagging might have on the jury.

Not only is it possible that the sight of shackles and gags might have a significant effect on the jury's feelings about the defendant, but the use of this technique is itself something of an affront to the very dignity and decorum of judicial proceedings that the judge is seeking to uphold.[29]

The Court noted that another problem with gagging is that this procedure prevents the defendant from meaningful contact with his attorney. For that reason, the Court refused to hold that the state must use this method in lieu of excluding the defendant from trial. Further, the Court emphasized the importance of maintaining decorum in the courtroom. "The flagrant disregard in the courtroom of elementary standards of proper conduct should not and cannot be tolerated." The Court continued with these words:

> [I]f our courts are to remain what the Founders intended, the citadels of justice, their proceedings cannot and must not be infected with the sort of scurrilous, abusive language and conduct paraded before the Illinois trial judge in this case.[30]

The Trial Process

In this section the stages or steps of a criminal trial are discussed in the order in which they generally occur. Spotlight 8.2 lists those steps, and the discussion follows the order in that list. These stages are not always distinct, and some of the procedures may occur at various stages. For example, motions might be made throughout the trial; an obvious motion is one to dismiss or to declare a mistrial made by defense counsel after the prosecutor or a prosecution witness has said something improper. A defense motion for change of venue (place of trial) might be made before and during the trial as increased media attention to the trial leads the defense to argue that it is impossible for the defendant to have a fair trial in that area.

Opening the Court Session

When it is time for the trial court session to begin, the bailiff arrives and calls the court to order with such words as "Hear ye, hear ye, the court of the Honorable Judge Decider is in session—all rise." At that point everyone in the courtroom should rise. The judge, usually dressed in a robe, enters the courtroom and sits. Then everyone else may sit. The judge announces the case, "The State of California versus John Jones, Case No. 45629-16." The judge asks whether the prosecution is ready; if so, he or she asks whether the defense is ready. If both are ready, the case begins with jury selection, assuming that the court has no additional business regarding the case, such as pretrial motions, that need to be heard prior to the beginning of the trial.

After the jury has been selected and sworn, the judge reads the indictment or information and informs the court that the defendant has entered a plea of not guilty (or not guilty by reason of insanity if that is permitted), and the trial begins with the opening statements. Variances may occur in these procedures; for example, the jury may be selected and sent home (or sequestered) while attorneys argue various motions before the judge.

Jury Selection

Jurisdictions differ in their procedures for selecting potential members of the pool. Persons included in the jury pool for a specific case (or cases; some jurisdictions select several juries at once before beginning one trial) are notified by means of a **summons**, a formal document issued by the court to notify a person that his or her presence is required for a particular reason in a particular court at a specified time and day. The potential juror, after arriving at the specified place, may sit

Spotlight 8.2

Stages in the Trial and appeal of a U.S. Criminal Case

1. Opening of the court session
2. Jury selection
3. Opening statement by the prosecutor
4. Opening statement by the defense attorney
5. Presentation of evidence by the prosecutor
6. Cross-examination by the defense
7. Redirect examination by the prosecutor
8. Cross-examination by the defense
9. Presentation of the defense's case by the defense attorney
10. Cross-examination by the prosecutor
11. Redirect by the defense
12. Cross-examination by the prosecutor
13. Rebuttal proof by the prosecutor
14. Closing statement by the prosecutor
15. Closing statement by the defense
16. Rebuttal statement by the prosecutor
17. Submitting the case to the jury
18. The verdict
19. Postverdict motions
20. Sentencing
21. Appeals and writs

all day and not be picked for a jury. If that happens, he or she may be required to return for jury selection the following day. This procedure may go on for days, but many judges try to avoid this inconvenience to potential jurors.

Usually, the members of the jury pool are seated in the courtroom before the judge enters for jury selection. After the formal opening of the court session, the judge instructs the jury pool about procedures. The minute clerk begins by selecting names from a jury wheel, drawing names out of a fish bowl, or using some other similar procedure. As each name is drawn, the minute clerk reads and spells the name. The first selected person sits in the first seat in the jury box, and so on until the jury box is filled or contains the number the judge wishes to process at one time. Questioning of the potential jurors follows, a process called ***voir dire***, which means "to tell the truth." The defense attorney and the prosecuting attorney *voir dire* the jury pool; that is, they question each potential juror and decide whether or not they would approve the selection of that person. Judges may question potential jurors, too. In the federal system, judges may refuse to permit attorneys to question prospective jurors. Normally, in the federal system jury selection takes only a few hours; in some states, the process may take weeks or even months.

After they are questioned, potential jurors may be excused from jury duty in two ways: If they are excused for *cause*, they are presumed to be biased in the case. Bias may be presumed on the basis of the potential juror's answers to the questionnaire or to questions in court, association with or knowledge of the defendant or some other person involved in the trial, personal financial interest in the case, or some particular background that might prejudice them. For example, a person whose spouse has been murdered might be presumed to be prejudiced against a defendant on trial for murder. Attorneys are entitled to an unlimited number of challenges for cause. The judge may exclude potential jurors for cause as well.

The second way a potential juror may be excused is by **peremptory challenge**, which means that the attorneys may excuse without cause. No reason need be given; that is the purpose of the challenge. In the federal system, the prosecution and the defense each have twenty peremptory challenges in a capital case and three in a misdemeanor case. In a felony case, the prosecution has six; the defense has ten. States vary in the number of peremptory challenges permitted.

Some attorneys retain consultants to assist them in the questioning and selection of jurors. Through empirical studies, social scientists have provided information on characteristics that are related to opinions and therefore may influence the decision of a juror. In a particular case a retained jury consultant may conduct a survey to determine factors that might influence a juror in that town on that case.

Opening Statements

After the jury is selected, attorneys may make opening statements. The prosecutor makes the first opening statement. This is the prosecution's chance to outline what he or she intends to prove during the trial. The opening statement is very important; it should be planned carefully and delivered convincingly.

The opening statement should be brief but long enough to present an adequate statement of the facts the prosecution expects to prove. It should be interesting but not overly dramatic. The prosecutor must be certain not to overstep his or her boundaries and raise the ire of the judge, the defense, and the jury. Inflammatory or prejudicial statements are not permitted.

The defense is permitted to follow the prosecution with an opening statement, and many defense attorneys do so. The same principles apply to the defense as to the prosecution. The opening statement should raise the interest of the jury to listen further but should not be too long or too dramatic. A defense attorney has the option of waiving the opening statement until the prosecution has presented its evidence. Some do so in order to hear that evidence before revealing the defense. Prosecutors, knowing that this may occur, may make comments in their opening statements that would lead the jury to expect the defense to make a statement or to be suspicious if the defense does not do so.

Presentation of the Evidence

Before looking at the types of evidence that may be presented by the prosecution and the defense, it is necessary to understand some general rules of evidence and to look at the categories of evidence that apply to both the prosecution and the defense. The rules of evidence in criminal cases are contained in statutory and case law. They are complex, and they differ from one jurisdiction to another; however, a few general rules are important to a basic understanding of the criminal trial.

Any evidence presented must be relevant, competent, and material to the case. The meaning of those words has been litigated in many cases because the meaning may differ, depending on the type of case being heard. In rape cases, historically the defense was permitted to ask the complainant about her prior sexual experiences, to imply that the alleged rape was a voluntary sexual act, not one of force. If she had sexual relationships with other men, particularly if it could be inferred that she was promiscuous, a rape conviction was unlikely. Today many jurisdictions have changed that rule. Some permit such questions only if the evidence is relevant to motive or conduct during the alleged crime. Other jurisdictions do not permit any questions about the victim's sexual experiences other than with the defendant and may limit that evidence to the case on trial. This change in what is defined as material evidence may affect not only the outcome of the case, but also make it much more likely that victims will report rapes and agree to testify at trial.

Attempts by the prosecution or the defense to introduce evidence or to ask questions thought by the opposing side to be incompetent, irrelevant, or immaterial may be countered by an objection by opposing counsel. If the objection is sustained, the evidence is not admitted. If the objection involves a question posed to the witness, the judge tells the witness not to answer the question. If the question has been answered already, the judge instructs the jury to disregard the answer, unless the information is so prejudicial that the judge declares a **mistrial**, which means the case cannot continue with that jury. A new trial must be scheduled or the charges dropped.

An important evidence rule is that of *discovery*, which refers to the ability of one side to obtain the information that will be used by the other side. The purpose of discovery is to prevent surprise in the trial and to enable each side to prepare adequately for its cross examination of the evidence of the other side. If discovery procedures are violated, the judge may impose fines or more severe sanctions, such as excluding the evidence in question.

Several types of evidence may be presented. **Demonstrative evidence** is evidence that is real to the senses, in contrast to evidence presented by the testimony of other people. Examples might be the weapon used in the crime, blood samples, hair samples, clothing, and so on. The integrity of demonstrative evidence may be, and often is, challenged.

Some evidence may be competent, relevant, and material to the case but be excluded because it has been secured in violation of the defendant's rights or because it is considered to be too prejudicial or inflammatory. Deciding which evidence to admit and which to exclude is the responsibility of the judge. He or she may be overruled on appeal, but many of the decisions made at the trial (or pretrial) stages will stand, and often they are crucial to the outcome of the case.

A second type of evidence that may be introduced at trial is that of witnesses, which is referred to as *testimonial evidence*. Witnesses may be called by the prosecution or by the defense, and they are sworn in before they are permitted to testify. If they do not tell the truth, they may be prosecuted for perjury. There are several types of witnesses.

The testimony of a *victim-witness* is a preferred type of testimonial evidence. In many cases, prosecutors drop charges if victims will not agree to testify against the accused. *Eyewitnesses* are prime candidates for being called to testify in criminal cases, although some psychologists question the use of eyewitnesses, finding evidence that some jurors place too much weight on their testimonies.[31]

Expert witnesses may be called by the defense or the prosecution. Expert witnesses testify regarding subjects on which they have expertise beyond that of the average person. For example, experts in ballistics may be called to testify about the specifics of when and where the gun was fired and what kind of gun was used. Medical experts might testify to the cause of death in a murder case. Psychiatrists might testify concerning the mental or emotional state of the defendant.

Before expert evidence may be admitted, the judge must rule that the science is advanced sufficiently to qualify. The second issue regarding expert testimony is whether a particular person is qualified to testify on the subject in question. The attorney who introduces the expert offers evidence to qualify that person. Typically, experts are asked where they received their education and training, how much experience they have had, and whether they have testified in the kind of case before the court. Opposing counsel may challenge these credentials, but in most cases they are accepted and after the expert testifies, opposing counsel will try to discredit him or her during cross examination. Both the prosecution and the defense might present experts from the same field. If they disagree, it is the jury's responsibility to determine credibility. A particular expert may be allowed to testify to some but not all issues about which the attorney wishes to question him or her.

Generally witnesses must testify to facts, not opinion, although in some instances opinions are allowed. But witnesses are not permitted to testify to the ultimate question of fact in a criminal case: the guilt or innocence of the defendant.

One way for counsel to get around the requirement of factual, not opinion, testimony is to ask hypothetical questions concerning facts similar to those in the case on trial. The expert witness may answer these hypothetical questions.

In most instances experts and other witnesses are permitted to testify only to what they know, not to what they have heard from others, which constitutes **hearsay evidence**. Hearsay evidence is not admissible because there is no opportunity to cross examine the source of the information and thus determine whether it is true. There are a number of exceptions to the hearsay evidence rule, such as the so-called *dying declaration*. Since it might be presumed that one who is dying has no reason to lie, courts may permit the individual to testify (either in a deposition or at trial) to information that otherwise would be considered hearsay.

One further distinction important to the presentation of evidence is the difference between direct and circumstantial evidence. For example, a witness who testifies that he or she saw the alleged weapon being used by the defendant, is providing **direct evidence**. Much evidence, however, is not direct; rather, it is *inferred* from a fact or series of facts and is called **circumstantial evidence**. In the Oklahoma City bombing trial, the prosecution was not able to present a witness who could testify that he or she saw Terry Nichols at the federal building in Oklahoma City when it was bombed. The evidence linking Nichols with that crime was inferred from other testimony, and that testimony did not even involve inferences that he was there but rather, that he had some involvement in the planning of the crime.

After the prosecution presents its witnesses, they may be questioned by the defense attorney. The prosecution questions its witnesses in a process called **direct examination**. The defense then conducts **cross examination** of that witness or reserves the right to do so later. If the defense cross examines, the prosecutor may follow with questions of the prosecution witness in a process called *redirect examination*. If that occurs, the defense may cross examine the witness again. The same process occurs in reverse after the defense has presented its evidence.

The Prosecution's Case

The prosecution is the first to present evidence in a criminal case. Its case may include the presentation of demonstrative evidence as well as the testimony of the victim, other witnesses, and experts. Usually, police officers involved in the arrest or the investigation of the case are called to testify. The prosecutor's presentation of evidence may consume days, weeks, even months in some trials. It may involve very complicated evidence.

After the defense has rested its case, the prosecutor has the option of presenting additional proof to rebut the case presented by the defense. Not all prosecutors choose to exercise this option to present what is called *rebuttal evidence*. Where it is exercised, the prosecution may call or recall police officers or others to testify regarding facts that have been in dispute among witnesses at the trial.

The Defense Attorney's Case

After the prosecution has presented its case and all cross examinations and redirect examinations have occurred, the defense presents its case. This, too, may consume considerable time, but some special issues arise here.

First, the defendant has a right not to testify (see Appendix A, Fifth Amendment). The reason is that even innocent persons might appear guilty if they take the stand. If the defendant does not testify, neither the prosecution nor the judge may make unfavorable comments about that fact.[32]

Some defendants choose to testify. In that case they are sworn in, and they may be prosecuted for perjury if they testify to falsehoods. They may be cross examined by the prosecutor. Rules vary, but generally whatever rules apply to other witnesses apply also to the defendant. In most jurisdictions this means that the cross examination may cover only those subjects covered on direct or redirect examination. Where that is the case, the defense attorney has the ability to limit the subject matter on which the prosecution may ask questions to the subjects covered on direct examination. Some jurisdictions, however, permit the prosecution to go beyond those subjects once the defendant takes the stand.

The defense may call *character witnesses*, who testify about the defendant's character. If the defense calls character witnesses, the prosecutor may call witnesses to testify to the defendant's bad character, but the prosecutor may not begin this line of evidence. Character witnesses, like all other witnesses, may be subjected to stringent cross examination. This is difficult for many people, and therefore it is important that attorneys who plan to call character or other kinds of witnesses spend time with those witnesses preparing them for trial.

Another important element of the case of the defense is the presentation of defenses. Commission of a criminal act, even with the required criminal intent, is not sufficient for a guilty verdict if the defense proves a legally acceptable reason why the law should not be applied in this case to this defendant. Many defenses might be raised. Infancy, intoxication, duress, involuntary action, entrapment, public duty, legal impossibility, self-defense or defense of others, acting under authority of law (for example, a justifiable killing by a police officer), and insanity are some examples. Jurisdictions differ in which of these defenses they will accept and the conditions under which they are acceptable. Differences exist in the type of proof required for the defense to be successful.

Closing Statements

After all of the evidence has been presented in the case, attorneys may offer closing statements. The closing statement is given first by the prosecution, then by the defense; this is followed with rebuttal by the prosecutor. Both attorneys must be careful not to go beyond the evidence and reasonable inferences from the evidence offered in the case.

In the closing statement, as in the entire trial, the prosecutor must be careful not to go too far. If he or she does so, the judge must determine whether the statements are so prejudicial or erroneous that they might have undue influence on the jury's determination of guilt. If so, they are considered **prejudicial errors**, and the judge orders a mistrial. If not, they are considered **harmless errors**. Harmless errors and prejudicial errors may be committed by defense or prosecution and may refer to actions or comments made at various stages in the criminal process.

The defense offers a closing statement after that of the prosecutor, unless the defense chooses to waive this step. The defense should be careful not to go beyond the evidence or be too emotional, but as a practical matter rarely are defense attorney's closing statements the subject of appeal. This is because the prosecution may not appeal an acquittal; if the defendant is convicted and the defense appeals, that appeal will be concerned only with alleged errors made by the prosecution or rulings made by the judge.

Submitting the Case to the Jury

After all of the preceding steps have been completed, most cases are submitted to a jury. The judge may not direct the jury to return a guilty verdict. However, in many jurisdictions trial judges, on their own or by granting a motion from the defense, may order a **directed verdict**, a direction to the jury to return a verdict of not guilty.

Why would a trial judge have that power? If the evidence is so weak that it is unreasonable to conclude beyond a reasonable doubt that the defendant is guilty, it would be a travesty of justice to send the case to the jury, let the jury return a verdict of guilty, and then make the defendant wait for an appeal to get justice.

Before the case is given to the jury for deliberation, the judge has the responsibility of charging the jury, which means instructing jurors on matters of law relating to the case they must decide. In many jurisdictions, patterned jury instructions are given for the most commonly raised issues. The judge accepts suggested instructions from the prosecution and the defense and usually schedules a conference with them on the proposed instructions. The judge determines the final instructions (which may be subject to appeal) and presents them orally to the jury. The charge of the judge is very important, for it can be influential, perhaps determinative in the jury's decision.

The jury charge should be as clear and as simple as possible without distorting the meaning of the law. The law as applied to many cases is complicated and difficult to understand, especially for people who are not legally trained. Yet it is the responsibility of the jury to apply that law to the case it has heard. It is the duty of the trial judge to explain the law in terms that the jury can understand. If the judge's charge is too complicated or is an inaccurate interpretation of the law in the case, the defense may appeal that issue. In some instances the case is reversed and requires a new trial.

The charge must explain to the jury the law that applies to the case, and it must clarify what the jury may do. For example, if the defendant has been charged with first-degree murder but the law permits the jury to return a verdict of guilty of second-degree murder, that must be explained, along with the elements that must be proved for conviction on each of those charges. The judge should explain the meaning of evidence and distinguish the types of evidence. If conflict exists in the testimonial evidence, the jurors need to understand that they are the final determiner of whose testimony is most credible. This is true particularly when expert opinions conflict. Jurors may expect conflict between the testimony of a victim and that of a defendant but be very confused when two physicians give different and conflicting statements. Experts do differ; the jury is to decide whom to believe. The jury may ignore the testimony of all experts if it so chooses.

The judge may instruct the jury to disregard certain evidence that has been admitted but that for some reason should not be considered. Research reveals that in these cases juries do not disregard the evidence and may use it unconsciously to create "facts" that were not presented but which they may need for their decision. The results of one study raise the critical question of whether a mistrial should follow the admission of such evidence.[33]

In the federal system and in some states, the judge is permitted to summarize and comment on the evidence when the charge is given to the jury. This is an immense responsibility, for the obligation of the judge to be a neutral party continues throughout the trial unless the right to a jury trial is waived and the judge is to determine guilt or innocence.

Many areas of law might be covered by the judge in the instructions. The nature of each charge depends on the nature of the case being tried. Two issues deserve further attention: the presumption of innocence and the burden and standard of proof. In U.S. criminal justice systems, the defendant is presumed innocent. The **presumption of innocence** is an important principle. It means that the prosecution has the responsibility of proving every element required for conviction and that the defendant does not have to prove innocence. The defendant can do nothing and still be acquitted if the government does not prove its case.

Most judges instruct the jury regarding the presumption of innocence, although the U.S. Supreme Court has held that it is not constitutionally required that an instruction be given. According to the Court, all circumstances must be examined to determine whether the defendant had a fair trial without an instruction on the presumption. If so, the case will not be reversed for failure to give the instruction.[34]

The presumption of innocence is essential in protecting those who are accused falsely. Innocent people are convicted in some cases, and these convictions may be devastating to their personal and professional lives. The criminal justice system is impaired when the rights of innocent persons are violated, particularly when that violation leads to a conviction.

The standard of proof in a criminal case is **beyond a reasonable doubt.** That burden is a heavy one; it means that when jurors look at all the evidence, they are convinced, satisfied to a moral certainty, that guilt has been established by the facts. Some judges refuse to define *beyond a reasonable doubt* on the assumption that not much more can be said. We all understand those words, and any attempt to define them further might be confusing or misleading.[35]

After the charge is read to the jury, the bailiff takes the jurors to the jury room to deliberate. These deliberations must be conducted in secret. It is the bailiff's responsibility to make certain that no one talks to the jurors; nor are the jurors permitted to seek advice. If they need further instruction, they may send the bailiff to ask the judge. That instruction may or may not be given, depending on the nature of the request.

If the jury is sequestered, they will be escorted by the bailiff (or another court person, such as deputy sheriff) not only in and out of the courtroom but to all meals and to the hotel rooms where they are staying. Access to television and newspapers will not be permitted unless special arrangements are made to avoid any possibility that jurors will be exposed to media accounts of the trial. For example, jurors might be offered newspapers only after the articles about the trial have been removed.

Normally, when the jurors deliberate, they have access to the demonstrative evidence that has been introduced during the trial. If they have been permitted to take notes during the trial, they may have their notes for the deliberation. Generally, it is left to the discretion of the trial judge whether jurors may take notes.

The jury may be given a copy of the charges against the defendant. Some judges give them a written copy of the judge's oral instructions. In some trials jurors deliberate for hours and do not reach verdicts. They report to the judge, who may tell them to go back and try again. The number of times a judge may send them back and how long they must deliberate is a matter of jurisdictional rules and judicial discretion, but the judge may not require jurors to deliberate for an unreasonable period of time. The definition of *reasonable* depends on the complexity of the trial. If they cannot reach a verdict, the jury is deadlocked, also called a *hung jury,* and the judge should declare a mistrial.

Mistrials may be declared under other circumstances, such as the serious illness or death of the judge or one of the attorneys or jurors. Mistrials may be declared during the trial as the result of a prejudicial error made by one of the parties involved in the trial. Other reasons may include prejudicial media publicity that comes to the attention of the jury or efforts of someone to bribe some or all of the jurors.

If the jury is not deadlocked and returns a verdict, the verdict may be not guilty. In that case the judge may order a verdict of acquittal, and the case is ended. The judge may not reverse a not guilty verdict. The judge may, but rarely does, reverse a guilty verdict. This may happen if the judge believes the evidence was not sufficient to support the guilty verdict. In addition, as noted in Chapter 6 (Spotlight 6.2, p. 154), the judge may find the defendant guilty of a lesser charge than the one on which the jury based its verdict. In that case, involving defendant Louise Woodward, the jury was instructed only on murder charges and found the defendant guilty of second-degree murder. Several days after the verdict the judge reduced that to manslaughter.

After the verdict and before sentencing, the attorneys may file post-verdict motions. If the jury returns a guilty verdict, the defense may make a motion for a judgment of acquittal. That motion may be made before the case goes to the jury and probably is more appropriately done at that time. The motion is based on the argument that the evidence is not sufficient to support a guilty verdict. The court may be more likely to grant that motion before the jury has returned a verdict, particularly in a close case.

The more common motion made by the defense after a guilty verdict is a motion for a new trial. This motion may be made on several specific grounds or on general grounds; that is, a new trial is in the interest of justice. Court rules or statutes may enumerate specific grounds on which this motion may be based.

Sentencing

After a guilty verdict the court imposes a sentence, which may or may not involve a jury recommendation to the judge. In some jurisdictions the jury determines the sentence. The situation may differ in death penalty cases. In the Oklahoma City bombing case, for example, only the jury was permitted to impose the death penalty. The jury deadlocked on the sentencing issue, sending the matter to the judge. In other cases the jury is permitted to make a sentencing recommendation, but the judge does not have to follow it.

Frequently, the sentencing process takes place at a later hearing to allow time for presentence reports. The court may hold an extensive sentencing hearing, or the judge may impose sentence without a hearing, depending on the rules of the jurisdiction and, in some cases, the preferences of the judge. Sentencing is an important stage, and in recent years it has come under intense scrutiny by the public and the media as well as by courts.

Increasing concern with rising crime rates in the United States, particularly the incidence of personal, violent crimes in which victims appear to be chosen randomly, along with the publicized recidivism of some criminals, have precipitated get-tough sentencing policies in most jurisdictions. This approach resembles the mechanical and harsh philosophy of Cesare Beccaria, who argued successfully in the eighteenth century that punishment should fit the crime. It was a philosophy that made sentencing easy. The legislature decided the sentence for each offense, and the court's only function was to determine whether the accused had committed the offense. That system was abolished in many countries because it did not take into account mitigating circumstances.[36]

An individualized treatment philosophy developed in the United States during the twentieth century, but in recent years the discretion of sentencing judges and parole boards has been decreased. It is argued that such discretion has led to sentence disparity, which could be reduced significantly if more definite sentencing provisions were established by the legislature. The assumption is that such provisions will decrease sentence disparity, limit or eliminate the early release of inmates from prison, and reduce crime. Such assumptions must be analyzed carefully, however, in light of overall criminal justice systems. This section of the chapter examines sentencing issues, procedures, and trends. In addition, it considers the effect that current reforms are having on the overall crime problem. During your study of this section, it is wise to recall the earlier discussion (Chapter 1) of punishment philosophies, which form the basis for sentencing. Consider how those philosophies relate to the topics discussed in this chapter.

A **sentence** is a term of punishment imposed by a court on a convicted offender. Sentencing is one of the most controversial topics in criminal justice systems. It can be one of the simplest or one of the most complex processes. Sentencing may involve numerous people, ranging from legislators who formulate sentencing laws to probation officers who compile the presentence reports that may be used by judges in making sentence decisions.

The Concept and Process of Sentencing

Sentence length may be affected by prison administrative authorities who may have discretion to determine how long inmates are incarcerated. They determine whether **good time credits**, where available, are extended to inmates for their exemplary behavior while incarcerated. They determine the removal of good time credits for unacceptable behavior. These administrative authorities may be influential with parole boards, which have the power to determine whether inmates are released early in those jurisdictions in which a parole system remains. Sentencing may be affected by the prosecutor's recommendations and by the reactions of victims or other witnesses who testify at the trial or who may be permitted to engage in discussions concerning the appropriate sentence.

An understanding of sentencing is complicated further because it differs significantly from state to state, from court to court within a state, from county to county, and even from time to time within any of these jurisdictions. Sentencing policies in the federal system differ from those in states. Finally, attitudes toward what is and is not appropriate in sentencing differ as well.

Sentencing Strategies

Four main strategies are used for sentencing: indeterminate, determinate, presumptive, and mandatory sentences. Most states use a combination of these. An **indeterminate sentence** involves legislative specifications of sentence ranges that permit judges to exercise discretion in determining actual sentences. In its purest form, the indeterminate sentence would be from one day to life. Usually, it involves legislative specification of a maximum and minimum term for each offense. For example, if the legislative sentence for armed robbery is not more than twenty-five nor less than ten years, judges have discretion to set the sentence at any point in between.

Another sentencing model involves the **presumptive sentence**. In presumptive sentencing the normal sentence is specified for each offense, but judges are permitted to deviate from that norm. Some jurisdictions require that any deviation from a presumptive sentence be accompanied by written reasons for the deviation. Furthermore, the law may specify which conditions and circumstances may be considered for deviating from the presumptive sentence.

Mandatory sentences may be confused with determinate sentences. *Mandatory sentence* means that the sentence must be imposed upon conviction. Mandatory sentences are specified by legislatures (or by Congress) and usually involve a prison term. The mandatory approach leaves the judge no discretion concerning sentencing. For example, if the provision is for a specific prison term, the judge may not suspend the sentence or impose a different term as an alternative to prison.

In a **determinate sentence** structure, although the legislature specifies a fixed term of incarceration for conviction of a particular offense, the judge may have the option of suspending that sentence or imposing probation (or some other sanction, such as work service) rather than a jail or prison term. But once the judicial sentence is imposed, the parole board does not have the discretion to reduce the sentence by offering early parole. The determinate sentencing scheme may involve a provision for mandatory parole after a specified portion of the determinate sentence has been served. It may include a provision for sentence reduction based on good time credits earned by the inmate.

Determinate sentences may include a provision for raising or lowering the sentence if there are mitigating or aggravating circumstances. For example, the determinate sentence for rape might be fifteen years; but if a weapon is used to threaten the victim, there may be a provision for increasing the penalty. Likewise, if there are circumstances that reduce the moral culpability of the offender, the sentence might be reduced. An example would be extreme passion in a homicide, as when the accused finds his or her spouse in bed with another and in a fit of anger kills that person.

In any of the sentencing models, the power to determine sentence length may be altered by other factors. Power may be given to the governor to commute a sentence of life to a specified term of years or to commute a death sentence to a life sentence. The governor may have the power to **pardon** an offender. (In the case of a federal crime, the pardoning power resides in the president of the United States).

In recent years many states, faced with severe prison overcrowding and federal court orders concerning acceptable prison capacity, have enacted legislation that enables the governor to order early release of some inmates to make room for new ones. This policy has come under increasing criticism, particularly when early releasees commit additional crimes, leading some jurisdictions to eliminate the policy.

The Sentencing Hearing

For less serious offenses, particularly when the case is not tried before a jury, the judge may pronounce sentence immediately upon finding the defendant guilty or upon accepting a guilty plea. Sentencing may be immediate when the judge has no option but to assess the statutory penalty. Sentencing may be set for a future date but not involve any special investigations, with the judge taking recommendations from the defense and the prosecution. However, the trend is toward having a separate sentencing hearing. After the trial verdict, the judge sets a formal date for sentencing, leaving sufficient time to consider appropriate presentence investigations. It is common in capital cases to have a separate hearing on the issue of whether the defendant will be sentenced to death, life, or a term of years.

The **presentence investigation (PSI)** may include information based on interviews with the defendant, family, friends, employers, or others who might have information pertinent to a sentencing decision. Medical, psychiatric, or other reports from experts may be included. Prior offenses, work records, school records, associates, pastime activities, attitudes, willingness to cooperate, and information on problems with alcohol or other drugs might be included as well.

If the PSI is conducted thoroughly, it is a time-consuming job. In some jurisdictions the reports are prepared by the Department of Corrections (DOC). Most of these departments have diagnostic facilities and may be better equipped to conduct the investigations than probation officers, who conduct the PSI in many jurisdictions and who may have access to fewer resources for the investigation.

The Sentencing Decision

Judges decide most sentences (unless the legislature has removed all judicial discretion), but in some cases (usually in serious offenses such as first-degree murder) juries have sentencing power. The judge is not required to follow the jury's recommendation in all jurisdictions.

Florida and Alabama illustrate two systems for jury input in capital cases, and the U.S. Supreme Court has considered both systems in recent years. In 1995 the Court upheld the Alabama system against an argument that the defendant's Eighth Amendment right to be free of cruel and unusual punishment (see Appendix A) was violated. Alabama requires the trial judge to *consider* the jury's sentencing recommendation in a capital case but does not specify the weight the judge must place on that recommendation. In *Harris* v. *Alabama* petitioner Harris was convicted of murder after her husband was killed in a murder-for-hire situation. Harris was having an affair with McCarter, whom she asked to find someone to kill her husband. McCarter asked a co-worker, who refused and reported the request, but McCarter found two willing accomplices, each of whom was paid $100.00, with a vague promise of more money later. Harris and McCarter were planning to share the $250,000 life insurance on the victim.[37]

The jury voted seven to five to recommend life without parole for Harris (a Sunday school teacher and mother of seven), but the judge imposed death. Harris argued that her constitutional rights were violated because the statute did not specify the weight the judge should give to the jury's recommendation. The statute left the decision to the discretion of the sentencing judge. Harris supported her argument with the statute and case law from Florida, in which the state supreme court has ruled that the trial judge must give "great weight" to the jury's recommendation in a capital case. In Florida the judge may not override the jury's advisory recommendation unless "the facts suggesting a sentence of death [are] so clear and convincing that virtually no reasonable person could differ."[38]

The U.S. Supreme Court has held the Florida capital punishment sentencing procedures to be constitutional.[39] The issue in *Harris* was whether the U.S. Constitution *requires* the sentencing judge to give any prescribed weight to the jury's recommendation. The Court held that it does not.

In 1990 the Court upheld the Arizona plan, which provides that after an individual is found guilty of first-degree murder a "separate sentencing hearing . . . shall be conducted before the court alone" to determine whether to impose life imprisonment or the death penalty. The statute specifies factors that are to be considered for and against leniency in making that decision.[40]

In jurisdictions in which the jury has sentencing power, the judge instructs the jury concerning the law and its application to sentencing. As the discussion of the PSI notes, many factors might be considered in the sentencing decision. Those factors may be designated by statute. Some states have formalized and restricted the factors that may be considered. One method is the use of sentencing formulas with weight given to specified factors such as prior history, nature of the crime, and so on.

If the defendant has been convicted of more than one offense, usually the judge has the authority to determine whether the sentences are to be imposed concurrently or consecutively. With **concurrent sentences**, the defendant satisfies the terms of all sentences at the same time. For example, if the defendant is sentenced to twenty years for each of three counts of armed robbery, the total number of years served will be twenty if the sentences are concurrent. With **consecutive sentences**, the defendant will have to serve sixty years (unless the term is reduced by parole or good time or is commuted or pardoned). Most multiple sentences are imposed concurrently.

After the sentence is determined, the judge reads the sentence to the defendant, and the sentence is recorded in court records. If the sentence involves incarceration, generally the defendant is taken into custody immediately (or returned to custody if he or she had not been released before trial). The judge may allow the defendant some time to prepare for incarceration, but that occurs rarely and generally applies only in the cases of government officials or other people who might, in the eyes of the judge, need time to get their affairs in order and who would not be a danger to society or flee the jurisdiction.

One final issue concerning the sentencing decision should be noted. In some jurisdictions, for example California, crime victims are permitted to express their concerns and opinions on issues such as sentencing.[41] The role of victims in sentencing was limited by the Supreme Court in a 1987 decision, *Booth* v. *Maryland*, in which the Court held that the defendant's constitutional rights are violated when Victim Impact Statements (VIS) contain information such as the severe emotional impact of the crime on the family, the personal characteristics of the victim, and the family members' opinions and characterizations of the crime and of the offender. When the issue arose in the sentencing phase of a capital case, the Court emphasized the concern that in such serious cases decisions should be based on reason, not on emotion. Thus, the jury should not hear this type of information, which "can serve no other purpose than to inflame the jury and divert it from deciding the case on the relevant evidence concerning the crime and the defendant."[42]

In 1991 the Court reversed itself on the ruling in *Booth* and another case. In *Payne* v. *Tennessee* the Court ruled that VISs may be used at capital sentencing hearings. "A state may legitimately conclude that evidence about the victim and about the impact of the murder on the victim's family is relevant to the jury's decision as to whether or not the death penalty should be imposed."[43] In 1995 the Washington Supreme Court upheld that state's provision for admitting victim impact evidence during the sentencing phase of a capital trial. The U.S. Supreme Court refused to hear an appeal.[44]

Types of Sentences

In some jurisdictions judges have numerous sentencing options. In addition to incarcerating defendants for short jail terms or for longer prison terms, judges may place offenders on probation or impose fines. Judges may employ a combination of these possibilities along with others, such as work assignments. Sentencing options differ from jurisdiction to jurisdiction, and vary by crimes, but it is possible to examine the *types* of sentences. They are listed and defined in Spotlight 8.3 and discussed briefly here.

The **fine** is a punishment in which the offender is ordered to pay a sum of money to the state in lieu of or in addition to other forms of punishment. "The fine is one of the oldest forms of punishment and is widely used in Western Europe as the sole sanction for the major portion of cases coming before the

Spotlight 8.3

Types of Sentences

Death penalty—In most States for the most serious crimes such as murder, the courts may sentence an offender to death by lethal injection, electrocution, exposure to lethal gas, hanging, or other method specified by State law.

Incarceration—The confinement of a convicted criminal in a Federal or State prison or a local jail to serve a court-imposed sentence. Confinement is usually in a jail, administered locally, or a prison, operated by the State or Federal Government. In many States offenders sentenced to 1 year or less are held in a jail; those sentenced to longer terms are committed to a State prison.

Probation—The sentencing of an offender to community supervision by a probation agency; often as a result of suspending a sentence to confinement. Such supervision normally entails specific rules of conduct while in the community. If the rules are violated a sentence to confinement may be imposed. Probation is the most widely used correctional disposition in the United States.

Split sentences, shock probation. and intermittent confinement—A penalty that explicitly requires the convicted person to serve a brief period of confinement in a local, State, or Federal facility (the "shock") followed by a period of probation. This penalty attempts to combine the use of community supervision with a short incarceration experience. Some sentences are periodic rather than continuous; for example, an offender may be required to spend a certain number of weekends in jail.

Restitution and victim compensation—The offender is required to provide financial repayment or, in some jurisdictions, services in lieu of monetary restitution, for the losses incurred by the victim.

Community service—The offender is required to perform a specified amount of public service work, such as collecting trash in parks or other public facilities.

Fines—An economic penalty that requires the offender to pay a specified sum of money within limits set by law. Fines often are imposed in addition to probation or as alternatives in incarceration.

Source: Bureau of Justice Statistics, *Report to the Nation on Crime and Justice: The Data*, 2d ed. (Washington, D.C.: U.S. Department of Justice, 1988), p. 96.

criminal courts." In Sweden, England, and West Germany "more than three-quarters of cases result in a fine." Fines are used in the United States in combination with probation and other alternatives to incarceration, but fines are relatively small.[45]

Historically, in the United States fines were used primarily in cases involving traffic violations or other nonviolent offenses. Recently, with the increasing interest in victim compensation, including compensation for violent and property crimes, some jurisdictions have begun to assess fines against offenders convicted of violent crimes. Fines are used in conjunction with incarceration as well, with the latter being extended beyond the original sentence if the fine has not been paid.[46]

Historically, it was common to incarcerate persons who were unable to pay their fines. The Court has held, however, that an indigent defendant may not be imprisoned for failure to pay a traffic violation fine when a fine is the only punishment provided for that offense.[47] In *Bearden* v. *Georgia* the Court held that when a defendant is placed on probation and ordered to pay restitution (discussed later) but cannot pay the full restitution, probation cannot be revoked automatically and the probationer incarcerated. The court must consider alternatives to incarceration to avoid depriving the "probationer of his conditional free-dom simply because, through no fault of his own, he cannot pay the fine. Such a deprivation would be contrary to the fundamental fairness required by the Four-teenth Amendment" (see Appendix A).[48]

In many European countries the *day fine* is used commonly. The day fine is based on the amount the offender earns per day, and the system contrasts to the traditional method used in the United States, which is to set the fine in terms of the crime for which it is imposed. Recent studies show that the day fine could be implemented successfully in U.S. courts as a substitute for fixed fines, and that the result would be an overall increase in revenue derived from fines.[49]

A second type of sentence that is growing in use is **restitution**, which requires offenders to reimburse victims financially or with services. Restitution has had a long history in other countries and in the United States, although it was not until 1913 that the issue arose before the U.S. Supreme Court, which approved of it.[50] The primary rationale for restitution is victim compensation; retribution is another. Third, it is argued that the state should assist crime victims, and restitu-tion provides one source of revenue at the expense of the offender. Fourth, there is some evidence, especially among juveniles, that there is a greater chance of reducing the number of **recidivists** if offenders participate in some form of resti-tution, either financial or work services.[51]

Restitution may be combined with work assignments. The work assignments may be designed to benefit only the victim or a larger group, as in the case of **community work service** assignments. Restitution and community work service programs have a long history, but little attention was given to these sentencing alternatives until the increasing emphasis on rehabilitation, especially of juveniles, gave restitution and community work service a much needed push in the 1960s and 1970s.[52] Many programs were developed in the past two decades, and the practice is common in European countries as well.[53]

Some administrative questions are left open by the statutes providing for restitution or community work service. Some are ambiguous about the kind of work that may be assigned. Others require work programs or restitution of a nature that aids the victim but also fosters rehabilitation of the offender. Usually, community work service orders impose strict rules on the offender and, in many cases, are combined with **probation**, which is the most frequently used sanction for criminal activity.

Probation is utilized nearly three times as often as incarceration. It is a sen-tence in which the defendant is released into the community for a specified period, theoretically at least, under supervision. It has been argued that probation is not a sentence, but it is in the sense that it may be imposed only by the judi-ciary, which may set terms and conditions for the sentence. These are discussed in more detail, along with other aspects of probation, in Chapter 11. It is important to understand at this point, however, that probation may be imposed in lieu of or in combination with a fine, restitution, or community service. It may be imposed in conjunction with a brief period of incarceration or with electronic monitoring, also discussed in Chapter 11.

Another type of sentencing, **corporal punishment**, is not a legal sentence in the United States at this time. The last statute to be repealed was the Delaware whipping statute in 1973. In the last two decades, however, some scholars have argued for a return to corporal punishment, considering it a less expensive and more humane punishment than incarceration.[54]

Another type of sentence that was used extensively in the past is **capital pun-ishment**. Over the years capital punishment has been in and out of favor, with abolition movements beginning in the eighteenth century, gaining momentum in the late 1800s, and leading to actual abolition of the death penalty in many states during this century, only to have it reinstated recently.[55]

In 1972 in *Furman* v. *Georgia*, the U.S. Supreme Court held that although capital punishment is not per se unconstitutional, it is unconstitutional when in its application it involves discrimination caused by arbitrary and capricious administration of the sentence. *Furman* invalidated most capital punishment statutes in existence at the time, but the Court left the door open for new legislation providing for capital punishment if it is applied without violating defendants' constitutional rights.[56]

By 1976 thirty-six states had responded with new capital punishment statutes, but some of those were challenged in the courts. In 1977 the constitutional issues were satisfied in the case of the Utah statute; that year, Gary Gilmore became the first person executed since 1967. In May 1979, after a long and complicated legal battle, John Spenkelink, convicted of murdering a man with a hatchet, was the first involuntary inmate to die of capital punishment in the United States since 1967 (Gilmore refused to appeal his sentences and asked that it be carried out). Spenkelink was executed in Old Sparky, Florida's electric chair.[57]

The movement toward capital punishment was highlighted in 1995 when New York revived the death penalty after eighteen years. Former New York governor Mario Cuomo vetoed death penalty legislation twelve times, but the current administration had no difficulty enacting death penalty legislation, making New York the thirty-eighth state with capital punishment. Governor George E. Pataki signed the bill with two pens owned by slain police officers.[58] Highlights of capital punishment in 1995 are contained in Spotlight 8.4, while Figure 8.1 graphs executions in the United States between 1930 and 1997.

A final major type of punishment is confinement or **incarceration**. Offenders may be incarcerated in a jail or in a prison or confined in a community treatment center. These facilities, along with the issues surrounding confinement and incarceration, are discussed in Chapters 9, 10, and 11.

Current Sentencing Issues

Two of the most critical current issues in sentencing are related. The first is the reduction of judicial discretion in the sentencing decision. The second is the use of longer, determinate sentences. Both are the result of a concern over the crime rates and alleged sentence disparity. Both are controversial, and both are related to perceived sentence disparity.

Sentence Disparity

There is great concern about sentence disparity, but its meaning is not clear. Some use the term to refer to any differences that they think are unfair or inappropriate. Thus, the differences between legislatively determined sentences in two jurisdictions might be viewed as disparate. Others limit the term to the differences in sentences imposed by different judges in similar cases. Some include any differences; others look to the circumstances surrounding the crime before determining whether sentences are disparate.

Sentence disparity may stem from legislative, judicial, or administrative decisions. Sentence length may vary from jurisdiction to jurisdiction because legislatures establish different terms for the same crime. Legislatures may differ in whether a defendant with multiple sentences serves them concurrently or consecutively. Legislative sentences may be disparate if within a system there are sentences that are considered unfair. Sentence disparity may result from decisions made by administrators. Prosecutors may have influence over the imposed sen-

Spotlight 8.4

Highlights: Capital Punishment 1995

Status of the Death Penalty, December 31, 1995

Executions During 1995		Number of Prisoners Under Sentence of Death		Jurisdictions Without a Death Penalty
Texas	19	California	420	Alaska
Missouri	6	Texas	404	District of Columbia
Illinois	5	Florida	362	Hawaii
Virgina	5	Pemsylvania	196	Iowa
Florida	3	Ohio	155	Maine
Oklahoma	3	Illinois	154	Massachusetts
Alabama	2	Alabama	143	Michigan
Arkansas	2	North Carolina	139	Minnesota
Georgia	2	Oklahoma	129	North Dakota
North Carolina	2	Arizona	117	Rhode Island
Pennsylvania	2	Georgia	98	Vermont
Arizona	1	Tennessee	96	West Virginia
Delaware	I	Missouri	92	Wisconsin
Louisiana	1	22 other jurisdIctions	549	
Montana	I			
South Carolina	1			
Total	56	Total	3,054	

- In 1995, 56 men were executed:
  33 were white
  22 were black
  1 was Asian
- The persons executed In 1995 were under sentence of death an average of 11 years and 2 months.
- At yearend 1995, 34 States and the Federal prison system held 3,054 prisoners under sentence of death, 5.1% more than at yearend 1994. All had committed murder.
- Of persons under sentence of death—
  1,730 were white
  1,275 were black
    22 were Native American
    19 were Asian
      8 were classified as "other race."

- Forty-eight women were under a sentence of death.
- The 237 Hispanic inmates under sentence of death accounted for 8.5% of inmates with a known ethnicity.
- Among inmates under sentence of death and with available criminal histories, 2 in 3 had a prior felony conviction; 1 in 12 had a prior homicide conviction.
- Among persons for whom arrest information was available, the average age at time of arrest was 28; about 2% of inmates were age 17 or younger.
- At yearend, the youngest inmate was 18; the oldest was 80.

Source: Bureau of Justice Statistics, *Capital Punishment 1995* (Washington, D.C.: U.S. Department of Justice, December 1996), p. 1.

tence. In the plea bargaining process, the prosecutor may offer a deal that involves a lesser penalty for one offense if the offender pleads guilty to another or to several others.

Juries also have considerable discretion, even when they are not empowered to determine sentences. If they think that the judge will be too harsh or if they perceive that the legislative sentence is unfair, jurors may refuse to convict. In that

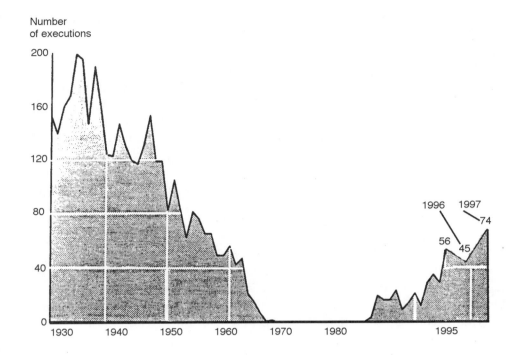

Figure 8.1
Persons Executed,
1930–1997

Source: Bureau of Justice Statistics,
Capital Punishment 1995 (Washington,
D.C.: U.S. Department of Justice,
December 1996), p. 2, updated from
Bureau of Justice Statistics,
http://www.ojp.usdj.gov/bjs/glance.
htm (April 1998).

case juries have the ultimate power to decide sentences. Although parole has been abolished in some states, where it does exist, parole authorities have great latitude in deciding actual time served. Even when the legislature specifies by statute the percentage of a term that must be served before an offender is eligible for parole, the parole board has the power to determine when, if ever, that person will be released before the end of the actual sentence.

Judicial sentences are another potential source of disparity. Most of the recent changes in sentencing laws have been aimed at controlling or removing judicial sentencing discretion, and most of the allegations of discrimination involved the variables of race and gender.

Earlier studies examining race and gender in sentencing did not agree on whether discrimination existed and if it did, to what extent and why. Modern scholars do not agree either, and the debates continues.[59]

Some criminologists argue that criminal justice systems are racist in sentencing. Michael J. Lynch and the late W. Byron Groves, in their explanation of radical criminology, referred to numerous studies that support this position.

> These studies show that minorities, particularly blacks, are discriminated against in
> the sentencing process. Blacks receive longer sentences than whites for the same
> crime, and blacks who victimize whites receive longer sentences than blacks who
> victimize blacks. Recent research . . . on rape indicates that this bias remains in force
> today.[60]

In a 1994 publication law professor Michael Tonry reports his analysis of jail and prison data and concludes that racial disparities in sentencing have "steadily gotten worse since 1980." Tonry attributes this to politically motivated decisions by Republican administrations to increase penalties for drug violations when they knew that such increases would impact minorities negatively and not have a significant impact on crime rates. Tonry gives several reasons for his conclusions. He charges that drug arrests are easier to make in inner-city minority areas than in areas dominated by middle and upper classes. Increased penalties have been aimed primarily at the illegal use of crack cocaine, used by minorities more frequently than powder cocaine, "a pharmacologically indistinguishable drug used primarily by middle-class Whites."[61]

The differences between African Americans and whites in drug sentences has been raised by some African American defendants who claim they are denied equal protection because of the higher sentences for the illegal distribution or possession of crack cocaine (approximately 100-to-1). With lower courts disagreeing on whether these differences constitute racial discrimination, the U.S. Supreme Court voted to decide the issue. In 1996 in *United States* v. *Armstrong* the Court held that the African American defendants had not shown racial discrimination. The fact that 88.3 percent of all federal prosecutions for crack cocaine violations are against African Americans does not in itself prove racial discrimination.[62] Despite this decision, the U.S. Sentencing Commission has recommended a change in the ratio of penalties for the two types of drug offenses, and President Clinton voiced some support for modified changes.

It has also been alleged that sentence disparity is related to the offender's gender.[63] Some researchers say that women are treated differentially at every stage in U.S. criminal justice systems and that this treatment is sexist; that is, women are discriminated against because of their gender. It is not uncommon to see such allegations in the popular media. The increasing number of women in jails and prisons is presumed to represent "unequal justice."[64]

Others say the system is more lenient toward women than toward men at every level and that, in particular, women receive lighter sentences than men for the same offenses. That, too, must be analyzed in terms of legal factors courts may consider in sentencing, such as prior convictions, seriousness of the current offense, and so on. It is argued that when these factors are analyzed, there is little or no evidence of gender bias in sentencing.[65]

In an earlier study, Darrell J. Steffensmeier reviewed the empirical evidence concerning differential sentencing of women and concluded that, although preferential treatment exists, it is of small magnitude. He argued that the "changing sex role definitions and the contemporary women's movement have had little impact on sentencing outcomes of either male or female defendants" and that the differentials by gender have been diminished recently.[66]

In a much later study Steffensmeier and his colleagues analyzed gender and imprisonment decisions during a two-year period in Pennsylvania. They found support for earlier research concluding that in general women received more lenient sentences than men. However, unlike some of their predecessors, these scholars concluded that the differences were due to "the type or seriousness of the crime committed and the defendant's prior record, not the defendant's gender (or, for that matter, age, race, or other background/contextual variables.)"[67]

These various conclusions, especially those based on research data, along with those concerning whether racial discrimination exists, are confusing to those who want definitive answers. The justice system discriminates or it does not, one or the other. The confusion in the scholarly literature is compounded by several recent court studies of gender bias reporting that it does exist in states such as New York, Massachusetts, and Florida and that the bias pervades most if not all phases of the court system, including bias against female attorneys.[68]

Many solutions to sentence disparity have been proposed, but most of the reform efforts have centered on two approaches: controlling judicial discretion and removing judicial discretion from the sentencing process. This is done primarily through the imposition of sentencing guidelines or requirements. Sentencing guidelines are seen as a way to control discretion without abolishing it, while correcting the extreme disparity that can result from individualized sentencing.[69]

Basically, guidelines work as follows: A judge has an offender to sentence. Without guidelines the judge may consider the offender's background, the nature of the offense, or other variables. When guidelines are available, presumably the relevance of these and other variables has been researched. Thus, the judge has a benchmark of an appropriate penalty in such circumstances. However, the judge may decide that it is reasonable in a given case to deviate from the guidelines; in that situation, reasons should be given.

Sentencing guidelines may be based on an empirical analysis of what *has* been done in the jurisdiction, not a philosophy of what *ought to be* done. Sentencing guidelines may be based on what it is thought *should* be done. This may occur in a variety of ways. The guidelines may be recommended by a committee and accepted and thus mandated by the legislature, or they may be adopted by judges to apply to their jurisdictions. Special attention is given to the federal guidelines because they are controversial and have produced extensive litigation, but it is important to understand that many states have adopted guidelines.[70]

Sentencing guidelines have been adopted in the federal system, too. After years of attempts, Congress revised the criminal code in 1984. Part of the revised code provided for the establishment of a federal sentencing commission, appointed by the president and charged with the responsibility of establishing sentencing guidelines. The federal sentencing guidelines became law on 1 November 1986. In the following months, many lawsuits were filed, challenging the guidelines. Some federal judges refused to enforce them. Others complained that the guidelines give the appearance of precision but only succeed in removing important judicial discretion. They do not achieve either of their goals: removing disparity and establishing sentences that are in proportion to the crimes for which they are assessed.

More critical, however, are the constitutional challenges to the federal sentencing guidelines. Lower federal courts split on the issues, but in 1989 the Supreme Court upheld the 1984 Sentencing Reform Act. In *Mistretta* v. *United States* the Court discussed the history of sentencing, noting that rehabilitation and the indeterminate sentence had failed; that parole was an inadequate device to overcome these problems; and that sentence disparity existed. The Sentencing Reform Act "rejects imprisonment as a means of promoting rehabilitation" and provides that "punishment should serve retributive, educational, deterrent, and incapacitative goals." The Court explained the details of the criminal code revision, including the establishing of the Sentencing Commission and the method provided for the adoption of sentencing guidelines. After analyzing Mistretta's arguments, the Court concluded that the sentencing guidelines did not violate any of his constitutional rights.[71]

Determinate Sentencing

The second major proposed solution to sentence disparity is the reduction or removal of judicial sentencing discretion, clearly the most popular approach in recent history. It is manifested primarily in the adoption of determinate sentencing, which began in the 1970s.

One of the most rigid of the new determinate sentencing statutes was that of California, the state that pioneered the indeterminate sentence and that used it most extensively. The California statute removed the rehabilitation philosophy and substituted punishment as the reason for incarceration. It specified that sentences are not to be disparate and that individuals charged with similar offenses should receive similar sentences. The judge may decide on the basis of aggravating or mitigating circumstances to raise or lower the presumed sentence, but written reasons must be given for deviating from the presumed sentence.

The California statute abolishes the parole board with its discretion to determine release, but it provides that all releasees be placed under parole *supervision* for one year upon release. Good time credits for good behavior in prison are available to reduce sentence length. The law permits sentencing judges to add up to three years to a sentence imposed on a defendant whose crime results in great bodily injury to the victim.[72]

The emphasis on determinate sentencing is manifested most severely in the national focus on the habitual offender, summarized in the 1994 political slogan, **"three strikes and you're out"**. The phrase figured prominently at the state as well as the national level, with statutes such as that enacted in California. The California statute, which went into effect on 7 March 1994, provides a mandatory sentence of from twenty-five years to life in prison for conviction of a third felony. The statute imposes tougher penalties on first and second offenders as well. The California statute includes a provision for **truth in sentencing**, which provides that anyone convicted of a violent or serious crime must serve at least 80 percent of the imposed sentence. This provision applies to all crimes and is designed to avoid the previous situation in which inmates could earn good-time credits and cut their sentences by one-half.[73]

Appeals and Writs

Spotlight 8.5 explains the appeals process, along with what might happen to a case after appeal. A successful appeal does not necessarily mean that the case is over and the defendant is released from the criminal justice system. Generally, a successful appeal means that the case is retried, and in most cases the defendant is convicted again. A successful appeal on a sentence, for example the death penalty, may result in another death sentence. The difference is that in the retrial (or resentencing), the state must not commit the errors made in the previous trial. As Spotlight 8.5 notes, it is possible that on appeal a defendant may be successful on some issues and not on others.

In addition to appeals, defendants may petition for a **writ**, which is an order from the court. It gives permission to do whatever was requested or orders someone to do something specific. A common writ filed for offenders is a writ of *habeas corpus*, which means "you have the body." Originally a writ of *habeas corpus* was an order from the court to someone like a sheriff or a jailer to have the person in court at a specified time and to state the legal theory under which the person was being held. Today it is more extensive, and its use is governed by statutes that differ from jurisdiction to jurisdiction. Often it is used by inmates who are questioning the legality of their confinement. It does not question the issue of guilt or innocence but asserts that some due process rights of offenders are being violated or have been violated.

Under some circumstances, sentences may be appealed. Occasionally, sentences are reversed, and the case is sent back for resentencing. In practice, this occurs rarely. Appellate courts have given judges wide discretion in sentencing. As long as the sentence is within the statutory provisions and the sentencing judge has not abused his or her discretion or shown undue prejudice, it is difficult for defendants to challenge a judicial sentence successfully. In rare cases, courts may declare a legislatively determined sentence to be in violation of the defendant's rights.

Spotlight 8.5

The Appeals Process

An appeal occurs when the defendant in a criminal case (or either party in a civil case) requests that a court with appellate jurisdiction rule on a decision that has been made by a trial court or administrative agency.

Appellate courts receive two basic categories of cases: appeals and writs. Appeals, by far the most time-consuming and important, occur when a litigant's case receives a full-scale review after losing at the trial level (or, in several States, after losing in certain administrative proceedings).

The appeal begins when the party losing the case in the trial court, the "appellant," files a notice of appeal, usually a month or two after the trial court decision. Then within a few months the appellant files the trial court record in the appellate court. The record, often bulky, consists of the papers filed in the trial court along with a transcript of the trial testimony. Next the appellant and the opposing party, the "appellee," file briefs that argue for their respective positions. The briefs are usually followed by short oral presentations to the judges. Finally, the judges decide the case and issue a written opinion. An increasing number of courts, but still a minority, decide some appeals without written opinions.

State supreme court decisions are usually issued by the full court; intermediate court decisions are generally issued by three-judge panels. The whole decision process takes roughly a year, although it ranges from six months in some courts to several years in courts with large backlogs.

In making its final disposition of the case, an appellate court may

- "Affirm," or uphold, the lower court ruling.
- "Modify" the lower court ruling by changing it in part, but not totally reversing it.
- "Reverse," or set aside, the lower court ruling and not require any further court action.
- "Reverse and remand" the case by overturning the lower court ruling but requiring further proceedings at the lower court that may range from conducting a new trial to entering a proper judgment.
- "Remand" all or part of the case by sending it back to the lower court without overturning the lower courts ruling but with instructions for further proceedings that may range from conducting a new trial to entering a proper judgment.

Thus, the termination of an appellate court case may or may not be the end of the case from the perspective of the parties involved in the case. They may be required to go back to the lower court for further proceedings. If federal law is involved, a party can petition for review in the U.S. Supreme Court. In criminal cases, defendants can file further petitions in a federal court or state court.

Source: Bureau of Justice Statistics, *Trends: The Growth of Appeals* (Washington, D.C.: U.S. Department of Justice, 1986), p. 3.

WiseGuide Wrap-Up

This chapter focuses on the criminal trial, sentencing, and appeal. The procedures and issues surrounding these aspects of U.S. criminal justice systems are extensive and complicated and are governed by numerous statutes and court decisions. It is not possible to state "the law" in many of these areas because often the judges of state courts and lower federal courts differ in their analyses of how statutes and constitutions apply to the facts before them.

Even when the Supreme Court agrees to hear and decide some of the controversies, often we do not know how these decisions will be applied in similar cases. Some of the Court's decisions are close. Many of the criminal procedure cases have been decided by a five-to-four vote. Thus, a change of one member of the Court may alter the direction of what has been called the revolution in criminal procedure of the past two decades.

It is possible, however, to state generally what happens in the trial of a criminal case and how the constitutional guarantees apply to any or all of the stages of that trial. This chapter begins with a brief overview of those constitutional rights discussed earlier in the text and gives closer attention to the rights that are more specific to the trial and appellate stages. The right to a speedy trial, the right to a public trial by an impartial jury, and the right to confrontation and cross examination of witnesses, along with defendants' right to remain silent and not be forced to testify against themselves, are crucial to understanding the implementation of the various stages of the trial. Although states have considerable freedom in establishing the procedures by which they will conduct criminal trials, they may not violate constitutional rights.

In that sense, every stage of the trial must be understood and analyzed in light of the federal constitutional requirements to which all criminal defendants are entitled. The right to a public trial by an impartial jury precludes selection of the jury in secret. It precludes implicit or explicit exclusion of people because of their race, gender, religion, or ethnic origin. Yet understanding the right to a jury of one's peers may seem elusive to most people who read this text; for most juries are not representative of young adults, and courts have held that lack of representation to be permissible in most cases.

The importance of constitutional rights that apply to the trial is underscored by the fact that when those rights are violated, with only a few exceptions, the demonstrative or testimonial evidence secured as a result of those violations should be excluded from the trial. In some cases it is not possible to prove guilt beyond a reasonable doubt without this tainted evidence; thus, the case must be dismissed.

This use of the exclusionary rule has led to considerable controversy concerning U.S. criminal justice systems. Its implications are extensive. Police may become discouraged and refuse to arrest in certain situations, thinking the case will not result in a conviction anyway. Society may become critical of a system that lets the guilty go free. Potential criminals may decide to commit crimes, thinking they will not be convicted even if arrested. On the other hand, those protections are to ensure that when people are convicted of crimes, those convictions occurred only after proper procedures were followed and constitutional safeguards were observed.

In this chapter, each stage of the criminal trial is explained and discussed, beginning with the opening of the court session in which charges against the defendant are read, through jury selection, the presentation of evidence, the final arguments, and the verdict. In all of these stages the defense, the prosecution, and the judge are primary figures in assuring that proper procedures are followed. But following proper procedures does not end the matter. It is important to consider and reconsider the issues involved in U.S. criminal justice systems.

Some of those important issues are raised in this chapter. The right of the public to know and of the media to tell may conflict with the right of the defendant to be tried fairly and impartially. Which right should give way when that occurs? The right of the defendant to a trial by jury creates enormous expenses and consumes considerable time of all participants in the criminal trial. At what point, if ever, should that right give way to cost?

The criminal trial has an enormous effect on the rest of the criminal justice system. Long criminal trials increase the backlog in civil and criminal courts and result in a greater likelihood that defendants are denied their right to a speedy trial and that society must spend more money to keep the system operating. Mistrials increase the amount of time and money devoted to trials. Failure to convict in numerous cases might lead the public to question the effectiveness of the system. Conviction of the innocent undermines the entire system, but acquittal of those whom most believe guilty has led to rioting. Repeated appeals lead many to question whether there is any finality in the law.

Throughout this discussion of the procedures and issues of the trial, however, it should be remembered that the vast majority of defendants do not go to trial. Therefore it is important not to let the issues of the trial overshadow the need to give attention to the pretrial stages of criminal justice systems. In addition, it is important to understand and analyze what happens after defendants plead guilty or are found guilty at trial. Sentencing is a critical stage of the system and is the focus of the next major section of the chapter.

The sentencing process, ranging from the sentencing hearing to the formal stage of imposing the actual sentence on the convicted defendant, involves numerous issues and problems. The major ones are discussed in this chapter, beginning with an overview of the various sentencing strategies. The sentencing hearing is noted, along with some of the processes and issues involved in the decision-making process of sentencing.

The various types of sentences, ranging from probation to the most severe, capital punishment, are noted, followed by a discussion of the current issues and trends in sentencing. The concern with alleged sentence disparity has led to a return to determinate sentences, many of which are longer than previously. The current concepts of truth in sentencing and three strikes and you're out embody this return to longer and more determinate sentences.

The final section of the chapter focuses on appeals and writs, both means by which individuals may challenge the legality of their incarceration or, in some cases, their sentences or even their convictions.

This chapter concludes our study of what happens in adult criminal court systems. As we have seen, most people accused of crimes do not go through the entire system. But for the small percentage who do, and for a society that needs and deserves protection from property offenders as well as from violent offenders, confinement and incarceration have become the solutions. Whether they are adequate solutions is the underlying issue in the next section of the text, which includes three chapters.

Apply It

1. Explain the importance of constitutional rights in a criminal trial.

2. What is the purpose of the Speedy Trial Act of 1974? What kinds of delays does it permit?

3. Why is the right to a public trial important to defendants? What are the legal problems and issues with public trials as far as the media are concerned?

4. Why is the jury system considered important in the United States? Should it be abolished? Why or why not? Do you think a fair and impartial jury can be selected in high publicity trials?

5. What are the requirements for jury size and the selection of names for the jury pool? What is meant by an impartial jury? A jury of peers?

6. What is the role of the judge in controlling the conduct of defendants at trial?

7. Should people who are chosen for the jury pool be permitted to be excused from jury duty at their own request or should all persons called be required to serve? If you think personal requests should be honored, for what reasons should they be honored? What reasons should not be considered?

8. What is the significance of *Batson* v. *Kentucky*? Does the case apply to gender?

9. How do opening statements differ from closing statements? Are both required for the prosecution and the defense?

10. Define *demonstrative evidence*. How does it differ from witness testimony as evidence?

11. What is the *hearsay rule*?

12. What is the difference between direct and circumstantial evidence?

13. What is meant by *direct examination, cross examination,* and *redirect*?

14. Contrast the prosecution's case with that of the defense.

15. Describe the role of the judge in presenting the case to the jury.

16. Describe and evaluate the role of the jury in a criminal trial.

17. Discuss the importance of sentencing and explain sentencing strategies.

18. Is a sentencing hearing necessary? Is it required? What occurs in a sentencing hearing? What is the value of a presentence investigation? Should the PSI be available to the prosecution and the defense as well as the judge? Why or why not?

19. Explain what *Harris* v. *Alabama* holds about sentencing.

20. What are the legal issues concerning the role of victims in the sentencing process? What is your opinion regarding the role they should be permitted to play?

21. Should capital punishment be abolished? Why? Why not?

22. What is meant by *sentence disparity*? Discuss the issue of gender and racial discrimination in sentencing.

23. What problems have arisen with federal sentencing guidelines?

24. What is the difference between *determinate* and *indeterminate sentences*?

25. What do you think will be the effect of "three strikes and you're out" legislation? "Truth in legislation?"

26. Explain the meaning of *appeals* and *writs*.

Notes

1. Klopfer v. North Carolina, 386 U.S. 213 (1967).
2. U.S. Code, Title 18, Sections 3161-3174 (1997).
3. Tex. Code Crim. Proc., Art. 32A.01 (1977).
4. Tex. Code Crim. Pro. Art. 32A.02, Section 1 (1977).
5. Sheppard v. Maxwell, 384 U.S. 333, 356 (1966), quoting 135 N.E.2d 340, 342 (1956).
6. "Sheppard Lawyers Can Argue for Suit against State," *Columbus Dispatch* (25 December 1997), p. 11D.
7. See, for example, Richmond Newspapers, Inc. v. Virginia, 448 U.S. 555 (1980), recognizing the right of the public and the press to attend a criminal trial. The Court did not address the issue of how this right might be limited, but see Press-Enterprise Co. v. Superior Court of California, 464 U.S. 501 (1984), involving a sexual abuse trial. The Court said that it would be appropriate to close the process of questioning potential jurors. In Press-Enterprise Co. v. Superior Court, a capital case, 478 U.S. 1 (1986), the Court held that the proceedings could not be closed to the public unless it could be shown that there is a "substantial probability" that the right to a fair trial would be prejudiced by publicity and that the right could not be protected by reasonable alternatives to closure. This case was supported by a subsequent decision, El Vocero de Puerto Rico v. Puerto Rico, 508 U.S. 147 (1993) (per curiam).
8. Globe Newspaper Co. v. Superior Court, 457 U.S. 596 (1982).
9. Duncan v. Louisiana, 391 U.S. 145 (1968).
10. Duncan v. Louisiana, 391 U.S. 145, 149 (1968).
11. Duncan v. Louisiana, 391 U.S. 145, 159 (1968).
12. See Ballew v. Georgia, 435 U.S. 223 (1978). See also Williams v. Florida, 399 U.S. 78 (1970). In Colgrove v. Battin, 413 U.S. 149 (1973), the Court held that a six-person jury is permissible in federal cases.
13. Burch v. Louisiana, 441 U.S. 130 (1979).
14. Apodaca v. Oregon, 406 U.S. 404 (1972).
15. See Andres v. United States, 333 U.S. 740, 748 (1948); and Johnson v. Louisiana, 406 U.S. 356, 369 (1973). The federal rules require a unanimous verdict. See Fed. Rules Crim. Procedure 31(a).
16. Smith v. Texas, 311 U.S. 128 (1940).
17. Taylor v. Louisiana, 419 U.S. 522, 523 (1975), footnotes and citations omitted.
18. Swain v. Alabama, 380 U.S. 202 (1965).
19. Batson v. Kentucky, 476 U.S. 79 (1986). For an analysis of race and jury selection, see the *American Criminal Law Review* 31 (Summer 1994), which contains a symposium on the subject.
20. See, for example, State v. Cantu, 750 P.2d 591, 595 (Utah 1988). In 1987 the U.S. Supreme Court held that *Batson* applies to all cases still pending on direct review: Griffith v. Kentucky, 479 U.S. 314 (1987).
21. See Powers v. Ohio, 499 U.S. 400 (1991).

22. See Government of the Virgin Islands v. Forte, 865 F.2d 59 (3d Cir. 1989), *cert. denied*, 500 U.S. 954 (1991); and Georgia v. McCollum, 505 U.S. 42 (1992).

23. Powers v. Ohio, 499 U.S. 400 (1991).

24. Edmonson v. Leesville Concrete Co., 500 U.S. 614 (1991).

25. J.E.B. v. Alabama *ex rel.* T.B., 511 U.S. 127 (1994).

26. Barber v. Ponte, 772 F.2d 982 (1st Cir. 1985), *cert. denied*, 475 U.S. 1050 (1986).

27. See Mary A. Lynch, "The Application of Equal Protection to Perspective Jurors with Disabilities: Will Batson Cover Disability-Based Strikes? *Albany Law Review* 57 (1993): 289–363.

28. Illinois v. Allen, 397 U.S. 337 (1970).

29. Illinois v. Allen, 397 U.S. 337 (1970).

30. Illinois v. Allen, 397 U.S. 337 (1970).

31. See Elizabeth F. Loftus, *Eyewitness Testimony* (Cambridge, Mass.: Harvard University Press, 1979). For a more recent analysis, see Marvin Zalman and Larry Siegel, "The Psychology of Perception, Eyewitness Identification, and the Lineup," *Criminal Law Bulletin* 27 (March/April 1991): 159–176.

32. See Griffin v. California, 380 U.S. 609 (1965).

33. See "Juries Often Disregard Judge's Word," *New York Times* (28 March 1988), p. 12; and "'The Jury Will Disregard . . .' But New Study Suggests That by Then It's Too Late," *American Bar Association Journal* 73 (1 November 1987): 34.

34. Kentucky v. Whorton, 441 U.S. 786 (1979).

35. See, for example, Sullivan v. Louisiana, 508 U.S. 275 (1993). The reasonable doubt standard was stated by the U.S. Supreme Court in *In re* Winship, 397 U.S. 358 (1970).

36. For a brief statement of Beccaria's contributions, see Sue Titus Reid, *Crime and Criminology*, 8th ed. (New York: McGraw-Hill, 1997), pp. 75–76. See also Cesare Beccaria, *On Crimes and Punishments*, trans. Henry Paolucci (Indianapolis: Bobbs-Merrill, 1963).

37. Harris v. Alabama, 513 U.S. 504 (1995). All of the conspirators were convicted of capital murder. Two were sentenced to life without parole. The triggerman was sentenced to death after the judge rejected the jury's seven-to-five vote for life in prison without possibility of parole.

38. Tedder v. State, 322 So.2d 908, 910 (Fla. 1975).

39. See Proffitt v. Florida, 428 U.S. 242 (1976).

40. Walton v. Arizona, 497 U.S. 639 (1990).

41. See Cal. Const. Art. I, Section 28 (1997).

42. Booth v. Maryland, 482 U.S. 496 (1987), *overruled in part*, Payne v. Tennessee, 501 U.S. 808 (1991).

43. Payne v. Tennessee, 501 U.S. 808 (1991). The other case that was overruled is South Carolina v. Gathers, 490 U.S. 805 (1989).

44. State v. Gentry, 888 P.2d 1105 (Wash. 1995), *cert. denied*, 516 U.S. 843 (1995).

45. George F. Cole, *Innovations in Collecting and Enforcing Fines* (Washington, D.C.: U.S. Department of Justice, July/August 1989), p. 3, footnotes omitted.

46. Williams v. Illinois, 399 U.S. 235 (1970).

47. Tate v. Short, 401 U.S. 395 (1971).

48. Bearden v. Georgia, 461 U.S. 660 (1983).

49. See Laura A. Winterfield and Sally T. Hillsman, *The Staten Island Day-Fine Project* (Washington, D.C.: National Institute of Justice, January 1993): 1. For a discussion of the possible impact of race on fines, see James F. Nelson, "A Dollar or a Day: Sentencing Misdemeanants in New York State," *Journal of Research in Crime and Delinquency* 31 (May 1994): 183–201.

50. See Bradford v. United States, 228 U.S. 446 (1913).

51. See, for example, National Center for Juvenile Justice, *Restitution and Juvenile Recidivism* (Rockville, MD: Juvenile Justice Clearinghouse, 1992).

52. See Richard C. Boldt, "Restitution, Criminal Law, and the Ideology of Individuality," *Journal of Criminal Law and Criminology* 77 (Winter 1986): 969–1022.

53. For further information on how these programs work, see Joe Hudson and Burt Galaway, "Community Service: Toward Program Definition," *Federal Probation* 54 (June 1990): 3–9.

54. See, for example, Graeme Newman, *Just and Painful: A Case for the Corporal Punishment of Criminals* (New York: Macmillan, 1983).

55. For an examination of modern capital murder statutes, see James R. Acker and Charles S. Lanier, "The Dimensions of Capital Murder," *Criminal Law Bulletin* 29 (September–October 1993): 379–417. For a history of capital punishment, see Raymond Paternoster, *Capital Punishment in America* (New York: Lexington Books, 1992).

56. Furman v. Georgia, 408 U.S. 238 (1972).

57. For a recent analysis of capital punishment statutes, see James R. Acker and Charles S. Lanier, "Matters of Life or Death: The Sentencing Provisions in Capital Punishment Statutes," *Criminal Law Bulletin* 31 (January–February 1995): 19–60.

58. "New York Revives Death Penalty After Eighteen Years," *New York Times* (8 March 1995), p. 1. See New York Penal Code, Section 60.06 (1997).

59. Consider, for example, the debate between William Wilbanks and Coramae Richey Mann, whose views are available in brief form in a publication entitled "Racism in the Criminal Justice System: Two Sides of a Controversy," *Criminal Justice Bulletin* 3, no. 5 (1987). See also Wilbanks, *The Myth of a Racist Criminal Justice System* (Monterey, Calif.: Brooks-Cole, 1987); and Coramae Richey Mann, *Unequal Justice: A Question of Color* (Bloomington, Indiana: Indiana University Press, 1993).

60. Michael J. Lynch and W. Byron Groves, *A Primer in Radical Criminology*, 2d ed. (New York: Harper and Heston, 1989), pp. 106–107, citations omitted.

61. Michael Tonry, "Racial Politics, Racial Disparities, and the War on Crime," *Crime & Delinquency* 40 (October 1994): 475, 483–488.

62. United States v. Armstrong, 517 U.S. 456 (1996).

63. See Rita James Simon, "American Women and Crime," *Annals of the American Academy of Political and Social Science* 423 (January 1976): 31–46. Simon's more recent publication on women and crime, coauthored by Jean Landis, *The Crimes Women Commit, The Punishments They Receive* (Lexington, Mass.: D. C. Heath, 1991), received a very critical review by Russ Immarigeon, who called the book "a disappointing, incomplete, and poorly researched update." See "Women and Crime Revisited," *Federal Probation* 55 (March 1991): 96.

64. See, for example, "Women in Jail: Unequal Justice," *Newsweek* (4 June 1990), p. 37.

65. See, for example, Ilene H. Nagel, "The Legal/Extra-Legal Controversy: Judicial Decisions in Pretrial Release," *Law and Society Review* 17 (1983): 481–515.

66. Darrell J. Steffensmeier, "Assessing the Impact of the Women's Movement on Sex-Based Differences in the Handling of Adult Criminal Defendants," *Crime & Delinquency* 26 (July 1980): 344–57.

67. Darrell Steffensmeier et al., "Gender and Imprisonment Decisions," *Criminology* 31 (August 1993): 411–446; quotation is on p. 435. See also Kathleen Daly and Rebecca L. Bordt, "Sex Effects and Sentencing: An Analysis of the Statistical Literature," *Justice Quarterly* 12 (March 1995): 141–176; and Daly, *Gender, Crime and Punishment* (New Haven, Conn.: Yale University Press, 1994).

68. "Sex Bias Is Found Pervading Courts," *New York Times* (2 March 1989), p. 8; "Task Forces in 27 States Studying Gender Bias in Courts," *Criminal Justice Newsletter* 20 (1 June 1989): 6; "California Panel Urges Reforms to Curb Gender Bias in Courts," *Criminal Justice Newsletter* 21 (1 May 1990): 4. For a series of articles on the subject of women and the law, see the symposium issue: "Women and the Law: Goals for the 1990s," *Florida Law Review* 42 (January 1990).

69. See Leslie T. Wilkins et al., *Sentencing Guidelines: Structuring Judicial Discretion: Report on the Feasibility Study* (Washington, D.C.: National Institute of Law Enforcement and Criminal Justice, Law Enforcement Assistance Administration, 1978); and Wilkins, "Sentencing Guidelines to Reduce Disparity?" *Criminal Law Review* 1980 (April 1980): 201–214.

70. See, for example, an account of the state that pioneered in the use of sentencing guidelines: Dale G. Parent, S*tructuring Criminal Sentences: The Evolution of Minnesota's Sentencing Guidelines* (Stoneham, Mass.: Butterworth, 1988). For a comparison and analysis of Minnesota's guidelines with those of two other states, see John H. Kramer et al., "Sentencing Guidelines: A Quantitative Comparison of Sentencing Policies in Minnesota, Pennsylvania, and Washington," *Justice Quarterly* 6 (December 1989): 565–587. For a more recent analysis, see Lisa Stolzenberg and Stewart J. D'Alessio, "Sentencing and Unwarranted Disparity: An Empirical Assessment of the Long-Term Impact of Sentencing Guidelines in Minnesota," *Criminology* 32 (May 1994): 301–310; and Stolzenberg and D'Alessio, "The Impact of Sentencing Guidelines on Jail Incarceration in Minnesota," *Criminology* 33 (May 1995): 283–302.

71. Mistretta v. United States, 488 U.S. 361 (1989).

72. Cal. Penal Code, Section 1170 *et seq.* (1997).

73. "States Embracing Tougher Measures for Fighting Crime," *New York Times* (10 May 1994), p. 1. See Cal. Penal Code, Section 667 (1997).

Confinement and Corrections

INTRODUCTION

After the processes of convicting and sentencing, society is faced with the issue of what to do with offenders. Historically, convicted offenders were treated informally by means of various psychological and physical punishments. Physical or corporal punishments became severe; however, and for humanitarian and other reasons, reformers decided corporal punishment should be replaced with confinement.

Confinement facilities—formerly used primarily for detaining the accused temporarily while they awaited trial or the convicted while they awaited corporal or other forms of punishment—were viewed as places for punishment and reformation. Although many reformers saw confinement facilities as replacements for corporal punishment, others saw

INTRODUCTION—Continued

them as an environment in which offenders would be reformed through work; have time for reflection; and, in some cases, be subjected to corporal punishment.

The history of the emergence of prisons and jails as places of punishment is a fascinating study, but it is laced with controversy, idealism, and unfulfilled promises. Part IV traces that development from its early beginning through modern times. Chapter 9 focuses on the history and structure of confinement, pointing out the differences between state and federal systems, the different levels of security that characterize confinement, and the emergence of prisons as places for punishment. The nature of private corrections is discussed along with the problems of prison and jail overcrowding. This chapter provides the background needed for an analysis of some of the issues surrounding modern correctional practices.

Chapter 10 examines the administration and inmate life of modern prisons, looking particularly at the ways in which the internal structure of the prison may be used to control inmates. That control is not always successful, however, as illustrated by the discussions on prison violence and the lawsuits filed as the result of alleged violations of inmates' constitutional rights. Section 4 closes with a chapter on probation, parole, and community corrections.

The History and Structure of Confinement

WiseGuide Intro

In the past, when confinement of offenders was necessary, it was not for long periods of time. Lengthy confinements would have been impractical in a less populated world where formal police protection did not exist and conditions were so unstable that populations moved from one place to another in search of food and shelter. Under those conditions, usually the punishment of persons who violated society's norms was carried out by quick methods such as corporal punishment, or in extreme cases, capital punishment. Generally, confinement was for very short periods while defendants awaited corporal punishment or trial.

Places of confinement for suspects or convicted defendants should reflect the purposes for which they are intended. If confinement is for holding a person until trial or corporal punishment, little attention need be paid to that confinement facility except to keep it secure. The architecture, conditions, and administration should reflect the security goal. If humanitarian concerns are not important, the conditions of confinement are relatively unimportant. Likewise, if the reason for confinement is to remove offenders from society and punish them for their criminal acts, then programming, treatment personnel, and prison conditions are unimportant. Prison is a place of custody and punishment; being there is the punishment. Offenders are getting what they deserve as a result of their criminal activities.

If the purpose of confinement is to rehabilitate **offenders,** more attention should be given to the total confinement program. Location of confinement facilities is important; facilities should be close enough to inmates' homes to enable family members to visit. Confinement conditions are important because they are related to inmates' rehabilitation. Treatment programs, educational and work opportunities, fairness in discipline, and many other activities behind prison walls are important. Administration and management must

Key Terms

classification
community-based corrections
custody
humanitarianism
inmates
jail
offenders
penitentiary
prison
reformatory
silent system
transportation
warden
workhouse

reflect a treatment-rehabilitation orientation and, at the same time, maintain security within the institution.

This chapter looks at the historical development of the incarceration of offenders in prisons and jails as a method of detention and punishment. Throughout the discussion, the purposes of confinement discussed earlier—retribution and just deserts, incapacitation, deterrence, and rehabilitation—should be kept in mind.[1] The focus on one or more of these purposes is not necessarily chronological in the history of prisons, but the purpose is tied to the type of prison that emerges.

Learning Objectives

Learning Objectives

After reading this chapter, you should be able to do the following:

- Explain the reasons given for the emergence of institutions for confining offenders.
- Explain the significance of the Walnut Street Jail.
- Distinguish the Pennsylvania and the Auburn systems and evaluate the contributions of each.
- Recall the contributions of Europeans to the emergence and development of prisons.
- Explain the relevance of the Elmira Reformatory.
- Summarize the development of the modern U.S. prison system.
- Distinguish jails, prisons, and community corrections.
- List and describe the purposes of prison security levels.

- Analyze the differences between prisons for men and women and compare to co-correctional institutions.
- Describe state and federal prison systems and evaluate the differences.
- Discuss the implications of the growth in jail and prison populations with particular attention to the negative effects of overcrowding.
- Discuss the distinguishing features of jails and analyze the role of the federal government in local jails.
- Explain *boot camps* and evaluate these programs.
- Analyze the role of privatization in correctional facilities.

The Emergence of Prisons for Punishment

Historical Development

The use of secure facilities for *confinement* is an ancient practice. Persons were confined awaiting trials or sentencing. But the use of secure facilities, such as prisons or jails, for *punishment* is a relatively recent practice.

The transition from corporal punishment to prison as punishment took place in the eighteenth century. In 1704 Pope Clement XI erected the papal prison of San Michele in Rome. In 1773 the prison in Ghent, Belgium, was established by Hippolyte Vilain XIII. In 1776 England was faced with a rising crime rate, the elimination of the need for galley slaves, and decreasing opportunities for **transportation** of criminals to her colonies. England legalized the use of hulks, usually broken-down war vessels. By 1828 at least 4,000 offenders were confined in English prison hulks. The ships were unsanitary, poorly ventilated, and vermin-infested. Contagious diseases killed many inmates. Punishments were brutal. There was little work for inmates, and idleness was demoralizing. Moral degeneration set in because of the "promiscuous association of prisoners of all ages and degrees of criminality.[2] This system of penal confinement in England lasted until the middle of the nineteenth century.

The spirit of **humanitarianism** that arose during the Enlightenment was among the reasons for the substitution of imprisonment for transportation, corporal, and capital punishment. People began to realize the horrors inherent in the ways offenders were treated, and the French prison built in Paris in the fourteenth century, the Bastille, became a symbol of prisons administered in tyrannical ways. French philosophers such as Voltaire, shocked by what they called judicial murders, sought changes in criminal justice systems. "Voltaire and the Encyclopedists prepared the ground for the later success of Beccaria, who accomplished the most 'effective work in the reform of criminal jurisprudence.'"[3]

Another important philosophical development in France during the French Revolution was the emphasis on rationalism. This approach was important in the history of prisons because of its influence on social and political philosophy. The philosophers believed that social progress and the greatest happiness for the greatest number would occur only through revolutionary social reform, which could be brought about only by applying reason.

It was logical that these reform ideas would flourish in the United States because many Frenchmen lived here during the French Revolution and many influential Americans had been to France. Because the Constitutional Convention was influenced significantly by the political philosophy of French philosophers, it is not unreasonable to assume that its members were aware of French social philosophy.

There are other important reasons for the rise of the prison system in America. The increasing emphasis on personal liberty meant that deprivation of liberty could be seen as punishment. In addition, after the Industrial Revolution there was an increasing need for labor that could be supplied by inmates. It has been argued, too, that prisons were developed by those in power for the purpose of suppressing persons who were not in power.[4]

John Howard's Reforms

One of the greatest prison reformers of all time was John Howard (1726–1790), an Englishman credited with the beginning of the **penitentiary** system. Howard traveled throughout Europe and brought to the world's attention the sordid conditions under which inmates were confined.

Howard's classic work, *State of Prisons,* published in 1777, was extremely influential in prison reform in Europe and the United States. Among his other ideas, Howard suggested that inmates should be housed alone in sanitary facilities and provided clean clothing. Women and children should be segregated. Jailers should be trained and well paid. Howard's role in the development and improvement of prisons was recognized in a 1991 publication on prisons. The collection of essays examines prison systems in several countries, including the United States, using the descriptive analysis characteristic of John Howard's work.[5]

The history of correctional institutions may be traced back to Roman, French, and English systems. An early English gaol (jail) is featured in Spotlight 9.1. The unique contribution of America was the substitution of imprisonment for corporal punishment, an innovation of the Quakers of West Jersey and Pennsylvania in the eighteenth century. They combined the prison and the **workhouse** to achieve a system of confinement at hard labor.

Emergence of American Penitentiaries

Spotlight 9.1

The First London Gaol

Built shortly after the Norman Conquest in 1066, the Fleet Prison was the first London facility constructed solely for the purpose of holding prisoners. It was called the Gaol of London until 1188, when that name was taken over by the Newgate Prison and the original gaol became known as the Fleet Prison. The early gaol was built of stone and surrounded by a moat, typical of many structures in those days, serving the dual purpose of keeping the inmates in and outsiders out.

This first London gaol was really a jail as we know that facility today, not a prison. Its primary purpose was detention of suspects awaiting trial, after which they were punished elsewhere. One exception was debtors, who were held until their debts were paid. On occasion they were permitted to leave the institution for limited periods, although generally a fee was charged for this privilege. Early physical conditions in the Fleet Prison were better than those in most English institutions, which is "not saying much since the state of the early English prisons was generally quite deplorable." Over time conditions deteriorated and "soon the Fleet had the reputation of being one of the worst in all the country."

The Fleet was burned in 1666, soon rebuilt, destroyed over one hundred years later, rebuilt again, and closed in 1842. "The Fleet Prison was demolished some four years later, thus ending the career of one of the oldest English institutions, the original Gaol of London."

Source: Paraphrased from J. M. Moynahan, "The Original Gaol of London," *American Jails* 1 (Winter 1988): 88.

In 1787 Pennsylvania enacted a statute reducing the number of capital crimes, substituting imprisonment for many felonies, and abolishing most corporal punishments. A 1794 statute abolished capital punishment except for first-degree murder and substituted fines and imprisonment for corporal punishment in the case of all other crimes. The Pennsylvania criminal code reform set the stage for similar developments in other states. The main feature of early Pennsylvania reform was the Walnut Street Jail.

Walnut Street Jail

In 1787 in Pennsylvania, Benjamin Rush, Benjamin Franklin, and others met to discuss punishment. Rush proposed a new system for the treatment of offenders. This system included classification, individualized treatment, and prison labor to make prisons self-supporting. A 1790 statute codified the principle of solitary confinement and established the Walnut Street Jail in which individual cells were provided for serious felons. Other inmates were separated by gender and by whether they had been sentenced or were being held for detention only. This law was the beginning of the modern prison system in the United States, and the Walnut Street jail is often cited as the first U.S. prison.

Some scholars have argued that the Walnut Street Jail was not the first American prison. Alexis M. Durham III has written extensively about the development of early prisons. According to Durham, the honor goes to Connecticut's Newgate Prison, the "first true colonial prison for the long-term punishment of serious offenders."[6] The prison was used for the incarceration and punishment of offenders who committed the following crimes: robbery, burglary, forgery, counterfeiting, and horse thievery. Unlike the Walnut Street Jail, Newgate was much more like the English houses of corrections and other early penal facilities, with an emphasis on punishment rather than rehabilitation.[7]

Offenders in the Walnut Street Jail worked an eight- to ten-hour day and received religious instruction. They labored in their cells and were paid for their efforts. Guards were not permitted to use weapons, and corporal punishment was forbidden. Inmates were allowed to talk only in the common rooms at night before retiring. With some variations, this plan was followed in other states. By 1800 problems with the system were obvious. Crowded facilities made work within individual cells impossible; there was not enough productive work for the large number of inmates, and vice flourished. Ultimately, the Walnut Street Jail failed as a result of politics, finances, lack of personnel, and crowding, but not before it had gained recognition throughout the world.

The Walnut Street Jail and other early prisons faced serious problems. Despite the thick walls and high security, **inmates** escaped. To combat that problem, some **wardens** required inmates to wear uniforms; in some prisons the color of the uniform symbolized whether the convict was a first-, second-, or third-time offender. Discipline was a major issue; some wardens reinstituted corporal punishment, while others used solitary confinement.

Funding was another problem in these early prisons, and facilities were needed for exercise. To alleviate these problems, work programs such as gardening were begun, but they were not effective. Inmates were neither reliable nor efficient, and administrators were not skilled in managing the labor situation. The result was that most prisons operated at a loss. By 1820 the viability of the entire prison system was in doubt, and its most dedicated supporters conceded a near total failure. Institutionalization had failed to pay its own way and had encouraged and educated the criminal to a life in crime.[8]

In response to these problems, two types of prison systems developed: the Pennsylvania, or separate, system, based on solitary confinement; and the New York, or Auburn, system, known as the **silent system.** These two systems were the subject of intense debate. Tourists flocked to see the prisons; foreign nations sent delegates to examine the two systems. By the 1830s the two American penitentiary systems were famous around the world.

The Pennsylvania System

With the demise of the Walnut Street Jail, solitary confinement at hard labor appeared a failure. Consideration was given to a return to corporal punishment. But in 1817 the Philadelphia Society for the Alleviation of the Miseries of Prisons began a reform movement that led to a law providing for the establishment of the separate system of confining inmates in solitary cells without labor.

The first separate system prison was opened in Pittsburgh in 1826 and subsequently was known as the Western Penitentiary. Due to the problems of idleness in this prison, the law was changed to permit work in solitary confinement before the establishment of the Eastern Penitentiary in Philadelphia. The design of its building became the basic architectural model for the Pennsylvania system.

The Eastern Penitentiary, or Cherry Hill as it was called because of its location in a cherry orchard, was established in 1829. It was the first large-scale attempt at implementing the philosophy of solitary confinement at all times with work provided for inmates in their cells. The law that authorized construction of this prison specified that although the commissioners could make some alterations and improvements in the plan used for the Western Penitentiary, the principle of solitary confinement must be incorporated.

John Haviland, the architect for Cherry Hill, was faced with the problem of creating a design that would permit solitary confinement but would not injure inmates' health or permit escapes. His solution was seven wings, each connected to a central hub by covered passageways. Each inmate had a single inside cell with an outside exercise yard. Inmates were blindfolded when taken to the prison and were not permitted to see other inmates. They were not assembled even for religious worship. The chaplain spoke from the rotunda with inmates remaining in their individual cells.

Before Cherry Hill was completed, it became the focus of discussion among prison reformers around the world. Although it was the architectural model for most of the new prisons in Europe, South America, and, later, Asia, the design was not popular in the United States. Despite that fact, John Haviland's contributions to prison architecture in American should not be minimized.

> Compared with the penitentiaries of their day, Haviland's prisons were overwhelmingly superior, both technically and stylistically. . . . Haviland's great service to penology would seem to be in establishing high standards of construction, standards which were to have an influence on almost all of the prison construction of the nineteenth century.[9]

Haviland should be remembered as well for the fact that his prison architecture embodied a treatment philosophy.

The Auburn System

The prison system that became the architectural model for the United States was the Auburn System. In 1796 New York enacted a statute that provided for the building of two prisons. Newgate in New York City was first occupied in 1797. That prison soon became so crowded that, to make room for new inmates, as many inmates had to be released as were admitted.

The Auburn Prison was similar to Newgate, with workshop groups during the day and several inmates to a cell at night. Discipline was a problem, however, so a new system, which became known as the Auburn System, developed. The Auburn System featured congregate work during the day, with an enforced silent system. Inmates were housed in individual cells at night. The architecture created a fortresslike appearance with a series of tiers set in a hollow frame, a much more economical system than that of Cherry Hill.

The silent system was enforced strictly at Auburn. The inmates ate face to back. They stood with arms folded and eyes down so they could not communicate with their hands. They walked in lockstep with a downward gaze. Strict regulation of letters and visits with outsiders and few or no newspapers isolated them further. Inmates were brought together for religious services, but each sat in a booth-like pew that prevented seeing anyone other than the speaker.

Discipline was enforced strictly at Auburn. The warden, Captain Elam Lynds, thought that the spirit of a person must be broken before reformation could occur. He was credited with the Auburn punishment philosophy. It is said that he changed discipline rules without legislative authority, instituted the silent system, fed inmates in their cells, and required lockstep in marching. A committee from the legislature visited the prison, approved of the way it was being run, and persuaded the legislature to legalize the new system.

In 1821 a system of **classification** was instituted. It placed dangerous offenders in solitary confinement. Solitary confinement led to mental illness, inmates' pleadings for work, and sometimes, even to death. A commission established to study prisons recommended abolishing solitary confinement and putting all inmates to work.

Comparison of the Pennsylvania and Auburn Systems

Architecture is important in distinguishing the Pennsylvania and Auburn systems. The latter emphasized the congregate but silent system, the former solitary confinement. Both emphasized the importance of a disciplined routine and isolation from bad influences. Both reflected the belief that, because the inmate was not inherently bad, but rather the product of defective social organization, he or she could be reformed under proper circumstances. The discussions of crime centered on the advantages and disadvantages of these two systems, but few questioned the premise on which both rested: that incarceration was the best way to handle criminals.[10]

The differences in architecture of the two systems resulted in cost differentials. The Auburn system was more economical to build, although the Pennsylvania system was more economical to administer. It was argued that the Auburn system was more conducive to productive inmate labor and less likely to cause mental illness. The silent system continued into the twentieth century, not for the original purpose of preventing cross-infection, but because it was easier to run an institution if the inmates were not allowed to speak to each other.

Both the Pennsylvania and the Auburn systems sound harsh today, but they must be viewed in historical perspective:

> The most that can be said for this period of American prison history is that, despite all its stupidities and cruelties, it was better than a return to the barbarities of capital and corporal punishment for crime. In the face of public indignation at the chaos existing in early American prisons in 1820, it maintained the penitentiary system.[11]

The Pennsylvania and Auburn systems were important also in that both were based on treatment philosophies, with architecture designed to accommodate those philosophies. The importance of architecture on treatment and programming within prisons should not be underestimated.

The disagreement over the Pennsylvania and Auburn systems led to a prison system that emphasized reformation, a system characterized by indeterminate sentences, parole, work training, and education. Before looking at the emergence of that system in the United States, it is important to look briefly at the European developments that influenced U.S. systems.

Emergence of the Reformatory Model

European Background

We look to the works of Captain Alexander Maconochie, an Englishman, and Sir Walter Crofton, an Irishman, for the beginnings of a reformatory movement. Maconochie began the movement in 1840 when he was placed in charge of the British penal colony on Norfolk Island, off the coast of Australia. Norfolk Island was used by England for the worst offenders who had been transported from England to mainland Australia, where they committed further crimes. Maconochie was critical of the use of transportation. Previously, England had transported her offenders to the American colonies. After the American Revolution, that was no longer an option; so many offenders were sent to Australia. The conditions of transportation were dreadful. Offenders were chained together and in some cases had only standing room on the ships. Fevers and diseases were rampant; food was meager; sanitary conditions were unbelievable; homosexual rape and other forms of violence were common.

Upon his arrival at Norfolk, Maconochie began to implement his reformation philosophy. He emphasized that he was not lenient, and that society has a right to punish those who break its laws, but

> We have no right to cast them away altogether. Even their physical suffering should be in moderation, and the moral pain framed so as, if possible, to reform, and not necessarily to pervert them. The iron should enter both soul and body, but not so utterly to sear and harden them.[12]

Maconochie's reform program was characterized by his advocacy of the indeterminate sentence and his belief that inmates should work, improve their conduct, and learn frugality of living before they were released. While in prison, they should earn everything they receive. Their work served to earn the required number of "marks." When they were qualified by discipline to do so, they should work in small groups of about six or seven, with all of the offenders answerable for the behavior of the entire group as well as of each member. Before they were released, while still required to earn their daily tally of marks, offenders should be given a proprietary interest in their labor. They should be subjected to less rigorous discipline in order to be prepared to live in society without the supervision of prison officials.

Maconochie never was given the authority that he thought he would have when he went to Norfolk. His ideas were controversial and not greatly appreciated by the British authorities, but he made many changes in the penal colony, and it was a more humane place when he left.

Maconochie described his accomplishments as follows: "I found a turbulent, brutal hell, and left it a peaceful well-ordered community." Evidence proved him right. But the controversy over his methods and philosophies led to his recall in 1844:

> He was replaced by Major Childs, an incompetent who sought to carry out instructions to restore the previous evil methods in place of Maconochie's reforms. This led, on 1 July 1846 to a revolt by some of the convicts, and four of the penal staff were murdered.[13]

Sir Walter Crofton, a disciple of Maconochie, applied Maconochie's reform ideas to the Irish prisons, where he served as chairman of the board of directors. The Irish system was recognized widely for its emphasis on the following:

1. A reward system—all advantages, including release, were based on rewards for good behavior.
2. Individual influence of the prison administrators on the inmates—prison populations were to be kept small (300 in ordinary prisons, 100 in intermediate prisons) to permit this influence.
3. Gradual release from restrictions—restrictions were gradually removed until during the last stage, the intermediate prison, one-half of the restrictions were removed.
4. A parole system involving strict supervision after release and revocation for infractions of the rules.[14]

The American Reformatory

American reformers visited the Irish prison system in the 1860s and returned with great enthusiasm for their reformation philosophy. On 12 October 1870 a meeting led by the penologist Enoch C. Wines was held in Cincinnati, Ohio, to settle the dispute between the Pennsylvania and Auburn systems. This meeting led to the organization of the American Correctional Association, then called the

National Prison Association. The group drafted thirty-seven principles calling for indeterminate sentences, cultivation of inmates' self-respect, classification of offenders, and advancement of the philosophy of reformation, not punishment.

The Elmira Reformatory, established in 1876, emerged from this meeting. This institution became the model for a **reformatory,** which was designed for young offenders. The architecture was similar to that of the Auburn system, but greater emphasis was placed on educational and vocational training. Indeterminate sentences with maximum terms, opportunities for parole, and the classification of inmates according to conduct and achievement were the greatest advances of this new institution.

It was predicted that Elmira would dominate U.S. prison systems. Elmira was established at the same time that other reforms, such as the juvenile court, probation, parole, and indeterminate sentences were emerging.[15]

From Reformation Back to Custody

The great contribution of the Elmira reformatory system was its emphasis on rehabilitation through education, which led to greater prison discipline, indeterminate sentences, and parole. The system declined eventually, mainly as a result of the lack of trained personnel to conduct the educational programs and to carry on the classification system adequately. Some scholars argue that the Elmira system was never intended to be a real reform but, rather, was developed for the purpose of controlling the lower class as well as women and minorities. The system promised benevolent reform but delivered only repression.[16]

An increase in the prison population in the late 1800s resulted in severe overcrowding. Eventually, new prisons were built, including Attica (New York) in 1931 and Stateville (Illinois) in 1925. Most of these followed the Auburn architectural plan and were characterized by increasing costs per inmate, Sunday services, a chaplain on duty most of the time, and insufficient educational and vocational training programs. The latter were based on the needs of institutions, not the interests or needs of inmates. Insufficient funds were available to hire and retain adequate personnel.

Those institutions provided work for some inmates, and the prison products were sold on the open market. This industrial period of prison history irritated those in private industries, who complained that competition from prisons was unfair because of the low wages. In 1929 the Hawes–Cooper Act was passed, followed in 1935 by the Ashurst–Summers Act to restrict the sale of prison goods.

These in turn were followed by state laws designed to do the same. With the passage of these laws, the Industrial Prison was eliminated. In 1935 for the great majority of prisoners the penitentiary system had again reverted to its original status: punishment and custody.[17]

Modern Prisons: An Overview

United States prisons emerged as a substitute for corporal punishment, but corporal punishment continued. Supposedly, prisons emerged as places in which inmates could be reformed.[18] However, the early reform approach was abandoned eventually in favor of a custody philosophy. According to David Rothman, reformation was abandoned for several reasons. The change was not inherent in prison designs. Some disappointment was to be expected because of the great expectations the founders had for the success of the prison movement. Change came about also as a result of the resources drained from prisons during the Civil War. Additionally, the rehabilitation goal promoted but also disguised the shift from reformation to custody. Too often prison administrators assumed that incarceration was reformation, and no one recognized that reformation programs were lacking. The administrators relaxed their reformative efforts, and abuses of power arose within the prisons.

The nature of the inmate was related to the change from a reformation to a custodial emphasis. The silent, segregated systems were not designed for hardened offenders serving long-term or life sentences. The founders who envisaged reformation of the offender had not contemplated what to do with the hardened offender or the juvenile already committed to a life of crime. When the situation arose, **custody** seemed the best answer. The public accepted that approach because of the need for safety and security.[19]

The custodial institution seemed the best way to handle changes in the composition of inmate populations. As cities became larger and their populations were more heterogeneous, including an influx of immigrants as well as distinct social classes, traditional methods of social control became ineffective. When those persons entered prison, custody seemed the best approach.

By the late 1800s it was clear that reformation was no longer a major punishment goal. Later studies reported corruption between correctional officers and inmates, cruel punishment of inmates, overcrowded prisons with financial problems, and severe criticism of both the Pennsylvania and the Auburn systems. But prisons remained long after the original goals were abandoned. As hardened offenders were held for long periods of time, prisons turned into holding operations where wardens were content if they could prevent riots and escapes.

Some reformers began to express dissatisfaction with incarceration per se, criticizing long sentences as counterproductive and large expenditures on prisons as foolish and unnecessary. Probation and parole were advocated but slow to be adopted. Most reforms and the public seemed content to incarcerate for the sake of security.

Why did the public stand for the decline of the original prison philosophy? David Rothman suggests that part of the explanation might be that usually it is easier to capture public interest "with predictions of success than with the descriptions of corruption." Some may have believed that incarceration was synonymous with rehabilitation. But, said Rothman, the reasons went deeper. Many persons saw the prison as performing an important social function, for they noted that the majority of inmates were from the lower social class and many were immigrants. Few upper- or upper-middle-class persons were incarcerated.[20]

In recent years reformation or rehabilitation has been dealt a severe blow by researchers who claim that empirical evidence shows that rehabilitation has failed. As previous discussions indicate, some evidence of the rehabilitative ideal remains, but no longer is it the dominant reason for punishment. It has been replaced by the just deserts model, with its emphasis on deterrence and retribution as the main reasons for punishment.

Many aspects of modern U.S. prisons are examined in this and the next chapter, which demonstrate that modern prisons are characterized by disruption, violence, monotonous daily routine, lack of work opportunities, and unconstitutional living conditions. Many jails and prisons are under federal court orders to improve inmates' living conditions and reduce inmate populations or be closed. Some readers may question whether these modern prisons are an improvement over the earlier ones. Others may say the question is not relevant; offenders should be punished—just what the system is doing.

Offenders may be confined in various types of institutions. These institutions are classified most commonly as jails, prisons, and community correctional facilities.

Although the terms **jail** and **prison** are used interchangeably, and the two types of institutions have many common characteristics, they may be distinguished by their purposes. Jails and detention centers are used for the confinement of persons awaiting trial. They are used for short-term detention of persons in need of care when no other facilities are available immediately. For example, a public drunk might be detained until sober or until arrangements are made for admittance to a treatment facility. Jails are used to detain witnesses to a crime if it is thought that otherwise they might not be available for trial. Jails are used for the incarceration of persons sentenced to short terms, usually less than one year.

Prisons are used for the incarceration of offenders sentenced for lengthy terms, usually over one year, and for more serious offenses, such as felonies. A third type of facility that is used for confinement is a **community-based corrections** facility that houses offenders but permits them to leave during part of the day to work, attend school, or engage in treatment programs. Offenders may be confined in special-purpose facilities such as treatment centers for abusers of alcohol or drugs, sex offenders, or the mentally ill.

Confinement Institutions

Prison security levels may be divided into three main categories: maximum, medium, and minimum security, as Spotlight 9.2 illustrates. The federal government and most states have all three types; most inmates are in maximum-security prisons. Characteristics of the security levels differ from one jurisdiction to another. As Spotlight 9.2 relates, levels differ in outside security and in architecture.

Many of the maximum-security prisons were built before 1925, and prior to that time most inmates were housed in maximum-security prisons, although many of them did not require that security level. Unfortunately, this occurs in some jurisdictions today. Maintenance of these old maximum-security facilities is difficult and costly; many of the complaints about prison conditions that are discussed subsequently are related to the problems of maintaining these old facilities.

Maximum-, medium-, and minimum-security prisons differ in the emphasis on treatment and related programs and in the freedom permitted inmates. In maximum-security prisons, inmates are detained in their cells for longer periods of time and given less freedom of movement within the cell blocks than those in the other security levels.

Another type of prison is the *open prison*. Open prisons make use of the natural environment for security. An example is Alcatraz Island, located in San Francisco Bay. Called "the Rock" because the island is mainly rock, Alcatraz has been used for numerous purposes, including a military prison and a maximum-security federal prison. Officially, it became a federal prison on 1 January 1934, and its purpose was to incarcerate the most dangerous federal offenders. The U.S. attorney general described the prison as one that would make no pretense at rehabilitation. Rather, it would be a place for "the ultimate punishment society could inflict upon men short of killing them; the point of no return for multiple losers." Alcatraz was described by one writer as "the great garbage can of San Francisco Bay, into which every federal prison dumped its most rotten apples."[21]

Alcatraz incarcerated some of the most notorious federal offenders, men such as George "Machine Gun" Kelly, a college-educated man from a prosperous family, convicted of bootlegging; and Robert F. Stroud, a young pimp who killed a customer after he attacked one of Stroud's prostitutes. Stroud became known as the "Birdman of Alcatraz" because of his knowledge of bird diseases. Men such as

Prison Security Levels

Spotlight 9.2

Prison Security Levels

Maximum-or close-custody prisons are typically surrounded by a double fence or wall (usually 18 to 25 feet high) with armed guards in observation towers. Such facilities usually have large interior cell blocks for inmate housing areas. In 1984, according to self-reports of superintendents, about 1 in 4 State prisons were classified as maximum security, and about 44 percent of the Nation's inmates were held in these facilities.

Medium-custody prisons are typically enclosed by double fences topped with barbed wire. Housing architecture is varied, consisting of outside cell blocks in units of 150 cells or fewer, dormitories, and cubicles. In 1984, according to self-reports of superintendents, 40 percent of all prisons were medium security and 44 percent of the Nation's inmates were held in such facilities.

Minimum-custody prisons typically do not have armed posts and may use fences or electronic surveillance devices to secure the perimeter of the facility. More than a third of the Nation's prisons are graded by superintendents as minimum-security facilities, but they house only about 1 of 8 inmates. This is indicative of their generally small size.

Source: Bureau of Justice Statistics, *Report to the Nation on Crime and Justice: the Data,* 2d ed. (Washington, D.C.: U.S. Department of Justice, 1988), p. 107.

Kelly and Stroud were sent to Alcatraz because it was considered the most secure prison in the United States. It was assumed that no one could survive in the icy waters and current long enough to swim to San Francisco. There are no records of successful escapes, although on 11 June 1962 three inmates escaped and their bodies were never found. In 1986 the grandson of one of the men claimed that his grandfather had escaped successfully and died a free man in Iowa. He claimed also that the other two men had been eaten by sharks, but in 1990 it was rumored that two of the three (including the one who allegedly died in Iowa) who were from Florida may have escaped alive and be living near Marianna, Florida. The alleged escape case was reopened, and U.S. marshals are looking for the men.[22]

The cost of keeping an offender at Alcatraz was three times as high as it was at any other federal prison, and costly capital improvements were needed. In early 1963 the U.S. attorney general, Robert F. Kennedy, flew to Alcatraz to announce that it would be closed as a federal penitentiary. On 21 March 1963 the prison was closed. Inmates were transferred to other federal prisons. After a period of occupation by Native Americans between 1969 and 1971, Alcatraz became a tourist attraction. Today it is the most frequently visited tourist attraction in the San Francisco area. In recent years it has been renovated and in 1991 a museum filled with "Alcatrivia" was opened on the island.[23]

Alcatraz illustrates some of the problems with open prisons. They may be more secure, but they are costly and inconvenient. Land is scarce, and finding appropriate places for prison colonies is difficult. It is unlikely, therefore, that the open prison will be used extensively in the future, although it has been suggested that drug offenders be sent to penal islands for incarceration.[24] The federal penitentiary on McNeil Island off the coast of Washington state remains in use although it is now part of the Washington state prison system.

In recent years special prisons for high security needs have been built. These secure facilities are referred to as *maxi-maxi prisons* or *supermaximum-security* prisons. Conditions within some have been questioned. A class action suit was filed against Pelican Bay State Prison, California's maxi-maxi prison. In January 1995 the U.S. District Court of Appeal for the Northern District of California appointed a neutral Special Master to oversee the prison and gave the parties

120 days to fashion remedies. The court will maintain jurisdiction over the case until the issues are resolved. The court's one-hundred-plus page opinion details numerous allegations of constitutional violations by inmates and denials by prison officials. Some of those issues are discussed in Chapter 11 of this text.[25]

A federal prison opened in 1994 in Colorado is referred to as the *new Alcatraz*. This prison is a state-of-the art prison designed and built specifically for predator inmates—those who have demonstrated that they cannot live in other prisons without causing trouble for inmates as well as staff and administration. The facility located at the foot of the Rockies was built for 400 inmates at a cost of $60 million. The inmates live in a "super-controlled environment that enforces a hard-edged solitude to contain the risk of social mixing and violence. Even the cell windows deny them all views of the outside except the sky above."[26] A British newspaper described this prison as looking "more like a chemical weapons installation than anything else" because of the obvious security measures, including fourteen-foot-high razor wire bundles and a "triangular ring of mirrored-glass towers guarding the new tomb-like highest security prison" that "can be seen from six miles across the prairie wastelands of Colorado's Rockies."[27]

In August of 1997 Texas began moving inmates into the state's latest facility for hard-core offenders. Inmates in the new maxi-maxi prison in Huntsville, Texas, spend twenty-three out of every twenty-four hours in their un-airconditioned cells. For one hour of each day they are led, while handcuffed and wearing only their undershorts, to an exercise area where they may exercise. Television, books, and newspapers are forbidden; interaction between inmates and anyone else, including correctional officers, is limited; and meals are taken to the inmates' cells.[28]

The problem of housing predatory offenders arose in the case of Jeffrey Dahmer, who killed and dismembered seventeen men and boys. Dahmer was incarcerated in Wisconsin's maximum-security facility at Columbia Correctional Institution, along with the state's other predatory felons. In late 1994 Dahmer was killed by another inmate, an act that, according to the mother of one of Dahmer's victims, "was not as brutal as what he did to our children." Despite the fact that Dahmer was attacked by another inmate earlier that year, officials did not think he was in any danger if he mingled with the general population. He was killed while he cleaned bathrooms.[29]

Despite how some may feel about this act of violence in comparison to those Dahmer committed, the state has a duty to protect its inmates from violence and inhumane conditions. In 1997 an organization that monitors prison conditions alleged that in two super-maximum security Indiana prisons inmates are being subjected to what amounts to torture as defined by international human rights law. According to a report issued by the New York-based group, at both the Maximum Control Facility (MCF) in Westville and the Secured Housing Unit (SHU) at the Wabash Valley Correctional Facility in Carlisle, many inmates are so mentally ill that it is difficult for them to comply with prison rules; some are incapable of doing so. Others are abusing themselves.

Specifically, it is alleged that the problems at these two institutions are obvious even to nonprofessionals. "Prisoners rub feces on themselves, stick pencils in their penises, stuff their eyelids with toilet paper, bite chunks of flesh from their bodies, slash themselves," and so on.[30]

Women's Prisons

Until the late nineteenth century, women, men, and children occupied the same dungeons, almshouses, and jails. The institutions were plagued with physical and sexual abuses. Prison reform led to segregated areas for women within the existing institutions. There were few female inmates, however, and that fact was used to justify not providing separate facilities. Some women's sections did not have a female matron. Vocational training and educational programs were not considered important.

In 1873 the first separate prison for women, the Indiana Women's Prison, was opened. Its emphases were rehabilitation, obedience, and religious education. Other institutions followed: in 1877 in Framingham, Massachusetts; a reformatory for women in 1891 in New York; the Westfield Farm (New York) in 1901; in 1913 an institution in Clinton, New Jersey.

In contrast to institutions for adult men, most institutions for women are more aesthetic and less secure. Generally, female inmates are not considered high security risks. Most are not as violent as male inmates. There are some exceptions, but on the whole the institutions are built and maintained to reflect the assumption that the occupants are not great risks to themselves or to others. Usually, female inmates are permitted greater privacy than incarcerated men.[31]

Historically, female inmates have had fewer educational, vocational, and treatment programs than their counterparts in all-male institutions. The movement toward inmates' rights in the 1970s led to a recognition of these discrepancies. Increasing populations of female inmates created overcrowding at the existing facilities. According to recent data, a record number of 74,730 women were incarcerated in U.S. prisons in 1996, representing a 9.1 percent increase over the previous year.[32]

Co-Correctional Institutions

As already noted, in earlier U.S. prisons men and women were not segregated, and in some facilities the two genders were not segregated within prisons either. In the late 1800s physical and sexual abuses led to a movement toward gender segregation in prisons, and by the mid-1950s, that was the norm. In 1971 the federal system opened a co-correctional facility in Fort Worth, Texas. It was followed by additional state co-correctional institutions and several in the federal system. One of the reasons for this development was the realization that women were not receiving equal treatment in correctional facilities. Women's prisons are less secure and physically more attractive and comfortable, but geographically they are more isolated than institutions for men. Correctional institutions for women have fewer facilities for educational and vocational training, as well as for medical, psychological, and psychiatric treatment.

It was argued that the gender roles exhibited in male and female institutions (aggressive macho in the former and family-related in the latter) might be counteracted by co-correctional institutions. Some of these, particularly in the federal system, were developed primarily to meet problems of overcrowding in other facilities.[33]

In their 1995 publication based on a survey of current literature, John Ortiz Smykla and Jimmy J. Williams reported that in 1994 there were fifty-two co-correctional institutions in the United States and U.S. territories, but that forty-one co-correctional institutions had been closed since 1971. Smykla and Williams found few evaluative studies of co-correctional incarceration.[34] Furthermore, the numbers are misleading, for as one researcher noted, in many of the co-correctional institutions no attempt is made at integration of the genders. "By 1988, the coed movement of the 1970s was all but dead at the state and federal levels."[35]

Smykla and Williams conclude that the available research reveals that co-correctional facilities have not provided improved opportunities for female inmates. To the contrary, the movement is viewed as having a negative impact. Co-correctional institutions provided more opportunities for male than for female inmates. Female inmates were subjected to greater security; expanded work opportunities did not materialize; and female inmates were not incarcerated closer to their homes, one of the alleged advantages of co-correctional institutions.[36]

Other attempts to combine incarcerated women and men have been made. For example, in 1993 Texas officials announced plans to build unisex jails. Officials stated that the experiment was being undertaken solely for economic reasons.[37]

State and Federal Prisons

Most U.S. prisons are state institutions, but the federal government has a large prison system as well.

The Federal System

The previous discussion of the emergence of U.S. prisons referred to state-supported prisons. The federal government, which did not have prisons until the 1900s, contracted with states to incarcerate federal inmates. One of the first acts of Congress was to pass a statute encouraging states to permit the incarceration of federal inmates, at the federal government's expense, in state prisons. Most federal inmates with less than a year to serve or those awaiting trial were kept in local jails.[38]

In 1870 Congress established the Justice Department, which had a general agent in charge of the federal inmates in local jails and state prisons. Later that position was called *superintendent of prisons*. The superintendent was in charge of the care and custody of federal inmates and reported to an assistant attorney general in the Department of Justice.

Overcrowding in state prisons after the Civil War made some states reluctant to house federal offenders; other states accepted only federal offenders from within their borders. Transporting federal offenders to other states was expensive. In 1891 Congress passed a statute authorizing the purchase of land for three federal prisons.

The first federal prison was taken over from the War Department at Fort Leavenworth, Kansas. The facility had been used to house military offenders. It was found to be inadequate for the federal system, and Congress authorized the building of a prison on the Fort Leavenworth military reservation. Federal offenders housed at Fort Leavenworth built the prison. On 1 February 1906, inmates were moved to the new prison, and Fort Leavenworth was returned to the War Department. Final work on Leavenworth was not completed until 1928. Leavenworth remains in use as a prison, but in August of 1997 inmates filed a lawsuit claiming that the prison was near collapse and unsafe. In 1992 one of the commanding officers at the institution warned that "the deterioration of structural members will continue and will likely result in catastrophic failure in 10 years."[39]

Leavenworth was followed by the construction of federal prisons—all for men—in Atlanta, Georgia, and McNeil Island, Washington (which is a state prison now). These prisons followed the architecture and philosophy of the Auburn system.

Prison overcrowding, poor conditions, and inconsistent administration of prisons that were run primarily by local wardens led to the need for more organization in the federal system. On 14 May 1930 President Herbert Hoover signed the law that created the Bureau of Prisons. Today that bureau is a complex system, headed by a director, Kathleen M. Hawk, who succeeded J. Michael Quinlan in December 1992. The director reports to the U.S. Department of Justice. The bureau has a prison industries division as well as a research arm, the National Institute of Corrections. The regional offices of the bureau facilitate the supervision and administration of the federal institutions, inmates, and staff members in the Federal Bureau of Prisons system.[40] The bureau has an extensive legal department as well as divisions overseeing programming, medical services, and administration.

In 1927 the federal system opened a prison for women in Alderson, West Virginia. In addition, female federal offenders are incarcerated in the Federal Correctional Institution at Morgantown, West Virginia. Women with special medical problems are assigned to the Federal Correctional Institution in Lexington, Kentucky. The Federal Correctional Institution at Pleasanton, California, has a Children's Center and Pregnant Women's Shelter Home for women who give birth while incarcerated in federal prisons.[41]

In recognition of the special needs of female inmates, in 1990 the Federal Bureau of Prisons formed a Female Offender Section at its Washington, D.C., headquarters. In 1994 it was announced that the Federal Bureau of Prisons was planning to spend $52 million to convert a 140-bed hospital at Carswell Air Force Base in Fort Worth, Texas, into a medical center for female inmates.[42] Currently, that institution is in use for female inmates as are other institutions throughout the country.

In comparison to state prisons, federal prisons are more costly. Officials of the federal system say the cost differential is justified by the increased educational, vocational, and recreational facilities and lower inmate-staff ratio of the federal system, a difference that results in easier control of inmates and a reduction in long-term operating costs. "The federal prisons use nearly a third fewer employees, including guards, than the states use."[43]

Information concerning careers in the federal correctional system is contained in Professions 9.1.

State Systems

All states have correctional systems; most are centralized and headed by a director who reports to the governor. The director is responsible for overseeing all correctional facilities. Most states have all levels of security—super-, maximum-, medium-, and minimum-security prisons—in addition to separate institutions for juveniles and women and treatment centers in the communities. Not all levels of security are available for women, however, because of the smaller number of female inmates.

States may contract with other states for the incarceration of some inmates. After a riot, it is not uncommon for inmates to be transferred to another state until the riot-damaged facilities are remodeled, repaired, or replaced. Such transfers may be made to remove the riot's leaders. States may contract with other states to house inmates whose lives might be in danger in their own states. Such arrangements might be made between a state and the federal system as well.

In recent years a few states, such as Florida and Texas, have overbuilt their prisons or jails and have contracted with other states to house their surplus of inmates. The arrangements have not always been satisfactory, however, as illustrated by the lawsuit filed in August 1997 against the Texas facilities. Eight inmates filed the suit in St. Louis, Missouri, alleging that they were abused physically while housed in a Texas county jail. Missouri brought 415 inmates back from Texas after a video of the alleged abuse surfaced. The video is reported to show excessive use of physical force by correctional officers against inmates.[44] Additional lawsuits were filed. One of the attorneys alleged that the inmates were "treated worse than dogs." Four officials were indicted as of 30 July 1998.[45]

State prison systems differ considerably in size and complexity as well as in prison conditions and administrative problems. Most of the topics discussed in

PROFESSIONS 9.1

A Career in Federal Corrections: Bureau of Prison Fundamentals

Mission Statement

The Federal Bureau of Prisons protects society by confining offenders in the controlled environments of prisons and community-based facilities that are safe, humane, and appropriately secure, and which provide work and other self-improvement opportunities to assist offenders in becoming law-abiding citizens.

Cultural Anchors/Core Values

- *Bureau Family*   The Bureau of Prisons recognizes that staff are the most valuable resource in accomplishing its mission, and is committed to the personal welfare and professional development of each employee. A concept of "family" is encouraged through healthy, supportive relationships among staff and organization responsiveness to staff needs. The active participation of staff at all levels is essential to the development and accomplishment of organizational objectives.

- *Sound Correctional Management*   The Bureau of Prisons maintains effective security and control of its institutions utilizing the least restrictive means necessary, thus providing the essential foundation for sound correctional management programs.

- *Correctional Workers First*   All Bureau of Prisons staff share a common role as correctional worker, which requires a mutual responsibility for maintaining safe and secure institutions and for modeling society's mainstream values and norms.

- *Promotes Integrity*   The Bureau of Prisons firmly adheres to a set of values that promotes honesty and integrity in the professional efforts of its staff to ensure public confidence in the Bureau's prudent use of its allocated resources.

- *Recognizes the Dignity of All*   Recognizing the inherent dignity of all human beings and their potential for change, the Bureau of Prisons treats inmates fairly and responsively and affords them opportunities for self-improvement to facilitate their successful re-entry into the community. The Bureau further recognizes that offenders are incarcerated as punishment, not for punishment.

- *Career Service Orientation*   The Bureau of Prisons is a career-oriented service, which has enjoyed a consistent management philosophy and a continuity of leadership, enabling it to evolve as a stable, professional leader in the field of corrections.

- *Community Relations*   The Bureau of Prisons recognizes and facilitates the integral role of the community in effectuating the Bureau's mission, and works cooperatively with other law enforcement agencies, the courts, and other components of government.

- *High Standards*   The Bureau of Prisons requires high standards of safety, security, sanitation, and discipline, which promote a physically and emotionally sound environment for both staff and inmates.

Source: *State of the Bureau: Accomplishments and Goals* (Washington, D.C.: U.S. Department of Justice, 1996), p. 5.

the following two chapters concern state prisons. State prisons differ also in the cost of maintaining inmates.

Most incarcerated persons are in local jails rather than state or federal prisons.

Local Systems: The Jail

Jails may be defined as "local (usually county) institutions used to confine individuals awaiting trial or other legal disposition, adults serving short sentences, or some combination of both."[46] Jails are the most important facilities in criminal justice systems because they affect the most people. The "jail is a major intake center not only for the entire criminal justice system, but also a place of first or last resort for a host of disguised health, welfare, and social problem cases."[47]

Jails may be traced far back into history, when they made their debut "in the form of murky dungeons, abysmal pits, unscaleable precipices, strong poles or trees, and suspended cages in which hapless prisoners were kept."[48] The primary purpose of those jails, also called *gaols* (see Spotlight 9.1), was to detain people awaiting trial, transportation, the death penalty, or corporal punishment. The old jails were not escape-proof, and frequently the person in charge received additional fees for shackling inmates. Inmates were not separated according to classification; physical conditions were terrible; food was inadequate; and no treatment or rehabilitation programs existed.

These early detention centers were followed in the fifteenth and sixteenth centuries in Europe by facilities characterized by work and punishment, called *workhouses*, or *houses of correction*. After the breakup of the feudal system, all of Western Europe experienced a significant increase in pauperism and public begging. To combat this problem, a workhouse called the *Bridewell* was established in London in 1557. The dominant philosophy at the Bridewell was a belief that if people had to work at hard and unpleasant tasks, they would abandon their wantonness and begging. The sordid conditions of jails and workhouses in Europe were brought to the attention of the world by John Howard, the prison reformer mentioned earlier. After his tour of European institutions, Howard said in 1773 that more inmates died of jail fever than of execution.[49]

The first jails in the American colonies were places of confinement used mainly to hold suspects awaiting trial, persons who could not pay their debts, and convicted offenders waiting to be taken to prison. Jails were used as punishment only rarely. Most of the offenses for which people may be sentenced to jail or prison today were handled in other ways then: by corporal punishment, capital punishment, fines, or publicly humiliating activities such as sitting in the stock or pillory, where people could jeer at the offenders. In the stocks, the victim's ankles were chained to holes in a wooden frame. The pillory was a device of varying shapes and sizes to which the offender was secured in several ways, one of which was to be nailed to boards. The pillory was driven through town so that people could throw rotten eggs or vegetables at the offenders.

In the 1600s, to replace such severe punishments, Pennsylvania Quakers suggested what they considered to be a more humane form of treatment, the use of jails as punishment. Thus, U.S. jails came to be used not only for the confinement of those awaiting trial but also as places for those serving short-term sentences.

The horrible conditions of American jails continued over the years. In 1923 Joseph Fishman, a federal prison inspector, investigator, and consultant, wrote a book, *Crucible of Crime*, in which he described U.S. jails. He based his descriptions and evaluations on visits to 1,500 jails. He said that some of the convicted would ask for a year in prison in preference to six months in jail because of the inhumane jail conditions.

According to Fishman, most jails were characterized by a lack of space; inadequate amenities such as meals, bathing facilities, hospitals; and no separate facilities for juveniles. Although Fishman said jail conditions were terrible nationwide, the facilities were worse in the South. Fishman's conclusion might be summarized by his definition of jails as

> an unbelievably filthy institution. . . . Usually swarming with bedbugs, roaches, lice, and other vermin; has an odor of disinfectant and filth which is appalling; supports in complete idleness thousands of able-bodied men and women, and generally affords ample time and opportunity to assure inmates a complete course in every kind of viciousness and crime. A melting pot in which the worst elements of the raw material in the criminal world are brought forth, blended and turned out in absolute perfection.[50]

The typical jail in the United States is small, built before 1970, and in need of renovation. It is located in a small town, usually the county seat of a predominantly rural county. These small rural jails constitute the majority of jails but house a minority of jail populations. Some are used infrequently, and many are not crowded, in contrast to jails in urban areas. The typical jail is financed and administered locally.

Some states have assumed partial control of their jails and established statewide minimum standards. Professional organizations have been involved with jail standards, too. In the 1980s the American Correctional Association sponsored the Commission on Accreditation for Corrections. That commission develops standards for jails and certifies jails that meet those standards, but supervision or evaluation by states or professional organizations may not be sufficient to raise jail standards to an acceptable level. Federal courts have become involved, and their actions are discussed in Chapter 10 in conjunction with court orders concerning jail and prison conditions.

The influence of the federal government on jails is seen in other areas such as federal technical assistance, financial assistance, and the imposing of standards. In addition, the federal government has provided states and local governments with assistance to build new correctional facilities and remodel existing ones.

Shock Incarceration: The Boot Camp Approach

One final recent approach to incarceration is gaining widespread attention. Military-style boot camps are used for shock incarceration of some offenders, usually young ones with their first prison term for drug offenses. A typical day at one New York boot camp begins at 5:30 A.M. with the flashing of bright lights and the sound of reveille blaring through the intercom. Inmates hop out of bed and begin strenuous exercises. Meals are consumed in eight minutes, with no talking allowed. Only one hour of talking is permitted per day. The entire day is packed with such activities as study, drug counseling, exercises, and work. Inmates are not permitted to look anyone in the eye; they run, not walk, and they stand at attention when ordered to do so.[51]

Although there was some initial criticism of boot camps, the concept spread quickly in the 1990s. By 1991 a private association that has been critical of the correctional system in New York praised the boot camp program and called for its expansion. According to the Correctional Association of New York, "In contrast to many other prisons, shock camps are safe, drug-free, and well-run institutions." The association continued:

> Their objective is not to warehouse prisoners—but to help inmates build new lives. Such a goal seems unrealistic to many skeptical students of prisoner rehabilitation, but most inmates clearly understand the difference between shock and other facilities, appreciate how shock can help them, and strive hard to fulfill the requirements of the program.[52]

Not everyone agrees with this positive assessment of boot camps. Some scholars note that the model is conducive to abuses of power as well as to aggressive behavior by both inmates and staff. Further, "research does not provide indications that there will be beneficial effects."[53] A 1994 National Institute of Justice (NIJ) study of boot camps concluded that "the boot camp experience in itself does not successfully reduce recidivism." On the other hand, graduates of boot camps were more likely than those released from prison to state that the experience had been a positive one. It is important, however, to control for the supervision factor, for there is evidence that close supervision within the community after release from boot camp is important to the success of the shock incarceration experience.[54]

A 1995 research article reporting on the NIJ data from eight state boot camp programs notes the variation in the programs and the difficulty of measuring all variables that might influence results. The authors suggest that programs should be evaluated on a state-by-state basis. They conclude that "those who complete boot camp do not inevitably perform either better or worse than their comparison group counterparts."[55]

Other scholars report that their initial research shows overall positive results from boot camps.[56] An evaluation of the New York boot camp program recognized some of its problems but concluded the following:

> Since shock incarceration graduates are confined for substantially shorter periods and fail at the same or lower rates than the comparison groups, DOCS officials believe the program is meeting the goals of reducing the need for prison beds without increasing the risk to public safety.[57]

In 1996 the New York program, which combines shock incarceration and boot camp training, was hailed by a state agency as a "rehabilitation model." According to the Correctional Association of New York, "With its intensive stress on both discipline and therapy, shock provides in six months a far better chance of rehabilitation than a sentence of one and one-half to three years in an ordinary prison."[58]

On the other hand, some jurisdictions have found that boot camps work—until youths leave. Researchers who evaluated boot camp programs for the NIJ reported in 1996 that, "What appeared to be a promising prognosis at the conclusion of boot camp disintegrated during aftercare."[59]

Other jurisdictions have experienced sufficient problems with boot camps that the programs have been eliminated.[60] Despite the difficulties and the controversy, the boot camp concept is spreading. Boot camps were a big issue in the 1994 Congressional debates over criminal law reform. They are a part of the Violent Crime Control and Law Enforcement Act of 1994,[61] and are supported as one solution to jail and prison overcrowding. The concept has grown to include boot camps for female offenders as well.[62] Finally, a recent evaluation by NIJ, of three boot camp programs for juveniles, concludes that despite the problems encountered in the programs, "[S]ignificant numbers of youth . . . demonstrated important positive outcomes."[63]

But boot camps alone do not solve the problems of overcrowding in correctional facilities; other efforts are necessary.

Prison and Jail Overcrowding

An earlier survey of state and local correctional administrators, conducted by NIJ, concluded that prison and jail overcrowding was seen as the most pressing problem for criminal justice systems.[64] The space crisis is greater today, and the effects of overcrowded facilities are enormous.

Populations of State and Federal Prisons

In the past decade, federal and state prisons have experienced dramatic population growth. Figure 9.1 graphs this growth from 1985–1997 by each type of facility, representing an average growth rate of 7.8 percent annually. At the end of 1996 one in every 163 U.S. residents were incarcerated, compared to one in every 319 at the end of 1985. By the end of 1997 the prison population had grown to 1,725,842, representing 645 inmates per 100,000 people. That was over twice the 1985 rate of incarceration. Jail populations increased by 9.4 percent over 1996, and that was twice the usual increase in jail populations. The number of state and

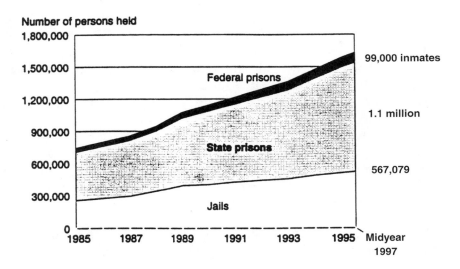

Number of persons held

1,800,000	
1,500,000	99,000 inmates
1,200,000	Federal prisons
900,000	1.1 million
600,000	State prisons
300,000	567,079
0	Jails

1985   1987   1989   1991   1993   1995   Midyear 1997

Figure 9.1
Number of Inmates Held in Prisons or Jails, 1985–1996.

Source: Bureau of Justice Statistics, *Prisoners in 1996* (Washington, D.C.: U.S. Department of Justice, June 1997), p. 2; AAP Neusfeed (19 January 1998), citing the U.S. Department of Justice.

federal inmates rose 4.7 percent, which was less than the average rate of increase in those populations between 1990 and 1996. In 1997 four states (California, Texas, Missouri, and Illinois) and the federal system combined for more than one-half of the 1997 increase in inmates.[65]

The number of female inmates increased by 9.1 percent between 1995 and mid-year 1996, compared to a 4.7 percent in male inmates. The cumulative increases over the years had resulted in the fact that state prisons were operating at between 16 percent and 24 percent over capacity by mid-year 1996, and federal prisons were 25 percent over capacity. Local jails were holding over 31,000 inmates who could not be admitted to prisons because of their overcrowding. The number of inmates sentenced to more than one year in prison show more dramatic increases for minorities than for whites, with the increase for African American males at 143 percent compared to a 103 percent increase for white males. The increase for African American females was 204 percent compared to 194 percent for white females. Changes were obvious when types of offenses were compared, too, with the number of inmates sentenced for drug offenses increasing, while the number for violent offenses decreased.[66]

Effects of Overcrowding

Social scientists and federal judges have noted the negative impact of jail and prison overcrowding on inmates. In the Texas prison case, litigated for almost fifteen years, the court concluded that "inmates are routinely subjected to brutality, extortion, and rape. . . . The overcrowding . . . exercises a malignant effect on all aspects of inmate life." The court noted that inmates are in the presence of other persons almost constantly, sleeping only with the knowledge that they might be attacked by cellmates. "There is little respite from these conditions, for . . . inmates have wholly inadequate opportunities to escape the overcrowding in their living quarters."[67]

In 1995 it was reported that the Cook County (Chicago) Jail was so overcrowded that one out of every seven inmates slept on the floor. The facility holds primarily accused persons awaiting trial, and thus it was not designed to provide educational or other rehabilitative facilities and programs. "The chronic tedium breeds violence, gang warfare, and drug trafficking," according to jail officials. A new facility was under construction, but officials said it would not solve the overcrowding problems, as more and more persons are arrested and tried. "We will never be able to build our way out of the problem," said one official at the John Howard Association, which serves as a watchdog on prisons.[68]

Also in 1995 Georgia officials reported severe overcrowding in jails and prisons, with the populace desiring locking up more criminals and curtailing or eliminating programs designed to facilitate rehabilitation. Experts warned that the approach would be extremely costly and would not reduce the crime rate significantly.[69] And in 1996 the executive director of the Oklahoma Sheriff's Association commented on the physical conditions of that state's jails by stating, "The world may be poised to enter the 21st century, but Oklahoma's rural county jails are barely in this century."[70]

Determinate and longer sentences have contributed to jail and prison overcrowding problems, and the current "three strikes and you're out" approach will only exacerbate the problem. In particular, drug arrests and convictions and longer sentences have swelled jail and prison populations.

Prison and Jail Expansion

One obvious way to cope with jail and prison overcrowding is to build new facilities, but this is an extremely costly measure. Some jurisdictions have responded to overcrowding by building new facilities; others have remodeled existing facilities, resulting in a corrections business that is one of the fastest growth industries in the United States.

Construction costs are not the only expenses to be considered. Operational costs of jails and prisons are high, and they continue to increase, outstripping the ability of many jurisdictions to cover them. Construction time is a factor as well. Because many jurisdictions are under federal court orders to reduce their prison and jail populations, they need available space quickly. As a result some jurisdictions have sought faster construction plans and methods.

Hasty planning and construction have created unanticipated difficulties. A national survey of correctional officials revealed that security problems, designs conducive to inmate suicides, and increased vulnerability to lawsuits regarding confinement conditions have resulted from the design of some new facilities and renovations. In addition, faulty architecture has "resulted in multi-million-dollar cost overruns."[71]

Private Correctional Facilities

One solution to prison problems has been to hire private firms to build and operate prisons.[72] The federal government utilizes some private contractors for management and operation of federal correctional facilities.

In March 1988 a White House commission recommended that the federal government turn over the operation of prisons, air traffic control facilities, mail delivery, and many other services to private businesses. The chair of the President's Commission on Privatization described the agencies that administered such services as "muscle-bound to the point of paralysis.[73] In 1990, however, it was reported that the efforts of the Office of Management and Budget (OMB) to privatize government jobs had run into resistance from the U.S. Department of Justice (DOJ), whose officials argued that some of its positions are too sensitive to place in private hands.[74] However, in 1990 the DOJ reported that its initial studies of correctional privatization drew some "positive conclusions," including cost savings and staff enthusiasm.[75]

In 1990 the U.S. Marshals Service announced that it had awarded a contract to two private companies to design, build, and operate a federal detention facility in Leavenworth, Kansas, representing the first private contract for a federal maximum-security facility. It was argued that the contract would save federal funds and release federal employees to perform "more productive law enforcement duties."[76]

Some states, such as California, have utilized privatization extensively, especially in juvenile facilities. Texas has many private facilities, although researchers emphasize that it is "still too early to tell whether privatization is a remedy or just another correctional fad."[77] The movement, thought by many to be a modern one, was utilized in the 1800s, in many cases for the same reasons as today, such as prison overcrowding. The recent emphasis on privatization may be attributed to "the failure of reform and rehabilitation, penal crowding, and concern with institutional costs."[78]

The new trend is distinguished from previous privatization of prisons in several ways. For a long time correctional facilities, particularly jails and juvenile and adult community correctional facilities, have relied on outside agencies to provide certain goods and services. Studies show this practice to be more cost-effective than each institution's providing every service and product that it needs. Medical service contracts are mentioned most frequently as more cost-effective than in-house services.[79]

The involvement of the private sector in corrections exists in three main areas: (1) prison work programs, (2) financing construction, and (3) managing facilities. A state or the federal government might contract for one, two, or all of these.

The involvement of the private sector in corrections raises many questions. First is the issue of whether private companies can deliver what they promise, such as "high-tech prisons that offer a full-range of rehabilitative programs, including college courses and job training, . . . pristine facilities that are efficiently managed without crowding problems" and at a lower cost than current facilities. These types of promises are made by companies such as Wackenhut Corrections Corporation and Corrections Corporation of America.[80] The issue is whether the companies can deliver.

Other issues arise as well. Politically, it is argued that corrections is a government function that should never be delegated. To do so increases problems, leading to lobbying for programs that might not be in the best interests of the public or corrections. The profit motive reduces the incentive to decrease the number of incarcerated people. The profit incentive encourages larger and larger private prisons. To make a profit, those facilities must be occupied. When the incentive for full prisons is combined with the public's call for longer and harsher sentences, the result may be more inmates serving more time.

Critics believe that the government will not realize long-term cost savings. In addition to paying the per-day fee for more inmates and for more days in confinement, eventually the government may be forced to pay increased daily fees. If the government does not have its own prisons, it may have no alternative but to pay the fees set by the private firms.

Many other questions arise concerning private correctional facilities. If an inmate sues, will the government be held liable along with the private business? Should the government be involved in internal discipline or staff training? Will the short-term relief offered by private prisons turn into long-term, costly government obligations? Will public employees accept the presence of private staff? Will corrections administrators allow transfer of inmate control to private business? Will the public lose its voice in determining the location of private prisons?[81]

The Texas facility mentioned on p. 254 as the defendant in a lawsuit brought by inmates from Missouri is managed by a private company, Capital Correctional Resources Inc. The company lost all of its contracts in Missouri. According to one newspaper, two of its jailers have criminal convictions, and a security chief had previously been "reprimanded and demoted for punching a shackled inmate."[82]

Although we do not know whether private prisons can exist successfully with traditional government programs, some believe there are definite advantages. The private sector can concentrate on special offenders. This may include women, juveniles, illegal aliens, or inmates who are at risk in the general prison population, such as child molesters, former law enforcement officials, or prison informants.

The private sector may provide an invaluable service simply by showing jail and prison officials that efficient and flexible management is possible in corrections, too. In most government facilities, competitive business principles, creative use of staff, adaptation of existing buildings and programs to meet changing needs, and experimentation with new ideas all seem to lag behind the private sector. Private involvement in corrections may encourage correctional administrators to modernize management styles, staff relations, and inmate care.[83]

WiseGuide Wrap-Up This chapter sets the stage for the next two chapters, which discuss life in prison and community corrections. It is important to understand the history of jails and prisons in order to evaluate what is happening today. The chapter begins with the European background of incarceration, emphasizing the reform efforts of John Howard. Howard was influential in America, but the Quakers led the movement toward incarceration, intended as a milder sanction to replace the death penalty and the inhumane methods of corporal punishment that prevailed in U.S. criminal justice systems.

Two systems that emerged in the United States, the Pennsylvania system with its emphasis on solitary confinement and the Auburn system with its emphasis on the silent system, competed for recognition in the United States and in Europe. The influence of the systems is seen today; many of our maximum-security prisons, built in the late 1800s and early 1900s, reflect an architecture typical of the Auburn system. In Europe many prisons built on the architectural model of the Pennsylvania system remain in use. The Elmira Reformatory did not survive long as a place of reformation, but it set the stage for the movement toward rehabilitation and established the reformatory model that became characteristic of institutions for juveniles.

It is impossible to talk about a prison system in the United States, because states have their own unique systems; the jail systems of local communities differ widely; and the federal government has a separate system. The federal system is considered the most efficient and effective. State prisons have been the sites of most of the riots and overcrowded conditions that are discussed in subsequent chapters. But many local jails also face problems of overcrowding and inadequate facilities, leading to the establishment of jail standards by the federal government, the American Correctional Association, and some states.

The use of military-style boot camps is popular currently, although the assessment of these programs is not consistent. The concept is supported, however, for it gives the appearance of punishment as well as some semblance of preparing inmates to live more productive lives.

Many of the problems of incarceration are related to overcrowding. There are two basic ways to solve this problem. First, we can build more facilities. The costs, however, are overwhelming. Perhaps even more important, if we build them, we fill them, and the problem of a lack of prison space remains. The second solution is to reduce prison populations. This has been done in some states by enacting statutes that permit governors to declare an emergency situation when notified that the prison population has reached 95 percent (or some other figure) of legal capacity. Problems occur, however, when the releasees commit new crimes.

The cost of building new facilities to handle the overcrowding of jails and prisons, coming at a time when many government budgets are being cut, has led to the involvement of the private sector in the financing and management of jails and prisons. This is a very recent and highly controversial innovation, as the chapter's discussion demonstrates.

Inadequate conditions, overcrowding, and management problems in jails and prisons increase the problems of living behind the walls, as we see in Chapter 10.

Apply It

1. Explain why prisons emerged in Europe and relate your discussion to the contributions of John Howard.

2. What characterized the emergence of prisons in the United States, and how did the Walnut Street Jail contribute to this development?

3. Compare and contrast the Pennsylvania and the Auburn systems.

4. What is a *reformatory*? Why were they developed? Explain the importance of European reformers to this development and compare that to the emergence of the Elmira Reformatory.

5. How do jails differ from prisons? From community correctional facilities?

6. What is the difference between prisons centered on a philosophy of custody and those that focus on rehabilitation?

7. Distinguish levels of prison security.

8. Explore the general and unique features of prisons for women and compare with those for men. How do co-correctional facilities fit into the scheme of incarceration?

9. Distinguish state and federal prison systems and analyze population growth in each. Compare with the growth of jail populations.

10. How does the present-day purpose of jail compare to its historical purpose? What are the problems of administering jails, and what role, if any, should the federal government play in the administration of local jails?

11. What are boot camps? How effective are they?

12. What are the effects of prison and jail overcrowding?

13. What is the place of the private sector in jails and prisons?

Notes

1. For a recent analysis of the purposes of punishment, see Alexis M. Durham III, *Crisis and Reform: Current Issues in American Punishment* (Boston: Little, Brown, 1994), pp. 7–40.

2. Harry Elmer Barnes, *The Story of Punishment* (Boston: Stratford, 1930), pp. 117, 122. The introductory material on the history of prisons is based on this source unless otherwise noted.

3. Stephen Schaefer, *Theories in Criminology* (New York: Random House, 1969), pp. 104–105. For an analysis challenging the belief that the penitentiary emerged as a by-product of the Enlightenment, see the work of law professor Adam J. Hirsch, *The Rise of the Penitentiary* (New Haven, Conn.: Yale Historical Publications, 1992).

4. Numerous sources may be utilized for these and other arguments for the development of prisons. A few are as follows: Barnes, *The Story of Punishment;* George Rusche and Otto Kircheimer, *Punishment and Social Structure* (New York: Russell and Russell, 1939); Benedict Alper, *Prisons Inside-Out* (Cambridge, Mass.: Ballinger, 1974); David J. Rothman, *The Discovery of the Asylum: Social Order and Disorder in the New Republic* (Boston: Little, Brown, 1971); and Rothman, *Conscience and Convenience* (Boston: Little, Brown, 1980).

5. Dick Whitfield, ed., *The State of the Prisons* (New York: Chapman and Hall, 1991).

6. Alexis M. Durham III, "Social Control and Imprisonment during the American Revolution: Newgate of Connecticut," *Justice Quarterly* 7 (June 1990): 293.

7. Alexis M. Durham III, "Newgate of Connecticut: Origins and Early Days of an Early American Prison," *Justice Quarterly* 6 (March 1989): 89–116.

8. Rothman, *The Discovery of the Asylum,* pp. 92–93.

9. Norman B. Johnston, "John Haviland," in *Pioneers in Criminology,* ed. Herman Mannheim (Montclair, N.J.: Patterson Smith, 1960), p. 122.

10. Rothman, *The Discovery of the Asylum,* p. 83.

11. Howard Gill, "State Prisons in America 1787–1937," in *Penology,* ed. George C. Killinger and Paul F. Cromwell (St. Paul, Minn.: West Publishing, 1973), p. 41.

12. Quoted in John Vincent Barry, "Alexander Maconochie," in *Pioneers in Criminology,* 2d enlarged ed., ed. Hermann Mannheim (Montclair, N.J.: Patterson Smith, 1972), p. 90.

13. Ibid., pp. 91, 95–97.

14. Ibid., pp. 99–100.

15. Orlando G. Lewis, *The Development of American Prisons and Prison Customs* (1922; reprint, Montclair, N.J.: Patterson Smith, 1967), p. 7.

16. See Alexander W. Pisciotta, *Benevolent Repression* (New York: New York University Press, 1994).

17. Gill, "State Prisons in America," p. 53.

18. See Michael Foucault, *Discipline and Punish: The Birth of the Prison,* trans. Alan Sheridan (New York: Pantheon, 1977).

19. Rothman, *The Discovery of the Asylum,* pp. 238–239.

20. Ibid., pp. 243–253.

21. Francis J. Clauss, *Alcatraz: Island of Many Mistakes* (Menlo Park, Calif.: Briarcliff, 1981), p. 35. The brief history of Alcatraz comes from this source.

22. "Report Raises Questions About Three Escapees from Alcatraz," *St. Petersburg Times* (24 December 1990), p. 3; "Escape from Alcatraz: Ex-Convict's New Clues Renew Jail-Break Tale," *Houston Chronicle* (5 December 1993), p. 14.

23. "Museum Traces History of a Renovated Alcatraz," *Tallahassee Democrat* (20 April 1991), p. 3.

24. "Penal Islands for Drug Dealers Debated by House Committee," *Miami Herald* (22 September 1990), p. 3.

25. See "Suicidal Inmates Often Ignored—Until Too Late," *San Francisco Chronicle* (4 October 1994), p. 1. The case is Madrid v. Gomez, 889 F.Supp. 1146 (N.D.Cal. 1995), *cert. denied,* 117 S.Ct. 1823 (1997). For a brief media discussion of this lengthy case, see "Judge Finds Inmate Abuse at Top-Security Prison in California," *New York Times* (13 January 1995), p. 21.

26. "A Futuristic Prison Awaits the Hard-Core 400," *New York Times* (17 October 1994), p. 1.

27. "There are Jails . . . ," *The Daily Telegraph* (10 August 1996), p. 22.

28. "Serving Superhard Time, "*USA Today* (4 August 1997), p. 1.

29. "Bloody Attack in Prison Kills Jeffrey Dahmer," *Orlando Sentinel* (29 November 1994), p. 1.

30. "Rights Group Alleges 'Torture' in Indiana Super-Max Prisons," *Criminal Justice Newsletter* 28 (1 October 1997): 1.

31. For a history of women's prisons, see the following sources: Joy Eyman, *Prisons for Women* (Springfield, Ill.: Charles C. Thomas, 1971); Rose Giallombardo, *Society of Women: A Study of a Women's Prison* (New York: John Wiley, 1966); Nicole Hahn Rafter, *Partial Justice: Women in State Prisons, 1800–1935* (Boston: Northeastern University Press, 1985); and Joycelyn M. Pollock-Byrne, *Women, Prison, and Crime* (Florence, Ky.: Wadsworth, 1990). For a recent overview of women's prisons, see Durham, *Crisis and Reform,* pp. 105–132.

32. Bureau of Justice Statistics, *Prisoners in 1996* (Washington, D.C.: U.S. Department of Justice, June 1997), p. 1.

33. J. G. Ross et al., *National Evaluation Program, Phase I Report, Assessment of Coeducational Corrections* (Washington, D.C.: National Institute of Law Enforcement and Criminal Justice, 1978). Unless otherwise indicated, the material in this section on coeducational institutions comes from this publication, which was based on the first nationwide assessment of such institutions.

34. John Ortiz Smykla and Jimmy J. Williams, "Co-Corrections in the United States of America, 1970–1990: Two Decades of Disadvantages for Women Prisoners," *Women and Criminal Justice* 8, no. 1 (1996): 61–76. For a history of co-corrections prior to 1980, see Smykla, ed., *Coed Prison* (New York: Human Sciences Press, 1980).

35. N. H. Rafter, *Partial Justice: Women, Prisons, and Social Control,* 2d ed. (New Brunswick, N.J.: Transaction, 1990), p. 184, quoted in Smykla and Williams, ibid.

36. Smykla and Williams, "Co-corrections in the United States."

37. "Unisex Units: State Plans Joint Jails; but Mingling Unlikely in Texas' First Male-Female Prisons," *Houston Chronicle* (25 September 1993), p. 1.

38. This history of the federal prison system comes from a publication by Norman A. Carlson, who at the time was director of the Federal Bureau of Prisons. See *The Development of the Federal Prison System,* supplied by the Federal Bureau of Prisons on request. For a detailed history of federal corrections from the Continental Congress through June 1987, see Paul W. Keve, *Prisons and the American Conscience: A History of U.S. Federal Corrections* (Carbondale, Ill.: Southern Illinois University Press, 1991).

39. "Inmates Say Military Prison Is Near Collapse," *New York Times* (17 August 1997), p. 19.

40. "Hawk Appointed BOP Director," *Corrections Today* 55 (February 1993): 35.

41. Norman A. Carlson, *Federal Bureau of Prisons: 1984* (Washington, D.C.: U.S. Department of Justice, 1985), p. 10.

42. "Regional News: Southwest," *Modern Healthcare* (21 February 1994), p. 18.

43. "Study: U.S. Prisons Cost More than States'," *Miami Herald* (1 November 1991), p. 9. The study was conducted by the General Accounting Office.

44. "Prisoners Sue over Treatment in Texas Jail," *Kansas City Star* (28 August 1997), p. 1.

45. "Inmates' Lawyers Huddle on Strategy in Texas Case," *St. Louis Post-Dispatch* (23 October 1997), p. 4C; "Four Indicted in Alleged Abuse . . . ," *Dallas Morning News* (30 July 1998), p. 17.

46. Advisory Commission on Intergovernmental Relations, *Jails: Intergovernmental Dimensions of a Local Problem: A Commission Report* (Washington, D.C.: U.S. Government Printing Office, May 1984), p. 2.

47. Hans Mattick, "The Contemporary Jails of the United States: An Unknown and Neglected Area of Justice," in *Handbook of Criminology,* ed. Daniel Glaser (Skokie, Ill.: Rand McNally, 1974), p. 781.

48. Edith Elisabeth Flynn, "Jails and Criminal Justice," in *Prisoners in America,* ed. Lloyd E. Ohlin (Englewood Cliffs, N.J.: Prentice Hall, 1973), p. 49.

49. Jerome Hall, *Theft, Law and Society* (Boston: Little, Brown, 1935), p. 108. See also John Howard, *State of Prisons,* 2d ed. (Warrington, England: Patterson Smith, 1792).

50. Joseph F. Fishman, *Crucible of Crime: The Shocking Story of the American Jail* (New York: Cosmopolis Press, 1923), pp. 13–14.

51. Thomas W. Waldron, "Boot Camp Prison Offers Second Chance to Young Felons," *Corrections Today* 52 (July 1990): 144–149, 169. For a history of boot camps, along with a discussion of their effectiveness, see Durham, *Crisis and Reform,* pp. 231–258.

52. "New York Correctional Group Praises Boot Camp Programs," *Criminal Justice Newsletter* 22 (1 April 1991): 4.

53. Merry Morash and Lila Rucker, "A Critical Look at the Idea of Boot Camp as a Correctional Reform," *Crime & Delinquency* 36 (April 1990): 204.

54. National Institute of Justice Update, *Researchers Evaluate Eight Shock Incarceration Programs* (Washington, D.C.: U.S. Department of Justice, October 1994), p. 2.

55. Doris Layton Mackenzie et al., "Boot Camp Prisons and Recidivism in Eight States," *Criminology* 33 (August 1995): 327–358; quotation is on p. 327.

56. See, for example, Doris Layton MacKenzie and James W. Shaw, "Inmate Adjustment and Change During Shock Incarceration: The Impact of Correctional Boot Camp Programs," *Justice Quarterly* 5 (March 1990): 125–147.

57. National Institute of Justice Program Focus, *Shock Incarceration in New York: Focus on Treatment* (Washington, D.C.: U.S. Department of Justice, August 1994), p. 10.

58. Quoted in "New York's Shock Incarceration Called a Rehabilitation Model," *Criminal Justice Newsletter* 27 (15 April 1996): 1.

59. "Boot Camps Seem to Work—Until Youths Leave, Study Finds," *Criminal Justice Newsletter* 27 (3 June 1996): 3.

60. See, for example, "Boot Camp Has So Many Problems that HRS Gives Up," *Orlando Sentinel* (8 May 1994), p. 7B; and "Connecticut Closes Boot Camp Built to Assist Troubled Youths," *New York Times* (11 June 1994), p. 8.

61. Violent Crime Control and Law Enforcement Act of 1994, Public Law 103-322 (13 September 1994).

62. See Doris Layton MacKenzie and Heidi Donaldson, "Boot Camp for Women Offenders," *Criminal Justice Review* 21 (Spring 1996): 21–43.

63. Michael Peters et al., *Boot Camps for Juvenile Offenders,* Office of Juvenile Justice and Delinquency Prevention (Washington, D.C.: U.S. Department of Justice, September 1997), p. 29.

64. Stephen Gettinger, National Institute of Justice, *Assessing Criminal Justice Needs* (Washington, D.C.: U.S. Department of Justice, June 1984), p. 1. For a more detailed discussion of prison overcrowding, see Durham, *Crisis and Reform,* pp. 31–66.

65. Bureau of Justice Statistics, *Prisoners in 1996,* pp. 1, 2; Bureau of Justice Statistics News Release (18 January 1998).

66. Ibid., pp. 1–2, 5, 6–7, 9.

67. Ruiz v. Estelle, 503 F.Supp. 1265, 1281–1282 (S.D. Texas, 1980), *aff'd. in part, vacated in part, modified, in part, appeal dismissed in part,* 679 F.2d 1115 (5th Cir. 1983), *cert. denied,* 460 U.S. 1042 (1982). Other proceedings occurred, resulting in the most recent ones, *later proceeding sub. nom.,* 981 F.2d 1256 (5th Cir. 1992), *dismissed without opinion,* 114 F.3d 1180 (5th Cir. 1997). For a history of the Texas prison system and especially this case, see Ben M. Crouch and James W. Marquart, *An Appeal to Justice: Litigated Reform of Texas Prisons* (Austin, Texas: University of Texas Press, 1989).

68. "Overcrowding Keeps the Fuse Lit at Jail: New Cells Won't Solve Problem, Experts Say," *Chicago Tribune* (7 February 1995), p. 1.

69. "Crime and Punishment Lock 'Em Up: It's the Rallying Cry of the '90s," *Atlanta Journal and Constitution* (26 March 1995), p. 1R.

70. "Escapees Plague Crumbling Structures," *Tulsa World* (14 October 1996), p. 13.

71. "Surveyed Officials Cite Errors in Design of Prisons and Jails," *Criminal Justice Newsletter* 21 (1 May 1990): 2, referring to a report by Juvenile and Criminal Justice International, Inc.: *Design, Equipment, Construction and Other Blunders in Detention and Correctional Facilities: Who Is to Blame?*

72. For a brief description of developments in privatization of prisons, see John J. Dilulio Jr., National Institute of Justice, *Private Prisons* (Washington, D.C.: U.S. Department of Justice, 1988); and Malcolm M. Feeley, "The Privatization of Prisons in Historical Perspective," *Criminal Justice Research Bulletin* 6, no. 2 (Huntsville, Texas: Sam Houston State University Criminal Justice Center 1991). For a collection of nine essays that examine privatization from a public policy perspective, see Douglas C. McDonald, *Private Prisons and the Public Interest* (New Brunswick, N.J.: Rutgers University Press, 1990).

73. "Panel Urges Broad Privatization," *Dallas Morning News* (19 March 1988), p. 3.

74. "Privatization of Federal Jobs Moving Slowly at Justice Department," *Criminal Justice Newsletter* 21 (16 January 1990): 6.

75. "Justice Department Cites Successes in Privatization," *Criminal Justice Newsletter* 21 (1 November 1989): 6.

76. "Privatization Advances with Marshals Service Jail Contract," *Criminal Justice Newsletter* 21 (2 July 1990): 4.

77. Phillip A. Ethridge and James W. Marquart, "Private Prisons in Texas: The New Penology for Profit," *Justice Quarterly* 10 (March 1993): 45.

78. Alexis M. Durham III, "Origins of Interest in the Privatization of Punishment: The Nineteenth and Twentieth Century American Experience," *Criminology* 27 (February 1989): 109. See also Durham, "Rehabilitation and Correctional Privatization: Observations on the 19th Century Experience and Implications for Modern Corrections," *Federal Probation* 53 (March 1989): 43–52.

79. See Camille G. Camp and George M. Camp, *Private Sector Involvement in Prison Services and Operations,* Criminal Justice Institute for the National Institute of Corrections (Washington, D.C.: U.S. Government Printing Office, February 1984), cited in *Corrections and the Private Sector,* Joan Mullen, National Institute of Justice (Washington, D.C.: U.S. Government Printing Office, March 1985), p. 2.

80. "Prisons Turn Profit for Private Firms: Lawmakers Seek OK to Buy Services," *St. Louis Post-Dispatch* (30 March 1995), p. 1 Illinois Section.

81. Joan Mullen, *Corrections and the Private Sector,* National Institute of Justice (Washington, D.C.: Department of Justice, March 1995), pp. 2–8.

82. "Jail's Security Chief Demoted in Earlier Job," *St. Louis Post-Dispatch* (29 August 1997), p. 1.

83. See Anthony P. Travisono, "Is 'For-Profit' a Wolf at the Door?" *Corrections Today* 47 (July 1985): 4.

Life in Prison

WiseGuide Intro

From the point of view of inmates, imprisonment is a series of status degradation ceremonies that serve two functions: to destroy their identities and to assign them new identities of a lower order.[1] The way offenders are treated when they enter prison exemplifies society's rejection; they are stripped of most of their personal belongings, given a number, searched, examined, inspected, weighed, and documented. To the inmates, these acts represent deprivation of their personal identities. The actions may be conducted in a degrading way that emphasizes their diminished status. They face the correctional officers, who have contacts and families in the outside world, but who are there to make sure inmates conform to institutional rules.

Gresham M. Sykes has referred to the psychological and social problems that result from the worst punishment, deprivation of liberty, as the "pains of imprisonment." In his classic study of male inmates in a maximum-security prison, Sykes discussed the moral rejection by the community, which is a constant threat to the inmate's self-concept; the deprivation of goods and services in a society that emphasizes material possessions; the deprivation of heterosexual relationships and the resulting threat to his masculinity; and the deprivation of security in an inmate population where he faces threats to his safety and sometimes to his health and life.[2]

In their attempts to adjust to the pains of imprisonment, inmates devise ways of manipulating the prison environment. Sometimes this manipulation creates serious control problems, thus presenting the correctional officers, staff, and administrators with their greatest problem: inmate control. Prison officials are charged with the ultimate responsibility of maintaining safety and order within the prison and keeping inmates from escaping. This is not an easy task, and the problems are becoming more serious. But at the same time federal courts have interpreted various constitutional amendments as providing standards for the treatment of inmates, along with reasonable accommodations while they are incarcerated.

Key Terms

building tenders
civil rights
commisary
conjugal visits
contraband
correctional officer
cruel and unusual
    punishment
deprivation model
guards
hands-off doctrine
importation model
norms
prisonization
social system

This chapter examines life in prison for inmates as well as for the prison administrators and correctional officers charged with the responsibility of maintaining prisons. These topics are discussed in the context of legal issues. We begin with an overview of life in prison before looking at the major legal issues connected with incarceration. The traditional approach to inmates' rights is contrasted with the modern approach as we analyze substantive and procedural issues raised by the U.S. Constitution and the modern cases interpreting that document.

The roles of the primary persons charged with administering prisons, administrators and correctional officers, are explored historically and in light of recent developments. Their respective roles are scrutinized, along with issues such as recruitment, training, and the importance of diversity.

The next major section of the chapter is devoted to an explanation of what it is like to live in prison. It focuses on how inmates adapt to prison life. A general discussion of inmate subcultures is followed by a look at the inmate social system as a method of social control. Special needs of female inmates, such as how to provide for their children as well as their unique health needs, are noted. Inmate sexual behavior is examined, with a comparison of male and female inmates. Among other critical issues associated with prison life are the subject of AIDS and how to deal with those who are infected as well as the growing concerns with disabled and aging inmates.

Prison programs, such as education, work, and recreation, are highlighted before the chapter closes with a discussion of prison violence, a growing concern in many institutions.

Learning Objectives

Learning Objectives

After reading this chapter, you should be able to do the following:

- Relate the historical position of federal courts on the issue of inmates' rights to the more recent approach.

- Explain how inmates may raise legal objections to their confinement.

- State the general criteria the Supreme Court uses to determine whether inmates' rights have been violated.

- Trace the evolution of prison management styles and compare with today's needs.

- Explain the functions of correctional officers, exploring ways in which correctional officers controlled inmates historically and how that has changed recently.

- Analyze correctional officer recruitment and training.

- Discuss gender and racial issues concerning correctional administrators.

- Identify some of the issues faced by new inmates and give a brief overview of inmate prison life.

- Explain what is meant by the *inmate subculture;* discuss its origin; and explore how subculture affects adjustments of male and female inmates.

- Analyze the social control role of the inmate system.

- Discuss the influence of prison gangs in men's prisons.

- Analyze the needs of female inmates and of those requiring special care and programs, and discuss how those needs are or are not accommodated.

- Contrast same-gender sexual behavior of female and male inmates.

- Discuss the impact of AIDS in a prison setting.

- Discuss briefly the nature and availability of prison programs.

- Analyze the impact of prison violence.

After offenders have been sentenced, official papers are prepared to turn them over to the custody of the state's Department of Corrections (or the Federal Bureau of Prisons in the federal system). They may be transported to prison immediately or retained in jail for a short period. In some states they are sent to a diagnostic center for a physical examination, psychological testing, and orientation. Assignment to a particular institution is made after a thorough evaluation of test results. In other states, the decision regarding placement may be made according to the seriousness of the offense, the age and gender of the offender, and whether the offender has a prior record (and, if so, the extent and nature of that record). In the case of women, there may be no choice; the state may have only one institution that must accommodate all security levels, unless the state contracts with another state or the federal system.

If the state has a central diagnostic unit, inmates must be transported from that unit to their individual assignments for incarceration. Upon arrival at the assigned institution, usually they are isolated from the general population for several days or even a week or longer. During that period they are told the rules or given a rule book to read. Physical exams are given. In most institutions they are strip searched for drugs and weapons. They may be required to take a bath with a disinfectant soap and shampoo. Urine samples may be taken to determine whether they are on drugs. Laxatives may be given to determine whether they are smuggling drugs.

The inmates' clothing may be taken and special prison clothing issued. In lower security institutions and often in women's prisons, inmates are permitted to wear their own clothing, although there may be restrictions concerning the type of clothing. The rules differ from state to state and even within states, depending on the institution's security level and other reasons. When inmates are not allowed to keep personal clothing, they may be required to pay to have the clothing shipped home or find upon release that it has been donated to a charity. When the inmate is released, most prisons issue only one new set of clothing.

During the orientation period inmates are required to complete numerous forms concerning their background, medical history, and lists of persons who might be visiting. They may be asked whether they fear any persons in the prison; it is necessary to place some inmates in protective custody for protection from the rest of the population. Other inmates and correctional officials may test the inmate during the orientation period; most inmates advise that it is wise to be respectful to the officers and to be careful about making friends among other inmates.

Generally, inmates are not permitted to have visitors during this orientation period. Phone calls are prohibited or limited. Thus, it is a lonely, frustrating time and may be quite stressful. Inmates may be interviewed for job assignments or educational programs in an effort to determine placement within the institution.

They are permitted to buy a few personal items from the **commissary,** but times for purchases and frequency of purchases are limited. Money may not be kept by inmates in most institutions; it is placed in a trust fund against which the inmate may draw for purchases. Money that may be received from outside is limited. Any or all of the rules in effect during the orientation period may apply also to the inmate's life in the general population.

Eventually, inmates are relocated in the facility to which they are assigned and "normal" prison life begins. Before looking at the details of adaptation to prison life, it is important to discuss the legal implications of incarceration.

Legal Implications of Incarceration

The recognition of inmates' legal rights has had a short history. The earlier position of courts on inmates' rights was expressed in an 1872 case in which a federal court declared bluntly that by committing a crime the convicted felon forfeits his liberty and "all his personal rights except those which the law in its humanity accords to him. He is for the time being the slave of the state."[3]

From 1872 until the past two decades, for the most part the federal courts observed a **hands-off doctrine** toward inmates and prisons, reasoning that prison administration is a part of the executive, not the judicial, branch of government. The doctrine has been expressed by courts at all appellate levels.[4]

In 1974, however, the U.S. Supreme Court held that although an incarcerated person loses some rights because of institutional needs, "a prisoner is not wholly stripped of constitutional protections when he is imprisoned for crime. There is no iron curtain drawn between the Constitution and the prisons of this country."[5]

But even before the 1974 decision, lower federal courts had begun looking into inmates' claims that they were being denied basic constitutional rights. By the 1980s numerous lawsuits had been filed by inmates, and federal courts had scrutinized prison conditions, particularly regarding overcrowding. Entire prison systems had been placed under federal court orders to reduce populations and to make other changes in prison conditions. By the 1990s extensive problems of jail and prison overcrowding had resulted in an explosion of federal lawsuits concerning incarceration conditions.[6]

What is responsible for the increasing recognition of inmates' rights in federal courts? Among other issues, the **civil rights** activism of the 1960s included the treatment of inmates, and during that period federal courts began to look at what was happening inside prisons. Many of the earlier cases involved allegations of physical brutality as well as questionable living conditions. For example, a federal district court heard evidence on the prison conditions in Arkansas and concluded that inmates were living under degrading and disgusting conditions and found the prison system unconstitutional. The need for judicial intervention into the administration of prisons was stated emphatically by the federal court. "If Arkansas is going to operate a Penitentiary System, it is going to have to be a system that is countenanced by the Constitution of the United States."[7]

Modern Litigation: An Overview

Since the 1970s federal courts have heard many cases on prison conditions. Federal intervention has been extended to jails as well. Some prison officials have been ordered to close facilities until conditions are corrected; others have been ordered to change specific conditions. Some officials who have defied these orders have been held in contempt of court. Judges continue to defer to prison authorities concerning day-to-day prison operations, but they intervene when federal constitutional rights are violated. It is important to look at those rights more closely, considering the differences between rights and privileges. It is important also to consider how actions are brought by inmates who seek legal remedies to alleged conditions.

In analyzing inmates' rights historically, prison officials spoke of the difference between *rights* and *privileges*. Rights require constitutional protection; privileges are there by the grace of prison officials and may be withdrawn at their discretion. In 1971 the Supreme Court rejected the position that "constitutional rights turn upon whether a governmental benefit is characterized as a 'right' or a 'privilege.'"[8] It is clear, however, that a hierarchy of rights is recognized. Some rights are considered more important than others and therefore require more extensive due process before they may be infringed upon. For example, an inmate's right to be released from illegal confinement is more important than the right to canteen privileges. Some of the other rights high in the hierarchy are the right to protection against willful injury, access to courts, freedom of religious belief, freedom of communication, and the right to be free of cruel and unusual punishment.

The recognition of inmates' rights and of the hierarchy of rights does not mean that the government (or prison officials acting as government agents) may not restrict those rights. Rights may be restricted if prison officials can show that the restriction is necessary for security or for other recognized penological purposes such as discipline and order. In analyzing whether prison officials have shown one or more of these purposes, the Court uses a reasonableness test articulated in 1987 in *Turner* v. *Safley*. "When a prison regulation impinges on inmates' constitutional rights, the regulation is valid if it is reasonably related to legitimate penological interests." The Court suggested several factors that should be considered when analyzing whether infringements on individual rights are appropriate within a prison:

1. Whether there is a logical connection between the regulation and the legitimate interest it is designed to protect
2. Whether inmates have other means of exercising that right
3. The impact that accommodating the right in question would have on other inmates, correctional officers, and prison administration and staff
4. The absence of readily available alternatives that fully accommodate the prisoner's rights at little or no cost to valid penological interests.[9]

There was concern that the Religious Freedom Restoration Act, enacted by Congress in 1993 in response to two Supreme Court decisions that were thought to be too restrictive of religious rights, erodes the Court's reasonableness test in areas other than religion. The act requires that freedom of religion may not be restricted except under circumstances that constitute a "compelling state interest" and that the invitation is accomplished by the "least restrictive means" available, tests that are much stricter than those required in *Safley*. Prison officials lobbied unsuccessfully for exemptions, arguing that the act would have devastating results in prisons.[10] Their concerns were soothed, however, in 1997, in *City of Boerne* v. *Flores*, when the Supreme Court held that Congress had exceeded its power in enacting the Religious Freedom Restoration Act of 1993.[11]

Another issue in this overview of the legal implications of prison life is to look at how inmates bring actions in federal courts. Most civil actions brought by inmates involve one of two types of legal actions: *habeas corpus* or a Section 1983 action. The first, **habeas corpus**, means "you have the body." There are several types of *habeas corpus* actions, but the one that is relevant to this chapter's discussions is the action brought by the inmate who is asking the court to grant a writ of *habeas corpus*, directing prison officials to release that inmate.

When inmates request a writ of *habeas corpus*, they are arguing that they are confined illegally. They may make this argument because prison conditions are alleged to be unconstitutional or because they have been disciplined without proper procedures being observed. The *habeas corpus* action means, "I am being held illegally in this prison because my rights have been violated. Therefore, I should be released." Few inmates are successful in their *habeas corpus* petitions, but multiple petitions have been filed by numerous inmates, although the Court has been restricting this in recent years.[12] In particular, *habeas* petitions are restricted by some of the provisions of the Antiterrorism and Effective Death Penalty Act of 1996, although the Court held in June of 1997 that the act cannot be applied retroactively, that is, to inmates' petitions that were pending before the act became effective on 24 April 1996.[13]

In 1995, however, the Supreme Court made it easier for inmates to win new trials on some *habeas corpus* writs. In *O'Neal* v. *McAninch* the Court held that convicted persons deserve the benefit of the doubt if federal courts are not sure whether errors committed by the trial court were harmless. Thus, the Court made it more difficult for federal judges to "excuse" the errors made by trial courts. If those errors are harmless, the convicted person is not entitled to a new trial. If they are prejudicial, that is, the errors could be viewed as making a difference in the outcome of the trial, the inmate is entitled to a new trial. The Court is saying that if the effect of those errors is not clear on appeal, the offender gets a new trial.[14]

A second and more frequently used method for petitioning federal courts is a Section 1983 action filed for monetary damages to compensate for illegal actions taken by prison (or law enforcement) officials against inmates. The name comes from the section number of the federal statute under which the action may be brought. It is a section of the Civil Rights Act, and it provides that

> Every person who, under color of any statute, ordinance, regulation, custom, or usage, of any State or Territory, subjects or causes to be subjected, any citizen of the United States or the person within the jurisdiction thereof to the deprivation of any rights, privileges, or immunities secured by the Constitution and laws, shall be liable to the party injured in an action at law, suit in equity, or other proper proceeding for redress.[15]

To come within this statute, inmates must show that prison officials have deprived them of their rights protected by the U.S. Constitution or by a federal statute. Section 1983 claims may cover almost any aspect of an inmate's life, and litigation under this statute is complex.

If the Section 1983 action is successful, inmates may be awarded damages for the deprivations they have suffered, as noted in Spotlight 10.1. The federal court may order prison officials to change the conditions that led to the constitutional violation. In cases of extreme violations, courts have ordered jails or prisons closed until conditions were corrected. In cases of overcrowded facilities, judges may order that the population be reduced.

Another issue important to this overview concerns the tests used for determining whether an inmate's constitutional rights have been violated. One right is illustrative—the Eighth Amendment's ban against **cruel and unusual punishment** (see Appendix A). Generally, the Court's tests are stated broadly and thus open to interpretation.

In 1976, in examining allegations of cruel and unusual punishment with regard to prison conditions, the Court held that an inmate may bring a successful Section 1983 action against prison officials who deny him or her adequate medical care for a serious medical problem only if it can be shown that the officials acted with *deliberate indifference* to the inmate's needs. In *Estelle* v. *Gamble* the Court stated that allegations of "inadvertent failure to provide adequate medical care," or of a "negligent . . . diagnos[is]" do not establish the requisite state of mind for a violation of the cruel and unusual punishment clause.[16]

In subsequent years the Court construed the cruel and unusual punishment issue further. In 1991 in *Wilson* v. *Seiter* the Court held that, "If the pain inflicted is not formally meted out *as punishment* by the statute or the sentencing judge,

Spotlight 10.1

Enforcing Inmate Rights through Civil Cases

In 1989 a New York court awarded a total of $1.3 million in seven lawsuits brought by inmates or their estates for damages caused by the actions of police in the 1971 Attica prison riots. These awards were granted to inmates who did not take part in the riots but were subjected to excessive force by authorities attempting to regain control of the prison. Police efforts during that uprising were described by a state investigating committee as constituting the "bloodiest encounter between Americans since the Civil War." Individual damage awards ranged from $35,000 to $473,000.[1]

In 1997 a federal judge awarded a former Attica inmate $4 million for damages sustained when he was beaten and tortured by correctional officers during the Attica riot. The suit, first filed in 1974, alleged that Frank Smith was "forced to walk over broken glass, beaten with batons, locked in his cell for four days, . . .[and] made to lie on a picnic table [naked] for hours with a football under his chin." During that time officers "struck his testicles with batons" and burned his body with cigarettes while threatening to kill him or castrate him if he allowed the ball to roll away. Mr. Smith commented after the verdict: "The jury has sent a message that people everywhere need to be treated like humans, not animals." The principal attorney for Mr. Smith, Elizabeth Fink, has spent her entire career representing inmates who were incarcerated in Attica at the time of the uprising, which resulted in forty-three deaths and ninety injuries.[2]

1. "Court Awards $l.3 Million to Inmates Injured at Attica," *New York Times* (26 October 1989), p. 14.
2. "Ex-Attica Inmate Wins $4 Million in Suit over Reprisals after 1971 Uprising," *New York Times* (6 June 1997), p. 20.

some mental element must be attributed to the inflicting officer before it can qualify." The Court interpreted the Constitution to require that when inmates question prison conditions, they must show a negative state of mind of officials in order to win their cases. Specifically, they must prove that prison officials harbor *deliberate indifference.* Dissenters noted correctly that in many cases this standard will be difficult if not impossible to prove.[17]

In 1994 the Court applied a subjective rather than an objective standard to determining whether prison officials have the required state of mind to constitute deliberate indifference. *Farmer* v. *Brennan* involved an inmate who is biologically male but has some characteristics of a woman. He alleged that he was raped by another inmate after he was incarcerated in an all-male prison. He argued that placing a transsexual in an all-male population constituted deliberate indifference to his safety. Officials knew or should have known of the risks involved. The Court rejected that objective standard, stating that prison officials may be held liable for unsafe prison conditions only if they "know that inmates face a substantial risk of serious harm and disregard that risk by failing to take reasonable measures to abate it."[18]

In 1992 in *Hudson* v. *McMillian,* the Court held that inmates may bring actions for cruel and unusual punishment against prison officials who engage in physical force that results in injuries even if those injuries are not significant. Justice Sandra Day O'Connor wrote the majority opinion, in which she stated that, "When prison officials maliciously and sadistically use force to cause harm, contemporary standards of decency always are violated."[19]

One final issue is that inmates should not be permitted to file frivolous lawsuits. A recent article noted a few. One inmate filed a suit claiming he was the victim of cruel and unusual punishment because he was served melted ice cream. Another alleged that he was served creamy peanut butter after ordering chunky, while another who had an ulcer claimed he should be provided with lamb, veal, and oysters. His physician said these foods were permitted but not required for his health.[20]

Frivolous lawsuits must be distinguished, however, from the issue of the magnitude of federal suits filed by inmates. It is true that the numbers have soared, representing an increase of 23,230 to 68,235 between 1980 and 1996, with only about 2 percent of inmates prevailing in their litigation.[21] But the fact that an inmate does not prevail does not mean the suit was frivolous, and often it is difficult to determine in advance which lawsuits are frivolous. On the other hand, some are easy. An example is that of the inmate who claimed that when he got drunk, committed a crime and was arrested, he violated his own civil rights. He asked the state to pay his expenses to sue himself for $5 million. His lawsuit was dismissed as frivolous.[22]

In an effort to curb frivolous lawsuits, the power of federal courts over prisons, and other issues concerning prisons, Congress enacted the Prison Litigation Reform Act (PLRA) in 1993 and amended it subsequently. Federal courts have disagreed on the constitutionality of the act, and eventually the Supreme Court will have to decide the various issues.[23]

The responsibility to protect inmates' rights lies with the same people who are assigned to maintain security in prisons: wardens or superintendents and correctional officers. Closer attention is given in the next section to prison administration.

Prison Administration

State prison systems have a director, who reports to the governor or a corrections board. In the federal system the director reports to the U.S. attorney general's office in the Department of Justice. Director Kathleen M. Hawk serves as commissioner of the Federal Prison Industries as well. Her rise to this position is featured in Professions 10.1. Serving as the chief prison administrator in a state or in the federal system is a high-pressure job and turnover is high.

Wardens or Superintendents

Prison directors hire and fire wardens or superintendents of the institutions within their respective jurisdictions and manage the correctional agency's central staff. Preparing and managing a budget is one of the director's most important functions. Directors must justify to the legislature the need for additional funds for running the prisons, a difficult problem today, with so many jurisdictions facing budget cuts while prison populations soar. But despite the importance of the director's position, the day-to-day administration of adult prisons is the responsibility of the warden or superintendent of each institution.

In early prisons wardens had great power. Although some exercised control as the result of strong personalities, most controlled their institutions with the authority that came from their positions. The strict chain of command from the warden down to the inmates was emphasized by the military atmosphere of most institutions: the wearing of uniforms, the use of job titles, lockstep marching, and total deference to the warden and his staff. Strict discipline, and in some cases, corporal punishment, were part of that traditional, authoritarian management style.

The wardens of earlier prisons exercised authoritarian management styles in their interactions with the staff, too. They had total authority to hire and fire the staff, and they required undivided loyalty; loyalty was a more important factor in staff selection than competence. The warden controlled the institution's resources as well. Most wardens lived on the grounds of the institutions, and the warden's household budget was included in that of the prison.

PROFESSIONS 10.1

Women in Corrections

During an internship at the Federal Correctional Institution in Morgantown, West Virginia, Kathleen M. Hawk decided on a career in corrections. Today Hawk, who holds a bachelor's degree in psychology and master's and doctoral degrees in counseling and rehabilitation, is the Director of the Federal Bureau of Prisons. Prior to assuming the highest position in the Bureau, Hawk served as the assistant director of the Federal Bureau of Prisons. She has also been a staff psychologist, chief of psychology services, an associate warden, and a warden. In her earlier years she served in training administration in the federal system. While she served as assistant director, she made this statement:

> I feel strongly that as women we should take full positive advantage of the marvelous career opportunities available to us today and pursue them not as our given right,

but rather as occasions to demonstrate our talents and abilities so that many more doors will be open for generations of women after us.[1]

Hawk's elevation to the highest position in the Federal Bureau of Prisons demonstrates that women are assuming administrative positions in the criminal justice field. Women have made contributions to corrections as well as to other criminal justice functions. "Beginning in the mid-1800s, they chaired, as well as served on, governing boards and citizen committees overseeing correctional agencies." They served as volunteers and later as correctional officers, assistant and associate wardens, and more recently, as wardens.[2] Today they serve as correctional officers in men's as well as women's prisons, and they have been appointed to some of the higher administrative positions as well, as Hawk's appointment illustrates.

1. Karen Carlo Ruhren, "Kathleen M. Hawk: Profile: BOP Programming Administrator Sees Opportunities for Women," *Corrections Today* 54 (August 1992): 132.
2. Joann B. Morton, "Looking Back on 200 Years of Valuable Contributions," *Corrections Today* 54 (August 1992), p. 76.

The authoritarian style dominated prison management until the middle of the twentieth century.[24] During the 1970s significant changes took place in many American prisons. First, there were demographic changes. Harsh drug laws led to the incarceration of more young people (some from the middle class) with drug problems. The percentage of the prison population that was poor, minority, and urban increased.[25]

Attempts to suppress gang activity have resulted in the incarceration of greater numbers of gang members, many of whom have maintained close ties to their members outside prison. Increased politicalization within prisons occurred as the younger, more radical prison population viewed incarceration as a political process. They looked with disdain on the traditional rewards the officers might offer in exchange for their cooperation.[26]

A second factor that precipitated change during the 1970s was the warden's decreased power. Many inmates and correctional officers were unwilling to accept the authoritarian governance style, and their rejection of that style has been supported by federal court orders. Court decisions that require changes in prison physical conditions as well as provisions for due process in some correctional proceedings have reduced the traditional power of prison administrators and correctional officers.

There are numerous obstacles to significant changes in prison management. First, the values of each social group within the prison may conflict. Second, the conflict between the goals of custody and rehabilitation remains. Third, there are insufficient facts on which to base decisions. Part of this results from a lack of research, limited evaluation of treatment programs, and insufficient knowledge of the applicability of new management techniques to prison settings. With a lack of knowledge of treatment and management, the prison administrator tends to fall back on rule books and manuals, which are likely to produce a more rigid and authoritarian type of organization.[27]

Finally, prisons continue to be faced with serious financial problems that have reduced expenditures for management training programs and have resulted in difficulties in recruiting trained persons at competitive salaries. Reduced funding has also reduced the degree to which prison managers can provide the resources that are needed for other programs within the institution as well as sufficient staff and officers.

Some signs of progress are evident in the area of corrections management. First, more institutions are implementing research techniques to measure the success of programs and evaluation strategies for personnel. Therefore, an increasing amount of information is available to correctional managers. Second, professional organizations are developing standards for criminal justice administration, including correctional administration. These standards reflect a general concern with effective management. More important, the standards being developed by correctional managers in the field may be more responsive to problems and more acceptable to administrators.[28]

A third and most important reform in prison administration is the increased attention to professionalism. More attention has been given to attracting more highly educated people to the correctional field. Management has sought to improve correctional training and introduce new management techniques. An issue arises, however, when professionalism is viewed as the *solution* to organizational problems, which may result in a better image of the organization without sufficient attention to underlying problems.

Some research suggests, for example, that more highly educated correctional officers do not have more positive and humane attitudes toward inmates than less educated officers. Furthermore, the more highly educated officer may be more frustrated in the job. Thus, the appearance of professionalism may be only that, unless adequate prior and on-the-job training programs are implemented to prepare correctional officers for the difficulties they will face. Important organizational changes must be made, too.[29]

Correctional Officers

The goals of the correctional institution and the management style of the warden or superintendent are very important in determining the success or failure of the institution. However, the individuals with the most extensive contact and perhaps the greatest effect on inmates are the **correctional officers,** or **guards.**

Correctional officers in maximum-security prisons spend almost all of their workdays behind bars in close contact with inmates. It is impossible to generalize the working conditions or the reactions of all correctional officers, but normally the job is monotonous and boring. Salaries are low; fringe benefits are limited; the risk is tremendous. Stress is high, and violence is increasing, with authorities citing the changing nature of the population and the overcrowding of the institutions as the main causes of increased prison violence.[30] The result is a high rate of turnover in most institutions.

The primary function of correctional officers is to maintain internal security and discipline. In the past, when corporal punishment was allowed, officers controlled inmates by physical force and, if necessary, brutality. Although courts have held that excessive force is not permitted constitutionally, there is recent evidence that some correctional officers have brutalized inmates. Spotlight 10.2 discusses some cases. In the Rikers Island case, inmates and correctional officers accused each other of being "younger, more aggressive, less respectful," with each side alleging that violence was the result of a power struggle for internal control of the prison.[31]

Spotlight 10.2

Correctional Officers Accused of Brutalizing Inmates

A "fairly serious disturbance" at Rikers Island Jail in New York City in 1990 was followed by two investigations of alleged administrative mismanagement, including failure to plan properly for such uprisings and brutality of inmates by correctional officers. One concluded that 140 inmates were injured, fifty-four of whom "exhibited clear evidence of blunt trauma inflicted from behind."[1]

In 1996 authorities were still investigating these and other allegations of brutality at Rikers Island Jail in the early 1990s, reporting the case of one inmate who asked to be moved to another area because he feared inmates would kill him. It was alleged that before that could happen, however, correctional officers beat the inmate severely. The following day he was found dead in his cell. A class action lawsuit against the city alleged that between 1990 and 1992 there were fifteen incidents in which inmates were beaten by officers, some being kicked and hit while officers dragged the handcuffed inmates by their feet.[2]

Seven county jail correctional officers in Charleston, West Virginia, were fired in 1990 after investigations concluded that without any provocation, the officers beat a handcuffed inmate who was arrested for public intoxication and resisting arrest. At the time of the beating, the suspect was so drunk that he could not even give his name to authorities.[3]

In the fall of 1992 fourteen former employees of the Georgia women's prison at Hardwick were indicted on charges of sexual abuse of female inmates. It was labeled the worst case of such abuse in prison history, with alleged offenders charged with trading sex for coerced abortions, prostitution rings, rape, and sodomy. The accused included men and women. One of the accused was a former deputy warden. The indictments stemmed from a 1984 lawsuit against the institution's officials. The recently appointed female warden, Mary Esposito, said the charges reflected the change in attitudes toward women's rights in prison.[4]

In March 1993, after a state prison employee was killed at the Hardwick prison, ABC News reported that the killing occurred to prevent the victim from testifying in the case of alleged sexual abuse. By that time, almost 200 female inmates at the Georgia Women's Correctional Institution and two other Georgia prisons had accused officers and other staff and former staff of sexual and other forms of abuse.[5] By July 1994 a former deputy warden accused of sexual molestation in the Georgia case was rehired, and all charges against him were dismissed. Cornelius Stanley was rehired as a lieutenant at the same salary he held formerly at the rank of captain. Stanley received more than $58,000 in back pay plus another $50,000 from the state. It was the second time Stanley had been rehired after a firing involving alleged misconduct. Of the fifteen men and women indicted in the Georgia prison sex case, charges against three were dropped because the statute of limitations had expired. Two entered guilty pleas and received probationary sentences. One officer was acquitted.[6]

1. Quote from the New York State Commission of Correction, cited in "Two Probes Yield Same Conclusion: Rikers Inmates were Brutalized," *Criminal Justice Newsletter* 22 (1 May 1991), p. 3.
2. "Prosecutors Investigating Claims of Prison Brutality," *New York Times* (23 January 1996), p. 15B.
3. "Guards Fired over Beating of Prisoner," *Tallahassee Democrat* (31 May 1990), p. 1B.
4. "Fourteen Are Charged with Sex Abuse in Women's Jail," *New York Times* (14 November 1992), p. 1.
5. "ABC: Prison Worker's Death May Be Part of Sex Scandal," *Orlando Sentinel* (16 March 1993), p. 6.
6. "Prison Guard Accused of Abusing Female Inmates Is Rehired," *Atlanta Journal and Constitution* (12 July 1994), p. 1.

Another method correctional officers have used to control inmates is to manipulate the inmates' **social system.** Correctional officers permit selected inmates to have positions of authority and control over other inmates. They are called **building tenders.** In recent years, federal courts have prohibited the practice of elevating certain inmates to positions of power over other inmates. In some cases, the changes resulting in the removal of inmate power over other inmates have occurred quickly without the addition of more correctional officers to fill the power void. In others, inmates have gained control of institutions for temporary periods, leading to devastating riots.

In some institutions, correctional officers' use of inmates to help control other inmates has led to corruption, including officers' acceptance of bribes from inmates. Some officers have brought **contraband** into prisons. Contraband is any forbidden material, such as drugs, alcohol, and weapons. In 1997, for example, twenty people, including eleven correctional officers, were arrested for allegedly attempting to turn the new federal jail in Brooklyn into a social club for organized criminals. The jail is used primarily for detaining persons awaiting trial. Some of these inmates are wealthy persons associated with organized crime, and it was alleged that officers accepted financial bribes to bring in the suspects' associates for planning crimes and other illegal activities.[32]

In this case some officials theorized that the low salaries of the officers ($25,000–$30,000 annually) made them susceptible to bribes. (It might be pointed out, however, that many individuals working in criminal justice systems make no more; some less; and they do not accept bribes). Lack of professionalism and training are issues as well. In many jurisdictions a high school diploma is sufficient for the entry-level officer, although it would be difficult today for someone without college experience to advance to an administrative position. Good health is required, for the duties of a correctional officer may involve strenuous physical work, particularly during a riot or other prison disturbance. Mental and emotional health are important, too, although many jurisdictions provide inadequate testing and training in this area.

Recruitment of correctional officers poses problems. The administrator in charge of the New York City jails blamed the violence at the Rikers facility, discussed earlier, on inadequate hiring practices of correctional officers.[33] New prisons in Georgia have faced a dearth of qualified persons for correctional officer positions in some areas; administrators cite lack of a high school diploma as a problem. Adult illiteracy and stress are problems, too, as is staff reduction caused by financial cutbacks.[34]

Stress among officers may be expected as a result of increased fear of violence within prisons. For example, in 1995 correctional officers in the federal penitentiary in Atlanta responded to the increasing violence in that facility by alleging that they were understaffed and that some officers lacked sufficient training. The president of a union that represents about one-half of the staff of that institution expressed his support of the "get tough on crime" approach that is popular currently, but he added, "But we can't just keep throwing so many people in prison and using 1920 tactics to try to control them." The previous year an officer was killed, the first federal officer killed within a prison since 1987. Five inmates were slain by other inmates in 1994 and 1995, and a female officer was beaten by an inmate. In January 1995 three inmates sustained wounds inflicted by the knife of another inmate. The warden, who denied claims of understaffing, noted that the prison population was younger and more violent than in previous years, "and they have less respect for the rights of people and property."[35]

In 1997 a court convicted Anthony Battle, inmate at Atlanta, of murder in the death of a correctional officer at the Atlanta Federal Penitentiary in 1994. Battle was sentenced to death. "The tormented defendant, already serving a life sentence for killing his wife, took the witness stand against the advice of his lawyers and confessed to the crime."[36]

Although concerns with violence will remain, attempts are being made to assist officers in adjusting to the stress caused by violence and other problems within prisons. Stress management is becoming an important element of officer training. The American Correctional Association (ACA) provides numerous publications to assist officers in dealing with the daily problems they face. The ACA provides correspondence courses; criminal justice institutes provide continuing education programs. Some prison systems are giving correctional officers a taste of life as an inmate by sending them to prison to be treated as inmates for a short period of time, but these programs are expensive and not used widely.

Initial formal training of correctional officers is critical, too. Usually, training is conducted at a central place within the prison system, and the nature of training varies from one system to another. Of necessity, it covers institutional security. In addition, officers must learn how to protect themselves from inmates who attack them physically, and how to react when inmates curse, spit, or urinate on them. Recruits are taught the rules and regulations that govern inmate behavior in prisons, and they must learn the rules and constitutional provisions that govern the behavior of correctional officers in relation to inmates.

Despite problems of high turnover, corruption and brutality, difficulties in recruiting, and stress, there is some evidence that correctional officers see themselves as correctional agents (not just as officers having the primary responsibility of maintaining security and order) with a belief that the system can have positive effects on inmates. "Most officers seek to enrich their work through a human services or rehabilitative orientation."[37]

Female and Minority Officers

It is important that women and minorities have opportunities to participate fully in all professions, and their perspectives are vital in corrections, which has a high representation of minorities and an increasing number of women. Despite the small number of female inmates in corrections overall, women have unique problems in the correctional setting, and those problems might be understood best by female officers. In addition, female officers allege that to gain parity with male officers, they must be able to work in prisons that house male inmates.

Several court cases have established the right of women to work in correctional institutions for men and affected their hiring and promotion, but these changes have occurred only within the past decade or so.[38] In 1997, for example, Arkansas hired 400 more female correctional officers to work in the state's prisons for men in order to settle a lawsuit.[39] In 1995 a federal court held that the Constitution does not prohibit the viewing of a male inmate by a female correctional officer. Thus, women may work in men's prisons even when those jobs involve monitoring the inmates in the nude. The court stated:

> How odd it would be to find in the eighth amendment a right not to be seen by the other sex. Physicians and nurses of one sex routinely examine the other. In exotic places such as California people regularly sit in saunas and hot tubs with unclothed strangers. . . . Women reporters routinely enter locker rooms after games. How could an imposition that male athletes tolerate be deemed cruel and unusual punishment?[40]

In spite of potential problems and some negative attitudes in their work environments, it appears that female correctional officers are able to establish and maintain personal authority in a prison setting; they are not manipulated by inmates any more often than male officers. One study reports that "the authority of women correctional officers is as legitimate as that of their male colleagues."[41]

Many women find the position of correctional officer to be rewarding and challenging. In fact, there is some survey evidence that male and female correctional officers do not view their jobs differently.[42] And there is recent evidence that female officers contribute to a reduction of violence in prisons. A Minnesota corrections consulting firm that secured data from one maximum security prison in each of the contiguous forty-eight states, the District of Columbia, and the federal prison system, reported that "over the course of a year, 12.3 percent of the male officers were assaulted by inmates, compared to 3.4 percent of female officers." The differences did not appear to be caused by female officers being too lenient with male inmates. The president of the firm concluded that the results suggest "That other facilities should consider employing more female officers. . . . It appears that if a greater percentage of women were employed, an overall reduction in assaults on officers might result."[43]

Prison Life

Life in prison is monotonous and routine. In maximum-security prisons, inmates are regulated for most of each day, beginning with the time for rising in the morning. Meal schedules may be unusual; for example, in some prisons inmates eat breakfast at 3 or 4 A.M. and then go back to bed for naps before beginning the regular workday. This is done because of the long time period required to feed a large population in a secure facility. Dinner may be served as early as 3 P.M. Some inmates are fed in their cells. During lock-down, when there has been internal trouble among inmates, and particularly after riots, inmates may be confined to their cells most of the day, with all meals served in their cells.

Most prisons do not have sufficient jobs for all inmates to work an eight-hour day, so many inmates must find ways to fill their time. The security needs of the institution determine how free they are to do so, but in some prisons they are permitted to move about rather freely within certain areas of the prison. Inmates may be out of their cells (or rooms) and permitted to mingle with other inmates.

Recreational facilities may be available in the prison's common areas. Ping-pong and basketball are examples. Some prisons have gyms; others have weight rooms or a provision for outdoor recreation such as baseball or basketball, but hours of use are limited. Some books are available for inmates to take to their cells or rooms. In large prisons, particularly maximum-security institutions, inmates are limited to a specified number of showers per week, for example, three; and they are marched to and from, and supervised during their showers. Privacy is nonexistent in most prisons. During the hours of the regular workweek, inmates may be assigned to jobs or be permitted to attend educational or vocational classes. Others may have no organized activities.

After dinner inmates may be permitted to socialize with other inmates in common areas. The institution may provide activities such as movies, Alcoholics Anonymous meetings, drug abuse seminars, or other self-help programs. Many institutions make television available; some permit inmates to have a television and radio in their cells, provided the equipment is purchased from the commissary to avoid the problem of contraband being brought into the institution by this means. But as prisons have become more crowded and more expensive in a society that is more punitive, television and other amenities have been eliminated in some prisons.

Part of the inmate's day may be spent writing letters to friends and family, although there may be limits on the number of letters that may be sent and received. Gifts are limited or excluded. Inmates may spend time taking care of their personal or prison-issued clothing and working at institutional assignments.

In minimum-security institutions, some inmates may be permitted to leave the institution from time to time for various purposes. For the most part, however, inmates are confined day and night for the duration of their sentences. During confinement, particularly in maximum-security prisons for men, inmates may be subjected to violence by other inmates; some are raped. Prison life is bleak for most inmates.[44]

Adaptation to Prison

How do inmates adapt to the prison environment? In earlier prisons they were not allowed to interact with other inmates. With the end of the segregated and silent systems came the opportunity for inmates to interact. One result of this has been the opportunity for inmates to form a prison subculture or community. The new inmate encounters this subculture through the process of socialization or, as it is called in prison, **prisonization.**

In 1940 Donald Clemmer reported his study of the male prison community of Illinois's maximum-security prison at Menard. The book has become recognized as one of the most thorough studies of a prison setting. Many of the more recent studies of prisons have been conducted as tests of Clemmer's theories, the most important of which was his concept of prisonization.[45]

Clemmer defined *prisonization* as "the taking on, in greater or lesser degree, of the folkways, mores, customs, and general culture of the penitentiary." The process begins as the newcomer learns his or her status as an inmate. The most important aspects of prisonization are "the influences which breed or deepen criminality and antisociality and make the inmate characteristic of the ideology in the prison community."

The degree to which prisonization is effective in a given inmate depends on several factors: (1) the inmate's susceptibility and personality; (2) the inmate's relationships outside the prison; (3) the inmate's membership in a primary group in prison; (4) the inmate's placement in the prison, such as which cell and cellmate; and (5) the degree to which the inmate accepts the dogmas and codes of the prison culture.

Clemmer contended that the most important of these factors is the primary group. Clemmer saw prisonization as the process by which new inmates become familiar with and internalize prison **norms** and values. He argued that once inmates become prisonized, they are, for the most part, immune to the influences of conventional value systems.

Other scholars have tested Clemmer's conclusions. Stanton Wheeler found strong support for Clemmer's position on prisonization in his study at the Washington State Reformatory. Wheeler found that the degree to which inmates became involved in prisonization varied by the length of time the inmate was in prison. Inmates were more receptive to the institutional values during the first and the last six months of incarceration. During their middle period of incarceration, they were more receptive to values of the inmate subculture.[46]

In comparing prisonization of male and female inmates, researchers have questioned the Wheeler hypothesis. Geoffrey P. Alpert and others found that although time spent in prison was related significantly to prisonization among female inmates, this was not the case among male inmates. In their study of inmates in the Washington State prison system, these researchers found that other variables were predictive of prisonization, too. Among women, attitudes toward race and the police were significant. Among men, age was a significant variable, as were attitudes toward law and the judicial system.[47]

The Inmate Subculture: Models for Analysis

In earlier studies, scholars analyzed the emergence and development of the inmate subculture and created two models for explaining the phenomenon: deprivation and importation. In the **deprivation model,** the inmate's pattern of behavior is an adaptation to the deprivations of his or her environment. The inmate social system is functional for inmates; it enables them to minimize the pains of imprisonment through cooperation. For example, inmate cooperation in the exchange of favors not only removes the opportunity for some to exploit others but enables inmates to accept material deprivation more easily. Their social system redefines the meaning of material possessions. Inmates come to believe that material possessions, so highly valued on the outside, result from connections instead of hard work and skill, which enables them to insulate their self-concepts from failures in work and skill.

In addition, those goods and services that are available may be distributed and shared if the inmates have a cooperative social system. Because of the pains of imprisonment and the degradation of inmates, which result in a threat to their self-esteem, inmates repudiate the norms of the staff, administration, and society and join forces with each other, developing a social system that enables them to preserve their self-esteem. By rejecting their rejecters, they avoid having to reject themselves.[48]

The more traditional approach to an understanding of the inmate subculture, according to John Irwin and Donald R. Cressey, is that patterns of behavior are brought with the men to prison. This constitutes the **importation model.** Irwin and Cressey argued that social scientists have overemphasized inside influences as explanations for the prison inmate culture. In reality, the prison subculture is a combination of several types of subcultures brought by inmates from past experiences and used within prison to adjust to the deprivations of prison life.[49]

Research on the deprivation and importation models was conducted by Charles W. Thomas at a maximum-security prison for men. Thomas's research was designed to show the importance of both importation and deprivation variables. When an inmate arrives at prison, both the formal organization and the inmate society compete for his allegiance; these two represent conflicting processes of socialization. Thomas calls the efforts of the formal organization *resocialization* and those of the inmate society *prisonization.* The success of one requires the failure of the other. The prison is not a closed system.

In explaining the inmate culture, one must examine all of these factors: preprison experiences, both criminal and noncriminal; expectations of prison staff and fellow inmates; quality of the inmate's contacts with persons or groups outside the walls; postprison expectations; and the immediate problems of adjustment that the inmate faces. Thomas found that the greater the degree of similarity between preprison activities and prison subculture values and attitudes, "the greater the receptivity to the influences of prisonization." Thomas found also that inmates from the lower social class are more likely to become highly prisonized as compared to the upper social class; those who have the highest degree of contact with the outside world had the lowest degree of prisonization; and those having a higher degree of prisonization were among inmates who had the bleakest post-prison expectations.[50]

Other researchers have concurred with one or the other of the models. In his study of race relations in a maximum-security prison for men, Leo Carroll found support for the importation model, although he concluded that it needed refinement. Carroll criticized the deprivation model as diverting attention from important factors within prison such as racial violence.[51] Support for both the importation and the deprivation models has been found in studies of prisons in other countries.[52]

Studies of jail inmates are important in determining whether the inmate subculture is imported into the institution or results from adaptations to the institutional setting. Findings from these studies support both the importation and the deprivation theories.[53]

The Inmate System as a Social Control Agency

The inmate social system may create problems for correctional officers and other prison personnel, for inmates upon release, and for society. The inmate social system serves as a social control agency within the prison, wielding a powerful influence over the inmate because it is the only reference group available. It is powerful because inmates need status. In addition, they may be more susceptible than usual to peer-group pressure and more prone to look to the peer group than to authority figures for social support. This form of social control is functional to the prison when it maintains order within the institution. To understand it, we must look more carefully at the problems of control faced by penal institutions.

Within the prison two powerful groups seek to control one another: the correctional officers, whose primary responsibilities are custody and security, and the inmates, who are interested in escaping as much as possible from the pains of imprisonment. Richard A. Cloward studied the power struggle between these two groups. Cloward noted that in most institutions inmates reject the legitimacy of those who seek to control them. A serious social control problem may result. In many ways the job of the custodian in prison is an impossible one. He or she is expected to maintain control and security within the institution but may not use the traditional method—force—of doing this. The new, more liberal philosophy of recognizing due process and other inmates' rights has increased problems of social control for correctional officers.[54]

Under the authoritarian regime of prison administration and management, inmate cooperation was necessary to maintain peace within institutions. The few officers could not have kept a disorganized body of inmates under control. Inmates ran the institutions, and the officers cooperated. For example, correctional officers permitted the leaders to take the supplies they needed. When a "surprise" search was conducted, they told the inmate leaders in advance. The leaders spread the word as a form of patronage. The officers were aiding certain inmates in maintaining their positions of prestige within the inmate system; in return, inmate leaders maintained order. The system was a fairly stable one with little disorder.

Federal court orders to abolish inmate power positions changed the traditional system of inmate-officer interaction and altered the role of the inmate social system in social control. The results are illustrated by the Texas prison system, which has been plagued with administrative attempts to maintain order. After a disturbance in late 1985, during which eight inmates were killed in eight days, Texas prison officials announced that they were declaring war on the prison system. They locked down 17,000 inmates in thirteen prisons. Sociologists studying the Texas prison system had reported earlier that the use of inmates as building tenders had kept racial tension in check, and little violence existed.[55] Inmates were removed from those powerful positions as the result of a federal court order. The consequence was a power vacuum that was filled by gangs, beginning with one in 1983 (the Texas Syndicate, fifty-six members) to eight gangs with a total of 1,400 members less than two years later. Violence increased, with gang warfare occurring between the Texas Syndicate and the Mexican Mafia, two of the largest prison gangs. In his analysis of the organizational structure of these two gangs, one scholar described them as similar. Among other characteristics, each follows a code of rules, called the *constitution*. The penalty for violating any of these rules is death.[56]

Gangs may be very influential in prison social control, with activities ranging from sex to murder. Effective control of gang influence demands knowledge of the gang members and their activities. Such knowledge is compiled and disseminated by computers. Gangs are difficult to control, and one administrator has emphasized that prisons do not create the gangs, "and they will not be eliminated no matter how successful our programs." The public needs to keep in mind that prisons are small societies, "temporary places of custody and control for individuals that society has chosen to reject from its membership."[57]

Courts have upheld some administrative attempts to combat gang activity. A federal court has upheld California's routine use of polygraph examinations, along with other measures, to determine whether inmates who claim they have renounced gang membership actually have done so.[58] A state court has upheld prison policies forbidding inmates to engage in ritualistic greetings to each other when those greetings signify gang membership. Handshakes, embraces, or kisses may be prohibited without violating the inmate's First Amendment rights (see Appendix A) when officials meet the tests established by the Supreme Court: The prohibition is necessary for security reasons; the policy is rationally related to security needs; other greeting methods are available (inmates may greet each other verbally); and the policy is not an exaggerated response to officials' concern about gang activity. "Gang symbolism helps to perpetuate the existence of gangs in the prison. Prohibiting gang symbolism is a reasonable response to the problem."[59]

In a recent case involving the California prison at Pelican Bay, a federal court acknowledged the problem that the California prison system has had with gangs but refused to hold that the system's procedure of assigning gang members to administrative segregation for indeterminate terms was done for punitive rather than for security reasons. Despite its findings that segregating gang members was done for appropriate administrative reasons, the court required that before the segregation occurs, the record must contain some facts establishing that the decision was based on reliable information.[60]

Collection of data on gang crime and analysis of gang activities and memberships has increased in recent years. Some of these studies include prison settings; others do not. Some of the research focuses on gangs and drugs.[61] A general review of the recent research on gangs led its author to conclude that there is evidence that violent youth gang problems have increased and gang members are committing more violent offenses. "However, it is unclear whether the growth in urban violence should be attributed largely to gangs, law-violating youth groups, or nongang youths." A number of gangs are appearing in smaller cities, but "family migration, not gang unit relocation, and local genesis appear to be the main explanatory factors." In short, there are a lot of unanswered questions about gang activity today.[62]

Despite the unanswered questions, it is clear that prison life has been affected by gangs. Gang formation has been cited by inmates as one of the reasons for the increased turmoil within prisons. The presence of gangs, along with administrative policies concerning gangs, adds to the increasingly unpredictable world in which inmates live. Some who have been in prison in the past, left, and returned, note that prison life "is no longer organized but instead is viewed as both capricious and dangerous," a world they no longer understand and one that is difficult to adjust to and to manipulate.[63]

Although young men beyond juvenile age participate in gangs, and many of the prison gang members fall into this category, gangs are thought of generally as a juvenile phenomenon. Thus, more attention is given to gangs in Chapter 12.

Female Inmates and Special Needs

Characteristics of the female offender may help to explain the nature of her adaptation to prison life and the differences between her methods of adapting and those of the typical male offender. Women constitute 6.3 percent of state and federal prison inmates, although their numbers have increased more rapidly than those of males in recent years. Women are more likely than men to be serving time for drug offenses and are more likely to have used crack. More than three-fourths of female inmates are mothers, with two-thirds having children under the age of eighteen. In comparison to male inmates, women are more likely to have been married and to have been unemployed at the time of incarceration.[64]

In her study of the Federal Reformatory for Women, Rose Giallombardo considered the issue of whether the female inmate subculture is an adaptation to the pains of imprisonment or is imported from outside experiences. Giallombardo concluded that the prison inmate culture or social system cannot be explained solely as a response to prison deprivations, although they may precipitate its development. She illustrates her point primarily by looking at gender roles within correctional institutions for women and girls. Those gender roles reflect the roles women play in society. Her point is that attitudes and values as well as roles and statuses are imported into the prison system. Prison deprivations provide the structure in which these roles are played.[65]

The evidence seems to suggest that although roles within the inmate systems of men and women differ, they reflect the differences in attitudes, values, and roles that have distinguished men and women traditionally. For example, in his study of a men's prison, Sykes suggested that loss of security is the greatest problem the male inmate faces. For the female inmate it appears that the loss of liberty and autonomy are the major deprivations. Women miss the freedom to go and come and resent the restrictions on communications with family and friends. In the institutions everything is planned for them. Furthermore, female inmates may be frustrated because they have no control over things that happen in the outside world: their children may be neglected; a loved one may become sick or die; husbands may be unfaithful.

For some female inmates prison life is a deprivation of goods and services to which they are accustomed. As soon as they enter the institution, they are stripped of most of their worldly possessions, a "kind of symbolic death." They must endure supervised baths and bodily examinations for drugs or contraband. They may have to give up their personal clothing and wear prison uniforms, although in some institutions female inmates are permitted to wear their own clothes. Generally, personal items such as jewelry, pictures, cosmetics, and other beauty products are banned or limited.[66]

Although some male inmates may have children, the issue of child care appears to be a more critical factor with female inmates. Not only do most have children, they were living with those children when they were incarcerated. Care for their children is a primary concern of many inmate mothers, and separation from them is one of the greatest pains of their incarceration.

An inmate mother must face her inability to care for her children, along with the loss of self-esteem that may come with incarceration. She must cope with the readjustment she and her children face when she is released from prison. She must deal with the lack of visitation opportunities for children and the difficulty of telling her children what is happening. Some may face lawsuits over the legal custody of their children. All may affect the ways that incarcerated mothers adapt to prison life.[67]

A social worker at a federal prison for women noted that 80 percent of female inmates are mothers. "What happens to the children . . . is devastating." She describes the tears in the prison visiting rooms. "It must be the most intense torture there is—the intense pain of being emotionally helpless."[68]

Some states are making special provisions for visits between female inmates and their children. For example, Missouri's Parents and Their Children (PATCH) helps arrange visits. PATCH is a private, nonprofit organization begun in 1984 and funded by grants and donations. PATCH officials help arrange and even pay for visits for children to see their mothers in prison.[69]

Another program designed to assist inmate mothers in their relationships with their children, "Girl Scouts Beyond Bars," is described in Spotlight 10.3. In 1997 it was announced that two facilities, the first in Illinois, would permit female inmates in community corrections facilities to live with their children. Among other eligibility requirements, the inmate must be within one release of her sentence for a nonviolent offense.[70]

Women have special medical needs, too. A California prison is experimenting with some "new age medicine" techniques for assisting female inmates with health care. Many female inmates are sexual abuse victims, and that abuse may have caused low self-esteem and depression. Some techniques used to combat these conditions are meditation, breathing techniques, and vocal expression, along with movement classes to improve physical strength. Inmates are taught to use methods other than violence to solve problems, and doctors say improvement in health has resulted from the approach. "Women on medication for depression are no longer on anti-depressants. Women with chronic pelvic pain no longer need narcotics."[71]

The issue of whether special medical care for women should be available in prisons, along with legal issues surrounding the differences in programs that are available to male as compared to female inmates, has led to numerous court cases. In a 1996 case, *Women Prisoners of the District of Columbia Department of Corrections* v. *District of Columbia,* a federal court of appeals held that the district court

Spotlight 10.3

Girl Scouts Beyond Bars

Children of prison inmates are the hidden victims of their parents' crimes. Like children of divorced or deceased parents, they often show signs of distress caused by the lack of a stable home life and parental separation, such as depression, aggression, poor school performance, and truancy. Many times they also follow their parents' criminal behavior patterns. To keep mothers and daughters connected and to enhance parenting skills, Girl Scouts Beyond Bars involves mothers in their daughters' lives through a unique partnership between a youth services organization and State and local corrections departments.

Girl Scouts Beyond Bars programs have been implemented in the following States:

- **Maryland** In 1992 the pilot program began at the Maryland Correctional Institution for Women. More than 30 girls now visit their mothers 2 Saturdays each month. On alternate Saturdays, they attend meetings at a community church, just as girls in other troops would. Before the Girl Scout program started, many of these girls rarely visited their incarcerated mothers.

- **Florida** Its first program started at the Jefferson Correctional Institution near Tallahassee in early 1994, and a second program soon followed in Fort Lauderdale. The Florida Department of Corrections hopes to expand the program to correctional facilities throughout the State. The program includes formal parenting instruction and transitional services for the mothers and monitoring of the children's school performance, and collaboration with mental health care providers.

- **Ohio** The Seal of Ohio Girl Scout Council launched the first program in a prerelease center, the Franklin Pre-Release Center in Columbus. When the Girl Scout council expanded the program to the Ohio reformatory for Women in 1994, Ohio became the first to connect the inprison program with the transition to home.

- **Arizona** Maricopa County (Phoenix) is the first jail site in the country to form a Girl Scouts Beyond Bars partnership. Parents Anonymous and Big Brothers/Big Sisters have also joined the effort.

Girl Scout councils in four other States have also begun Girl Scouts Beyond Bars programs with their corrections partners. While the partnership has demonstrated its ability to increase mother-daughter visitation time, the long-term effect of breaking the cycle of criminal behavior will require a more comprehensive approach on the part of the correctional institution, the Girl Scout council, and the mothers involved.

The program, however, may be used as a model to involve more youth service organizations in crime prevention. Partnerships should include many community service organizations that can provide the range of support services for incarcerated parents and their children to stop negative social behaviors and to break intergenerational cycles of involvement in crime.

Source: National Institute of Justice, *Keeping Incarcerated Mothers and their Daughters Together: Girl Scouts Beyond Bars* (Washington, D.C.: U.S. Department of Justice, October 1995), p. 2.

had gone too far in its orders for the plaintiffs in a class action suit. The court noted that if all prisons were required to provide *identical* programs for men and women, prison administrators might not provide programs at all, especially with current budget problems in most prisons. The court held that using physical restraints on women during the third trimester of pregnancy, sexual harassment by correctional officers, lack of adequate fire safety provisions, and general living conditions at the institution in question constituted cruel and unusual punishment and thus must be changed. But with regard to programs and work opportunities, the court emphasized that there is no constitutional right to these programs; some are available only for women, some for men. This is not unconstitutional, especially given the differences in the sizes of the institutions involved. A specific program provided for men but not for women does not in and of itself violate equal protection.[72]

The issue of sexual harassment by correctional officers is one that distinguishes female from male inmates, and the problem appears to be increasing. As one official said, "There is a possibility it may get worse, and it's already bad." Several out-of-court settlements have been reached in recent cases of alleged sexual harassment, and the Department of Justice won seven convictions of male employees in the federal system between 1990 and 1996.[73]

The Women's Rights Project of Human Rights Watch, based in New York City, alleges that the abuse of female inmates by male correctional officers is common. "Male officers vaginally, anally, and orally rape and sexually assault and abuse female prisoners. . . . They use mandatory pat-frisks to grope women's breasts, buttocks, and vaginal areas, view them inappropriately while in a state of undress, and engage in constant verbal harassment of female prisoners."[74] It is difficult, however, to prove many of these allegations.

Sexual Behavior

Sexual harassment of inmates by correctional officers may be limited primarily to female inmates, but male inmates have been attacked by prison administrators or officers. In 1997 a federal court affirmed a case in which the lower court found that a male inmate was sexually assaulted by a prison official. The court upheld the $250,000 award for compensatory damages but reduced the punitive damage award from $500,000 to $200,000.[75]

Inmates also face sexual harassment and abuse from other inmates, and this occurs more frequently among male than among female inmates. The issue of same-gender sex and especially rape has been a topic of research in male prisons for years.

Isolation from the opposite gender implies abstinence from the satisfaction of heterosexual relationships at a time when the sex drive is strong. Some inmates turn to same-gender behavior not by preference but because they need an expression for sexual outlet. Earlier studies reported that between 30 and 40 percent of male inmates had some homosexual experiences while in prison. These estimates were discussed at a conference on prison homosexuality in the early 1970s. Peter C. Buffum wrote a synthesis of the five working papers presented at that conference, and he concluded that the evidence suggests that many of the beliefs about prison homosexuality are myths.

According to Buffum, some important myths are that there is a high incidence of homosexual rape in prisons and that rape is the main form of prison homosexuality. He contended that the belief that we can solve the problem by establishing outlets for sexual drives is a myth.[76] Others have not agreed, and the subject deserves greater attention.

Male homosexuality in prison seldom involves a close relationship between the parties. In some cases, a man who is vulnerable to sexual attacks enters into a relationship with another man who agrees to protect him from the attacks of others. Earlier studies found that homosexual acts of male inmates seemed to be a response to their sexual needs coupled with their socialization. Men are taught to be aggressive, and playing the male role (the wolf) in a homosexual act may enable the inmate to retain this self-concept. Further, male inmates may see a prison homosexual relationship as little more than a search for a casual, mechanical act of physical release.[77]

Male homosexuality and the forms it takes in prison should be viewed in light of the previous discussion of the importation versus deprivation theories. Prison presents the inmate with a problem of sexual deprivation, but "the meaning, amount, and character of these adjustments will be strongly dependent on the meaning that these same behaviors had for the inmate before he or she was incarcerated."[78]

Some researchers have found that most male homosexuality is not the result of violence, with prostitution being the most frequent type of homosexual relationship, but that when violence occurs, it has racial implications.[79] It is a power play, which some compare to the rape of a woman by a man in society. It represents the need to dominate, to control, to conquer.[80]

Daniel Lockwood, who reported on his analysis of male inmates in New York prisons, interviewed men designated as targets of sexual propositions or sexual abuse, as well as those who were identified as sexual aggressors. He found that many verbal threats of sexual aggression did not result in actual aggression.[81]

Most inmate homosexual rape victims do not report the acts, primarily because of the fear of reprisal by other inmates. Some fear for their lives if they cooperate with officials in trying to solve violent acts. These fears may not be unreasonable.

Inmates have filed lawsuits over homosexual rape. The standard used by courts in analyzing these claims is whether officials were "deliberately indifferent" to the needs of inmates and the situations in which they were placed. This standard was illustrated in a 1991 case in which a heterosexual jail detainee alleged that he was raped by a homosexual with whom he was forced to share a cell. An appellate court held that the inmate had stated a sufficient claim that his due process rights were violated when he showed that prison officials engaged in a custom or policy of placing aggressive homosexuals in the general population while isolating passive homosexuals. This action permits aggressive homosexuals to prey on other inmates, especially in an overcrowded facility. Defendants in the case argued unsuccessfully that inmates should have to prove that prison officials showed a "reckless indifference" to their welfare or that officials acted with "callous disregard."

The appellate court rejected those standards and held that the same standard required for cases involving lack of medical treatment should be used: that of deliberate indifference. According to the court, this standard is an appropriate balance between the right of jail officials to manage the facility and maintain security and the right of pretrial detainees to personal security. Although the case involves pretrial detainees (who have not been convicted and thus cannot be punished), it is reasonable to expect the same standard to be applied in prisons.[82]

In a more recent case, heard by the U.S. Supreme Court and sent back to the lower court for reconsideration, an inmate who considered herself a woman, but whom the prison officials classified as a man, sued for rape by a male inmate in a men's prison. Dee Farmer alleged that on April Fool's Day in 1989 she was raped in her cell in a high-security federal prison in Terre Haute, Indiana, where she was incarcerated for credit card fraud. Subsequently, Farmer was transferred to a low- and medium-security prison at Butner, North Carolina. Farmer claimed that federal officials purposely put her at risk. Her suit for $200,000 and placement in a facility that houses both genders was dismissed by a federal court in Wisconsin and by a federal appeals court. Farmer, who has a penis, had enhanced her female appearance through silicone breast implants and hormone injections.

In deciding Farmer's case, the Court focused on the meaning of *deliberate indifference*, defining the term for the first time. The term is similar to criminal negligence and calls for subjective rather than objective knowledge. "The officials must both be aware of facts from which the inference could be drawn that a substantial risk of serious harm exists, and he must also draw the inference." The case was sent back to determine more facts.[83]

In contrast to the homosexual behavior of male inmates, same-gender sexual behavior among female inmates may develop out of mutual interest to alleviate the depersonalization of the prison and to gain status.[84] For a female inmate, a lesbian relationship may take the place of the primary group relationship for some male inmates. Talk of loyalty, sharing, trust, and friendship among female inmates may refer to the same-gender relationship, not to primary groups per se. Lesbian relationships represent an attempt to simulate the family found outside the prison and are not primarily for sexual gratification. One study reports that same-gender relationships are the most important relationships among female inmates.[85]

For female inmates, pseudofamilies may compensate for the lack of the close family environment on the outside. They permit the exercise of dominant and submissive roles that the women have learned outside of prison. Within these pseudofamilies there is an opportunity for sexual behavior, but the primary reason for forming family relationships appears not to be for that purpose.[86]

Another characteristic of the sexual behavior of female inmates distinguishes their behavior from that of male inmates' sexual involvement. Whereas in most cases male sexual behavior, especially rape, is manifested in actual physical sexual contact (oral or anal sex), for female inmates sexual relationships may involve only a strong emotional relationship with some bodily contact that would be acceptable outside prison (for example, embracing upon seeing one another). On the other hand, some women may hold hands or fondle breasts whereas others engage in more serious forms of sexual contact, such as oral-genital contact and bodily contact that attempts to simulate heterosexual intercourse.[87]

AIDS in Prison

The acquired immune deficiency syndrome (AIDS) has become a household word in the United States, as educational efforts to alert people to the deadly and rapidly spreading disease have had some success. Thousands of people have died of AIDS, and to date there is no known cure. There is evidence that AIDS is spread primarily through sexual contacts and intravenous drug use.

AIDS is a major concern in correctional facilities as well as in other areas of criminal justice systems. Studies report that AIDS is growing in prisons but not at a rampant rate. A 1997 Bureau of Justice Statistics (BJS) publication, based on 1995 prison data, revealed that 2.3 percent of inmates in state and federal prisons were HIV-positive (human immunodeficiency virus, which causes AIDS). AIDS was confirmed in 5,099 inmates (0.5% of the total). In 1995 slightly over 1,000 inmates died of AIDS-related causes, and between 1991 and 1995 "about one in three inmate deaths were attributable to AIDS-related causes." The changes in the data between 1991 and 1995, along with other information, are contained in Spotlight 10.4.

In 1991 the Eleventh Circuit upheld a segregation policy in the Alabama prisons. The court noted that this policy is a reasonable means for limiting behavior that might cause the rapid spread of the disease. The lawsuit was brought by

Spotlight 10.4

HIV in Prisons and Jails, 1995

HIV-Positive State and Federal Prison Inmates

Year	Number	Percent of Custody Population
1991	17,551	2.2%
1992	20,651	2.5
1993	21,475	2.4
1994	22,717	2.4
1995	24,226	2.3

- Between 1991 and 1995 the number of HIV-positive prisoners grew at about the same rate (38%) as the overall prison population (36%).

- At yearend 1995, 4.0% of all female State prison inmates were HIV positive, compared to 2.3% of male State prisoners.

HIV-Positive Prison Inmates

Jurisdiction	Number	Percent of Custody Population
New York	9,500	13.9%
Florida	2,193	3.4
Texas	1,890	1.5
California	1,042	.8
New Jersey	847	3.7
Georgia	828	2.4
Federal system	822	.9
Connecticut	755	5.1
Maryland	724	3.4

Based on jurisdiction with more than 700 HIV-positive inmates.

- New York held more than a third of all inmates (9,500 inmates) known to be HIV positive at yearend 1995.

- Of all HIV-positive prison inmates, 21% were confirmed AIDS cases. In State prisons, 21% of HIV-positive inmates had AIDS; in Federal prisons, 16%.

- The overall rate of confirmed AIDS among the Nation's prison population (0.51%) was more than 6 times the rate in the U.S. population (0.08%).

- Inmates in local jails, who have been tested for HIV, report similar HIV-infection rates:

Tested Jail Inmates Who Reported Results

	Number	Percent HIV Positive
All inmates	289,991	2.2%
Male	258,019	2.1
Female	31,972	2.4
White	110,023	1.4%
Black	125,259	2.6
Hispanic	45,759	3.2
Age 24 or younger	81,228	.7%
25–34	116,532	2.1
35–44	70,776	3.8
45 or older	21,455	3.0

From the 1995–96 Survey of Inmates in Local Jails.

- Jail officials in the last national Census of Jails (conducted in 1993) reported that 6,711 inmates were known to be HIV positive and 1,888 had confirmed AIDS. The infection rate was highest in the largest jail jurisdictions.

Source: Bureau of Justice Statistics, *HIV in Prisons and Jails, 1995* (Washington, D.C.: U.S. Department of Justice, August 1997), p. 1.

150 inmates with AIDS or who were HIV-positive who sought to have the policy eliminated. The court held that the lower court should reassess the plaintiffs' argument that by being segregated they were denied equal access to educational and recreational programs as well as legal assistance to which they had access before they were segregated.[88]

The following year the Fifth Circuit upheld a Mississippi State Penitentiary policy of identifying and segregating HIV-positive inmates.[89] On the other hand, a federal district court in New York ruled that a policy of identifying and segregating an HIV-positive inmate violated her privacy and due process rights. Louise Nolley, who was confined for three months at the Erie County Holding Center, was incarcerated in a cell block reserved for mentally ill inmates as well as those with contagious diseases. Special red identifying marks were placed on her files, her transportation documents, and her clothing bag. The court held that the red sticker served no purpose other than to publicize Nolley's medical condition to prison officials as well as inmates serving in custodial positions and constituted an overreaction to AIDS hysteria; that Nolley did not constitute a threat to the general population; and that she was in greater danger by being placed in a cell block with persons who have contagious diseases. On appeal, the punitive damage award of $20,000 was reversed.[90]

Some prison systems are looking more closely into the general conditions under which HIV-positive inmates are confined. California inmates protested their conditions and won some concessions, such as enhanced programs, improved medical care, and training of correctional officers to handle the problems of HIV-positive inmates.[91] Some other restrictions on HIV-positive inmates may be upheld, however.

One final point concerning AIDS in prisons is the issue of contact visits between inmates and their families. In 1987 New York's highest court upheld prison officials' decision to prohibit **conjugal visits** between an inmate infected with AIDS and his wife. The court held that this refusal was not an unreasonable interference with the rights of the inmate or of his spouse.[92] Prison officials rescinded that policy. In 1994 a federal court in California upheld that state's policy forbidding inmates with the HIV virus from working in food service jobs. The court held that other inmates might fear the HIV-infected inmates would bleed or spit on the food. This might cause violence, thus creating a security risk. Therefore, the policy is "reasonably related to legitimate penological interests."[93]

In 1997 an Illinois inmate, Michael Blucker, filed suit in federal court alleging that he became HIV-positive as the result of repeated prison rapes. He alleged that he reported these acts but the officials did not respond. The case was tried in August, 1997, with Blucker testifying that he became a "sex slave" to inmates who threatened to kill him if he did not submit. Blucker, who is white, alleged that the black inmates, who were gang members, had knives. Prison officials testified that the plaintiff was engaging in voluntary sexual acts in order to obtain drugs in prison and subsequently lied to obtain monetary damages in court. After a week's trial the jury rejected Blucker's claims against five defendants but could not reach verdicts against the other two. The case was scheduled for retrial. Blucker was paroled in 1996 and lives with his wife.[94]

Disabled and Older Inmates

Another characteristic of changing prison life is the increase in the number of disabled and older inmates. The incarceration of persons with disabilities had taken place for years, but recently some courts have held that the Americans with Disabilities Act (ADA) and its predecessor, the 1973 federal Rehabilitation Act, apply to inmates in some cases. The Ninth Circuit has held that in its administration of programs prison officials may not discriminate against disabled inmates who are "otherwise qualified" (a requirement of the statute).[95] It has been held, however, that the statutes do not apply to inmate employment.[96]

The aging of the prison population presents new challenges, too. In the United States the inmate population aged fifty-five or older grew from 9,500 in 1980 to 30,000 in 1997. Approximately two-thirds of those older inmates were convicted of violent crimes, and 68 percent of them have been incarcerated for less than five years. In some states, such as Florida, the increased costs of a large aging inmate population are leading officials to question how the costs will be financed.[97]

The special needs of female inmates as well as of inmates who are HIV-positive or have already contracted AIDS; older inmates; and those who are physically or mentally disabled should not be ignored. But neither should the mental, social, and physical needs of other inmates who do not fall into these categories. This discussion delves into the programs that might be utilized for the well-being of all inmates. In particular, education, work, and recreation are examined.

Despite the importance of education, insufficient attention is given to educational opportunities in correctional institutions. It is estimated that as many as 50 to 75 percent of American adult inmates are illiterate. Over 50 percent have not completed high school, and there is evidence that whatever grade they have completed, their skills are lower than those of non inmates who have completed that grade. If these inmates are to return to society as law-abiding individuals, they must have skills, and formal education provides some of those important skills. Most prisons provide some educational opportunities; some provide college courses. Jails lag far behind prisons in this as well as in many other areas.[98]

Of course, one cannot learn without the desire to do so, and it is argued by some that inmates do not care about learning. One professor who taught a course in a prison in the early 1990s disagreed. He reported that his students were so enthusiastic and eager to learn that at times he forgot that he was teaching in a prison.[99]

Despite the evidence of the beneficial effects of education for inmates,[100] those who argue that prisons should be for punishment and that state or federal government money should not be wasted on educating inmates, may be winning in some jurisdictions. For example, the 1994 revision of the federal criminal code eliminated grants that were used to provide college courses in prisons. And some jurisdictions, faced with budget cuts, may find that education and other programs not essential to prison security must be cut.

Even if education programs are not deleted or reduced in availability, the number of inmates who may complete the programs is affected by the growth reduction plans of some prisons. A number of educators studied the Windham School System in Texas. This system is said to be one of the most outstanding education programs for inmates in the United States. The investigators found that with early release, many inmates were not in the system long enough to complete a grade level or the requirements for a vocational certificate. They concluded, "Attempts to control prisoner population levels can have negative unintended consequences for entire prison organizations and individual inmates alike."[101]

There is evidence that education is therapeutic for inmates,[102] but courts have not ruled that inmates have a right to any educational opportunities they may choose, and some courts have ruled that inmates do not have a right to a free college education.[103] In the past, the lack of educational or work opportunities, combined with a lack of other opportunities, has been cited by courts as evidence that the overall prison system did not meet minimum constitutional requirements. Recall, however, our earlier discussions in this chapter, indicating that in 1991 the Court ruled that to prevail on allegations of unconstitutional conditions within the prison, inmates must show deliberate indifference on the part of prison officials.

Prison Programs

A second area of important focus in programming is work. It has been said that, "the most difficult prison to administer is the one in which prisoners languish in idleness. Absence of work leads to moral and physical degradation and corrupts institutional order."[104] Work has been an important part of U.S. prisons historically, and some of the early industries were profitable economically. State laws prohibiting the sale of prison-made goods to the general public, along with federal laws prohibiting shipping prison-made goods across state lines into states with these statutes, changed the nature of prison labor. Prisons were confined primarily to making goods for state (or federal) use.

In recent years additional attempts have been made to introduce meaningful vocational opportunities into prisons, along with "just plain work" to keep inmates busy and provide needed services for state and federal institutions. The Federal Bureau of Prisons has led the way, and in 1994 officials announced the need to expand the Federal Prison Industries. All federal inmates are required to work, but the increase in population is outstripping available jobs. Furthermore, most of the inmates work in jobs that maintain the institution and thus may not have marketable skills for their release from prison. Federal prisons are limited to producing goods for federal institutions in order to avoid competition, and some suggest a change in that policy.[105]

Inmates may but do not have to be paid for their work. A 1990 federal court ruling stated that, "Compelling an inmate to work without pay is not unconstitutional."[106] Inmates' wages are very low (some as low as 25 cents an hour), and it has been suggested that inmates should be paid the minimum wage and required to pay for "room and board." A study published in 1993 concluded that paying inmates in the federal system a minimum wage would cost the government hundreds of millions of dollars even if they imposed substantial fees for room and board.[107]

In 1995 the Federal Bureau of Prisons finalized its regulations concerning collecting fees from inmates. The regulations apply to all inmates convicted after 1 January 1995.[108] Legal issues have been raised concerning imposing on inmates the requirement of paying costs of their incarceration, and courts are not uniform in their reactions to these issues.[109]

Some states have made arrangements with private companies to hire inmates. One of the most extensive of these programs received approval in March 1995. The Virginia program employs inmates to work in the manufacturing of eyeglasses and copier parts. A portion of their earnings is used to compensate their victims and to pay for their own incarcerations. Inmates pay for visits to the infirmary as well.[110]

A final area of focus on programming is recreational. It is in this area that many budget cuts have been made in recent years. In particular federal prisons are described as "Club Feds," with some providing pool tables, cable television, miniature golf, handball courts, daily movies, even swimming pools. A Princeton professor calculates that about 40 percent of prison expenses go to these amenities and treatment programs, with the implication being that if they were eliminated prisons would be far less costly. The U.S. House of Representatives agrees, having introduced a "No Frills Prison Act" in 1995. Under this bill inmates would have no better living conditions than army recruits. "At a time when many Americans are struggling to make ends meet, and Congress is struggling to eliminate the deficit, we should not be spending money to pamper those who neither respect nor obey our laws."[111] The bill remains in the House Judiciary Committee.[112]

Prison officials are warning that one of the results of reducing or eliminating prison programs may be increased violence, manifested in escapes or riots that may result in serious property damage, injuries, or deaths. Prison violence in the form of riots commands the immediate attention of the public and the media, and if some inmates cannot gain satisfaction otherwise (for example, through the courts) they may resort to rioting. Although few in number, prison riots are serious in their injuries to humans—injuries that in some cases result in death—and in their destruction of property.

Two of the most destructive and highly publicized U.S. prison riots occurred in 1971 in Attica, New York, and in 1980 in Santa Fe, New Mexico. The Attica riot is summarized in a 1985 opinion of a federal judge whose court heard allegations of violations of constitutional rights in that facility. The judge noted that forty-three persons (thirty-two inmates and eleven correctional employees) were killed during the riot, the "bloodiest one-day encounter between Americans since the Civil War." Prior to the riot, the prison was overcrowded, with 2,200 inmates in a facility built for 1,700. Although 54 percent of the inmates were African American and 9 percent were Puerto Rican, all officers were white. The institution had no meaningful programs for inmates.[113]

On 2 February 1980, a riot as devastating as the Attica riot occurred at the state prison in Santa Fe, New Mexico. Estimates of damage ranged from $20 million to repair, to $60 or $80 million, to replace the prison. At least ninety persons required hospitalization, and thirty-three inmates were killed. Characteristic of the killings was the torture and incredible brutality of inmates toward inmates, which led national guardsmen to regurgitate on the scene and firemen who had fought in Vietnam to proclaim that they had not seen such atrocities as those that were committed during the riot.[114]

More recent prison riots are featured in Spotlight 10.5. Again we see brutality, physical injury, death, and destruction of property. We see inmates protesting prison conditions and demonstrating their anger at prison officials who have not changed those conditions.

One final form of violence is less obvious but very important, and that is inmate self-inflicted violence. Self inflicted violence may not be reported in jails and prisons for a variety of reasons, but when that violence leads to suicide, the acts become known and may trigger investigations by public officials and law suits by survivors. Suicides are more common in jails than in prisons, and little is known about the reasons for inmate death by suicide. The issue gained national attention in 1993 when Attorney General Janet Reno ordered a federal investigation of the forty-six hanging deaths that had occurred in Mississippi jails since 1987. Some argued that the deaths of young blacks were lynchings, not suicides. After an eight-month investigation, the state was ordered by federal investigators to correct "gross deficiencies" in Mississippi jails or face closure of the facilities. In 1995, after almost two years of additional investigation, the FBI reported that it found no evidence of misconduct on the part of jail officials. Not all agreed with that finding, with some alleging that the FBI did not talk to all of the witnesses.[115]

The reasons for self-inflicted violence and suicide in jails and prisons are various. They have been linked to overcrowded institutions, the extended use of solitary confinement, and the psychological consequences of being a victim in jail or prison. Some inmates who are threatened with rape or other violence become depressed and desperate about their physical safety, because their only options are

Spotlight 10.5

Selected Disturbances/Riots in American Prisons, 1985–1995

McAlester, Oklahoma—Oklahoma State Penitentiary, 17 December 1985

Three officers were stabbed, in serious condition; another officer, a woman, was in good condition; seven officers were taken hostage; the prison was under inmate control for twenty hours. Estimated property damage: $375,000. Prison's capacity was 496; population at the time of the riot was 610. The immediate precipitating factor, according to the superintendent, was his firing of five inmates in chief work positions. These inmates had considerable control over other inmates; the superintendent was trying to get the control back into the hands of the administration. Twenty inmates were transferred to prisons in other states; inmate freedom inside the prison was restricted.

The OSP was the scene of a major riot in 1973. At that time, the prison was overcrowded. A later court order found conditions unconstitutional and placed the prison under court order to eliminate those conditions. Considerable progress was made. The prison was removed from the order in 1984, but some claimed that it was slipping back into unconstitutional conditions.

Moundsville, West Virginia—West Virginia Penitentiary, 1 January 1986

Inmates wielding homemade weapons took correctional officers hostage and seized control of the prison; three inmates were killed; sixteen hostages were taken; the prison was held by inmates for forty-three hours. Officers taken hostage were forced to watch inmates brutalize, torture, and then kill inmates thought to be snitches. The body of one inmate, a convicted murderer and child molester, was dragged up and down a cellblock as other inmates spat on him. The riot was triggered by inmate anger over restrictions on contact visits with family and friends and the cancellation of a Christmas open house.

Officials in the state blamed each other for the problems. The current governor and the former governor "traded charges of accusing each other of cowardice and misguided policies." The current governor said the killed inmates were accused of being informants for the administration and that the informant policy was started by the previous governor, who retorted that during the three-day crisis the current governor was not available. On 16 January 1986 inmates began a work strike to protest continued restrictions of their activities since the riot. In February, twenty-five inmates who had been placed in isolation since the New Year's Day riot broke out of their cells. Correctional officers persuaded twenty-three of the inmates to surrender and then captured the other two. Sixty-eight inmates were in isolation as a result of the riot.

The West Virginia Penitentiary had been placed under court order in 1983 after the court found unconstitutional conditions, including maggot-infested food and raw sewage in living areas. The prison at that time was overcrowded, and officials were ordered to reduce the population.

Source: Summarized by the author from media sources unless otherwise noted.

---

fight or flight. If they submit to violence, they are branded as weak and forced to face further violent attacks from aggressive inmates. If they seek help from the prison administration, they are branded as snitches or rats. Furthermore, the inmate social system rewards violence against weaker inmates.[116]

WiseGuide Wrap-Up   In 1984 the Supreme Court said that the continuing guarantee of substantial rights to prison inmates "is testimony to a belief that the way a society treats those who have transgressed against it is evidence of the essential character of that society."[117] This chapter explores life in prison historically and currently, looking at the legal as well as other issues. It begins with a

Spotlight 10.5 *continued*

Maryland and New York Prisons, 1991

Fourteen correctional officers and forty-four inmates were injured when Maryland inmates rioted in the Correctional Institution at Hagerstown on 25 May 1991. Of the 1,600 inmates at the institution, approximately 1,000 were involved in the riot, "which officials described as the most serious disturbance at the prison in decades." Inmates caused over $1 million of damage before the riot was quelled. The prison was approximately 60 percent overcrowded at the time of the riot.[1]

On 28 May 1991 a disturbance began at the Southport Correctional Facility at Pine City, New York. This facility is a maxi-maxi prison designed to house the state's most serious and dangerous offenders. Three correctional officers, taken hostage by approximately fifty inmates, were held for twenty-six hours before being released. Although there were no deaths in this riot, several officers were stabbed or beaten. Inmates were protesting the institution's lock-down policy, which kept them in their cells twenty-three hours a day with only one hour out for supervised exercise; poor living conditions and food; and some of the restrictions on visitation.[2]

Lucasville, Ohio—Southern Ohio Correctional Facility, April 1993

In March 1995 Jason Robb, an inmate accused of helping lead the 1993 riot that resulted in the deaths of nine inmates and one correctional officer, was convicted of killing the officer and one inmate. Robb was convicted of six of seven charges against him, including aggravated murder and kidnapping. The riot began on Easter Sunday when a fight broke out as inmates returned from the recreation yard to their cell blocks. It lasted eleven days. Inmates surrendered after they agreed with prison officials on twenty-one issues including numerous improvements in prison conditions. Officials agreed that inmates would not be subjected to retaliations by correctional officers, although it was made clear that those who committed crimes, such as murder, would be subject to prosecution.

Phoenix, Arizona—Durango Jail, November 1996

Eleven correctional officers were held hostage for almost three hours when hundreds of inmates at the Durango Jail protested being housed in tents, complained about inadequate medical care, bad food, and brutality by officers. Sheriff Joseph M. Arpaio met with inmates who then released the hostages. The sheriff is known for his tough tactics with inmates, including banning cigarettes and putting women as well as men on chain gangs.[3]

In 1997 Sheriff Arpaio announced that since he was so short of correctional officers he had secured four specially trained German shepherd dogs, who will wear miniature video cameras and monitor the perimeter of "Tent City," which serves as the area jail for 1,100 inmates.[4]

1. "Maryland and New York Prisons Suffer Serious Disturbances," *Criminal Justice Newsletter* 22 (3 June 1991), p. 5.
2. Ibid.
3. "Jail Inmates Riot, but then Talk to Sheriff," *New York Times* (19 November 1996), p. 7.
4. "Tent City Going to the Dogs: Jail Getting Canines with Video Cameras," *Arizona Republic* (9 February 1997), p. 1.

brief look at the events that might accompany an inmate's arrival at prison and proceeds to the legal issues.

The Supreme Court has made it clear that some rights are forfeited by inmates and that security needs may justify the restriction of rights normally recognized in prison. This chapter surveys the historical and current approaches to inmates' legal rights, beginning with a look at the traditional hands-off doctrine, in which federal courts refused to become involved in daily prison administration and maintenance. As a result of recognized abuse of inmates and the civil rights movement, which brought the nation's attention to the problems not only of minorities in society but also of the conditions under which inmates lived, courts began to abandon the hands-off policy. Courts continue to defer to prison officials, but they no longer tolerate violations of basic rights.

An introduction to modern litigation in the area of constitutional rights introduces us to the concept of rights versus privileges as well as the problem of how to evaluate and test alleged infringements on constitutional rights. The guidelines handed down in *Turner* v. *Safley* provided the background for discussing the avenues for pursuing legal challenges to incarceration: filing a writ of *habeas corpus* or a Section 1983 civil rights suit. The discussion continues with a brief look at Supreme Court decisions of this decade in which the Court has established the tests for a successful lawsuit.

The chapter focuses next on prison administration and its relationship to security goals. In the earlier days, authoritarian prison wardens or superintendents and correctional officers maintained security by keeping inmates separate; by not permitting them to talk to each other; or by using fear and force, often involving corporal punishment. Those methods are not permitted today; new management techniques are necessary.

Correctional officers are crucial to prison management. They have primary responsibility for maintaining internal discipline, order, and security. Their jobs are difficult and at times boring, but the position is challenging and rewarding to many who have chosen the profession of correctional officer. The chapter emphasizes the importance of selecting and training officers carefully and of including women and minorities within their ranks.

When we think of life behind bars, however, we think mainly of inmates serving time in those facilities. This chapter notes how inmates adjust to prison life through the prisonization process. The resulting subculture is discussed in view of its origin: whether inmates develop the subculture as a method of adapting to the deprivations of prison, or whether they have acquired the values of the subculture previously and import them into prisons.

The male inmate subculture is characterized by social roles that assist inmates in maintaining some self-esteem and positive self-concepts. Some accomplish these goals at the expense of other inmates: social control through economics, through racial and gang violence, and through homosexual attacks. Prison gangs play a critical role in these interactions.

Female inmates develop patterns of adaptation to prison life, too, but their adaptations are less violent than those of male inmates. Their social roles mirror the roles they have played in society. Women face many of the same deprivations as male inmates, but they face the additional problems of adjusting to daily life without their children. Mothers behind bars have become a subject of research only recently, and even today few provisions are made for them to interact with their children. Women also face special medical needs, and some institutions are attempting to accommodate those needs.

The sexual behavior of male and female inmates is contrasted and discussed in the context of a relatively recent complication of prison life: AIDS. The complications are increasing, too, as officials must determine how to cope with AIDS without violating inmates' constitutional rights. Other special needs exist in prison settings, and brief attention is given to those needs, in particular those of disabled and aging inmates.

Adaptations to prison are made more difficult by the lack of activities, including education, work, and recreational programs and facilities. Recent attention to the need for such programs is discussed.

The final section looks at the impact of prison violence, with particular attention given to the major prison riots of recent times. The Attica riot of 1971 and subsequent studies of the riot illustrate the devastation of riots regarding personal injury, death, and property damage as well as the slowness with which meaningful changes are made. The 1986 West Virginia riot illustrates the torture and brutality of which inmates are capable. The more recent riots remind us that serious prison disturbances still happen.

Another type of violence in prison is self-inflicted violence, apparently the only way some inmates find to adjust. In some cases suicide results.

This chapter's discussion of the problems of controlling inmates within prison looks at the issues historically and in terms of recent events. Perhaps in closing it is important to consider a 1995 report by a Mississippi state official who investigated corruption in that state's prisons. The state auditor referred to one prison in particular, Parchman Prison in the Delta, concluding that the prison is controlled by inmates. "It's the corporate headquarters of crime in Mississippi. Much of the drug activity and much of the gang activity in the state is . . . being conducted and led from Parchman under the auspices of the state of Mississippi. . . . The bottom line is the inmates are running the penitentiaries."[118]

Apply It

1. What is the *hands-off doctrine* and to what extent (and why) has it been abandoned?

2. What is meant by a *hierarchy of rights*?

3. Compare and contrast a writ of *habeas corpus* and a Section 1983 action.

4. What were the characteristics of the authoritarian warden? What do you think would be the characteristics of the ideal warden or prison superintendent?

5. What changes have occurred within prisons during the past two decades that have forced changes in prison administration?

6. How did early correctional officers control inmates? If allowed, would those techniques be effective today?

7. Discuss recruitment and training issues with regard to correctional officers. Note the issues regarding gender and race.

8. Describe some of the daily aspects of inmate life in prison.

9. Define *prisonization* and *subculture*, and explain the development and importance of each in a prison setting. Would the importance be different in prisons for women as compared to those for men?

10. Distinguish the *importation* and *deprivation* models and explain the social control role of inmate social systems.

11. What is the significance of prison gangs? What could be done to lessen their influence in prisons?

12. What provisions do you think should be made for incarcerated women who have children at home or for women who give birth during incarceration? What provisions should be made for incarcerated fathers to visit with their children? Do female inmates have special problems other than child care, and if so, how should they be handled?

13. Distinguish male and female prison homosexuality. Would co-correctional prisons be a solution?

14. What has been the impact of AIDS on prisons? How should the problems be handled?

15. Discuss the situations faced by prison officials as the result of an aging inmate population. What are the special needs of disabled inmates?

16. If most inmates are relatively poorly educated, why do we not make a greater effort to provide education classes in prisons?

17. Should inmates have to work? If there is a lack of jobs, how should that problem be solved?

18. What policies would you recommend to prison administrators if they asked you how to prevent prison riots? Jail or prison suicides?

Notes

1. See Harold Garfinkel, "Conditions of Successful Degradation Ceremonies," *American Journal of Sociology* 61 (March 1956): 420–424.

2. Gresham M. Sykes, *The Society of Captives* (Princeton, N.J.: Princeton University Press, 1958), pp. 63–83.

3. Ruffin v. Commonwealth, 62 Va. 790, 796 (1872).

4. See, for example, Bell v. Wolfish, 441 U.S. 520 (1979).

5. Wolff v. McDonnell, 418 U.S. 539 (1974).

6. For a discussion of the law on inmates' rights, see John W. Palmer, *Constitutional Rights of Prisoners,* 5th ed. (Cincinnati, Oh.: Anderson, 1997).

7. Holt v. Sarver, 309 F.Supp. 362 (E.D.Ark. 1970). This case has a long history of remands and reversals leading to the Supreme Court case, Hutto v. Finney, 437 U.S. 678 (1978). A good source for the history up to 1977 is found in Finney v. Hutto, 548 F.2d 740 (8th Cir. 1977). See also Thomas O. Murton, *The Dilemma of Prison Reform* (New York: Holt, Rinehart & Winston, 1976).

8. Graham v. Richardson, 313 F.Supp. 34 (D.Ariz 1970), *aff'd.,* 403 U.S. 365, 375 (1971).

9. Turner v. Safley, 482 U.S. 78, 88–90 (1987).

10. Campos v. Coughlin, 854 F.Supp. 194 (S.D.N.Y. 1994). See also "Religious Freedom Act Worries AGs," *American Bar Association* 80 (February 1994): 20. The Act is codified at U.S. Code, Title 42, Sections 2000bb et seq. (1997)

11. City of Boerne v. Flores, 117 S. Ct. 2157 (1997).

12. See, for example, McCleskey v. Zant, 499 U.S. 467 (1991), *cert. denied sub nom.,* 501 U.S. 1282 (1991).

13. Antiterrorism and Effective Death Penalty Act of 1996, U.S. Code, Title 28, Section 2254 *et seq.* (1997). The case is Lindh v. Murphy, 117 S.Ct. 2059 (1997).

14. O'Neal v. McAninch, 513 U.S. 432 (1995).

15. U.S. Code, Title 42, Section 1983 (1997).

16. Estelle v. Gamble, 429 U.S. 97, 106 (1976).

17. Wilson v. Seiter, 501 U.S. 294 (1991).

18. Farmer v. Brennan, 511 U.S. 895 (1994).

19. Hudson v. McMillian, 503 U.S. 1 (1992).

20. "Flood of Prisoner Rights Suits Brings Effort to Limit Filings," *New York Times* (21 March 1994), p. 1.

21. Bureau of Justice Statistics, *Prisoner Petitions in the Federal Courts, 1980–96* (Washington, D.C.: U.S. Department of Justice, October 1997), p. iii.

22. "Prisoner Sues Himself But Neither Side Wins Suit," *Orlando Sentinel* (10 April 1995), p. 8.

23. The Prison Litigation Reform Act of 1993, as amended, is codified at U.S. Code, Title 42, Section 1997e(e) (1997). See also Hampton v. Hobbs, 106 F.3d 1281 (6th Cir. 1997), upholding the filing fee provisions of the act; Zehner v. Trigg, 952 F.Supp. 1318 (S.D.Ind. 1997), *aff'd.,* 133 F. 3d 459 (7th Cir. 1997), upholding the requirement that inmates must show a physical injury in a case claiming mental or emotional injury; and Hadix v. Johnson, 933 F.Supp. 1362, *mot. granted sub nom.,* 1996 U.S. Dist. LEXIS 16719

(W.D.Mich. 1 October 1996), striking the provision of the act concerning consent decrees. The appeal of this case was dismissed without an opinion, 134 F. 3d 371 (6th Cir. 1998). In 1997 a federal court held that the Prison Litigation Reform Act is not retroactive, thus, it does not apply to actions filed before its passage. See Nanayakkara v. Krug, 1997 U.S. Dist. LEXIS 19168 (E.D.Pa. 4 December 1997). For a discussion of the issue of prison oversight by courts, see "Courts Now Out of Job as Jailers," *American Bar Association* 82 (August 1996): 40–41.

24. Norman Holt, "Prison Management in the Next Decade," *Prison Journal* 57 (Autumn/Winter 1977): 17–19. For a classic study of the role of the warden in earlier prison, see James B. Jacobs, *Stateville: The Penitentiary in Mass Society* (Chicago: University of Chicago Press, 1977).

25. For a recent look at the problems created by long-term inmates, see Ernest L. Cowles and Michael J. Sabath, "Changes in the Nature and Perception of the Long-Term Inmate Population: Some Implications for Prison Management and Research," *Criminal Justice Review* 21 (Spring 1996): 44–61. See also Lawrence A. Greenfeld et al., "Prisons: Population Trends and Key Issues for Management," in the same journal, pp. 4–20.

26. This discussion is based on Holt, "Prison Management." For a recent statement on racial gangs in one jail system, see "Racial Tensions on the Rise in Los Angeles Jail System," *New York Times* (6 February 1995), p. 8.

27. For recent analyses of prison management problems and issues, see Alvin W. Cohn, "The Failure of Correctional Management: Recycling the Middle Manager," *Federal Probation* 59 (June 1995): 10–16; and James Houston, *Correctional Management: Functions, Skills, and Systems* (Chicago: Nelson-Hall, 1994).

28. Alvin W. Cohn, "The Failure of Correctional Management— Revisited," *Federal Probation* 43 (March 1979): 13–14.

29. Nancy C. Jurik and Michael C. Musheno, "The Internal Crisis of Corrections: Professionalization and the Work Environment," *Justice Quarterly* 3 (December 1986): 477. See also James B. Jacobs, *New Perspectives on Prisons and Imprisonment* (Ithaca, N.Y.: Cornell University Press, 1983).

30. "Inmate Violence Is on Rise As Federal Prisons Change," *New York Times* (9 February 1995), p. 1.

31. "Inside Rikers Island: A Bloody Struggle for Control," *New York Times* (1 September 1990), p. 1.

32. "U.S. Says Bribed Guards Turned Jail into a 'Badfellas' Social Club," *New York Times* (23 May 1997), p. 1.

33. "Correction Chief Faults Hiring Methods at Rikers," *New York Times* (25 August 1990), p. 11.

34. For example, see "Layoffs This Week for 600 Employees of New York State," *New York Times* (26 December 1990), p. 16; and "Guard Layoff Plans Put Fear in 'Prison Town,'" *Miami Herald* (11 February 1991), p. 6B.

35. "Inmate Violence Is On Rise," p. 1.

36. "Violence, Drugs Way of Life Behind Bars," *Atlanta Journal and Constitution* (21 March 1997), p. 4F.

37. Francis T. Cullen et al., "The Correctional Orientation of Prison Guards: Do Officers Support Rehabilitation?" *Federal Probation* 53 (March 1989): 40.

38. See, for example, Dothard v. Rawlinson, 433 U.S. 321 (1977); and Washington v. Gunther, 452 U.S. 161 (1981).

39. "Female Guards at Men's Prisons," *Orlando Sentinel* (20 June 1997), p. 10.

40. Johnson v. Phelan, 69 F.3d 144 (7th Cir. 1995), *cert. denied,* 117 S.Ct. 506 (1996).

41. Rita J. Simon and Judith D. Simon, "Female COs: Legitimate Authority," *Corrections* 50 (August 1988): 132.

42. See Kevin N. Wright and William G. Saylor, "Male and Female Employees' Perceptions of Prison Work: Is There a Difference?" *Justice Quarterly* 8 (December 1991): 520–521.

43. "Female Correctional Officers Said to Reduce Prison Violence," *Criminal Justice Newsletter* 27 (1 April 1996): 2.

44. For a study of inmate victimization see Angela S. Maitland and Richard D. Sluder, "Victimization in Prisons: A Study of Factors Related to the General Well-Being of Youthful Inmates," *Federal Probation* LX (June 1996): 24–31.

45. This discussion of Clemmer's concept of prisonization comes from his book, *The Prison Community* (New York: Holt, Rinehart and Winston, 1958), pp. 298–301.

46. Stanton Wheeler, "Socialization in Correctional Communities," *American Sociological Review* 26 (October 1961): 697–712.

47. Geoffrey P. Alpert et al., "A Comparative Look at Prisonization: Sex and Prison Culture," *Quarterly Journal of Corrections* 1 (Summer 1977): 29–34. For an analysis of prisonization among Polish inmates, see Mark M. Kaminski and Don C. Gibbons, "Prison Subculture in Poland," *Crime & Delinquency* 40 (January 1994): 105–119.

48. See Sykes, *Society of Captives;* and Gresham M. Sykes and Sheldon L. Messinger, "The Inmate Social System," in *Theoretical Studies in Social Organization of the Prison,* ed. Richard A. Cloward et al. (New York: Social Science Research Council, 1960).

49. See John Irwin and Donald R. Cressey, "Thieves, Convicts and the Inmate Culture," *Social Problems* 10 (Fall 1962): 142–155.

50. Charles W. Thomas, "Prisonization or Resocialization: A Study of External Factors Associated with the Impact of Imprisonment," *Journal of Research in Crime and Delinquency* 10 (January 1975): 13–21.

51. Leo Carroll, "Race and Three Forms of Prisoner Power Confrontation, Censoriousness, and the Corruption of Authority," in *Contemporary Corrections: Social Control and Conflict,* ed. C. Ronald Huff (Beverly Hills, Calif.: Sage Publications, 1977), pp. 40–41, 50–51.

52. Ronald L. Akers et al., "Prisonization in Five Countries: Type of Prison and Inmate Characteristics," *Criminology* 14 (February 1977): 538.

53. See James Garofalo and Richard D. Clark, "The Inmate Subculture in Jails," *Criminal Justice and Behavior* 12 (December 1985): 431. For a general analysis of inmate coping, see Edward Zamble and Frank J. Porporino, *Coping, Behavior, and Adaptation in Prison Inmates* (Secaucus, N.J.: Springer-Verlag, 1988). For an analysis of the coping mechanisms of problem inmates, see Hans Toch et al., *Coping: Maladaptation in Prisons* (New Brunswick, N.J.: Transaction, 1989).

54. Richard A. Cloward, "Social Control in the Prison," in *Theoretical Studies,* ed. Cloward et al.

55. James W. Marquart and Ben M. Crouch, "Coopting the Kept: Using Inmates for Social Control in a Southern Prison," *Justice Quarterly* 1, no. 4 (1984): 491–509. The use of building tenders in the Texas prison system is discussed in numerous places in a book about that system: Steve J. Martin and Sheldon Ekland-Olson, *Texas Prisons: The Walls Came Tumbling Down* (Austin: Texas Monthly Press, 1987).

56. Robert S. Fong, "The Organizational Structure of Prison Gangs," *Federal Probation* 54 (March 1990): 36–43. See also Fong and Salvador Buentello, "The Detection of Prison Gang Development: An Empirical Assessment," *Federal Probation* 55 (March 1991): 66–69.

57. Michael P. Lane, "Inmate Gangs," *Corrections Today* 51 (July 1989): 98–102.

58. Toussaint v. McCarthy, 926 F.2d 800 (9th Cir. 1990), *cert. denied,* 502 U.S. 874 (1991).

59. State *ex rel* Whiting v. Kolb, 461 N.W.2d 816 (Wis.App. 1990). The U.S. Supreme Court case is Turner v. Safley, 482 U.S. 78 (1987).

60. Madrid v. Gomez, 889 F.Supp. 1146 (N.D.Cal. 1995), *cert. denied,* 117 S.Ct. 1823 (1997), *rev'd., remanded,* 1998 U.S. App. LEXIS 148 57 (9th Cir. Cal. 1998).

61. See, for example, John M. Hagedorn, "Neighborhoods, Markets, and Gang Drug Organization," *Journal of Research in Crime and Delinquency* 31 (August 1994): 264–294; and Malcolm W. Klein et al., "Crack, Street Gangs, and Violence," *Criminology* 29 (November 1991): 623–650.

62. James C. Howell, "Recent Gang Research: Program and Policy Implications," *Crime & Delinquency* 40 (October 1994): 494–515; quotation is on p. 509. For a study of gang migration, see Malcolm W. Klein, *The American Street Gang* (New York: Lexington Free Press, 1994).

63. Geoffrey Hunt et al., "Changes in Prison Culture: Prison Gangs and the Case of the 'Pepsi Generation'," *Social Problems* 40 (August 1993): 398–409; quotation is on p. 407.

64. Bureau of Justice Statistics, *Prisoners in 1996* (Washington, D.C.: U.S. Department of Justice, June 1997), p. 5; Bureau of Justice Statistics, *Women in Prison* (Washington, D.C.: U.S. Department of Justice, March 1991), pp. 2, 3.

65. Rose Giallombardo, *The Social World of Imprisoned Girls: A Comparative Study of Institutions for Juvenile Delinquents* (New York: John Wiley, 1974).

66. David A. Ward and Gene G. Kassebaum, "Women in Prison," in *Correctional Institutions,* ed. Robert M. Carter, Daniel Glaser, and Leslie T. Wilkins (Philadelphia: J. B. Lippincott, 1972), p. 215. For a more recent account of prison life among female inmates, see the books by Jean Harris, who was incarcerated for killing her lover, the "Scarsdale Diet" doctor. Jean Harris, *Stranger in Two Worlds* (New York: Macmillan, 1986); and Harris, *They Always Call Us Ladies* (New York: Charles Scribner's Sons, 1988).

67. Phyllis Jo Baunach, "You Can't Be a Mother and Be in Prison . . . Can You? Impacts of the Mother-Child Separation," in the *Criminal Justice System and Women,* ed. Barbara Raffel Price and Natalie J. Sokoloff (New York: Clark Boardman, 1982), pp. 155–169.

68. "Women in Prison: Sisterhood Sometimes Penetrates the Bars; At Isolated Federal Institute in W. Va., Inmates Miss Family," *Los Angeles Times* (13 November 1988), p. 2.

69. "Imprisoned Moms Get Family Time," *Chicago Tribune* (7 October 1993), p. 8.

70. "DOC Facility First to Hold Female Inmates with Babies," *Copley News Service* (1 August 1997), State and Regional Section.

71. "California Prison Takes Holistic Approach to Health," CNN (31 March 1994), Transcript no. 417–8. For a recent discussion of the medical needs of female inmates, see Joanne Belknap, "Access to Programs and Health Care for Incarcerated Women," *Federal Probation* LX (December 1996): 34–39.

72. Women Prisoners of the District of Columbia Department of Corrections v. District of Columbia, 899 F.Supp. 659 (D.D.C. 1995), *vacated, in part, remanded,* 93 F.3d 910 (D.C.Cir. 1996), *cert denied,* 117 S.Ct. 1552 (1997).

73. "With More Women in Prison, Sexual Abuse by Guards Becomes a Troubling Trend," *New York Times* (27 December 1996), p. 10.

74. "Sex Abuse of Female Inmates Is Common, Rights Group Says," *Criminal Justice Newsletter* 27 (16 December 1996), p. 2.

75. Mathie v. Fries, 121 F.3d 808 (2d Cir. 1997).

76. Peter C. Buffum, *Homosexuality in Prisons* (U.S. Department of Justice et al., Washington, D.C.: U.S. Government Printing Office, 1972), p. 13.

77. Sykes, *Society of Captives,* p. 97.

78. Buffum, *Homosexuality in Prisons,* p. 9.

79. Leo Carroll, *Hacks, Blacks, and Cons: Race Relations in a Maximum Security Prison* (Lexington, Mass.: D.C. Heath, 1974), p. 194.

80. Susan Brownmiller, *Against Our Will: Men, Women and Rape* (New York: Simon & Schuster, 1975), p. 258.

81. Daniel Lockwood, *Prison Sexual Violence* (New York: Elsevier Science Publishing, 1980), p. 21.

82. Redman v. San Diego County, California, 942 F.2d 1435 (9th Cir. 1991), *cert. denied,* 502 U.S. 1074 (1992).

83. Farmer v. Brennan, 511 U.S. 825 (1994).

84. Ward and Kassebaum, "Women in Prison," pp. 217–219.

85. Rose Giallombardo, *Society of Women: A Study of a Woman's Prison* (New York: John Wiley, 1966).

86. John Gagnon and William Simon, "The Social Meaning of Prison Homosexuality," *Federal Probation* 32 (March 1968): 27–28.

87. David Ward and Gene Kassebaum, "Sexual Tensions in a Women's Prison," in *Crime and Justice: The Criminal in Confinement,* ed. Leon Radzinowicz and Marvin E. Wolfgang (New York: Basic Books, 1971), pp. 146–155. For other studies of women in prison, see Nicole Hahn Rafter, *Partial Justice: Women in State Prisons,* 1800–1935 (Boston: Northeastern University Press, 1985); and Estelle B. Freedman, *Their Sisters' Keepers: Prison Reform in America,* 1830–1930 (Ann Arbor: University of Michigan Press, 1981). See also James G. Fox, "Women in Prison: A Case Study in the Social Reality of Stress," in *The Pains of Imprisonment,* ed. Robert Johnson and Hans Toch (Beverly Hills, Calif.: Sage Publications, 1982), pp. 205–220.

88. "Court Backs Policy To Separate Inmates with the AIDS Virus," *New York Times* (20 September 1991), p. 4. See Harris v. Thigpen, 941 F.2d 1495 (11th Cir. 1991).

89. Moore v. Mabus, 976 F.2d 268 (5th Cir. 1992).

90. Nolley v. County of Erie, 776 F.Supp. 715 (W.D.N.Y. 1991), *supplemental opinion,* 802 F.Supp. 898 (W.D.N.Y. 1992), *set aside, on reconsideration, remanded,* 798 F.Supp. 123 (W.D.N.Y. 1992).

91. For a discussion see "California Inmates Win Better Prison AIDS Care," *New York Times* (25 January 1993), p. 7. For a recent analysis of HIV-related behavioral issues among inmates, see Robert F. Schilling et al., "HIV-Related Behaviors in Transitional Correctional Settings," *Criminal Justice and Behavior* 24 (June 1997): 256–277.

92. Doe v. Coughlin, 523 N.Y.S.2d 782 (N.Y.Ct.App. 1987), *cert. denied,* 488 U.S. 879 (1988).

93. Gates v. Rowland, 39 F.3d 1439 (9th Cir. 1994), *cert. denied,* 117 S.Ct. 2454 (1997).

94. "Word for Word/Prison Rape; From Thief to Cellblock Sex Slave: A Convict's Testimony," *New York Times* (19 October 1997), p. 7, Section 4.

95. Bonner v. Lewis, 857 F.2d 559 (9th Cir. 1988). *cert. denied,* 111 S. Ct. 799 (1991). The ADA is the Americans with Disabilities Act of 1990, Public Law 101-336, U.S. Code, Title 42, Section 12101 *et seq.* (1997). See also Inmates of the Allegheny County Jail v. Wecht, 1996 U.S. App. LEXIS 24921 (3d Cir. 1996); Crawford v. Indiana Department of Corrections, 115 F.3d 481 (7th Cir. 1997); and Harris v. Thigpen, 941 F.2d 1495 (11th Cir. 1991), *cert. denied sub nom.,* 516 U.S. 1071 (1996), all holding that either the ADA or the Rehabilitation Act or both apply to prisons or jails.

96. See Torcasio v. Murray, 57 F.3d 1340 (4th Cir. 1995), *cert. denied,* 516 U.S. 1071 (1996).

97. America's Aging, Violent Prisoners," *New York Times* (6 July 1997), p. 3E. See also "Elderly Inmate Population Grows, Raising Prison Costs," *Miami Herald* (24 August 1997), p. 8.

98. For an overview of the literature regarding education in prisons and jails, see the article by Richard A. Tewksbury and Gennaro F. Vito, "Improving the Educational Skills of Jail Inmates: Preliminary Program Findings," *Federal Probation* 53 (June 1994): 55–59.

99. Ahmad Tootoonchi, "College Education in Prisons: The Inmates' Perspectives," *Federal Probation* 52 (December 1993): 34–40.

100. See Hans Toch, "Regenerating Prisoners Through Education," *Federal Probation* 51 (September 1987): 61–66.

101. James W. Marquart et al, "A Limited Capacity to Treat: Examining the Effects of Prison Population Control Strategies on Prison Education Programs," *Crime & Delinquency* 40 (October 1994): 516–531; quotation is on p. 529.

102. See Hans Toch, "Regenerating Prisoners Through Education," *Federal Probation* 51 (September 1987): 61–66.

103. See Hernandez v. Johnston, 833 F.2d 1316 (9th Cir. 1987).

104. Elmer H. Johnson, *Crime, Correction, and Society,* rev. ed. (Homewood, Ill: Dorsey, 1968), p. 559.

105. "Bureau of Prisons Cites Need to Expand Prison Industries," *Criminal Justice Newsletter* 25 (16 May 1994): 4.

106. Murray v. Mississippi Department of Corrections, 911 F.2d 1167 (5th Cir. 1990), *cert. denied,* 498 U.S. 1050 (1991).

107. *Prisoner Labor: Perspectives on Paying the Federal Minimum Wage* (Washington, D.C.: U.S. Government Accounting Office, 1993), cited in "Cost of Inmate Minimum Wage Would Be Prohibitive, GAO Finds," *Criminal Justice Newsletter* 24 (15 June 1993): 7.

108. The statute providing for such fees is Public Law 102-395, Section 111, enacted in 1992. These new regulations will be codified as 28 CFR Part 505.1-9. They are published in full at 59 Fed.Reg. 64780 (15 December 1994).

109. See Comment, "Prisoners Paying for the Costs of Their Own Incarceration: United States Circuit Courts of Appeal Spar Over the Validity and Application of United States Sentencing Guideline Section 5E1.2(i)," *Dickason Law Review 99* (Fall 1994): 221–264.

110. "Allen Seeks More Work for Inmates: Virginia Prisoners to Get Private Industry Jobs," *Washington Post* (10 March 1995), p. 1D.

111. "Prison Is No Place for 'Extras,'" *Christian Science Monitor* (28 February 1995), p. 20, quoting a Republican representative.

112. The "No Frills Prison Act," which would amend the Violent Crime Control and Law Enforcement Act of 1994 by preventing luxurious conditions in prisons, was referred to the House Judiciary Committee on 28 October 1997.

113. Abdul Wali v. Coughlin, 754 F.2d 1015 (2d Cir. 1985).

114. Cited in Joseph W. Rogers, "Postscripts to a Prison Riot" (paper presented at the Annual Meeting of the Academy of Criminal Justice Sciences, Louisville, Ky., 25 March 1982).

115. See, for example, "After Mississippi Hangings, Feds Order Jails to Shape Up," *Atlanta Journal and Constitution* (31 December 1993), p. 1; "Around the South: Mississippi Jail Deaths Probe Ends; FBI Finds No Evidence of Civil Rights Violated," *Atlanta Journal and Constitution* (26 January 1995), p. 3.

116. See Garvin McCain et al., *The Effect of Prison Crowding on Inmate Behavior* (Washington, D.C.: U.S. Government Printing Office, 1980), pp. 113–115. For a more recent analysis, see John D. Wooldredge and L. Thomas Winfree Jr., "An Aggregate-Level Study of Inmate Suicides and Deaths Due to Natural Causes in U.S. Jails," *Journal of Research in Crime and Delinquency* 29 (November 1992): 466–479.

117. Hudson v. Palmer, 468 U.S. 517, 523, 525 (1984).

118. "State Official Says Inmates Are Running Prisons in Mississippi," *Orlando Sentinel* (5 February 1995), p. 6.

Probation, Parole, and Community Corrections

WiseGuide Intro

Supervison of offenders in the community is a frequent alternative to imprisonment, although the conditions placed on offenders may be severe. Parole and probation violations are common and may result in revocation, but statutes and constitutions require that proper procedures be followed before revocation occurs.

This chapter focuses on probation, parole, and community treatment of offenders. It begins with an overview of community-based corrections, noting the historical development and discussing problems offenders face when they enter these programs. It examines how problems might be minimized by preparation before release from prison and by provision of resources in the community.

Probation, the most frequently imposed sentence, and **parole**, until recently a major form of release from prison, are discussed in their historical contexts and with their modern changes. Both have been the focus of considerable attention in recent years. Frequently, crimes committed by probationers and parolees receive widespread publicity, leading to public pressure to reduce the use of probation and parole. In some cases, these pressures have been successful.

Like other changes in criminal justice systems, however, changes in the use of probation and parole must be viewed in terms of their effects on the rest of the system. A significant reduction in the use of one or both places severe strain on correctional systems, increasing prison overcrowding and all of its consequences. In addition, it may result in the incarceration of offenders who do not need such severe restraints. On the other hand, crimes committed by probationers and parolees reduce the safety and security of society. It is not possible to predict with great accuracy who will harm society while on probation or parole.

Key Terms

community-based corrections
diversion
furlough
house arrest
intensive probation supervision (IPS)
pardon
parole
parole board
parole officer
parole revocation
probation
probation officer
probation revocation
recidivist
reintegration
work release

Learning Objectives

After reading this chapter, you should be able to do the following:

- Explain the meaning of *community corrections* and state the advantages of using this approach.
- Explain *furlough, work release,* and *prerelease* programs.
- Distinguish *probation* and *parole.*
- Explain *felony probation* and analyze recent approaches to its use.
- Analyze the use of electronic monitoring and house arrest.
- Discuss the legal limitations on probation and parole conditions.
- Recognize the advantages and disadvantages of intensive probation supervision.

- Analyze search and seizure of parolees.
- Identify three organizational models of parole systems.
- Explain the parole process with particular attention given to due process.
- Explain the legal controls on parole and probation revocation.
- Analyze the future of probation and parole.
- Assess the impact of Megan's laws and analyze the constitutional issues raised by these statutes.

Supervision of Offenders in the Community: An Overview

Earlier discussions describe some methods used in the past to permit the accused or the convicted offender to remain in the community. Family members, friends, or attorneys served as sureties to guarantee the presence of the accused at trial. Later sureties were replaced by a variety of methods of posting bond. Early reformers such as John Augustus were successful in their efforts to have convicted persons placed on probation in the community. In the late 1880s in New York City, halfway houses were used to permit inmates a gradual readjustment to the community.

The major impetus for the modern movement toward supervision of the offender within the community was given by the Federal Prisoner's Rehabilitation Act of 1965 and by the President's Crime Commission, which stated in its 1967 report that the new direction in corrections recognized that crime and delinquency are community as well as individual failures. The commission saw the task of corrections as one of reintegrating offenders into the community, restoring family ties, assisting offenders to get an education or employment, and securing for them a place in the normal functioning of society. That requires changes in the community and in offenders. The Commission described the traditional methods of institutionalizing offenders as fundamentally deficient. It concluded that **reintegration** is likely to be more successful if we work with offenders in the community rather than confine them in prisons.[1]

In 1973 the National Advisory Commission on Criminal Justice Standards and Goals called for an increased emphasis on probation. The commission concluded, "The most hopeful move toward effective corrections is to continue to strengthen the trend away from confining people in institutions and toward supervising them in the community."[2]

Reintegration of the offender into the community is not a one-way process, however. The community must take an active role in the process of treating the offender. It might not be sufficient to try to reintegrate the offender into the community; the latter may need to change along with the offender. For example, if resources for reintegration are not available, they must be developed.

Some punishments that do not involve incarceration do not fall within the definition of **community-based corrections.** Fines and restitution are alternatives to incarceration, but they are not community-based corrections. The important factor in community-based corrections is the relationship between those involved in the program, both clients and staff, and the community. Community-based programs involve an element of supervision aimed at assisting the offender to reintegrate into the community. In some programs supervision may not be adequate, but it is the effort to supervise and improve that distinguishes community-based programs from fines and restitution, both of which could be combined with community-based corrections.

Community-based corrections should be distinguished from **diversion,** a process of directing the offender away from the criminal (or juvenile) systems and into other programs. Diversion occurs instead of, not in addition to, criminal court processing. Diversion has been used primarily in the processing of juveniles, but it may be used for adult offenders as well. The alcoholic or drug addict who is apprehended for petty theft might be counseled to enter a drug and alcohol treatment program in the community and told that successful completion of that program will result in criminal charges being dropped. That program could be a community-based treatment program.[3]

Diversion programs are not the focus of this chapter, in which the term *community-based corrections* refers to that process of involving convicted offenders in supervised programs aimed at reintegrating them into the community. These programs may be offered within prisons to prepare offenders for release. They may be programs outside the prisons to which offenders report on a part-time basis before their release from prison, or they may be programs provided for convicted offenders who are placed on probation or released on parole.

Community-based programs and supervision may be provided in residential facilities, such as community treatment centers, group homes, foster homes, or halfway houses. Foster homes and group homes may be used for juveniles who do not need specialized treatment programs but who have experienced difficulties living in their own homes. They may house juveniles who do need specialized programs, which may be provided in nonresidential community treatment centers, schools, or other institutions.

Halfway houses may be viewed as places for offenders nearing the end of their terms to live during a period of gradual reentry into society. The offender lives in a supervised environment but may leave that facility during the day to work or to participate in vocational, treatment, or educational programs.

Residential programs may be used for more than halfway programs. Some are viewed as long-term programs for offenders, usually juveniles, who need intensive treatment and supervision. Programs may be designed for offenders having particular needs. For example, some programs are limited to first offenders; others are limited to repeat offenders who do not function effectively without intensive supervision. Residential programs may include community treatment centers that provide housing and supervision for persons who have not been to prison, such as those who are on probation and need more supervision than may be provided in a nonresidential environment.

Some community treatment programs are nonresidential. Offenders live in their own homes or with relatives or friends but come to the treatment centers for individual or group therapy and for participation in seminars and other programs designed to assist them with adjustment problems.

Problems of Offenders on Release

The number of offenders involved in community-based programs has been increasing, with legislation indicating various reasons for providing such programs. One of the most important goals of community corrections, however, is rehabilitation, a concept that has ceased to be a primary goal of incarceration.[4]

Each year approximately 400,000 persons are released from prisons back into the community. Approximately 40 percent of those individuals will be apprehended again within three years.[5] Before offenders are placed in community corrections following time in prison, attention should be given to problems they will face. The problems vary considerably, but some are common. Inmates need street clothing when they are released from prison. Although most prisons provide clothing or permit inmates to receive clothing from home, usually this is insufficient. The prison may provide only one set of clothing; the inmate may not have family or friends who provide additional clothing. Even a prearranged job may not be much help, for the inmate will not get a paycheck for a week or longer.

Many prison systems give inmates a small amount of money upon release if they do not have any money. The amount varies from state to state but may be as low as $50. Usually, inmates get a bus ticket home. Out of these provisions, inmates who have no other financial resources must pay for additional clothing, room and board, and in many cases, debts incurred before incarceration and restitution. They may have families to support.

Employment is another problem faced by the released offender. Institutions may or may not provide offenders assistance in seeking employment. Inmates face social adjustments upon release. The day of release may be characterized by a sense of optimism, the belief that life will be different and more pleasant now. Release from prison has been called a positive life change, but people experience uncertainty, loneliness, depression, and disorganization as well.

For many ex-offenders, release from prison means frustration and anxiety over how to act and what to say in social situations and on the job. Feelings of helplessness, insecurity, fear, indecision, and depression may result in physical problems such as loss of appetite, chronic exhaustion, problems in sleeping, or sexual difficulties. Fear of the unknown may be particularly acute for the inmate who has not been able to maintain close ties with his or her family during incarceration.[6]

Relationships with family members may create problems for ex-offenders. Spouses and children suffer as a result of the offender's incarceration; anger and hostility may greet the offender who returns home. Years of absence, with few opportunities for family members to visit their loved ones in prison, may create interpersonal problems that are beyond repair. Financial hardships created by the absence of the offender may compound the interpersonal tensions.

Financial, economic, social, and other difficulties that inmates encounter on release from prison may be eased if adequate services are provided for ex-offenders by the community, but adequate preparation for release is important. Preparation may be made in various types of programs; those used most frequently are discussed briefly. Unfortunately, many prison systems do not provide sufficient preparation for inmates upon release from prison.

Furlough or Work Release

The first **work release** law was the Huber Law, passed in Wisconsin in 1913. The next statute was not passed until 1957 in North Carolina. The first **furlough** program was introduced by legislation in Mississippi in 1918. A few states passed laws providing for work release or furloughs before 1965, but most of the programs in existence today were established by state laws after the passage of the 1965 federal law, the Prisoner Rehabilitation Act.

It is necessary to distinguish work release programs from furlough programs. A furlough involves permitting the inmate to leave the institution once or occasionally for a specified purpose other than work or study. The offender may be given a furlough to visit a sick relative, to attend a family funeral, or to look for a job. The leave is temporary and is granted for a short period of time.

In work release programs, inmates are released from incarceration to work or to attend school. Inmates may participate in work study, take courses at an educational institution, or work at jobs in the community. Work release is referred to by other names as well: day parole, outmate program, day work, daylight parole, free labor, intermittent jailing, and work furlough. Work release is used more frequently than study release.

State legislation varies regarding who decides which inmates are placed on work release and whether inmates may retain any or all of the money they earn. Most legislation permits states to contract with other political subdivisions for housing of inmates who cannot find work near the institution. Some provide halfway houses or work-release centers, and some use county jails. Generally, inmates may not work in areas where there is a surplus of labor. They must be paid the same as others doing the same jobs. If a union is involved, it must be consulted, and the releasee may not work during a labor dispute.

Furlough and work release programs are important for several reasons. Work release programs enable offenders to engage in positive contacts with the community, assuming, of course, that work placement is satisfactory. They permit offenders to provide some support for themselves and their families. This can eliminate the self-concept of failure that may be the result of the loss of the supporter role, which is so important in American society. The offender may obtain more satisfying jobs than the prison could provide.

Work release and furlough programs provide a transition for the incarcerated inmate from a closely supervised way of life in prison to a more independent life within society. These programs give the community a transition period to accept offenders back into society. These programs have permitted some states to close one or more correctional facilities, thus decreasing the cost to taxpayers.

Problems with work release involve the selection process, finding sufficient jobs, gaining community acceptance, and most important, ensuring that inmates do not commit crimes while they are on release. There is no guarantee, of course, that offenders placed on furlough or work release will not commit crimes. In fact, the possibility that they will has led to community action to eliminate these methods of early release, but according to one survey several states reported a success rate of from 95 to 100 percent in their furlough programs.[7]

Over forty U.S. correctional systems have work release programs, and over thirty have educational release programs. Inmates participating in many of these programs are required to pay room and board, help support their families, pay fines and costs, or contribute to victims' compensation funds.[8]

One work release program was the focus of a recent report by the National Institute of Justice. The key findings of the study of the Washington system are

Spotlight 11.1

Washington State's Work Release Program: Key Findings

- Nearly a quarter of all prisoners released in Washington made a successful transition to the community through work release.

- Less than 5 percent of the work releasees committed new crimes while on work release, 99 percent of which were less serious property offenses, such as forgery or theft. However, with heightened supervision under strict conditions, many work releasees incurred infractions (most for rule violations and drug possession), and a quarter returned to prison. Thus, when one considers the reincarceration time spent by work release "failures," the time under correctional supervision was as long or longer for work release participants as for nonparticipants. And there were no differences in corrections costs between work releasees and inmates completing their full terms in prison. . . .

- Middle-aged offenders and offenders convicted of property crimes were most likely to participate in work release. Hispanic offenders were less likely to go to work release than white or African American offenders.

- Fifty-six percent of the 965 work releasees in the cohort studied were termed "successful"; they incurred no program infractions or arrests. Another 13.5 percent were "moderately successful"; their infractions were not serious enough to return them to prison. Almost 30 percent were "unsuccessful"; they returned to prison.

- Older offenders were more successful than younger ones, and whites were more successful than either Hispanics or African Americans. Success was also associated with having no prior criminal record.

Source: National Institute of Justice, *Work Release: Recidivism and Corrections Costs in Washington State* (Washington, D.C.: U.S. Department of Justice, December 1996), p. 1–2.

reported in Spotlight 11.1. The report noted that many work release programs were deleted because of the demise of federal funds once funneled to states through the now defunct Law Enforcement Assistance Administration. In Washington, however, the problem was eased by turning to private industry. Pioneer Human Services (PHS) works closely with the Washington Department of Corrections to provide and supervise jobs for inmates. PHS operates several facilities in which work release inmates live while involved in the program. Inmates are provided job training, housing, electronic monitoring, and employment. "PHS is highly regarded nationally and in the State and was recognized by President Bush in 1992 as one of the Nation's "Points of Light.""[9]

Prerelease Programs

Before release, all inmates should have an opportunity to participate in prerelease programs. It is unreasonable to expect that the difficulties faced by releasees will be solved by inmates without any assistance from counselors and other professionals.

Prerelease centers are another solution for preparing inmates who have serious adjustment problems but who are being released because they have completed their terms. In a residential environment that provides more supervision than offenders would have under probation or parole but less than they experienced in prison, releasees may be able to make the adjustment to freedom gradually enough to succeed upon final release. In these cases, for a specified period before their release, inmates would be transferred to prerelease facilities to finish their terms. The housing facility alone, however, is not sufficient for most inmates. Ideally, those facilities would provide the full range of services needed to prepare inmates for release, including meaningful work opportunities.

Preparation of inmates for release is not sufficient to ensure that they will make adequate adjustments when they leave prison. Their families need to be prepared for the adjustments that they must make upon the return of the inmates. Counseling for families should be provided. Despite the need for preparing inmates and their families for release, many prison systems are releasing inmates early to provide room for others ready for incarceration. Little if any efforts are made to prepare these inmates or their families for release.

Probation and parole are the most frequently used alternatives to prison and probably the most controversial. Probation is a sentence that does not involve confinement but may involve conditions imposed by the court, usually under the supervision of a **probation officer.**

The term *probation* is used also to refer to the status of a person placed on probation, to refer to the subsystem of the criminal justice system that handles this disposition of offenders, and to designate a process that refers to the activities of the probation system: preparing reports, supervising probationers, and providing or obtaining services for probationers.

Parole refers to the release of persons from correctional facilities after they have served part of their sentences. It is distinguished from *unconditional release,* which occurs when the full sentence (or the full sentence minus time reduced for good time credits) has been served. Parolees are placed under supervision, and conditions are imposed on their behavior.

Probation and parole permit a convicted person to live in the community under supervision. Probation and parole are based on the philosophy that the rehabilitation of some individuals might be hindered by imprisonment (or further imprisonment) and may be aided by supervised freedom. The processes differ in that parole is granted after a portion of the prison term is served, whereas probation is granted in lieu of incarceration. Probation is granted by the judge. Usually, parole is granted by a **parole board** appointed or elected specifically for that purpose.

In recent years probation and parole have come under severe attack, and many attempts have been made to reduce the number of people who are permitted to participate. However, the programs have not been cut back as severely as some had hoped, primarily because of overcrowded prisons and jails. Problems arise; security of the community and supervision cost are the two biggest.

Despite these problems, probation and parole are important elements of criminal justice systems, with probation the most widely used sentence. Almost four million of the 5.5 million adults under correctional supervision in the United States in 1996 were on probation or parole. Perhaps even more surprising was that 60 percent of all convicted sex offenders under the control of correctional authorities were on probation or parole.[10]

Figure 11.1 graphs the distribution of persons under correctional supervision from 1980–1996, showing the differences between those on probation and those incarcerated in prisons. Note how the differences between these two categories increased significantly during that period.

The gender and race distributions of those on probation and parole should be noted as well. Although men constitute the greatest percentage on probation and parole, the number of women is growing faster as the number of women arrested grows significantly. In 1996 women constituted 21 percent of all probationers and 11 percent of those on parole, up from 18 percent and 8 percent, respectively, in

Probation and Parole: An Overview

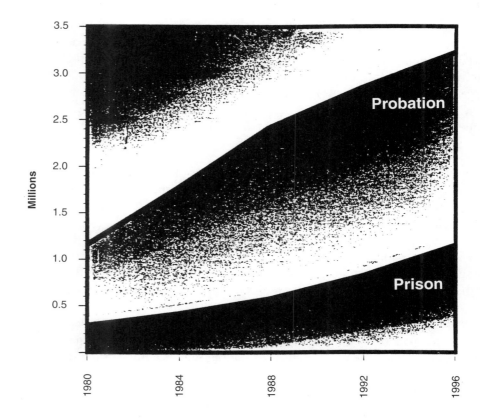

Figure 11.1 Probation and Prison Populations in the United States: 1980–1996.
Source: National Institute of Justice Journal, *Probation in the United States: Practices and Challenges* (Washington, D.C.: U.S. Department of Justice (September 1997), front cover.

1990. African Americans constituted a little over one-third of all probationers and almost one-half of all parolees in 1996, with Hispanics constituting 15 percent of probationers and 20 percent of parolees.[11]

Probation

Scholars do not agree on the origins of probation, but some trace it to English common law. The earliest use of a system that resembled probation was the concept of *benefit of clergy*. The church maintained that it had sole jurisdiction over members of the clergy. If the clergy committed crimes, they were not to be subjected to the criminal courts but were to be handled by the church courts.

Henry II objected to this system and insisted that clerics suspected of crimes should be tried in secular courts. A compromise was worked out, providing that clergy accused of crimes would be tried in secular courts but with benefit of clergy. That meant that their bishops could claim dispensation for them. The charge would be read, but the state would not present evidence against the accused cleric, who was permitted to give his view of the accusation and bring witnesses. With the only evidence coming from witnesses chosen by the accused, it is understandable that most cases resulted in acquittals.

Benefit of clergy was extended later to all church personnel as protection against capital punishment, and eventually to all people who could read. The ability to read signified the person's association with the church. To test the clerical character, the accused was given a psalm, usually the fifty-first, to read. Those who demonstrated an ability to read were released from secular courts and turned over to the ecclesiastical courts. This procedure was used to mitigate the harsh sentences of the criminal law, but due to severe abuse it fell into disfavor. Subsequently, parliament declared that certain acts would be felonies "without benefit of clergy." Eventually, the procedure was abandoned.

In the United States probation is traced to John Augustus, a prosperous Boston shoemaker. He asked that offenders be given their freedom within the community under his supervision. Massachusetts responded with a statute in 1878. By 1900 six states had probation statutes; by 1915, thirty-three states had statutes providing for adult probation; and by 1957 all states had probation statutes. In 1925 a statute authorizing probation in federal courts was passed.[12]

Types of Probation

We have noted that probation is the sentence used most frequently, but it is important to look more closely at the types of probation. This discussion considers felony probation, house arrest, and shock probation combined with periodic sentencing.

Although generally probation is considered appropriate only for offenders convicted of minor offenses, in some jurisdictions probation is used for *serious* offenders, a process referred to as *felony probation.*

Earlier studies by the Rand Corporation disclosed that many felony probationers committed crimes while on probation. Thus, they are **recidivists.** In 1985 the Rand Corporation published the results of its study of 16,000 felons on probation. Over a forty-month period, the research team tracked 1,671 felons; a total of 2,608 criminal charges had been filed against them. Of the felony probationers, 65 percent were arrested, 51 percent were convicted, and 34 percent were returned to jail or prison. Most of the offenses committed by the probationers were serious. The director of the Rand study warned that this information should not be used to abolish probation. Rather, it should be used to assess the problems we have created by increasing the use of probation rapidly without adequate increases in funds and staff. "No single human can adequately evaluate, report on, and supervise 300 criminals at a given time."[13]

The Rand Corporation study concluded that probation in its current form was not successful, but the researchers emphasized that sending felons to overcrowded prisons would not solve the problem either. They suggested alternatives:

> The answer may be intensive surveillance programs that include intense monitoring and supervision, real constraints on movement and action, requirement of employment, mechanisms to immediately punish infractions, and added requirements of community service, education, counseling, and therapy.[14]

Studies in other states reveal that some felony probation programs are more successful than those evaluated by Rand. After reviewing the Rand research and studies of more successful programs, such as those in Kentucky and Missouri, one scholar used data from New Jersey to examine the effectiveness of felony probation programs. He recommended that more attention be given to such problems of probationers as drug abuse and employment and that the studies of felony probation be scrutinized more carefully:

> The major conclusion is that probation is an acceptable sentencing alternative for some felony offenders in some states but that recidivism rates can be alarmingly high for particular categories of offenders.[15]

Probation may be combined with **house arrest** (or home detention or confinement), a relatively recent development in the United States, dating back only a couple of decades.[16] Offenders who are confined by house arrest are placed under specific restrictions. They may live at home or in another designated facility, but they may leave only under specified conditions.

In some jurisdictions house arrest is accompanied by electronic monitoring, in which monitors are attached to the offender, usually to the ankle or the wrist. The devices are monitored by probation officers or other personnel who can determine whether the probationer leaves home (or another area of confinement, such as place of employment) during restricted hours.[17] Although electronic monitors were not developed until 1984, when they were first used in Florida,[18] by 1990 they were utilized in all fifty states.[19]

Some empirical research is available on the use of electronically monitored home confinement. An earlier study concluded that the operation of electronic equipment was successful; most local criminal justice personnel accepted the program; no serious legal problems appeared to develop when the plan was used as an alternative to detention. A significant savings resulted when the cost of electronic monitoring was compared to that of detention.[20]

Social scientists emphasize that more time and experience are required for thorough evaluation of the benefits of this approach and that it is dangerous to assume that electronic monitoring will alleviate prison overcrowding:

> Although the technology may be a useful tool in the repertoire of the criminal justice system, it is not the sole remedy for the overcrowding problem and cannot serve as a substitute for sound correctional policy making.[21]

In a recently published analysis of three electronic monitoring programs, researchers emphasize that there are significant differences in the behavior of program administrators as well as participants of each program. Thus, any evaluations must take into account these differences, such as the ability of administrators to detect and apprehend violators. The types of participants involved and the nature of the programs are other issues that must be considered.[22]

Electronic monitoring is used extensively with abusers of alcohol and other drugs. It has been noted already in this text that substance abuse violations have increased in number and swelled prison populations as well as court dockets. Many jurisdictions have turned to treatment alternative programs combined with electronic monitoring in these cases. One problem is that the dropout rate is high for drug treatment programs, an issue that should be addressed.[23]

The use of electronic monitoring with driving-while-intoxicated offenders has been studied by several scholars who report that the program is cost effective; most of the clients completed their respective programs successfully; but the probation success rates declined during the period after the program was completed.[24]

Another problem with electronic monitoring is that it may be utilized without sufficient inquiry into the legal implications of this type of surveillance. Two recent lawsuits illustrate the civil implications of recidivism among offenders released with electronic monitoring. In both of these cases plaintiffs alleged that the equipment was not maintained properly and that officials knew the bracelets broke down repeatedly. Some judges in the districts in which the cases occurred stopped ordering electronic monitoring as a result of these crimes, stating that they had lost faith in the system. In the first case, a Chicago jury awarded $3 million to the estate of a fireman, a brother of Philadelphia 76ers all-star Maurice Cheeks. Cheeks was murdered by a gang, one of whom had succeeded in removing his electronic bracelet.[25]

The second case involves the murder of Holly Staker, an eleven-year-old babysitter. The suit claims she was attacked by a convicted burglar, Juan Rivera, who had slipped off his electronic monitor. Rivera was convicted of stabbing the sitter twenty-seven times and raping her as she died and the child looked on. He was sentenced to life in prison, but the conviction was overturned for technical reasons. Prosecutors announced in September of 1997 that they would seek the death penalty, although it was unclear whether it is legal to seek a stiffer sentence on retrial.[26] Rivera's trial was scheduled to begin 14 September 1998.

One final argument against house arrest (electronic monitoring) is that the sentence is too lenient, but, with or without electronic monitoring, house arrest may be accompanied by **intensive probation supervison (IPS),** discussed on p. 320. And probation may be combined with fines or restitution as well as house arrest. It may also be combined with brief sentences, which constitutes the third type of system.

Some statutes permit sending offenders to prison for a short period of time and then placing them on probation. It is assumed that this procedure will shock the offender into appropriate behavior. This process is called *shock probation,* although technically that term is incorrect because probation is an *alternative* to incarceration. The purpose of shock probation is to expose offenders to the shock of prison before placing them on probation and to release them before they are influenced negatively by the prison experience.

Shock probation programs have existed for a couple of decades, but most of today's programs are called *boot camps,* which were discussed in Chapter 9. The concept is relevant here, too, as frequently it is combined with supervision after release.[27]

Probation may be combined with a jail term, a procedure called *periodic sentencing.* The offender may be confined to jail during the night but be permitted to go to work or school during the day. The jail term might be served on weekends only, with the offender, although under some probation terms, free to move about in the community during the week. The weekend alternative has been used frequently for offenders who have been convicted of driving while intoxicated, particularly in jurisdictions in which jails are crowded and the offender has a steady job.

Probation Administration

In most jurisdictions probation administration is a court function, meaning that it is located in the judicial branch of government. It is possible, however, that various courts within a particular jurisdiction will have probation departments, resulting in an overlap of services and other administrative problems. Other jurisdictions may have a statewide probation system with branches at the city and county levels.[28]

Probation departments may be found in the executive branch, too, reporting to the governor in the case of statewide systems. Probation departments differ in size and complexity and in the extent and quality of services that they provide for clients. Thus, it is not possible to define a typical probation department.

One division of the probation department provides services to courts. Usually, the presentence investigation (PSI) is prepared by the probation department through interviewing clients and related parties, investigating and compiling materials relevant to each case, and developing recommendations for the sentencing body. In addition, the department provides the court with processing and reporting services for probation cases. This section keeps records of all persons on probation, the status of their probation, whether probation has been revoked, and other pertinent data.

Probation departments provide services for probation clients, too. Counseling, referral to other community sources, and supervision are the most common services provided by probation departments to their clients. Counseling alcoholics and the families of alcoholics is a service offered by some probation departments.[29]

Many probation departments are headed by a chief probation officer who has functions typical of a chief executive officer of any organization. The primary responsibility for hiring, training, and firing probation officers and for managing all sections of the probation department is in the hands of this officer. The chief probation officer has public relations functions as well, working with community leaders, attorneys, police officers, and court personnel.

If the probation department is large enough, it may have an assistant chief probation officer, who reports to the chief probation officer and may be assigned such responsibilities as coordinating volunteer efforts and administering the department. A supervisor might be in charge of coordinating the efforts of those who prepare the PSIs, assign cases, and handle other administrative functions.

Probation officers work directly with probationers. These officers should have training in the various aspects of probation work, including skills in interpersonal relationships. They provide counseling for probationers and perform the function of surveillance to determine whether their clients are violating probation conditions.

Probation officers do most of the investigative work in preparing the PSI and may be required to make a sentence recommendation to the judge before sentencing. This function of being involved in the sentencing decision and then in supervising the probationer may present problems. Probationers may resent the position the probation officer has in relationship to the judge. Furthermore, it is questionable whether probation officers can be effective counselors while being responsible for surveillance as well.

Average beginning salaries for probation officers are not high enough to attract many well-qualified people, particularly if the goal is to attract people who have baccalaureate degrees, as the National Advisory Commission recommended in its report. Efforts must be made to raise salaries and to improve working conditions for probation officers. Opportunities to work in federal probation systems are discussed in Professions 11.1.

Probation Conditions

The purpose of probation is to assist offenders in making social adjustments and in reintegrating into society as law-abiding citizens. Therefore the policy has been to impose restrictions on the offender's freedom. Restrictions differ from jurisdiction to jurisdiction, but some are common to all.

It is customary to require probationers to report to an officer periodically at specified times and places; the officer may visit the client, too. Probationers may change residence only with the permission of the supervising officer. They must work (or attend school or some other approved activity); if those plans are changed, the changes must be reported. In some cases they will not be allowed to make changes without prior permission of the supervising officer or court.

Most probationers are required to submit periodic reports of their activities and progress. They may be restricted in the use of alcoholic beverages (or prohibited from using them) and appearance in bars or other questionable places. They may be required to submit to periodic drug testing if the facts of their cases suggest drug violations.[30] They are not permitted to use drugs. They are not permitted to own, possess, use, sell, or have deadly weapons or firearms under their control. Their associations are restricted.

In some jurisdictions, probationers are not permitted to drive an automobile; in others, driving is permitted only with prior permission of the supervising officer. Normally, they may not leave the county or state without permission, which is granted infrequently and only for extraordinary reasons. Probationers are required to refrain from violating laws, and they must cooperate with their probation officers. In some cases curfews or restrictions on where they may live are imposed. Their civil rights may be affected as well. Usually, they are not permitted to marry, engage in business, or sign contracts without permission.

PROFESSIONS 11.1

Federal Probation Services

Most people who are under the supervision of criminal justice systems are on probation. Theoretically, they are supervised by probation officers. These officers perform a variety of functions and offer young people interesting and challenging career choices. This Professions focuses on the federal probation system, which was the subject of a 1997 issue of *Federal Probation*. Reference is made to several specialities within the federal probation system.

The Function of Federal Probation Officers[1]

Probation officers have two basic duties: presentence investigations and the supervision of offenders. Both require written and oral skills, a broad understanding of criminal justice systems, knowledge of federal probation and parole systems, knowledge of the federal prison system, federal sentencing guidelines, federal case law, and an ability to work with diverse populations.

Presentence investigations require a probation officer to prepare for the court a document that includes information on the offense in question, the offender's history and personal characteristics, sentencing options, and the application of federal sentencing guidelines. Collecting and analyzing the data may require extensive time by the officer, who must make recommendations regarding the potential risk of the offender as well as the need for restitution, treatment, or other options. Probation officers engage in these reports by interviewing the offender and other persons and reading available documents and analyzing other evidence.

The Function of Federal Pretrial Services Officers[2]

Federal pretrial services officers also have two main functions: investigation and supervision. They investigate each offender in order to recommend to the court whether the individual should be released pending trial.

If the offender is released, they provide supervision for some but not all offenders. The court may determine that some offenders do not pose a threat to themselves or to society and can be predicted to show up for trial; thus, they need no supervision.

Pretrial services officers also attend court sessions concerned with pretrial services and detention. They prepare release status reports for the courts. These reports summarize the offender's compliance with prerelease orders and make recommendations for release or detention if the offender is released after sentencing and pending an appeal. Supervision may include meeting with offenders to counsel them about the details of their release, the need to attend treatment programs for the abuse of alcohol or other drugs, other treatment programs, job opportunities, and so on.

To be eligible for the position, an applicant must have a bachelor's degree in an academic subject such as sociology, criminology or criminal justice, psychology, or some other social science, although occasionally those with majors in other disciplines, such as business, are hired. Many individuals working as pretrial services officers have graduate degrees, and many of the federal officers have had experience at the local or state levels.

Substance Abuse Specialists[3]

Most probation officers must deal with offenders who have abused alcohol or other drugs, but the substance abuse specialist is a senior-level officer "whose job is to oversee (or assist . . .) and manage the offices' substance abuse program." This person is in charge of the budget for substance abuse, which includes the contracts for substance abuse treatment programs. He or she may provide in-service training for those who supervise offenders with drug problems: the individual may or may not have his or her own case load.

1. Adapted from John P. Storm, "What United States Probation Officers Do," *Federal Probation* 61 (March 1997): 13–18.
2. Adapted from Thomas J. Wolf, "What United States Pretrial Services Officers Do," *Federal Probation* 61 (March 1997): 19–24.
3. Adapted from Edward M. Read, "Challenging Addiction: The Substance Abuse Specialist," *Federal Probation* 61 (March 1997): 25–26.

Probation conditions may be severe, but in the past they were considered by most offenders to be preferable to prison. Today, however, with actual prison time reduced in some jurisdictions due to prison overcrowding, some inmates choose a prison term over probation. In making that choice, one offender stated that he did not believe he could comply with his probation conditions for a three-year period. His lawyer advised that if he took the fifteen-month prison term instead, he would "probably just ride the bus up there (to prison), get my paperwork done and then come back home. It made sense to me."[31]

Legal Limits on Probation Conditions

Just as courts have been reluctant to interfere with daily prison administration, traditionally they have taken a hands-off policy toward the imposition of probation conditions as well. In recent years, however, courts have rejected some restrictions as constituting improper restraints on probationers' rights.

Two recent cases illustrate constitutional issues with regard to probation conditions. A federal court in Illinois has held that it was reasonable for a court to order a probationer to get a paying job rather than become a missionary. The probationer had been ordered to pay restitution and fines after conviction of a series of religious scams. A federal court in New York has held that it is unconstitutional to require a convicted drunk driver to attend Alcoholics Anonymous (AA) meetings while on probation. The court noted the spiritual and religious nature of AA meetings and held that requiring one to attend them violated the probationer's First Amendment rights (see Appendix A).[32]

In contrast, a California court held that it is permissible to require a probationer to attend non-spiritual programs aimed at assisting with substance-abuse programs.[33]

Other recent cases demonstrate varying probation conditions approved by courts. The key is whether the conditions are reasonably related to the offense for which the individual is on probation. For example, normally a court could not require that a probationer abstain from sexual relations, especially if that requirement was not related to the crime at issue, but if the probationer is HIV-positive, the prohibition might be reasonable. A Texas judge placed an offender on probation for five years and required him to get a signed consent prior to a sexual relationship. The consent form, drafted by the judge, specified that the prospective sexual partner had been told by the probationer that he was HIV-positive and might transmit that virus to a sexual partner. The offender was convicted of stealing a car, for which he could have received a two-year prison term. A few months later the offender, who was given permission to go to Louisiana to settle personal problems and get medication, left Texas before completing his court-ordered community service and reporting to his probation officer. He was arrested in Louisiana and returned to Texas, where the judge who sentenced him originally found him guilty of violating two terms of his probation and sentenced him to twenty months in jail.[34]

An order requiring that a probationer "make every attempt to avoid being in contact with children," was held reasonable in a case involving an offender who was convicted of a sex crime against a twelve-year-old. The court held that the condition not only fell within the statutory provision "as the court, in its discretion, deems reasonably necessary to insure that the defendant will lead a law-abiding life or to assist him [or her] to do so." It met the provision that the court has discretion to require a defendant to "[s]atisfy any other conditions reasonably related to his [or her] rehabilitation."[35]

A probation order designed solely to embarass or humiliate an offender may not be upheld. A California judge "whose penchant for innovative sentencing has made him a media darling"[36] ordered an offender to wear a T-shirt proclaiming "I am on felony probation for theft." That condition was held to be a violation of the offender's right to privacy. The appellate court noted that the statute states that a purpose of probation is rehabilitation, but the condition in question was designed to expose the offender to public ridicule and humiliation. Further, the order would make it impossible for the offender to fulfill another probation condition, which was to get a job. The court stated that the condition

> could adversely affect [the probationer]'s ability to carry on activities having no possible relationship to the offense for which he was convicted or to future criminality. . . . The condition was unreasonably overbroad and as such was invalid.[37]

Likewise, requiring that one convicted of aggravated battery erect a large sign on his property stating, "WARNING! A violent felon lives here. Enter at your own risk," was held to be unreasonable. The condition might hinder the offender's rehabilitation as well as cause psychological problems for him and for the innocent members of his family. The sign was viewed as a "drastic departure" from the state's sentencing provisions.[38] Warnings might be appropriate, however, in some cases, such as those involving sex offenders, as the discussion on p. 330 notes.

One of the primary functions of the probation officer is to supervise probationers. The type and degree of supervision vary. In some probation departments it is the probation officer's job to counsel probationers. In other departments, a probation officer is expected to supervise only the activities of probationers, and that supervision may be limited. Which of these models is chosen may depend on the availability of resources, the caseloads of probation officers, their professional training, probationers' needs, and many other factors. Essentially, the officer's function is to assist the probationer in making important transitions—from law-abiding citizen to convicted offender; from free citizen to one under supervision; and finally, back to free citizen.

Probation Supervision

Some probation officers may prefer to have a close interpersonal relationship with the clients they are assisting. The literature contains numerous articles discussing ways in which probation officers may improve their supervisory relationships with their clients. Many articles discuss the expectation that probation officers will go beyond supervision and serve as treatment agents for their clients. Treatment of probationers may be multidimensional. Many probationers need to learn the social skills involved in successful interpersonal relationships. Most offenders have long histories of personal failures, and probation officers are crucial people in helping them build up their confidence in themselves and acquire the social skills and habits necessary for successful interpersonal relationships.

When probation officers go beyond supervision of their clients and begin a treatment process, some problems may occur. Many officers lack sufficient training in treatment techniques. Even if probation officers are trained and skilled in treatment techniques and are licensed for such work, the very nature of the position may preclude successful treatment. Because of the legal nature of probation work, realistically, probation officers may not promise the confidentiality that an effective treatment relationship needs. In reality, probation officers have a conflict of interest. The officers represent not only the interests of the state in taking action against violations of probation agreements or of the law, but they also represent the interests of clients in treatment and supervision.

Two recent developments present further problems for probation (and parole) supervision. The discovery and rapid spread of AIDS creates a need for additional education of supervisors as well as policy developments within probation departments. Some progress is being made in this area, but it is slow for many reasons such as low finances and lack of knowledge about the spread of HIV.[39]

A second area of concern is the legal liability issue. As Rolando V. del Carmen states, "The 'hands off' judicial doctrine is dead. In its place is a 'hands on' policy, which means the courts will consider cases brought by the public" against probation and parole officers as well as others who make decisions within criminal justice systems. Probation and parole officers should be trained in the legal issues of civil liability for the actions of their clients.[40]

Two areas of probation supervision are explored in more detail: intensive probation supervision, and issues relating to the search and seizure of probationers.

Intensive Probation Supervision

In the past, researchers debated the effect of the officer's caseload size on the success or failure of probationers. That issue is not settled, and many factors are important in determining what type of caseload is most efficient. Today the focus of probation has shifted in many jurisdictions. No longer is rehabilitation the primary purpose of probation. The function of probation is to divert from prison persons who might not need that intensive security and supervision, and through that diversion process, reduce the populations that are swelling prisons. It is argued that many offenders can succeed on probation if they are under intensive probation supervision (IPS).

Although there are a variety of models in use, IPS programs are available in all states and the federal government.[41] Intensive probation supervision programs developed in the 1960s. The earlier programs were studied, and two researchers have suggested that three conclusions may be drawn from those analyses:

1. Intensive supervision is difficult to achieve.
2. Close contact does not guarantee greater success.
3. Intensive supervision produces an interactive effect.

The third conclusion refers to the evidence that although IPS appears to assist some offenders, "it is entirely reasonable that intensive supervision might interfere with the functionings of some clients who would otherwise be successful."[42]

In a comparison of IPS clients with regular probation clients, it was found that the former had more technical probation violations, but that probably is the result of the fact that they are watched more closely. The IPS probation clients, however, were not more likely to be rearrested or incarcerated. But if IPS does not result in lower recidivism, why continue with the program, given its higher costs over minimal-supervision probation? Further research needs to be conducted, but one consideration is that probation conditions for IPS may be too severe. "We believe that these early results call for serious reconsideration of the conditions that ISP [Internal Supervision Program, another term for IPS] impose and monitor."[43]

In a later publication, the Rand Corporation researchers concluded the following about IPS:

> [I]f judged by a standard of zero risk, all [intensive supervision probation and parole] programs fail to protect public safety. However, what most of these programs try to achieve is a more stringent punishment for at least some of the serious offenders who now receive only nominal supervision. Judged by that criterion, virtually all of the sites succeeded.[44]

A research monograph that contains several articles on IPS, including a review of several specific programs and the research findings concerning those and other programs, concludes that we need more research on the effectiveness of IPS. Although there is some evidence that increased supervision decreases recidivism among some offenders, "there is mounting evidence that increased supervision of low-risk offenders actually increases their rate of failure." The researchers conclude that the "research issues are complex, but society can ill afford to let them go unanswered."[45]

IPS is expensive, and in order to provide better probation supervision for the most difficult probationers, New York City instituted a new probation supervision policy in 1993. Those most in need of supervision are required to attend four or more hours of therapy a week, while less risky probationers are required only to report regularly to automated kiosks.[46]

Search and Seizure

One of the most controversial aspects of probation (or parole) supervision is search and seizure. In 1987 in *Griffin* v. *Wisconsin* the U.S. Supreme Court ruled that probation officers may search probationer's homes without a search warrant if they have the approval of the probation supervisor and if there are reasonable grounds to believe that the probationer is in possession of contraband. In *Griffin* the probation officer received a tip that his probationer had a gun in his home, in violation of one of Wisconsin's probation conditions: probationers may not possess firearms without receiving advance approval from a probation officer. The Court held that the officer's subsequent search was permissible.[47]

Griffin involved a search under a state regulatory scheme, but in a more recent case the First Circuit Court of Appeals held that a state regulatory scheme is not necessary despite the fact that the state provisions would provide guidance to probation officers. "Similar guidance and constraints . . . are provided where . . . . a sentencing judge narrowly tailors the need for and scope of any problem search conditions to the circumstances of an individual case."[48] Similarly, in 1991 the Pennsylvania Superior Court held that based on an unwritten "pattern and practice," it is permissible for a parole officer to search the residence of any parolee arrested for violating parole conditions. The U.S. Supreme Court refused to hear the case on appeal.[49]

On the other hand, a 1994 decision by a federal court in New York held that parole officers acted improperly when they forced their way into a parolee's home and seized ammunition they had seen during an earlier visit to that home. The officers could have seized the items during their earlier visit, but they had no right to a subsequent forcible entry and seizure. In this case there were no federal statutes or regulations permitting the forced entry; nor had the parole commission imposed any search conditions on the parolee.[50]

One final area of search and seizure involves drug testing. A 1994 case decided by the Ninth Circuit held that it was improper for the lower court to require a defendant awaiting sentencing on a conviction of theft from a military base to submit to a urine test for drugs. There was no information that the defendant used or was otherwise involved with illegal drugs. The court held that in order to impose drug testing, there must be some indication that the testing is warranted. This case did not involve a probationer, but the rule of the case might be applied in that setting.[51]

Parole

Parole is an administrative decision to release an offender after he or she has served time on a sentence to a correctional facility. It may be distinguished from other methods of release from prison. Some inmates are released before serving their full sentences because they have accumulated good time credits given for good behavior during incarceration. The amount of prison time that may be reduced for good time credits is determined by prison policies or by legislation. Some offenders are not released from prison until they serve the full term imposed at sentencing; at the end of that term, they must be released. In addition, offenders may be released by means of a **pardon** granted by the governor of the state or the president of the United States.

Rehabilitation, justice, prison overcrowding: these are the three main reasons for parole in the United States, although any one of these has been emphasized in different places at different times. Some systems developed for the primary purpose of relieving prison overcrowding; some were for the purpose of rehabilitation. Ironically, the movement to abolish parole, a movement that paralleled the movement toward determinate sentencing in the late 1970s and 1980s, was propelled by the cry for justice, disillusionment with rehabilitation, and the argument that the lack of justice in the parole decision process hindered rehabilitation. Parole was called the "never-knowing system" by many inmates who argued that it was granted for arbitrary and capricious reasons.

Parole has come under severe attack in the United States primarily as the result of violent crimes committed by persons released on parole, as for example, the one discussed in Spotlight 11.2. After a decade of attempts, the federal criminal code was revised when President Reagan signed the Comprehensive Crime Control Act of 1984. That act abolished early release by parole in the federal system and, over a five-year period, phased out the U.S. Parole Commission. Under the new statute, inmates in the federal system may receive only a maximum of 15 percent good time credit on their sentences. Under the former statute, they were eligible for parole after serving only half of their sentences.[52]

Many states have abolished parole. In 1994 Virginia enacted a major overhaul of its criminal sentencing system and abolished parole, while requiring sentenced inmates to serve 85 percent of their time.[53] Some states that abolished parole have reinstituted parole release or other methods of release to cope with prison overcrowding. In 1995 the American Probation and Parole Association (APPA) and the Association of Paroling Authorities International (APAI) began an effort to counteract the public view that parole means the system is too lenient. These organizations emphasize that abolition of parole means that when offenders are released automatically (as they must be at the end of their terms), they are released without supervision, a situation far worse potentially than release on parole. Officials of the APPA and the APAI state emphatically that, "The abolition of parole has been tried and has failed on a spectacular scale."[54]

Organization of Parole Systems

The organization of parole is complex. One reason for this complexity is the variety of sentencing structures under which parole systems must operate. Sentencing structure is related to the parole system. In jurisdictions where sentences are long with little time off for good behavior, parole may involve a long supervision period. In jurisdictions where sentences are short, parole may be unimportant as a form of release, and supervision is for shorter periods.

Despite the wide variety of parole programs, three organizational models may be identified: the institutional, the independent, and the consolidated models. Under the *institutional model* found mainly in the juvenile field, the decision to release is made by the correctional staff. The assumption is that those who work closely with the offender are in the best position to make a decision concerning his or her release. Arguments against this model are that institutions may make decisions in their own best interests, not in the best interests of the offender or the

Spotlight 11.2

Paroled Murderer Convicted of Rape and Murder

In December 1969 Reginald McFadden and three other men were accused of killing a sixty-year-old woman during a burglary. McFadden was convicted and sentenced to life without parole. In 1992 McFadden's sentence was commuted by a four-to-one vote of the Pennsylvania Board of Parole, but the board required that he spend two years in a halfway house program. Due to mistakes in paperwork and a long delay by the governor's office in signing the appropriate papers, McFadden did not enter a halfway house; nor did he receive any other type of supervised release.

By October of 1994 McFadden was back in custody, charged with raping a fifty-five year old woman, who was kidnapped from her home while taking out the garbage, beaten, and raped repeatedly. On 27 March 1995 he was indicted for the murder of Robert Silk, who was abducted from his home and killed. He was convicted of these crimes and sentenced to prison.

In 1997 McFadden sued the Department of Corrections for $1.05 million in damages, claiming that through "gross negligence" they failed to rehabilitate him, thus causing the crimes he committed after his release. His case was dismissed and led to passage later in the year of Senate legislation that limits frivolous lawsuits filed by inmates. Pennsylvania's attorney general, in praising the bill, noted that the state is sued an average of ninety times a week, and many of those lawsuits are filed by inmates.[1]

After McFadden's rape conviction the victim, Jeremy Brown, made a public statement. Brown described herself as the "only living victim" of the defendant. She promised to work to change the state's parole law. Brown spoke angrily about the trial in which McFadden served as his own attorney. "I think it is perfectly ludicrous that I was tortured by this man for five hours and then to have to sit there and answer his ridiculous questions. . . . I think it's crazy."[2]

When he was sentenced in 1996, McFadden told the judge he was proud that he is the symbol of "everything that is wrong with society" and that he would take the life of the judge "as quick as you can blink your eye. . . . Think about that." In a sentencing the previous year McFadden told the judge not to give him any mercy. "If I was sitting where you are at, I wouldn't show you a bit of mercy."[3]

It is expected that McFadden will spend the rest of his life in prison.

Source: Summarized by the author from media sources.

1. "Pennsylvania Attorney General Fisher Applauds Legislation Limiting Frivolous Lawsuits," PR Newswire, State and Regional News (4 June 1997).
2. "Rape Victim Takes Spotlight and Aims It at Parole System," *New York Times* (25 August 1995), p. 1.
3. "Why We Need the Death Penalty," *The Record* (Bergen Record Corp. 15 April 1996), p. 16.

community. Decisions may be based on institutional overcrowding. Staff members may be less objective in the decisions because they are involved closely with the offender. Abuse of discretion may be a greater possibility under this model than in the independent authority model.

As a result of those two problems, many parole boards for adult correctional facilities follow the *independent authority model,* where the parole board is established as an agency independent of the institution. This model has been criticized severely. Often, the parole board is composed of people who know little or nothing about corrections. The board is removed from the institution and may not understand what is taking place there. Decisions may be made for inappropriate reasons, and as a result, parole boards may release those who should not be paroled and retain those who should be released.

Recently, a new model has emerged, a *consolidated model* of organization for parole boards, and there is a trend toward adopting it. This trend accompanies a move toward consolidating correctional facilities into one common administration, usually a department of corrections. Under the consolidated model, the parole-granting board is within the administration of the department of corrections but possesses independent powers.

It is important for parole board members to have an understanding of all correctional programs in the system. It is more likely that such understanding will occur under the consolidated model than under the other two models. However, the board should possess independence so that it can act as a check on the rest of the system.

With the exception of the institutional model, most parole systems are located in the executive branch of government and are administered at the state level. Most systems have one parole board, whose members are appointed by the executive branch. In most states that board has final authority to decide who is granted parole. In other states the board makes recommendations to someone else who has the final decision-making authority. That person might be the governor.

Some parole board members serve full-time; others serve part-time. They may or may not have specific qualifications for the position. As political appointees, they may be appointed for reasons unrelated to expertise in the kind of decision making that is the board's function. The board may have the authority to revoke as well as to grant parole.

The parole system has a division responsible for parole services, which includes parole supervision. Parole services may be delegated to smaller divisions throughout the state. Generally, the parole system provides some parole services at the institutions in which inmates are incarcerated. Often one person has the responsibility of interviewing all those eligible for parole and making written recommendations to the parole board.

Parole officers should have the same qualifications as probation officers. Increasingly, professional organizations and commissions are recommending that parole and probation officers hold a bachelor's degree, and some recommend that additional education should be required. In-service training is very important as well and should be continued throughout the officer's period of work and evaluated periodically. "Aspiring probation and parole professionals should obtain a broad, liberal arts education, augmented with productive employment in the system."[55]

The Parole Process

The parole process is very important, and adequate preparation should be made for the parole hearing. The ability of the inmate to convey an improved self-image and to demonstrate an ability to work with others and stick with a job may influence the board's decision. Inmates who have maintained strong family ties may have an edge in the decision-making process. Inmates who have had successful experiences on work release, education release, or furlough may have an advantage. A good behavior record in the institution may be viewed favorably.

Inmates should be told what to expect regarding timing of the decision and what kinds of questions they might anticipate. Demeanor and behavior are important; some inmates are put through mock decision-making situations to prepare them for the parole board hearing. It is important also to prepare the inmate for the parole board's decision. A negative decision may have a disastrous effect on an inmate who has not been prepared adequately for that result.

Eligibility for Parole

The determination of eligibility for parole varies, but usually there are statutory specifications such as requiring that inmates serve a certain percentage of their sentences before they are eligible for parole. Good time credits may reduce that period. Many jurisdictions require that inmates have job commitments before parole is granted; others grant parole on the condition that the inmate has a job by the time of parole release.

The Parole Hearing

The candidate may appear before the entire board or only a committee of the parole board. Larger boards may split into smaller groups to process paroles faster. Usually, the parole hearing is held at the institution where the inmate is incarcerated. However, if only a few are eligible, those inmates might be transported by the state to a central location for the hearing.

Many parole systems allow the inmate to participate in the hearings, although that participation might be very short. This gives inmates a greater sense of fairness in that they have an opportunity to express to the board members their perceptions of their chances for success.

Numerous factors may be considered in a parole decision. Those factors require information from the past, present, and future. They include statements made by the sentencing judge concerning the reasons for sentencing, as well as the inmate's plans for the future. They include disciplinary action, if any, that has occurred during the inmate's incarceration. Documentation on changes in attitude and ability are important. The crime for which the inmate is serving time, along with any prior experience on parole or probation, is considered as well. Family relationships, ability to get along with others, and jobs are important, too.

Parole Board Discretion

Historically, parole boards have had almost total discretionary power in determining parole. Parole was viewed as a privilege, not a right. Because parole was not a right, no reasons had to be given for denial. Elements of due process were not required at the time the decision was made.[56] Courts reasoned that due process was not required at the determination of parole because parole granting is not an adversary proceeding. Parole granting is a complicated decision, and the parole board must be able to use evidence that would not be admissible in an adversary proceeding such as a trial.

The general lack of due process at the parole decision stage resulted in bitter complaints from inmates. Perhaps the late Justice Hugo Black of the U.S. Supreme Court best summarized the view of many inmates toward the parole board:

> In the course of my reading—by no means confined to law—I have reviewed many of the world's religions. The tenets of many faiths hold the deity to be a trinity. Seemingly, the parole boards by whatever names designated in the various states have in too many instances sought to enlarge this to include themselves as members.[57]

Due Process and the Parole Hearing

The Fourteenth Amendment (see Appendix A) prohibits the denial of life, liberty, or property without due process of law. Claims by inmates for due process at the parole decision are based on the argument that they have a liberty interest in parole. The Supreme Court has held that, although there is no constitutional right to parole, statutes may create a protected liberty interest. When that is the case, parole may not be denied if the conditions of those statutes are met.

How do we know whether a protected liberty interest has been created and therefore due process is required? According to the Court, if the state creates a parole system and provides that, if certain conditions are met by inmates, they are entitled to parole, a liberty interest has been created. Under those circumstances, the state has created a presumption that inmates who meet certain requirements will be granted parole. If the statute is general, however, giving broad discretion to the parole board, no liberty interest is created.

In *Greenholtz* v. *Nebraska* the U.S. Supreme Court examined the Nebraska statute, which provided for two hearings before a final parole decision. At the first hearing, an informal one, the inmate is interviewed, and all relevant information in the files is considered. If the board decides the inmate is not ready for parole, parole is denied and the inmate is given reasons. If the board finds evidence that the inmate might be ready for parole, it notifies the inmate of a formal hearing, at which time the inmate may present evidence, call witnesses, and be represented by retained counsel.

In *Greenholtz* the Court found that a liberty interest was created by the Nebraska statute but that the procedures required by the statute met due process requirements. "The Nebraska procedure affords an opportunity to be heard and when parole is denied it informs the inmate in what respects he falls short of qualifying for parole; this affords the process that is due under these circumstances. The Constitution does not require more."[58]

In 1987, while analyzing the Montana parole statute, the Court reaffirmed its holding in *Greenholtz* that, although the existence of a parole system does not by itself give rise to an expectation of parole, states may create that expectation or presumption by the wording of the statute. In *Board of Pardons* v. *Allen,* the Court held that the Montana statute, like the Nebraska statute examined in *Greenholtz,* creates an expectation of parole, provided certain conditions are met. Thus, if those conditions are met, parole must be granted.[59]

In both of these cases, the Supreme Court emphasized that the language—the use of the word *shall* rather than *may*—creates the presumption that parole will be granted if certain specified conditions are met. Thus, the Court injected some procedural requirements into the parole-granting process in those states that use mandatory language in their parole statutes.

Control of Parole Decisions

Parole boards are criticized by inmates, and many scholars find some parole decisions to be arbitrary and capricious. Criticism of parole decisions has led to the suggestion that some restrictions be placed on this important decision-making process.

In the 1920s sociologists developed prediction scales to be used in situations such as predicting success in marriage. Some of the scales were adapted for the parole decision. Charts involved factors such as age, education, and prior criminal record to predict whether most inmates with those characteristics would be successful if paroled. The application of prediction scales yielded conflicting results, although the various approaches are difficult to compare.[60] The only general conclusion that might be drawn from statistical prediction studies is that it may be easier to predict nonviolent than violent crime.

Social scientists have used the clinical approach to prediction as well, looking at the specific characteristics of a particular inmate and trying to predict whether that person would be successful on parole. Generally, this approach has led to overprediction of dangerousness, which means that fewer inmates who are thought to be dangerous actually are.[61]

Another method of control over parole is to require written reasons for denying parole. In the past most parole boards did not give reasons for denial, and courts did not require them to do so. Today some jurisdictions that have retained parole require that reasons be given for its denial. Although the result may be only a checklist given to the inmate, this information lets the inmate know what is required for a successful parole hearing in the future.

Parole guidelines are used as a method of control over parole decision making. Not only has the use of system-wide guidelines given inmates a feeling of greater fairness in the parole process, but also, in some states, guidelines have had the advantage of being used to reduce prison overcrowding. Critics of objective guidelines for parole decision making argue that they do not result in greater fairness and may actually increase prison overcrowding.

Parole Conditions

Parole conditions are an essential element of the release process. The Supreme Court has stated

> The essence of parole is release from prison, before the completion of sentence, on the condition that the prisoner abide by certain rules during the balance of the sentence. . . .

> [T]he conditions of parole . . . prohibit, either absolutely or conditionally, behavior that is deemed dangerous to the restoration of the individual into normal society.[62]

Parole conditions vary from jurisdiction to jurisdiction and are similar to probation conditions. Many parole conditions have been challenged in court. They are valid, however, if they are reasonably related to the crimes in question, not against public policy, and if it is reasonably possible for the parolee to comply with them.

Parole Supervision

When inmates are released from prison on parole, they must report to a parole supervisor or **parole officer.** They are told the circumstances under which they are to report, how often, when and where to file reports, and what to expect regarding visits from parole officers.

Parole supervision has come under attack. The surveillance function of parole officers may be undermined by large caseloads; officers may not have time for anything more than brief contacts with their parolees. Because of this, some argue that home visits and monthly reports are costly and useless devices for control of parolee behavior and that this function would be better performed by police. Changing the conditions of parole supervision is another suggested reform. Conditions that have only slight relevance to criminal behavior could be eliminated. This change would leave parole officers free to concentrate on the service aspect of supervision: helping with employment, housing, and other adjustments in the community.[63]

Probation and Parole Revocation

Historically, **probation** or **parole revocation** occurred without due process hearings. In probation cases in which the offender had been sentenced to prison but the judge suspended the sentence and placed the offender on probation, violation of probation conditions resulted in incarceration to serve the original sentence.

In 1967 in *Mempa* v. *Rhay,* the Supreme Court held that when sentencing has been deferred and the offender placed on probation, revocation of that probation and determination of a sentence of incarceration require the presence of counsel. The Court reasoned that this situation, in which in reality the offender is being sentenced, invokes the requirement that "at every stage of a criminal proceeding where substantial rights of a criminal accused may be affected" counsel is required. This case and others pertinent to probation and parole revocation are summarized in Spotlight 11.3. Probation revocation that does not involve deciding a sentence, however, does not always require counsel, although there are some due process requirements, which are discussed later.

Like probation, historically parole revocation was conducted with little concern for due process. Lack of due process was justified on the basis that parole was a privilege, not a right, or that it involved a contract. The inmate contracted to behave in exchange for freedom from incarceration. If that contract were broken, the inmate could be returned to prison. Others argued that parole is a status of continuing custody, during which the offender is subject to prison rules and regulations; thus revocation requires no greater due process than that required for any action against the inmate while incarcerated.

In 1972 in *Morrissey* v. *Brewer,* the Supreme Court looked at parole revocation in the case of two offenders, Morrissey and Booher. Morrissey's parole was revoked for these allegations:

1. He bought a car under an assumed name and operated it without permission.
2. He gave false statements to police concerning his address and insurance company after a minor accident.
3. He obtained credit under an assumed name.
4. He failed to report his place of residence to his parole officer.

Booher's parole was revoked because allegedly he had

1. Violated the territorial restriction of his parole without consent.
2. Obtained a driver's license under an assumed name.
3. Operated a motor vehicle without permission.
4. Violated the employment condition of his parole by failing to keep himself in gainful employment.[64]

No hearing was held before parole was revoked in these two cases. In its discussion of the cases, the Court made several findings. According to the Court, the purpose of parole is rehabilitation. Until parole rules are violated, an individual may remain on parole, and parole should not be revoked unless those rules are violated. Parole revocation does not require all due process rights of a criminal trial, but some due process elements must be observed. Informal parole revocation hearings are proper, and the requirements of due process for parole revocation change with particular cases.

In *Morrissey* the Court enumerated the minimum requirements for revocation; they are reproduced in Spotlight 11.3. The Court ruled also that there should be two hearings before the final decision is made. The first is to determine whether there is probable cause to support a parole violation. At the second and more formal hearing, the final decision is made whether to revoke parole.

One year after *Morrissey* the Court extended these minimum due process requirements to probation revocation, but in *Gagnon* v. *Scarpelli,* in addition, the Court discussed the issue of whether counsel would be required at probation and parole revocation. The Court had not decided that issue in *Morrissey.* In *Gagnon* the Court held that there might be some cases in which counsel is necessary in order for the offender to have a fair hearing, but counsel is not constitutionally required in all revocation cases.[65]

Two other cases of significance to revocation hearings are summarized in Spotlight 11.3. Taken together, *Bearden* v. *Georgia* and *Black* v. *Romano* demonstrate that there are some restrictions on probation revocation. In *Bearden* the Court held that it was improper to revoke the probation of an indigent who had not paid a fine and restitution unless there was a finding that the indigent had not

Spotlight 11.3

Due Process and Parole and Probation Revocation: The Supreme Court Responds

Mempa v. *Rhay,* 389 U.S. 128 (1967)

A probationer is entitled to be represented by appointed counsel at a combined revocation and sentencing hearing. This is because sentencing is a stage of the actual criminal proceeding, "where substantial rights of a criminal accused may be affected."

Morrissey v. *Brewer,* 408 U.S. 471 (1972)

Before parole can be revoked, the parolee is entitled to two hearings. The first is a preliminary hearing at the time of arrest and detention, and is for the purpose of determining whether there is probable cause to believe that parole has been violated. The second hearing is a more comprehensive hearing that must occur before making a decision to revoke parole.

Minimum due process requirements at that second hearing are

1. Written notice of the alleged violations of parole
2. Disclosure to the parolee of the evidence of violation
3. Opportunity to be heard in person and to present evidence as well as witnesses
4. Right to confront and cross-examine adverse witnesses unless good cause can be shown for not allowing this confrontation
5. Right to judgment by a detached and neutral hearing body
6. Written statement of the reason for revoking parole, and of the evidence used in arriving at that decision

The court did not decide whether retained or appointed counsel is required at a parole revocation hearing.

Gagnon v. *Scarpelli,* 411 U.S. 778 (1973)

The minimum due process requirements enumerated in *Morrissey* v. *Brewer* apply to revocation of probation. A probationer is entitled to the two hearings before revocation.

The Court considered the issue of whether counsel is required and held that there is no constitutional right to counsel at revocation hearings, and that the right to counsel should be determined on a case-by-case basis. The Court left the matter of counsel to the discretion of parole and probation authorities and indicated in part that an attorney should be present when required for fundamental fairness. An example might be a situation in which the parolee or probationer is unable to communicate effectively.

Bearden v. *Georgia,* 461 U.S. 660 (1983)

The state may not revoke probation in the case of an indigent who has failed to pay a fine and restitution, unless there is a determination that the probationer has not made a bona fide effort to pay or that there were not adequate alternative forms of punishment. "Only if alternate measures are not adequate to meet the state's interests in punishment and deterrence may the court imprison a probationer who has made sufficient bona fide efforts to pay."

Black v. *Romano,* 471 U.S. 606 (1985)

The due process clause generally does not require a sentencing court to indicate that it considered alternatives to incarceration before revoking probation. This case did not involve the indigency issue regarding failure to pay a fine and restitution, as did the *Bearden* case.

---

made a sufficient effort to pay. Even then, the court must look at other alternatives before revoking probation and incarcerating the offender. But in *Romano,* when the offender's probation was revoked because he was charged with leaving the scene of an automobile accident (a felony), the Court held that due process did not require that, before incarcerating the offender on the original sentence, other sentencing alternatives be considered.[66]

It is clear from these decisions, read in conjunction with those involving the decision whether to grant parole, that the Court sees a significant difference between granting parole and revoking parole. The Court states it this way:

> The Court has fashioned a constitutional distinction between the decision to revoke parole and the decision to grant or to deny parole. Arbitrary revocation is prohibited by *Morrissey* v. *Brewer* . . . whereas arbitrary denial is permitted by *Greenholtz* v. *Nebraska Panel Inmates*.[67]

One final probation issue of significant importance arose in a recent case in which the U.S. Supreme Court heard oral arguments and then refused to decide the case, stating, "The writ of certiorari is dismissed as improvidently granted." The case involved an offender who was convicted of committing a sex crime against a minor. One condition of his probation was the successful completion of a therapy program in which he would have been required to admit responsibility for the crime for which he was convicted. Therapy was terminated when the offender refused to admit his crime, and his probation was revoked. The Montana Supreme Court held that the revocation order was improper as it violated the Fifth Amendment privilege against self-incrimination (see Appendix A).[68]

Megan's Laws

Another measure taken in some jurisdictions to avoid recidivism by offenders released from prison or parole or otherwise is to require registration and notice. In 1994 New Jersey enacted a community notification statute, commonly called *Megan's Law*. The name refers to Megan Kanka, who was sexually assaulted and murdered earlier in 1994. Jessee K. Timmendequas, a neighbor with two sex offender convictions, was charged, convicted, and sentenced to death.[69]

Megan's parents turned the tragedy into a national effort to enact legislation requiring that when sex offenders are released from prison notification must be given to the law enforcement officers in the areas in which the offenders plan to live. New Jersey's statute was followed by others, and today most states have some type of notification statute as does the federal system. They vary in their requirements, but many require that residents must be notified of the presence of a sex offender in the neighborhood. One (Louisiana) requires offenders to do the notification and to register for ten years after their convictions. In Louisiana ex-offenders may be required to wear designated articles of clothing; their cars may be marked with stickers indicating their criminal histories; mailings may be sent to their neighbors. In Oregon ex-offenders may be required to place signs reading "Sexual Offender Residence" in the windows of their residences. Additionally, in its 1994 criminal code revision, Congress included a section that permits withholding federal funds for states that fail to devise public notification systems and register sex offenders.[70]

Megan's Laws may require that schools, community organizations, and entire neighborhoods be notified when sex offenders move into the area. Notification includes the offender's name, address, description, picture, license plate number, and place of employment, depending on the assessment assigned to the offender by the prosecutor's office. That office is required to assess whether the released sex offender is considered a low, moderate, or high risk for subsequent sex crimes, a difficult task that is requiring much prosecutorial time. A *New York Times* editorial referred to that state's Megan's Law as an "irresistible invitation to vigilantes and self-proclaimed protectors of community safety" after two men were charged with assault when they broke into a home in which they had been told a sex offender was living. One recommendation for revising the statute is to provide that only law enforcement officers be notified.[71]

Courts have upheld some of these notification statutes and declared others unconstitutional. In 1994 the Washington Supreme Court upheld that state's registration statute.[72] In August of 1997 a federal court upheld the New York statute, along with its provision of making public the names and addresses of sex offenders, and officials made plans to begin the notification process.[73] Also in 1997 a federal court upheld an amendment to Michigan's sexual registration law. The amendment provides that the public may have access to police information on sexual offenders. The court held that this provision does not violate the offender's right to be free of cruel and unusual punishment, double jeopardy, ex post facto laws, and bills of attainder.[74]

On the other hand, in 1997 a provision of the Massachusetts statute, providing that any adult may have access to information on sexual offenders, was held to be unconstitutional.[75]

Ironically, the New Jersey version of Megan's Law is one of the most restrictive in the country, primarily as the result of constitutional challenges to the statute. Prosecutors and law enforcement officials began making the names and addresses of sex offenders available at the end of January 1998, but those lists included only about one-third of the actual offenders living in the community. Some of the restrictions on the statute were ordered by the New Jersey Supreme Court, which was striving for a balance between the rights of convicted persons who have served their terms and been released and the rights of citizens to be protected from crime. For example, notification is permitted only to persons "likely to encounter" the offender. Factors to be considered in making that determination are: nearness to the offender's home or workplace or any other place the offender frequents. Offenders must be classified as low, medium, or high risk, but the state must bear the burden of proving those categories in any given case. The courts did hold, however, that the New Jersey Megan's Law does not constitute unconstitutional punishment.[76]

The legal challenges to Meagan's Laws may be expected to continue, along with local and state efforts to publicize information on sexual offenders. In California, for example, the names, photographs, physical descriptions, criminal histories, and zip codes of almost 64,000 sexual offenders are available on CD-ROM and may be accessed on home computers. In September 1997 the material, available at the Los Angeles County Fair, was one of the more popular attractions. Ten persons found that sexual offenders were living in their neighborhoods.[77]

The popularity of Megan's Laws in the United States has spread to some other countries. In 1997, for example, Britain announced a version of the laws, requiring sex offenders to register their names and addresses and any changes in those to local law enforcement authorities. Those authorities may pass that information on to employers, community organizations, and the public if the offenders are considered a threat. Full disclosure of the information, however, is not permitted without that designation. Failure to register carries a possible penalty of up to six months in jail and a fine of $8,000.[78]

In addition to the legal challenges to sex offender registration laws, treatment-oriented persons have noted the burden the laws place on sex offenders who committed their crimes many years ago and have been rehabilitated. Since the laws generally apply to all sex offenders, they sweep within their coverage teenagers who impregnated their underage lovers, whom they plan to marry, gay males convicted of sodomy, and so on. Critics of the statutes refer to them as the swift reaction to a high-profile case and a lack of attention to the details by which the statutes are implemented.[79]

Supporters argue that by making the public more aware of the location of sexual predators in their neighborhhoods, the statutes will deter additional sexual offenses. The only other alternative, they argue, is to confine sex offenders for longer periods of time. They cite the Kansas Sexually Violent Predator Act, which was enacted in 1994 and upheld by the U.S. Supreme Court in 1997. This act permits the potentially indefinite confinement of "sexually violent predators." But the act reaches only those offenders who have "been convicted of or charged with a sexually violent offense" and who suffer from a "mental abnormality or personality disorder which makes the person likely to engage in . . . predatory acts of sexual violence."[80]

It may be expected that the laws in this area might change even before this text is published. As the endnotes detail, several of the cases are on appeal to the United States Supreme Court, with those appeals having been filed late in 1997 and not yet decided by that Court.

WiseGuide Wrap-Up   This chapter covers some critical areas of criminal justice. Despite the current public demand for stricter reactions to criminals, the crisis of overcrowded jails and prisons forces most jurisdictions to use some type of community corrections. Despite the retreat from rehabilitation as a purpose for punishment and corrections, offenders are (and will continue to be) in the community, usually with limited supervision. The issue is not whether we wish to have community corrections; the issue is how much attention and funding we will provide to make sure the use of community corrections does not impair the goal of security.

This chapter begins with an overview of community-based corrections: it considers the history of this approach to corrections, along with the cost. Financing is a real problem, particularly with the cutbacks in federal and state budgets; but the costs for corrections in the community are far less than the costs of incarceration, and that is true even when intensive supervision is provided for those offenders residing in the community. The problems that offenders face when they live in the community are discussed, along with the need for services in assisting them to cope with these adjustments. In particular, attention is given to furlough, work release, and prerelease programs.

Probation and parole are discussed in greater depth than other community corrections because they are the methods used most frequently. Probation is the sentence imposed most often and is used today for serious as well as minor offenders, primarily because of prison overcrowding. The prognosis for success is not great, although it is thought that, with intensive probation supervision, the probability for success improves. Special attention is given to felony probation, house arrest, and shock probation.

Brief attention is given to the administration of probation systems before focusing on probation conditions. Courts uphold most restrictions on the daily lives of probationers provided the imposed conditions are reasonably related to the offenses in question and do not interfere with constitutional rights. The final section on probation gives attention to the supervision of probationers and in particular, the process of search and seizure.

Parole has been the most frequently used method of release from prison, but its use for early release has been restricted in recent years. The various methods of organizing parole systems are discussed, along with the parole process, including eligibility for parole and the parole hearing. The due process requirements for the parole decision-making hearings are discussed as well. Attempts to decrease the perceived arbitrariness of parole decisions have involved the use of parole guidelines. Due process in the revocation of probation and parole has helped to remove the arbitrariness and unfairness of those important processes.

The movement away from rehabilitation has resulted in problems for community corrections. Perhaps the most bitter criticisms have been hurled at parole, resulting in action in many states to abolish or, at least, curtail its use. Despite the call for parole abolition, it has become obvious that some form of discretion in the release of offenders must be retained, especially if sentences are long.

No one can say which is the real problem: the failure of parole per se or the abuse of discretion by parole-granting authorities. In 1975 Maurice H. Sigler, chairman of the U.S. Board of Parole, argued that parole "has now become the scapegoat of all of corrections' ills." He suggested that the system deserves the same objective, dispassionate analysis that its critics demand of parole decisions:

> To those who say "let's abolish parole," I say that as long as we use imprisonment in this country we will have to have someone, somewhere, with the authority to release people from imprisonment. Call it parole—call it what you will. It's one of those jobs that has to be done.[81]

The abolition of parole may result only in shifting discretion to another area such as prosecution. Prosecutors may refuse to prosecute; juries may refuse to convict in cases involving long mandatory sentences with no chance of parole. Efforts to control discretion within the parole system may be a more reasonable approach than the total abolition of the system.

The final section of the chapter analyzes Megan's Laws, now enacted in most states and by Congress. The discussion details the types of notification that are required and looks at the constitutional issues raised by these statutes, which were passed after the 1994 rape and murder of Megan Kanka, aged seven, of New Jersey. We can expect continued controversy over these sex offender registration laws as courts balance society's rights against those of ex-offenders.

Apply It

1. Define *community-based corrections* and give reasons why some argue that it is to be preferred over incarceration of offenders.

2. What problems do offenders face when they return to the community from incarceration? What is being done to assist them in coping with those problems? Evaluate *furlough, work release,* and *prerelease* programs.

3. What is the difference between *probation* and *parole*? Which is used more frequently and why?

4. What are the arguments for and against the use of house arrest?

5. What is *electronic monitoring*? Should its use be increased?

6. Discuss and evaluate *shock probation.*

7. What typical restrictions or conditions are placed on probationers? What should be the guidelines, legally or practically, for such restrictions?

8. What is meant by *intensive probation supervision?* How does it compare in effectiveness to traditional methods of supervision?

9. Describe and analyze recent trends in parole systems.

10. What effect do due process requirements have on parole granting? On parole revocation?

11. Explain and discuss the implications of Megan's Laws. Comment on the legality of these laws.

Notes

1. President's Commission on Law Enforcement and Administration of Justice, *The Challenge of Crime in a Free Society* (Washington, D.C.: U.S. Government Printing Office, 1967), p. 121.

2. National Advisory Commission on Criminal Justice Standards and Goals, *A National Strategy to Reduce Crime* (Washington, D.C.: U.S. Government Printing Office, 1973), p. 121.

3. For a discussion, see Elizabeth Mauser et al., "The Economic Impact of Diverting Substance-Abusing Offenders into Treatment," *Crime & Delinquency* 40 (October 1994): 568–588. For a discussion of the federal system, see Sharon D. Stewart, "Community-Based Drug Treatment in the Federal Bureau of Prisons," *Federal Probation* 58 (June 1994): 24–28.

4. For an analysis of legislative goals for community-based correctional programs, see W. Wesley Johnson et al., "Goals of Community-Based Corrections: An Analysis of State Legal Codes," *American Journal of Criminal Justice* 18, no. 1 (1994): 79–93.

5. Bureau of Justice Statistics, *Correctional Populations in the United States 1992* (Washington, D.C.: U.S. Department of Justice, 1995), Table 5.12a.

6. See Sheldon Ekland-Olson et al., "Postrelease Depression and the Importance of Familial Support," *Criminology* 21 (May 1983): 254–257.

7. "Number of Prison Furloughs Increases," *On the Line* 15 (March 1992): 5. See also "Prisons Grant More Furloughs, but Eligibility Is Tighter," *Criminal Justice Newsletter* 23 (2 January 1992): 4.

8. "Most Systems Now Have Work Release Programs," *Corrections Today* 55 (July 1993): 16.

9. National Institute of Justice, *Work Release: Recidivism and Corrections Costs in Washington State* (Washington, D.C.: U.S. Department of Justice, December 1996), p. 3.

10. Bureau of Justice Statistics News Release, reported in the *Washington Post* (18 August 1997), p. 13. See also, "Sixty Percent of Convicted Sex Offenders Are on Parole or Probation," *PR Newswire* (2 February 1997), Washington Dateline, reporting on a release from the Bureau of Justice Statistics.

11. *Probation in the United States,* ibid., p. 4.

12. See Sanford Bates, "The Establishment and Early Years of the Federal Probation System," *Federal Probation* 51 (June 1987): 4–9.

13. Joan Petersilia, "Rand's Research: A Closer Look," *Corrections Today* 47 (June 1985): 37.

14. *Criminal Justice Research at Rand* (Santa Monica, Calif.: Rand Corp., January 1985), p. 11.

15. John T. Whitehead, "The Effectiveness of Felony Probation: Results from an Eastern State," *Justice Quarterly* 8 (December 1991): 525–543.

16. For a brief history of home confinement as well as a discussion of specific programs, see Alexis M. Durham III, *Crisis and Reform: Current Issues in American Punishment* (Boston: Little, Brown, 1994), pp. 187–191. See also, "House Arrest and Electronic Monitoring," in *Community Corrections* by Marilyn D. McShane and Wesley Krause (New York: Macmillan, 1993), pp. 115–148.

17. For a brief description of its use in one state, see Joseph E. Papy and Richard Nimer, "Electronic Monitoring in Florida," *Federal Probation* 55 (March 1991): 31–33.

18. Annesley K. Schmidt and Christine E. Curtis, "Electronic Monitors," in *Intermediate Punishments: Intensive Supervision, Home Confinement and Electronic Surveillance,* ed. Belinda R. McCarthy (Monsey, N.Y.: Willow Tree Press, 1987), pp. 137–152.

19. Terry L. Baumer et al., "A Comparative Analysis of Three Electronically Monitored Home Detention Programs," *Justice Quarterly* 10 (March 1993): 121.

20. Daniel Ford and Annesley K. Schmidt, "Electronically Monitored Home Confinement," *National Institute of Justice Report* (November 1985), p. 2. For a more recent discussion of electronic monitoring, see Darren Gowen, "Electronic Monitoring in the Southern District of Mississippi," *Federal Probation* 59 (March 1995): 10–13.

21. Joseph B. Vaughn, "Planning for Change: The Use of Electronic Monitoring as a Correctional Alternative," in *Intermediate Punishments,* ed. McCarthy, p. 153.

22. Baumer, "A Comparative Analysis of Three Electronically Monitored Home Detention Programs," pp. 121–142.

23. For a discussion, see Annette Jolin and Brian Stipak, "Drug Treatment and Electronically Monitored Home Confinement," *Crime & Delinquency* 38 (April 1992): 158–170.

24. J. Robert Lilly et al., "Electronic Monitoring of the Drunk Driver," *Crime & Delinquency* 39 (October 1993): 462–484.

25. "Electronic Bracelets Flawed, Suits Claim," *American Bar Association Journal* 81 (April 1995): 30.

26. "Death Penalty May Be Sought During Retrial," *Chicago Tribune* (16 September 1997), p. 1.

27. For a discussion of some of the problems with shock incarceration, see Mark W. Osler, "Shock Incarceration: Hard Realities and Real Possibilities," *Federal Probation* 55 (March 1991): 34–42.

28. For information on the federal probation system, see the series of articles in *Federal Probation* LXI (March 1997).

29. See, for example, Eric T. Assur et al., "Probation Counselors and the Adult Children of Alcoholics," *Federal Probation* 51 (September 1987): 41–51; and Edward M. Read, "The Alcoholic, the Probation Officer, and AA: A Viable Team Approach to Supervision," *Federal Probation* 51 (March 1987): 11–15.

30. See State v. Morris, 806 P.2d 407 (Hawaii 1991).

31. "Defendants Choosing Prison Time," *St. Petersburg Times* (18 February 1990), p. 1B.

32. United States v. Myers, 864 F.Supp. 794 (N.D.Ill. 1994); Warner v. Orange County Department of Probation, 870 F.Supp. 69 (S.D.N.Y. 1994), *vacated, remanded,* 115 F.3d 1068 (2d Cir. 1997), *on remand,* 968 F.Supp. 917 (S.D.N.Y. 1997). The case was sent back to the lower court for a determination regarding whether the probationer had consented to attend spiritual meetings. The court adhered to its earlier judgment that he had not done so as he did not know the meetings were of a religious nature.

33. See O'Connor v. California, 855 F.Supp. 303 (C.D.Cal. 1994).

34. "A Man Must Get Written Consent for Sex," *New York Times* (10 March 1996), p. 11; "Admission Spurs Jail," *Houston Chronicle News Service* (23 August 1996), p. 38.

35. People v. Griffith, 657 N.Y.S.2d 823 (App.Div.3d Dept. 1997).

36. Stephanie B. Goldberg, "No Baby, No Jail: Creative Sentencing Has Gone Overboard, A California Court Rules," *American Bar Association Journal* 78 (October 1992): 90.

37. People v. Hackler, 13 Cal.App.4th 1049 (5th Dist. 1993).

38. People v. Meyer, 680 N.E.2d 315 (Ill. 1997).

39. See Eugene Griffin et al., "HIV Policy for Probation Departments," *Crime & Delinquency* 37 (January 1991): 36–47; and Arthur J. Lurigio et al., "HIV Education for Probation Officers: An Experimentation and Evaluation Program," *Crime & Delinquency* 37 (January 1991): 125–134.

40. Rolando V. del Carmen, "Facing Today's Tough Liability Issues," *Corrections Today* 52 (August 1990): 34. See also Richard D. Sluder and del Carmen, "Are Probation and Parole Officers Liable for Injuries Caused by Probationers and Parolees?" *Federal Probation* 54 (December 1990): 3–12.

41. For a description and analysis of three programs, see Mark Jones, "Intensive Probation Supervision in Georgia, Massachusetts, and New Jersey," *Criminal Justice Research Bulletin* 6, no. 1 (Huntsville, Tex.: Sam Houston State University Criminal Justice Center, 1991).

42. Todd R. Clear and Patricia L. Hardyman, "The New Intensive Supervision Movement," *Crime & Delinquency* 36 (January 1990): 42–44. The entire journal is devoted to issues on IPS.

43. Joan Petersilia and Susan Turner, "Comparing Intensive and Regular Supervision for High-Risk Probationers: Early Results from an Experiment in California," *Crime & Delinquency* 36 (January 1990): 87–111.

44. Quoted in *Criminal Justice Newsletter* 24 (1 July 1993): 1. For more details, see Joan Petersilia and Susan Turner, *Evaluating Intensive Supervision Probation/Parole: Results of a Nationwide Experiment* (Washington, D.C.: U.S. Department of Justice, May 1993). For a discussion of the evaluation of IPS with drug offenders, see Susan Turner et al., "Evaluating Intensive Supervision Provation/Parole (ISP) for Drug Offenders," *Crime & Delinquency* 38 (October 1992): 539–556.

45. James M. Byrne et al., "The Effectiveness of the New Intensive Supervision Programs," *Research in Corrections* 2 (September 1989): 42. For a discussion of the evaluation of IPS with juveniles, see Henry Sontheimer and Lynne Goodstein, "An Evaluation of Juvenile Intensive Aftercare Probation: Aftercare Versus System Response Effects," *Justice Quarterly* 10 (June 1993): 197–228.

46. "Some New Yorkers on Probation Will Begin Reporting to Machines," *New York Times* (24 May 1993), p. 1.

47. Griffin v. Wisconsin, 483 U.S. 868 (1987).

48. United States v. Giannetta, 909 F.2d 571 (1st Cir. 1990).

49. Commonwealth v. Green, 591 A.2d 1079 (Pa.Super. 1991), *cert. denied sub nom.*, 503 U.S. 964 (1992).

50. United States v. Trzaska, 866 F.Supp. 98 (E.D.N.Y. 1994).

51. Portillo v. United States, 15 F.3d 819 (9th Cir. 1994).

52. The Sentencing Reform Act was passed as part of the Comprehensive Crime Control Act of 1984, Pub.L.No. 98-473, 98 Stat. 1837, 1976 (1984), and is codified with its subsequent amendments in U.S. Code, Title 18, Sections 3551 *et seq.* (1997) and U.S. Code, Title 28, Sections 991–998 (1997).

53. See "Virginia OKs Tougher Sentences, Ends Parole in Landmark Bill," *Criminal Justice Newsletter* 25 (3 October 1994): 5. The statute is Va. Code Ann., 53.1-165.1 (1997).

54. "Parole Groups Launch Campaign to Curb Abolition Efforts," *Criminal Justice Newsletter* 26 (3 April 1995), p. 6.

55. Harry E. Allen et al., *Probation and Parole in America* (New York: Free Press, 1985), p. 165.

56. See, for example, Tarlton v. Clark, 441 F.2d 384 (5th Cir. 1971), *cert. denied,* 403 U.S. 934 (1971).

57. Quoted in Jessica Mitford, *Kind and Usual Punishment: The Prison Business* (New York: Alfred A. Knopf, 1973), p. 216.

58. Greenholtz v. Nebraska, 442 U.S. 1 (1979).

59. Board of Pardons v. Allen, 482 U.S. 369 (1987).

60. See U.S. Department of Justice, *Sentencing and Parole Release Classification Instruments for Criminal Justice Decisions,* vol. 4 (Washington, D.C.: U.S. Government Printing Office, 1979), p. 7.

61. See John S. Carroll, "Judgments of Recidivism Risk: The Use of Base-Rate Information in Parole Decision," in *New Directions in Psycholegal Research,* ed. Paul D. Lipsitt and Bruce B. Sales (New York: Van Nostrand Reinhold, 1980), pp. 66–86; and Don M. Gottfredson et al., *Guidelines for Parole and Sentencing: A Policy Control Method* (Lexington, Mass.: D. C. Heath, 1978).

62. Morrissey v. Brewer, 408 U.S. 471, 478 (1972).

63. Andrew von Hirsch and Kathleen J. Hanrahan, *Abolish Parole?* (Washington, D.C.: U.S. Government Printing Office, 1978), p. 21.

64. Morrissey v. Brewer, 408 U.S. 471 (1972).

65. Gagnon v. Scarpelli, 411 U.S. 778 (1973).

66. Black v. Romano, 471 U.S. 606 (1985); and Bearden v. Georgia, 461 U.S. 660 (1983).

67. Jago v. Van Curen, 454 U.S. 14 (1981).

68. State v. Imlay, 813 P.2d 979 (Mont. 1992), *cert. granted,* 503 U.S. 905 (1992), *cert. dismissed,* 506 U.S. 5 (1992).

69. The statute is codified in N.J.Stat., Section 2C:7-1 *et seq.* (1997).

70. "A Scarlet Letter for Sex Offenders," *Baltimore Sun* (6 April 1995), p. 17. The federal provision is part of the Violent Crime Control and Law Enforcement Act of 1994, Public Law 103-323 (13 September 1994), Section 20417. See also Rev. Code Wash. 9A.44.130 (1996); La. Rev. Stat., Title 15, Section 540 *et seq.* (1997); and Ore. Rev. Stat. 181.519 (1996).

71. "Megan's Law Needs Fixing," *New York Times* (13 January 1995), p. 14; "Sex-Offender Disclosure Law Hitting Snags in New Jersey," *New York Times* (9 January 1995), p. 1.

72. State v. Ward, 869 P.2d 1062 (Wash. 1994). See also the Ninth Circuit decision in 1997, upholding the statute against challenges that it violates due process, privacy, and the federal constitutional provision prohibiting ex post facto laws: Russell v. Gregoire, 124 F.3d 1079 (9th Cir. 1997), *cert. denied,* 118 S. Ct. 1191 (1998).

73. Doe v. Pataki, 120 F.3d 1263 (2d Cir. 1997), *cert. denied,* 118 S. Ct. 1066 (1998).

74. Doe v. Kelley, 961 F.Supp. 1105 (W.D.Mich. 1997).

75. Doe v. Attorney General, 680 N.E.2d 97 (Mass. 1997).

76. See E.B. v. Verniero, 119 F.3 1077 (3d Cir. 1997), *cert. denied,* 118 S. Ct. 1039 (1998).

77. "California Releases CD with Sex convicts' Data," *Miami Herald* (2 July 1997), p. 7; "Lundgren Hails Success of Sex Offender List," *Los Angeles Times* (16 September 1997), p. 1B.

78. "British Impose a 'Megan's Law' of their Own on Child Molesters," *New York Times* (12 August 1997), p. 7.

79. "Registry Laws Tar Sex-Crime Convicts with Broad Brush," *New York Times* (1 July 1997), p. 11.

80. Kan. Stat. Ann., Section 59-29aO1 *et seq.* (1994). The case is Kansas v. Hendricks, 117 S.Ct. 2072 (1997).

81. Maurice H. Sigler, "Abolish Parole?" *Federal Probation* 39 (June 1975): 48.

Juvenile Justice:
A Special Case

Chapter 12
Juvenile Justice Systems

INTRODUCTION

Juvenile court systems emerged as separate systems for processing juveniles who engage in criminal and delinquent activities or who are dependent or neglected. These special courts and systems were viewed as being concerned with the welfare of children who did not need the procedural safeguards characteristic of criminal court systems.

In recent years that orientation has changed. Some but not all procedural safeguards have been extended to juvenile court systems. The result is systems that are far less distinguishable from criminal courts than was the case originally. Whether these are positive

INTRODUCTION—Continued

or negative changes is debatable. The increased attention given to the involvement of juveniles in violent crimes has resulted in efforts to change juvenile justice systems or process violent juveniles in criminal court systems.

Chapter 12 discusses the early development and the recent changes that have been made in juvenile court systems, along with the development and changes that have occurred in juvenile correctional systems.

Juvenile Justice Systems

Criminal responsibility in adversary systems is based on the premise that the accused has the ability to understand and control his or her behavior. Most people are presumed to have this ability, but among the exceptions have been persons of tender years. Separate systems for them emerged in the late 1800s in the United States. In recent years these systems have gone through significant changes, including the transfer of some juveniles to criminal courts. For those who remain in juvenile court systems, the Supreme Court requires some procedural safeguards.

This chapter begins with a brief historical overview of the background of U.S. juvenile justice systems. The origin of juvenile courts is discussed, along with the dispute over the purposes of juvenile justice systems. Data on delinquency are analyzed, with particular emphasis on violent crimes. The chapter examines how U.S. Supreme Court decisions have changed traditional juvenile justice systems before looking more closely at how those systems operate today. Juvenile justice systems are contrasted with the processing of juveniles in criminal court systems. In addition the chapter gives brief attention to juveniles in corrections as well as to the issue of capital punishment and juveniles. A final section contains a brief assessment of criminal and juvenile justice systems.

Key Terms

adjudication
aftercare
certification
custody
delinquency
detention center
detention
disposition
diversion
intake decision
juvenile
juvenile delinquent
parens patriae
petition
status offense
training school

Learning Objectives

After reading this chapter, you should be able to do the following:

- List and explain the basic procedural and philosophical differences between juvenile and criminal courts historically and currently
- Discuss current data on delinquency, especially data on violent crimes.
- List and explain the major Supreme Court cases regarding juveniles' constitutional rights.
- List and explain the purpose and practice of juvenile curfews and discuss the legal issues involved.
- Explore the racial and gender issues of juvenile justice systems.

- Discuss the general procedures of juvenile courts.
- Discuss the role of attorneys in juvenile courts.
- Discuss the processing of juvenile offenders in adult criminal courts and relate this discussion to persistently violent juvenile offenders.
- Summarize recent changes in juvenile corrections, emphasizing the impact of deinstitutionalization.
- Evaluate capital punishment of juveniles.
- Assess the future of juvenile court systems.

Juvenile Justice Systems: An Overview

Special justice systems for children rest on the belief that children and **juvenile delinquents** should be treated separately and differently from adults. They need special handling and processing when they engage in delinquent or criminal acts. Children are considered amenable to treatment, to change, and to rehabilitation.

Although the first discussion of juvenile problems of which we have record dates back 4,000 years to the Code of Hammurabi, the treatment of children in the United States may be traced to the philosophy of the English, who in the eleventh and twelfth centuries developed the practice of treating children differently from adults. A child under the age of seven was considered incapable of forming the intent required for criminal prosecutions. A child between the ages of seven and fourteen years was presumed to be incapable of forming the intent, but that presumption could be refuted. A child over fourteen was treated as an adult.

During this earlier period of English history, when the death penalty was provided for many crimes, children were not exempted from capital punishment, although few children were executed. Later in England, the chancery or equity courts were established for the purpose of avoiding the harshness of the strict technicalities of the English common law. Equity courts were to decide cases on the principles of justice and fairness. These courts were called *chancery courts* because they were under the jurisdiction of the king's chancellor. Equity courts had jurisdiction over many types of cases, including those involving children.[1]

The English king could exercise the power of a parent over children and others, a concept called ***parens patriae,*** literally meaning the "parent of the country." In time this concept became so important that England enacted statutes permitting the legal rights of parents and other family members to be terminated in the cases of persons who needed the legal guardianship of the king.

Parens patriae was interpreted in England to mean that the sovereign had the responsibility to oversee any children in his kingdom who might be neglected or abused. The court exercised this duty only when it was thought necessary for the welfare of the child, and that occurred rarely. Protection of society and punishment of parents were not considered to be sufficient reasons to invoke the responsibility. In the English system and in the system as adopted during the early period of American history, the *parens patriae* doctrine applied only to children who were in need of supervision or help because of the actions of their parents or guardians, not to children who were delinquent. These children are called by various names, such as *children in need of supervision* (CINS), *persons in need of supervision* (PINS), or *dependent* or *neglected children*. The extension of juvenile court jurisdiction over delinquent children was an innovation adopted in Illinois in 1899.[2]

In the United States juvenile court jurisdiction was extended to children considered incorrigible because they would not obey their parents or other adults. Even if they were not violating the law, these juveniles could be accused of committing **status offenses.** The trend in recent years has been to remove status offenses from juvenile court jurisdiction, but where jurisdiction remains, generally the status offender is included within the definition of juvenile delinquent. Some states have a minimum age for juvenile court jurisdiction, but as a practical matter, most courts do not decide cases involving very young children.

Prior to the emergence of the juvenile court, children in the United States were treated as adults. Capital punishment was permitted but seldom used; however, many children were deprived of food, incarcerated with adults, or subjected to corporal punishment. Some institutions were established to separate incarcerated juveniles from adults. The New York House of Refuge, established in 1824, was the first and served as a model. These early institutions eliminated some of the evils of imprisoning children with adult criminals, although scholars have questioned whether they provided much improvement in the treatment of juveniles.[3]

By the middle 1800s in the United States, probation for juveniles had been established and separate **detention centers** had been built. The 1800s saw the evolution of progressive ideas in the care and treatment of dependent and neglected children, too. Protective societies, such as the Society for the Prevention of Cruelty to Children (developed in New York in 1875), paved the way for juvenile courts. Illinois gets credit for establishing the first **juvenile court** in 1899. Other states followed quickly.

Spotlight 12.1 lists some of the historical differences between U.S. criminal and juvenile courts. The juvenile court, with its emphasis on individualized treatment, was visualized as a social agency or clinic rather than a court of law, a vision that has encountered much criticism in subsequent years. The court was to be a social institution designed to protect and rehabilitate the child rather than determine the child's guilt or innocence. Juvenile courts were to be treatment—not punishment—oriented. The purpose of juvenile courts was to prevent children from becoming criminals by catching them in the budding stages and by giving them the protection and love that a parent would be expected to provide.

The vocabulary of juvenile and criminal courts differed, too. Children would not be arrested but, rather, summoned or apprehended; they would not be indicted, but a petition would be filed on their behalf. If **detention** were necessary, they would be placed in facilities separate from adults, not in jails. They would not have a public trial but a private hearing, in which juries and prosecuting attorneys would rarely, if ever, be used. In most cases they would not have an attorney.

The juvenile hearing would be informal, for the ordinary trappings of the courtroom would be out of place. Judges would not act as impartial observers, as was their function in criminal courts. Rather, they would act as wise parents disciplining their children with love and tenderness and deciding in an informal way what was best for those children. Juveniles would not be sentenced as the concept is known in criminal courts. Rather, after the hearing they would be adjudicated. A disposition would be made only after a careful study of the juvenile's background and potential, and the decision would be made in the best interests of the child.

Spotlight 12.1

The Criminal and the Juvenile Courts: Some Historically Important Contrasts

Adult Criminal Court	Juvenile Court
Court of law	Social institution, agency, clinic
Constitutional rights	*Parens patriae* approach—supra constitutional rights
Purpose to punish, deter	Purpose to salvage, rehabilitate
Begins with arrest	Begins with apprehension, summons; process of intake
Indictment or presentment	Petition filed on behalf of child
Detained in jails or released on bail	Detained in detention centers or released to family or others
Public trial	Private hearing
Strict rules of evidence	Informal procedures
Right to trial by jury	No right to trial by jury
Right to counsel	No right to (or need for) counsel
Prosecuted by state	Allegations brought by state
Plea bargaining	No plea bargaining; state would act in child's best interests
Impartial judge	Judge acting as a wise parent
Pleads guilty, innocent, or *nolo contendere*	Admits or denies petition
Found guilty or innocent	Adjudicated
Sentenced	Disposition of the case
Probation	Probation
Incarcerated in jail or prison	Placed in reformatory, training school, or foster home, etc.
Released on parole	Released to aftercare

The juvenile court hearing differed from that of the criminal court in procedure as well as in philosophy. Rules of evidence required in criminal courts were not applied to juvenile courts. Criminal court procedural safeguards were set aside in the interest of treatment and the welfare of children. Because the state, in recognizing its duty as parent, was helping, not punishing, children, no constitutional rights were violated. The emphasis in juvenile court was not on what the child did but what the child was. Juvenile courts were to be concerned with the children as individuals, and this enabled judges to save children from criminal careers through proper treatment. In contrast, the criminal court was concerned at trial with the narrow issue of the guilt or innocence of the accused.

Early advocates of juvenile courts believed that law and humanitarianism were not sufficient for the treatment of juveniles. They expected juvenile courts to rely heavily on the findings of the physical and social sciences. It was anticipated that these research findings would be applied scientifically in the **adjudication** and disposition of juveniles. The failure of the social sciences to develop sufficient research to implement this philosophy adequately, the failure of the legal profession to recognize and accept those findings that would be of assistance, and the abuse of discretion by correctional officials contributed to the tensions that developed over the lack of procedural safeguards in juvenile courts.

The dream of the rehabilitative ideal of the founders of juvenile courts has not been realized. In reality, many juveniles receive punishment, not treatment. In reality, being processed through juvenile rather than criminal courts does not remove the stigma of *criminal*.

Not only may a juvenile suffer the "worst of both worlds," but some scholars take the position that this was the intent. Disputing the benevolent motives of the

PROFESSIONS 12.1

Careers in Juvenile Justice

The increase in juvenile crime, especially violent crimes has led officials to pay greater attention to research into juvenile crime. Research provides numerous job opportunities for those who are trained in research methodology. The opportunities exist in all areas of criminal justice, but juvenile justice is one area that often appeals to young people. The desire to find out why it happens and what to do—how to treat—may lead to intriguing days at the office.

Those who prefer the "hands–on" approach will also find numerous chances to become involved in juvenile justice. Jobs are available in juvenile detention and correctional facilities, juvenile probation and parole, school service personnel, community treatment programs, court services, and many other areas. Students may be interested in teaching positions that focus on children with behavior problems as well as those who have already committed juvenile or criminal offenses.

Another area of service to juveniles is in victimization, as larger numbers of children, some very young, become crime victims, often at the hands of other children or juveniles. The government has developed an action plan to deal with breaking the cycle of juvenile crime and victimization, with the U.S. attorney general, Janet Reno, concluding:

More and more of our Nation's children are killing and dying. The only way we can break the cycle of violence is through a truly national effort implemented one community at a time. Everyone has a role—businesses, schools, universities, and especially parents. Every community and every citizen can find practical steps in the Action Plan to do something now about youth violence.[1]

The implementation of the government's plan provides various career and job opportunities for those interested in focusing their work on juveniles.

1. Attorney General Janet Reno, quoted in Sarah Ingersoll, "The National Juvenile Justice Action Plan: A Comprehensive Response to a Critical Challenge," *Juvenile Justice: Kids and Guns: From Playgrounds to Battlegrounds* (Washington, D.C.: U.S. Department of Justice, Office of Juvenile Justice and Delinquency Prevention, September 1997), p. 11.

founders of juvenile courts, scholars have argued that juvenile courts diminish the civil liberties and privacy of juveniles and that the child-saving movement was promoted by the middle class to support its own interests.[4]

Others have contended that the development of juvenile courts represented neither a great social reform nor an attempt to diminish juveniles' civil liberties and to control them arbitrarily. Rather, it represented another example of the trend toward bureaucratization and an institutional compromise between social welfare and the law. The juvenile court "was primarily a shell of legal ritual within which states renewed and enacted their commitment to discretionary social control over children."[5]

Changes have occurred in the juvenile court philosophy and procedures. But before discussing those, it is appropriate to take a brief look at delinquency data, an area of research that provides interesting job opportunities, as noted in Professions 12.1.

Juvenile Delinquency Data

It is impossible to get accurate data on the amount of delinquency. Jurisdictions differ in their definitions of delinquency. Theoretically, **delinquency** does not refer to children processed through juvenile courts because they are in need of supervision, because they are dependent or neglected, or because they are abused. Nevertheless, some jurisdictions include in delinquency data all categories of juveniles over which juvenile courts have jurisdiction.

Methods of collecting delinquency data vary, too, and in most cases juvenile records are considered confidential; some states require that the records be destroyed or sealed. How, then, do we know about juvenile offenses? Chapter 2 discusses the use of self-report studies, in which respondents are asked to state the

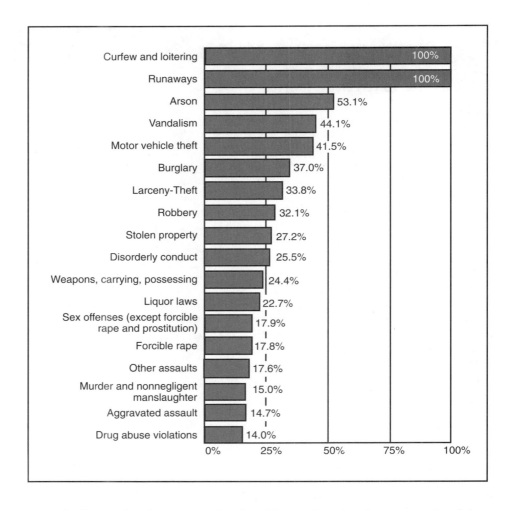

Figure 12.1

Percentage of Total Arrests in 1996 Involving Youths Under Eighteen Years of Age.

Source: Federal Bureau of Investigation, *Uniform Crime Reports, 1996* (Washington, D.C.: U.S. Government Printing Office, 1997), p. 230.

types of offenses they have committed and how often they have committed them. From carefully selected samples of the population, predictions may be made on the overall extent of delinquency.

Official arrest rates recorded by age brackets and published by the FBI are another source of data. The official data reveal that in 1995, persons under eighteen accounted for 18.7 percent of the arrests for violent crimes and 35.2 percent of arrests for property crimes. Figure 12.1 graphs the percentage of total arrests in 1996 of persons under eighteen for all serious offenses and several other crimes. The figure demonstrates that according to official data, juveniles under the age of eighteen do not commit most of the violent crimes. If the age is extended from eighteen to twenty-five, however, the picture is different. In 1996 those under twenty-five constituted 46.1 percent of all arrestees for violent crimes and 59.5 percent of all arrestees for property offenses.[6]

Some experts claim that over time the rise in arrest rates for violent crimes among the young is startling. For example, between 1992 and 1996, the percentage of persons under eighteen who were arrested for serious crimes increased in four of the eight crimes: robbery, up 16.9 percent; aggravated assault, up 1.7 percent; arson, up 6.8 percent; and larceny-theft, up 8.7 percent. During that period forcible rape arrests of those under eighteen decreased by 6.6 percent; murder and nonnegligent arrests were down 18.4 percent; burglary, down 6.5 percent; and motor vehicle theft, down by 20.5 percent. The overall percentage of arrests for property crimes was down by 1.7 percent in the age group under eighteen, but arrests for violent crimes were up by 2.8 percent in that age group.[7]

It is the amount of violence by juveniles, often with juvenile victims, that raises great concern, along with the types of violent crimes that have been committed. Consider a few recent examples.

In April 1998 the cover of *Time* pictured a young toddler, smiling broadly and bearing a rifle. The headline, "Armed & Dangerous," referred to the deaths of five school children in Jonesboro, Arkansas. The cover also contained recent pictures of the two students who are charged with the murders: Mitchell Johnson, aged 13, and Andrew Golden, aged 11. Golden is the featured toddler. The boys waited in jail, one reading a Bible, the other staring out the window, as one of the victims was eulogized by hundreds of mourners. Authorities allege that the boys, who are charged with five counts of murder and ten of battery, began the shooting spree because Mitchell was rejected by a girl he liked.[8]

Also in 1998 Daphne Abdela, aged 15, admitted that she participated in the murder of Michael McMorrow, aged 44, in Central Park in New York City. Abdela and her boyfriend stabbed McMorrow, cut his throat, and dumped his body in the lake. The teens and others partied and drank in the park, and they knew their victim, whom they killed after he drank with them.[9] Abdela pleaded guilty to first-degree manslaughter and was sentenced to ten years in prison.

In August of 1997 Ray DeFord, aged eleven at the time of his crime, was found guilty of one count of arson and eight counts of felony murder for the deaths of eight people in a fire started by the youth in a Portland, Oregon, suburb. The mentally disabled boy was sentenced to thirteen years of state custody. The judge said, "I'm still convinced he has no idea what he did. . . . That's precisely what makes Ray so dangerous."[10]

Also in 1997 an eighteen-year-old, Robert Dingman, was found guilty of two counts of murder in the death of his parents and one count of conspiracy with his brother in those murders. Prosecutors introduced evidence at trial that Robert persuaded his fifteen-year-old brother to steal the gun from the father's locked cabinet. The younger brother entered a guilty plea to one count of second–degree murder and testified against Robert. The brothers wanted more money from their parents, who left an estate valued at $200,000. Robert was sentenced to the mandatory penalty: life in prison without an opportunity for parole. The younger brother could be paroled in eighteen years, and because he agreed to testify this sentence may be reviewed in twelve years.[11]

In addition to murder, youths are committing sex crimes, usually against other youths or children. In 1997 in Texas City, Texas, two boys, aged ten and fourteen, were held in the rape of a four-year-old girl. The boys were caught assaulting the little girl, whom they allegedly lured into a school bus by telling her they would take her to a carnival. The fourteen-year-old was found guilty of kidnapping and sexually assaulting the victim, who at the age of five, testified at his trial. She would not say what happened on the bus, but she did identify the defendant, who faces up to forty years in prison. The other youth awaits trial. He was released from custody pending his trial but ordered to leave the community, in which the victim still lives.[12]

In July of 1997 Joseph Corcoran was accused of killing his brother, his sister's fiancé, and two others whom he claimed were talking about him. Five years earlier, when Corcoran was seventeen, he was accused of shooting his parents, but a jury acquitted him.[13]

Recent crimes by youths are not confined to the United States. In 1997 a Japanese teenager confessed to beheading eleven-year-old Jun Hase and placing his head on a school gate; subsequently, he admitted that he killed a ten-year-old girl by beating her to death with a steel pipe and that he attacked three other teenage girls, one of whom almost bled to death. The offender cannot be imprisoned under Japanese law, which prohibits trying children as adults for crimes they commit before the age of sixteen. The offender was fourteen when he committed the crimes. He will be placed on probation or sent to a reform school. Japanese law forbids publishing the name and picture of young offenders, but one paper violated that law. There was a public outcry of criticism, and most papers refused to publish the article.[14]

The relationship between the crimes of young people and school has been explored. A study released by the National Center for Juvenile Justice in the fall of 1997 disclosed that the rates of juvenile violence triple during the hour after the school day ends, between 3 and 4 P.M., as compared to the hour between 1 and 2 P.M. The data reveal that 57 percent of all violent crimes committed by juveniles occur on school days. The report is being used to encourage the government to provide after-school programs for juveniles.[15]

Juvenile Gangs

Gang membership is not limited to juveniles, and especially in prison, gang members may be older. But juvenile gangs are a major focus in today's efforts to combat crime, especially violent crimes. Research on gangs and delinquency is not a new phenomenon,[16] but the nature of gang activities has changed in recent years.

Although violence might have characterized some early gangs, it appears to be the focal point of today's gangs. Whereas the gangs that were the focus of early sociological research may have fought over turf, today's gangs "have become a form of urban guerrilla warfare over drug trafficking. Informers, welchers, and competitors are ruthlessly punished, many have been assassinated."[17]

In a 1995 hearing on Capitol Hill, the administrator of the Drug Enforcement Administration (DEA) testified about teen violence, noting that violent crime rates for teens aged fourteen to seventeen are twice as high as adult levels. Violence among teens can be expected to increase as the proportion of the population who are teenagers increases. Much of it is connected with illegal drug trafficking, with gangs such as the Bloods and Crips, formerly confined to cities like Los Angeles, moving into other communities, even small towns and villages throughout the United States. "The core of their violence is related to protecting and expanding their lucrative drug trade."[18]

A recent study of juvenile violence and gangs disclosed that most juvenile crime is committed by gang members. The study tracked 808 children for seven years and found that 85 percent of robberies by youths were committed by the 15 percent of the youths who joined gangs. These gang members committed 54 percent of the felony thefts; 58 percent of the juvenile crime; and 62 percent of drug sales committed by the surveyed youths. Data were obtained from self-report studies of those surveyed as well as from juvenile courts records; both sources showed that most crimes committed by youths were by those who joined gangs. Other conclusions were that with the exception of drug involvement, youth crimes dropped when the teens left the gangs. The following facts were found to be associated with joining gangs: "poverty, unstable family living conditions, the availability of drugs and alcohol, parents who tolerate or commit violence, falling behind or failing in school, and 'hanging out' with delinquents."[19]

Some examples of gang violence have received national publicity in recent years. Here are a few examples. In 1997 three gang members involved in the Los Angeles killing of Stephanie Kuhen, aged three, were sentenced to prison terms of fifty-four years and eight months to life. Two of the gang were not teens, but one, Hugo Gomez, was under eighteen at the time of the killing. Stephanie was a passenger, along with her brothers and her mother, in a car driven by her mother's boyfriend. When he took a wrong turn and drove into the gang territory, gang members began firing at the car. One of Stephanie's brothers, Christopher, aged 5 at the time of the shooting, was not injured but appears to have sustained serious psychological problems as a result of the crime.[20]

After two fourteen-year-olds were killed in drive-by shootings in Chicago in 1995, the Chicago Crime Commission declared gang violence to be the worst public threat. The following month a twenty–six-year-old gang member became the first person in the United States to be convicted of compelling a person to join an organization. Robert Piggott was sentenced to the maximum term, seven years in prison, for beating a sixteen-year-old boy in an effort to force him to join a gang.[21]

Considerable efforts are being made to intervene in gang activity and to prosecute the extreme cases, but district attorneys report that their efforts are being met with serious problems. They complain about the leniency of the juvenile justice system and the intimidation of victims and witnesses by gang members. Prosecutors complain that many gang members "pass through the system without serving any sentence." Prosecution efforts are hindered further by the changing roles of the persons involved. "In gang crime, today's victim may become tomorrow's perpetrator seeking revenge."[22]

Current gangs and gang activities are not limited to male members. Sociological researchers report that female juveniles participate in gangs, too, and that they do so for some of the same reasons as their male counterparts: to find a sense of belonging that they have not found otherwise. One researcher found that female gang members do not view themselves as criminals, even when they engage in behavior that violates the law. They rationalize their behavior by saying that it is necessary in their society or by denying responsibility for what they do. Female gang members are aggressive against other women but not against men.[23]

Constitutional Rights of Juveniles

The Supreme Court has held that the U.S. Constitution extends some but not all of the rights of adult defendants to juveniles. In most situations, juveniles have a right to counsel (and to have counsel appointed if they cannot afford private defense counsel), the right not to be tried twice for the same offense, and the right to have the allegations against them proved by the same standard that is used in a criminal trial (beyond a reasonable doubt). They do not have a constitutional right to a trial by jury, although some states provide by statute for a jury trial.

The Supreme Court has not decided the issue of whether juveniles have the right to a public trial, but it has held that the press may not be punished criminally for publishing the name of a juvenile delinquent when it obtains it by lawful means.[24] Some states have statutes permitting the press to attend juvenile hearings. Others leave the decision to the discretion of the judge or prohibit the press entirely. The issue of whether juveniles have a federal constitutional right to a speedy trial has not been decided, but many states have provided by statute for limitations on the period of time the state may take to process a juvenile case.

Supreme Court Cases

Recognition of the constitutional rights of juveniles has occurred in a limited number of cases decided by the U.S. Supreme Court, beginning with *Kent* v. *United States,* decided in 1966.[25] Technically, this case does not apply to juvenile courts in other jurisdictions because it involved the interpretation of a District of Columbia statute. The case is important, however, because it signaled the beginning of the movement to infuse juvenile court proceedings with some due process elements.

Kent, a sixteen-year-old, was arrested and charged with rape, six counts of housebreaking, and robbery. In accordance with a Washington, D.C., statute, the juvenile court waived its jurisdiction over Kent, who was transferred to the adult criminal court for further proceedings. Kent requested a hearing on the issue of whether he should be transferred, and his attorney requested the social service file used by the court in the transfer decision. Both requests were denied.

Although the D.C. statute required a full investigation prior to waiver of a juvenile to adult court, the juvenile court judge did not state any findings of facts; nor did he give reasons for his decision to transfer Kent to the criminal court, which might lead one to think a full investigation did not occur.

Kent was indicted by a grand jury and tried in a criminal court. A jury found him not guilty by reason of insanity on the rape charge and guilty on the other charges. He was sentenced to serve from five to fifteen years on each count, for a total of thirty to ninety years in prison. Kent appealed his case. The first appellate court affirmed; the Supreme Court reversed. The Court agreed that juvenile courts need great latitude in juvenile cases; it affirmed the doctrine of *parens patriae*, but the Court concluded that the doctrine does not constitute "an invitation to procedural arbitrariness." The Court suggested that the "original laudable purpose of juvenile courts" had been eroded and that there "may be grounds for concern that the child receives the worst of both worlds; that he gets neither the protection accorded to adults nor the solicitous care and regenerative treatment postulated for children."[26]

The first juvenile case from a state court to be heard by the U.S. Supreme Court was *In re Gault*. On 8 June 1964 fifteen-year-old Gerald Gault and a friend were taken into custody in Arizona after a Mrs. Cook complained that two boys were making lewd phone calls to her. Gault's parents were not notified that, in effect, their son had been arrested. When they returned home from work that evening and found that Gerald was not there, they sent his brother to look for him and were told that he was in police custody.

Gault's parents were not shown the petition that was filed the next day. At the first hearing, attended by Gerald and his mother, Mrs. Cook did not testify; no written record was made of the proceedings. At the second hearing, Mrs. Gault asked for Mrs. Cook, but the judge said that Mrs. Cook's presence was not necessary. The decision of the judge was to commit Gerald to the state industrial school until his majority. When the judge was asked on what basis he adjudicated Gerald delinquent, he said he was not sure of the exact section of the code. The section of the Arizona Criminal Code that escaped his memory defined as a misdemeanant a person who "in the presence or hearing of any woman or child . . . uses vulgar, abusive, or obscene language." For this offense a fifteen-year-old boy was committed to a state institution until his majority. The maximum legal penalty for an adult was a fine of $5 to $50 or imprisonment for a maximum of two months. In contrast to an accused juvenile, an adult charged with this crime would be afforded due process at the trial.

The case was appealed to the U.S. Supreme Court, which reversed. The late Justice Abe Fortas delivered the opinion for the majority. Counsel had raised six basic rights: notice of the charges, right to counsel, right to confrontation and cross-examination, privilege against self-incrimination, right to a transcript, and right to appellate review. The Supreme Court ruled on the first four of these issues. The Court limited the extension of procedural safeguards in juvenile courts to those proceedings that might result in the commitment of juveniles to an institution in which their freedom would be curtailed. Justice Fortas excluded from the Court's decision the preadjudication and the postadjudication, or dispositional, stages. Justice Fortas reviewed the humanitarian philosophy of juvenile courts, but he said that the reality of juvenile courts is an unfulfilled dream. Courts that had been designed to act in the best interests of the child had become courts in which arbitrary and unfair procedures occurred frequently.

The Court explained the importance of due process and of the procedural rules that protect due process, comparing procedure in law to scientific method in science. The Court noted that Gault was "committed to an institution where he may be restrained of liberty for years." The fact that the institution was called an industrial school made no difference. The fact was that the juvenile's world became "a building with whitewashed walls, regimented routine and institutional hours . . . in which his world is peopled by guards, custodians, state employees, and 'delinquents' confined with him for anything from waywardness to rape and homicide." In light of the seriousness of this confinement, it would be "extraordinary if our Constitution did not require the procedural regularity and the exercise of care implied in the phrase 'due process.' Under our Constitution, the condition of being a boy does not justify a kangaroo court."[27]

In 1970 in *In re Winship*, the Supreme Court considered whether juvenile court proceedings require the same standard of proof as required in adult criminal courts or whether a lesser standard could be used. The Court applied the criminal court standard, concluding that "the observance of the standard of proof beyond a reasonable doubt will not compel the States to abandon or displace any of the substantive benefits of the juvenile process."[28]

In 1971 in *McKeiver* v. *Pennsylvania*, the Court refused to extend to juvenile court proceedings the right to a trial by jury. The Court emphasized that the underlying reason for its decisions in *Gault* and *Winship* was the principle of fundamental fairness. When the issue is one of fact-finding, elements of due process must be present. But a jury is not a "necessary component of accurate fact-finding." The Court concluded that juvenile courts should not become full adversary courts like criminal courts. The Court left open the possibility for state courts to experiment, inviting them to try trial by jury in juvenile proceedings, but refusing to require them to do so.[29]

In 1975 in *Breed* v. *Jones*, the Court held that the constitutional provision that defendants may not be tried twice for the same offense applies to juveniles. Breed, seventeen, was apprehended for committing acts while armed with a deadly weapon. He was adjudicated in the juvenile court, which found the allegations to be true. At the hearing to determine disposition, the court indicated that it intended to find Breed "not . . . amenable to the care, treatment and training program available through the facilities of the juvenile court," as required by the statute. He was transferred to criminal court, where he was tried and found guilty of robbery in the first degree. Breed argued on appeal that the transfer after a hearing and decision on the facts in juvenile court subjected him to two trials on the same offense. The Court agreed.[30]

In 1984 in *Schall* v. *Martin*, the Court upheld the New York statute that permitted preventive detention of juveniles. The Court held that preventive detention fulfills a legitimate state interest of protecting society and juveniles by detaining those who might be dangerous to society or to themselves. The Court reiterated its belief in the doctrines of fundamental fairness and *parens patriae*, stating that it was trying to strike a balance between the juvenile's right to freedom pending trial and the right of society to be protected. The juveniles in this case were apprehended for serious crimes. According to the Court, the period of preventive detention was brief and followed proper procedural safeguards. Three justices disagreed with the Court's decision.[31]

In 1994 the California Supreme Court interpreted *Schall* v. *Martin* as not requiring that juveniles be granted a probable cause hearing within forty-eight hours after arrest, as is required for adults. The court recognized significant differences in the detention of juveniles as compared to adults, noting that in many cases it is in the juvenile's best interest that detention occur. The court cited specific sections in the California statute that provide adequate safeguards for detained juveniles. For example, a juvenile may not be detained for more than twenty-four hours without written review and approval. The U.S. Supreme Court refused to hear the case, thus leaving the California decision intact.[32]

In 1992 in *United States* v. *R.L.C*, the Court held that juveniles may not be punished more harshly in sentencing than they would have been had they been charged and convicted of the same crime as an adult.[33]

Juvenile Curfews

Constitutional issues have arisen in recent years with the imposition of curfews in an attempt to reduce crime by keeping juveniles who are unaccompanied by an adult off the streets after specified hours. An example of this trend, which is being adopted by more and more cities, is the Dallas, Texas, ordinance. This ordinance provides that youths under seventeen must be off the street from 11 P.M. to 6 A.M. During those hours juveniles may not be in "public places" or "establishments." There are some exceptions: youths who are running errands for their parents or other adults, returning from school, civic, or religious functions, passing time on sidewalks in front of their homes, or exercising First Amendment rights (see Appendix A). Violations may result in a fine not to exceed $500 for each offense.

The U.S. Court of Appeals for the Fifth Circuit upheld the Dallas ordinance, noting that the ordinance is tailored narrowly to further the city's compelling interest in reducing and preventing juvenile crime and victimization. The U.S. Supreme Court refused to hear the case, thus allowing the decision of the Fifth Circuit to stand.[34]

An Arizona court has upheld a juvenile curfew despite its recognition that most courts that have considered the issue have refused to hold that the city or state has a legitimate interest in such ordinances or statutes. The Arizona court quoted the U.S. Supreme Court in its rejection of the notion that juveniles have no rights.

> Constitutional rights do not mature and come into being magically only when one attains the state-defined age of majority. Minors, as well as adults, are protected by the constitution and possess constitutional rights.[35]

The Arizona court emphasized that the U.S. Supreme Court recognizes the right of states to exercise greater control over juveniles than over adults. The Court has articulated three factors that should be considered in determining whether the state's proposed exercise of power over juveniles involves a significant state interest: "the peculiar vulnerability of children; their inability to make critical decisions in an informed, mature manner; and the importance of the parental role in child rearing."[36] According to the Arizona court, "If the state does not have a significant interest that is unique to children in terms of one of these factors, then the state must treat adults and children the same." The court found that the Arizona statute met those requirements, was not vague or too broad, and thus did not violate the constitutions of Arizona or of the United States.[37]

In contrast, in 1997 a federal appellate court in California held that the San Diego ordinance that makes it illegal for minors to "loiter, idle, wander, stroll or play" after 10 P.M. is unconstitutional.[38]

A separate issue is whether we should have juvenile curfew laws. If the research cited earlier, which shows that most juvenile violent crimes are committed during the hour after school dismisses for the day, is correct, forbidding juveniles to be on the streets late at night will not have a significant impact on juvenile crime rates.

A study of Missouri's juvenile justice systems disclosed discrimination against youths based on gender and race. "Evidence exists that decision processes are systematically disadvantaging youths who are either black, female, or both." The study found that even with controlling other relevant variables (such as the nature of the offense), African American youths were far more likely than whites to be processed through every phase of court systems. The study disclosed that the discrimination was much more likely to occur in rural than in urban courts, with rural courts being described as taking a "pre *Gault* approach" to juveniles.[39]

A study published in 1994 disclosed that even after controlling for the influence of social factors and the seriousness of the offense in question, "African American and Latino youth were more likely to be detained at each decision point in the juvenile justice system."[40] Another study of African American youths had similar findings with regard to differential treatment but found the differences varied among jurisdictions. This suggests the need for a more careful analysis of variables other than race that might be involved in producing the differences.[41]

Another issue crucial to an analysis of differential reactions within juvenile justice systems is that of gender. The 1974 Juvenile Justice and Delinquency Prevention Act (JJDPA) encouraged states to find means other than incarceration for juveniles who had committed nonserious offenses (status offenders, most of whom were girls) and for juveniles who were dependent or neglected but who had not committed any offenses. The statute called for an end to incarcerating juveniles with adults.[42]

Subsequent studies indicate that far fewer girls and boys have been incarcerated for status offenses recently than in the past, but that girls are more likely than boys to be incarcerated for status or other minor offenses. Studies show also that there is a wide range of differences in incarceration practices by gender in the various states.[43]

Race and Gender Issues

Juvenile Court Organization and Procedures

Court Procedures

Juvenile courts differ somewhat from jurisdiction to jurisdiction, but this discussion involves the organization and procedures that are found in most U.S. juvenile court systems. Figure 12.2 diagrams a typical organizational model and should be used as a reference for this discussion.

Juveniles may be referred to a juvenile justice system in various ways. Whereas 84 percent are referred by law enforcement agencies, other referrals come from parents, relatives, schools, probation officers, other courts, and miscellaneous other sources. As Figure 12.2 notes, juveniles may be counseled and released to their parents. Some may be diverted to social services or other programs. **Diversion** means to turn aside or alter the nature of things. In juvenile systems originally diversion was thought to be a process that would divert juveniles from official juvenile or criminal proceedings. They would be referred out of those systems before a hearing. The diagram in Figure 12.2 shows that after investigation by a police officer, one of the alternatives is to refer and divert juveniles to community resources.

Diversion in the juvenile field gained momentum after the 1967 President's Commission emphasized the need for this approach. In the 1970s, however, critics began to see the need for careful evaluation of diversion programs, noting that in many cases this resulted in net widening rather than in diversion. Juveniles who would not have been processed in the system previously were being brought in under the disguise of diversion.

If a decision is made not to divert the juvenile to some other agency or to the parents, other dispositions must be made. In some cases, after a referral has been made and the police have observed delinquent behavior, or an offense has been

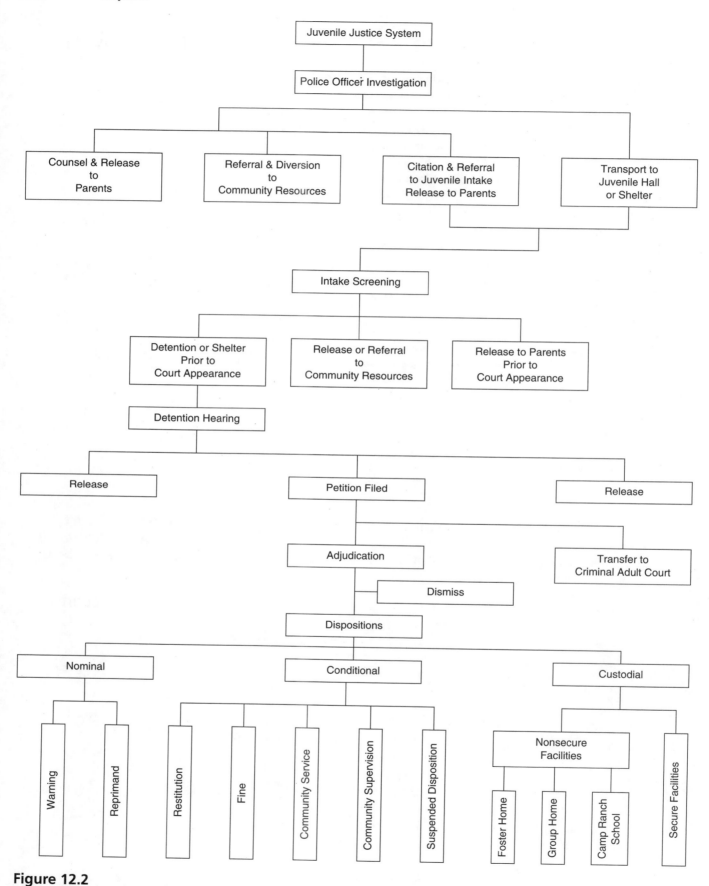

Figure 12.2

Organizational Model for Juvenile Justice Systems.

Source: National Advisory Committee on Criminal Justice Standards and Goals, *Juvenile Justice and Delinquency Prevention: Report of the Task Force on Juvenile Justice and Delinquency Prevention* (Washington, D.C.: U.S. Government Printing Office. 1976). P. 9.

reported and juveniles are suspected, the police may begin surveillance and investigation. There is no way of knowing how many cases are handled by the police without any formal action being taken, but most juveniles are not taken into **custody** upon apprehension by police. Police are not the only people who may take children into custody. Officials in child protective services, probation officers, family services, and youth services may take children into custody in many jurisdictions.

Historically, there were few guidelines for taking juveniles into custody. In the *Gault* case, the Supreme Court excluded prejudicial activities (activities, such as police apprehension, that occur prior to a court appearance) from the due process requirements of that case. Some lower courts have held that taking a juvenile into custody is not an arrest, and therefore the due process requirements that must be observed in the arrest of an adult are not applicable. But most courts appear to consider the process of taking a juvenile into custody an arrest that should be accompanied by due process requirements.[44]

If a juvenile is taken into custody, the issue of search and seizure may arise. Most state courts have interpreted *Gault's* fundamental fairness test to mean that the constitutional prohibition against unreasonable searches and seizures applies to juvenile proceedings. Some states have incorporated exclusionary rules into their statutes; thus, evidence seized illegally in juvenile cases may not be admitted as evidence against the offenders.[45]

Whether or not a search is conducted, there may be a decision to detain the juvenile. Most often juveniles are taken into custody without a summons or a warrant. Police must then decide what to do with the juveniles in their custody.

Most juveniles who are taken into custody are released to their parents. When that is not possible or reasonable, most jurisdictions require that juveniles be placed in special juvenile detention centers. As noted earlier in this chapter, in *Schall* v. *Martin* the Supreme Court upheld preventive detention for juveniles. After noting that juveniles have a substantial interest in liberty, the Court said, "But that interest must be qualified by the recognition that juveniles, unlike adults, are always in some form of custody." The Court reiterated its belief that courts have special powers over children as compared to adults. "[C]hildren, by definition, are not assumed to have the capacity to take care of themselves" and therefore, according to the Court, they need additional protection. Preventive detention of juveniles may be appropriate to protect the juveniles themselves, not just to protect society, as in the case of preventive detention of adults, which the Court upheld in 1987.[46]

The power to detain juveniles does not mean the power to detain them in jails rather than in special juvenile detention facilities. The Juvenile Justice and Delinquency Prevention Act, passed by Congress in 1974 and amended in subsequent years, provides that funds be provided for juvenile justice and delinquency projects and programs to those states that comply with the statute's mandates. Among other provisions is the phasing out of juvenile detention in adult jails, a mandate that had been met by thirty-nine states by 1992.[47]

Some states have taken measures to correct the problem of incarcerating juveniles in adult jails. For example, in 1994 Delaware agreed to a settlement in the lawsuit brought by the ACLU against the state, with regard to alleged unconstitutional conditions in detention and correctional institutions for juveniles. In agreeing to the settlement, state officials did not admit fault with regard to the allegations, which ranged from overcrowding to beatings, but they did agree to implement specific policies and programs.[48]

Placing juveniles in adult prisons is an even more serious and controversial measure. In 1997 the Washington Supreme Court upheld that state's provision that juveniles deemed to constitute a "continuing and serious threat to the safety of others at the institution" may be transferred administratively from a juvenile facility to an adult prison. The juvenile argued that since his juvenile court hearing did not provide him with all of the procedural protections of an adult court, he was denied his constitutional rights. The court responded that changing the location of detention did not alter the system: the juvenile remained under the juvenile system and retained the benefits of that system.[49]

To the contrary, in 1998 the Indiana Supreme Court rejected the practice of incarcerating juveniles in adult prisons and ordered the Department of Corrections to transfer a sixteen-year-old female from the adult prison to an institution for young offenders. As a result of this decision, Donna Ratliff, aged sixteen, must be moved, and probably the other eighty-five youth under age eighteen who are housed in adult prisons will have to be moved. At the time it was estimated that approximately 6,500 persons under age eighteen were being held in U.S. adult jails and prisons. Ratliff was fourteen when she burned down the house, killing her mother and sixteen-year-old sister. She claimed that she had been beaten repeatedly by her mother and sexually molested by another older sister and an uncle.[50]

One final issue with regard to detention is that of bail. Some states have granted juveniles the right to release on bail; others have denied that right, and still others have decided that it is not an issue because of the provision of special facilities for juvenile detention.

Another issue in juvenile court systems is whether juveniles should be interrogated by police. Originally, it was assumed that it would be therapeutic for children to confess; thus, juveniles had few procedural protections concerning police interrogation. Today the rule is that juvenile confessions may be used against them in court, provided those confessions are made voluntarily.

Certain procedures conducted by police may not be applicable in juvenile cases. Most statutes covering juvenile proceedings attempt to protect juveniles from some of the harshness of the criminal court and therefore prohibit publication of the pictures of suspects and the taking of fingerprints. The use of lineups and showups, however, has been left to the courts, most of which have held that the same standards applicable to adults must be applied in juvenile proceedings.

If a decision is made to detain a juvenile, the individual will be taken to intake screening, as indicated in Figure 12.2. Intake screening is designed to screen out the juveniles who should be diverted if that decision was not made earlier. A decision could be made at this stage to refer the juvenile to another agency or to his or her parents to await a hearing. A third alternative is to detain (or continue to detain) the juvenile before the hearing.

Intake decisions are made by intake officers, many of whom are probation officers. Theoretically, they conduct an investigation before making the intake decision, but with heavy caseloads, this may not be conducted thoroughly, if at all. Some states have placed statutory requirements on the intake officer regarding referrals out of the system or dismissals. For example, in some jurisdictions the intake officer may not dismiss a case without the prosecutor's written permission. In others, the case may not be dismissed or diverted if the complaining witness insists that formal action proceed beyond this stage.

If the juvenile is detained with the intent that a petition will be filed to bring formal procedures, usually a hearing is held to determine whether there is reason to continue with the case. This is true whether the juvenile is being held as a dependent and neglected child or for alleged delinquency. The hearing must be held within a reasonable period after detention begins, but it does not involve all of the specific procedural safeguards.

After the preliminary inquiry or hearing, the juvenile may be released from detention, or the case may be dismissed. If the case is not dismissed, it may proceed only with the filing of a **petition,** the formal document for initiating a case in the juvenile system. This petition is in contrast to a grand jury indictment or a prosecutor's presentment in adult criminal courts.

The *Gault* case requires that juveniles and their parents be given adequate notice of the charges and of the proceedings to follow. Most states require that the adjudicatory hearing be held within a specified period after the petition is filed. If this does not occur, in some jurisdictions the case must be dismissed.

Juveniles may admit or deny guilt; most admit that they committed the acts of which they are accused. This plea must be a knowing and voluntary one, and juveniles have the right to counsel if they are involved in proceedings that could lead to confinement in an institution.

Since *Kent* some jurisdictions have enacted statutes to permit juveniles some discovery procedures. Discovery involves the right to find out what the opposing side is going to use in the case. This information is necessary for the juvenile and his or her attorney to know how best to proceed with the case, and it might affect the juvenile's decision to admit or deny the allegations.

Role of Attorneys

In traditional juvenile court systems, there was no place for attorneys. The proceedings were not considered adversarial; all parties were thought to be acting in the child's best interests, and no need was seen for attorneys.

Prosecutors were not needed because the decision to proceed was made by intake officers. In reality, however, whether the person is called an intake officer or a prosecutor, a person permitted to decide who will or will not be processed in the system has considerable power. The question is not whether prosecutors have power but how much power they have. Some jurisdictions restrict their power to dismiss the case after the petition is filed, but even then prosecutors retain considerable discretion over determining in the first place whether to proceed with cases referred by the police or others.

The defense attorney's primary function in a juvenile case is to ensure that the juvenile's constitutional rights are protected during all of the proceedings. The attorney should be familiar with all the facts of the case and be prepared to present the defense at the hearing. The lack of formality in the hearing does not mean the defense is any less important in a juvenile than in a criminal court hearing.

An important issue in juvenile court cases is whether a right to counsel exists. In 1971 when the Court decided *McKeiver,* it stated in a footnote that although it had not ruled that the *Miranda* case applies to juveniles, it was assuming the *Miranda* principles were applicable to the proceedings in *McKeiver,* despite the Court's holding in *McKeiver* that the juvenile is not entitled to all procedures applicable to criminal trials. Most courts ruling on the issues have held that *Miranda* applies to juvenile cases.[51] The issues arise over whether juveniles may waive their *Miranda* rights. Some courts have refused to accept a juvenile waiver without parental guidance.[52] Others have held that children may not waive complicated legal rights, and thus it is permissible for police to question children in custody provided they do so in a fair manner.[53]

The interaction between those who serve as prosecutors and those who serve as defense attorneys is as important in juvenile as in criminal court systems. The relationship between prosecutors and defense attorneys in juvenile systems is similar to the relationship they share in criminal court systems. They may serve as checks on the potential abuse of power, or they may cooperate to the point of violating juveniles' rights. They may serve diligently and competently, with the best interests of juveniles as their goals. But in some cases those who take that perspective find their goals thwarted by a system that has inadequate resources and insufficient personnel.

Another interaction that occurs between prosecutors and defense attorneys in criminal court proceedings is applicable also to juvenile proceedings. Plea bargaining does occur, and some have argued that "plea bargaining and the best interests of the child are not necessarily mutually exclusive."[54]

The juvenile hearing is less formal than that of the criminal court, but the same general procedures occur. The prosecutor presents the evidence against the juvenile; the defense has an opportunity to cross-examine the witnesses, and some rules of evidence apply. Hearsay evidence may be presented in a juvenile hearing, in contrast to an adult trial. Evidence is presented to the judge and not to a jury unless the jurisdiction provides for a trial by jury and the juvenile did not waive the right.

At the end of the presentation of evidence, there is an **adjudication** of whether the juvenile did what he or she was accused of doing. Technically, the terms *guilty* and *not guilty* are not used in juvenile proceedings, although the obvious purpose is to determine whether the alleged acts were committed. To support a finding of responsibility, the evidence must be sufficient to convince the judge beyond a reasonable doubt.

In traditional language, juveniles are not sentenced; **dispositions** are made. Dispositions tend to be indeterminate, although the court loses jurisdiction over the child when the child reaches the age of majority. Several types of dispositions are available. Figure 12.2 illustrates that the court may take one of three routes. Nominal dispositions such as warnings and reprimands may be made. Conditional dispositions are similar to those in criminal courts: restitution, fine, community service, suspended disposition, or community supervision (probation). A final method of disposition is to place juveniles in secure or nonsecure facilities. Frequently, juveniles are ordered to make restitution for the damages they have caused.

What procedures must be followed at the disposition hearing? In *Gault*, the Supreme Court stated that it was not answering the question of which federal constitutional due process rights apply to the pre- or post-adjudicatory hearing stages of the juvenile process. Therefore, the required procedures are established by state statutes or by state court decisions, and they vary from state to state. Because most juvenile cases do not involve a dispute over the facts, the disposition hearing becomes the most significant part of the process, and the right to counsel is important. Normally, it is a separate hearing from that of adjudication, and it is preceded by an investigative report, or social report, on which the disposition may be based.

The social report is crucial to the philosophy that juveniles are to be treated individually and that it is possible to rehabilitate them. The social study should include any information that might have a bearing on assessing the needs of the particular child. The types of evidence that may be admitted at the dispositional stage are much broader than those permitted at the adjudicatory hearing.

After the disposition, the juvenile may have grounds for an appeal. In *Gault*, the Court refused to rule that there is a constitutional right to appeal from a juvenile court decision, but since *Gault* all jurisdictions have made some statutory provisions for appeal.[55]

Juveniles in Criminal Courts

Concern with what appears to be an increasing number of juveniles involved in violent crimes has resulted in a push for more stringent treatment of such persons. Most states provide that in certain cases juveniles may be tried in criminal courts. This may be permitted because both courts have jurisdiction; the offenses

Spotlight 12.2

Juveniles Prosecuted in State Criminal Courts

A 1997 publication by the Bureau of Justice Statistics (BJS) presents data from their 1994 National Survey of Prosecutors and other BJS statisticians as well as data from the National Center for Juvenile Justice. Following are the Highlights of that publication.

- Nationwide, 94% of State court prosecutors' offices had responsibility for handling juvenile cases.

- Among prosecutors' offices handling juvenile cases, almost two-thirds transferred at least one juvenile case to criminal court in 1994. Of these offices, 37% transferred at least one aggravated assault case, 35% at least one burglary case, 34% at least one robbery case, and 32% at least one murder case.

- 19% of prosecutors' offices handling juvenile cases had a specialized unit that dealt with juvenile cases transferred to criminal court.

- 16% of prosecutors' offices handling juvenile cases had written guidelines about the transfer of juveniles to criminal court.

- States have developed several mechanisms to permit proceeding against alleged juvenile offenders as adults in criminal court. These mechanisms include judicial waiver, concurrent jurisdiction statutes, and statutorily excluding certain offenses from juvenile court jurisdiction.

- The percentage of petitioned cases judicially waived to criminal court has remained relatively constant at about 1.4% since 1985. In 1994, 12,300 juvenile cases were judicially waived.

- From 1985–91 property offenses comprised the largest number of cases judicially waived. Since 1991 violent offenses have outnumbered property offenses as the most serious charge.

- Currently no national data describe the number of juvenile cases processed in criminal court under concurrent jurisdiction or statutory exclusion provisions.

Source: Bureau of Justice Statistics, *Juveniles Prosecuted in State Criminal Courts* (Washington, D.C.: U.S. Department of Justice, March 1997), p. 1.

are excluded from the jurisdiction of juvenile courts; or there is a waiver from the juvenile to the criminal court. This last procedure, also called *transfer* or **certification,** means just what the words say: the juvenile court waives jurisdiction; the case is transferred from the juvenile to the criminal court; or the court certifies that the juvenile should be tried as an adult. When certification occurs, the juvenile goes through the same procedures and has the same constitutional rights as adults tried in criminal courts. Spotlight 12.2 contains additional information on juveniles prosecuted in state criminal courts.

Certification to a criminal court is important because it may result in more severe consequences to the juvenile, although this is not always the case. The procedures that must be followed differ from state to state. In some states the prosecutor makes the decision; in others the decision is made by the juvenile court judge.

The procedural requirements for waiver were articulated by the Supreme Court in the *Kent* case, discussed on p. 347. Although that case applied only to the statute in question in Washington, D.C., most courts have interpreted *Kent* as stating the minimum due process requirements for transfer from the juvenile to the criminal court. The juvenile is entitled to a hearing on the question of transfer, and the right to counsel attaches to that hearing. Upon request, counsel must be given access to the social record that the court has compiled on the juvenile. If jurisdiction is waived, the juvenile must be given a statement of the reasons for the waiver.

Some statutes give jurisdiction to criminal courts over juveniles who commit specified serious crimes such as murder but permit the criminal court to transfer the case to juvenile court. New York is an example. Under the New York statute, children aged thirteen or older who are charged with second-degree murder and children fourteen or older who are charged with any one of a number of serious crimes (including burglary, sodomy in the first degree, aggravated sexual abuse, manslaughter in the first degree, murder, rape, and robbery) are under the exclusive jurisdiction of criminal courts. But criminal courts may transfer the cases to juvenile courts by a process known as *reverse certification*.[56]

The Colorado Court of Appeals has held that when a juvenile is transferred to adult court, due process does not require that the evidence supporting transfer be clear and convincing. Under the Colorado statute, a juvenile who is fourteen or older and is accused of an act that would be a felony if committed by an adult, may be transferred to adult criminal court at the request of the prosecutor, provided the juvenile court conducts an investigation. The purpose of that investigation is to determine whether there is probable cause to believe that the juvenile committed the act and, if so, whether it is in the interests of society and of the accused juvenile that the case be transferred. The court noted that the decision of whether or not to transfer is more analogous to a sentencing hearing than to a trial to determine guilt. The court emphasized that there is no constitutional right to be tried as a juvenile and that the risk to society of not trying the juvenile as an adult may outweigh any reasons for leaving the case in the juvenile court.[57]

Waiver of juveniles to criminal courts with judicial discretion or legislative provisions for trying them in criminal courts has been criticized severely by juvenile court judges. According to the National Council of Juvenile and Family Court Judges, the "assumption is that . . . criminal courts will be tougher and can serve as a more effective deterrent for juvenile crime. . . . This assumption is not borne out by the facts."[58]

Two scholars who tested the results of Idaho's automatic waiver statute found that the change did not result in a reduction of violent juvenile crime. The authors concluded that their results were similar to those of a study of New York's automatic waiver statute: "There does not appear to be a deterrent effect of legislative waiver on rates of juvenile violent crimes." They note that the finding is interesting particularly in light of the vast differences between the two states, one a highly urbanized state with high crime rates, the other much more rural with low crime rates.[59]

Successful constitutional challenges have been made to some automatic waivers from juvenile to criminal courts. For example, the Delaware provision that a juvenile who turns eighteen before trial should be transferred to criminal court automatically if one or more enumerated crimes were charged, was held to violate the state and federal constitutions because it removed from the judiciary the authority to make the transfer decision. In essence, the decision was made by the prosecutor, who had the power to effect a transfer by bringing charges of an enumerated offense.[60]

There are a number of factors that might influence the decision to transfer a juvenile to criminal court. A study of these factors in Virginia reported that age, current offense, and prior delinquency record were the most frequent factors accounting for waiver.[61] In contrast, a study of an upstate New York city disclosed that in a jurisdiction providing for automatic transfers, accused juveniles from single-parent families are more likely than those from dual-parent families to be indicted by a grand jury, suggesting that "nonoffense-related considerations were not eliminated by legislative or automatic forms of waiver."[62]

There are a number of reasons for and against certification or waiver. One of the strongest arguments in favor of waiver is that it sends a message to juveniles and thus serves as a deterrent. It serves as notice to society that we are getting tough on juvenile crime. On the other hand, there is evidence that the get-tough approach is not working, giving only the *appearance* of toughness and deterrence. Earlier discussions of discretion are important here. If the system is too severe, police may not arrest; prosecutors may not prosecute or will charge lesser offenses; juries may not convict. But as one scholar notes, "Criminal court leniency does not indicate that transfer was unnecessary."[63]

Despite this reaction, the move is toward harsher treatment of violent juveniles no matter how young they are. In addition to the "three strikes and you're out" theme that permeates legal reactions to adult criminals, proposals for transferring serious juvenile cases to criminal court and prohibiting juveniles from using handguns continue. Several state legislatures have followed Colorado, which bans the possession of a handgun by a person under eighteen. The first offense is a misdemeanor; subsequent offenses are felonies. Furnishing a handgun for a juvenile is a felony, too.[64]

Illinois enacted legislation designed to crack down on juvenile crime. That legislation, which became effective on 1 January 1995, is aimed particularly at gang- and drug-related crimes involving firearms. The legislation makes it easier for fifteen-and sixteen-year-olds who are involved in these crimes to be tried in criminal rather than in juvenile courts.[65]

Finally, Congress has given attention to efforts to combat serious crimes by juveniles. The House of Representatives passed a bill in May of 1997, voting overwhelmingly to provide $1.5 billion to states that enact legislation requiring juveniles aged fifteen and over accused of violent crimes to be tried in criminal courts automatically or to give prosecutors discretion to make that decision. Further, the state must provide escalating penalties for repeat offenders and allow juvenile court judges to sanction parents and other guardians who do not provide proper supervision for delinquents. President Clinton opposed the bill, stating that it does not provide a comprehensive plan for combatting youth gangs and violence.[66] The federal legislation might not be helpful anyway, as it applies only to federal crimes, which constitute only a small part of juvenile crime.

Juveniles In Corrections

Placement of juveniles in closed institutions is a relatively new practice. In the 1700s and early 1800s, it was thought that the family, the church, and other social institutions should handle juvenile delinquents. Jail was the only form of incarceration, and it was used primarily for detention pending trial. From 1790 to 1830, the traditional forms of social control began to break down as mobility and town sizes increased. Belief in sin as the cause of delinquency was replaced by a belief in community disorganization. Some method was needed whereby juveniles could be put back into orderly lives. It was decided that the institution—the house of refuge, the well-ordered asylum patterned after the family structure—was the answer.

The institutional model was used for juveniles, adult criminals, elderly persons, the mentally ill, orphans, unwed mothers, and vagrants. By institutionalizing these persons, their lives could become ordered as they were removed from the corruption of society. Life in the total institution was characterized by routine, head counts, bells to signal the beginnings and the ends of activities, and marching to all activities.[67]

By the 1850s many people were admitting that custody was all the institutions offered. Problems such as overcrowding, lack of adequate staff, and heterogeneous populations led to the realization that institutionalization was not accomplishing its purpose. The next concept for juveniles was the **training school,** typically built around a cottage system. It was thought that cottage parents would create a homelike atmosphere. Hard work, especially farm work, was emphasized.

In recent years overcrowding, shortness of staff, and lack of resources, along with due process violations have characterized juvenile corrections. The first nationwide investigation of juvenile institutions, published in 1993, disclosed that 75 percent of juveniles were housed in institutions that violated at least one standard relating to living space. Forty-seven percent lived in overcrowded institutions, up from 36 percent in 1987. Overcrowding was described as a "pervasive and serious problem across the nation."[68]

The study, mandated by Congress in 1988, found that only 27 percent of juvenile facilities met security standards; only 25 percent of juveniles were in facilities that met standards for controlling suicidal behavior, and 11,000 youths committed more than 17,000 suicidal acts in a year, although only ten were complete in 1990. The study led Attorney General Janet Reno to declare, "This study puts an exclamation point on the obvious conclusion that America must take better care of its children before they get into trouble and not abandon them once they are in trouble."[69]

The study disclosed that between 1987 and 1991 the proportion of confined juveniles who are minorities increased from 53 percent to 63 percent, with Hispanics increasing from 13 percent to 17 percent and African Americans from 37 percent to 44 percent.[70]

Types of Institutions for Juveniles

Despite the movement toward diversion of juveniles from closed institutions, today most juveniles who are under the care and custody of the state are confined in public institutions or in traditional training schools. Detention centers and shelters are used to confine those who have been referred to juvenile courts and are awaiting disposition by those courts. These facilities are used for detaining juveniles who cannot be detained in their own homes. A child who is to be placed in a correctional institution may be held temporarily in a reception or diagnostic center, pending a decision concerning which institution would be the best placement for the child. Our primary concern here is with the facilities in which the juveniles are placed for their more lengthy confinement, and those are of three basic types.

Generally the training school, which houses most confined juveniles, is the largest of the facilities. It was the first type of facility accepted widely for the confinement of juveniles, and it is the most secure. Some jurisdictions operate other types of facilities that are less secure, such as ranches, forestry camps, or farms. Most of these facilities are located in rural areas and permit greater contact with the community than the training school provides.

Boot camps, discussed in greater detail in Chapter 9, are becoming widely used as well. In the boot camp atmosphere the offender must participate in a strongly regimented daily routine of physical exercise, work, and discipline, which resembles military training. Most of the programs include rehabilitative measures such as drug treatment and educational programs.

The least physically secure facilities are group homes. Unlike foster homes, which are community-based facilities in which juveniles live with families, many group homes are small institutions. Most are operated by a staff, not a family. The cost per juvenile resident is twice as high for staff-operated group homes as for foster care. Group homes have been criticized as a poor substitute for foster care homes because they remove the positive influence of the family atmosphere.[71]

Many juvenile institutions attempt to make the facility as homelike as possible. A campuslike environment or cottage setting is not uncommon, with a small number of juveniles housed in each building along with cottage or house parents. Despite these efforts, the architecture of many juvenile facilities reflects the premise that all who are confined there must face the same type of security as those few who need the secure environment. Security is very important, but the facilities should not preclude rehabilitation opportunities.

Originally special facilities were established to isolate juveniles from the harmful effects of society and from incarcerated adults. Later, with the development of juvenile courts, the philosophy of treatment became dominant. During the past century, however, various commissions have pointed out the failure of juvenile corrections to provide adequate services and programs to enable the successful implementation of a treatment philosophy. As noted earlier, in recent years courts have entered the picture. Courts have required some elements of due process in the adjudication of juveniles, changes in the disciplinary handling of institutionalized juveniles, and changes in the degree and kinds of services provided in those institutions.

The assignment of juveniles to special facilities for the purpose of treatment after they have been through proceedings that do not involve all elements of due process raises a critical issue. Do juveniles have a constitutional right to treatment? Recall that the original reason for not infusing the juvenile court with due process requirements was that, unlike adult offenders, juveniles were not being punished. They were being treated; juvenile judges acted in the best interests of the child. Thus, juveniles did not need due process requirements to protect them from governmental action.

The Supreme Court has discredited the practice of using the philosophy of rehabilitation to deny juveniles their basic constitutional rights, and it has acknowledged that rehabilitation has failed. Yet the Court has indicated its support for retention of at least part of the *parens patriae* philosophy in juvenile proceedings while applying some but not all due process requirements. This has left a somewhat confusing result.

Scholars and many courts have taken the position that, under the doctrine of *parens patriae*, juveniles have given up some of their constitutional rights in order to be processed through a system that is based on treatment rather than punishment. Therefore, the state must provide that treatment or relinquish custody of the child. The right to treatment is based on cases involving the rights of the confined mentally ill, too.

The Supreme Court has not decided a case on the constitutional right to treatment for juveniles, although in *O'Conner* v. *Donaldson,* a case involving confinement of the mentally ill, the opinion of the Court implies that the justices might not hold that juveniles have a constitutional right to treatment.[72] Some lower courts have held that juveniles have a statutory or constitutional right to treatment, but most of those cases that have not been reversed were decided before *O'Conner.*[73]

Some of the earlier cases decided before *O'Conner* have been reversed on appeal. An example is *Morales* v. *Turman,* a Texas case that began in a lower federal court in 1973, when the court found numerous violations of statutory and constitutional rights of the children confined in Texas juvenile systems. The

Treatment and Juvenile Corrections

lower court held that the children had a constitutional right to treatment, but that conclusion was questioned by the federal appellate court, and in most subsequent decisions, the case has been interpreted as not recognizing a *constitutional* right to treatment.[74]

In 1983 a federal court rejected the constitutional right to treatment argument:

> We therefore agree . . . that, although rehabilitative training is no doubt desirable and sound as a matter of policy and perhaps of state law, plaintiffs have no constitutional right to that rehabilitative training.

The Supreme Court refused to hear the case, thus permitting the decision to stand.[75]

On the other hand, some constitutional rights for incarcerated juveniles are being recognized. For example, the Sixth Circuit Court of Appeals has held that the right to counsel applies to incarcerated juveniles when they raise claims involving constitutional rights and for civil rights actions that relate to their incarceration. If they cannot afford counsel, the state must provide it for them in these cases. The issue arose in a class action suit in Tennessee and involved incarcerated youths who claimed that they were being denied access to courts.[76]

There is some reason for encouragement with regard to juvenile corrections. For example, in 1994 the Colorado governor announced that the Metropolitan State College of Denver would be taking over the educational program in the state's juvenile correctional system. Remedial and vocational training programs as well as secondary and postsecondary academic programs are provided on a five-year basis.[77]

Studies show that generally those youths who get into trouble with the law have performed poorly in school. Many have difficulty with reading, and literacy skills are the focus of one of the projects of the Office of Juvenile Justice and Delinquency Prevention (OJJDP). "Designed to teach illiterate youth to read and write, these programs offer a nontraditional, motivational approach that provides students with immediate positive feedback and then encourages them to strive for success."[78]

Juveniles in the Community

Juveniles may be released from institutions and placed on parole, usually called **aftercare.** Historically, juveniles have had no right to early release, but most do not remain in confinement for long periods of time. Usually, they are released to aftercare, but if they violate the terms of that release they may be returned to confinement. Many of the rules that the Supreme Court has applied to adult parole and probation revocation have been applied to juveniles.

The type of aftercare of juveniles is important. Aftercare should begin with prerelease programs while the juvenile is in confinement. There are two kinds of prerelease programs in juvenile institutions. In the first type, juveniles may be given furloughs or weekend passes to visit their families, which permit gradual reentry into society. In the second type, the inmates may be moved to special cottages within the institution, where they live for a period of time with other inmates who are almost ready to be released, and where special programs are provided to prepare them for that release. The length of the aftercare period depends on the needs of each child.

Another procedure for keeping the juvenile in the community is probation. Earlier discussions note that probation is the most frequently used sanction for adults; the same is true of juveniles. And the same issues are raised. As with adults, the key issue with juveniles is whether serious offenders may be placed in the community without causing unreasonable harm to others. There is some evidence to indicate that intensive probation supervision of serious juvenile offenders is an effective alternative to incarceration but that the cost-effectiveness of IPS is difficult to achieve without widespread use of diversion.[79]

The National Advisory Commission on Criminal Justice Standards and Goals advocated that where possible, juvenile delinquents should be diverted from institutionalization. The commission concluded:

> The failure of major juvenile and youth institutions to reduce crime is incontestable. Recidivism rates, imprecise as they may be, are notoriously high. The younger the person when entering an institution, the longer he is institutionalized, and the farther he progresses into the criminal justice system, the greater his chance of failure.[80]

The advisory commission emphasized that these institutions are places of punishment, and they do not have a significant effect on deterrence. They remove juveniles from society temporarily. In that sense society is protected, but the changes in the offender during that incarceration are negative, not positive. The institutions are isolated geographically, which hinders delivery of services from outside the institution, decreases visits from families and friends, reduces opportunities for home furloughs, and limits the availability of staff. Many of these institutions have outlasted their functions. Because of their architecture, the institutions are inflexible at a time when flexibility is needed. They were built to house too many people for maximum treatment success. The large numbers have resulted in an excessive emphasis on security and control. The advisory commission maintained that these institutions are dehumanizing and that they create an unhealthy need for dependence.

The traditional juvenile correctional institution must change. It should not continue to warehouse failures and release them back into society without improvement. It must share a major responsibility for the successful reintegration of those juveniles into society, but as institutions change their goals, the public must bear its share of responsibility. No longer may it be assumed that the major responsibility for institutionalized juveniles lies with the officials at those institutions. The public must be involved in the planning, the goals, and the programs, as well as in the efforts toward reintegration into the community. Most importantly, the public must give full acceptance to these institutional and community programs for juveniles. The advisory commission concluded its discussion of juvenile corrections by saying, "It is no surprise that institutions have not been successful in reducing crime. The mystery is that they have not contributed even more to increasing crime."[81]

Effect of Institutionalization on Juveniles

Deinstitutionalization

Dissatisfaction with closed institutions has led to several movements. One is diversion. Another is community corrections. A third movement, related to diversion and community corrections, is deinstitutionalization. This movement began with an emphasis on probation, foster homes, and community treatment centers for juveniles. The establishment of the California Youth Authority in the early 1960s and the closing of Massachusetts's juvenile institutions in 1970 and 1971 gave impetus to the movement.

What caused this movement toward deinstitutionalization for juveniles? Some say it started in the early 1960s when the government began granting money to localities to improve conditions in the processing and treatment of delinquency. Others say it emerged when social scientists began to assume the role of clinicians and became involved in policy decision making at local and federal levels. Still others point to the interest of lawyers in the 1960s and 1970s in reforming juvenile courts.

Some scholars take the position that the movement came primarily from a desire to save the costs of constructing new facilities and repairing existing ones.[82] Whatever the reasons, it is clear that this movement is unlike most others in the field. It involves a major change: abandoning the large institution and replacing it with a different concept of corrections. The era of the large institution may be over, with some jurisdictions abolishing them. An example is that of Massachusetts.

In 1969 Jerome G. Miller took charge of the Department of Youth Services in Massachusetts. At first he attempted to reform the system, but "after fifteen months of bureaucratic blockades, open warfare with state legislators, and sabotage by entrenched employees, Miller abandoned reform and elected revolution."[83] Between 1969 and 1973, Miller closed the state juvenile institutions, placing juveniles in community-based facilities.

The Massachusetts experiment with deinstitutionalization has been evaluated by a team of social scientists from Harvard University. In the early stages of evaluation, they concluded guardedly that the experiment was a success. In 1977 the tentative conclusions were questioned. The recidivism rates of the youth had not increased or decreased; therefore, it might be concluded that deinstitutionalization, though no better, was no worse than institutionalization and was certainly more humane. However, the evaluators reported a crisis in the reaction of the public, the courts, and the police.

Public concern in Massachusetts was over the need for more secure facilities. A task force appointed to consider the issue concluded:

> We are left with a picture of the reformed agency showing clear signs of difficulty and crisis in the political structure that supports it and some suggestions of difficulty in its actual operations.

The evaluators were looking specifically at the results of the use of extreme tactics in effecting reform.[84] Empirical studies of the Massachusetts system conducted in the 1980s to determine the success of deinstitutionalization were contradictory.

More recently, Jerome Miller has written a book about the Massachusetts deinstitutionalization program. For this scholarly effort Miller was awarded the prestigous Edward Sagarin Prize in criminology by the American Society of Criminology. One reviewer has described the book as one that "deserves many prizes because it contains the substance of monumental criminology."[85]

In 1994 it was announced that the National Juvenile Justice Reform Project, established by the Robert F. Kennedy Memorial with an $800,000 grant from the Robert Wood Johnson Foundation, would provide funds for five jurisdictions to participate in a project to replicate the Massachusetts experience.[86]

Deinstitutionalization may be the government's reponse to court pressures or orders to improve juvenile institutions. In 1988 Maryland closed the Montrose School, a secure facility for juveniles. Among other reasons, threatened lawsuits over conditions, an environmental group's threat to sue because of the facility's sewer system, and two suicides led to closing this facility. Youths were placed in alternative programs, an appropriate move because many of the confined juveniles were being incarcerated for status offenses.[87] A subsequent study of this closing has mixed results, much like those of other studies, leading its authors to conclude that "neither institutional programs nor community-based programs are uniformly effective or ineffective."[88]

In evaluating deinstitutionalization, we must raise the issue of whether the negative effects of institutionalization, at least to some extent, will crop up in community treatment centers or other forms of handling juveniles as well. In responding to the argument that large juvenile institutions should be abolished because they are schools for crime, one researcher points out that in many cases those large institutions are confining juveniles who previously were in the smaller institutions. Thus, the smaller institutions must take responsibility for part of the failure of the correctional system to rehabilitate juveniles. Furthermore, replacing the large institutions with smaller facilities "may not really change the amount of teaching and learning that takes place among offenders."[89] If juveniles who already have a strong orientation toward crime are confined together, they may continue to infect and teach each other.

In 1994 five Houston, Texas, teens were sentenced to death for the vicious rapes and murders of two young women, reportedly showing no remorse for their actions.[90] Also in 1994 a poll of juvenile justice judges revealed that two out of five believe that the death penalty is appropriate for some juveniles. Forty percent of the respondents thought the minimum age should be fourteen or fifteen, while 17 percent thought twelve or thirteen should be the minimum age.[91]

Juveniles and Capital Punishment

The 1986 execution of James Terry Roach, then twenty-five, but executed for a crime he committed when he was sixteen, raised the issue of whether capital punishment should be imposed on juveniles. In an earlier case, Monty Lee Eddings, who was fifteen when he murdered the Oklahoma highway patrol officer who stopped him for a traffic violation, was successful in the appeal of his death sentence to the Supreme Court. Eddings's attorney argued that capital punishment for a crime committed while the offender was a juvenile constituted cruel and unusual punishment. The Supreme Court did not decide that issue but sent the case back for resentencing on the grounds that at the sentencing hearing, the lower court did not consider mitigating circumstances. The trial court considered the mitigating circumstances and resentenced Eddings to death. Before his case reached the Supreme Court a second time, Oklahoma's Court of Criminal Appeals changed his sentence from death to life imprisonment.[92]

In 1985 the Court upheld the death sentence of a defendant who was eighteen at the time he committed his atrocious capital crime.[93] In 1988 the Court decided *Thompson* v. *Oklahoma*, in which it reversed the capital sentence of William Wayne Thompson, who was fifteen when he committed the crime for which he was given the death penalty. In *Thompson* a majority of the Court agreed that execution of an individual who was fifteen at the time he committed a capital crime is cruel and unusual punishment even though the crime was heinous. In deciding the issue, the Court used the standard established in *Trop* v. *Dulles,* decided in 1958. The standard is "the evolving standards of decency that mark the progress of a maturing society."[94]

But how does a judge decide whether that standard has been met? The Court looked at legislative enactments and jury decisions (only 5 of the 1,393 persons sentenced to death between 1982 and 1986 were less than sixteen when they committed the crimes for which they were sentenced) and decided that the "evolving standards of decency" preclude executing one so young.[95]

The Court's decision in *Thompson* bans capital punishment for youths who are under sixteen when they commit a capital offense. It does not answer the question of whether capital punishment is cruel and unusual when imposed on youths between the ages of sixteen and eighteen at the time the capital murder is committed. The Court makes this very clear in its opinion, noting that it has been asked to declare capital punishment unconstitutional for all youths under eighteen:

> Our task today, however, is to decide the case before us; we do so by concluding that the Eighth and Fourteenth Amendments prohibit the execution of a person who was under sixteen years of age at the time of his or her offense.[96]

Subsequently, the Supreme Court decided the cases of two other death row inmates who had committed murders while they were juveniles. One was approximately seventeen years and four months old when he raped and sodomized a twenty-year-old woman repeatedly, before he killed her with a bullet in the front and another in the back of her head. The second was approximately sixteen years and six months of age when he killed a twenty-six-year-old mother of two by multiple stab wounds in her chest. The Court held that capital punishment for these youths does not constitute cruel and unusual punishment.[97]

Juvenile and Criminal Justice Systems: An Assessment

She appeared to be a "perfect" candidate for Harvard University, which granted her early admission for the fall class of 1995. Gina Grant, an orphan, had high grades in an excellent school, an IQ of 150, excellent references, and a high score on entrance exams. She was co-captain of the tennis team and tutored underprivileged kids. But after a published article about her and other orphans, an anonymous source sent Harvard information about her previous life in South Carolina. When she was fourteen, Grant entered a plea of no contest to manslaughter in the death of her mother, whose skull was smashed by at least thirteen blows of a candlestick. Harvard revoked her early admission letter after notification of this incident.

Grant's case drew reactions from all over the nation, with forces lining up in support and in opposition of Harvard's decision. Harvard officials said little other than to state that the early admission of Grant had been rescinded. Some alleged that Grant lied on her application; her attorney denied that, indicating that juvenile records are sealed and that she was not under an obligation to reveal that her six months of incarceration was followed by probation until she was eighteen. Some alleged that Grant misrepresented her situation, used her status as an orphan to gain advantages as well as sympathy, and showed no remorse. It was alleged that she and her boyfriend at the time plunged a knife into her mother's throat to give the appearance of a suicide.

Others argued that Grant committed the killing in self-defense of an alcoholic mother who had abused her for years, and whose blood-alcohol level was three times the state limit for intoxication at the time of her death. It was alleged that Grant is an extraordinary young woman who had achieved great success despite her troubled background and that she deserved a chance at a Harvard education, for which she was qualified. A *New York Times* editorial referred to Harvard's decision to rescind the offer as a mistake done in haste and urged a reconsideration of that decision, noting that Grant's record indicated that she has been rehabilitated.[98] Grant enrolled at Tufts University in the fall of 1995, but she faced opposition from some in the university.

The case of Gina Grant is an excellent one to note in closing this text's study of criminal and juvenile justice systems, for it raises many of the issues those systems face today. Although she was accused of a violent crime, Grant was processed through the juvenile justice system. She was given only a short term and placed on probation. Her records were sealed, and she was given a chance at rehabilitation. Many argue that she was successful; she served her time; she deserved a chance for a new life; that is the purpose of the juvenile system.

Others argue that the case illustrates that juveniles are becoming more violent and that juvenile justice systems are soft on crime. Grant should have been processed through the criminal justice system and sentenced to a long term, and Harvard should have revoked its offer of admission.

Grant's case and others like it focus on many of the issues facing justice systems today. Should we continue to preserve juvenile justice systems; or should all serious crimes be processed through criminal justice systems? If we retain juvenile systems, how closely should they mirror criminal systems in structure and in procedure? Most importantly, will crime rates be affected by changing the current systems?

WiseGuide Wrap-Up Juvenile justice systems held the highest hopes for success in rehabilitation, reformation, and reintegration; but they contained some of the greatest deprivations of constitutional rights. In the name of "the best interests of the child," the state took away liberty without due process of law. Under the guise of treatment and rehabilitation, not punishment, juvenile court systems swept into their clutches many who otherwise would not have been processed by court systems.

There is a need to treat juveniles differently from adults; there is a need to segregate them from adults in confinement; there is a need to offer them opportunities for improvement so they can succeed in a competitive world. Those needs may not be met by violating their rights.

This chapter looks at the historical treatment of juveniles, traces the development of juvenile courts, and examines the current procedural requirements for those courts. The chapter reviews the major Supreme Court and lower court decisions concerning juveniles' rights.

The discussion shows that although not all procedural requirements of criminal courts have been applied to juveniles, many due process rights have been extended to juvenile courts. No longer is it sufficient to say that juveniles are not arrested, they are apprehended. They are not found guilty, they are adjudicated. They are not sentenced, but dispositions are made of their cases. The change in wording does not compensate for a lack of due process. In many respects present-day criminal and juvenile courts are similar. On the other hand, states have some room to experiment in their juvenile systems. Trial by jury is not required by the federal Constitution but has been extended by statute to juvenile courts in some states.

Violent crimes by juveniles appear to be committed by a few, but those violent few commit a large percentage of the total crimes committed by juveniles. Concern with this violence and with recidivism has led some states to pass statutes giving criminal courts jurisdiction over juveniles who commit serious crimes. In other states, after a proper hearing, juvenile courts may waive jurisdiction over juveniles who have committed serious crimes.

All reforms have problems, and one problem with the get-tough laws concerning juveniles has been the unwillingness of courts and juries to convict if they know there will be an automatic penalty that they consider too severe. Thus, in some cases the get-tough policy results in less, not more, protection for the community. It is important to evaluate changes carefully for that reason. Insufficient attention has been given to evaluating legislative changes in juvenile systems.

Juveniles have received differential treatment in corrections, too, although it is not at all clear that those differences are positive. Indefinite detention of juveniles under the guise that they are being treated when they are being detained without treatment has been held by courts to be inappropriate. Unfortunately, disillusionment with treatment and rehabilitation in many jurisdictions has resulted in a decreased emphasis on treatment, even in the case of juveniles. At the other extreme has been the position that institutionalization is bad for juveniles and therefore should be abandoned, with juveniles being cared for in community treatment facilities.

It is possible that other significant changes will be made, too. Some scholars are questioning the wisdom and efficiency of retaining juvenile court systems if most of the procedures of adult court systems become a part of juvenile systems. Others note the unfairness of a system that is moving toward criminal court sentences without all of the elements of due process provided in those courts. One law professor stated the issue as follows:

> As juvenile courts' sentencing practices resemble increasingly those of their criminal counterparts, does any reason remain to maintain a separate court whose sole distinguishing characteristic is its persisting procedural deficiencies?[99]

Another scholar commented that juvenile court systems are old enough that we should consider whether it is time for them to die. But after considering carefully the pros and cons for abolishing juvenile courts, he decided that on balance we should keep them.[100]

It may be that the future of criminal justice is related to what we do with juvenile court systems. Certainly, this is an area to follow closely as the Supreme Court ponders and decides whether to continue the march toward greater due process and equal protection or to retract from that path into a more conservative approach to the interpretation of the U.S. Constitution.

Apply It

1. How were juveniles treated historically?

2. What events led to the emergence of juvenile courts in the United States?

3. What are the basic ways in which juvenile courts and adult criminal courts differ?

4. Briefly describe what the Supreme Court held in each of the following cases: *Kent, Gault, Winship, McKeiver, Breed, Schall,* and *R.L.C.*

5. Explain the recent use of juvenile curfews, giving an example and discussing the legal implications.

6. What are the major gender and racial issues today regarding juvenile offenders?

7. What is the relationship of the police to juveniles?

8. Define and discuss intake proceedings in juvenile systems.

9. Describe the role of the prosecutor and of the defense attorney in juvenile proceedings.

10. Discuss the disposition of a juvenile case and the appeal process.

11. Why are some juveniles tried in adult criminal courts, and how is this accomplished?

12. Why did separate institutions for juveniles develop? Are they successful? Should they be continued? What is meant by *deinstitutionalization?*

13. Should juveniles ever be sentenced to capital punishment? What are the issues? What is the current legal status of capital punishment of juveniles?

Notes

1. F. Nicholas, "History, Philosophy, and Procedures of Juvenile Courts," *Journal of Family Law* 1 (Fall 1961): 158–159.

2. Orman Ketcham, "The Unfulfilled Promise of the American Juvenile Courts," in *Justice for the Child,* ed. Margaret Keeney Rosenheim (New York: Free Press, 1962), p. 24.

3. See Alexander W. Pisciotta, "*Parens Patriae,* Treatment and Reform: The Case of the Western House of Refuge, 1849–1907," *New England Journal of Criminal and Civil Confinement* 10 (Winter 1984): 65–86.

4. See Anthony Platt, *The Child Savers* (Chicago: University of Chicago Press, 1969).

5. John R. Sutton, "The Juvenile Court and Social Welfare: Dynamics of Progressive Reform," *Law and Society Review* 19, no. 1 (1985): 142.

6. Federal Bureau of Investigation, *Crime in the United States: Uniform Crime Reports 1996* (Washington, D.C.: U.S. Government Printing Office, 1997), p. 230.

7. Ibid., p. 220.

8. "Execution to be Sought in Pizza Killings," *New York Times* (14 August 1997), p. 4B. *Time* (6 April 1998), front cover; "Arkansas City Begins Burying Its Young Dead," *New York Times* (28 March 1998), p.1.

9. "Fifteen-Year-Old Girl Pleads Guilty to Manslaughter in Central Park Killing," *New York Times* (12 March 1998), p. 23.

10. "Boy, Twelve, Is Found Guilty of Murder in Fire," *New York Times* (27 August 1997), p.13; "Mentally Disabled Boy Sentenced," *Atlanta Journal and Constitution* (24 September 1997), p.6.

11. "Youth Is Guilty in the Slaying of His Parents," *New York Times* (29 May 1997), p. 11.

12. "Two Youths Held on Charge of Raping Four-Year-Old Girl," *Orlando Sentinel* (27 June 1997), p. 5; "Boy Guilty of Assaulting Girl, Four," *Houston Chronicle* (14 October 1997), p. 15.

13. "Five Years after Acquittal, Man Accused of Killing Again," *St. Petersburg Times* (29 July 1997), p. 4.

14. "Japanese Teen-Ager Charged in Second Murder," *New York Times* (16 July 1997), p. 7; "Child Crime Unnerving Japanese," *New York Times* (28 August 1997), p. 8.

15. "Juvenile Crime Soars when Afternoon Bell Rings," *Miami Herald* (11 September 1997), p. 1.

16. See, for example, Frederic M. Thrasher, *The Gang* (1963; abridged ed., Chicago: University of Chicago Press, 1972); James F. Short, *Delinquency and Society* (Englewood Cliffs, N.J.: Prentice Hall, 1990); Short, ed., *Delinquency, Crime, and Society* (Chicago: University of Chicago Press, 1976); Short and Fred L. Strodtbeck, *Group Process and Gang Delinquency* (Chicago: University of Chicago Press, 1965); Malcolm Klein, *Street Gangs and Street Workers* (Englewood Cliffs, N.J.: Prentice-Hall, 1976); and Klein and Cheryl Maxson, "Street Gang Violence," in *Violent Crime, Violent Criminals,* ed. Neil Alan Weiner and Marvin E. Wolfgang (Newbury Park, Calif.: Sage Publications, 1989), pp. 198–234.

17. "The Drug Gangs," *Newsweek* (28 March 1988), p. 23.

18. "Testimony 30 March 1995", Thomas A. Constantine, Administrator, Drug Enforcement Administration, *Federal Document Clearing House Congressional Testimony* (30 March 1995). For information on gangs and drugs, see John M. Hagedorn, "Neighborhoods, Markets, and Gang Drug Organization," *Journal of Research in Crime and Delinquency* 31 (August 1994): 264–294.

19. "Most Juvenile Crime Committed by Gang Members, Study Finds," *Criminal Justice Newsletter* 28 (2 January 1997): 5.

20. "Three Gang Members Sentenced in '95 Slaying," *New York Times* (3 August 1997), p. 18; "Family in 'Wrong Turn' Killing Feels Justice," *USA Today* (4 August 1997), p. 3.

21. "Gang Member Gets Prison for Coercion," *Chicago Tribune* (10 February 1995), p. 3 Metro Northwest.

22. "Prosecutors Cite Difficulties in Prosecuting Gang Members," *Criminal Justice Newsletter* 26 (3 April 1995), p. 3, referring to *Prosecuting Gangs: A National Assessment* (Rockville, Md.: National Criminal Justice Reference Service).

23. Anne Campbell, "Self Definitions by Rejection: The Case of Gang Girls," *Social Problems* 34 (December 1987): 451–466. See also Campbell, *The Girls in the Gang* (New York: Basil Blackwell, 1984).

24. Smith v. Daily Mail Publishing Co. 443 U.S. 97 (1979).

25. Kent v. United States, 383 U.S. 541 (1966).

26. Kent v. United States, 383 U.S. 541, 554–555 (1966).

27. *In re* Gault, 387 U.S. 1, 19–21, 26–28 (1967).

28. *In re* Winship, 397 U.S. 358 (1970), quoting *in re* Gault.

29. McKeiver v. Pennsylvania, 403 U.S. 528 (1971).

30. Breed v. Jones, 421 U.S. 519 (1975).

31. Schall v. Martin, 467 U.S. 253 (1984).

32. Alfredo A. v. Superior Court, 849 P.2d 1330 (Cal. 1994), *subsequent opinion on reh'g.*, 865 P.2d 56 (Cal. 1994), *cert. denied,* 513 U.S. 822 (1994).

33. United States v. R.L.C. 503 U.S. 291 (1992).

34. Qutb v. Strauss, 11 F.3d 488 (5th Cir. 1993), *cert. denied,* 511 U.S. 1127 (1994).

35. Planned Parenthood v. Danforth, 428 U.S. 52, 74 (1976), *overruled in part as stated in* Oliverson v. West Valley City, 1994 Dist. LEXIS 19383 (D.Utah 1994).

36. Bellotti v. Baird, 443 U.S. 622, 634 (1979).

37. *In re* Appeal in Maricopa County Juvenile Action # JT9065297, 887 P.2d 599 (Ariz. App. 1994).

38. Nunez by Nunez v. City of San Diego, 114 F.3d 935 (9th Cir. 1997).

39. "Race, Sex, Demographics Said to Affect Missouri Case Outcomes," *Criminal Justice Newsletter* 22 (17 September 1991): 5.

40. Madeline Wordes et al., "Locking Up Youth: The Impact of Race on Detention Decisions," *Journal of Research in Crime and Delinquency* 31 (May 1994): 149. See also Darlene J. Conley, "Adding Color to a Black and White Picture: Using Qualitative Data to Explain Racial Disproportionality in the Juvenile Justice System," *Journal of Research in Crime and Delinquency* 31 (May 1994): 135–148.

41. Edmund F. McGarrell, "Trends in Racial Disproportionality in Juvenile Court Processing: 1985–1989," *Crime & Delinquency* 39 (January 1993): 19–48.

42. Juvenile Justice and Delinquency Prevention Act, U.S. Code, Title 42, Section 5633 (1997).

43. Ira M. Schwartz et al., "Federal Juvenile Justice Policy and the Incarceration of Girls," *Crime & Delinquency* 36 (October 1990): 503–520.

44. See Lanes v. State, 767 S.W.2d 789 (Tex.Crim.App. 1989), requiring probable cause to arrest a juvenile.

45. For a case involving searches of school lockers, see New Jersey v. T.L.O., 469 U.S. 325 (1985).

46. Schall v. Martin, 467 U.S. 253, 265 (1984). The adult preventive detention case is United States v. Salerno, 481 U.S. 739 (1987).

47. "Thirty-Nine States Meet Federal Mandate to Halt Juveniles' Jail Detention with Adults," *NCJA Juvenile Justice* (March 1992), p. 1. The statute is codified at U.S. Code, Title 18, Section 5031 et seq. (1997).

48. "Delaware Agrees to Reforms in Juvenile Institution Conditions," *Criminal Justice Newsletter* 25 (18 May 1994): 5.

49. Monroe v. Soliz, 939 P.2d 205 (Wash. 1997).

50. "Indiana Court Bars Mixing of Young and Adult Inmates," *New York Times* (15 May 1997), p. 10. See Ratliff v. Cohn, 693 N.E. 2d 530 (Ind. 1998).

51. See, for example, State v. Whatley, 320 So.2d 123 (La. 1975).

52. *In re* E.T.C., 449 A.2d 937 (Vt. 1982).

53. See *In re* H., 293 A.2d 181 (N.J. 1972).

54. Joseph B. Sanborn Jr., "Philosophical, Legal, and Systemic Aspects of Juvenile Court Plea Bargaining," *Crime & Delinquency* 39 (October 1993): 509–527; quotation is on p. 522.

55. See Robert E. Shepherd Jr., "Juvenile Justice," *Criminal Justice* (a publication of the American Bar Association) 5 (Fall 1990): 31–33.

56. New York CLS Family Court Act, Section 301.2 (1997).

57. *In re* A.D.G., 895 P.2d 1067 (Colo.Ct.App. 1994), *cert. denied sub nom.*, 1995 Colo.App. LEXIS 423 (Colo. 5 June 1995).

58. "Judges' Group Criticizes Trend toward Waiver to Adult Court," *Criminal Justice Newsletter* 25 (1 March 1994): 1.

59. Eric L. Jensen and Linda K. Mitsger, "A Test of the Deterrent Effect of Legislative Waiver on Violent Juvenile Crime," *Crime & Delinquency* 40 (January 1994): 102.

60. Hughes v. State, 653 A.2d 241 (Del. 1994), *clarified, reh'g. denied,* 1995 Del. LEXIS 36 (Del. 30 January 1995).

61. Tammy Meredith Poulos and Stan Orchowsky, "Serious Juvenile Offenders: Predicting the Probability of Transfer to Criminal Court," *Crime & Delinquency* 40 (January 1994): 3–17.

62. Simon I. Singer, "The Automatic Waiver of Juveniles and Substantive Justice," *Crime & Delinquency* 39 (April 1993): 258.

63. Joseph B. Sanborn Jr., "Certification to Criminal Courts: the Important Policy Questions of How, When, and Why," *Crime & Delinquency* 40 (April 1994): 276.

64. "Juvenile Crime Measures Top State Legislative Agendas," *Criminal Justice Newsletter* 25 (18 January 1994): 5. The Colorado statute is C.R.S. 18-12-108.5 (1996).

65. "Illinois Legislature Passes Tough Juvenile Crime Bill," *Criminal Justice Newsletter* 23 (1 December 1994), p. 6. See Ill. Code, Chapter 705, Section 405/5-4 (1997).

66. "House of Representatives Passes Bill Aimed at Juvenile Crime," *Criminal Law Reporter* 61 (14 May 1997): 1155. The bill has not passed in the Senate. See Juvenile Crime Control Act of 1997, 105 H.R. 3 (1997).

67. See David J. Rothman, *The Discovery of the Asylum* (South Salem, N.Y.: Criminal Justice Institute, 1988), pp. 50, 51.

68. "Crowding of Juvenile Facilities Is 'Pervasive,' Study Finds," *Criminal Justice Newsletter* 24 (15 April 1993): 4.

69. Ibid, p. 5.

70. Dale G. Parent et al., *Conditions of Confinement: Juvenile Detention and Corrections Facilities. Research Summary* (Washington, D.C.: U.S. Department of Justice, February 1994), p. 1. This publication is a summary of the Congressionally mandated study, and it was prepared by Abt Associations, Inc., under a grant from the Office of Juvenile Justice and Delinquency, Office of Justice Programs, U.S. Department of Justice.

71. Joseph R. Rowan and Charles J. Kehoe, "Let's Deinstitutionalize Group Homes," *Juvenile and Family Court Journal* 36 (Spring 1985): 1–4.

72. O'Conner v. Donaldson, 422 U.S. 563 (1975).

73. See, for example, Nelson v. Heyne, 355 F.Supp. 451 (N.D.Ind. 1972), *aff'd.*, 491 F.2d 352 (7th Cir. 1974), *cert. denied*, 417 U.S. 976 (1974).

74. This case has had a long history that cannot be detailed here, but the citations and decisions may be traced through Morales v. Turman, 569 F.Supp. 332 (E.D.Tex. 1983).

75. Santana v. Collazo, 714 F.2d 1172, 1177 (1st Cir. 1983), *cert. denied,* 466 U.S. 974 (1984).

76. Shookoff v. Adams, 750 F.Supp. 288 (M.D.Tenn. 1990, *aff'd. sub nom.*, 969 F.2d 228 (6th Cir. 1992). The Supreme Court case on which the decision relies concerns the right of adult offenders to access to courts. See Bounds v. Smith, 430 U.S. 817 (1977).

77. "Denver College to Take Over Juvenile Corrections Education," *Criminal Justice Newsletter* 25 (1 March 1994): 3. For more

78. Jane Hodges et al., *Improving Literacy Skills of Juvenile Detainees* (Washington, D.C.: U.S. Department of Justice, Office of Juvenile Justice and Delinquency Prevention, October 1994), p. 5.

79. See, for example, Richard G. Wiebush, "Juvenile Intensive Supervision: The Impact on Felony Offenders Diverted from Institutional Placement," *Crime & Delinquency* 39 (January 1993): 68–89.

80. The National Advisory Commission on Criminal Justice Standards and Goals, *Corrections* (Washington, D.C.: U.S. Government Printing Office, 1973), p. 350.

81. Ibid., pp. 350–352.

82. For example, see Andrew T. Scull, *Decarceration: Community Treatment and the Deviant: A Radical View,* 2d ed. (New Brunswick, N.J.: Rutgers University Press, 1984).

83. *Time* (30 August 1976), p. 63.

84. Alden D. Miller et al., "The Aftermath of Extreme Tactics in Juvenile Justice Reform: A Crisis Four Years Later," in *Corrections and Punishment*, ed. David F. Greenberg, Sage Criminal Justice System Annuals (Beverly Hills, Calif.: Sage Publications, 1977), p. 245.

85. Mark S. Hamm, Book review essay, "Reforming Juvenile Corrections," *Justice Quarterly* 10 (December 1993): 699. The book by Jerome G. Miller is *Last One Over the Wall: The Massachusetts Experiment in Closing Reform Schools* (Columbus, Ohio: Ohio State University Press, 1991).

86. "Project Aims to Replicate 'Massachusetts Experiment,'" *Criminal Justice Newsletter* 25 (15 June 1994): 2.

87. "Closing of Training School in Maryland Cited as Model Reform," *Criminal Justice Newsletter* 19 (15 November 1988): 5.

88. Denise C. Gottfredson and William H. Barton, "Deinstitutionalization of Juvenile Offenders," *Criminology* 31 (November 1993): 605.

89. Maynard L. Erickson, "Schools for Crime?" *Journal of Research in Crime and Delinquency* 15 (January 1978): 32–33.

90. "Fifth Youth Sentenced to Death in Killings of Two Teen-Age Girls," *New York Times* (25 September 1994), p. 15.

91. "Tougher Treatment Urged for Juveniles," *New York Times* (2 August 1994), p. 13.

92. Eddings v. Oklahoma, 455 U.S. 104 (1982).

93. Baldwin v. Alabama, 472 U.S. 372 (1985).

94. Trop v. Dulles, 356 U.S. 86, 101 (1958) (plurality opinion).

95. Thompson v. Oklahoma, 487 U.S. 815 (1988). For a discussion of capital punishment and juveniles, see Comment, "Reflections on the Juvenile Death Penalty: Contravention of Precedent and Public Opinion," *In the Public Interest* 15 (1996–1997): 113–127.

96. Thompson v. Oklahoma, 487 U.S. 815 (1988). See also Allen v. State, 636 So.2d 494 (Fla. 1994), in which the Florida Supreme Court held that it would be cruel and unusual punishment under that state's constitution as well as the federal constitution to execute a person who was fifteen when he committed murder. The Florida court emphasized that no person under sixteen had been sentenced to death and executed in Florida in over fifty years.

97. Stanford v. Kentucky, 492 U.S. 361 (1989).

98. "Harvard's Unseemly Haste," *New York Times* (13 April 1995), p. 14.

99. Barry C. Feld, "The Punitive Juvenile Court and the Quality of Procedural Justice: Disfunctions Between Rhetoric and Reality," *Crime & Delinquency* 36 (October 1989): 443.

100. Robert O. Dawson, "The Future of Juvenile Justice: Is It Time to Abolish the System?" *Journal of Criminal Law and Criminology* 81 (Spring 1990): 136–155.

information on educational programs in juvenile correction facilities, see Robert J. Gemignani, *Juvenile Correctional Education: A Time for Change* (Washington, D.C.: U.S. Department of Justice, October 1994).

Selected Amendments to the United States Constitution

Amendment I (1791)

Congress shall make no law respecting an establishment of religion, or prohibiting the free exercise thereof; or abridging the freedom of speech, or of the press; or the right of the people peaceably to assemble, and to petition the Government for a redress of grievances.

Amendment IV (1791)

The right of the people to be secure in their persons, houses, papers, and effects, against unreasonable searches and seizures, shall not be violated, and no Warrants shall issue, but upon probable cause, supported by Oath or affirmation, and particularly describing the place to be searched, and the persons or things to be seized.

Amendment V (1791)

No person shall be held to answer for a capital, or otherwise infamous crime, unless on a presentment or indictment of a Grand Jury, except in cases arising in the land or naval forces, or in the Militia, when in actual service in time of War or public danger; nor shall any person be subject for the same offence to be twice put in jeopardy of life or limb; nor shall be compelled in any criminal case to be a witness against himself, nor be deprived of life, liberty, or property, without due process of law; nor shall private property be taken for public use, without just compensation.

Amendment VI (1791)

In all criminal prosecutions, the accused shall enjoy the right to a speedy and public trial, by an impartial jury of the State and district wherein the crime shall have been committed, which district shall have been previously ascertained by law, and to be informed of the nature and cause of the accusation; to be confronted with the witnesses against him; to have compulsory process for obtaining witnesses in his favor, and to have the Assistance of Counsel for his defence.

Amendment VIII (1791)

Excessive bail shall not be required, nor excessive fines imposed, nor cruel and unusual punishments inflicted.

Amendment IX (1791)

The powers not delegated to the United States by the Constitution, nor prohibited by it to the States, are reserved to the States respectively, or to the people.

Amendment XIV (1868)

Section 1   All persons born or naturalized in the United States, and subject to the jurisdiction thereof, are citizens of the United States and of the State wherein they reside. No State shall make or enforce any law which shall abridge the privileges or immunities of citizens of the United States; nor shall any State deprive any person of life, liberty, or property, without due process of law; nor deny to any person within its jurisdiction the equal protection of the laws.

Section 5   The Congress shall have power to enforce, by appropriate legislation, the provisions of this article.

Appendix B

How to Read a Court Citation

Pugh v. Locke, 406 F.Supp. 318 (M.D.Ala. 1976), *aff'd., remanded,* Newman v. Alabama, 559 F.2d 283 (5th Cir. 1977), *reh'g. denied,* 564 F.2d 97 (5th Cir. 1977), *and rev'd. in part sub nom.,* 438 U.S. 781 (1978), *later proceeding sub nom.,* 466 F.Supp. 628 (M.D.Ala. 1979), *later proceeding,* 688 F.2d 1312 (11th Cir. 1982), *cert. denied,* 460 U.S. 1083 (1983), *later proceeding sub nom.,* 740 F.2d 1513 (11th Cir. 1984), *dismissed,* 1988 U.S.Dist LEXIS 18634 (M.D.Ala., 28 December 1988).

This case has a number of citations, and that is not common among all cases but is common among cases involving unconstitutional conditions in prisons and jails. The case is used here because it illustrates so many elements of case citations, some of which are omitted because of their length.

Original Citation

[Pugh v. Locke][1] [406][2] [F.Supp.][3] [318][4] [M.D.Ala.][5] [1976][6].

1. Name of case
2. Volume number of reporter in which case is published
3. Name of reporter; see Abbreviations for Commonly Used Reporters.
4. Page in the reporter where the decision begins
5. Court deciding the case
6. Year decided

Additional Case History

[*aff'd., remanded*][7] [Newman v. Alabama][8] [559][9] [F.2d][10] [283][11] [(5th Cir. 1977)][12] [*and rev'd, in part*][13] [438][14] [U.S.][15] [781][16] [1978][17] [*later proceeding*] or [*later proceeding*][18] [*cert. denied*][19] [*dismissed*][20]

7. Affirmed and remanded (sent back for further proceedings). The appellate court told the lower court that it agreed with part of its decision but that some aspect of the decision needed to be reconsidered.
8. The name under which the case was affirmed and remanded. In some cases the name will be omitted, and the citation will carry the notation *sub nom.,* which means "by another name." Several times that occurs in this case, but they are omitted here.
9. Volume number of the reporter in which case is published
10. Abbreviated name of reporter (Federal Reporter, second series)
11. Page number on which the opinion begins
12. The court deciding the case and the date decision was given
13. Additional history—appeal to U.S. Supreme Court, which reversed the lower court in part, under another name
14. Volume number of reporter in which Supreme Court decision is published
15. Abbreviated name of reporter

16. Page number on which Supreme Court decision begins
17. Year in which Supreme Court decided the case
18. The case had a later proceeding under a different name before the Middle District of Alabama court (in 1979) and another before the Eleventh Circuit in 1982
19. The U.S. Supreme Court refused to grant *certiorari;* thus, the case was not heard by that Court.
20. The case was dismissed by the Middle District of Alabama court in 1988.

Abbreviations for Commonly Used Reporters for Court Cases

Decisions of the U.S. Supreme Court

S.Ct.: Supreme Court Reporter

U.S.: United States Reports

Decisions from Other Courts: A Selected List

A., A.2d: Atlantic Reporter, Atlantic Reporter Second Series

Cal.Rptr: California Reporter

F.2d: Federal Reporter Second Series

F.3d: Federal Reporter Third Series

F.Supp: Federal Supplement

N.Y.S.2d: New York Supplement Second Series

N.W., N.W.2d: North Western Reporter, North Western Reporter Second Series

N.E., N.E.2d: North Eastern Reporter, North Eastern Reporter Second Series

P., P.2d: Pacific Reporter, Pacific Reporter Second Series

S.E., S.E.2d: South Eastern Reporter, South Eastern Reporter Second Series

Definitions

Aff'd Affirmed; the appellate court agrees with the decision of the lower court.

Aff'd sub nom. Affirmed under a different name; the case at the appellate level has a different name from that of the trial court level.

Aff'd per curium. Affirmed by the court. The opinion is written by "the court" instead of by one of the judges; a decision affirmed but no written opinion is issued.

Cert. denied *Certiorari* denied; the U.S. Supreme Court refuses to hear and decide the case. Some state supreme courts use this terminology; others use *review denied.*

Concurring opinion An opinion agreeing with the court's decision but offering different reasons.

Dismissed The court dismissing the case from legal proceedings, thus refusing to give further consideration to any of its issues.

Dissenting opinion An opinion disagreeing with the reasoning and result of the majority opinion.

Later proceeding Any number of issues could be decided in a subsequent proceeding.

Reh'g. denied Rehearing denied; the court's refusal to rehear a case.

Remanded The appellate court sending a case back to the lower court for further action.

Rev'd Reversed, overthrown, set aside, made void. The appellate court reverses the decision of the lower court.

Rev'd. and remanded Reversed and remanded; the appellate court reverses the decision and sends the case back for further action.

Vacated. Abandoned, set aside, made void. The appellate court sets aside the decision of the lower court.

Glossary

Glossary

A

Acquired immune deficiency syndrome (AIDS) A deadly disease that attacks the immune system; communicated through exchange of bodily fluids, especially during sexual activity and blood transfusions but also may be transmitted in other ways.

Acquittal Legal verification of the innocence of a person in a criminal trial.

Adjudication The process of decision making by a court. Normally used to refer to juvenile proceedings.

Administrative law Rules and regulations made by agencies to which power has been delegated by the legislature. Administrative agencies investigate and decide cases concerning potential violations of these rules.

Adversary system One of two primary systems for settling disputes in court. The accused is presumed to be innocent. A defense attorney and a prosecuting attorney attempt to convince a judge or a jury of their versions of the case. *See* **Inquisitory system.**

Aftercare Providing continued supervision of juveniles after they are released from a correctional facility; similar to the term *parole* in criminal court systems.

Aggravated assault Technically, an assault is a threat to commit a battery, but often the term is used to refer to a battery. Aggravated assault involves a battery inflicted by use of a deadly weapon.

Appeal A stage in a judicial proceeding in which a higher court is asked to review the case decided by a lower court.

Appellant The loser in a court case, who seeks a review of that case in a higher court.

Appellee The winning party in a lower court, who argues on appeal against reversing the lower court's decision.

Arraignment A hearing before a judge during which the defendant is identified, hears the formal reading of the charges, is read his or her legal rights, and enters a plea to the charges.

Arrest The act of taking a person into custody in order to make a criminal charge against that person.

Arson The willful and malicious burning of the structure of another with or without the intent to defraud. Burning of one's own property with the intent to defraud is included in some definitions. Many modern statutes carry a more severe penalty for the burning of a dwelling than of other real property.

Assault *See* **Aggravated assault.**

Assigned counsel An attorney appointed and paid by the court to represent a defendant who does not have funds to retain a private attorney.

B

Bail Money or property posted by the defendant (or a surety) to guarantee that he or she will appear for trial, sentencing, or imprisonment. If the defendant does not appear, the money or property may be forfeited.

Battered person syndrome A syndrome arising from a cycle of abuse by a special person, often a parent or a spouse, that leads the battered person to perceive that

375

violence against the offender is the only way to end the abuse. In some cases the battered person murders the batterer.

Beyond a reasonable doubt The standard for evidence required for conviction in a criminal case; means a lack of uncertainty; the facts presented to the judge or jury are sufficient to lead a reasonable person to conclude without question that the defendant committed the act for which he or she is charged. In contrast is the standard required in a civil case: a preponderance of the evidence, meaning that the facts indicate that, more probably than not, the facts are as the plaintiff has argued.

Bond A written document stating that the defendant or his/her sureties assure the presence of that defendant at a criminal proceeding, and that if the defendant is not present, the security posted for the bond will be forfeited.

Booking The official recording of the name, photograph, and fingerprints of a suspect, along with the offense charged and the name of the officer who made the arrest.

Bow Street Runners Mid-eighteenth century London system that gave police powers of investigation and arrest to constables who were given some training and paid a portion of the fines in successfully prosecuted cases.

Building tenders Inmates who gain supervisory control in exchange for assisting prison officials with maintenance of the institution and control of other inmates.

Burglary Illegally or forcibly entering any enclosed structure in order to commit a crime, usually theft.

C

Capital punishment Punishment by death for those convicted of capital crimes.

Case law Legally binding court interpretations of written laws or rules made by the courts. *See* **common law.**

Causation Requirement in criminal law that the criminal act must be the cause of the harmful consequence.

Certification Process used to remove juveniles from the jurisdiction of the juvenile court to that of the criminal court; also called *transfer* or *waiver.*

Circumstantial evidence Evidence that may be inferred from a fact or a series of facts. *See also* **Direct evidence**

Civil law Distinguished from criminal law as that law pertaining to private rights.

Civil rights Sometimes called civil liberties; refers to all the natural rights guaranteed by the Constitution, such as free speech and the right to religious beliefs and practices; also refers to the body of law concerning natural rights.

Classification The assignment of new inmates to the housing, security status, and treatment programs that best fit their needs.

Commissary Refers both to the prison store and to the incidental items sold to inmates. May also be an inmate's account, which is debited when an item is purchased.

Common law Broadly defined, the legal theory and law that originated in England and are common in the United States as well. More specifically, common law consists of the guidelines, customs, traditions, and judicial decisions that courts use in decision making. It is contrasted to constitutions and written laws.

Community-based corrections Punishment that emphasizes assimilation into the community. Instead of imprisonment, the offender may be put on probation or placed in programs such as work release, foster homes, halfway houses, parole, and furlough.

Community work service Punishment assigning the offender to community service or work projects. Sometimes it is combined with restitution or probation.

Concurrent sentences Term of imprisonment for more than one offense that is served at the same time. If an offender receives a three-year term for robbery and a five-year term for assault to be served concurrently, the total sentence is five years.

Concurring opinion A judge's written opinion agreeing with the result in a case, but disagreeing with the reasoning of the majority opinion.

Conjugal visiting Permitting inmates to engage in sexual and other social contacts with their spouses in an unsupervised, private setting.

Consecutive sentences Term of imprisonment for more than one offense that must be served one following the other. If an offender receives a three-year term for robbery and a five-year term for assault, the consecutive sentence adds to a total of eight years.

Constable An officer of a municipal corporation who has duties similar to those of a sheriff, such as preserving the public peace, executing papers from the court, and maintaining the custody of juries.

Contempt of court An act done to embarrass, humiliate, or undermine the power of the court; may be civil or criminal; often is declared by a judge whose order has been violated.

Continuance An adjournment of a trial or other proceeding until a later date.

Contraband Any item such as weapons, drugs, or alcohol, possession of which is illegal or violates prison rules.

Corporal punishment Physical punishment such as beatings or whippings.

Correctional officer A corrections employee with supervisory power over a suspect or convicted offender in custody.

Crime An illegal act of omission or commission that is punishable by law.

Crime rate The number of crimes per 100,000 population.

Crimes known to the police   All serious criminal offenses that have been reported to the police for which the police have sufficient evidence to believe the crimes were committed.

Criminal   A person found guilty of an act that violates the criminal law.

Criminal justice system   The entire system of criminal prevention, detection, apprehension, trial, and punishment.

Criminal law   Statutes defining acts so offensive that they threaten the well-being of the society and require that the accused be prosecuted by the government. Criminal laws prescribe punishments that may be imposed on offenders.

Cross examination   The questioning of a witness by adversary counsel after one attorney concludes the direct examination.

Cruel and unusual punishment   The punishments prohibited by the Eighth Amendment to the U.S. Constitution, as interpreted by the courts. Some examples are torture, prison conditions that "shock the conscience," excessively long sentences, and the death penalty for rape but not murder of an adult woman.

Curtilage   Enclosed ground and buildings immediately around a dwelling.

Custody   Legal control over a person or property; physical responsibility for a person or thing.

D

Deadly force   Force likely to cause serious bodily injury or death.

Defendant   The person charged with a crime and against whom a criminal proceeding has begun or is pending.

Defense   A response by the defendant in a criminal or civil case. It may consist only of a denial of the factual allegations of the prosecution (in a criminal case) or of the plaintiff (in a civil case). If the defense offers new factual allegations in an effort to negate the charges, there is an affirmative defense.

Defense attorney or counsel   The counsel for the defendant in a criminal proceeding, whose main function is to protect the legal rights of the accused.

Delinquency *See* **Juvenile delinquent.**

Demonstrative evidence   Real evidence; the kind of evidence that is apparent to the senses, in contrast to evidence presented by the testimony of other people.

de novo   Literally means "anew" or "fresh." A trial *de novo* refers to a case that is tried again, as if no decision had been rendered previously. In some jurisdictions a first appeal from a lower court may be a trial *de novo*. The term may be used to refer to other proceedings, such as hearings.

Depositions   Oral testimony taken from the opposing party or a witness for the opposing party. Depositions are taken out of court but under oath. They are recorded verbatim, usually by a court reporter.

Attorneys for both sides are present. Depositions may be used when the deposed is not able to appear in court. They may be used also to impeach the testimony of a witness in court.

Deprivation model   A model of prisonization based on the belief that the prison subculture stems from the way inmates adapt to the severe psychological and physical losses imposed by imprisonment.

Detention *See* **Pretrial detention.**

Detention center   A facility for the temporary confinement of juveniles in custody who are awaiting court disposition.

Determinate sentence   Length of a sentence for a specific crime is determined by the legislature; the parole board, correctional officials, or judge cannot make changes in the sentence length. The judge may have the power to suspend the sentence or to impose probation rather than a term of years.

Deterrence   Punishment philosophy based on the assumption that the acts of potential offenders can be prevented. *Individual deterrence* refers to the prevention of additional criminal acts on the part of the specific individual being punished; *general deterrence* refers to the presumed effect that punishing one offender will have on other potential offenders.

Dicta   Written portions of a judge's opinion that are not part of the actual ruling of the court and are not legally binding precedents for future court decisions.

Direct evidence   Evidence offered by an eyewitness who testifies to what he or she saw, heard, tasted, smelled, or touched.

Direct examination   Examination conducted by the attorney who called the witness to testify.

Directed verdict   Upon a finding of insufficient evidence to convict a defendant, the judge may direct the jury to return a verdict of not guilty. The judge may not direct a verdict of guilty.

Discovery   A legal motion requesting the disclosure of information held by the opposing counsel. In criminal law the defense counsel files a discovery motion to obtain information from the police and the prosecutor.

Discretion   In the criminal justice system, authority to make decisions based on one's own judgment rather than on specified rules. The result may be inconsistent handling of offenders as well as positive actions tailored to individual circumstances.

Disposition   The final decision of a court in a criminal proceeding to accept a guilty plea, to find the defendant guilty or not guilty, or to terminate the proceedings against the defendant.

Diversion   Removal of the offender from the criminal proceeding before or after guilt is determined, and disposition through other procedures such as work release, drug treatment, or community service.

Domestic violence   Causing serious physical harm or threatening such harm to a member of the family or household, including spouses, ex-spouses, parents, children, persons otherwise related by blood, persons living in the household, or persons who lived there formerly. May include relationships of persons who do not live together but who have had close intimate relationships.

Due process Constitutional principle that a person should not be deprived of life, liberty, or property without reasonable and lawful procedures that must be made available in any criminal action, including postconviction procedures such as prison disciplinary hearings or parole revocations.

E

Entrapment A defense asserting that a crime has been instigated by a government agent who offers inducements to commit a crime or makes false representations.

Equal protection All persons under like circumstances must receive the same treatment in the criminal justice system; they may not be discriminated against because of race, gender, minority status, or religion.

Exclusionary rule Evidence excluded from a criminal trial that was secured as the result of illegal actions by law enforcement officers.

Expert witness Person with extensive training or education in a particular field such as medicine who testifies at depositions or at trial concerning a critical issue of that case, such as what caused the death of the deceased.

F

Felony A serious offense such as murder, armed robbery, or rape. Punishments range from probation to imprisonment in a state or federal institution or execution.

Fine Payment of a sum of money to a court by the convicted person in addition to or instead of other punishment.

Fleeing felon rule Common law rule that permitted police to shoot at any fleeing felon. The rule has been modified to require circumstances involving (1) the threat of serious injury or death of the officer or others, (2) the prevention of an escape if the suspect threatens the officer with a gun, or (3) the officer's having probable cause to believe the suspect has committed or threatened to commit serious bodily harm.

Forcible rape *See* **Rape.**

Frisk Action by law enforcement officer or correctional officer, consisting of patting down or running one's hands quickly over a person's body to determine whether the suspect or inmate has a weapon or other contraband. This is in contrast to a search, which is a more careful and thorough examination.

Frankpledge system In old English law, a system whereby the members of a tithing had corporate responsibility for the behavior of all members over fourteen years old.

Furlough An authorized, temporary leave from a correctional facility in order to attend a funeral, visit the family, attempt to secure employment, or engage in any other approved activity.

G

General deterrence *See* **Deterrence.**

Good faith exception Provision that illegally obtained evidence will not be excluded from a subsequent trial if it can be shown that the police secured the evidence in good faith, meaning that they had a reasonable belief that they were acting in accordance with the law.

Good time credits Days subtracted from an inmate's prison term, awarded for satisfactory behavior during incarceration.

Grand jury A group of citizens, convened by legal authority, who evaluate evidence to ascertain whether a crime has been committed and whether there is sufficient evidence against the accused to justify prosecution. If so, the grand jury returns an indictment. Grand juries may conduct investigations into alleged criminal activities in some jurisdictions.

Guard The traditional term for correctional employees, who supervise suspects or convicted offenders in custody. *See also* **Correctional officer.**

H

Habeas corpus, **writ of** Technically, a written court order requiring that the accused be brought to court to determine the legality of custody and confinement. Refers also to writs filed by inmates regarding the alleged illegality of their confinement.

Hands-off doctrine A policy used by courts to justify nonintervention in the daily administration of correctional facilities.

Harmless error Minor or trivial errors not deemed sufficient to harm the rights of the parties who assert the errors. Cases are not reversed on the basis of harmless errors.

Hate crime Defined in the federal criminal code as a crime "that manifests evidence of prejudice based on race, religion, disability, sexual orientation, or ethnicity, including where appropriate the crimes of murder, non-negligent manslaughter, forcible rape, aggravated assault, simple assault, intimidation, arson, and destruction, damage or vandalism of property."

Hearsay evidence Secondhand evidence of which the witness does not have personal knowledge, but merely repeats something the witness says he or she heard another person say. Hearsay evidence must be excluded from trial unless it meets one of the exceptions to the hearsay rule.

House arrest A form of confinement, usually on probation, in which the offender is permitted to live at home but is restricted in his or her movements to and from the home. Curfew may be imposed, and the offender may be subject to unannounced visits from a probation officer. In some cases, electronic devices are used to monitor the probationer's location.

Humanitarianism In penal philosophy, the doctrine advocating the removal of harsh, severe, and painful conditions in penal institutions.

Hundred In English law, a combination of ten tithings as part of the frankpledge system. *See also* **Tithing** and **Frankpledge system.**

I

Importation model A theory of prisonization based on the assumption that the inmate subculture arises not only from internal prison experiences, but also from the external patterns of behavior the inmates bring to prison.

Incapacitation A punishment theory usually implemented by imprisoning an offender to prevent the commission of any other crimes by that person. In some countries (and in earlier days in the United States), incapacitation involved mutilation, such as removing the hands of thieves or castrating sex offenders.

Incarceration Imprisonment in a jail, prison, or other type of penal institution.

Indeterminate sentence Sentence to confinement without a definite term. Parole boards or professionals determine when the offender should be released.

Index offenses or crimes The FBI's *Uniform Crime Reports* of the occurrences of the eight crimes considered most serious: murder and nonnegligent manslaughter, forcible rape, robbery, aggravated assault, burglary, larceny-theft, motor vehicle theft, and arson.

Indictment The written accusation of a grand jury, formally stating that probable cause exists to believe that the suspect committed a felony.

Individual deterrence *See* **Deterrence.**

Inevitable discovery rule States that evidence secured illegally by police will not be excluded from the suspect's trial, provided it can be shown that the evidence would have been discovered anyway under legal means.

Informant A person who gives information to law enforcement officials about a crime or planned criminal activity.

Information A formal written document used to charge a person with a specific offense. Prosecutors issue informations, in contrast to indictments, which are issued by grand juries.

Initial appearance The first appearance of the accused before a magistrate; if the accused is detained in jail immediately after arrest, he or she must be taken quickly to a magistrate for the initial appearance. At that point the magistrate decides whether there is probable cause to detain the suspect and, if so, tells the suspect of the charges and of his or her constitutional rights, including the right to an attorney.

Inmate A person whose freedom has been replaced by confinement in a prison, mental ward, or similar institution.

Inquisitory system A system in which the defendant must prove his or her innocence, in contrast to the adversary system, which has a presumption of innocence requiring the state to prove the defendant's guilt.

Intake decision In prosecution, the first review of a case by an official in the prosecutor's office. Weak cases may be weeded out at this stage. In juvenile court, the reception of a juvenile against whom complaints have been made. Decision to dismiss or proceed with the case is made at this stage.

Intensive probation supervision (IPS) With small caseloads, probation officers provide more careful supervision than they could provide with larger caseloads; probationers are supervised carefully.

Interrogatories A set of questions given to a party thought to have pertinent information that may be used at trial. The party completing the interrogatories must sign an oath that the statements are correct.

INTERPOL A world police organization that was established for the purpose of cooperation among nations involved in common policing problems.

J

Jail A local, regional, or federal facility used to confine persons awaiting trial as well as those serving short sentences.

Judge An elected or appointed officer who presides over a court of law; the final and neutral arbiter of law who is responsible for all court activities.

Judicial review The authority of a court to check the power of the executive and legislative branches of government by deciding whether their acts defy rights established by the state and federal constitutions.

Jurisdiction The lawful exercise of authority; the area within which authority may be exercised, such as the geographical area within which a particular police force has authority. Courts may have *original* jurisdiction to hear the case; if more than one court has authority to hear the case, jurisdiction is *concurrent*. *Appellate* jurisdiction refers to the power of a court to hear the case on appeal. *Exclusive* jurisdiction means that only one court may hear the case.

Jury In a criminal case, a group of people who have been sworn in at court to listen to a trial and decide whether the defendant is guilty or not guilty. In some jurisdictions, juries may determine or recommend sentence.

Just deserts The belief that those who commit crimes should suffer for those crimes; also the amount or type of punishment a particular offender deserves to receive.

Juvenile A young person under age for certain privileges such as voting or drinking alcoholic beverages. If accused of a criminal or juvenile offense, usually a juvenile is not tried by a criminal court but is processed in the juvenile court.

Juvenile court The court having jurisdiction over juveniles who are accused of delinquent acts or offenses or criminal acts, or who are in need of supervision because they are being neglected or mistreated by their parents or guardians.

Juvenile delinquent A person under legal age (the maximum age varies among the states from sixteen to twenty-one, but eighteen is the most common) whom a juvenile court has determined to be incorrigible or in violation of a criminal statute.

L

Larceny-theft The unlawful removal of someone else's property with the intention of keeping it permanently. Historically, small thefts were categorized as *petit larceny* and large thefts as *grand larceny*. The latter was punished by the death penalty, a punishment no longer permitted for larceny in the United States. Most modern theft laws do not distinguish between the two types of larceny.

Law Enforcement Assistance Administration (LEAA) Agency established by Congress in 1965, provided funding for development of police departments, police techniques, police education, and police training. It was abolished in 1982. Money for education was provided through the Law Enforcement Education Program (LEEP).

Law Enforcement Education Program (LEEP) *See* **Law Enforcement Assistance Administration (LEAA).**

Lineup A procedure in which a group of people are placed together in a line to allow the complainant or an eyewitness to point out the alleged offender.

M

Magistrate A judge from the lower courts of the state or federal court system. Usually magistrates preside over arraignments, preliminary hearings, bail hearings, and minor offenses.

Mala in se Actions that are intrinsically immoral, such as murder, forcible rape, and robbery.

Mala prohibita Actions that are wrong because legislation prohibits them, although there may not be general agreement that they are wrong in themselves.

Mandamus Literally means "we command." A writ of mandamus is an order from a higher court to a lower court (or to other organizations or persons within its jurisdiction) commanding that specified acts be performed. The writ is an extraordinary one and is not used frequently.

Mandatory sentence Sentences having lengths imposed by the legislature when no discretion is given the judge concerning the sentence. If the defendant is convicted, the specified sentence must be imposed. This is in contrast to determinate sentencing, in which the judge may have discretion to impose probation or suspend the specified sentence.

Manslaughter The unlawful killing of a human being by a person who lacks malice in the act. Manslaughter may be *involuntary* (or negligent), the result of recklessness while committing an unlawful act such as driving while intoxicated; or *voluntary,* an intentional killing committed in the heat of passion.

Marshal Sworn law enforcement officer who performs civil duties of the courts, such as the delivery of papers to begin civil proceedings. In some jurisdictions marshals may serve papers for the arrest of criminal suspects and escort inmates from jail to court or into the community when they are permitted to leave the jail or prison temporarily.

Mens rea The guilty or criminal intent of the accused at the time the criminal act is committed.

Miranda **warning** The rule stemming from *Miranda* v. *Arizona,* which stipulates that anyone in custody for an offense that might result in a jail or prison term must be warned of certain rights before any questioning by law enforcement officials occurs. These rights include the right to remain silent and the right to counsel, which will be appointed if the suspect cannot afford to retain private counsel. If the warning is not given or is given and violated, any information obtained from the suspect may be inadmissible as evidence at trial.

Misdemeanor A less serious offense, punishable by a fine, probation, or a short jail term; in contrast to a felony, a more serious crime.

Mistrial A trial that cannot stand; is invalid. Judges may call a mistrial for such reasons as an error on the part of counsel, the death of a juror or counsel, or the inability of the jury to reach a verdict.

Molly Maquires A powerful secret police organization in the 1870s in Pennsylvania.

Moot The term used to describe a controversy that has ended or evolved to the stage where a court decision on that particular case no longer is relevant or necessary; this is a limitation on the power of courts to decide a case.

Motion A document submitted to the court asking for an order or a rule.

Motor vehicle theft Stealing an automobile, in contrast to stealing an automobile part, or larceny-theft from an automobile.

Murder The unlawful killing of another person either with express or implied malice aforethought.

N

National Crime Victimization Survey (NCVS) Crime data collected by the Bureau of Justice Statistics (BJS) and based on surveys of people to determine who has been victimized by crime.

National Incident-Based Reporting System (NIBRS) A new reporting system utilized by the FBI in collecting crime data. In this system, a crime is viewed along with all its components, including type of victim, type of weapon, location of the crime, alcohol/drug influence, type of criminal activity, relationship of victim to offender, residence of victims and arrestees, and a description of property and its value. This system includes twenty–two crimes, rather than the eight that constitute the FBI's Part I Offenses of serious crimes.

National Youth Survey (NYS) Program for gathering data on crime by interviewing adolescents over a five-year period. The program has been structured to overcome many of the criticisms of other self-report studies.

Nolo contendere Literally means "I will not contest it." In a criminal case this plea has the legal effect of a guilty plea, but the plea cannot be used against the defendant in a civil action brought on the same act. It might be used in a case involving a felony charge of driving while intoxicated. A guilty plea could be used as evidence of liability in a civil action of wrongful death filed by the family of the victim who died in the accident, whereas a *nolo* plea requires that the plaintiff in the civil action prove liability.

Norms The rules or standards of behavior, shared by members of a social group that define appropriate behavior.

O

Offender A person who has committed a criminal offense.

P

Pardon An act exempting a convicted offender from punishment. The pardon may be complete or partial, exempting only part of the punishment.

Parens patriae "Parent of the country;" doctrine from English common law that was the basis for allowing the state to take over guardianship of the child. In the United States, the doctrine forms the basis for the juvenile court. The doctrine presumes that the state acts in the best interests of the child.

Parole The status of an offender who is released before the completion of the sentence but who must be supervised in the community by a parole officer.

Parole board A panel at the state or federal level that decides whether an inmate is released from an institution before the expiration of the sentence.

Parole officer Government employee who supervises and counsels inmates paroled in the community.

Parole revocation The process of returning a released offender to an institution for technical violations of parole conditions or for violating the criminal law.

Penitentiary Historically, an institution intended to isolate convicted offenders from one another, giving them time to reflect on their bad acts and become penitent. Later, synonymous with prison.

Peremptory challenge A challenge that may be used by the prosecution or the defense to excuse a potential juror from the jury panel. No reason need be given. Each attorney gets a specified number of these challenges.

Petition The formal document for filing an action in juvenile court, in contrast to a grand jury indictment or prosecutor's presentment in the criminal court.

Petit jury Literally means small, minor, or inconsiderate; used to distinguish a trial jury from a grand jury.

Plea bargaining The process of negotiation between the defense and the prosecution before or during the trial of a defendant. The process may involve reducing or dropping of some charges or a recommendation for leniency in exchange for a plea of guilty on another charge or charges.

Police A government official authorized to enforce the law and to maintain order, using physical force if necessary.

Posse Rural police system in which the sheriff may call into action any number of citizens over a certain age if they are needed to assist in law enforcement.

Posttraumatic stress syndrome (PTSD) A severe disorder caused by stress experienced by people returning from war (or who have experienced some other severe stress, such as rape) who have such severe nightmares or guilt that they lose their orientation and kill someone (or engage in other violent or otherwise inappropriate behavior), thinking they are back in war (or another experience that caused severe stress). It is argued that victims of this disorder should not be held criminally responsible for crimes committed as a result of PTSD.

Prejudicial errors Errors that affect the rights of parties substantially and thus may result in the reversal of a case.

Preliminary hearing An appearance before a lower-court judge to determine whether there is sufficient evidence to submit to the grand jury or to the trial court. Preliminary hearings may include the bail decision.

Presentence investigation (PSI) Investigation of the background and characteristics of the defendant; may include information that would not be admissible at the trial; presented to the judge to be used in determining sentence.

Presentment A document issued by a grand jury that states that probable cause exists to believe that the suspect committed the crime. Presentments are issued without the participation of the prosecutor. *See also* **Indictments.**

Presumption of innocence A cornerstone of the adversary system; says a defendant is innocent unless and until the prosecution proves guilt beyond a reasonable doubt.

Presumptive sentence The normal sentence is specified by statute for each offense; judges are permitted to deviate from that sentence but usually may do so only under specified circumstances or must give reasons for the deviation.

Pretrial detention Detention of a defendant in jail between arrest and trial, either because the judge has refused bail or the defendant cannot meet the requirements of bail. Generally, the purpose is to assure the presence of the accused at trial. May refer also to *preventive detention* of defendants thought to present a danger to themselves, to others, or to both if released pending trial.

Preventive detention *See* **Pretrial detention.**

Prison Federal or state penal facility for detaining adults sentenced to a year or longer after conviction of a crime.

Prisonization The process of an inmate's becoming accustomed to the subculture of prison life.

Private security forces Persons employed by private agencies instead of governmental ones to provide security from criminal activity.

Proactive Process in which police take the initiative in finding criminals rather than depending on the reports of citizens.

Probable cause In search warrant cases, a set of facts and circumstances that lead to the reasonable belief that the items sought are located in a particular place. In arrest cases, the facts and circumstances lead to the reasonable belief that the suspect has committed a crime.

Probation A type of sentence that places the convicted offender under the supervision of a probation officer within the community instead of in prison. The term refers also to the part of the criminal justice system that is in charge of all aspects of probation.

Probation officer Government official responsible for supervising persons on probation and for writing the presentence reports on offenders.

Probation revocation Process of declaring that a sentenced offender violated the terms of probation. If probation involved a suspended prison or jail sentence, the revocation may mean that the original sentence is invoked and the individual is sent to prison or jail.

Pro bono Literally means "for the good." Generally, the term is used to refer to professional services, especially in law, performed without compensation.

Property crimes Crimes aimed at the property of another person rather than at the person. Serious property crimes include arson, larceny-theft, motor vehicle theft, and burglary.

Pro se "On behalf of self;" acting as one's own attorney.

Prosecution The process that occurs when the state (or federal government) begins the formal process in a criminal case. The action is taken by a prosecuting attorney, a government official whose duty is to initiate and maintain criminal proceedings on behalf of the government against persons accused of committing crimes.

Prosecutor or prosecuting attorney A government official responsible for representing the state against an offender in criminal proceedings.

Public defender An attorney retained and paid by the government to represent indigent defendants in criminal proceedings.

R

Rape Historically, unlawful vaginal intercourse with a woman; called *forcible rape* if obtained against the will of the woman by the use of threats or force; called *statutory rape* if the sexual intercourse is consensual between a man and a woman who is under the age of consent. More recently some rape statutes have been rewritten to include male victims, as well as penetration of any bodily opening by any instrument, including but not limited to the male sexual organ.

Reactive Process in which police depend on the reports of citizens to find criminal suspects, rather than working independently; an important process because police are not in a position to observe most criminal behavior.

Recidivist One who commits crimes repeatedly.

Recusal To remove oneself from a proceeding, such as a judge who has a conflict of interest in a case.

Reformatory Early correctional facility that was less physically secure, and which emphasized changing or reforming the offender. Usually used to refer to institutions.

Rehabilitation Punishment philosophy based on a belief that the offender can and will change to a law-abiding citizen through treatment programs and facilities. Rehabilitation may be most likely to occur in community-based programs rather than during incarceration in penal institutions. The "rehabilitative ideal" was embodied in probation, parole, the indeterminate sentence, and the juvenile court.

Reintegration Punishment philosophy emphasizing the return of the offender to the community so that employment, family ties, and education may be restored.

Restitution Punishment that requires an offender to repay the victim with services or money. This punishment may be imposed instead of or in addition to other punishment or fines. It may be a requirement of parole, too.

Retribution *See* **Just deserts.**

Right to counsel The right to be represented by an attorney at crucial stages in the criminal justice system; indigent defendants have the right to counsel provided by the state.

Robbery The use of force or fear to take personal property belonging to another against that person's will.

S

Sanction A penalty or punishment that is imposed on a person in order to enforce the law.

Search and seizure Examining a person or a person's property and taking items that may be evidence of criminal activity. Generally requires a search warrant. Unreasonable searches and seizures are prohibited.

Search warrant *See* **Warrant.**

Self-report data (SRD) The process of collecting crime data by asking people about their criminal activity, usually by use of anonymous questionnaires.

Sentence The punishment imposed by the court on a convicted offender.

Sentence disparity Inequalities and differences that result when people found guilty of the same crime receive sentences varying in length and type, without reasonable justification for those differences.

Sheriff The chief law enforcement officer in a county, usually chosen by popular election.

Showup Identification procedure during police investigation; involves showing the alleged victim only one person rather than several as in a lineup. Permitted only in extraordinary circumstances.

Silent system In penitentiaries, the historical practice of not allowing offenders to speak with one another.

Social system Interrelationship of roles, acts, and statuses of people who make up the social structure; a social group or set of interacting persons or groups considered a unitary whole because it reflects the common values, social norms, and objectives of the individuals whom it comprises, even though the group is considered distinct from those individuals.

Specific deterrence *See* **Deterrence.**

Standing In the legal system, the doctrine mandating that courts may not recognize a party to a suit unless that person has a personal stake or direct interest in the outcome of the suit.

Stare decisis "Let the decision stand." The doctrine that courts will abide by or adhere to the rulings of previous court decisions when deciding cases having substantially the same facts.

Status offense A class of crime that does not consist of proscribed action or inaction, but of the personal condition or characteristic of the accused, for example, being a vagrant. In juvenile law, may refer to a variety of acts that would not be considered criminal if committed by an adult. Examples are being insubordinate or truant, or running away from home.

Statutory law Law that the legislature has originated and passed by a written enactment.

Statutory rape *See* **Rape**

Subculture A group of significant size whose behavior differs significantly from the behavior of the dominant groups of society.

Subpoena A command issued by the court, ordering a person to appear in court at a specified time and place for the purpose of giving testimony on a specified issue. Persons may be ordered to bring documents pertinent to the case; that order is called a subpoena *duces tecum.*

Summons A formal document issued by a court to notify a person that his or her presence is required for a particular reason in a particular court at a specified day and time.

T

Theft *See* **Larceny–theft.**

Three strikes and you're out Legislation enacted in most states and in the federal government in recent years and designed to impose long sentences on persons who commit three or more serious crimes.

Tithing In English history, a system of ten families who had responsibility for the behavior of members over the age of fourteen. Tithings were important in protecting the group from outsiders, too.

Torts Noncriminal (civil) wrongs or injuries arising from a breach of legal duty for which one may be sued in civil court for damages to person or property, or for wrongfully causing a death. Some actions may constitute both torts and crimes.

Training school A secure correctional facility to which juveniles are confined by court order.

Transportation Historically, the practice of punishing criminals by exiling them to another country, usually far away.

Trial In criminal law, court proceedings during which a judge, a jury, or both listen to the evidence as presented by the defense and the prosecution and determine whether the defendant is guilty beyond a reasonable doubt.

True bill The prosecutor's indictment returned with the approval of the grand jury. After hearing the prosecutor's evidence, the grand jury determines that the indictment is accurate; that is, it is a true bill.

Truth in sentencing A concept requiring that actual time served by offenders is closer to the time allocated for the sentence. Many jurisdictions are establishing 85 percent as their goal, meaning that offenders may not be released for any reasons until they have served 85 percent of their sentences.

U

Uniform Crime Reports (UCR) Official crime data, collected and published by the Federal Bureau of Investigation (FBI) and based on "crimes known to the police"—crimes that are reported to or observed by the police and that the police have reason to believe were committed.

V

Venire   Literally means "to come." A venire is the pool of persons summoned for jury duty in a particular case or cases and from which juries for those cases are selected.

Venue   Location of the trial; *change of venue* refers to the removal of the trial from the location where it would be held normally to another location, either to avoid public pressure or to obtain an impartial jury.

Victim compensation programs   Plans for assisting crime victims in making social, emotional, and economic adjustments.

Victimology   The discipline that studies the nature and causes of victimization as well as programs for aiding victims and preventing victimization.

Victim precipitation   A criminal act that may have been brought on by the victim's actions.

Vigilante or vigilantism   Literally, means *watchman;* a person who is alert and on guard, cautious, suspicious, ready to take action to maintain and preserve peace. Refers to citizens who take the law into their own hands in an effort to catch and punish criminals.

Violent crimes   Those crimes defined by the FBI's *Uniform Crime Reports* as serious crimes against the person. They include forcible rape, robbery, murder and nonnegligent manslaughter, and aggravated assault.

Voir dire   To speak the truth; the process of questioning prospective jurors to determine their qualifications and desirability for serving on a jury.

W

Waiver   The giving up or relinquishing of one's rights, such as the right to counsel or to a jury trial. Waivers must be knowing and intelligent; that is, the defendant must understand what is being relinquished. Some rights may not be waived.

Warden   Historical term for the chief administrative officer in a correctional facility.

Warrant   A court-issued writ authorizing an officer to arrest a suspect or to search a person, personal property, or place.

Watch system   A system charged with the duties of overseeing, patrolling, or guarding an area or a person. Watchmen were prominent in the early watchsystem of policing.

White-collar crime   The illegal actions of corporations or individuals, committed while pursuing their legitimate occupations. Examples are consumer fraud, bribery, and embezzlement.

Workhouse   English institution used for the purpose of confining offenders who were forced to work at unpleasant tasks; offenders were punished physically as well. The concept is used in some places today to refer to institutions that emphasize reformation or rehabilitation through work.

Work release   Release of an inmate to attend school or to work outside the institution, but requiring that person to return to the institution at specified times.

Writ   An order from the court. *See* **Writ of *certiorari*** and ***Habeas corpus.***

Writ of *certiorari*   *Certiorari* literally means "to be informed of." A *writ* is an order from a court giving authority for an act to be done or ordering that it be done; a writ of *certiorari* is used by courts that have discretion to determine which cases they will hear. It is used most commonly today by the U.S. Supreme Court when cases are appealed from lower courts.

Case Index

Name Index

General Index